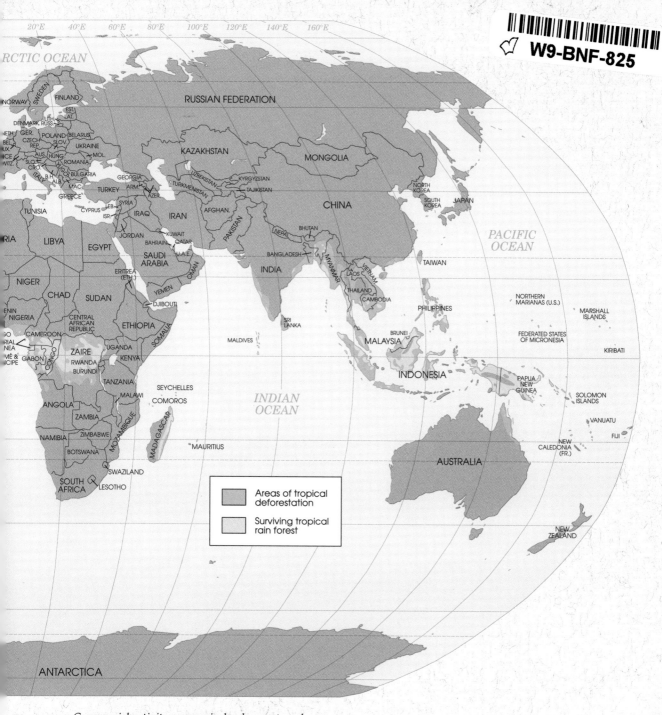

W9-BNF-825

Commercial activity, economic development, and
population growth threaten habitats and ecosystems
throughout the world. The forest degradation that often
accompanies cash cropping, logging, ranching, road
building, and drilling endangers plants, animals, peoples,
and cultures. Lost along with trees are songs, myths,
words, ideas, artifacts, and techniques—the cultural
knowledge and practices of the world's indigenous
peoples. This map shows the extent of recent tropical
deforestation—a major problem in global environmental
change. The map compares estimated original tropical rain
forest cover with surviving forests.

ANTHROPOLOGY

THE
EXPLORATION
OF HUMAN DIVERSITY

SIXTH EDITION

ANTHROPOLOGY
THE
EXPLORATION
OF HUMAN DIVERSITY

Conrad Phillip Kottak

The University of Michigan

McGRAW-HILL, INC.

New York   St. Louis   San Francisco   Auckland   Bogotá
Caracas   Lisbon   London   Madrid   Mexico City   Milan   Montreal
New Delhi   San Juan   Singapore   Sydney   Tokyo   Toronto

This book was set in Palatino by Waldman Graphics, Inc.
The editors were Sylvia Shepard and Bob Greiner;
the designer was Joan E. O'Connor;
the production supervisor was Friederich W. Schulte.
The photo editor was Barbara Salz.
Von Hoffmann Press, Inc., was printer and binder.

Cover photo: David Lainé / Actuel

**ANTHROPOLOGY:
THE EXPLORATION OF HUMAN DIVERSITY**

Copyright © 1994, 1991, 1987, 1982, 1978, 1974 by McGraw-
Hill, Inc. All rights reserved. Printed in the United States of
America. Except as permitted under the United States
Copyright Act of 1976, no part of this publication may be
reproduced or distributed in any form or by any means, or
stored in a data base or retrieval system, without the prior
written permission of the publisher.

Acknowledgments appear on pages 555–559, and on this page
by reference.

This book is printed on acid-free paper.

1 2 3 4 5 6 7 8 9 0   VNH VNH   9 0 9 8 7 6 5 4 3

ISBN 0-07-035918-0

Library of Congress Cataloging-in-Publication Data

Kottak, Conrad Phillip.
    Anthropology: the exploration of human diversity /
Conrad Kottak.—6th ed.
        p.   cm.
    Includes bibliographical references and index.
    ISBN 0-07-035918-0 (acid-free paper)
    1. Anthropology.   I. Title.
GN25.K67   1994
301—dc20   93-1127

ABOUT THE AUTHOR

Conrad Phillip Kottak (A.B. Columbia College 1963; Ph.D. Columbia University, 1966) is Professor of Anthropology at the University of Michigan, were he has taught since 1968. In 1991 he was honored for his teaching by the University and the state of Michigan. In 1992 he received an excellence in teaching award from the College of Literature, Sciences, and the Arts of the University of Michigan.

From 1990 to 1992 Kottak chaired the General Anthropology Division of the American Anthropological Association and served on the AAA executive committee. He has done field work in cultural anthropology in Brazil (since 1962), Madagascar (since 1966), and the United States. His general interests are in the processes by which local cultures are incorporated into larger systems. This interest links his earlier work on ecology and state formation in Africa and Madagascar to his more recent research on economic development, global change, deforestation, national and international culture, and the mass media.

The second edition of Kottak's case study *Assault on Paradise: Social Change in a Brazilian Village*, based on his field work in Arembepe, Bahia, Brazil from 1962 through 1992, was published in 1992 by McGraw-Hill. In a project during the 1980s, collaborating with Brazilian and North American researchers, Kottak blended ethnography and survey research in studying "Television's Behavioral Effects in Brazil." That research is the basis of Kottak's book *Prime-Time Society: An Anthropological Analysis of Television and Culture* (Wadsworth 1990)—a comparative study of the nature and impact of television in Brazil and the United States.

Kottak's other books include *The Past in the Present: History, Ecology and Cultural Variation in Highland Madagascar, Researching American Culture: A Guide for Student Anthropologists* (both University of Michigan Press) and *Madagascar: Society and History* (Carolina Academic Press).

Conrad Kottak's articles have appeared in academic journals including *American Anthropologist, Journal of Anthropological Research, American Ethnologist, Ethnology, Human Organization*, and *Luso-Brazilian Review*. He has also written for more popular journals, including *Transaction/SOCIETY, Natural History*, and *Psychology Today*.

Kottak is now directing research projects on "Ecological Awareness and Risk Perception in Brazil" and "An Integrated Approach to Deforestation in relation to Variant Land-Use Patterns, using Satellite Images" (in Madagascar). In summer 1990 he did an applied anthropological study directed at preserving biodiversity in Madagascar. In summers 1991 and 1992 he did research on ecological issues in Brazil.

The sixth editions of Kottak's texts *Anthropology: The Exploration of Human Diversity* and *Cultural Anthropology* are being published by McGraw-Hill in August, 1993.

Conrad Kottak appreciates comments about his textbook from professors and students. He can be easily reached at the following internet address:

Conrad.Kottak@um.cc.umich.edu

To my mother,
Mariana Kottak Roberts

CONTENTS IN BRIEF

CONTENTS

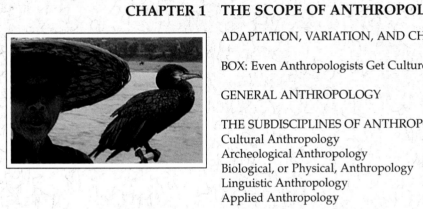

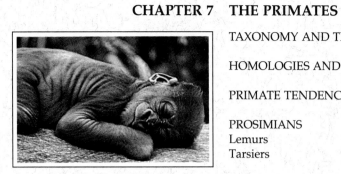

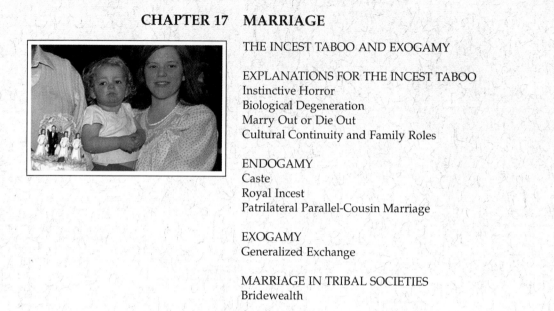

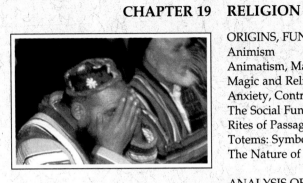

LIST OF BOXES

ISSUES BOXES

IN THE NEWS BOXES

PREFACE

Having done a substantial revision in the fifth edition of *Anthropology: The Exploration of Human Diversity*, I didn't plan to change as much as I ended up doing for the sixth. But the subfields of anthropology—reflecting the world itself—seem to change at an increasing pace with each new edition. I added two new chapters (and changed several old ones) to reflect recent changes in the world. These include the demise of the Soviet Union, the growing significance of multiculturalism in the United States and Canada, and anthropology's increasingly transnational, multilocal, and longitudinal perspectives.

I also made some organizational changes. I merged the two primates chapters into one (7). The food production chapter (10) now logically follows the discussion of the Mesolithic in Chapter 9. In this edition, the Gender chapter (18) comes after, rather than before, the chapters on Kinship and Descent (16) and Marriage (17). Some of the material in Applied Anthropology (17) has been moved to the Colonialism and Development chapter (18), and vice versa. Reorganization is intended to make the themes of globalization, cultural and ecological adaptation, change, variation, and diversity—unifying anthropology's subdisciplines—as clear as possible. (However, other approaches are also discussed and respected.)

A new feature in the sixth edition is the inclusion of several **In-the-News boxes** along with the **issues boxes** of previous editions. These In-the-News boxes describe recent discoveries (e.g., the Alpine "Iceman") or topics of anthropological relevance that are drawing increased public attention. Both kinds of boxes give students a chance to consider anthropology's relevance to today's multicultural world and to their own lives. Some boxes examine current events or debates. Others are personal accounts of field experiences, which add human feeling to the presentation of anthropology's subject matter. Many boxes illustrate a point by bringing in an example familiar to students from their enculturation or everyday experience.

All chapters have been updated. As with the fifth edition, the entire book was scanned into a computer, allowing me to scrutinize every word, sentence, paragraph, and caption—to attend to style, content, and organization. I have been able to respond to hundreds of suggestions from users and reviewers as I did for the last edition, which got favorable comments in terms of readability and interest. The result, I hope, is a well-organized, interesting, and "user-friendly" introduction to anthropology.

WHAT ABOUT CONTENT REVISION?

Besides **updating** in all chapters, there are two new chapters: "Ethnicity and Ethnic Relations" (4) and "Cultural Exchange and Survival" (24). To keep the book from getting too big, I had to make some cuts for new material and chapters. For example, the previous edition's two chapters on primates have been collapsed into one, and information from the chapter "The Future" has been moved to other chapters. Many chapters, especially the chapter on **Race** have **new sections**. These respond to users' and reviewers' suggestions and to my recent teaching experience.

Retained from the previous edition is the unifying world system perspective, and the related focus on social change and ecological adaptation (including the human dimension of global environmental change).

The special theme of this new edition is **Preserving Cultural Diversity in the Face of Globalization**. Globalization describes the accelerating links between nations and people in a world system connected economically, politically, and by modern media and transportation. I recognize and try to show how linkages in the modern world system have both enlarged and erased old boundaries and distinctions as described in standard anthropology textbooks. People travel more than ever, but migrants maintain their ties with home, so that they live multilocally. With so many people "in motion," the unit of anthropological study expands from the local community to the transnational diaspora.

Different degrees of destruction, domination, resistance, survival, adaptation, and modification of native cultures have followed contact between cultures and ethnic groups. Today's world is marked by ethnocide, genocide, and attacks on native landscapes and their traditional management systems. Indigenous peoples and traditional cultures have devised various strategies to resist attacks on their autonomy, identity, and livelihood. New forms of political mobilization and cultural expression have emerged from the interplay of local, regional, national, and international cultural forces. I examine new and changing social and cultural forms, contexts, identities, and creations throughout this book.

In considering ethnic and national cultural identities, Chapter 4 examines multiculturalism in North America and the revival of ethnic expression and conflict in eastern Europe and the former Soviet Union. Chapter 24 focuses on issues of cultural exchange and survival in a global culture driven by flows of people, technology, finance, images, information, and ideology. Chapter 24 shows that contemporary cultural diffusion is a creative process in which people and cultures survive by revising, reworking, resisting, or rejecting the messages they get from external systems.

This edition's theme, *Preserving Diversity in the Face of Globalization*, is illustrated by the new end paper map, illustrating global deforestation, a growing threat to the survival of indigenous peoples (and primates), especially in the tropics. Several chapters examine human dimensions of global environmental change and other environmental issues. There are discussions of endangered primates, ecocide, ethnocide, genocide, resistance and cultural survival (especially in Chapters 24).

I am pleased to have been one of the textbook authors chosen to participate in the **Gender in the Curriculum** Project of the American Anthropological Association. In that project I was paired with Yolanda Moses, who commented extensively on, and met with me to discuss, the treatment of gender issues in previous editions. Responding to suggestions and comments by Dr. Moses and others, gender issues are the focus of a separate Chapter (18) and also receive expanded treatment throughout the text.

The following **annotated outline** summarizes, by chapter, the main changes in *Anthropology: the Exploration of Human Diversity*, 6e:

Chapter
1. The Scope of Anthropology—updated.
2. Field Methods—organizational change: the discussion of ethnographic procedures has been expanded and placed before survey research.
3. Culture—greater attention to how individuals use culture creatively (see also Chapter 24).
4. **New chapter: ETHNICITY AND ETHNIC RELATIONS.**
   This chapter discusses models of ethnic relations, including multiculturalism in North America and the resurgence of nationalism and ethnic conflict in eastern Europe and the former Soviet Union.
   Major headings: ETHNIC GROUPS AND ETHNICITY; ETHNIC GROUPS, NATIONS, AND NATIONALITIES; ETHNIC TOLERANCE AND ACCOMMODATION; ROOTS OF ETHNIC CONFLICT.
   Sections on: Nationalities and Imagined Communities, Acculturation and Assimilation, The Plural Society and Pluralism, Multiculturalism and Ethnic Identity, Prejudice and Discrimination, Chips in the Mosaic, Aftermaths of Oppression.
   Boxes: A Handbook of Ethnic Interaction, Ethnic Nationalism Run Wild.
5. The Cultural Construction of Race—new discussion of racial categories and relations in **Japan**, including Koreans and *burakumin*; expanded discussion of the relation between

ethnic and racial categories in the **United States** and **Latin America**.

6. Evolution, Genetics, and Biological Adaptation—updated, with expanded discussion of adaptation.

7. The Primates—updating, new tables and charts; two chapters have been collapsed into one, which surveys primate classification, anatomy, adaptation, behavior, and society; box on endangered primates in the context of global deforestation.

8. Early Hominids—updated, new section on taphonomy, expanded discussion of dating techniques, including thermoluminescence (TL) and electron spin resonance (ESR); implications of recent Miocene ape discoveries.

9. The Emergence of Modern Humans—thoroughly updated; implications of new dating methods for understanding the relation between Neandertals and moderns; box on mitochondrial Eve; recent cave painting discoveries.

10. Early Food Production—updated; new evidence for early food production in Africa and Asia; the significance of the Alpine "Iceman."

11. Cultural Change and Adaptation—updated, new discussion of the authenticity of the hunter-gatherer mode of production and the position of foragers in the world system; new box on "The Great Forager Debate."

12. Bands and Tribes—updated.

13. Chiefdoms and States—updated with new tables.

14. The World System, Industrialism, and Stratification—updated, with new information on Indian caste.

15. Economic Systems—updated, with new discussion of Native American fishing rights.

16. Kinship and Descent—updated.

17. Marriage—updated, with new information on the role of love in marriage.

18. Gender Roles—updated; reorganized to give greater emphasis to gender stratification and variation in male and female status and activities.

19. Religion—updated.

20. Personality and Worldview—updated.

21. Language—updated, with In-The-News box on preserving linguistic diversity.

22. Applied Anthropology—updated and reorganized along with Chapter 23; expanded discussion of medical and urban anthropology (both academic and applied dimensions).

23. Colonialism and Development—updated and reorganized along with Chapter 22.

24. **New chapter: CULTURAL EXCHANGE AND SURVIVAL.**
This chapter discusses several examples of culture contact, mobility, exchange, resistance, and survival in the modern world system. It considers the implications of a changing, transnational world for cultural identities and for anthropology.
Major headings: PEOPLE IN MOTION; DOMINATION; RESISTANCE AND SURVIVAL; SYNCRETISMS, BLENDS, AND ACCOMMODATION; MAKING AND REMAKING CULTURE; THE CONTINUANCE OF DIVERSITY.
Sections on: Cultural Contact in Larger Systems; Development and Environmentalism; Religious Domination; Weapons of the Weak; Nongovernmental Organizations; Tribal and Human Rights; Cultural Imperialism, Stimulus Diffusion, and Creative Opposition; Indigenizing Popular Culture; A World System of Images; A Transnational Culture of Consumption.
Boxes: Voices of the Rainforest, Rigoberta Menchu.

Appendix

American Popular Culture—updated; new discussion of the creative role of the individual in interpreting popular culture.

WHAT ABOUT DESIGN, PEDAGOGY, AND STUDY AIDS?

The McGraw-Hill staff and I take suggestions by users and reviewers seriously in planning illustrations. We've increased the number of illustrations, choosing many new photos, most in color.

We've retained the pedagogical devices at the end of each chapter: **summary, study questions,** a **glossary** defining terms boldfaced in the chapter, and a list of **suggested reading**. In addition, a complete **bibliography** appears at the end of the book.

The new **instructor's manual** contains a list of **films**, organized by topic. The instructor's manual also contains a huge selection of multiple-choice, true-or-false, and essay questions. These are also available on diskette for use with the **computerized testmaker**.

Available for the first time with the sixth edition is a new **Ethnographic Case Studies** book written by Dr. Holly Peters-Golden. This supplement has case studies of ten of the cultures discussed in the textbook. Dr. Peters-Golden has taught introductory anthropology at the University of Michigan, using my textbook for several years.

ACKNOWLEDGMENTS

I thank many colleagues at McGraw-Hill. Sylvia Shepard, anthropology editor since 1992, and former developmental editor, read and commented on several chapters of the new edition—especially the new chapters. She helped me conceptualize the new chapters (and the entire sixth edition) and improve the organization, scope, and content of all the chapters she read. I thank Sylvia for her help in planning and realizing both the fifth and sixth editions. Phil Butcher and Barry Fetterolf also provided valuable input in planning the fifth and sixth editions. Barry, who has been associated with this book since its first edition, heads McGraw-Hill's social sciences publishing.

Bob Greiner did his usual conscientious, considerate, and efficient job as project editor. Without him I might not have met my deadlines and kept on schedule. It's been a pleasure to work again with Barbara Salz, photo researcher, and Kathy Bendo, photo manager. I also thank Marci Nugent, for her copyediting; Joan O'Connor, for conceiving and executing the attractive design; Fred Schulte, for shepherding the manuscript through production; and Sally Constable, marketing project manager. I am especially grateful to the McGraw-Hill sales representatives who wore their ribbons proudly and made sure instructors get to sample *Anthropology: The Exploration of Human Diversity*.

I thank the following reviewers of the fifth edition and the sixth edition as it progressed: Eric J. Bailey, Indiana University; William O. Beeman, Brown University; Edward Bendix, CUNY, Hunter College; Thomas W. Collins, Memphis State University; Linda J. DiLaura, Wayne State University; Chantal Ferraro, CUNY, Flushing; James G. Flanagan, Uni-

versity of Southern Mississippi; Brian L. Foster, Arizona State University; John W. Fox, Baylor University; David W. Frayer, University of Kansas; Luther Gerlach, University of Minnesota; Dru C. Gladney, University of California, Los Angeles; Robert Bates Graber, Northeast Missouri State University; Nancy L. Hamblin, University of Nebraska, Lincoln; Dale Hutchinson, East Carolina University; H. Edwin Jackson, University of Southern Mississippi; Barbara K. Larson, University of New Hampshire; Nancy B. Leis, Central Michigan University; William Leons, University of Toledo; Patrick McKim, California Polytechnic University; Beth Misner, University of Georgia; Richard H. Moore, Ohio State University; Alan J. Osborn, University of Nebraska, Lincoln; Rene Peron, Santa Rosa Junior College; Susan J. Rasmussen, University of Houston; Alan Rogers, University of Utah; John Alan Ross, Eastern Washington University; Lynn A. Schepartz, University of Michigan; Mary Jo Schneider, University of Arkansas; Andrei Simic, University of Southern California; Marcella H. Sorg, University of Maine; Leslie E. Sponsel, University of Hawaii at Manoa; Norman E. Whitten, Jr., University of Illinois at Urbana-Champaign; and Linda Wolfe, East Carolina University.

I again extend my special gratitude to Yolanda Moses, who worked closely with me for the AAA Gender in the Curriculum Project. Professor Thomas Collins of Memphis State University provided me with the prototype for Table 1.1. I thank all my colleagues who use the book and send me their comments, corrections, and suggestions—personally or through the sales representatives. Anyone—student or teacher—with access to email (internet) can now send me messages and suggestions at the following address:
Conrad.Kottak@um.cc.umich.edu

As always, my wife, children, and mother offered support and inspiration during the preparation of a new edition. I renew my dedication of this book to my mother, Mariana Kottak Roberts, for kindling my interest in the human condition, reading and commenting on what I write, and for the insights about people and society she continues to provide.

After thirty years in anthropology and twenty-five years of teaching, I have benefitted from the knowledge, help, and advice of so many friends, colleagues, teaching assistants, and students that I can no longer fit all their names into a short preface.

I hope they know who they are and accept my thanks.

Annually since 1968 I've taught Anthropology 101 (Introduction to Anthropology) to a class of 500–600 students, with the help of 8-12 teaching assistants each time. Feedback from students and teaching assistants keeps me up-to-date on the interests, needs, and views of the people for whom this book is written. I continue to believe that effective textbooks have to be based in enthusiasm and in practice—in the enjoyment of one's own teaching experience. I hope that this product of my experience will be helpful to others.

Conrad Phillip Kottak

CHAPTER 1

THE SCOPE OF ANTHROPOLOGY

1

That's just human nature." "People are pretty much the same all over the world." Such opinions, which we hear in conversations, in the mass media, and in a hundred scenes in daily life, promote the erroneous idea that people in other countries have the same desires, feelings, and aspirations that we do. Such statements proclaim that because people are essentially the same, they are eager to receive the ideas, beliefs, institutions, values, practices, and products of an expansive North American culture. Often this assumption turns out to be wrong.

Anthropology offers a broader view—a distinctive comparative, crosscultural perspective. Most people think that anthropologists study fossils and nonindustrial cultures, and they do. My research has taken me to remote villages in Brazil and Madagascar, a large island off the southeast coast of Africa. In Brazil I sailed with fishermen in simple sailboats on Atlantic waters. Among Madagascar's Betsileo people I worked in rice fields and took part in ceremonies in which I entered tombs to rewrap the corpses of decaying ancestors.

However, anthropology is much more than the study of nonindustrial peoples. It is a comparative science that examines all societies, ancient and modern, simple and complex. Most of the other social sciences tend to focus on a single society, usually an industrial nation such as the United States or Canada. Anthropology, however, offers a unique cross-cultural perspective, constantly comparing the customs of one society with those of others. Exemplifying cross-cultural comparison and anthropology's increasing focus on modern society is my own recent research on the cultural context and impact of television in the United States and Brazil (Kottak 1990).

To become a cultural anthropologist, one normally does ethnographic field work. This usually entails spending a year or more in another culture, living with the local people and learning about their customs. No matter how much the anthropologist discovers about that culture, he or she remains an alien there. That experience of alienation has a profound impact. Having learned to respect other customs and beliefs, anthropologists can never forget that there is a wider world. There are normal ways of thinking and acting other than our own.

ADAPTATION, VARIATION, AND CHANGE

Humans are the most adaptable animals in the world. In the Andes of South America, people awaken in villages 17,500 feet above sea level and then trek 1,500 feet higher to work in tin mines. Tribes in the Australian desert worship animals and discuss philosophy. People survive malaria in the tropics. Men have walked on the moon. The model of the *Starship Enterprise* in Washington's Smithsonian Institution symbolizes the desire to seek out new life and civilizations, to boldly go where no one has gone before. Wishes to know the unknown, control the uncontrollable, and bring order to chaos find expression among all peoples. Flexibility and adaptability are basic human attributes, and human diversity is the subject matter of anthropology.

Students are often surprised by the breadth of anthropology, which is a uniquely **holistic** science. It studies the whole of the human condition: past, present, and future; biology, society, language, and culture. People share **society**—organized life in groups—with other animals. Culture, however, is distinctly human. **Cultures** are traditions and customs, transmitted through learning, that govern the beliefs and behavior of the people exposed to them. Children *learn* these traditions by growing up in a particular society.

Cultural traditions include customs and opinions, developed over the generations, about proper and improper behavior. Cultural traditions answer such questions as: How should we do things? How do we interpret the world? How do we tell right from wrong? A culture produces consistencies in behavior and thought in a given society.

The most critical element of cultural traditions is their transmission through learning rather than biological inheritance. Culture is not itself biological, but it rests on hominid biology. (**Hominids** are members of the zoological family that includes fossil and living humans.) For more than a million years, hominids have had at least some of the biological capacities on which culture depends. These abilities are to learn, to think symbolically, to use language, and to employ tools and other cultural features in organizing their lives and adapting to their environments.

Bound neither by time nor by space, anthropology ponders and confronts major questions of human existence. By examining ancient bones and tools, anthropologists solve the mysteries of hominid origins. When did our own ancestors separate from those remote great-aunts and great-uncles whose descendants are the apes? Where and when did *Homo sapiens* originate? How has our species changed? What are we now and where are we going? How have changes in culture and society influenced biological change? Our genus, *Homo,* has been changing for more than 1 million years. Cultural and biological adaptation and evolution have been interrelated and complementary, and humans continue to adapt both biologically and culturally.

Human **adaptation** (the process by which organisms cope with environmental stresses) involves an interplay between culture and biology. As an illustration, consider four different ways in which humans may cope with low oxygen pressure. Pressurized airplane cabins equipped with oxygen masks illustrate *cultural* (technological) adaptation. Natives of highland Peru seem to have certain *genetic* advantages for life at very high altitudes, where air pressure is low. However, human adaptation to high altitudes is not limited to culture and genes.

People who have grown up at a high altitude are physiologically more efficient there than are genetically similar people who have not. Human biological plasticity (the ability to change) permits such *long-term physiological* adaptation during growth and development. We also have the capacity for *immediate physiological* adaptation. Thus, lowlanders arriving in the highlands immediately increase their breathing rate, often doubling their usual rate at sea level. Hyperventilation increases the oxygen in their arteries and lungs, and, as the pulse also increases, blood reaches their tissues more rapidly. All these varied adaptive responses—cultural and biological, voluntary and involuntary, conscious and unconscious—are directed at a single goal: increasing the supply of oxygen in the human organism.

Much of the diversity we see in cultures, as in nature, reflects adaptation to varied environments and circumstances. People creatively manipulate their environment; they are not just determined by it. Recognizing this, John Bennett (1969, p. 19) has defined cultural adaptation as "the problem-solving, creative or coping element in human behavior" as people get and use resources and solve the immediate problems confronting them. This is the first dimension of adaptive behavior: It involves "goal-satisfaction: if coping is successful, the people realize their objectives" (Bennett 1969, p. 13). In a modern market economy these objectives include production, income, and consumption wants or needs.

Besides satisfaction of such *individual* goals, a second and equally important dimension of cultural adaptation is conservation of resources. "An economy that realizes economic gain but does so at the cost of exhausting or abusing its resources may be adapting in one dimension (the first) but can be said to be *maladaptive* [emphasis added] along the other." In other words, behavior that benefits individuals may harm the environment and threaten the group's long-term survival. Societies "must attempt to balance conservation of resources against economic success if they hope for a permanent or indefinite settlement [of their environment]" (Bennett 1969, p. 13).

As hominid history has unfolded, social and cultural means of adaptation have become increasingly important. In this process, humans have devised diverse ways of coping with the range of environments and social systems (local, regional, national, and global) they have occupied in time and space. The rate of cultural change has accelerated, particularly during the past 10,000 years. For millions of years, hunting and gathering of nature's bounty—*foraging*—was the sole basis of hominid subsistence. However, it took only a few thousand years for **food production** (cultivation of plants and domestication of animals), which originated in the Middle East 10,000 to 12,000 years ago, to supplant foraging in most areas. People started producing their own food, planting crops and stockbreeding animals, rather than simply taking what nature had to offer.

Between 6000 and 5000 B.P. (before the present), the first civilizations arose in the Middle East. (**Civilizations, nation-states,** or, most simply, **states** are complex societies with a central government and social classes.) Much more recently, industrial production has profoundly influenced people throughout the world. Today's global economy and communications link all contemporary people, di-

EVEN ANTHROPOLOGISTS GET CULTURE SHOCK

I first lived in Arembepe (Brazil) during the (North American) summer of 1962. That was between my junior and senior years at New York City's Columbia College, where I was majoring in anthropology. I went to Arembepe as a participant in a now-defunct program designed to provide undergraduates with experience doing ethnography—firsthand study of an alien society's culture and social life.

Brought up in one culture, intensely curious about others, anthropologists nevertheless experience culture shock, particularly on the first field trip. *Culture shock* refers to the whole set of feelings about being in an alien setting, and the ensuing reactions. It is a chilly, creepy feeling of alienation, of being without some of the most ordinary, trivial (and therefore basic) cues of one's culture of origin.

As I planned my departure for Brazil in 1962, I could not know just how naked I would feel without the cloak of my own language and culture. My sojourn in Arembepe would be my first trip outside the United States. I was an urban boy who had grown up in Atlanta, Georgia, and New York City. I had little experi-

ence with rural life in my own country, none with Latin America, and I had received only minimal training in the Portuguese language.

New York City direct to Salvador, Bahia, Brazil. Just a brief stopover in Rio de Janeiro; a longer visit would be a reward at the end of field work. As our propjet approached tropical Salvador, I couldn't believe the whiteness of the sand. "That's not snow, is it?" I remarked to a fellow field team member. . . .

My first impressions of Bahia were of smells—alien odors of ripe and decaying mangoes, bananas, and passion fruit—and of swatting ubiquitous fruit flies I had never seen before, although I had read extensively about their reproductive behavior in genetics classes. There were strange concoctions of rice, black beans, and gelatinous gobs of unidentifiable meats and floating pieces of skin. Coffee was strong and sugar crude, and every tabletop had containers for toothpicks and manioc (cassava) flour, to sprinkle, like Parmesan cheese, on anything one might eat. I remember oatmeal soup and a slimy stew of beef tongue in tomatoes. At one meal a disintegrating fish head, eyes still attached, but barely, stared

up at me as the rest of its body floated in a bowl of bright orange palm oil. . . .

I only vaguely remember my first day in Arembepe. Unlike ethnographers who have studied remote tribes in the tropical forests of interior South America or the highlands of Papua–New Guinea, I did not have to hike or ride a canoe for days to arrive at my field site. Arembepe was not isolated relative to such places, only relative to every other place *I* had ever been. . . .

I do recall what happened when we arrived. There was no formal road into the village. Entering through southern Arembepe, vehicles simply threaded their way around coconut trees, following tracks left by automobiles that had passed previously. A crowd of children had heard us coming, and they pursued our car through the village streets until we parked in front of our house, near the central square. Our first few days in Arembepe were spent with children following us everywhere. For weeks we had few moments of privacy. Children watched our every move through our living room window. Occasionally one made an incomprehensible

rectly or indirectly, in the modern world system. People in local settings must cope with forces generated by progressively larger systems—region, nation, and world. The study of such contemporary adaptations generates new challenges for anthropology: "The cultures of world peoples need to be constantly *re*discovered as these people reinvent them in changing historical circumstances" (Marcus and Fischer 1986, p. 24).

Over the course of human history, major innovations have spread at the expense of earlier ones. Each economic revolution has had social and cultural repercussions. This book will examine behav-

ior and institutions, beliefs, customs, and practices associated with several economic systems: foraging, food production, industrialism, and the modern world system.

GENERAL ANTHROPOLOGY

The academic discipline of anthropology, also known as **general anthropology,** includes four main subdisciplines: sociocultural, archeological, biological, and linguistic anthropology. (From here on, I will use the shorter term *cultural anthropology*

An ethnographer at work. During a 1980 visit, the author, Conrad Kottak, catches up on the news in Arembepe, a coastal community in Bahia state, northeastern Brazil, that he has been studying since 1962.

remark. Usually they just stood there. Sometimes they would groom one another's hair, eating the lice they found. . . .

The sounds, sensations, sights, smells, and tastes of life in northeastern Brazil, and in Arembepe, slowly grew familiar. I gradually accepted the fact that the only toilet tissue available at a reasonable price had almost the texture of sandpaper. I grew accustomed to this world without Kleenex, in which globs of mucus habitually drooped from the noses of village children whenever a cold passed through Arembepe. A world where, seemingly without effort, women with gracefully swaying hips carried 18-liter kerosene cans of water on their heads, where boys sailed kites and sported at catching houseflies in their bare hands, where old women smoked pipes, storekeepers offered *cachaça* (common rum) at nine in the morning, and men played dominoes on lazy afternoons when there was no fishing. I was visiting a world where human life was oriented toward water—the sea, where men fished, and the lagoon, where women communally washed clothing, dishes, and their own bodies.

This description is adapted from my ethnographic study *Assault on Paradise: Social Change in a Brazilian Village*, 2nd ed. (New York: McGraw-Hill, 1992).

as a synonym for "sociocultural anthropology.") Most American anthropologists, myself included, specialize in cultural anthropology. However, most are also familiar with the basics of the other subdisciplines. Major departments of anthropology usually include representatives of each.

There are historical reasons for the inclusion of four subdisciplines in a single field. American anthropology arose a century ago out of concern for the history and cultures of the native populations of North America ("American Indians"). Interest in the origins and diversity of Native Americans brought together studies of customs, social life, language, and physical traits. Such a unified anthropology did not develop in Europe, where the subdisciplines tend to exist separately.

There are also logical reasons for the unity of American anthropology. Each subdiscipline considers variations in time and space (that is, in different geographic areas). Cultural and archeological anthropologists study (among many other topics) changes in social life and customs. Biological anthropologists examine changes in physical form. Linguistic anthropologists may reconstruct the basics of ancient languages by studying modern ones. This concern with variation in time may be

Industrial production has profoundly influenced people throughout the world. Today's global economy and communications link all contemporary people, directly or indirectly, in the modern world system. Here children in rural Niger are fascinated by a solar-powered TV.

stated differently: An interest in **evolution** unifies anthropology's subdisciplines. Defined simply, evolution is change in form over generations. Charles Darwin called it "descent with modification."

The subdisciplines influence each other as anthropologists talk, read professional books and journals, and associate in professional organizations. General anthropology explores the basics of human biology, psychology, society, and culture and considers their interrelationships. Anthropologists share certain key assumptions. One is that sound conclusions about "human nature" can't be drawn from a single cultural tradition.

We often hear "nature-nurture" and "genetics-environment" questions. For example, consider gender differences. Do male and female capacities, attitudes, and behavior reflect biological or cultural variation? Are there universal emotional and intellectual contrasts between the sexes? Are females less aggressive than males? Is male dominance a human

Cross-cultural comparison shows that many differences between the sexes arise from cultural training rather than biology. Here men in Kenya do the laundry in the river.

universal? By examining diverse cultures, anthropology shows that many contrasts between men and women arise from cultural training rather than from biology.

Anthropologists also use their knowledge of biological and cultural diversity to evaluate assertions about intellectual differences. They have found no evidence for biologically determined contrasts in intelligence between rich and poor, black and white, or men and women.

Anthropology is not a science of the exotic carried on by scholars in ivory towers but a discipline with a lot to tell the public. One of its contributions is its broadening, liberating role in a college education. Anthropology's foremost professional organization, the American Anthropological Association, has formally acknowledged a public service role by recognizing a fifth subdiscipline, **applied anthropology**—the application of anthropological data, perspectives, theory, and methods to identify, assess, and solve contemporary social problems. More and more anthropologists from the four main subdisciplines now work in such "applied" areas as public health, family planning, and economic development.

THE SUBDISCIPLINES OF ANTHROPOLOGY

Cultural Anthropology

Cultural anthropologists study society and culture, describing and explaining social and cultural similarities and differences. In considering diversity in time and space, anthropologists must distinguish between the universal, the generalized, and the particular. Certain biological, psychological, social, and cultural features are *universal*—shared by all human populations. Others are merely *generalized*—common to several but not all human groups. Still others are *particular*—not shared at all.

Cultural anthropology has two aspects: ethnography (based on field work) and ethnology (based on cross-cultural comparison). **Ethnography** provides an "ethnopicture" of a particular group, society, or culture. During ethnographic field work the ethnographer gathers data, which he or she organizes, describes, analyzes, and interprets to build and present the *ethnopicture* (e.g., a book, article, or

film). Traditionally, ethnographers have lived in small communities and studied local behavior, beliefs, customs, social life, economic activities, politics, and religion.

The resulting anthropological perspective often differs radically from that of economics or political science. Those disciplines focus on national and official organizations and often on elites. However, the groups that anthropologists have traditionally studied have usually been relatively poor and powerless. Ethnographers often observe discriminatory practices directed toward such people, who experience food shortages, dietary deficiencies, and other aspects of poverty. The anthropological perspective is different—not necessarily better. Political scientists study programs that national planners develop, and anthropologists see how these programs work on the local level. Both perspectives are necessary to understand human life in the late twentieth century.

Anthropologists recognize that cultures are not isolated. As Franz Boas (1940/1966) noted many years ago, contact between neighboring tribes has always existed and has extended over enormous areas. A *world-system perspective* recognizes that many local cultural features reflect the economic and political position that a society occupies in a larger system. "Human populations construct their cultures in interaction with one another, and not in isolation" (Wolf 1982, p. ix). Villagers increasingly participate in regional, national, and world events.

There are many sources of exposure to external forces, including mass media, migration, and modern transportation. City and nation increasingly invade local communities in the guise of tourists, development agents, government and religious officials, and political candidates. Such **linkages,** or interconnections, are prominent components of regional, national, and international systems of politics, economics, and information. These larger systems increasingly affect the people and places that anthropology has traditionally studied. The study of such linkages and systems is a prominent part of the subject matter of modern anthropology.

Ethnology, the other aspect of cultural anthropology, examines and compares the results of ethnography—the data gathered in different societies. Ethnologists try to identify and explain cultural differences and similarities, to distinguish between universality, generality, and particularity (see the chapter "Culture"). Ethnology gets data for comparison not just from ethnography but also from the other subdisciplines, particularly from archeological anthropology, which reconstructs the social systems of the past.

Archeological Anthropology

Archeological anthropology (more simply, "archeology") reconstructs, describes, and interprets human behavior and cultural patterns through material remains. Archeologists are best known for studying **prehistory** (the period before the invention of writing less than 6,000 years ago). However, archeologists also study historical and even living cultures. Through a research project begun in 1973 in Tucson, Arizona, for example, archeologist William Rathje has learned much about contemporary life by studying modern garbage. The value of "garbology," as Rathje calls it, is that it provides "evidence of what people did, not what they think they did, what they think they should have done, or what the interviewer thinks they should have done" (Harrison, Rathje, and Hughes 1992, p. 103). What people report can contrast strongly with their real behavior as revealed by garbology. For example, the garbologists discovered that the three Tucson neighborhoods that reported the lowest beer consumption had the highest number of discarded beer cans

per household (Podolefsky and Brown, eds. 1992, p. 100).

Using material remains as primary data, and informed by ethnographic knowledge and ethnological theory, archeologists analyze cultural processes and patterns. Several kinds of remains interest archeologists. Garbage tells stories about consumption and activities. Wild and domesticated grains have different characteristics which allow archeologists to distinguish between gathering and cultivation. Examination of animal bones reveals the ages of slaughtered animals and provides other information useful in determining whether species were wild or domesticated.

Analyzing such data, archeologists answer several questions about ancient economies. Did the group being studied get its meat from hunting, or did it domesticate and breed animals, killing only those of a certain age and sex? Did plant food come from wild plants or from sowing, tending, and harvesting crops? At sites where people live or have lived, archeologists find **artifacts,** material items that humans have manufactured or modified. Did the residents make, trade for, or buy particular items? Were raw materials available locally? If not, where did they come from? From such information, archeologists reconstruct patterns of production, trade, and consumption.

Archeologists have spent much time studying

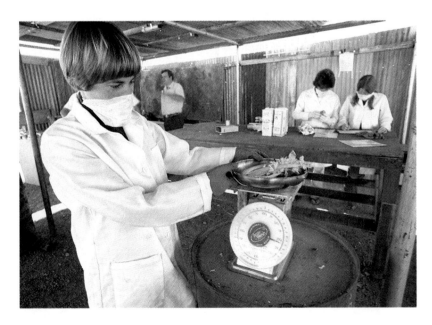

Archeological anthropology reconstructs, describes, and interprets human behavior through material remains. Besides prehistory, archeologists also study living cultures. In Tucson, University of Arizona archeologists learn about contemporary life by analyzing recent garbage.

potsherds, fragments of earthenware. Potsherds are more durable than many other artifacts, such as textiles and wood. The pottery types at a site can suggest its technological complexity. The quantity of pottery fragments allows estimation of population size and density. The discovery that potters used materials that were not locally available suggests systems of trade. Similarities in manufacture and decoration at different sites may be proof of cultural connections. Groups with similar pots may be historically related. Perhaps they shared common cultural ancestors, traded with each other, or belonged to the same political system.

Many archeologists examine paleoecology. **Ecology** is the study of interrelationships among living things in an environment. The organisms and environment together constitute an **ecosystem,** a patterned arrangement of energy flows and exchanges. Human ecology, or **cultural ecology,** studies ecosystems that include people, focusing on the ways in which human use "of nature influences and is influenced by social organization and cultural values" (Bennett 1969, pp. 10–11). **Paleoecology** looks at the ecosystems of the past. In studying either past or present societies, an ecological approach examines interrelationships among population, culturally styled needs and wants, the division of labor, technology, methods of production, and ways of dividing natural resources among those who need and use them. An ecological analysis cannot be limited to local production but must also study how local people react to informational and economic inputs from external sources.

In addition to reconstructing ecological patterns, archeologists infer cultural evolution, for example, from changes in the size and type of sites and the distance between them. A city develops in a region where only towns, villages, and hamlets existed a century earlier. The number of settlement levels (city, town, village, hamlet) is a measure of social complexity. Buildings offer clues about political and religious features. Special-purpose structures such as temples and pyramids suggest that an ancient society had a central authority capable of marshaling team labor, slave or free. The presence or absence of certain structures reveals differences in function between settlements. For example, some towns were ceremonial centers with prominent architecture. Others were burial sites; still others were farming communities.

Archeologists also document cultural patterns and processes by *excavating* (digging through a succession of levels) at particular sites. In a given area, through time, particular settlements may change in terms of form and purpose, as may the connections between settlements. Excavation can document changes in economic, social, and political activities.

To learn about prehistoric populations—those with no written records—archeology is essential. Comparison of archeological sequences in different areas has enabled anthropologists to formulate laws of development. For example, certain environments or economies correlate with particular types of social groups or political systems. Comparative archeology and ethnography both contribute to the understanding of social processes.

Biological, or Physical, Anthropology

The subject matter of **biological,** or **physical, anthropology** is human biological diversity in time and space. A combination of genetic and environmental features produces much of this variation. Relevant environmental stresses include heat and cold, moisture, sunlight, altitude, and disease. The focus on human variation unites five special interests within biological anthropology:

1. Hominid evolution as revealed by the fossil record (**paleoanthropology**)
2. Human genetics
3. Human growth and development
4. Human biological plasticity (the body's ability to cope with stresses, such as heat, cold, and altitude)
5. The biology, evolution, behavior, and social life of monkeys, apes, and other nonhuman primates

These interests link physical anthropology to other fields: biology, zoology, geology, anatomy, physiology, medicine, and public health. **Osteology**—the study of bones—helps paleoanthropologists, who examine skulls, teeth, and bones, to identify hominid ancestors and chart changes in anatomy. Biological anthropologists collaborate with archeologists in reconstructing biological and cultural aspects of human evolution. Fossils and tools are often found together. Tools suggest the

A paleoanthropologist—the late Louis B. Leakey—at work. The Leakey family—Louis, Mary, and their son, Richard—working with African collaborators, have made many important hominid fossil finds in East Africa.

habits, customs, and life styles of the hominids who used them.

More than a century ago, Charles Darwin noticed that the variety that exists within any population permits some individuals (those with the favored, or adaptive, characteristics) to do better than others at surviving and reproducing. Genetics, which developed later, enlightens us about the causes and transmission of this variety. However, it isn't just genes that cause variety. During any individual's lifetime, the environment works along with heredity to develop biological features. For example, people with a genetic tendency to be tall will be shorter if they are poorly nourished during childhood. Thus biological anthropology investigates the influence of environment (nutrition, altitude, temperature, and disease) on the body as it develops. As noted earlier, human biological and cultural evolution

have been interrelated and complementary, and humans continue to adapt both biologically and culturally. This is why both subdisciplines are studied within general anthropology.

Biological anthropology (along with zoology) also includes **primatology.** The **primates** include our closest relatives—apes and monkeys. Primatologists study their biology, evolution, behavior, and social life, often in their natural environments. Primatology assists paleoanthropology, because many anthropologists believe that primate behavior sheds light on early hominid behavior (and thus on our origins) and on issues of human nature and human universals.

Linguistic Anthropology

We don't know (and probably never will) when hominids began to speak. However, well-developed, grammatically complex languages have existed for thousands of years. **Linguistic anthropology** offers additional illustration of anthropology's interest in comparison, variation, and change. Linguistic anthropologists study language in its social and cultural context, in space and through time. Some make inferences about universal features of language, linking them to uniformities in the human brain. Others reconstruct ancient languages by comparing their contemporary descendants and in so doing make discoveries about history. Still others study linguistic differences to discover varied perceptions and patterns of thought in a multitude of cultures. The study of linguistic variation in its social context is called *sociolinguistics.* Sociolinguists examine diversity in a single language to show how speech reflects social differences. Linguistic techniques are also useful to ethnographers because they permit the rapid learning of unwritten languages.

Descriptive linguistics studies sounds, grammar, and meaning in particular languages. *Historical* linguistics considers variation in time, such as the changes in sounds, grammar, and vocabulary between Middle English (spoken in Chaucer's time) and modern English. There is also variation among the speakers of any language at any given time. One reason for variation is geography, as in regional dialects and accents. Linguistic variation is also associated with social divisions. Examples include the bilingualism of ethnic groups and speech patterns associated with particular social classes. Linguistic and cultural anthropologists collaborate in studying links between language and other aspects of culture.

Applied Anthropology

In its most general sense, applied anthropology includes any use of the knowledge and/or techniques of the four subdisciplines to identify, assess, and solve practical problems. Because of anthropology's breadth, it has many applications. For example, the growing field of **medical anthropology** considers the sociocultural context and implications of disease and illness. Cross-cultural research shows that perceptions of good and bad health, along with actual health threats and problems, vary among cultures. Different societies and ethnic groups recognize different illnesses, symptoms, and causes and have developed different health-care systems and treatment strategies. Medical anthropologists are both biological and cultural, and both theoretical and applied. Applied medical anthropologists have, for example, served as cultural interpreters in public health programs, which must fit into local culture and be accepted by local people.

Other applied anthropologists work for development agencies, assessing the social and cultural features that influence economic development and change. Anthropologists are experts on local cultures. As such, they often can identify specific social conditions and local needs that will influence the failure or success of development schemes. Planners in Washington or Paris often know little about, say, the labor necessary for rice cultivation in rural Africa. Forecasts and estimates of project success are often unrealistic if no one consults an anthropologist familiar with the rural scene. Development funds are often wasted if an anthropologist is not asked to identify the local political figures whose support for a program is critical. Such considerations have led development organizations to include anthropologists as well as agronomists, economists, veterinarians, geologists, engineers, and health specialists on planning teams.

Anthropologists also apply their skills in studying the human dimension of environmental degradation (e.g., deforestation, pollution) and global climate change. Anthropologists examine how the environment influences humans and how human activities affect the biosphere and the earth itself. Applied anthropologists also work in North America. Garbologists help the Environmental Protection Agency, the paper industry, and the packaging and trade associations. Many archeologists now work in cultural resource management—applying their knowledge and skills to interpret, inventory, and preserve archeological, historic, and paleontological resources for local, state (provincial), and federal governments. Forensic (physical) anthropologists work with the police, medical examiners, and the courts to identify victims of crimes and accidents. From skeletal remains they determine age, sex, size,

Both biological and cultural anthropologists contribute to the growing field of medical anthropology. Here Richard Wrangham and Robert Bailey watch Elizabeth Ross measure an Efe "pygmy" man in the Ituri forest of Zaire, Central Africa. This team research investigated Efe health and nutrition, along with social, cultural, economic, and ecological dimensions of Efe life.

Applied anthropology is the use of anthropological data, perspectives, theory, and methods to identify, assess, and solve contemporary problems that affect humans, such as deforestation. One threat to forests is charcoal production, to provide fuel for rapidly growing Third World cities. Here charcoal is sold along a road near one of Madagascar's burgeoning urban centers.

race, and number of victims. Applied physical anthropologists link injury patterns to design flaws in aircraft and vehicles.

Ethnographers have influenced social policy by showing that strong kin ties exist in city neighborhoods whose social organization was previously considered "fragmented" or "pathological." Suggestions for improvements in the education system emerge from ethnographic studies of classrooms and surrounding communities. Linguistic anthropologists show the influence of dialect differences on classroom learning. In general, applied anthropology aims to find humane and effective ways of helping the people whom anthropologists have traditionally studied. Table 1.1 summarizes the relationships among the subdisciplines of anthropology.

ANTHROPOLOGY AND THE OTHER HUMAN SCIENCES

As mentioned above, the basic difference between anthropology and the other fields that study people is *holism*, anthropology's unique blend of biological, social, cultural, linguistic, historical, and contemporary perspectives. Paradoxically, while distinguishing anthropology, this breadth also links it to many other disciplines. Techniques used to date fossils and artifacts have come to anthropology from physics, chemistry, and geology. Because plant and

animal remains are found with human bones and artifacts, anthropologists collaborate with botanists, zoologists, and paleontologists.

Cultural anthropology has ties to the other social sciences and the humanities. Thus contemporary sociology is experiencing an "opening to culture." Interpretive anthropology (Geertz 1973, 1983), which approaches cultures as texts whose meaning the anthropologist must decipher, links anthropology to the humanities and to history. More and more historians are interpreting historical narratives as texts, paying attention to their cultural meaning and the social context of their creation. Interdisciplinary collaboration is a hallmark of contemporary academic life, with ready borrowing of ideas and methods between disciplines (Geertz 1980). This is especially true for anthropology.

Cultural Anthropology and Sociology

Cultural anthropology and sociology share an interest in social relations, organization, and behavior. However, important differences between these disciplines arose from the kinds of societies each traditionally studied. Initially sociologists focused on the industrial West; anthropologists, on nonindustrial societies. Different methods of data collection and analysis emerged to deal with those different kinds of societies. To study large-scale, complex nations, sociologists came to rely on questionnaires and other means of gathering masses of quantifiable

Table 1.1 The Subfields of Anthropology: The Comparative Study of Humanity in Time and Space. *Anthropology studies variation in time and space in humans and our nearest relatives (the other primates). Starting on the **left** side of this table, we see that all the subfields of anthropology study variation in time. Biological anthropologists study primate and human evolution (paleoanthropology). Archeologists generally study the past (although archeological techniques—garbology, for example—can be used to study the present). Cultural anthropologists often study ethnohistory, using written records such as archives and oral historical accounts, to reconstruct the history of a social group. Historical linguists study change in language(s) over time.*

*The **right** side of this table shows that the subfields of anthropology also study variation in space. Biological anthropologists study the physical and social characteristics of nonhuman primates. Biological anthropologists also study contemporary human biological variation, including genetics and physiological adaptation. Sociocultural anthropologists do ethnographic studies of different cultures and social groups. Linguistic anthropologists study variation in language and speech in social and cultural contexts.*

*The **center** of this table represents the comparative and theoretical aspect of anthropology. Thus biological anthropologists use the modern synthetic theory of evolution, combining known principles of evolution and genetics, to understand biological variation in time and space. Ethnology examines and generalizes about social and cultural similarities and differences in time and space. Useful data for ethnological comparison and theory have come from ethnography, ethnohistory, archeology, and linguistics. Linguistic anthropologists consider features of language, as they vary (or do not vary) in time and space. Languages may be compared in order to reconstruct relationships between ancient and modern languages, or universal features shared by all languages.*

Some fields, like medical anthropology, have both biological and sociocultural components (as well as time-space dimensions). Also, although Table 1.1 does not show this, anthropology includes both research and application. Applied anthropology is the use of data, perspectives, theory, and methods from general anthropology and all its subfields to identify, assess, and solve problems that affect humans.

Time	Comparison/Theory	Space
Primate evolution	Evolutionary theory	Primatology
		Human genetics
Paleoanthropology		Human physiological adaptation
Biological Dimension (above)		
Co-evolution of culture and disease		Medical anthropology
Cultural Dimension (below)		
Archeology	Ethnology	Ethnography
Ethnohistory		
Historical linguistics	Comparative linguistics Linguistic universals	Descriptive linguistics Language and culture Sociolinguistics

SOURCE: Developed from a prototype provided by Thomas Collins, Professor of Anthropology, Memphis State University.

MARGARET MEAD: PUBLIC ANTHROPOLOGIST

Margaret Mead (1901–1978), the most famous anthropologist who ever lived, was one of my teachers at Columbia University. A full-time staff member at the American Museum of Natural History (also in New York City), Mead taught as an adjunct professor at Columbia for many years.

In winter 1962 I took Mead's course on the peoples and cultures of the Pacific. It was a large lecture, held at night. Mead made dramatic entrances and usually brought along an entourage of admirers. By that time Mead, a short woman with a commanding presence, had taken to walking with a shepherd's staff. Almost as tall as she, the forked rod made her resemble a mature Bo Peep.

Mead was known as a well-organized ethnographer. For example, she used a color-coded note system; into the field she took packs of large index cards of various colors. She used specific colors for notes on different topics, such as economics, religion, and social organization. Her meticulous methods for field work extended to everything she did. Mead's students had to fill out 6- by 8-inch index cards and attach photos. She wanted information on their background and interests, including their previous course work in anthropology. Mead and I never knew each other well. However, she used the information from my class card to write me letters of recommendation for graduate school and fellowships.

During her entire professional life Mead was a public anthropologist. She wrote for social scientists, the educated public, and the popular press. She had a column in *Redbook* and often appeared with Johnny Carson on *The Tonight Show*. Mead wrote several popular books about culture and personality (now usually called *psychological anthropology*). She was heavily influenced by Franz Boas (1858–1942), her mentor at Columbia and a "father" of American anthropology. Mead eventually did ethnography in the South Pacific, including Samoa and New Guinea. From her first field work emerged the popular book *Coming of Age in Samoa* (1928/1961).

Mead embarked for Samoa with a research topic that Boas had suggested: contrasts between female adolescence in Samoa and the United States. She shared Boas's assumption that different cultures train children and adolescents to have different personalities and behavior. Suspicious of biologically determined universals, she assumed that Samoan adolescence would differ from the same period in the United States and that this would affect adult personality. Using her Samoan ethnographic findings, Mead contrasted apparent sexual freedom and experimentation there with repression of adolescent sexuality in the United States.

Her findings supported the Boasian view that culture, not biology or race, determines variation in human behavior and personality. Derek Freeman (1983) has offered a severe critique of Mead's Samoan work. Freeman's critique has, in turn, been criticized (Brady, ed. 1983). Holmes (1987) offers a balanced view based on his own field work in Samoa.

data. For many years sampling and statistical techniques have been basic to sociology, whereas statistical training has been less common in anthropology (although this is changing as anthropologists increasingly work in modern nations).

Traditional ethnographers studied small, non-literate (without writing) populations and relied on methods appropriate to that context. "Ethnography is a research process in which the anthropologist closely observes, records, and engages in the daily life of another culture—an experience labeled as the fieldwork method—and then writes accounts of this culture, emphasizing descriptive detail" (Marcus and Fischer 1986, p. 18). One key method described in this quote is **participant observation**—taking part in the events one is observing, describing, and analyzing.

With increasing interdisciplinary communication, anthropology and sociology are converging. The "opening to culture" movement is a more qualitative and interpretive approach to sociological issues and data. As the modern world system grows, sociologists pursue research topics in Third World countries and in places that were once almost exclusively within the anthropological orbit. As industrialization spreads, many anthropologists work in industrial societies, where they study diverse topics, including rural decline, inner-city life, and the role of the mass media in creating national culture patterns. Anthropologists and sociologists also share

Mead's later field work among the Arapesh, Mundugumor, and Tchambuli of New Guinea resulted in *Sex and Temperament in Three Primitive Societies* (1935/1950). That book documented variation in male and female personality traits and behavior across cultures. She offered it as further support for cultural determinism.

Mead's reputation rested on her adventurous spirit, intellect, insight, forceful personality, writing ability, and productivity, along with the topics she chose to address. She made primitive life relevant to her time and her own society. Thus, *Coming of Age in Samoa* was subtitled *A Psychological Study of Primitive Youth* for Western Civilization [emphasis added]. *Growing Up in New Guinea* (1930) was subtitled *A Comparative Study of Primitive Education.*

The public viewed Margaret Mead as a romantic, exotic, and controversial figure. She lived an unorthodox life for her time and gender. She was an early feminist. She married three times. Her last two husbands, Reo Fortune and Gregory Bateson, were anthropologists. She

Margaret Mead, then Associate Curator of Ethnology at the American Museum of Natural History, holds two samples of Manus art brought back from a seven-month visit to the Manus of the Admiralty Islands. Mead helped anthropology flourish, using her research in the South Sea islands as lessons in alternative life styles.

was a small, lone, daring, and determined woman who journeyed to remote areas, lived with the natives, and survived to tell of it. Accounts of Mead's life include her autobiography, *Blackberry Winter* (1972), and a biography by her only daughter, Mary Catherine Bateson (1984).

Mead's clear, forceful, and vivid writing captured prominent themes of the Depression era. Her books fueled a revolution in the discussion of human sexuality spurred by Freudian psychology. The preoccupations of Depression-era society included issues that Americans still discuss: family breakdown, teenage sex, the "New Woman," birth control, an increasing divorce rate, and extramarital affairs. Anthropology flourished as South Sea islands offered lessons in romance, sexuality, and alternative life styles. "Free love" in Samoa and the Trobriand Islands (as described by Bronislaw Malinowski [1927, 1929*b*]) provided models for a new sexual order (Stocking 1986).

an interest in issues of race, ethnicity, social class, gender, and popular or mass culture in modern nations, including the United States and Canada.

Anthropology, Political Science, and Economics

Political science and economics developed to investigate particular domains of human behavior—as with sociology, mainly in modern nations. In the small-scale societies where ethnography grew up, politics and economics usually don't stand out as distinct activities amenable to separate analysis, as they do in a modern society. Rather, they are sub-

merged, or *embedded*, in the general social order. Anthropologists have expanded our comparative understanding of political systems by showing, for example, that law and crime are not cultural universals and by examining such matters as the expression and resolution of conflict in societies without governments.

The subject matter of economics has been defined as economizing—the *rational* allocation of scarce means (resources) to alternative ends (uses). The goal of maximizing profit is assumed to be the force behind such rational allocation. However, the sociologist Max Weber (1904/1958), whose work has also influenced anthropology, drew an important distinction between formal rationality and substantive rationality. *Formal rationality* refers to abstract standards of rational procedure based on the profit motive. *Substantive rationality* refers to standards of efficient procedure adjusted to cultural values. In other words, motivations vary cross-culturally and guide the kinds of decisions people make in different cultures. Following Weber's lead, anthropologists have contributed to *comparative* economics by showing that different principles propel the economy in other cultures. Through ethnography and cross-cultural comparison, the findings of economists and political scientists, usually based on research in Western nations, can be placed in a broader perspective.

Anthropology and the Humanities

The humanities study art, literature, music, dance, and other forms of creative expression. Traditionally (but this has changed—see below), they focused on highbrow "fine arts," knowledge of which was considered basic to a "cultured" person. Anthropology has always extended the definition of *cultured* beyond the elitist meaning of cultivated, sophisticated, college-educated, proper, and tasteful. For anthropologists, culture is not confined to elites or to any single social segment. Everyone acquires culture through **enculturation,** the social process by which culture is learned and transmitted across the generations. All creative expressions, therefore, are of potential interest as cultural products and documents. Growing acceptance of this view has helped broaden the study of the humanities from fine art and elite art to popular and folk art and the creative expressions of the masses.

Anthropology has influenced and is being influenced by the humanities—another example of *convergence*, the process of interdisciplinary communication and collaboration mentioned earlier. Adopting a characteristic anthropological view of creativity in its social and cultural context, current "postmodern" (Jameson 1984, 1988) approaches in the humanities are shifting the focus toward "lowbrow," mass, and popular culture and local creative expressions. Another area of convergence between anthropology and the humanities is the view of cultural expressions as patterned texts (Ricoeur 1971; Geertz 1973). Thus "unwritten behavior, speech, beliefs, oral tradition, and ritual" (Clifford 1988, p. 39) are interpreted in relation to their meaning within a particular cultural context. A final link between anthropology and the humanities is the study of ethnographic accounts as a form of writing (Clifford 1988; Marcus and Fischer 1986).

Anthropology and Psychology

Like sociologists and economists, most psychologists do research in their own society. Anthropology again contributes by providing cross-cultural data. Statements about "human" psychology cannot be based solely on behavior in a single type of society. The area of cultural anthropology known as psychological anthropology, or **culture and personality** (the study of variation in psychological traits and personality characteristics between cultures), links up with psychology. Margaret Mead, in her many books (1928/1961, 1930), attempted to show that psychological traits vary widely among cultures. Societies instill different values by training children differently. Adult personalities reflect a culture's child-rearing practices.

An early contributor to the cross-cultural study of psychology was Bronislaw Malinowski, who did research among the Trobriand Islanders of the South Pacific. The Trobrianders reckon kinship matrilineally. They consider themselves related to the mother and her relatives, not to the father. The relative who disciplines the child is not the father but the mother's brother, the maternal uncle. One inherits from the uncle rather than the father. Trobrianders show a marked respect for the uncle, with whom a boy usually has a cool and distant relationship. In contrast, the Trobriand father-son relationship is friendly and affectionate.

Malinowski's work among the Trobrianders suggested modifications in Sigmund Freud's famous theory of the universality of the Oedipus complex (Malinowski 1927). According to Freud (1918/1950), boys around the age of five become sexually attracted to the mother. The Oedipus complex is resolved, in Freud's view, when the boy overcomes his sexual jealousy of, and identifies with, his father. Freud lived in patriarchal Austria during the late nineteenth and early twentieth centuries—a social milieu in which fathers were strong authoritarian figures. The Austrian father was the child's primary authority figure and the mother's sexual partner, but in the Trobriands the father had only the sexual role.

If, as Freud contended, the Oedipus complex always creates social distance based on jealousy toward the mother's sexual partner, this would have shown up in the Trobriands. It *did not*. Malinowski concluded that the authority structure did more to influence the father-son relationship than did sexual jealousy. Like many later anthropologists, Malinowski showed that individual psychology depends on its cultural context. Anthropologists continue to provide cross-cultural perspectives on psychoanalytic propositions (Paul 1989) as well as on issues of developmental and cognitive psychology.

Anthropology and History

Convergence between history and anthropology was noted above in relation to the trend toward interdisciplinary communication. Historians increasingly interpret historical documents and accounts as texts requiring placement and interpretation within specific cultural contexts. Anthropologists and historians collaborate in the study of issues such as colonialism and the development of the modern world system (Cooper and Stoler 1989).

Despite this convergence, I think that it is useful to maintain a distinction between history (change in personnel) and evolution (change in form) as two aspects of change that involve people. In this sense *history* focuses on individuals. In a stable social system, people enter at birth and leave through death and migration. If there is true stability, people come and go but the system stays the same. There are changes in the *personnel*—in individuals—but not in the system's basic form. The second aspect of change (*evolution*) requires a larger perspective. A stable social system can become unstable. *A social system can change its structure or form.* Evolution is the study of such changes in form. (Although individual action always propels such systemic change, the focus here is on the system.)

Although there are still historians who focus on individual names and dates without much concern

An early contributor to the comparative study of psychology was Bronislaw Malinowski, who did ethnographic research among the Trobriand Islanders of the South Pacific. Here a Trobriand woman prepares dinner as her kin and neighbors watch.

for process or social context, the distinction between personnel change and formal change certainly doesn't pit all, or even most, historians against anthropologists. An increasing number of historians study changes in social form—social transforma- tions. Indeed, the growing collaboration of histori- ans and anthropologists has been institutionalized in joint programs in history and anthropology at several universities.

SUMMARY

Anthropology, a uniquely holistic discipline, studies hu- man biological and cultural diversity. It attempts to ex- plain similarities and differences in time and space. Cul- ture, which is passed on through learning rather than through biological inheritance, is a major reason for hu- man adaptability.

Anthropology is characterized by an interest in the origins of and changes in biology and culture. The four subdisciplines of general anthropology are (socio)cul- tural, archeological, biological, and linguistic anthropol- ogy. All share an interest in variation in time and space and in adaptation—the process by which organisms cope with environmental stresses. All study evolution: change in form over the generations. Anthropology attempts to identify and explain universal, generalized, and distinc- tive aspects of the human condition.

Cultural anthropology examines the cultural diversity of the present and the recent past. Archeology recon- structs social, economic, religious, and political patterns, usually of prehistoric populations. Biological anthropol- ogy relates biological diversity in time and space to vari- ation in environment. It studies fossils, genetics, growth and development, bodily responses, and nonhuman pri- mates. Linguistic anthropology documents diversity among contemporary languages. It studies ways in which speech changes in different social situations and over time. Applied anthropology uses anthropological knowl- edge and methods to identify and solve social problems in North America and abroad.

Concerns with past and present and with biology, so- ciety, culture, and language link anthropology to many other fields. The main difference between cultural anthro- pology and sociology is that sociologists have tradition- ally studied urban and industrial populations whereas an- thropologists have studied rural, non-Western peoples. Anthropologists bring a comparative perspective to eco- nomics and political science. Anthropologists also study art, music, and literature across cultures. However, their concern is as much with the creative expressions of com- mon people as with art commissioned and appreciated by elites. Anthropologists examine creators and products in their social context. Despite these traditional contrasts, in- terdisciplinary collaboration is a hallmark of contempo- rary academic life, with ready borrowing of ideas and methods between disciplines. This is especially true for anthropology because of its breadth and topical diversity.

Psychological anthropology, which relates human psy- chology to social and cultural variation, links anthropol- ogy and psychology. Anthropologists and historians col- laborate increasingly in placing historical events in their social and cultural context.

GLOSSARY

adaptation: The process by which organisms cope with environmental stresses.

applied anthropology: The application of anthropologi- cal data, perspectives, theory, and methods to identify, assess, and solve contemporary social problems.

archeological anthropology (prehistoric archeology): The study of human behavior and cultural patterns and processes through their material remains.

artifacts: Material items that humans have manufactured or modified.

biological anthropology: The study of human biological variation in time and space; includes evolution, genetics, growth and development, and primatology.

civilization: A complex society with a central government and social classes; synonyms are *nation-state* and *state*.

cultural ecology: The study of ecosystems that include people, focusing on how human use of nature influences and is influenced by social organization and cultural values.

culture: Distinctly human; transmitted through learning; traditions and customs that govern behavior and beliefs.

culture and personality: A subfield of cultural anthro- pology; examines variation in psychological traits and personality characteristics between cultures.

ecology: The study of interrelationships among living things in an environment.

ecosystem: A patterned arrangement of energy flows and exchanges; includes organisms sharing a common environment and that environment.

enculturation: The social process by which culture is learned and transmitted across the generations.

ethnography: Field work in a particular culture.

ethnology: Cross-cultural comparison; the comparative study of ethnographic data, of society and culture.

evolution: Descent with modification; change in form over generations.

food production: Cultivation of plants and domestication (stockbreeding) of animals; first developed in the Middle East 10,000 to 12,000 years ago.

general anthropology: The field of anthropology as a whole, consisting of cultural, archeological, biological, and linguistic anthropology.

holistic: Interested in the whole of the human condition: past, present, and future; biology, society, language, and culture.

hominids: Members of the zoological family (Hominidae) that includes fossil and living humans.

linguistic anthropology: The descriptive, comparative, and historical study of language and of linguistic similarities and differences in time, space, and society.

linkages: Interconnections between small-scale and large-scale units and systems; political, economic, informational, and other cultural links between village, region, nation, and world.

medical anthropology: Field including biological and cultural, theoretical and applied, anthropologists concerned with the sociocultural context and implications of disease and illness.

nation-state: See *civilization.*

osteology: The study of bones; useful to biological anthropologists studying the fossil record.

paleoanthropology: The study of hominid evolution as revealed by the fossil record.

paleoecology: The study, often by archeologists, of ecosystems of the past.

participant observation: A characteristic ethnographic technique; taking part in the events one is observing, describing, and analyzing.

potsherds: Fragments of earthenware; pottery studied by archeologists in interpreting prehistoric life styles.

prehistory: The period before the invention of writing less than 6,000 years ago.

primates: Monkeys, apes, and prosimians; members of the zoological order that includes humans.

primatology: The study of the biology, behavior, social life, and evolution of monkeys, apes, and other nonhuman primates.

society: Organized life in groups; typical of humans and other animals.

state: See *civilization.*

STUDY QUESTIONS

1. What does it mean to say that anthropology is global and holistic?
2. What are the subdisciplines of general anthropology? What unifies them into a single discipline?
3. How does cultural anthropology differ from sociology?
4. How is anthropology related to other human sciences, and what has it contributed to them?

SUGGESTED ADDITIONAL READING

BURLING, R.
1970 *Man's Many Voices.* New York: Harcourt Brace Jovanovich. Nontechnical yet comprehensive introduction to the role of language in culture and society.

CLIFFORD, J.
1988 *The Predicament of Culture: Twentieth-Century Ethnography, Literature, and Art.* Cambridge, MA: Harvard University Press. Literary evaluation of classic and modern anthropologists and discussion of issues of ethnographic authority.

FAGAN, B. M.
1990 *Archeology: A Brief Introduction.* 4th ed. New York: HarperCollins. Introduction to archeological theory, techniques, and approaches, including field survey, excavation, and analysis of materials.
1991 *People of the Earth: An Introduction to World Prehistory.* 7th ed. New York: HarperCollins.

Introduction to the archeological study of pre-historic societies, using examples from all areas.

HARRIS, M.
1989   *Our Kind: Who We Are, Where We Came From, Where We Are Going.* New York: Harper-Collins. Fascinating popular anthropology; origins of humans, culture, and major socio-political institutions.

MARCUS, G. E., AND M. M. J. FISCHER
1986   *Anthropology as Cultural Critique: An Experimental Moment in the Human Sciences.* Chicago: University of Chicago Press. Different types of ethnographic accounts as forms of writing, a vision of modern anthropology, and a consideration of anthropologists' public and professional roles.

NASH, D.
1993   *A Little Anthropology.* 2nd ed. Englewood Cliffs, NJ: Prentice-Hall. Short introduction to societies and cultures, with comments on developing nations and modern America.

PFEIFFER, J. E.
1985   *The Emergence of Humankind.* 4th ed. New York: HarperCollins. Introduction to human biological evolution and the primates.

PODOLEFSKY, A., AND P. J. BROWN, EDS.
1992   *Applying Anthropology: An Introductory Reader.* 2nd ed. Mountain View, CA: Mayfield. Forty-four essays focusing on anthropology's relevance to contemporary life; a readable survey of the current range of activities in applied anthropology.

FIELD METHODS

Anthropology differs from other fields that study human beings because it is comparative, holistic, and global. Anthropologists study biology, language, and culture, past and present, in ancient and modern societies. This chapter compares the field methods of cultural anthropology with those of the other social sciences.

Anthropology started to separate from sociology around the turn of the twentieth century. Early students of society, such as the French scholar Emile Durkheim, were among the founders of both sociology and anthropology. Comparing the organization of simple and complex societies, Durkheim studied the religions of Native Australia (Durkheim 1912/1961) as well as mass phenomena (such as suicide rates) in modern nations (Durkheim 1897/1951). Eventually anthropology would specialize in the former, sociology in the latter.

ETHNOGRAPHY: ANTHROPOLOGY'S DISTINCTIVE STRATEGY

Anthropology developed into a separate field as early scholars worked on Indian (Native American) reservations and traveled to distant lands to study small groups of foragers and cultivators. This type of firsthand personal study of local settings is called *ethnography*. Traditionally, the process of becoming a cultural anthropologist has required a field experience in another society. Early ethnographers lived in a small-scale, relatively isolated societies, with simple technologies and economies.

Ethnography thus emerged as a research strategy in societies with greater cultural uniformity and less social differentiation than are found in large, modern, industrial nations. In such nonindustrial settings, ethnographers have needed to consider fewer paths of enculturation to understand social life. Traditionally, ethnographers have tried to understand the whole of an alien culture (or, more realistically, as much as they can, given limitations of time and perception). To pursue this holistic goal, ethnographers adopt a free-ranging strategy for gathering information. They move from setting to setting, place to place, and subject to subject to discover the totality and interconnectedness of social life.

Ethnography, by expanding our knowledge of the range of human diversity, provides a foundation for generalizations about human behavior and social life. Ethnographers draw on varied techniques to piece together a picture of otherwise alien life styles. Anthropologists usually employ several (but rarely all) of the techniques discussed here.

ETHNOGRAPHIC TECHNIQUES

The characteristic *field techniques* of the ethnographer include the following:

1. Direct, firsthand observation of daily behavior, including *participant observation*
2. Conversation with varying degrees of formality, from the daily chitchat that helps maintain rapport and provides knowledge about what is going on to prolonged *interviews*, which can be unstructured or structured
3. *Interview schedules* to ensure that complete, comparable information is available for everyone of interest to the study
4. The *genealogical method*
5. Detailed work with *well-informed informants* about particular areas of community life
6. In-depth interviewing, often leading to the collection of *life histories* of particular people
7. **Emic** (actor-oriented) research strategies that focus on local (native) beliefs and perceptions and **etic** (observer-oriented) approaches that give priority to the ethnographer's perceptions and conclusions
8. Problem-oriented research of many sorts
9. Longitudinal research—the continuous long-term study of an area or site

Observation

Ethnographers must pay attention to hundreds of details of daily life, seasonal events, and unusual happenings. They must observe individual and collective behavior in varied settings. They should record what they see as they see it. Things will never seem quite as strange as they do during the first few days and weeks in the field. The ethnographer eventually gets used to, and accepts as normal, cultural patterns that were initially alien.

Many ethnographers record their impressions in a personal *diary*, which is kept separate from more formal *field notes*. Later, this record of early impressions will help point out some of the most basic aspects of cultural diversity. Such aspects include distinctive smells, noises people make, how they cover their mouths when they eat, and how they gaze at others. These patterns, which are so basic as to seem almost trivial, are part of what Bronislaw Malinowski called "the imponderabilia of native life and of typical behavior" (Malinowski 1922/1961, p. 20). These features of culture are so fundamental that natives take them for granted. They are too basic even to talk about, but the unaccustomed eye of the fledgling anthropologist perceives them. Thereafter they are submerged in familiarity and fade to the periphery of consciousness. This is why initial impressions are valuable and should be recorded. First and foremost, ethnographers should be accurate observers, recorders, and reporters of what they see in the field.

Participant Observation

Ethnographers don't study animals in laboratory cages. The experiments that psychologists do with pigeons, chickens, guinea pigs, and rats are very different from ethnographic procedure. Anthropologists don't systematically control subjects' rewards and punishments or their exposure to certain stimuli. Our subjects are not speechless animals but human beings. It is not part of ethnographic procedure to manipulate them, control their environments, or experimentally induce certain behaviors.

One of ethnography's characteristic procedures is *participant observation*, which means that we take part in community life as we study it. As human beings living among others, we cannot be totally impartial and detached observers. We must also take part in many of the events and processes we are observing and trying to comprehend. During the fourteen months I lived in Madagascar in 1966–67, for example, I simultaneously observed and participated in many occasions in Betsileo life. I helped out at harvest time, joining other people who climbed atop—in order to stamp down on and compact—accumulating stacks of rice stalks. One September, for a reburial ceremony, I bought a silk shroud for a village ancestor. I entered the village tomb and watched people lovingly rewrap the bones and decaying flesh of their ancestors. I accompanied Betsileo peasants to town and to market. I observed their dealings with outsiders and sometimes offered help when problems arose.

In Arembepe, I sailed on the Atlantic in simple boats with Brazilian fishermen. I gave Jeep rides into the capital to malnourished babies, to pregnant mothers, and once to a teenage girl possessed by a spirit. All those people needed to consult specialists outside the village. I danced on Arembepe's festive occasions, drank foul-tasting libations commemorating new births, and became a godfather to a village girl. Most anthropologists have similar field experiences. The common humanity of the student and the studied, the ethnographer and the researched community, makes participant observation inevitable.

Conversation, Interviewing, and Interview Schedules

Participating in local life means that ethnographers constantly talk to people and ask questions about what they observe. As their knowledge of the native language increases, they understand more. There are several stages in learning a field language. First is the naming phase—asking name after name of the objects around us. Later we are able to pose more complex questions and understand the replies. We begin to understand simple conversations between two villagers, and if our language expertise proceeds far enough, we eventually become able to comprehend rapid-fire public discussions and group conversations. The special oratory of political events and ceremonial or ritual occasions often contains **liturgies,** set formal sequences of words and actions that we can record for later analysis with a local expert.

One data-gathering technique I have used in both Arembepe and Madagascar involves an ethnographic survey that includes an interview schedule. In 1964, my fellow field workers and I attempted to complete an interview schedule in each of Arembepe's 160 households. We entered almost every household (fewer than 5 percent refused to participate) to ask a set of questions on a printed form.

Our results provided us with a census and basic information about the village. We wrote down the name, age, and sex of each household member. We gathered data on family type, political party, reli-

Ethnographers strive to establish rapport—a good, friendly relationship based on personal contact—with informants. These women in Guatemala are pleased with this anthropologist's gift—photos of themselves.

gion, present and previous jobs, income, expenditures, diet, possessions, and many other items on our eight-page form.

Although we were doing a survey, our approach differed from the survey research design routinely used by sociologists and other social scientists working in large, populous, industrial nations. That survey research, discussed below, involves sampling (choosing a small, manageable study group from a larger population) and impersonal data collection. We did not select a partial sample from the total population. Instead, we tried to interview in all households in the community we were studying (that is, to have a total sample). We used an interview schedule rather than a questionnaire. With the **interview schedule,** the ethnographer talks face to face with informants, asks the questions, and writes down the answers. **Questionnaire** procedures tend to be more indirect and impersonal; the respondent often fills in the form.

Our goal of getting a total sample allowed us to meet almost everyone in the village and helped us

establish rapport. Arembepeiros still talk warmly about how, three decades ago, we were interested enough in them to visit their homes and ask them questions. We stood in sharp contrast to the other outsiders the Arembepeiros had known who considered them too poor and backward to be taken seriously.

Like other survey research, however, our interview-schedule survey did gather comparable quantifiable information. It gave us a basis for assessing patterns and exceptions in village life. Our home visits also provided opportunities to do informal and follow-up interviewing. Our schedules included a core set of questions that were posed to everyone. However, some interesting side issues often came up during the interview.

We would pursue these leads into many dimensions of village life. One woman, for instance, a midwife, became the "well-informed informant" we consulted later, when we wanted detailed information about local childbirth. Another woman had done an internship at an Afro-Brazilian cult (*can-*

Working in natural communities, anthropologists form personal relationships with informants as we study their lives. Sometimes ethnographers become fictive or "adoptive" relatives of informants to whom they are especially close. Here David Maybury-Lewis, host of the "Millennium" TV series shown on PBS in 1992, sits with his Xavante brother, Sipuba.

Kinship and descent are important social building blocks in nonindustrial cultures. Without writing, genealogical information may be preserved in art. Here carvings on a tomb built by the Tanosy people of Ampanihy, Madagascar, depict their ancestors.

domblé) house in the city. She still went there regularly to study, dance, and get possessed. She became our *candomblé* expert.

Thus, our interview-schedule survey provided a structure that *directed but did not confine* us as researchers. It enabled our ethnography to be both quantitative and qualitative. The quantitative part consisted of the basic information we gathered and later analyzed statistically. The qualitative dimension came from our follow-up questions, open-ended discussions, pauses for gossip, and work with well-informed informants.

The Genealogical Method

Another ethnographic technique is the **genealogical method.** Early ethnographers developed genealogical notation to deal with principles of kinship, de-

scent, and marriage, which are the social building blocks of nonindustrial cultures. In contemporary North America most of our contacts outside the home are with nonrelatives. However, people in nonindustrial cultures spend their lives almost exclusively with relatives. Anthropologists must record genealogical data to reconstruct history and understand current relationships. In societies without a central government, these links are basic to social life and to political organization. Anthropologists even classify such societies as **kin-based.** Everyone is related to, and spends most of his or her time with, everyone else, and rules of behavior attached to particular kin relationships are basic to everyday life. Marriage is also crucial in organizing nonindustrial societies because strategic marriages between villages, tribes, and clans create political alliances.

All communities have well-informed informants, natives who can provide the best information about particular areas of life. Here the researcher (right) collects folklore from a well-informed informant.

Well-Informed Informants

Every community has people who by accident, experience, talent, or training can provide the most complete or useful information about particular aspects of life. These people are **well-informed informants.** In Ivato, the Betsileo village where I spent most of my time, a man named Rakoto was a particularly good informant about village history. However, when I asked him to work with me on a genealogy of the fifty to sixty people buried in the village tomb, he called in his cousin Tuesdaysfather, who knew more about this subject. Tuesdaysfather had survived an epidemic of Spanish influenza that ravaged Madagascar, along with much of the world, around 1919. Immune to the disease himself, Tuesdaysfather had the grim job of burying his kin as they died. He kept track of everyone buried in the tomb. Tuesdaysfather helped me with the tomb genealogy. Rakoto joined him in telling me personal details about the deceased villagers.

Life Histories

In nonindustrial societies as in our own, individual personalities, interests, and abilities vary. Some villagers prove to be more interested in the ethnographer's work and are more helpful, interesting, and pleasant than others. Anthropologists develop likes and dislikes in the field as we do at home. Often, when we find someone unusually interesting, we collect his or her **life history.** This recollection of a lifetime of experiences provides a more intimate and personal cultural portrait than would be possible otherwise. Life histories reveal how specific people perceive, react to, and contribute to changes that affect their lives. Such accounts can illustrate diversity, which exists within any community, since the focus is on how different people interpret and deal with some of the same problems.

Emic and Etic Research Strategies

To study cultures, anthropologists have used two approaches, emic (actor-oriented) and etic (observer-oriented). An *emic* approach instigates how natives (or one native, in the case of a life history) think. How do they perceive and categorize the world? What are their rules for behavior and thought? What has meaning for them? How do they imagine and explain things? The anthropologist seeks the "native viewpoint" and relies on the culture bearers—the actors in a culture—to determine whether something they do, say, or think is significant.

However, natives aren't scientists. They may think that spirits cause illnesses that come from germs. They may believe political leaders who tell them that missiles are peacemakers. The *etic* (observer-oriented) approach shifts the focus of research from native categories, expressions, explanations, and interpretations to those of the anthropologist. The etic approach realizes that culture bearers are often too involved in what they are doing to interpret their cultures impartially. The etic ethnographer gives more weight to what he or she (the observer) notices and considers important. As a trained scientist, the anthropologist should try to bring an objective and comprehensive viewpoint to the study of other cultures. Of course, the anthropologist, like any other scientist, is also a human being with cultural blinders that prevent complete objectivity. As in other sciences, proper training can reduce but not totally eliminate the observer's bias. But anthropologists do have special training to compare behavior between different societies.

In practice, most anthropologists combine emic and etic strategies in their field work. Native statements, perceptions, and opinions help ethnographers understand how cultures work. Native beliefs are also interesting and valuable in themselves and broaden the anthropologist's view of the world. However, natives often fail to admit, or even recognize, certain causes and consequences of their behavior. This is as true of North Americans as it is of people in any other society. To describe and interpret culture, ethnographers should recognize the biases that come from their own culture as well as those of the people being studied.

Problem-Oriented Ethnography

Although anthropologists are interested in the whole context of human behavior, it is impossible to study everything, and field research usually addresses specific questions. Most ethnographers enter the field with a specific problem to investigate, and they collect data about variables deemed relevant to that problem. And informants' answers to questions are not the only data source. Anthropologists also gather information on factors like population density, environmental quality, climate, physical geography, diet, and land use. Sometimes this involves direct measurement—of rainfall, temperature, fields, yields, dietary quantities, or time allocation (Bailey 1990; Johnson 1978). Often it means that we consult government records or archives.

The information of interest to ethnographers is not limited to what informants can and do tell us. For much that is significant we can rely neither on participant observation nor intensive local interviews. In an increasingly interconnected world, local informants lack knowledge about many factors (regional, national, and international) that affect their lives. Our informants may be as mystified as we are with the exercise of power from regional, national, and international centers.

Longitudinal Research

Geography limits anthropologists less now than in the past, when it could take months to reach a field site, and return visits were rare. New systems of transportation allow anthropologists to widen the area of their research and to return repeatedly. Ethnographic reports now routinely include data from two or more field stays. **Longitudinal research** is the long-term study of a community, region, society, culture, or other unit, usually based on repeated visits. One example of such research is the longitudinal study of the interplay of social and economic forces in Gwembe District, Zambia. This study, planned in 1956 as a longitudinal project by Elizabeth Colson and Thayer Scudder, continues with Colson, Scudder, and their associates of various nationalities. The Gwembe research project is both longitudinal (multitime) and multisite (considering several local field sites), because no single village or neighborhood could adequately represent Gwembe's diversity (Colson and Scudder 1975; Scudder and Colson 1980). Four villages, in different areas, have been followed for four decades. Periodic village censuses (1956–57, 1962–63, 1965, 1972–73, 1981–82, and 1987–88) provide basic data on population, economy, and other variables chosen to monitor changes in kinship and religious behavior. Censused people who have moved are traced and interviewed (if possible) to see how their lives compare with those of people who have stayed in the village. Information on labor migration, visits between town and country, and other linkages show the extent to which rural and urban belong to a single system.

Zambian assistants have kept records of local events and diaries of food bought and eaten. From field notes it is possible to reconstruct prices for different periods. Shifts in preferences for products are documented by shopping lists provided by villagers. Field notes also contain observations from attendance at courts, village and district meetings, church services, funerals, and ceremonies.

This information is supplemented by interviews with traders and officials, technical workers, political leaders, and foreigners who work for religious missions and *nongovernmental organizations* (NGOs). The anthropologists have also consulted government and other records, both published and unpublished. Zambian social scientists who have worked in the district also provide insights about the changes taking place.

THE EVOLUTION OF ETHNOGRAPHY

The Polish anthropologist Bronislaw Malinowski (1884–1942), who spent most of his professional life in England, is generally considered the father of ethnography. Like most anthropologists of his time, Malinowski did *salvage ethnography,* in the belief that the ethnographer's job is to study and record cultural diversity threatened by westernization. Early ethnographic accounts (*ethnographies*), including Malinowski's classic *Argonauts of the Western Pacific* (1922/1961), were similar to earlier traveler and explorer accounts in describing the writer's discovery of unknown people and places. However, the *scientific* aims of ethnographies set them apart from books by explorers and amateurs.

The style that dominated "classic" ethnographies was *ethnographic realism.* The writer's goal was to present an accurate, objective, scientific account of a different way of life, written by someone who knew it firsthand. This knowledge came from an "ethnographic adventure" involving immersion in an alien language and culture. Ethnographers derived their authority—both as scientists and as voices of "the native" or "the other"—from this personal research experience.

Malinowski wrote *functionalist* ethnographies, guided by the assumption that all aspects of culture are linked (functions of each other). A functionalist ethnography begins with *any* aspect of a culture, such as a Trobriand Islands sailing expedition. The ethnographer then follows the links between that entry point and other areas of the culture, such as magic, religion, myths, kinship, and trade. Contemporary ethnographies tend to be less inclusive, focusing on particular topics, such as kinship or religion.

According to Malinowski, a primary task of the ethnographer is "to grasp the native's point of view, his relation to life, to realize *his* vision of *his* world (1922/1961, p. 25—Malinowski's italics). Since the 1970s *interpretive anthropology* has considered the task of describing and interpreting that which is meaningful to natives. Interpretivists such as Clifford Geertz (1973) view cultures as meaningful texts which natives constantly "read" and which ethnographers must decipher. According to Geertz, anthropologists may choose anything in a culture that interests them, fill in details, and elaborate to inform their readers about meanings in that culture. Meanings are carried by public symbolic forms, including words, rituals, and customs. In the interpretive view, cross-cultural understanding emerges through "dialogues" between natives, anthropologist, and reader, who are all parties to a conversation.

A current trend in ethnographic writing is to question traditional goals, methods, and styles, including salvage ethnography and ethnographic realism (Marcus and Cushman 1982; Clifford 1982, 1988). Marcus and Fischer argue that anthropology has reached "an experimental moment." Experimentation is needed because all people and cultures have already been "discovered" and must now be "*re*discovered . . . in changing historical circumstances" (1986, p. 24).

These experimental anthropologists recognize that ethnographies are works of art as well as works of science. Ethnographic texts are lite-

Successively different questions have come to the fore, while basic data on communities and individuals continue to be collected. The first focus of study was the impact of a large hydroelectric dam, which flooded much of the Zambezi River plain and subjected the Gwembe people to forced resettlement. However, the dam also spurred road building and other activities that brought the people of Gwembe more closely in touch with the rest of Zambia (Colson 1971; Scudder 1972; Scudder and Habarad 1991).

By the late 1960s education had become a major concern at Gwembe and was playing an important role in changes then taking place. Accordingly, Scudder and Colson (1980) designed research to examine the role of education in providing access to new opportunities and in increasing social differentiation within the district and nation. At the same time, it was evident that alcohol consumption was a growing problem. A third major study then examined the role of changing markets, transportation, and exposure to town values in the transformation of domestic brewing and a radical change in drinking patterns (Colson and Scudder 1988).

rary creations in which the ethnographer, as mediator, communicates information from the "natives" to readers. Some recent experimental ethnographies are "dialogic," presenting ethnography as a dialogue between the anthropologist and one or more native informants (e.g., Dwyer 1982). These works draw attention to ways in which ethnographers, and by extension their readers, communicate with other cultures.

Ethnographers interpret and mediate between cultures in two ways. During field work they must interpret from native categories to their own, and in writing they must interpret for their readers. However, some dialogic ethnographies have been criticized as being too confessional, spending too much time on the anthropologist and too little on the natives and their culture.

The dialogic ethnography is one genre within a larger experimental category—*reflexive ethnography.* Here the ethnographer-writer puts his or her personal feelings and reactions to the field situation right in the text. An experimental writing strategy is prominent in reflexive accounts. The ethnographer may adopt some of the conventions of the novel, including first-person narration, conversations, dialogues, and humor.

Marcus and Fischer (1986) caution that the desire to be personal can be overplayed to the point of exhibitionism. Nevertheless, experimental ethnographies, using new ways of showing what it means to be a Samoan or a Brazilian, may convey to the reader a richer and more complex understanding of human experience. The result may be to convince readers that culture matters more than they might otherwise have thought.

Recent ethnographic writers have also attempted to correct the deficiency of *romanticized timelessness,* which is obvious in the classics. Linked to salvage ethnography was the idea of the *ethnographic present*—the period before westernization, when the "true" native culture flourished. This notion gives classic ethnographies an eternal, timeless quality. The cultures they describe seem frozen in the ethnographic present. Providing the only jarring note in this idealized picture are occasional comments by the author about traders or missionaries, suggesting that in actuality the natives were already part of the world system.

Anthropologists now recognize that the ethnographic present is a rather unrealistic and romantic construct. Cultures have been in contact—and have been changing—throughout history. Most native cultures had at least one major foreign encounter before any anthropologist ever came their way. Most of them had already been incorporated in some fashion into nation-states or colonial systems.

The classic ethnographies neglected history, politics, and the world system, but contemporary ethnographies usually recognize that cultures constantly change and that an ethnographic account applies to a particular moment. A current trend in ethnography is to focus on the ways in which cultural ideas serve political and economic interests. Another trend is to describe how particular "natives" participate in broader historical, political, and economic processes (Shostak 1981).

SURVEY RESEARCH

As anthropologists work increasingly in large-scale societies, they have developed innovative ways of blending ethnography and survey research (Fricke 1986). Before considering such combinations of field methods, I must describe survey research and the main differences between survey research and ethnography as traditionally practiced. Working mainly in large, populous nations, sociologists, social psychologists, political scientists, and economists have developed and refined the **survey research** design, which involves sampling, impersonal data collection, and statistical analysis. Survey research usually draws a **sample** (a manageable study group) from a much larger population. By studying a properly selected and representative sample, social scientists can make accurate inferences about the larger population.

In smaller-scale societies, ethnographers get to know most of the people, but given the greater size and complexity of nations, survey research cannot help being more impersonal. Survey researchers call the people they study **respondents.** (Ethnographers

For research in large, populous nations, sociologists, social psychologists, and political scientists have developed and refined survey research, which is indispensable for the scientific study of such societies. A typical social survey relies on sampling, questionnaires, and statistical analysis. Survey research is also used in political polling and market research, as in this photo.

work with **informants.**) Respondents are people who respond to questions during a survey. Sometimes survey researchers personally interview them. Sometimes, after an initial meeting, they ask respondents to fill out a questionnaire. In other cases researchers mail printed questionnaires to randomly selected sample members or have graduate students interview or telephone them. (In a **random sample**, all members of the population have an equal statistical chance of being chosen for inclusion. A random sample is selected by randomizing procedures, such as tables of random numbers, which are found in many statistics textbooks.)

Anyone who has grown up recently in the United States or Canada has heard of sampling. Probably the most familiar example is the polling used to predict political races. The media hire agencies to estimate outcomes and do exit polls to find out what kinds of people voted for which candidates (Table 2.1). During sampling, researchers gather information about age, gender, religion, occupation, income, and political party preference. These characteristics (**variables**—attributes that vary among members of a sample or population) are known to influence political decisions.

We may distinguish between a **predictor variable** (a predictor) and a **dependent variable** (any variable that is to be predicted or explained). Predictor variables work separately and together in influencing a dependent variable. For example, in predicting "risk of heart attack" (the dependent variable), predictors include sex, age, family history, weight, blood pressure, serum cholesterol, exercise, and cigarette smoking. Each predictor contributes separately to the risk of heart attack, and some have more impact than others. However, predictors also work together. Someone with many "risk factors" (particularly the most significant ones) has a greater risk of suffering a heart attack than does someone with few predictors.

In social science, predictor variables help us guess how people think, feel, and behave. Gender, for instance, is a useful predictor of political party affiliation and voting behavior. More women than men claim to be Democrats, and women are more likely to vote for candidates of that party than men are (Table 2.1). Survey research is indispensable in the study of large, populous nations, in which we must pay particular attention to variation.

Besides gender, more complex societies have role

Table 2.1. *Social indicators and the 1992 American Presidential vote. These exit poll data were collected by Voter Research and Surveys, based on written questionnaires filled out by 15,490 voters leaving 300 polling places in the United States on election day 1992.*

Overall By Social Category (Selected)	PERCENTAGE OF VOTE		
	Clinton 43	Bush 38	Perot 19
Men	41	38	21
Women	46	37	17
Whites	39	41	20
Blacks	82	11	7
Hispanics	62	25	14
Asians	29	55	16
Married	40	40	20
Unmarried	49	33	18
18–29 years old	44	34	22
60 and older	50	38	12
White Protestant	33	46	21
Catholic	44	36	20
Jewish	78	12	10
Union household	55	24	21
From the East	47	35	18
From the Midwest	42	37	21
From the South	42	43	16
From the West	44	34	22

(SOURCE: *The New York Times,* November 5, 1992, p. B9.)

specializations based on age, profession, social class, and many other variables. The number of variables influencing social identity and behavior increases with, and can be considered a measure of, social complexity. Many more variables affect social identities, experiences, and activities in a modern nation than is the case in the small communities and local settings where ethnography grew up. In the contemporary United States or Canada hundreds of factors influence social behavior and attitudes. These social predictors include our religion; the region of the country we grew up in; whether we come from a town, suburb, or inner city; and our parents' professions, ethnic origins, and income levels.

DIFFERENCES BETWEEN SURVEY RESEARCH AND ETHNOGRAPHY

There are several differences between survey research and ethnography:

1. In survey research, the object of study is usually a sample chosen (randomly or otherwise) by the researcher. Ethnographers normally study whole, functioning communities.
2. Ethnographers do firsthand field work, establishing a direct relationship with the people they study. Ethnographers strive to establish **rapport**, a good, friendly working relationship based on personal contact, with informants. Often, survey researchers have no personal contact with respondents. They may hire assistants to interview by phone or ask respondents to fill out a printed form or write answers to a questionnaire.
3. Ethnographers get to know their informants and usually take an interest in the totality of their lives. Often, a social survey focuses on a small number of variables, such as the ones that influence voting, rather than on the totality of people's lives.
4. Survey researchers normally work in modern nations, where most people are literate, permitting respondents to fill in their own questionnaires. Ethnographers are more likely to study people who do not read and write.
5. Because survey research deals with large and diverse groups and with samples and probability, its results must be analyzed statistically. Because the societies that anthropologists traditionally study are smaller and less diverse, many ethnographers have not acquired detailed knowledge of statistics.

ANTHROPOLOGICAL RESEARCH IN COMPLEX SOCIETIES

During World War I Malinowski spent several years studying the Trobriand Islanders. In his classic ethnographic **monograph** (a book based on ethnographic field work) *Argonauts of the Western Pacific,* Malinowski describes how an ethnographer "sets up shop" in another society. Like Malinowski's research in the Trobriands, my field work in Arembepe focused on a single community as the object of intensive study. I could get to know everyone in Arembepe because its population was small and its social system was uncomplicated. However, unlike the Trobriands, Arembepe was not a tribal society but part of a large, populous, and diverse nation.

Particularly since the 1950s, anthropologists have investigated contemporary life styles, including urban problems and social contrasts in North America. Here the rich meet the poor—tourists and homeless people exchange an awkward glance on the palm-lined waterfront of Santa Barbara, California.

The Trobriand Islands are small enough for an ethnographer to visit every village. Malinowski might well have managed to talk with every Trobriander. I could never hope to visit every Brazilian community or meet every Brazilian.

Malinowski used his field site as a basis for describing Trobriand society as a whole. Anthropologists have been criticized for generalizing about an entire culture on the basis of research in just one community, a practice which is somewhat more defensibly for small-scale, homogeneous societies than for complex nations. My study of Arembepe, a rural community in a particular region of an urbanized nation, could never encapsulate Brazil as a whole. Thus I viewed my Arembepe field study as part of a larger research program. I was just one ethnographer among many, each working separately in different Brazilian communities. Eventual compar-

ison of those studies would help reveal the range of diversity in Brazil.

One way of using ethnography in modern nations is to do such a series of **community studies.** Field sites in different regions can be used to sample different economic adaptations, degrees of participation in the modern world, and historical trends. However, even a thousand rural communities cannot constitute an adequate sample of national diversity. We must also consider urban life and social contrasts that are absent in small communities. The range of variation encountered in any nation makes the social survey an obligatory research procedure.

Nevertheless, ethnography can be used to supplement and fine-tune survey research. Anthropologists can transfer the personal, direct, observation-based techniques of ethnography to social groups and social networks in *any setting*. A combination of

One of ethnography's characteristic procedures is participant observation—taking part in community life as we study it. The common humanity of the observer and the observed, the ethnographer and the researched community, makes participant observation inevitable. Here Arlene Burns joins in a wedding dance in Nepal.

survey research and ethnography can provide new perspectives on life in **complex societies** (large and populous societies with social stratification and central governments). Preliminary ethnography can also help develop relevant and culturally appropriate questions for inclusion in national surveys.

Urban Anthropology

A series of community studies in a nation reveals variation in its small-town and rural life. However, there is much more to national life than small communities. One response to this problem has been **urban anthropology**—the anthropological study of cities. Particularly since the 1950s, anthropologists have systematically investigated urban problems

and life styles in the United States, Canada, and abroad. A common illustration of urban anthropology is the practice of having students do local field work for an anthropology course (assuming that the college is in an urban setting).

In my own courses in Ann Arbor, Michigan, undergraduates have done research on sororities, fraternities, teams, campus organizations, and the local homeless population. Other students have systematically observed behavior in public places. These include racquetball courts, restaurants, bars, football stadiums, markets, malls, and classrooms. Other "modern anthropology" projects use anthropological techniques to interpret and analyze mass media. Anthropologists have been studying their own cultures for decades, and anthropological research in the United States and Canada is booming today. (The Appendix, "American Popular Culture," provides several examples.) Wherever there is patterned human behavior, there is grist for the anthropological mill.

Anthropology in Complex Societies

Anthropologists can use field techniques such as participant observation and firsthand data collection in any social setting. However, for contemporary societies, anthropologists increasingly supplement traditional techniques with new procedures, many borrowed from survey research. During studies of urban life, modern anthropologists routinely gather statistical data. In any complex society, many predictor variables (*social indicators*) influence behavior and opinions. Because we must be able to detect, measure, and compare the influence of social indicators, many contemporary anthropological studies have a statistical foundation. Even in rural field work, more anthropologists now draw samples, gather quantitative data, and use statistics to interpret them (see Bernard 1988). Quantifiable information may permit a more precise assessment of similarities and differences between communities. Statistical analysis can support and round out an ethnographic account of local social life.

However, in the best studies, the hallmark of ethnography remains: Anthropologists enter the community and get to know the people. They participate in local activities, networks, and associations, in the city or in the countryside. They observe and experience social conditions and problems. They watch the effects of national policies and programs on local life. I believe that the ethnographic method and the emphasis on personal relationships in social research are valuable gifts that anthropology brings to the study of a complex society.

SUMMARY

Ethnography has several characteristic field procedures, including observation, establishing rapport, participant observation, conversation, listening to native accounts, formal and informal interviewing, the genealogical method, work with well-informed informants, life histories, emic and etic research strategies, problem-oriented ethnography, and longitudinal research. Recording the imponderabilia of daily life is particularly useful early in field work. That is when the most basic, distinctive, and alien features of another culture are most noticeable. Ethnographers do not systematically manipulate their subjects or conduct experiments. Rather, they work in natural communities and form personal relationships with informants as they study their lives.

Interview schedules are forms that ethnographers fill in by visiting many households. The schedules guide formal interviews, ensuring that the ethnographer collects comparable information from everyone. These interviews also introduce the researcher to many people. The schedule organizes the interview. However, ethnographers may also pursue additional topics in accordance with the particular interests and attributes of the interviewee.

Ethnographers work closely with well-informed informants to learn about particular areas of native life. Many ethnographers work long hours with particular informants. Life histories dramatize the fact that culture bearers are also individuals and document personal experiences with culture and culture change. The collection and analysis of genealogical information is particularly important in societies in which principles of kinship, descent, and marriage organize and integrate social and political life. Emic approaches focus on native perceptions and explanations of behavior. Etic approaches give priority to the ethnographer's own observations and conclusions. Anthropologists do many kinds of problem-oriented ethnography, and people are not our only data source. Measurements are made as well. Longitudinal research is the systematic study of an area or site over time.

Traditionally, anthropologists worked in small scale societies; sociologists, in modern nations. Different field techniques emerged for the study of different types of societies. Sociologists and other social scientists who work in complex societies use survey research to sample variation.

There are several contrasts between survey research and ethnography. With more literate respondents, sociologists employ questionnaires, which the research subjects fill out. Anthropologists are more likely to use interview schedules, which the ethnographer fills in during a personal interview. Anthropologists do their field work in communities and study the totality of social life. Sociologists study samples to make inferences about a larger population. Sociologists are often interested in causal relationships between a limited number of variables. Anthropologists are more typically concerned with the interconnectedness of all aspects of social life.

Anthropologists use modified ethnographic techniques to study complex societies. The diversity of social life and subcultural variation in modern nations and cities requires social survey procedures. However, anthropologists add the intimacy and firsthand investigation characteristic of ethnography. Community studies in regions of modern nations provide firsthand, in-depth accounts of cultural variation and of regional historical and economic forces and trends. Anthropologists may use ethnographic procedures to study urban life, but they also make greater use of statistical techniques and analysis of the mass media in their research in complex societies.

GLOSSARY

community study: Anthropological method for studying complex societies. Small communities are studied ethnographically as being (partially) representative of regional culture or particular contrasts in national life.

complex societies: Nations; large and populous, with social stratification and central governments.

dependent variable: Any variable to be explained or predicted.

emic: The research strategy that focuses on native explanations and criteria of significance.

etic: The research strategy that emphasizes the observer's rather than the natives' explanations, categories, and criteria of significance.

genealogical method: Procedures by which ethnographers discover and record connections of kinship, descent, and marriage, using diagrams and symbols.

informants: Subjects in ethnographic research; people the ethnographer gets to know in the field, who teach him or her about their culture.

interview schedule: Ethnographic tool for structuring a formal interview. A prepared form (usually printed or mimeographed) that guides interviews with households or individuals being compared systematically. Contrasts with a *questionnaire* because the researcher has personal contact with the informants and records their answers.

kin-based: Characteristic of many nonindustrial societies. People spend their lives almost exclusively with their relatives; principles of kinship, descent, and marriage organize social life.

life history: Of an informant; provides a personal cultural portrait of existence or change in a culture.

liturgies: Set formal sequences of words and actions; common in political events and rituals or ceremonies.

longitudinal research: Long-term study of a community, region, society, culture, or other unit, usually based on repeated visits.

predictor variables: Factors (e.g., sex, age, religion) that help predict other behavior—dependent variables (e.g., voting, occupation).

questionnaire: Form (usually printed) used by sociologists to obtain comparable information from respondents. Often mailed to and filled in by research subjects rather than by the researcher.

random sample: A sample in which all members of the population have an equal statistical chance of being included.

rapport: A good, friendly working relationship between people, for example, ethnographers and their informants.

respondents: Subjects in sociological research; the people who answer questions in questionnaires and other social surveys.

sample: A smaller study group chosen to represent a larger population.

survey research: Characteristic research procedure among social scientists other than anthropologists. Studies society through sampling, statistical analysis, and impersonal data collection.

urban anthropology: The anthropological study of cities.

variables: Attributes (e.g., sex, age, height, weight) that differ from one person or case to the next.

well-informed informant: Person who is an expert on a particular aspect of native life.

STUDY QUESTIONS

1. What are the characteristic field techniques of the ethnographer?
2. What are the imponderabilia of daily life, and when are they most obvious to the ethnographer?
3. What is participant observation?
4. What is the genealogical method, and why did it develop in anthropology?
5. What are the advantages for ethnography of life histories and working with well-informed informants?

6. What is the difference between emic and etic research strategies? Must anthropologists choose one of these approaches and reject the other?
7. Do all ethnographic data come from informants?
8. What is longitudinal research, and why is it of increasing importance in anthropology?
9. What is survey research design, and how does it differ from ethnography?
10. What are examples of predictor and dependent variables?
11. What are the differences between questionnaires and interview schedules?
12. What are the problems and advantages of community study research?
13. What techniques do anthropologists use to study urban life?

SUGGESTED ADDITIONAL READING

AGAR, M. H.
  1980 *The Professional Stranger: An Informal Introduction to Ethnography.* New York: Academic Press. Basics of ethnography, illustrated by the author's field experiences in India and among heroin addicts in the United States.

BERNARD, H. R.
  1988 *Research Methods in Cultural Anthropology.* Newbury Park, CA: Sage. The most complete and up-to-date survey of methods of data collection, organization, and analysis in cultural anthropology.

BRIM, J. A., AND D. H. SPAIN
  1974 *Research Design in Anthropology.* New York: Harcourt Brace Jovanovich. Discusses hypothesis testing and anthropological research design.

GEERTZ, C.
  1988 *Works and Lives: The Anthropologist as Author.* Stanford, CA: Stanford University Press. A prominent cultural anthropologist considers ethnography as a form of writing.

HARRIS, M.
  1979 *Cultural Materialism: The Struggle for a Science of Culture.* New York: Vintage. Theories of culture, including an extended discussion of emic and etic research strategies.

KOTTAK, C. P., ED.
  1982 *Researching American Culture: A Guide for Student Anthropologists.* Ann Arbor: University of Michigan Press. Advice for college students doing field work in the United States. Includes papers by undergraduates and anthropologists on contemporary American culture.

PELTO, P. J., AND G. H. PELTO
  1978 *Anthropological Research: The Structure of Inquiry.* 2nd ed. New York: Cambridge University Press. Discusses data collection and analysis, including the relationship between theory and field work, hypothesis construction, sampling, and statistics.

SPRADLEY, J. P.
  1979 *The Ethnographic Interview.* New York: Harcourt Brace Jovanovich. Discussion of the ethnographic method, with emphasis on discovering native viewpoints.

CHAPTER 3

CULTURE

Humans are animals with a difference. That difference is culture, a major reason for our adaptability and success. Social and cultural means of adaptation have been crucially important in hominid evolution. *Society* is organized life in groups. Like humans, many other animals, including apes, monkeys, wolves, and ants, live in organized groups. For example, many monkeys live in social groups called **troops,** composed of multiple adult males and females and their offspring, in which dominance hierarchies, juvenile play groups, and various coordinated movements and activities regulate contacts between members. Human populations, however, are organized not only by their habitual social activities and relationships but also by exposure to a common cultural tradition. Cultural traditions or, more simply, cultures are transmitted through learning and language.

The idea of culture has long been basic to anthropology. More than a century ago, in his classic book *Primitive Culture*, British anthropologist Edward Tylor proposed that systems of human behavior

Many monkeys live in organized societies, in which dominance relationships and coordinated activities, such as grooming, govern their social contacts. Humans, by contrast, are organized not only by habitual social activities and relationships, but also by exposure to a common cultural tradition. Culture is transmitted through learning and through language. Contrast the West African Guinea baboons with the Tuareg boys learning Islam by studying the Koran.

and thought are not random. Rather, they obey natural laws and therefore can be studied scientifically. Tylor's definition of culture still offers a good overview of the subject matter of anthropology and is widely quoted.

"Culture . . . is that complex whole which includes knowledge, belief, arts, morals, law, custom, and any other capabilities and habits acquired by man as a member of society" (Tylor 1871/1958, p. 1). The crucial phrase here is "acquired by man as a member of society." Tylor's definition focuses on beliefs and behavior that people acquire not through biological heredity but by growing up in a particular society where they are exposed to a specific cultural tradition. Enculturation is the process by which a child learns his or her culture.

Illustrating social situational learning, a cheetah uses a hartebeest calf to teach its young how to hunt and kill.

WHAT IS CULTURE?

Culture Is All-Encompassing

For anthropologists, culture includes much more than refinement, taste, sophistication, education, and appreciation of the fine arts. Not only college graduates but all people are cultured. The most interesting and significant cultural forces are those which affect people every day of their lives, particularly those which influence children during enculturation. *Culture,* as defined anthropologically, encompasses features that are sometimes regarded as trivial or unworthy of serious study, such as "popular" culture. To understand contemporary North American culture, we must consider television, fast-food restaurants, sports, and games. As a cultural manifestation, a rock star may be as interesting as a symphony conductor, a comic book as significant as a book-award winner.

Culture Is General and Specific

All human populations have culture, which is therefore a generalized possession of the genus *Homo.* This is **Culture** (capital C) in the **general** sense, a capacity and possession shared by hominids. However, anthropologists also use the word *culture* to describe the different and varied cultural traditions of specific societies. This is **culture** in the **specific** sense (small c). Humanity shares a capacity for culture, but people live in particular cultures, where they are enculturated along different lines. All people grow up in the presence of a particular set of cultural rules transmitted over the generations. These are the specific cultures or cultural traditions that anthropologists study.

Culture Is Learned

The ease with which children absorb any cultural tradition reflects the uniquely elaborated hominid capacity to learn. There are different kinds of learning, some of which we share with other animals. One kind is **individual situational learning,** which occurs when an animal learns from, and bases its future behavior on, its own experience, for example, avoiding fire after discovering that it hurts. Animals also exhibit **social situational learning,** in which they learn from other members of the social group, not necessarily through language. Wolves, for example, learn hunting strategies from other pack members. Social situational learning is particularly important among monkeys and apes, our closest relatives. Finally there is **cultural learning.** This depends on the uniquely developed human capacity to use *symbols,* signs that have no necessary or natural connection with the things for which they stand.

A critical feature in hominid evolution is dependence on cultural learning. Through culture people create, remember, and deal with ideas. They grasp and apply specific systems of symbolic meaning.

TOUCHING, AFFECTION, LOVE, AND SEX

Comparing the United States with Brazil—or virtually any Latin nation—we can see a striking cultural contrast between a culture that discourages physical contact and demonstrations of affection and one in which the contrary is true. We can also see rampant confusion in American culture about love, sex, and affection. This stands in sharp contrast to the more realistic Brazilian separation of the three.

"Don't touch me." "Take your hands off me." These are normal statements in American culture that are virtually never heard in Brazil, the Western Hemisphere's second most populous country. Americans don't like to be touched. The world's cultures have strikingly different opinions about matters of personal space. When Americans talk, walk, and dance, they maintain a certain distance from others—their personal space. Brazilians, who maintain less physical distance, interpret this as a sign of coldness. When conversing with an American, the Brazilian characteristically moves in as the American "instinctively" retreats. In these body movements, neither Brazilian nor American is trying consciously to be especially friendly or unfriendly. Each is merely executing a program written on the self by years of exposure to a particular cultural tradition. Because of different ideas about proper social space, cocktail parties in international meeting places such as the United Nations can resemble an elaborate insect mating ritual as diplomats from different cultures advance, withdraw, and sidestep.

One of the most obvious differences between Brazil and the United States involves kissing, hugging, and touching. Middle-class Brazilians teach their children—both boys and girls—to kiss (on the cheek, two or three times, coming and going) every adult relative they ever see. Given the size of Brazilian extended families, this can mean hundreds of people. Females continue kissing throughout their lives. They kiss male and female kin, friends, relatives of friends, friends of relatives, friends of friends, and, when it seems appropriate, more casual acquaintances. Males go on kissing their female relatives and friends. Until they are adolescents, boys also kiss adult male relatives. Thereafter, Brazilian men greet each other with hearty handshakes and a traditional male hug (*abraço*). The closer the relationship, the tighter and longer-lasting the embrace. These comments apply to brothers, cousins, uncles, and friends. Many Brazilian men keep on kissing their fathers and uncles throughout their lives.

Like other Americans who spend time in a Latin culture, I miss these kisses and handshakes when I get back to the United States. After several months in Brazil, I find North Americans rather cold and impersonal. Many Brazilians share this opinion. I have heard similar feelings expressed by Italian-Americans describing Americans with different ethnic backgrounds.

Many Americans fear physical contact and confuse love and affection with sex. According to clinical psychologist David E. Klimek, who has written about intimacy and marriage, "in American society, if we go much beyond simple touching, our behavior takes on a minor sexual twist" (Slade 1984). Americans define demonstrations of affection with

---

Anthropologist Clifford Geertz defines culture as ideas based on cultural learning and symbols. Cultures are sets of "control mechanisms—plans, recipes, rules, constructions, what computer engineers call programs for the governing of behavior" (Geertz 1973, p. 44). These programs are absorbed by people through enculturation in particular traditions. People gradually internalize a previously established system of meanings and symbols which they use to define their world, express their feelings, and make their judgments. Thereafter, this system helps guide their behavior and perceptions throughout their lives.

Every person begins immediately, through a process of conscious and unconscious learning and interaction with others, to internalize, or incorporate, a cultural tradition through the process of enculturation. Sometimes culture is taught directly, as when parents tell their children to say "thank you" when someone gives them something or does them a favor.

Culture is also transmitted through observation. Children pay attention to the things that go on around them. They modify their behavior not just because other people tell them to but as a result of their own observations and growing awareness of what their culture considers right and wrong. Culture is also absorbed unconsciously. North Ameri-

The world's cultures have strikingly different opinions about personal space—how far apart people should be in normal encounters and interactions. Contrast the gap between the two American men with the closeness of the Egyptian Bedouins.

reference to marriage. Love and affection are supposed to unite the married pair, and they blend into sex. When a wife asks her husband for "a little affection," she may mean, or he may think she means, sex. Listening as Americans discuss love and sex on talk shows and in other public forums, it's obvious that American cul-

ture confuses these needs and feelings.

This confusion between love, affection, and sex is clear on Valentine's Day, which used to be just for lovers. Valentines used to be sent to wives, husbands, girlfriends, and boyfriends. Now, after years of promotion by the greeting card industry, they also go to mothers, fathers, sons, daughters, aunts, and uncles. Valentine's Day "personals" in the local newspaper also illustrate this blurring of sexual and nonsexual affection, which is a source of so much confusion in contemporary American culture. In Brazil, Lovers' Day retains its autonomy. Mother, father, and children have their own separate days.

It is true, of course, that in a good marriage love and affection exist alongside sex. Nevertheless, affection does not imply sex. Brazilian culture shows that there can be rampant kissing, hugging, and touching without sex—or fears of improper sexuality. In Brazilian culture, physical demonstrations help cement several kinds of close personal relationships that have no sexual component.

cans acquire their culture's notions about how far apart people should stand when they talk not by being told to maintain a certain distance but through a gradual process of observation, experience, and conscious and unconscious behavior modification. No one tells Latins to stand closer together than North Americans do, but they learn to do so anyway as part of their cultural tradition.

Culture Is Symbolic

Symbolic thought is unique and crucial to humans and to culture. Anthropologist Leslie White defined culture as

an extrasomatic (nongenetic, nonbodily), temporal continuum of things and events dependent upon symbolling.... Culture consists of tools, implements, utensils, clothing, ornaments, customs, institutions, beliefs, rituals, games, works of art, language, etc. (White 1959, p. 3)

For White, culture originated when our ancestors acquired the ability to symbol, or

freely and arbitrarily to originate and bestow meaning upon a thing or event, and, correspondingly, ... to grasp and appreciate such meaning. (White 1959, p. 3)

A **symbol** is something verbal or nonverbal, within a particular language or culture, that comes to stand for something else. There is no obvious, natural, or necessary connection between the symbol and what it symbolizes. A pet that barks is no more naturally a *dog* than a *chien, Hund,* or *mbwa,* to use the words for the animal we call "dog" in French, German, and Swahili. Language is one of the distinctive possessions of *Homo sapiens.* No other animal has developed anything approaching the complexity of language.

Symbols are usually linguistic. However, there are also nonverbal symbols, such as flags, which stand for countries, as arches do for hamburger chains. Holy water is a potent symbol in Roman Catholicism. As is true of all symbols, the association between a symbol (water) and what is symbolized (holiness) is arbitrary and conventional. Water is not intrinsically holier than milk, blood, or other liquids. Holy water is not chemically different from ordinary water. Holy water is a symbol within Roman Catholicism, which is part of an international cultural system. A natural thing has been arbitrarily associated with a particular meaning for Catholics, who share common beliefs and experiences that are based on learning and are transmitted across the generations.

For hundreds of thousands of years, people have shared the abilities on which culture rests. These abilities are to learn, to think symbolically, to manipulate language, and to use tools and other cultural products in organizing their lives and coping with their environments. Every contemporary human population has the ability to symbol and thus to create and maintain culture. Our nearest relatives—chimpanzees and gorillas—have rudimentary cultural abilities. However, no other animal has elaborated cultural abilities—to learn, to communicate, and to store, process, and use information— to the same extent as *Homo.*

Culture Seizes Nature

Culture imposes itself on nature. I once arrived at a summer camp at 5 P.M. I was hot and wanted to swim in the lake. However, I read the camp rules and learned that no swimming was permitted after five. A cultural system had seized the lake, which is part of nature. Natural lakes don't close at five, but cultural lakes do.

Culture takes the natural biological urges we share with other animals and teaches us how to express them in particular ways. People have to eat, but culture teaches us what, when, and how. In many cultures people have their main meal at noon, but Americans prefer a large dinner. English people eat fish for breakfast, but Americans prefer hot cakes and cold cereals. Brazilians put hot milk into strong coffee, whereas Americans pour cold milk into a weaker brew. Midwesterners dine at five or six, Spaniards at ten. Europeans eat with the fork in the left hand and the knife in the right. Meat cut by the knife is immediately conveyed to the mouth with the fork, which Americans switch to the right hand before eating.

For the Betsileo of Madagascar, there is no way of saying "to eat" without saying "to eat rice," their favorite and staple food. So strong is their preference for rice that they garnish it with beans, potatoes, and other starches. Eels cooked in their own grease are a delicacy for the Betsileos' honored visitors, a category in which I feared being included because of my cultural aversion to eel meat (although I did tolerate grasshoppers cooked in peanut oil; they tasted like peanuts). In northeastern Brazil I grew to like chicken cooked in its own blood, a favorite there.

Like the lake at summer camp, human nature is appropriated by cultural systems and molded in hundreds of directions. All people must eliminate wastes from their bodies. However, some cultures teach people to defecate standing up, while others tell them to do it sitting down. Frenchmen aren't embarrassed to urinate in public, routinely stepping into barely shielded *pissoirs* in Paris streets. Peasant women in the Peruvian highlands squat in the streets and urinate into gutters. They get all the privacy they need from their massive skirts. All these habits are parts of cultural traditions that have converted natural acts into cultural customs.

Culture Is Shared

Culture is an attribute not of individuals per se but of individuals as members of *groups.* Culture is transmitted in society. We learn our culture by observing, listening, talking, and interacting with other people. Shared cultural beliefs, values, memories, expectations, and ways of thinking and acting override differences between people. Enculturation unifies people by providing us with common experiences.

People in the United States sometimes have trouble understanding the power of culture because of the value that American culture places on the idea of the individual. Americans are fond of saying that everyone is unique and special in some way. However, in American culture individualism itself is a distinctive shared value that is transmitted through hundreds of statements and settings in our daily lives. From daytime TV's Mr. Rogers to "real-life" parents, grandparents, and teachers, our enculturative agents insist that we are all "someone special."

Today's parents were yesterday's children. If they grew up in American culture, they absorbed certain values and beliefs transmitted over the generations. People become agents in the enculturation of their children, just as their parents were for them. Although culture constantly changes, certain fundamental beliefs, values, world views, and child-rearing practices endure. Consider a simple American example of enduring shared enculturation. As children, when we didn't finish a meal, our parents reminded us of starving children in some foreign country, just as our grandparents had done a generation earlier. The specific country changes (China, India, Bangladesh, Ethiopia). Still, American culture goes on transmitting the peculiar idea that by eating all our brussels sprouts or broccoli, we can somehow help a Third World child.

Culture Is Patterned

Cultures are not haphazard collections of customs and beliefs but integrated, patterned systems. Customs, institutions, beliefs, and values are interrelated; if one changes, others change as well. During the 1950s, for example, most American women expected to have domestic careers as homemakers and mothers. Today's college women expect to get jobs when they graduate.

As women enter the work force in increasing numbers, attitudes toward marriage, family, and children change. Outside work places strains on marriage and the family. Late marriage, "living together," and divorce become more common. These social changes reflect economic changes as the U.S. economy shifts from heavy goods manufacture toward services and information processing. Economic changes have produced changes in attitudes

Cultures are integrated, patterned systems: when one custom, belief, or value changes, others change as well. During the 1950s most American women expected to have domestic careers. With women entering the work force in increasing numbers over the past three decades, attitudes toward work and family have changed. Most of today's college graduates plan to balance jobs and family responsibilities. Contrast the "fifties Mom" with a modern career woman—Illinoisan Carol Moseley Braun, the first African-American woman to be elected to the United States Senate.

and behavior in regard to work, gender roles, marriage, and the family.

Cultures are integrated not simply by their dominant economic activities and social patterns but also by enduring themes, values, configurations, and world views. Cultures train their individual members to share certain personality traits. Separate elements of a culture can be integrated by key symbols, such as fertility or militarism. A set of characteristic central or **core values** (key, basic, or central values) integrates each culture and helps distinguish it from others. For instance, the work ethic, individualism, achievement, and self-reliance are core values that have integrated American culture for generations. Different value sets pattern other cultures.

People Use Culture Creatively

Although cultural rules tell us what to do and how to do it, we don't always do what the rules dictate. People can learn, interpret, and manipulate the same rule in different ways. People use their culture creatively, rather than blindly following its dictates. Even if they agree about what should and shouldn't be done, people don't always do as their culture directs or as other people expect. Many rules are violated, some very often (for example, automobile speed limits). Some anthropologists find it useful to distinguish between ideal and real culture. The *ideal culture* consists of what people say they should do and what they say they do. *Real culture* refers to their actual behavior as observed by the anthropologist. This contrast is like the emic-etic contrast discussion in the Field Methods chapter.

Culture Is Adaptive and Maladaptive

To cope with or adapt to environmental stresses, humans can draw on both biological traits and learned, symbol-based behavior patterns. Besides biological means of adaptation, human groups also employ "cultural adaptive kits" containing customary patterns, activities, and tools. Although humans continue to adapt biologically as well as culturally, reliance on social and cultural means of adaptation has increased during hominid evolution.

We saw in Chapter 1 that although adaptive behavior offers short-term benefits to individuals, it may harm the environment and threaten the group's long-term survival. Creative manipulation of culture and the environment by men and women can foster a more secure economy, but it can also deplete strategic resources (Bennett 1969, p. 19). Thus, despite the crucial role of cultural adaptation in human evolution, cultural traits and patterns can also be **maladaptive,** threatening the group's continued existence (survival and reproduction). Many modern cultural patterns, such as policies that encourage overpopulation, inadequate food distribution systems, overconsumption, and pollution, appear to be maladaptive in the long run.

Furthermore, practices that are adaptive or harmless for one culture may be maladaptive for another with which the first culture trades or which it dominates politically. Besides valuing subsistence resources, people may also esteem items (jewelry, for example) that lack subsistence or utilitarian value but are considered aesthetically pleasing or enhance social status. Given the modern world system of international trade and communication, the prestige demands of one culture can deplete the local ecosystems of others. For example, animals may be slaughtered for products that have no local value for food, dress, or ornamentation.

Many African animals are going extinct as poachers respond to the demands of collectors in other nations. Gorillas are killed, and their hands are sold to foreign collectors as ashtrays. Poachers slaughter elephants and export their ivory, which is used to make signature stamps (popular in Asia), jewelry, ornamental carvings, billiard balls, and piano keys. The main importers have been Japan and Hong Kong, which accounted for 75 percent of world ivory imports in 1988. The African elephant population declined from 1.5 million to 500,000 during the 1980s. An international ivory ban may yet save the elephant from the rapacious demands of foreign cultures. However, it may be too late for the rhinoceros, of which only a few thousand survive. Rhino horn is used for ceremonial dagger hilts in Yemen and is ground up to make aphrodisiac powder in Asia (Shabecoff 1989*a* and *b*).

Levels of Culture

The destruction of resources and biodiversity in order to gratify cultural appetites proceeds in a world in which we may distinguish different levels of culture: national, international, and subcultural. **Na-**

tional culture refers to the experiences, beliefs, learned behavior patterns, and values shared by citizens of the same nation. **International culture** is the term for cultural traditions that extend beyond national boundaries. Because culture is transmitted through learning rather than genetically, cultural traits can diffuse from one group to another. Two biological species cannot share their genetically transmitted means of adaptation. However, two cultures *can* share cultural experiences and means of adaptation through borrowing or diffusion.

Borrowing of culture traits has gone on throughout human history. **Diffusion** is direct when two cultures intermarry, wage war on, or trade with each other or when they watch the same TV program. Diffusion is indirect when products and patterns move from population A to population C via population B without any firsthand contact between A and C.

Through diffusion, migration, and multinational organizations, many culture traits and patterns have international scope. Roman Catholics in different countries share experiences, symbols, beliefs, and values transmitted by their church. Contemporary United States, Canada, Great Britain, and Australia share culture traits they have inherited from their common linguistic and cultural ancestors in Great Britain.

Cultures can also be smaller than nations. Although people in the same society or nation share a cultural tradition, all cultures also contain diversity. Individuals, families, villages, regions, classes, and other subgroups within a culture have different learning experiences as well as shared ones. **Subcultures** are different symbol-based patterns and traditions associated with subgroups in the same complex society. In a complex nation such as the contemporary United States or Canada, subcultures originate in ethnicity, class, region, and religion. The religious backgrounds of Jews, Baptists, and Roman Catholics create subcultural differences between them. Although they share the same national culture, northerners and southerners exhibit differences in beliefs and customary behavior as a result of regional subcultural variation. French-speaking Canadians contrast on the subcultural level with English speakers in the same country. Italian-Americans have ethnic traditions different from those of Irish-, Polish-, and African-Americans.

Despite characteristic American notions that peo-ple should "make up their own minds" and "have a right to their opinion," little of what we think is original or unique. We share our opinions and beliefs with many other people. Illustrating the power of shared cultural background, we are most likely to agree with and feel comfortable with people who are socially, economically, and culturally similar to ourselves. This is one reason why Americans abroad tend to socialize with each other, just as French and British colonials did in their overseas empires. Birds of a feather flock together, but for people the familiar plumage is culture.

Ethnocentrism and Cultural Relativism

One of anthropology's main goals is to combat **ethnocentrism,** the tendency to apply one's own cultural values in judging the behavior and beliefs of people raised in other cultures. Ethnocentrism is a cultural universal. People everywhere think that familiar explanations, opinions, and customs are true, right, proper, and moral. They regard different behavior as strange or savage. The tribal names that appear in anthropology books often come from the native word for *people.* "What are you called?" asks the anthropologist. "Mugmug," reply informants. *Mugmug* may turn out to be synonymous with *people,* but it also may be the only word the natives have for themselves. Other tribes are not considered fully human. The not-quite-people in neighboring groups are not classified as *Mugmug.* They are given different names that symbolize their inferior humanity.

The opposite of ethnocentrism is **cultural relativism,** the argument that behavior in a particular culture should not be judged by the standards of another. This position can also present problems. At its most extreme, cultural relativism argues that there is no superior, international, or universal morality, that the moral and ethical rules of all cultures deserve equal respect. In the extreme relativist view, Nazi Germany is evaluated as nonjudgmentally as Athenian Greece.

How should anthropologists deal with ethnocentrism and cultural relativism? I believe that anthropology's main job is to present accurate accounts and explanations of cultural phenomena. The anthropologist doesn't have to approve customs such as infanticide, cannibalism, and torture to record their existence and determine their causes. However, each anthropologist has a choice about where to do field work. Some anthropologists choose not to study a particular culture because they discover in advance or early in field work that behavior they consider morally repugnant is practiced there. Anthropologists respect human diversity. Most ethnographers try to be objective, accurate, and sensitive in their accounts of other cultures. However, objectivity, sensitivity, and a cross-cultural perspective don't mean that anthropologists have to ignore international standards of justice and morality.

UNIVERSALITY, PARTICULARITY, AND GENERALITY

Anthropologists agree that cultural learning is uniquely elaborated among hominids, that culture is the major reason for human adaptability, and that the capacity for culture is shared by all humans. Anthropologists also unanimously accept a doctrine originally proposed in the nineteenth century: "the psychic unity of man." Anthropology assumes **biopsychological equality** among human groups. This means that although *individuals* differ in emotional and intellectual tendencies and capacities, all human *populations* have equivalent capacities for culture. Regardless of physical appearance and genetic composition, humans can learn *any* cultural tradition.

To understand this point, consider that contemporary Americans and Canadians are the genetically mixed descendants of people from all over the world. Our ancestors were biologically varied, lived in different countries and continents, and participated in hundreds of cultural traditions. However, the earliest colonists, later immigrants, and their descendants have all become active participants in American and Canadian life. All now share a common national culture.

To recognize biopsychological equality is not to deny differences between populations. In studying human diversity in time and space, anthropologists distinguish between the universal, the generalized, and the particular. Certain biological, psychological, social, and cultural features are **universal,** shared by all human populations in every culture. Others are merely **generalities,** common to several but not all human groups. Still other traits are **particularities,** unique to certain cultural traditions.

Universality

Universal traits are the ones that more or less distinguish *Homo sapiens* from other species (see Brown 1991). Biologically based universals include a long period of infant dependency, year-round (rather than seasonal) sexuality, and a complex brain that enables us to use symbols, languages, and tools. Psychological universals arise from human biology and from experiences common to human development in all cases. These include growth in the womb, birth itself, and interaction with parents and parent substitutes.

Among the social universals is life in groups and in some kind of family. In all human societies culture organizes social life and depends on social interactions for its expression and continuation. Family living and food sharing are universals. Among the most significant cultural universals are **exogamy** and the **incest taboo** (prohibition against marrying or mating with a close relative). Humans everywhere consider some people (various cultures differ about *which* people) too closely related to mate or marry. The violation of this taboo is *incest*, which is discouraged and punished in a variety of ways in different cultures. If incest is prohibited, exogamy—marriage outside one's group—is inevitable. Because it links human groups together into larger networks, exogamy has been crucial in hominid evolution. Exogamy elaborates on tendencies observed among other primates. Recent studies of monkeys and apes show that these animals also avoid mating with close kin and often mate outside their native groups.

Particularity

Many cultural traits are widely shared because of diffusion and independent invention and as cultural universals. Nevertheless, different cultures emphasize different things. Cultures are patterned and integrated differently and display tremendous variation and diversity. Uniqueness and particularity stand at the opposite extreme from universality.

Unusual and exotic beliefs and practices lend distinctiveness to particular cultural traditions. Many cultures ritually observe such universal life-cycle events as birth, puberty, marriage, parenthood, and death. However, cultures vary in just which event merits special celebration. Americans regard expensive weddings as more socially appropriate than lavish funerals. However, the Betsileo of Madagascar take the opposite view. The marriage ceremony is a minor event that brings together just the couple and a few close relatives. However, a funeral is a measure of the deceased person's social position and lifetime achievement, and it may attract a thousand people. Why use money on a house, the Betsileo say, when one can use it on the tomb where one will spend eternity in the company of dead relatives? How different from contemporary Americans' growing preference for quick and inexpensive funerals and cremation, which would horrify the Betsileo, whose ancestral bones and relics are important ritual objects.

Cultures vary tremendously in their beliefs and practices. By focusing on and trying to explain alternative customs, anthropology forces us to reappraise our familiar ways of thinking. In a world full of cultural diversity, contemporary American culture is just one cultural variant, no more natural than the others.

Generality

Between universals and uniqueness is a middle ground that consists of cultural generalities: regularities that occur in different times and places but not in all cultures. One reason for generalities is diffusion. Societies can share the same beliefs and customs because of borrowing or through (cultural) inheritance from a common cultural ancestor. Other generalities originate in **independent invention** of the same culture trait or pattern in two or more different cultures. Similar needs and circumstances have led people in different lands to innovate in parallel ways. They have independently come up with the same cultural solution or arrangement.

One cultural generality that is present in many but not all societies is the **nuclear family,** a kinship group consisting of parents and children. Although many middle-class Americans ethnocentrically view the nuclear family as a proper and "natural" group, it is not universal. It is totally absent, for example, among the Nayars, who live on the Malabar Coast of India. The Nayars live in female-headed households, and husbands and wives do not coreside. In many other societies, the nuclear family is submerged in larger kin groups, such as extended families, lineages, and clans. However, the nuclear family is prominent in many of the technologically simple societies that live by hunting and gathering. It is also a significant kin group among contemporary middle-class North Americans and Western Europeans. Later, an explanation of the nuclear family as a basic kinship unit in specific types of society will be given.

SUMMARY

Culture, a distinctive possession of humanity, is acquired by all humans through enculturation. Culture encompasses rule-governed, shared, symbol-based learned behavior and beliefs transmitted across the generations. Everyone is cultured, not just people with elite educations. The genus *Homo* has the capacity for Culture (in a general sense), but people live in specific cultures where they are raised according to different traditions. Culture rests on the hominid capacity for cultural learning. *Culture* refers to customary beliefs and behavior and to the rules for conduct internalized in human beings through enculturation. These rules lead people to think and act in certain consistent, distinctive, and characteristic ways.

Other animals learn, but only humans have cultural learning, which depends on symbols. Cultural learning rests on the universal human capacity to think symbolically, arbitrarily bestowing meaning on a thing or event. By convention, a symbol, which may be linguistic or non-verbal, stands for something else with which it has no necessary or natural relation. Symbols have a particular meaning and value for people in the same culture. People share experiences, memories, values, and beliefs as a result of common enculturation. People absorb cultural lessons consciously and unconsciously.

Cultural traditions seize natural phenomena, including biologically based desires and needs, and channel them in particular directions. Cultures are patterned and integrated through their dominant economic forces, social patterns, key symbols, and core values. Cultural rules do not always dictate behavior. There is room for creativity, flexibility, and diversity within cultures. Anthropologists distinguish between what people say they do and what they actually do. Cultural means of adaptation have been crucial in hominid evolution, although aspects of culture can also be maladaptive.

There are different levels of cultural systems. Diffusion

and migration carry the same cultural traits and patterns to different areas. These traits are shared across national boundaries. Nations include subcultural differences associated with ethnicity, region, and social class.

Anthropology finds no evidence that genetic differences explain cultural variation. Adopting a comparative perspective, anthropology examines biological, psychological, social, and cultural universals and generalities. It also considers unique and distinctive aspects of the human condition. In examining cultural elaborations on the fundamental biological plasticity of *Homo sapiens*, anthropology shows that American cultural traditions are no more natural than any others.

GLOSSARY

biopsychological equality: The premise that although individuals differ in emotional and intellectual capacities, all human populations have equivalent capacities for culture.

core values: Key, basic, or central values that integrate a culture and help distinguish it from others.

cultural learning: Learning based on the human capacity to think symbolically.

cultural relativism: The position that the values and standards of cultures differ and deserve respect. Extreme relativism argues that cultures should be judged solely by their own standards.

Culture, general: Spelled with a capital C; culture in the general sense as a capacity and possession shared by hominids.

culture, specific: Spelled with a small c; a culture in the specific sense, any one of the different and varied cultural traditions of specific societies.

diffusion: Borrowing between cultures either directly or through intermediaries.

ethnocentrism: The tendency to view one's own culture as best and to judge the behavior and beliefs of culturally different people by one's own standards.

exogamy: Mating or marriage outside one's kin group; a cultural universal.

generality: Culture pattern or trait that exists in some but not all societies.

incest taboo: Universal prohibition against marrying or mating with a close relative.

independent invention: Development of the same culture trait or pattern in separate cultures as a result of comparable needs and circumstances.

individual situational learning: Type of learning in which animals learn from and base their future behavior on personal experience.

international culture: Cultural traditions that extend beyond national boundaries.

maladaptive: Harmful to survival and reproduction.

national culture: Cultural experiences, beliefs, learned behavior patterns, and values shared by citizens of the same nation.

nuclear family: Kinship group consisting of parents and children.

particularity: Distinctive or unique culture trait, pattern, or integration.

social situational learning: Learning from other members of the social group, not necessarily through language.

subcultures: Different cultural symbol-based traditions associated with subgroups in the same complex society.

symbol: Something, verbal or nonverbal, that arbitrarily and by convention stands for something else, with which it has no necessary or natural connection.

troop: Basic unit of social organization among nonhuman primates; composed of multiple adult males and females and their offspring.

universal: Something that exists in every culture.

STUDY QUESTIONS

1. What does it mean to say that culture is all-encompassing?
2. What is the difference between culture in the general sense and the specific sense?
3. What are the different kinds of learning? On which is culture based?
4. What does it mean to say that culture is symbolic?
5. What does it mean to say that culture is shared?
6. What does it mean to say that culture is patterned or integrated?
7. How is culture adaptive?
8. How are human adaptability and culture related?
9. What does it mean to say that there are levels of culture?

10. What is ethnocentrism?
11. What is cultural relativism, and what are its potential problems?
12. How does North American culture (of the United States or Canada) illustrate the idea of psychic unity?
13. What is meant by cultural universals, generalities, and particularities?
14. How is the idea of cultural particularity related to the notion of cultural patterning or integration?

SUGGESTED ADDITIONAL READING

BROWN, DONALD
  1991 *Human Universals.* New York: McGraw-Hill. Surveys the evidence for "human nature" and explores the roles of culture and biology in human variation.
GAMST, F.C., AND E. NORBECK, EDS.
  1976 *Ideas of Culture: Sources and Uses.* New York: Harcourt Brace Jovanovich. Surveys various aspects and definitions of culture. Contains both classic and original essays.
GEERTZ, C.
  1973 *The Interpretation of Cultures.* New York: Basic Books. Essays about culture viewed as a system of symbols and meaning.
HALL, EDWARD T.
  1990 *Understanding Cultural Differences.* Yarmouth, ME: Intercultural Press. Focusing on business and industrial management, this book examines the role of national cultural contrasts between France, Germany, and the United States.

  1992 *An Anthropology of Everyday Life: An Autobiography.* New York: Doubleday. A prominent student of language and culture examines his own life in the context of intercultural communication.
HARRIS, M.
  1987 *Why Nothing Works: The Anthropology of Daily Life.* New York: Simon & Schuster. Social consequences of the continuing economic shift from goods manufacture toward services and information processing.
KROEBER, A.L., AND C. KLUCKHOLN
  1963 *Culture: A Critical Review of Concepts and Definitions.* New York: Vintage. Discusses and categorizes more than a hundred definitions of culture.
WAGNER, R.
  1981 *The Invention of Culture.* rev. ed. Chicago: University of Chicago Press. Culture, creativity, society, and the self.

ETHNICITY AND ETHNIC RELATIONS

We know from the last chapter that culture is shared, learned, symbolic, patterned, all-encompassing, adaptive, and maladaptive. Now we consider the relation between culture and ethnicity. Ethnicity is based on cultural similarities and differences in a society or nation. The similarities are with members of the same ethnic group; the differences are between that group and others.

ETHNIC GROUPS AND ETHNICITY

As with any culture, members of an **ethnic group** *share* certain beliefs, values, habits, customs, and norms because of their common background. They define themselves as different and special because of cultural features. This distinction may arise from language, religion, historical experience, geographic isolation, kinship, or race (see the next chapter on race). Markers of an ethnic group may include a collective name, belief in common descent, a sense of solidarity, and an association with a specific territory, which the group may or may not hold (Ryan 1990, pp. xiii, xiv).

Ethnicity means identification with, and feeling part of, an ethnic group, and exclusion from certain other groups because of this affiliation. Ethnic feeling and associated behavior vary in intensity within ethnic groups and countries and over time. A change in the degree of importance attached to an ethnic identity may reflect political changes (Soviet rule ends—ethnic feeling rises) or individual life-cycle changes (young people relinquish, or old people reclaim, an ethnic background).

We saw in the last chapter that people participate in various levels of culture. Subgroups within a culture (including ethnic groups in a nation) have different learning experiences as well as shared ones. Subcultures originate in ethnicity, class, region, and religion. Individuals often have more than one group identity. People may be loyal (depending on circumstances) to their neighborhood, school, town, state or province, region, nation, continent, religion, ethnic group, or interest group (Ryan 1990, p. xxii). In a complex society like the United States or Canada people constantly negotiate their social identities. All of us "wear different hats," presenting ourselves sometimes as one thing, sometimes as another.

The term **status** can be used to refer to such "hats"—to any position that determines where someone fits in society (Light, Keller, and Calhoun 1994). Social statuses include parent, professor, student, factory worker, Democrat, shoe salesperson, labor leader, ethnic group member, and thousands of others. People always occupy multiple statuses (e.g., Hispanic, Catholic, infant, brother). Among the statuses we occupy, particular ones dominate in particular settings, such as son or daughter at home and student in the classroom.

Some statuses are **ascribed:** people have little or no choice about occupying them. Age is an ascribed status; people can't choose not to age. Race and ethnicity are usually ascribed; people are born members of a certain group and remain so all their lives. **Achieved** statuses, by contrast, aren't automatic but come through traits, talents, actions, efforts, activities, and accomplishments.

In many societies an ascribed status is associated with a position in the social-political hierarchy. Certain groups, called **minority groups,** are subordinate. They have inferior power and less secure access to resources than do **majority groups** (which are superordinate, dominant, or controlling). Often ethnic groups are minorities. When an ethnic group is assumed to have a biological basis, it is called a **race.** Discrimination against such a group is called **racism.** The next chapter considers race in social and biological perspective.

Minority groups are obvious features of stratification in the United States. The 1989 poverty rate was 10.0 percent for whites, 30.7 percent for blacks, and 26.2 percent for Hispanics (*Statistical Abstract* 1991, p. 462). Census data confirm the inequality that continues to deny African-Americans and Hispanics full access to advantages that most other Americans enjoy. In 1989, 43 percent of American black children and 35.5 percent of Hispanic children lived in households with subpoverty incomes. This was true for just 14 percent of American white children. Inequality shows up consistently in unemployment figures.

Minorities need not have fewer members than the majority group does. Women in the United States and blacks in South Africa are numerical majorities but minorities in terms of income, authority, and power. In 1992 ethnic Albanians, who are Moslems, were a political minority, although an overwhelming numerical majority (90 percent of the population), in Kosovo, a region of the former Yugoslavia (now Serbia and Montenegro) bordering Albania.

Status Shifting

Sometimes statuses, particularly ascribed ones, are mutually exclusive. It's hard to bridge the gap between black and white, or male and female (although some rock stars seem to be trying to do so). Sometimes, taking a status or joining a group requires a conversion experience, acquiring a new and overwhelming primary identity, such as becoming a "born again" Christian.

Some statuses aren't mutually exclusive, but contextual. People can be both black and Hispanic, or both a mother and a senator. One identity is used in certain settings, another in different ones. We call this the *situational negotiation of social identity*. When ethnic identity is flexible and situational (Moerman 1965), it can become an achieved status. Benedict (1970), Despres (ed. 1975), and Williams (1989) all stress the fluidity and flexibility of ethnicity.

Hispanics, for example, may move through levels of culture (shifting ethnic affiliations) as they negotiate their identities. "Hispanic" is an ethnic category based mainly on language. It includes whites, blacks, and "racially" mixed Spanish speakers and their ethnically conscious descendants. (There are also "Native American," and even "Asian," Hispanics). "Hispanic" lumps together millions of people of diverse geographic origin—Puerto Rico, Mexico, Cuba, El Salvador, Guatemala, the Dominican Republic, and other Spanish-speaking countries of Central and South America and the Caribbean. "Latino" is a broader category, which can also include Brazilians (who speak Portuguese).

Mexican-Americans (Chicanos), Cuban Americans, and Puerto Ricans may mobilize to promote general Hispanic issues (e.g., opposition to "English-only" laws), but act as three separate interest groups in other contexts. Cuban-Americans are richer on average than Chicanos and Puerto Ricans are, and their class interests and voting patterns differ. Cubans often vote Republican, but Puerto Ricans and Chicanos generally favor Democrats. Some Mexican-Americans whose families have lived in the United States for generations have little in common with new Hispanic immigrants, such as those from Central America. Many Americans (especially those fluent in English) claim Hispanic ethnicity in some contexts but shift to a general "American" identity in others.

As social categories—including ethnic labels—proliferate in our increasingly diverse society, some people have trouble deciding on their social identity, on a label that fits. One day a Korean-American student asked me, following my lecture on the social construction of race and ethnicity (see the next chapter), what she was, in ethnic terms. She had been born and raised in the United States by parents from Korea. She told me about visiting Korea, meeting her relatives there, and being considered by them—

The ethnic label "Hispanic" lumps together millions of people of diverse geographic origin—Puerto Rico, Mexico, Cuba, El Salvador, Guatemala, the Dominican Republic, and other Spanish-speaking countries of Central and South America and the Caribbean. Hispanics of diverse national backgrounds, like these Cuban-Americans in Miami, may mobilize to promote general Hispanic issues (such as opposition to "English-only" laws), but act as separate interest groups in other contexts. Images of Cuba decorate this restaurant in Miami's "Little Havana."

and feeling herself—American. She finds it hard to feel "Korean." In the United States she is labeled "Asian," "Oriental," or "Asian-American." But she doesn't feel much in common with other "Asians" and Asian-Americans, like Chinese, Japanese, Vietnamese, Laotians, and Cambodians. After our discussion, we concluded that a reasonable ethnic label for her was "Korean-American." Happily, she had found an ethnic identity, important in the contemporary United States.

ETHNIC GROUPS, NATIONS, AND NATIONALITIES

What is the relation between an ethnic group and a nation? The term **nation** was once synonymous with "tribe" or "ethnic group." All three of these terms referred to a single culture sharing a single language, religion, history, territory, ancestry, and kinship. Thus one could speak interchangeably of the Seneca (American Indian) nation, tribe, or ethnic group. Now *nation* has come to mean a **state**—an independent, centrally organized political unit, or a government. *Nation* and *state* have become synonymous. Combined in **nation-state** they refer to an autonomous political entity, a "country"—like the United States, "one nation, indivisible."

Because of migration, conquest, and colonialism (see below), most nation-states are not ethnically homogeneous, and the term *nation-state* is then a misnomer. Another reason for ethnic diversity is that states sometimes manipulate ethnicity and encourage ethnic divisions for political and economic ends. For example, analyzing nineteenth-century Guatemala, Carol Smith (1990) challenged the previously accepted notion that a coercive state arose there to curb and control ethnic conflict. Instead, she shows that the Guatemalan elites used the idea of ethnic contrasts to divide the masses and thus discourage peasant solidarity. This policy of "divide and rule" fostered economic development that benefitted the elite.

No more than one-fourth of all countries are ethnically homogeneous. Of 132 nation-states existing in 1971, Connor (1972) found just 12 (9 percent) to be ethnically homogeneous. In another 25 (19 percent) a single ethnic group accounted for more than 90 percent of the population. Forty percent of

the countries contained more than five significant ethnic groups.

In a later study, Nielsson (1985) classified 45 of 164 states as "single nation-group" (i.e., ethnic group) states (with one ethnic group accounting for more than 95 percent of the population). Identified as the three most homogeneous were North Korea, South Korea, and Portugal. Nielsson's study actually underestimates the ethnic diversity of modern states. There is reason to question the ethnic homogeneity of some of the countries on his list, such as Japan (see the next chapter) and Madagascar (see below). Further, many of the countries he lists are now multiethnic because of increased immigration.

Nationalities and Imagined Communities

Ethnic groups that once had, or wish to have or regain, autonomous political status (their own country) are called **nationalities.** In the words of Benedict Anderson (1991), they are "imagined communities." Even when they become nation-states, they remain imagined communities, because most of their members, though feeling deep comradeship, will never meet (Anderson 1991, pp. 6–10). They can only imagine that they all participate in the same unit.

Anderson traces Western European nationalism, which arose in imperial powers like England, France, and Spain, back to the eighteenth century. He stresses that language and print played a crucial role in the growth of European national consciousness. The novel and the newspaper were "two forms of imagining" communities (consisting of all the people who read the same sources and thus witnessed the same events) that flowered in the eighteenth century (Anderson 1991, pp. 24–25).

Making a similar point, Terry Eagleton (1983, p. 25) describes the vital role of the novel in fomenting English national consciousness and identity. The novel gave the English "a pride in their national language and literature; if scanty education and extensive hours of labor prevented them personally from producing a literary masterpiece, they could take pleasure in the thought that others of their kind—English people—had done so."

Print spurred national consciousness in three unique ways. First, the national print language carved a new level of culture: It created a unified (*national*) field of *mass* communication between Latin (by then an *international elite* language) and the regional dialects. Second, printing gave a new fixity to language. Being able to put and "see it in print" helped build an idea of permanent recorded history, which became essential to the idea of the nation. Third, the print industry established certain dialects (the ones used in print form) as new languages of power (Anderson 1991, pp. 42–45).

Over time, political upheavals and wars have divided many imagined national communities that arose in the eighteenth and nineteenth centuries. The German and Korean homelands were artifically divided after wars, and according to Communist and capitalist ideologies. World War I split the Kurds, who remain an imagined community, forming a majority in no state. Kurds are a minority group in Turkey, Iran, Iraq, and Syria. Similarly, Azerbaijanis, who are related to Turks, were a minority in the former Soviet Union, as they still are in Iran.

Migration is another reason certain ethnic groups live in different nation-states. Massive migration in the decades before and after 1900 brought Germans, Poles, and Italians to Brazil, Canada, and the United States. Through migration Chinese, Senegalese, Lebanese, and Jews have spread all over the world. Some of these (e.g., descendants of Germans in Brazil and the United States) have assimilated to their host nations and no longer feel attached to the imagined community of their origin.

World War I split the Kurds. They remain an imagined community, lacking their own nation-state and forming a majority in no state. Kurds are a minority group in Turkey, Iran, Iraq, and Syria. This photo shows Kurdish women in Turkey baking bread in an outdoor oven.

ETHNIC TOLERANCE AND ACCOMMODATION

Ethnic diversity may be associated with positive group interaction and coexistence or with conflict—discussed in another section. There are nation-states in which multiple cultural groups live together in reasonable harmony, including some less-developed countries. Linguistic and cultural similarity facilitates such harmony. The island nation of Madagascar provides one example. Under French colonial rule (1895–1960), and continuing after its independence, Madagascar has been a multiethnic country. Its population consists of about a dozen commonly recognized cultural groups (called *eth-nies* in French), with many smaller groups and subgroups. However, most of these groups speak closely related dialects and descend from the same ancestral culture, the Proto-Malagasy. This was a mixed Indonesian-African group, which began to settle Madagascar around A.D. 500.

Despite their common ancestry, an opposition has arisen between the people of the coasts and those of the central highlands. The main reason for this division is historical and political: The Merina, the most populous highlands ethnic group, conquered much of the island, including many coastal areas, in the nineteenth century. The opposition between highlands and coasts also correlates with some physical differences. Coastal people tend to have darker skin and more African features than the highlanders do. The highlanders on average look more Indonesian than the coastal people do, but the contrast between the highlands and the coasts is not usually phrased in racial terms.

Despite the opposition between highlands and coasts, Madagascar has less linguistic and ethnic diversity than most African countries do. (Most African "nations" are artificial political units created by colonialism, usually incorporating diverse cultures and languages). Unifying political and cultural factors run deep in Madagascar's history. The nation has had two centuries of experience with political centralization. First, the Merina conquered much of the island. Next, a French colonial administration ruled Madagascar from 1895 to 1960, until the Malagasy Republic was born. The government has been fairly stable since independence. Recent unrest has been based on policy disputes and economic issues rather than ethnic factors. A fairly uniform system of education, inherited from French colonial rule, has also contributed to national unity, despite the ethnic contrasts.

In Indonesia, a common language and colonial school system also promoted ethnic harmony, national identity, and integration, as Anderson (1991, pp. 120–123, 132) describes. Indonesia, a large and populous nation, spans about 3,000 islands. Its national consciousness straddles religious, ethnic, and linguistic diversity. Indonesia contains Muslims, Buddhists, Catholics, Protestants, Hindu-Balinese, and animists. Despite these contrasts, more than 100 distinct ethnolinguistic groups have come to view themselves as fellow Indonesians.

Under Dutch rule (which ended in 1949), the school system extended over the islands. Advanced study brought youths from different areas to Batavia, the colonial capital. The colonial educational system offered Indonesian youths uniform textbooks, standardized diplomas, and teaching certificates. It created a "self-contained, coherent universe of experience" (Anderson 1991, p. 121). Literacy acquired through the school system also paved the way for a single national print language. Indonesian developed as the national language out of an ancient lingua franca (common language) used in trade between the islands.

Most former colonies haven't been as lucky as Madagascar and Indonesia in terms of ethnic harmony and national integration. In creating multitribal and multiethnic states, colonialism often erected boundaries that corresponded poorly with preexisting cultural divisions. But colonial institutions also helped create new "imagined communities" beyond nations. A good example is the idea of **négritude** ("African identity") developed by African intellectuals in Francophone (French-speaking) West Africa. *Négritude* can be traced to the association and common experience of youths from Guinea, Mali, the Ivory Coast, and Senegal at the William Ponty school in Dakar, Senegal (Anderson 1991, pp. 123–124).

Acculturation and Assimilation

Globalization refers to the accelerating interdependence of nations in a world system linked economically and through mass media and modern transportation systems. Globalization promotes intercultural communication and migration, bringing people from different cultures into direct contact.

Such contact causes changes in one or both cultures. **Acculturation** is the exchange of cultural features that results when groups come into continuous firsthand contact; the original cultural patterns of either or both groups may be altered by this contact (Redfield, Linton, and Herskovits 1936). We usually speak of acculturation when the contact is *between* nations or cultures; elements of the cultures change, but each group remains distinct. Exemplifying acculturation are **pidgins**—mixed languages that develop to ease communication between members of different cultures in contact, usually in situations of trade or colonial domination. Pidgin English, for example, is a simplified form of English that blends English grammar with those of native languages in several world areas. Pidgin English was first used in commerce in Chinese ports; similar languages developed later in Melanesia, Papua–New Guinea, and West Africa. Repeatedly, in situations of continuous contact, cultures have exchanged and blended their languages, foods, recipes, music, dances, clothing, tools, techniques, and a host of other practices and customs.

Assimilation describes the process of change that a minority ethnic group may experience when it moves to a country where another culture dominates. By assimilating, the minority adopts the patterns and norms of its host culture. It is incorporated into the dominant culture to the point that it no longer exists as a separate cultural unit. Some countries, like Brazil, are more assimilationist than others are. Germans, Italians, Japanese, Mid-Easterners, and East Europeans started migrating to Brazil late in the nineteenth century. These immigrants have assimilated to a common Brazilian culture, which has Portuguese, African, and Native American roots. The descendants of these immigrants speak the national language (Portuguese) and participate in national culture. (During World World II, Brazil, which was on the allied side, forced assimilation by banning instruction in any language other than Portuguese—especially in German.)

Brazil has been more of a "melting pot" than have the United States and Canada, in which ethnic groups retain more distinctiveness and self-identity. I remember my first visit to the southern Brazilian city of Porto Alegre, the site of mass migration by Germans, Poles, and Italians. Transferring an expectation derived from my North American culture to Porto Alegre, I asked my tour guide to show me his city's ethnic neighborhoods. He couldn't understand what I was talking about. Except for a Japanese-Brazilian neighborhood in the city of São Paulo, the idea of an ethnic neighborhood is alien to Brazil.

The Plural Society and Pluralism

Assimilation isn't inevitable, and there can be ethnic harmony without it. Ethnic distinctions can persist despite generations of interethnic contact. Through a study of three ethnic groups in Swat, Pakistan, Fredrik Barth (1958/1968) challenged an old idea that interaction always leads to assimilation. He showed that ethnic groups can be in contact for generations without assimilating and can live in peaceful coexistence.

Barth (1958/1968, p. 324) defines **plural society** (an idea he extends from Pakistan to the entire Middle East) as a society combining ethnic contrasts and economic interdependence. He borrows the term from J. S. Furnivall (1944) who first used it to describe a different context—the Netherlands East Indies, now Indonesia. The term has also been used for Caribbean societies (M. G. Smith 1965). Furnivall, describing Dutch colonialism, saw plural societies as less harmonious than Barth did. Furnivall's plural society consisted of three main ethnic groups: the colonialists (the Dutch), the dominated natives (the Indonesians), and a middle group of merchants and small-scale business people (Chinese immigrants). The comparable groups in the Caribbean were European colonialists, African slaves and their descendants, and Asian (especially Indian) immigrants. Furnivall saw domination, conflict, and instability as inevitable features of plural societies. In his view, plural societies were creations of Western expansion, which brought different ethnic groups together in colonial states and the marketplace. Furnivall thought that plural societies would shatter when colonial rule ended, because the harmony between the ethnic groups was politically enforced,

Germans, Italians, Japanese, Mid-Easterners, and East Europeans started migrating to Brazil late in the nineteenth century. All have assimilated to a common Brazilian culture, which has Portuguese, African, and Native American roots. The descendants of the immigrants speak the national language (Portuguese) and participate in national culture. Here a Japanese-Brazilian woman reminds her grandson of his heritage by teaching him Japanese script. Except for certain Japanese-Brazilian areas of São Paulo, the idea of an ethnic neighborhood is alien to Brazil.

Furnivall described the Dutch East Indies (now Indonesia) as a plural society with three main ethnic groups: the colonialists (the Dutch), the dominated natives (the Indonesians), and a middle group of merchants and small-scale business people (Chinese immigrants). Furnivall saw conflict as inevitable in the plural society. But this Chinese merchant family has assimilated to Indonesian culture by converting to Islam.

and the ties between them were only economic—not buttressed by social links.

Barth had a more optimistic view of plural societies. Consider his description of the Middle East (in the 1950s): "The 'environment' of any one ethnic group is not only defined by natural conditions, but also by the presence and activities of the other ethnic groups on which it depends. Each group exploits only part of the total environment, and leaves large parts of it open for other groups to exploit." The ecological interdependence (or, at least, the lack of competition) between ethnic groups may be based on different activities in the same region, or on long-time occupation of different regions in the same nation-state.

In Barth's view, ethnic boundaries are most stable and enduring when the groups occupy different ecological niches. That is, they make their living in different ways and don't compete. Ideally, they should depend on each other's activities and exchange with one another. When different ethnic groups exploit the *same* ecological niche, the militarily more powerful group will normally replace the weaker one. If they exploit more or less the same niche, but the weaker group is better able to use marginal environments, they may also coexist (Barth 1968/1958, p. 331). Given niche specialization, ethnic boundaries, distinctions, and interdependence can be maintained although the specific cultural features of each group may change. By shifting the analytic focus from individual cultures

or ethnic groups to *relationships* between cultures or ethnic groups, Barth (1958/1968 and 1969) has made important contributions to ethnic studies.

The sociological term **pluralism** is used to describe a democratic political system (like Belgium, the Netherlands, and Switzerland) where the major ethnic groups share power through a coalition of their political leaders (Lijphart 1977). All those countries include diverse languages (e.g., in Belgium French, Dutch, and German; in Switzerland German, French and Italian), and historic and cultural variation associated with the linguistic differences. These contrasts tend to be regionally based, like the contrasts in the Netherlands between Protestants and Catholics and between majority Dutch and Frisians (who live in the north—Friesland—and speak a language closely related to English). Canadians, whose country is officially bilingual, continue to negotiate the political relationship between English speakers and French speakers, who live mainly in Quebec. Almost an equal number of Canadians claim British (25 percent) and French (24 percent) ancestry. Sixteen percent claim "other European" and 28 percent "mixed" ancestry (*The World Almanac and Book of Facts* 1992, p. 746).

Multiculturalism and Ethnic Identity

The view of cultural diversity in a country as something good and desirable is called **multiculturalism.** The multicultural model is the opposite of the assimilationist model, in which minorities are expected to abandon their cultural traditions and values, replacing them with those of the majority population. The multicultural view encourages the practice of cultural-ethnic traditions. A multicultural society socializes individuals not only into the dominant (national) culture but also into an ethnic culture. Thus in the United States millions of people speak both English and another language, eat both "American" (apple pie, steak, hamburgers) and "ethnic" foods, celebrate both national (July 4, Thanksgiving) and ethnic-religious holidays, and study both national and ethnic group histories. Multiculturalism succeeds best in a society whose political system promotes freedom of expression and in which there are many and diverse ethnic groups.

In the United States and Canada multiculturalism is of growing importance. This reflects an awareness that the number and size of ethnic groups have grown dramatically in recent years. If this trend continues, the ethnic composition of the United States will change dramatically (Figure 4.1).

Because of immigration and differential population growth, whites are now outnumbered by minorities in many urban areas. For example, of the 7,323,000 people living in New York City in 1990, 28.7 percent were black, 24.4 percent Hispanic, 7.0 percent Asian, 0.4 percent Native American, and 39.5 percent other—including non-Hispanic whites. The comparable figures for Los Angeles (3,485,000 people) were 14.0 percent black, 39.9 percent Hispanic, 9.8 percent Asian, 0.5 percent Native American, and 35.8 percent non-Hispanic whites (*Statistical Abstract* 1991, pp. 34–35).

One response to ethnic diversification and awareness has been for many whites to reclaim ethnic identities (Italians, Albanian, Serbian, Lithuanian, etc.) and to join ethnic associations (clubs, gangs). Some such groups are new. Others have existed for decades, although they lost members during the assimilationist years of the 1920s through the 1950s.

Multiculturalism seeks ways for people to understand and interact that don't depend on sameness but on respect for differences. Multiculturalism stresses the interaction of ethnic groups and their contribution to the country. It assumes that each group has something to offer and learn from the others.

We see evidence of multiculturalism all around us. Seated near you in the classroom are students whose parents were born in other countries. Islamic mosques have joined Jewish synagogues and Christian churches in American cities. To help in exam scheduling, colleges inform professors about the

Figure 4.1 *The proportion of the American population that is white and non-Hispanic is declining. Consider two projections of the ethnic composition of the United States in A.D. 2080. The first assumes an annual immigration rate of 500,000; the second assumes 1 million immigrants per year. With either projection the Hispanic and Asian segments of the population grow dramatically (much more so than do blacks and non-Hispanic whites). (From Bouvier and Davis 1982, p. 40)*

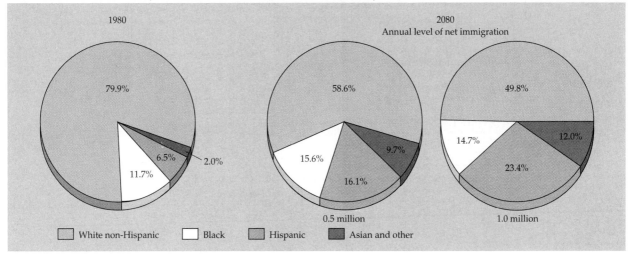

main holidays of many religions. You can attend ethnic fairs and festivals, watch ethnically costumed dancers on television, eat ethnic foods, even outside ethnic restaurants, and buy ethnic foods at your supermarket. Some such foods (e.g., bagels, pasta, tacos) have become so familiar that their ethnic origin is fading from our memories. There is even a popular shrine celebrating the union of diversity and globalization: At Disneyland and Walt Disney World we can see and hear a chorus of ethnically correct dolls drone on that "it's a small world after all." All these exemplify growing tolerance and support of ethnic communities in the United States and Canada.

Several forces have propelled North America away from the assimilationist model toward multiculturalism. First, multiculturalism reflects the fact of recent large-scale migration, particularly from the "less-developed countries" to the "developed" nations of North America and Western Europe. The global scale of modern migration introduces unparalleled ethnic variety to host nations. Multiculturalism is related to globalization: People use modern means of transportation to migrate to nations whose life styles they learn about through the media and from tourists who increasingly visit their own countries.

Migration is also fueled by rapid population growth, coupled with insufficient jobs (both for educated and uneducated people), in the less-developed countries. As traditional rural economies decline or mechanize, displaced farmers move to cities, where they and their children are often unable to find jobs. As people in the less-developed countries get better educations, they seek more skilled employment. They hope to partake in an international culture of consumption that includes such modern amenities as refrigerators, televisions, and automobiles.

Contrary to popular belief, the typical migrant to the United States or Canada isn't poor and unskilled but middle-class and fairly well educated. Educated people migrate for several reasons. Often they can't find jobs to match their skills in their countries of origin (Grasmuck and Pessar 1991). Also, they are knowledgeable enough to manipulate international regulations. Many migrants have been raised to expect a life style that their own nations can offer to just a few. On arrival in North America or Western Europe, immigrants find themselves in democracies where citizens are allowed (or even encouraged) to organize for economic gain and a "fair share" of resources, political influence, and cultural respect. The most educated immigrants often become political organizers and particularly effective advocates of multiculturalism.

In a world with growing rural-urban and transnational migration, ethnic identities are used increasingly to form self-help organizations focused mainly on enhancing the group's economic competitiveness (Williams 1989). People claim and express ethnic identities for political and economic

In the United States and Canada, multiculturalism is of growing importance. Especially in large cities like Montreal (shown here), people of diverse backgrounds attend ethnic fairs and festivals and feast on ethnic foods.

reasons. Michel Laguerre's (1984) study of Haitian immigrants in New York City shows that they make no conscious decision to form an ethnic group. Rather, they have to mobilize to deal with the discriminatory structure (racist in this case, since Haitians tend to be black) of American society. Ethnicity (their common Haitian creole language and cultural background) is an evident basis for their mobilization. Haitian ethnicity then helps distinguish them from Afro-Americans and other ethnic groups who may be competing for the same resources and recognition. In studying ethnic relations, it's not enough to look at the cultural content of the ethnic group. Equally important are the structural constraints and the political-economic context in which ethnic differentiation develops.

Although ethnic groups often face discrimination (see below), their members should not be viewed as passive victims of oppressive systems. Immigrants especially tend to be dynamic, creative, and courageous people, determined to enhance their chances in the modern world system. Ethnic groups mobilize for political action, often with economic goals. Their members also consciously manipulate multiple identities. Individual choice and purpose are evident in everyday expressions of ethnicity.

Kathryn Woolard (1989) has studied the role of language choice in negotiating ethnic identity in the Spanish Mediterranean region of Catalonia (where the port city of Barcelona is located). The people of Catalonia have a choice of two languages. Catalan (a close relative of Provençal, a Romance language spoken in southern France) is the traditional language of the local economic elite. The use of Catalan recalls Catalonia's former autonomy from the Spanish state and its history of economic prominence, based on Mediterranean trade. Castilian (Spanish) has become the dominant language of the legal order, official institutions, educational systems, and the mass media. This is an unusual situation. Usually the language of the economic elite is also the language of official power. In their everyday lives most Catalans and Castilians view their native language as the defining feature of their ethnic identity. But, as Woolard shows, that identity is not fixed but continually signaled and enacted in daily interactions. The people of Catalonia regularly manipulate ethnic identities and conduct political debates by shifting from one language to the other.

Similarly, in a study of Yemeni (from Yemen) Arabs in New York City, Staub (1989) stresses that Yemini immigrant ethnicity isn't static but achieved, situational, and flexible. Still, specific cultural content is also evident: traditional concepts (e.g., honor and shame), ethnic poetry, distinctive foods, dialects, local and regional history, exclusive ethnic social and political clubs, ethnic political events (called *festivals*), and dancing. These people prefer Yemeni ethnic identity to the more general label "Arab."

Herbert Lewis (1989), a long-time student of Yemeni Jews in Israel, also stresses the cultural characteristics of the ethnic group: Different patterns and values lead members of different groups to act in particular ways, to have different goals, and to make different choices. Yemeni Jews are very aware of how their values, attitudes, and behavior differ from those of their European and North African Jewish neighbors in Israel.

In contemporary North America one side-effect of the new immigration and the rise of the multicultural model has been to inspire old ethnic groups to strengthen their identity and fight for their rights. One example is Native American success—in the United States and Canada—in reclaiming traditional property rights. In Michigan and Wisconsin, Indians have used the court system to establish their privileged hunting and fishing rights, at the expense of sportspeople and commercial fishers. In 1992 Canadian Eskimos, or Inuit, won the right to administer part of their traditional homeland, which they call Nunavut, "Our Land." They will get title to about 20 percent of the land in Nunavut. Fights for the rights of ethnic groups also produce losers. The Inuit voted overwhelmingly for the Nunavut agreement, but their neighbors, the Dene Indians, opposed it. The new boundary cuts through some Dene hunting and burial grounds (Farnsworth 1992).

In the face of globalization, much of the world, including the entire "democratic West," is experiencing an "ethnic revival." The new assertiveness of long-resident ethnic groups extends to the Basques and Catalans in Spain, the Bretons and Corsicans in France, and the Welsh and Scots in the United Kingdom. The United States and Canada are becoming increasingly multicultural, focusing on their internal diversity. "Melting pots" no longer, they are better described as ethnic "salads" (each ingredient remains distinct, although in the same bowl, with the same dressing). In 1992 New York mayor David Dinkins called his city a "glorious mosaic."

A document of the University of Michigan American Culture Program published in 1992 offers a good exposition of the multicultural model. It recognizes "the multiplicity of American cultures." It presents multiculturalism as a new approach to the central question in American studies: What does it mean to be an American? The document suggests a shift from the study of core myths and values, and people's relationships to them as generalized Americans, to "recognizing that 'America' includes people of differing community, ethnic, and cultural histories, different points of view and degrees of empowerment." Such a perspective spurs studies of specific ethnic groups rather than the country as a whole (Internal Review document of the Program in American Culture of the University of Michigan—3/12/92).

What is the difference between multiculturalism and pluralism? Pluralism is a political concept based on a belief in equal power for the major ethnic groups. Multiculturalism originated as a cultural concept that places a value on understanding all cultures in a society, without a specific political agenda. However, successful politicians have to acknowledge the demographics of a growing ethnic population with voting rights and increasing power to affect elections. In a democracy where multiculturalism is valued, the political structure will eventually accommodate these groups.

ROOTS OF ETHNIC CONFLICT

Ethnicity, based on perceived cultural similarities and differences in a society or nation, can be expressed in peaceful pluralism and multiculturalism, or in discrimination or violent interethnic confrontation. Culture is both adaptive and maladaptive. The perception of cultural differences can have disastrous effects on social interaction.

The roots of ethnic differentiation—and therefore, potentially, of ethnic conflict—can be political, economic, religious, linguistic, cultural, or "racial." We may hypothesize that the potentiality for ethnic conflict is proportional to the number and degree of contrasts—particularly in situations of competition for resources and power. Why do ethnic differences

often lead to conflict and violence? The causes include a sense of injustice because of resource distribution, economic and/or political competition, and reaction to discrimination, prejudice, and other expressions of threatened or devalued identity (Ryan 1990, p. xxvii).

Prejudice and Discrimination

Ethnic conflict often arises in reaction to prejudice (attitudes and judgments) or discrimination (action). **Prejudice** means devaluing (looking down on) a group because of its assumed behavior, values, capabilities, or attributes. People are prejudiced when they hold stereotypes about groups and apply them to individuals. (**Stereotypes** are fixed ideas—often unfavorable—about what the members of a group are like.) Prejudiced people assume that members of the group will act as they are "supposed to act" (according to the stereotype) and interpret a wide range of individual behaviors as evidence of the stereotype. They use this behavior to confirm their stereotype (and low opinion) of the group.

A well-publicized American example comes from the 1992 trial, in California's Simi Valley, of four Los Angeles police officers accused of beating an African-American motorist, Rodney King. The jurors seem to have stereotyped King as a black criminal, and the white men who beat him as public servants doing their duty. Jurors' stereotypes led them to blame the victim: Rodney King was, they said, "in control." In other words, he caused his own beating. The jurors' prejudices affected their interpretation of the evidence (despite a judge's admonition to be objective). Their verdict was acquittal of the police officers, which led to the Los Angeles riot of spring 1992.

Discrimination refers to policies and practices that harm a group and its members. Discrimination may be *de facto* (practiced, but not legally sanctioned) or *de jure* (part of the law). An example of *de facto* discrimination is the harsher treatment that American minorities (compared with other Americans) tend to get from the police and the judicial system. This unequal treatment isn't legal, but it happens anyway. Segregation in the southern United States and *apartheid* in South Africa provide two examples of *de jure* discrimination, which are no longer in existence. In the United States *de jure* segregation has been illegal since the 1950s, and the South African *apartheid* system was abandoned in 1991. In both systems, by law, blacks and whites had different rights and privileges. Their social interaction ("mixing") was legally curtailed. Slavery, of course, is the most extreme and coercive form of legalized inequality; people are treated as property.

We can also distinguish between attitudinal and institutional discrimination. With **attitudinal discrimination,** people discriminate against members of a group because they are prejudiced toward that group. For example, in the United States members of the Ku Klux Klan have expressed their prejudice against blacks, Jews, and Catholics through verbal, physical, and psychological harassment.

The most extreme form of anti-ethnic (attitudinal) discrimination is **genocide,** the deliberate elimination of a group through mass murder. The United Nations defines *genocide* as acts "committed with intent to destroy, in whole or in part, a national, ethnical, racial, or religious group, as such" (Ryan 1990, p. 11). Strongly prejudicial attitudes (hate) and resulting genocide have been directed against people viewed as "standing in the way of progress" (e.g., Native Americans) and people with jobs that the dominant group wants (e.g., Jews in Hitler's Germany, Chinese in Indonesia).

In other examples of genocide, dictator Joseph Stalin's assault on ethnic groups in the Soviet Union led to their forced relocation, mass starvation, and murder. Twenty million people died. The Turks massacred 1.8 million Armenians during World War I. Nazis murdered 6 million Jews. In Burundi, East Africa, Tutsis massacred 200,000 Hutus in 1972. More recently, the Indonesian government waged a genocidal campaign against the people of East Timor (Ryan 1990).

Institutional discrimination refers to programs, policies, and institutional arrangements that deny equal rights and opportunities to, or differentially harm, members of particular groups. This form of discrimination is usually less personal and intentional than attitudinal discrimination is, but it may be based on a long history of inequality that also includes attitudinal bias. One example of institutional discrimination is what Bunyan Bryant and Paul Mohai (1991, p. 4) call **environmental racism**—"the systematic use of institutionally based power by whites to formulate policy decisions that will lead to the disproportionate burden of environmen-

tal hazards in minority communities." Thus, toxic waste dumps tend to be located in areas with nonwhite populations (Williams 1987).

Environmental racism is discriminatory but not always intentional. Sometimes toxic wastes *are* deliberately dumped in areas whose residents are considered unlikely to protest (because they are poor, powerless, "disorganized," or "uneducated"). In other cases property values fall after toxic waste sites are located in an area. The wealthier people move out, and poorer people, often minorities, move in, to suffer the consequences of living in a hazardous environment.

African-Americans and Hispanics on average have shorter lives, greater infant mortality, and higher murder rates than whites do for institutional reasons. They are more likely than whites are to live in impoverished, high-crime areas with inadequate access to health care—and to opportunities and services generally. This current lack of access reflects a long history of discrimination—both attitudinal and institutional.

Another example of institutional discrimination is the fact that social and economic shifts harm certain groups more than others. African-Americans have been hurt especially by the change from a manufacturing economy to one based on services and information processing. Factories, where people with a high school education used to find well-paid (usually unionized) employment, were traditionally located in cities. Now they have moved to the suburbs, necessitating a difficult and costly commute for city dwellers, including many African-Americans. The service jobs that are available to comparably educated people in urban areas pay half of what the old manufacturing jobs did. Many minorities haven't benefitted as much from a changing American society as majority groups—or even new immigrants—have.

Chips in the Mosaic

Although the multicultural model is increasingly prominent in contemporary North America, ethnic competition and conflict are just as evident. We hear increasingly of conflict between new arrivals, like Central Americans and Koreans, and long-established ethnic groups, like African-Americans. Ethnic antagonism flared in South-Central Los Angeles in spring 1992, in rioting that followed the acquittal of the four white police officers who were tried for the videotaped beating of Rodney King.

Angry blacks attacked whites, Koreans, and Hispanics. This violence expressed frustration by African-Americans about their prospects in an increasingly multicultural society. A *New York Times*/CBS News poll conducted May 8, 1992, just after the Los Angeles riots, found that blacks had a bleaker outlook than whites did about the effects of immigration on their lives. Only 23 percent of the blacks felt they had more opportunities than recent immigrants, compared with twice that many whites (Toner 1992).

South-Central Los Angeles, where most of the 1992 rioting took place, is an ethnically mixed area, which used to be mainly African-American. As blacks have moved out, there has been an influx of Latin Americans (Mexicans and Central Americans—mainly recent and illegal immigrants). The Hispanic population of South-Central Los Angeles increased by 119 percent in a decade, as the number of blacks declined by 17 percent. By 1992 the neighborhood had become 45 percent Hispanic and 48 percent black. Many store owners in South-Central Los Angeles are Korean immigrants.

Korean stores were hard hit during the 1992 riots, and more than a third of the businesses destroyed were Hispanic-owned. A third of those who died in the riots were Hispanics. These mainly recent migrants lacked deep roots to the neighborhood and, as Spanish speakers, faced language barriers (Newman 1992). Many Koreans also had trouble with English.

Koreans interviewed on ABC's *Nightline* on May 6, 1992, recognized that blacks resented them and considered them unfriendly. One man explained, "It's not part of our culture to smile; in Asia people who smile are considered airheads" (he hesitantly chose the word). African-Americans interviewed on the same program did complain about Korean unfriendliness. "They come into our neighborhoods and treat us like dirt."

These comments suggest a shortcoming of the multicultural perspective: Ethnic groups (blacks here) expect other ethnic groups in the same nation-state to assimilate to some extent to a shared (national) culture. The African-Americans' comments invoked a general American value system that includes friendliness, openness, mutual respect, community participation, and "fair play." Los Angeles blacks want their Korean neighbors to act more like generalized Americans—and good neighbors. They assume that those who profit from a community should give something back to it.

Whatever their ethnic background, people can't hope to live in social isolation from the communities from which they derive their livelihoods. They have to take steps to adapt. Some African-Americans jointly interviewed with a few Koreans by ABC told the store owners they could improve relations in the neighborhood by hiring one or two local people. The Koreans said they couldn't afford to hire nonrelatives.

Asian immigrants, including Koreans, are often considered a "model minority" because of the educational and economic success many of them achieve in North America. One way in which Koreans in cities like New York and Los Angeles have succeeded economically is through family enterprise. Family members work together in small grocery stores, like those in South-Central Los Angeles, pooling their labor and their wealth. Korean culture also stresses the value of education; children, supervised and encouraged by their parents, study hard to do well in school. In a society whose economy is shifting from manufacturing toward specialized services and information processing, good jobs demand education beyond high school. Asian family values and support systems encourage children to plan, study, and work hard, with such careers in mind.

These values also fit certain general American ideals. Work and achievement are American values that the Korean-Americans being interviewed invoked to explain their behavior. (Family solidarity is also a general American value, but the specific meaning of "family" varies between groups.) The Koreans also felt that they couldn't succeed financially if they had to hire nonrelatives.

The key question is whether such groups can prosper in impoverished multiethnic areas like South-Central Los Angeles if they don't try harder to fit into their host communities. Providing an economic service is not enough. Without efforts designed to gain social acceptance, storekeepers (of whatever ethnic group) will continue to face looting, boycotts, and other **leveling mechanisms.** This term refers to customs or social actions that operate to reduce differences in wealth and bring standouts in line with community norms. Leveling mechanisms surface when there is an expectation of community solidarity and economic similarity—especially

IN THE NEWS: A HANDBOOK FOR INTERETHNIC INTERACTION

Appreciation of multiculturalism is growing in contemporary North America. Still, ethnic groups expect other ethnic groups to assimilate to some extent to a shared (national) culture. This item describes efforts by an Asian-American businesswoman, Glenda Joe, to sensitize Vietnamese, Korean, Chinese, and Cambodian immigrants to general American norms about how business owners should treat their customers. Ms. Joe has written a handbook designed to enhance cross-cultural understanding and communication and to reduce interethnic tensions and conflicts that have recently erupted in North American cities.

Easing the Cultural Tension
At the Neighborhood Store

Deadly confrontations at stores owned by Asian-Americans in minority neighborhoods have become a sad fact of life from New York to Los Angeles. In Houston, Glenda Joe thinks it doesn't have to be.

After a young black man was killed there by a Vietnamese store-keeper in a dispute over a stolen beer and then, two weeks later, an Asian merchant was shot to death in a robbery, Ms. Joe knew she had to try to do something. A business owner and community activist, Ms. Joe, 40 years old, wrote an 11-page handbook for Asian-American merchants.

"At the core of the problem were cultural differences that had not been explained to the merchants or customers," she said. "Those differences, combined with the rage that followed the killings, meant increased racial tensions."

The booklet explains the cultural differences that recent immigrant merchants often face when dealing with customers.

Some Koreans, for example, do not speak to strangers, Ms. Joe said. While Korean culture frowns on what is considered overfamiliarity, Americans can interpret this as rudeness.

She also said some Asians "tend not to show appreciation," adding, "This too can be read the wrong way."

Ms. Joe, 40 years old, president of General Wall Enterprises, a public relations firm, said she began working in her father's grocery store at age 8.

"So I've been in that situation before. And it was clear to me that no one had tried to provide this type of communication between the two groups."

The handbook lists the most frequent complaints made by customers about the merchants. Rudeness was at the top. It also lists the types of behavior that could make shoppers feel uncomfortable. One is the failure to thank a customer for shopping at the store or the tendency of some merchants to act suspicious of black shoppers.

The guide also suggests ways to deal with problem customers. It is being translated into Vietnamese, Korean, Chinese and Cambodian and has been distributed to 200 businesses in Houston.

Copies can be obtained from Glenda Joe, 1714 Tannehill Drive, Houston, Texas 77008. *Veronica Byrd*

Source: Veronica Byrd, "Easing the Cultural Tension at the Neighborhood Store," *The New York Times,* October 25, 1992, sec. 3, p. F8.

---

shared poverty—and some people are profiting more than, or at the expense of, others.

Leveling mechanisms tend to discourage people from surpassing their peers—punishing those who do, pushing them back to the common level. Such mechanisms, according to Max Weber (1904/1958), were common in European peasant communities before the rise of capitalism. Peasants, Weber believed, worked just hard enough to satisfy their immediate needs. Then they quit, mistrusting people who needlessly worked more than others. The individualism associated with capitalism had to surmount the collectivism of the peasant community, in which gossip and other social pressures brought overachievers back in line.

Anthropologist George Foster (1965) stresses the importance of leveling mechanisms in "classic" peasant societies throughout the world. According to Foster, peasants have an "image of limited good," according to which all valued things are finite. They regard the total amount of health, wealth, honor, or success available to community members as limited. Thus, one person can excel only at the expense of others. Unless good fortune clearly comes from outside (for example, external wage work or a lottery) and unless the fruits of success are shared with others, successful people face ostracism through leveling mechanisms including gossip, avoidance, insults, and physical attack.

Leveling mechanisms are found not only in peas-

ETHNIC NATIONALISM RUN WILD

The Socialist Federal Republic of Yugoslavia, although Communist, was a nonaligned country outside the Soviet Union. But like the U.S.S.R., Yugoslavia fell apart, mainly along ethnic and religious lines, in the early 1990s. Among Yugoslavia's nationalities were Roman Catholic Croats, Eastern Orthodox Serbs, Muslim Slavs, and ethnic Albanians. Citing ethnic and religious differences, several republics broke away from Yugoslavia in 1991–92. These included Slovenia, Croatia, and Bosnia-Herzegovina (see map). Of Yugoslavia, with Belgrade as its capital, only Serbia and Montenegro remained in 1992, with Serbs as the dominant ethnic group.

Ethnic differentiation in Yugoslavia was based on religion, culture, and political and military history, rather than race or language. Serbo-Croatian is a South Slavic language spoken (with dialect variation) by Serbs, Croats, and Muslim Slavs. But Croats and Serbs use different alphabets. The Croats have adopted our Roman alphabet, but the Serbs use the Cyrillic alphabet, which they share with Russia and Bulgaria. The two alphabets help promote ethnic differentiation and nationalism. Serbs and Croats, who share speech, are divided by writing—by literature, newsprint, and political manifestos. With print (like religion) uniting some people while separating them from others, literate Serbs and Croats belong to different imagined communities (Anderson 1991).

Yugoslav Serbs reacted vio-

The former Yugoslavia, although Communist, was a nonaligned country outside the Soviet Union, but like the U.S.S.R. Yugoslavia disintegrated in the early 1990s. The breakaway portions included Slovenia, Croatia, and Bosnia-Herzegovina. Of Yugoslavia, with Belgrade as its capital, only Serbia, Montenegro, and Kosovo remained in 1992.

lently—with military intervention—after a February 1992 vote for the independence of Bosnia-Herzegovina, whose population is one-third Serbian. Nationalist Serbs (from both Bosnia and Yugoslavia) began a policy, in secessionist Bosnia-Herzegovina, of forced expulsion—"ethnic purification"—against Croats, but mainly against Muslim Slavs. United Nations sanctions were applied after Serbs in Yugoslavia, who controlled the National Army, lent their support to the Bosnian Serbs in their "ethnic-cleansing" campaign, which recalled the policies of Adolf Hitler.

Backed by the Yugoslav army, Serbian militias rounded up Muslims, killed groups of them, and burned and looted their homes.

ant communities but also in many other societies anthropologists have studied. The 1992 Los Angeles riots show that leveling mechanisms continue to operate in urban, stratified, multiethnic America.

Aftermaths of Oppression

Also fueling ethnic conflict are such forms of discrimination as forced assimilation, ethnocide, and

Thousands of Slavs fled. Hundreds of thousands of Muslims became involuntary refugees in tent camps, school gyms, and parks. According to the United Nations High Commission for Refugees, the Serbian campaign in Bosnia created Europe's worst refugee crisis since World War II.

The Serbs sought to end the interethnic coexistence that Yugoslav socialism had encouraged. They also wanted to avenge historic affronts by Muslims and Croats. In the fifteenth-century Muslim Turks (from the Ottoman Empire) had overthrown the medieval Serbian ruler, persecuted the Serbs, and—eventually—converted many local people to Islam during their centuries of rule in this area. Bosnian Serbs still resent all Muslims—including the converts, the ancestors of the Muslim Slavs—for the Turkish conquest.

In 1992 Bosnian Serbs claimed to be fighting to resist the new, Muslim-dominated, government of Bosnia-Herzegovina. They feared that a policy of Islamic fundamentalism (like that in Iran) might threaten the Serbian Orthodox Church and other expressions of Serbian identity. The Serbs' goal was to carve up Bosnia-Herzegovina along ethnic lines, and they wanted two-thirds of it for themselves.

The Serbs also sought vengeance against the Croats for arrests, deportations, and executions of Serbs by Croatian fascists during World War II. A stated aim of ethnic purification was to ensure that the Serbs would never again be dominated by another ethnic group (Burns 1992*a*).

In other break-away areas of Yugoslavia, Muslim Slavs and Croats also forced deportations, but the Serbian campaign was the widest and the most systematic. By mid-1992, with the military support of Croatia, Bosnian Croats (following the example of the Serbs) had declared their own separate minirepublic next to Croatia. With the Muslim Slavs caught in the middle and with Bosnia's capital, the multiethnic city of Sarajevo, under siege, the conflict was unresolved as of this writing.

How can we explain Bosnia's ethnic conflict and its nationalism run wild? According to Fredrik Barth (1969), ethnic differences are most secure and enduring where the groups occupy different ecological niches: They make their livings in different ways or places and don't compete. In Barth's view, peaceful coexistence is most likely when the ethnic groups are mutually dependent. In Bosnia-Herzegovina Serbs, Croats, and Muslim Slavs were more mixed than in any other former Yugoslav Republic (Burns 1992*f*). The boundaries between the three groups may not have been sharp enough to keep them together by keeping them apart.

United Nations sanctions were applied after Serbs in Yugoslavia, who controlled the National Army, lent their support to Bosnian Serbs in an ''ethnic cleansing'' campaign that recalled the policies of Adolf Hitler. According to the United Nations High Commission for Refugees, this produced Europe's worst refugee crisis since World War II.

cultural colonialism. A dominant group may try to destroy the cultures of certain ethnic groups (**ethnocide**) or force them to adopt the dominant culture (**forced assimilation**). Many countries have penalized or banned the language and customs of an ethnic group (including its religious observances). One example of forced assimilation is the anti-Basque campaign that the dictator Francisco Franco (who ruled between 1939 and 1975) waged in Spain. Franco banned Basque books, journals, newspapers, signs, sermons, and tombstones and imposed fines for using the Basque language (Eskedun) in schools. His policies led to the formation of a Basque terrorist group and spurred strong nationalist sentiment in the Basque region (Ryan 1990).

Resistance to forced assimilation may culminate in a policy of expulsion, as Bulgaria illustrates. Beginning in 1984 an Islamic Turkish-speaking minority, 10 percent of the national population, was subjected to a campaign of Bulgarization. This involved closing mosques (Islamic temples), bans on the Turkish language, ethnic clothing, printing and import of the Koran, Islamic burial, and circumcision (Ryan 1990, p. 7). When the Turks resisted these measures, the government started confiscating their land and expelled their leaders.

A policy of **ethnic expulsion** aims at removing groups who are culturally different from a country. There are many examples, including Bosnia-Herzegovina in 1992 (see box). Uganda expelled 74,000 Asians in 1972. The neofascist parties of contemporary Western Europe advocate repatriation (expulsion) of immigrant workers (West Indians in England, Algerians in France, and Turks in Germany) (Ryan 1990, p. 9).

A policy of expulsion may create **refugees**—people who have been forced (involuntary refugees) or who have chosen (voluntary refugees) to flee a country, to escape persecution or war. For example, Palestinian refugees moved to camps in Egypt, Jordan, and Lebanon after the Arab-Israeli wars of 1948 and 1967 (Ryan 1990).

Colonialism, another form of oppression, refers to the political, social, economic, and cultural domination of a territory and its people by a foreign power for an extended time (Bell 1981). The British and French colonial empires are familiar examples of colonialism, but we can extend the term to the former Soviet empire, formerly known as "the Second World."

Using the labels "First World," "Second World," and "Third World" is a common way of categorizing nations that may be introduced here. The **First World** refers to the "democratic West"—traditionally conceived in opposition to a "Second World" ruled by "communism." The First World includes Canada, the United States, Western Europe, Japan, Australia, and New Zealand. The **Second World** refers to the Warsaw Pact nations, including the former Soviet Union, the Socialist and once-Socialist countries of Eastern Europe and Asia. Proceeding with this classification, the "less-developed countries" (LDCs) make up the **Third World.** Some even assign the poorest nations to a **Fourth World.** This usage would, for example, distinguish Bangladesh (Fourth World) from India (Third World).

The frontiers imposed by colonialism (in the Second through Fourth Worlds) weren't usually based on, and often didn't reflect, preexisting cultural units. In many countries, colonial nation-building left ethnic strife in its wake. Thus, over a million Hindus and Moslems were killed in the violence

For decades the Soviet Union suppressed ethnic expression. Cultural colonialism refers to domination by one group and its culture/ideology over others. One example is the privileged position of the Russian people, language, and culture in the former Soviet Union. Ethnic Russian colonists were sent (as were tanks) to many areas, such as Tajikistan (shown here), to diminish the cohesion and clout of the local people—but there was resistance.

that accompanied the division of the Indian subcontinent into India and Pakistan. Problems between Arabs and Jews in Palestine began during the British mandate period. Ethnic conflicts in the less-developed countries have proliferated since the early 1960s, when decolonization reached its height. There have been bitter ethnic conflicts in Zaire, Nigeria, Bangladesh, Sudan, India, Sri Lanka, Iraq, Ethiopia, Uganda, Rwanda, Burundi, Lebanon, and Cyprus. Few of these have been resolved.

Like other colonial powers, the Soviet Union politically suppressed ethnic expression, including potential and actual conflict, for decades. Multiculturalism may be growing in the United States and Canada, but the opposite is happening in the disintegrating Second World, where ethnic groups (nationalities) want their own nation-states. The flowering of ethnic feeling and conflict as the Soviet empire disintegrated illustrates that years of political repression and ideology provide insufficient "common ground" for lasting unity.

Cultural colonialism refers to internal domination—by one group and its culture/ideology over others. One example is the domination over the former Soviet empire by Russian people, language, and culture, and by Communist ideology. The dominant culture makes itself the official culture. This is reflected in schools, the media, and public interaction. Under Soviet rule ethnic minorities had very limited self-rule in republics and regions controlled by Moscow. All the republics and their peoples were to be united by the oneness of "socialist internationalism."

One common technique in cultural colonialism is to flood ethnic areas with members of the dominant ethnic group. Thus, in the former Soviet Union, ethnic Russian colonists were sent to many areas, like Tajikistan (Figure 4.2), to diminish the cohesion and clout of the local people. Tajikistan is a small, poor state (and former Soviet republic) in central Asia, near Afghanistan, with 5.1 million people. In Tajikistan, as in central Asia generally, most people are Muslims. Today Islam, as an alternative way of ordering spiritual and social life, is replacing the ideology of Soviet Communism. This comes after more than seventy years of official atheism and suppression of religion. The Soviet empire limited Islamic teaching and worship, converting and destroying mosques, discouraging religious practice by the young, but allowing it for old people. Still, Islam was taught at home, around the kitchen table, so it has been called "kitchen Islam."

Now, as the Russians leave Tajikistan, the force of Russian culture and language are receding. Islamic influence is growing. Women have started covering their arms, legs, and hair. More and more

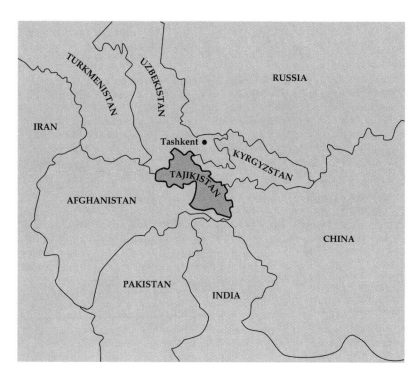

Figure 4.2 *Former Soviet Socialist Republics of Central Asia, including Tajikistan.*

people speak and pray in Tajik, a language related to Persian (which is spoken in Iran) (Erlanger 1992).

"The Commonwealth of Independent States" is all that remains of the Soviet Union. In this group of new nations, ethnic groups (nationalities) like the Tajiks are seeking to establish separate and viable nation-states based on cultural boundaries. This celebration of ethnic autonomy is an understandable reaction to the Soviet Union's years of suppressing diversity: historic, national, linguistic, ethnic, cultural, and religious. It is part of an ethnic florescence that—as surely as globalization and transnationalism—is a trend of the late twentieth century.

SUMMARY

Ethnicity is based on cultural similarities (among members of the same ethnic group) and differences (between that group and others). Ethnic distinctions can arise from language, religion, history, geography, kinship, or "race." A race is an ethnic group assumed to have a biological basis. Usually race and ethnicity are ascribed statuses; people are born members of a group and remain so all their lives.

The term *nation* was once synonymous with "ethnic group." Now *nation* has come to mean a state—a centrally organized political unit, a government. *Nation* and *state* have become synonymous. Combined in *nation-state*, they refer to such an autonomous political entity, a "country." Because of migration, conquest, and colonialism, most nation-states are not ethnically homogeneous. States sometimes encourage ethnic divisions for political and economic ends.

Ethnic groups that once had, or wish to have or regain, autonomous political status (their own country) are called *nationalities*. Language and print have played a crucial role in the growth of national consciousness. But over time, political upheavals, wars, and migrations have divided many imagined national communities.

Ethnic diversity may be associated with positive group interaction and coexistence (harmony) or with conflict. In creating multitribal and multiethnic states, colonial regimes often erected boundaries that corresponded poorly with preexisting cultural divisions. But certain colonial policies and institutions also helped create new "imagined communities."

Globalization refers to the accelerating interdependence of nations in a world system linked economically and through modern media and transportation. *Acculturation* is the exchange of cultural features that results when groups come into continuous firsthand contact. Elements of the cultures change, but each group remains distinct.

Assimilation describes the process of change that an ethnic group may experience when it moves to a country where another culture dominates. By assimilating, the minority adopts the patterns and norms of its host culture. Assimilation isn't inevitable, and there can be ethnic harmony without it.

A plural society combines ethnic contrasts and economic interdependence. Such interdependence (or, at least, the lack of competition) between ethnic groups may be based on different activities in the same region, or on long-time occupation of different regions in the same country.

The view of cultural diversity in a nation-state as good and desirable is multiculturalism. The multicultural model is the opposite of the assimilationist model, in which minorities are expected to abandon their cultural traditions and values, replacing them with those of the majority population. A multicultural society socializes individuals not only into the dominant (national) culture but also into an ethnic culture. Multiculturalism succeeds best in a society whose political system promotes freedom of expression and in which there are many and diverse ethnic groups.

In studying ethnic relations, it is not enough to look at the cultural content of the ethnic group. Equally important are the structural constraints and the political-economic context in which ethnic differentiation develops. In a world with growing migration, ethnic identities are used increasingly to mobilize for political action, often with economic goals.

Ethnicity can be expressed in peaceful multiculturalism, or in discrimination or violent interethnic confrontation. Ethnic conflict often arises in reaction to prejudice (attitudes and judgments) or discrimination (action). *Prejudice* means devaluing (looking down on) a group because of its assumed behavior, values, capabilities, or attributes. *Discrimination* refers to policies and practices that harm a group and its members. Discrimination may be *de facto* (practiced, but not legally sanctioned) or *de jure* (part of the law). With *attitudinal discrimination*, people discriminate because they are prejudiced toward a group. The most extreme form of antiethnic discrimination is genocide, the deliberate elimination of a group through mass murder. *Institutional discrimination* refers to programs, policies, and arrangements that deny equal rights and opportunities to, or differentially harm, particular groups.

Although the multicultural model is increasingly prominent in North America, ethnic competition and conflict are also evident. One shortcoming of the multicultural perspective is that ethnic groups may expect other ethnic groups who live in the same country to assimilate to some extent to a more general, supposedly shared, national culture and value system.

A dominant group may try to destroy the cultures of certain ethnic groups (ethnocide), or force them to adopt the dominant culture (forced assimilation). A policy of ethnic expulsion may create refugees—people who have been forced (involuntary refugees) or who have chosen (voluntary refugees) to flee a country. *Colonialism* refers to the political, social, economic, and cultural domination of a territory and its people by a foreign power for an extended time. In many countries, colonial nation-building left ethnic strife in its wake. *Cultural colonialism* refers to internal domination—by one group and its culture and/or ideology over others. One example is the domination of the former Soviet empire by the Russian people, language, and culture. The flowering of ethnic feeling and conflict as the Soviet empire disintegrated illustrates that years of political repression provide insufficient common ground for lasting unity. Celebration of ethnic autonomy is an understandable reaction to years of suppressing diversity: historic, national, linguistic, ethnic, cultural, and religious. It is part of an ethnic florescence that is a trend of the late twentieth century.

GLOSSARY

acculturation: The exchange of cultural features that results when groups come into continuous firsthand contact; the original cultural patterns of either or both groups may be altered, but the groups remain distinct.

achieved status: Social status that comes through talents, actions, efforts, activities, and accomplishments, rather than ascription.

ascribed status: Social status (e.g., race or gender) that people have little or no choice about occupying.

assimilation: The process of change that a minority group may experience when it moves to a country where another culture dominates; the minority is incorporated into the dominant culture to the point that it no longer exists as a separate cultural unit.

attitudinal discrimination: Discrimination against members of a group because of prejudice toward that group.

colonialism: The political, social, economic, and cultural domination of a territory and its people by a foreign power for an extended time.

cultural colonialism: Internal domination—by one group and its culture/ideology over others; for example, Russian domination of the former Soviet Union.

discrimination: Policies and practices that harm a group and its members.

environmental racism: The systematic use of institutionally based power by a majority group to make policy decisions that create disproportionate environmental hazards in minority communities.

ethnic expulsion: A policy aimed at removing groups who are culturally different from a country.

ethnic group: Group distinguished by cultural similarities (shared among members of that group) and differences (between that group and others); ethnic group members share beliefs, values, habits, customs, and norms, and a common language, religion, history, geography, kinship, and/or race.

ethnicity: Identification with, and feeling part of, an ethnic group, and exclusion from certain other groups because of this affiliation.

ethnocide: Destruction by a dominant group of the cultures of an ethnic group.

First World: The "democratic West"—traditionally conceived in opposition to a "Second World" ruled by "communism."

forced assimilation: Use of force by a dominant group to compel a minority to adopt the dominant culture—for example, penalizing or banning the language and customs of an ethnic group.

Fourth World: The very poorest of the less-developed countries—for example, Madagascar, Bangladesh.

genocide: The deliberate elimination of a group through mass murder.

globalization: The accelerating interdependence of nations in a world system linked economically and through mass media and modern transportation systems.

institutional discrimination: Programs, policies, and arrangements that deny equal rights and opportunities to, or differentially harm, members of particular groups.

leveling mechanisms: Customs and social actions that operate to reduce differences in wealth and thus to bring standouts in line with community norms.

majority groups: Superordinate, dominant, or controlling groups in a social-political hierarchy.

minority groups: Subordinate groups in a social-political hierarchy, with inferior power and less secure access to resources than majority groups.

multiculturalism: The view of cultural diversity in a country as something good and desirable; a multicultural society socializes individuals not only into the dominant (national) culture but also into an ethnic culture.

nation: Once a synonym for "ethnic group," designating a single culture sharing a language, religion, history, territory, ancestry, and kinship; now usually a synonym for "state" or "nation-state."

nationalities: Ethnic groups that once had, or wish to have or regain, autonomous political status (their own country).

nation-state: An autonomous political entity; a country like the United States or Canada.

négritude: African identity—developed by African intellectuals in Francophone (French-speaking) West Africa.

pidgins: Mixed languages that develop to ease communication between members of different cultures in contact, usually in situations of trade or colonial domination.

plural society: A society that combines ethnic contrasts and economic interdependence of the ethnic groups.

pluralism: Sociological term used to describe a democratic political system where the major ethnic groups share power through a coalition of their political leaders.

prejudice: Devaluing (looking down on) a group because of its assumed behavior, values, capabilities, or attitudes.

race: An ethnic group assumed to have a biological basis.

racism: Discrimination against an ethnic group assumed to have a biological basis.

refugees: People who have been forced (involuntary refugees) or who have chosen (voluntary refugees) to flee a country, to escape persecution or war.

Second World: The Warsaw Pact nations, including the former Soviet Union, the Socialist and once-Socialist countries of Eastern Europe and Asia.

state: An independent, centrally organized political unit; a government.

status: Any position that determines where someone fits in society; may be ascribed or achieved.

stereotypes: Fixed ideas—often unfavorable—about what the members of a group are like.

Third World: The less-developed countries (LDCs); used in combination with "Fourth World," "Third World" refers to the better-off LDCs (e.g., Brazil, India) compared with poorer LDCs (Bangladesh, Madagascar).

STUDY QUESTIONS

1. How is ethnicity based on cultural similarities and differences?
2. What does it mean to say that we "wear different hats" and negotiate our social identities?
3. What is the difference between ascribed and achieved status?
4. Is ethnicity ever an achieved status?
5. What is a minority group? Must it be a numerical minority?
6. What is the relation between an ethnic group, a nation, and a nation-state?
7. Are most nation-states ethnically homogeneous, and why or why not?
8. What is an imagined community, and how does it relate to ethnicity and nationality?
9. What role have print and language played in the rise of national consciousness?
10. How may linguistic and cultural similarities contribute to ethnic harmony, national identity, and integration?
11. What roles did colonialism play with respect to nationalism and ethnic unity and diversity?
12. What role does globalization play in ethnic relations?
13. What is the difference between acculturation and assimilation?
14. What is the difference between pluralism and a plural society?
15. What is multiculturalism, and how does it differ from the assimilationist model?
16. What does it mean to say that ethnic relations involve not just cultural content but also the political-economic context in which ethnic differentiation occurs?
17. How does prejudice differ from discrimination? Give examples of each?
18. Do you see any problems with the multicultural perspective?
19. What are various forms of ethnic discrimination? What is the difference between ethnocide and genocide?
20. What role did the former Soviet Union play in ethnic differentiation?
21. What are the main forms of "ethnic florescence" in the modern world?

SUGGESTED ADDITIONAL READING

ANDERSON, B.
   1991   *Imagined Communities: Reflections on the Origin and Spread of Nationalism*, rev. ed. London: Verso. The origins of nationalism in Europe and its colonies, with special attention to the role of print, language, and schools.

BARTH, F.
   1969   *Ethnic Groups and Boundaries: The Social Organization of Cultural Difference*. London: Allyn and Unwin. Classic discussion of the prominence of differentiation and boundaries (versus cultural features per se) in interethnic relations.

DESPRES, L., ED.
   1975   *Ethnicity and Resource Competition*. The Hague: Mouton. Ethnicity in the context of socioeconomic stratification and economic differentiation.

FOX, R. G., ED.
   1990   *Nationalist Ideologies and the Production of National Cultures*. American Ethnological Society Monograph Series, no. 2. Washington, D.C.: American Anthropological Association. A series of papers about ethnicity and nationalism in Israel, Romania, India, Guatemala, Guyana, Burundi, and Tanzania.

GELLNER, E.
   1983   *Nations and Nationalism*. Ithaca, NY: Cornell University Press. Industrialism and nation-building.

HOBSBAWM, E. J.
   1990   *Nations and Nationalism since 1780: Programme, Myth, Reality*. New York: Cambridge University Press. The making of modern nation-states.

LAGUERRE, M.
   1984   *American Odyssey: Haitians in New York*. Ithaca, New York: Cornell University Press. Interesting case study of the role of "race" and competition in ethnic differentiation in contemporary urban America.

RYAN, S.
   1990   *Ethnic Conflict and International Relations*. Brookfield, MA: Dartmouth. Cross-national review of the roots of ethnic conflict.

YETMAN, N.
   1991   *Majority and Minority: The Dynamics of Race and Ethnicity in American Life*, 5th ed. Boston: Allyn and Bacon. A wide-ranging anthology focusing on the United States.

THE CULTURAL CONSTRUCTION OF RACE

SOCIAL RACE
Hypodescent: Race in the United States
Not Us: Race in Japan
Phenotype and Fluidity: Race in Brazil

BIOLOGICAL RACE: A DISCREDITED CONCEPT
Explaining Skin Color

STRATIFICATION AND "INTELLIGENCE"

Box: Culture, Biology, and Sports

embers of an ethnic group may define themselves—and/or be defined by others—as different and special because of their language, religion, geography, history, ancestry, or physical traits. When an ethnic group is assumed to have a biological basis (shared "blood" or genetic material), it is called a *race*. This chapter will examine "race" both as a cultural construct and as a discredited biological term. Examples from different cultures will show that race, like ethnicity in general, is a cultural category rather than a biological reality. That is, ethnic groups, including "races," derive from contrasts perceived and perpetuated in particular societies, rather than from scientific classifications based on common genes.

It is not possible at this time to define races biologically. Only cultural constructions of race are possible—even though the average citizen conceptualizes "race" in biological terms. The belief that races exist and are important is much more common among the public than it is among scientists. Most Americans, for example, believe that their population includes biologically based "races" to which various labels have been applied. These labels include "white," "black," "yellow," "red," "Caucasoid," "Negroid," "Mongoloid," "Amerindian," "Euro-American," "African-American," "Asian-American," and "Native American."

We hear the words *ethnicity* and *race* frequently, but American culture doesn't draw a very clear line between them. As illustration, consider two articles in *The New York Times* of May 29, 1992. One, discussing the changing ethnic composition of the United States, states (correctly) that Hispanics "can be of any race" (Barringer 1992, p. A12). In other words, "Hispanic" is an ethnic category that crosscuts "racial" contrasts such as that between "black" and "white." The other article reports that during the Los Angeles riots of spring 1992, "hundreds of Hispanic residents were interrogated about their immigration status on the basis of their *race* alone [emphasis added]" (Mydans 1992*a*, p. A8). Use of "race" here seems inappropriate because "Hispanic" is usually perceived as referring to a linguistically based (Spanish-speaking) ethnic group, rather than a biologically based race. Since these Los Angeles residents were being interrogated because they were Hispanic, the article is actually reporting on ethnic, not racial, discrimination. However, given the lack of a precise distinction between race and ethnicity, it is probably better to use the "ethnic group" instead of "race" to describe *any* such social group, for example, African-Americans, Asian-Americans, Irish-Americans, Anglo-Americans, or Hispanics. (Table 5.1 lists the main ethnic groups in the United States.)

SOCIAL RACE

Races are ethnic groups assumed (by members of a particular culture) to have a biological basis, but ac-

"Hispanic" is an ethnic category that cross-cuts "racial" contrasts such as that between "black" and "white." This photo shows physical diversity among residents of Spanish Harlem, New York.

Table 5.1 *Ethnic Groups in the United States,*
1990 Census Data

Claimed Identity	Millions of People
Whites, German ancestry	57.9
Whites, Irish ancestry	38.7
Whites, English ancestry	32.6
Blacks	30.0
Asians and Pacific Islanders	7.3
American Indians, Eskimos, and Aleuts	1.9
Hispanics (any "race")	22.3
Others	58.0
Total population	248.7

Source: Barringer 1992, p. A12.

tually race is socially constructed. The "races" we hear about every day are cultural, or social, rather than biological categories. In Charles Wagley's terms (Wagley 1959/1968), they are **social races** (groups assumed to have a biological basis but actually defined in a culturally arbitrary, rather than a scientific, manner). Many Americans mistakenly assume that "whites" and "blacks," for example, are biologically distinct and that these terms stand for discrete races. But these labels, like racial terms used in other societies, really designate culturally perceived rather than biologically based groups.

Hypodescent: Race in the United States

How is race culturally constructed in the United States? In American culture, one acquires his or her racial identity at birth, as an ascribed status, but race isn't based on biology or on simple ancestry. Take the case of the child of a "racially mixed" marriage involving one black and one white parent. We know that 50 percent of the child's genes come from one parent and 50 percent from the other. Still, American culture overlooks heredity and classifies this child as black. This rule is arbitrary. From genotype (genetic composition), it would be just as logical to classify the child as white.

American rules for assigning racial status can be even more arbitrary. In some states, anyone known to have any black ancestor, no matter how remote, is classified as a member of the black race. This is a rule of **descent** (it assigns social identity on the basis of ancestry), but of a sort that is rare outside the contemporary United States. It is called **hypodes-**

cent (Harris and Kottak 1963) (*hypo* means "lower") because it automatically places the children of a union or mating between members of different groups in the minority group. Hypodescent divides American society into groups that have been unequal in their access to wealth, power, and prestige.

Millions of Americans have faced discrimination because one of their ancestors happened to belong to a minority group. We saw in Chapter 4 that governments sometimes manipulate ethnicity and encourage ethnic divisions for political and economic ends. The following case from Louisiana is an excellent illustration of the arbitrariness of the hypodescent rule and of the role that governments (federal, or state in this case) play in legalizing, inventing, or eradicating ethnicity (B. Williams 1989). Susie Guillory Phipps, a light-skinned woman with "Caucasian" features and straight black hair, discovered as an adult that she was "black." When Phipps ordered a copy of her birth certificate, she found her race listed as "colored." Since she had been "brought up white and married white twice," Phipps challenged a 1970 Louisiana law declaring anyone with at least one-thirty-second "Negro blood" to be legally black. Although the state's lawyer admitted that Phipps "looks like a white person," the state of Louisiana insisted that her racial classification was proper (Yetman, ed. 1991, pp. 3–4).

Cases like Phipps's are rare because "racial" identity is usually ascribed at birth and doesn't change. The rule of hypodescent affects blacks, Asians, Native Americans, and Hispanics differently. It's easier to negotiate Indian or Hispanic identity than black identity. The ascription rule isn't as definite, and the assumption of a biological basis isn't as strong.

To be considered "Native American," one ancestor out of eight (great-grandparents) or four (grandparents) may suffice. This depends on whether the assignment is by federal or state law, or an Indian tribal council. The child of a Hispanic may (or may not, depending on context) claim Hispanic identity. Many Americans with an Indian or Latino grandparent consider themselves "white" and lay no claim to minority-group status.

Something like hypodescent even works with the classification of sexual orientation in the United States. Bisexuals are lumped with gays and lesbians, rather than with heterosexuals. These statuses (sexual orientations) are viewed by many people as ascribed (no choice) rather than achieved (ambivalent or changing sexual preference possible).

The controversy that erupted in 1990–91 over the casting of the Broadway production of the musical *Miss Saigon* offers a final illustration of the cultural construction of race in the United States. The musical had opened a few years earlier in London, where the Filipina actress Lea Salonga played Kim, a young Vietnamese woman. Another major role is that of the Eurasian (half-French, half-Vietnamese) pimp known as the "Engineer." For the New York production the producer, Cameron Mackintosh, wanted Salonga to play Kim and the English actor Jonathan Pryce, who had originated the part in London, to play the Engineer. Actors' Equity must approve the casting of foreign stars in New York productions. The union voted that Mackintosh couldn't cast Pryce, a "Caucasian," in the role of a Eurasian. The part should go to an Asian.

In this case the American hypodescent rule was being extended from the offspring of black-white unions to "Eurasians" (in this case French-Vietnamese). Again, the cultural construction of ethnicity is that children get their social identity from the minority parent—Asian rather than European. This cultural construction of ethnicity also assumes that all Asians (e.g., Vietnamese, Chinese, and Filipinos) are the same. Thus it's okay for Filipinos to play Vietnamese (or even Eurasians), but an English actor can't play a half-French Eurasian.

In fact, Vietnamese and Filipinos are further apart in language, culture, and ancestry than French and English are. It would be "more logical" (based on language, culture, and common ancestry) to give the Engineer's part to an English actor than to a Filipino one. But Actors' Equity didn't see it that way. (The most "correct" choices for the part would have been a French man, a Vietnamese man, or a Eurasian of appropriate background.)

When Actors' Equity vetoed Pryce, Mackintosh canceled the New York production of *Miss Saigon*. Negotiations continued, and *Miss Saigon* eventually opened on Broadway, with a well-integrated cast, starring Pryce and Salonga (whose demanding part was shared, for two performances per week, with a Chinese-American actress). A year after the opening, Pryce and Salonga had left the production, and the three main "Asian" (Vietnamese) parts (including the Eurasian Engineer) were being played by Filipinos.

The culturally arbitrary hypodescent rule—not logic—is behind the notion that an Asian is more appropriate to play a Eurasian than a "Caucasian" is. But, the protest over the casting of Miss Saigon *illustrates that what has been used against a group can also be used to promote the interests of that group. There has been a shortage of parts for Asian and Asian-American actors. In this case they used the hypodescent rule as a basis for political action—to stake their claim to "Eurasian" as well as "Asian" parts.*

The culturally arbitrary hypodescent rule—not logic—is behind the motion that an Asian is more appropriate to play a Eurasian than a "Caucasian" is. Hypodescent governs ethnic ascription in the United States and channels discrimination against offspring of mixed unions, who are assigned minority status. But, as the case of *Miss Saigon* illustrates, what has been used against a group can also be used to promote the interests of that group. There has been a shortage of parts for Asian and Asian-American actors. In this case they used the hypodescent rule as a basis for political action—to stake their claim to "Eurasian" as well as "Asian" parts.

Not Us: Race in Japan

American culture ignores considerable diversity in biology, language, and geographic origin as it socially constructs race in the United States. North Americans also overlook diversity by seeing Japan as a nation that is homogeneous in race, ethnicity, language, and culture—an image the Japanese themselves cultivate. Thus in 1986 former Prime Minister Nakasone created an international furor by contrasting his country's supposed homogeneity (responsible, he suggested, for Japan's success in international business) with the ethnically mixed

United States. To describe Japanese society, Nakasone used *tan'itsu minzoku*, an expression connoting a single ethnic-racial group (Robertson 1992).

Japan is hardly the uniform entity Nakasone described. Some dialects of Japanese are mutually unintelligible, and scholars estimate that 10 percent of the national population of 124 million are minorities of various sorts. These include aboriginal Ainu, annexed Okinawans, outcast *burakumin*, children of mixed marriages, and immigrant nationalities, especially Koreans, who number more than 700,000 (De Vos et al. 1983).

Americans tend to see Japanese and Koreans as alike, but the Japanese stress the difference between themselves and Koreans. To describe racial attitudes in Japan, Jennifer Robertson (1992) uses Kwame Anthony Appiah's (1990) term "intrinsic racism"—the belief that a (perceived) racial difference is a sufficient reason to value one person less than another.

In Japan the valued group is majority ("pure") Japanese, who are believed to share "the same blood." Thus, the caption to a printed photo of a Japanese-American model reads: "She was born in Japan but raised in Hawaii. Her nationality is American but no foreign blood flows in her veins" (Robertson 1992, p. 5). Something like hypodescent also operates in Japan, but less precisely than in the United States, where mixed offspring automatically become members of the minority group. The children of mixed marriages between majority Japanese

and others (including Euro-Americans) may not get the same "racial" label as their majority parent, but they are still stigmatized for their non-Japanese ancestry (De Vos and Wagatsuma 1966).

How is race culturally constructed in Japan? The (majority) Japanese define themselves by opposition to others, whether minority groups in their own nation or outsiders—anyone who is "not us." Aspects of phenotype (detectable physical traits, such as perceived body odor) are considered part of being *racially different by opposition*. Other races don't smell as "we" do. The Japanese stigmatize Koreans by saying they smell different (as Europeans also do). The Japanese contend that Koreans have a pungent smell, which they mainly attribute to diet—Koreans eat garlicky foods and spicy kimchee. Japanese also stereotype their minorities with behavioral and psychological traits. Koreans are seen as underachievers, crime-prone, and working class, in opposition to dominant Japanese, who are positively stereotyped as harmonious, hard-working, and middle class (Robertson 1992).

The "not us" should stay that way; assimilation is generally discouraged. Cultural mechanisms, especially residential segregation and taboos on "interracial" marriage, work to keep minorities "in their place." (Still, many marriages between minorities and majority Japanese do occur.) However, perhaps to give the appearance of homogeneity, people (e.g., Koreans) who become naturalized

Japan's stigmatized burakumin *are physically and genetically indistinguishable from other Japanese. In response to* burakumin *political mobilization, Japan has dismantled the legal structure of discrimination against* burakumin *and has worked to improve conditions in their neighborhoods, which are called* buraku. *This Sports Day for* burakumin *children is one kind of mobilization.*

Japanese citizens are expected to take Japanese-sounding names (Robertson 1992; De Vos et al. 1983).

In its construction of race, Japanese culture regards certain ethnic groups as having a biological basis, when there is no evidence that they do. The best example is the *burakumin*, a stigmatized group of at least 4 million outcasts, sometimes compared to India's untouchables. The *burakumin* are physically and genetically indistinguishable from other Japanese. Many of them "pass" as (and marry) majority Japanese, but a deceptive marriage can end in divorce if *burakumin* identity is discovered (Aoki and Dardess, eds. 1981).

Burakumin are perceived as standing apart from the majority Japanese lineage. Through ancestry, descent (and thus, it is assumed, "blood," or genetics) *burakumin* are "not us." Majority Japanese try to keep their lineage pure by discouraging mixing. The *burakumin* are residentially segregated in neighborhoods (rural or urban) called *buraku*, from which the racial label is derived. Compared with majority Japanese, the *burakumin* are less likely to attend high school and college. When *burakumin* attend the same schools, they face discrimination. Majority children and teachers may refuse to eat with them because *burakumin* are considered unclean.

In applying for university admission or a job, and in dealing with the government, Japanese must list their address, which becomes part of a household or family registry. This list makes residence in a *buraku*, and likely *burakumin* social status, evident. Schools and companies use this information to discriminate. (The best way to pass is to move so often that the *buraku* address eventually disappears from the registry.) Majority Japanese also limit "race" mixture by hiring marriage mediators to check out the family histories of prospective spouses. They are especially careful to check for *burakumin* ancestry (De Vos et al. 1983).

The origin of the *burakumin* lies in a historic tiered system of stratification (from the Tokugawa period—1603–1868). The top four ranked categories were warrior-administrators (*samurai*), farmers, artisans, and merchants. The ancestors of the *burakumin* were below this hierarchy, an outcast group who did unclean jobs, like animal slaughter and disposal of the dead. *Burakumin* still do related jobs, including work with animal products, like leather. The *burakumin* are more likely than majority Japa-nese are to do manual labor (including farm work) and to belong to the national lower class. *Burakumin* and other Japanese minorities are also more likely to have careers in crime, prostitution, entertainment, and sports (De Vos et al. 1983).

Like blacks in the United States, the *burakumin* are class-stratified. Because certain jobs are reserved for the *burakumin*, people who are successful in those occupations (e.g., shoe factory owners) can be wealthy. *Burakumin* have also found jobs as government bureaucrats. Financially successful *burakumin* can temporarily escape their stigmatized status by travel, including foreign travel.

Today most discrimination against the *burakumin* is *de facto* rather than *de jure*. It is strikingly like the discrimination—attitudinal and institutional—that blacks have experienced in the United States. The *burakumin* often live in villages and neighborhoods with poor housing and sanitation. They have limited access to education, jobs, amenities, and health facilities. In response to *burakumin* political mobilization, Japan has dismantled the legal structure of discrimination against *burakumin* and has worked to improve conditions in the *buraku*. Still, Japan has yet to institute American-style affirmative action programs for education and jobs. Discrimination against nonmajority Japanese is still the rule in companies. Some employers say that hiring *burakumin* would give their company an unclean image and thus create a disadvantage in competing with other businesses (De Vos et al. 1983).

By contrast with the *burakumin*, who are citizens of Japan, most Japanese Koreans, who form one of the nation's largest minorities (about 750,000 people), are not. Koreans in Japan continue, as resident aliens, to face discrimination in education and jobs. They lack citizens' health-care and social-service benefits, and government and company jobs don't usually go to non-Japanese.

Koreans started arriving in Japan, mainly as manual laborers, after Japan conquered Korea in 1910 and ruled it through 1945. During World War II, there were more than 2 million Koreans in Japan. They were recruited to replace Japanese farm workers who left the fields for the imperial army. Some Koreans were women (numbering 70,000 to 200,000) forced to serve as prostitutes ("comfort women") for Japanese troops. By 1952 most Japanese Koreans had been repatriated to a divided Korea. Those who stayed in Japan were denied citizenship. They became "resident aliens," forced, like Japanese criminals, to carry an ID card, which resentful Koreans call a "dog tag." Unlike most nations, Japan doesn't grant automatic citizenship to people born in the country. One can become Japanese by having one parent born in Japan and living there three successive years (Robertson 1992).

Like the *burakumin,* many Koreans (who by now include third and fourth generations) fit physically and linguistically into the Japanese population. Most Koreans speak Japanese as their primary language, and many pass as majority Japanese. Still, they tend to be segregated residentially, often in the same neighborhoods as *burakumin,* with whom they sometimes intermarry. Koreans maintain strong kin ties and a sense of ethnic identity with other Koreans, especially in their neighborhoods. Most Japanese Koreans qualify for citizenship but choose not to take it because of Japan's policy of forced assimilation. Anyone who naturalizes is strongly encouraged to take a Japanese name. Many Koreans feel that to do so would cut them off from their kin and ethnic identity. Knowing they can never become majority Japanese, they choose not to become "not us" twice.

Phenotype and Fluidity: Race in Brazil

There are more flexible, less exclusionary ways of constructing social race than those used in the United States and Japan. Along with the rest of Latin America, Brazil has less exclusionary categories, which permit individuals to change their racial classification. Brazil shares a history of slavery with the United States, but it lacks the hypodescent rule. Nor does Brazil have racial aversion of the sort found in Japan. The history of Brazilian slavery dates back to the sixteenth century, when Africans were brought as slaves to work on sugar plantations in northeastern Brazil. Later, Brazilians used slave labor in mines and on coffee plantations. The contributions of Africans to Brazilian culture have been as great as they have been to American culture. Today, especially in areas of Brazil where slaves were most numerous, African ancestry is evident.

The system that Brazilians use to classify biological differences contrasts with those used in the United States and Japan. First, Brazilians use many more racial labels [over 500 have been reported—Harris (1970)] than Americans or Japanese do. In

northeastern Brazil I found forty different racial terms in use in Arembepe, a village of only 750 people (Kottak 1992). Through their classification system Brazilians recognize and attempt to describe the physical variation that exists in their population. The system used in the United States, by recognizing only three or four races, blinds Americans to an equivalent range of evident physical contrasts. Japanese races, remember, don't even originate in physical contrasts. *Burakumin* are physically indistinguishable from other Japanese but are considered to be biologically different.

The system that Brazilians use to construct social race has other special features. In the United States one's race is an ascribed status; it is assigned automatically by hypodescent and doesn't usually change. In Japan race is also ascribed at birth, but it can change when, say, a *burakumin* or a naturalized Korean passes as a majority Japanese. In Brazil racial identity is more flexible, more of an achieved status. Brazilian racial classification pays attention to phenotype. **Phenotype** refers to an organism's evident traits, its "manifest biology"—anatomy and physiology. There are thousands of evident (detectable) physical traits, ranging from skin color, hair form, and eye color (which are visible), to blood type, colorblindness, and enzyme production (which become evident through testing). A Brazilian's phenotype, and racial label, may change due to environmental factors, such as the tanning rays of the sun.

For historical reasons, darker-skinned Brazilians tend to be poorer than lighter-skinned Brazilians are. When Brazil's Princess Isabel abolished slavery in 1889, the freed men and women received no land or other reparations. They took what jobs were available. For example, the freed slaves who founded the village of Arembepe, which I have been studying since 1962, turned to fishing. Many Brazilians (including slave descendants) are poor because they lack a family history of access to land or commercial wealth and because upward social mobility is difficult. Continuing today, especially in cities, it is poor, dark-skinned Brazilians, on average, who face the most intense discrimination.

Given the correlation between poverty and dark skin, the class structure affects Brazilian racial classification, so that someone who has light skin and is poor will be perceived and classified as darker than a comparably colored person who is rich. The racial term applied to a wealthy person who has dark skin will tend to "lighten" the skin color, which gives rise to the Brazilian expression "money whitens." In the United States, by contrast, race and class are correlated, but racial classification isn't changed by class. Because of hypodescent, racial identity in the United States is an ascribed status—fixed and lifelong—regardless of phenotype or economic status. One illustration of the absence of hypodescent in Brazil is the fact that (unlike the United States) full siblings there may belong to different races (if they are phenotypically different).

Arembepe has a mixed and physically diverse population, reflecting generations of immigration and intermarriage between its founders and outsiders. Some villagers have dark, others, light, skin color. Facial features, eye and hair color, and hair type also vary. Although physically heterogeneous, Arembepe is economically homogeneous—local residents have not risen out of the national lower class. Given such economic uniformity, wealth contrasts don't affect racial classification, which Arembepeiros base on the physical differences they perceive between individuals. As physical characteristics change (sunlight alters skin color, humidity affects hair form), so do racial terms. Furthermore, racial differences are so insignificant in structuring community life that people often forget the terms they have applied to others. Sometimes they even forget the ones they've used for themselves. To reach this conclusion, I made it a habit to ask the same person on different days to tell me the races of others in the village (and my own). In the United States I am always "white" or "Euro-American," but in Arembepe I got lots of terms besides *branco* ("white"). I could be *claro* ("light"), *louro* ("blond"), *sarará* ("light-skinned redhead"), *mulato claro* ("light mulatto"), or *mulato* ("mulatto"). The racial term used to describe me or anyone else varied from person to person, week to week, even day to day. My best informant, a man with very dark skin color, changed the term he used for himself all the time—from *escuro* ("dark") to *preto* ("black") to *moreno escuro* ("dark brunet").

The American and Japanese racial systems are creations of particular cultures, rather than scientific—or even accurate—descriptions of human biological differences. Brazilian racial classification is also a cultural construction, but Brazilians have developed a way of describing human biological diversity that is more detailed, fluid, and flexible than the systems used in most cultures. Brazil lacks Japan's racial aversion, and it also lacks a rule of descent like that which ascribes racial status in the United States (Harris 1964; Degler 1970).

The operation of the hypodescent rule helps us understand why the populations labeled "black" and "Indian" (Native American) are growing in the United States but shrinking in Brazil. American culture places all "mixed" children in the minority category, which therefore gets all the resultant population increase. Brazil, by contrast, assigns the offspring of mixed marriages to intermediate categories, using a larger set of ethnic and racial labels. A Brazilian with a "white" (*branco*) parent and a "black" (*preto*) parent will almost never be called *branco* or *preto* but instead by some intermediate term (of which dozens are available). The United States lacks intermediate categories, but it is those categories that are swelling in Brazil. Brazil's assimilated Indians are called *cabôclos* (rather than *indíos*, or a specific tribal name, like Kayapó or Yanomami). With hypodescent, by contrast, someone may have just one of four or eight Indian grandparents or great-grandparents and still "feel Indian," be so classified, and even have a tribal identity.

For centuries the United States and Brazil have had mixed populations, with ancestors from Native America, Europe, Africa, and Asia. Although "races" have mixed in both countries, Brazilian and American cultures have constructed the results differently. The historic reasons for this contrast lie mainly in the different characteristics of the settlers of the two countries. The mainly English early settlers of the United States came as women, men, and families, but Brazil's Portuguese colonizers were mainly men—merchants and adventurers. Many of these Portuguese men married Native American women and recognized their "racially mixed" children as their heirs. Like their North American counterparts, Brazilian plantation owners had sexual relations with their slaves. But the Brazilian landlords more often freed the children that resulted—for demographic and economic reasons. (Sometimes these were their only children.) Freed offspring of master and slave became plantation overseers and foremen and filled many intermediate positions in the emerging Brazilian economy. They were not classed with the slaves, but allowed to join a new intermediate category. No hypodescent rule ever developed in Brazil to ensure that whites and blacks remained separate (see Harris 1964; Degler 1970).

BIOLOGICAL RACE: A DISCREDITED CONCEPT

Clearly, races are culturally constructed categories that may have little to do with actual biological differences. Furthermore, the validity of *race* as a biological term has been discredited. Historically, scientists have approached the study of human biological diversity from two main directions: racial classfication, an approach which has been rejected, and the current explanatory approach, which focuses on understanding specific differences. I'll briefly review each approach, first considering the problems with racial classification, then providing an example of the explanatory approach to human biological diversity.

Racial classification is out of favor in biology for several reasons. The main reason is that scientists have trouble grouping specific groups of people into isolated and distinct racial units. A race is supposed to reflect shared *genetic* material, but early scholars used *phenotypical* traits (usually skin color) for racial classification. There are several problems with a phenotypical approach to race. First, which traits should be primary in assigning people who look different to different races? Should races be defined by height, weight, body shape, facial features, teeth, skull form, or skin color? Like their fellow citizens, early European and American scientists gave priority to skin color. The phenotypic features, for example, skin color, that were most apparent to those early scientists were also the very characteristics that have been assigned arbitrary cultural value for purposes of discrimination. Genetic variation (e.g., differences in blood types or groups) that was not directly observable was not used in cultural ways—nor did it figure in early racial classification.

Many school textbooks and encyclopedias still proclaim the existence of three great races: the white, the black, and the yellow. Such simplistic racial classification was compatible with the political use of race as a power device during the colonialist period of the late nineteenth and early twentieth centuries. The tripartite scheme kept white Europeans neatly separate from their African and Asian subjects. Colonial empires began to break up,

The photos in this chapter illustrate just a small part of the range of human biological diversity. Traditional racial classification, now discredited, would classify this young woman from Beijing, China as "Mongoloid."

and scientists began to question established racial categories, after World War II.

Politics aside, one obvious problem with "color-based" racial labels is that the terms don't accurately describe skin color. "White" people are more pink, beige, or tan than white. "Black" people are various shades of brown, and "yellow" people are tan or beige. But these terms have also been dignified by more scientific-*sounding* synonyms: Caucasoid, Negroid, and Mongoloid.

Another problem with the tripartite scheme is that many human populations don't neatly fit into any one of the three "great races." For example, where does one put the Polynesians? **Polynesia** is a triangle of South Pacific islands formed by Hawaii to the north, Easter Island to the east, and New Zealand to the southwest. Does the "bronze" skin color of Polynesians place them with the Caucasoids or the Mongoloids? Some scientists, recognizing this problem, enlarged the original tripartite scheme to include the Polynesian "race." Native Americans present an additional problem. Are they red or yellow? Again, some scientists add a fifth race—the "red," or Amerindian—to the major racial groups.

Many people in southern India have dark skins, but scientists have been reluctant to classify them with "black" Africans because of their "Caucasoid" facial features and hair form. Some, therefore, have created a separate race for these people. What about

This Native Australian boy has brown skin, light hair, large front teeth, and a broad nose. There is no evidence that Native Australians are genetically closer to either Europeans or Africans than to Asians.

the Australian aborigines, hunters and gatherers native to the most isolated continent? By skin color, one might place some Native Australians in the same race as tropical Africans. However, similarities to Europeans in hair color (light or reddish) and facial features have led some scientists to classify them as Caucasoids. But there is no evidence that Australians are closer genetically or historically to either of these groups than they are to Asians. Recognizing this problem, scientists often regard Native Australians as a separate race.

Finally, consider the San ("Bushmen") of the Kalahari Desert in southern Africa. Scientists have perceived their skin color as varying from brown to yellow. Those who regard San skin as "yellow" have placed them in the same category as Asians. In theory, people of the same race share more recent common ancestry with each other than they do with

any others. But there is no evidence for recent common ancestry between San and Asians. Somewhat more reasonably, some scholars assign the San to the Capoid (from the Cape of Good Hope) race, which is seen as being different from other groups inhabiting tropical Africa.

Similar problems arise when any single trait is used as a basis for racial classification. An attempt to use facial features, height, weight, or any other phenotypical trait is fraught with difficulties. For example, consider the Nilotes, natives of the upper Nile region of Uganda and the Sudan. Nilotes tend to be tall and to have long, narrow noses. Certain Scandinavians are also tall, with similar noses. Given the distance between their homelands, to classify them as members of the same race makes little sense. There is no reason to assume that Nilotes and Scandinavians are more closely related to each other than either is to shorter (and nearer) populations with different kinds of noses.

Would it be better to base racial classifications on a combination of physical traits? This would avoid some of the problems mentioned above, but others would arise. First, skin color, stature, skull form, and facial features (nose form, eye shape, lip thickness) don't go together as a unit. For example, people with dark skin may be tall or short and have hair ranging from straight to very curly. Dark-haired populations may have light or dark skin, along with various skull forms, facial features, and body sizes and shapes. The number of combinations is very large, and the amount that heredity (versus environment) contributes to such phenotypical traits is often unclear.

There is a final objection to racial classification based on phenotype. The phenotypical characteristics on which races are based supposedly reflect genetic material that is shared and that has stayed the same for long time periods. But phenotypical similarities and differences don't necessarily have a genetic basis. Because of changes in the environment that affect individuals during growth and development, the range of phenotypes characteristic of a population may change without any genetic change. There are several examples. In the early twentieth century, the anthropologist Franz Boas (1940/1966) described changes in skull form among the children of Europeans who had migrated to the United States. The reason for this was not a change in genes, for the European immigrants tended to marry among themselves. Some of their children had been born in Europe and merely raised in the United States. Something in the new environment, probably in the diet, was producing this change. We know now that changes in average height and weight produced by dietary differences in a few generations are common and have nothing to do with race or genetics.

Explaining Skin Color

Traditional racial classification assumed that biological characteristics were fixed by heredity and stable (immutable) over long periods of time. We now know that a biological similarity doesn't necessarily indicate recent common ancestry. Dark skin color, for example, can be shared by tropical Africans and Native Australians for reasons other than common ancestry. It is not possible at this time to *define races* biologically. Still, scientists have made much progress in *explaining* variation in human skin color— once thought to be of primary significance for defining races—along with many other expressions of human biological diversity. We shift now from classification to *explanation,* in which natural selection plays a key role.

Originally formulated by Charles Darwin and Alfred Russell Wallace, **natural selection** is the process by which nature selects the forms most fit to survive and reproduce in a given environment— such as the tropics. Over the years, the less fit organisms gradually die out; the favored types survive by producing more offspring. The role of natural selection in producing variation in skin color will illustrate the explanatory approach to human biological diversity. Comparable explanations have been provided for many other aspects of human biological variation, but there is not space to discuss them here.

Skin color is a complex biological trait, influenced by several genes—just how many isn't known. **Melanin** is a chemical substance manufactured in cells in the epidermis, or outer skin layer. The melanin cells of darker-skinned people produce more and larger granules of melanin than do those of lighter-skinned people. By screening out (ultraviolet) radiation from the sun, melanin protects people against a variety of maladies, including sunburn and skin cancer.

Before the sixteenth century, almost all the very dark-skinned populations of the world lived in the **tropics,** a belt extending some 23 degrees north and south of the equator, between the Tropic of Cancer and the Tropic of Capricorn. The association between dark skin color and a tropical habitat existed throughout the Old World, where hominids have lived for millions of years. The darkest populations of Africa evolved not in shady equatorial forests but in sunny open grassland, or savanna, country.

Leaving the tropics, skin color becomes lighter. Moving north in Africa, there is a gradual transition from dark brown to medium brown. Skin color continues to lighten as one moves through the Middle East, into southern Europe, through central Europe, and to the north. South of the tropics skin color is also lighter (Figure 5.1). In the Americas, by contrast, tropical populations don't have very dark skin. This is because the settlement of the New World, by light-skinned Asian ancestors of Native Americans, was relatively recent, probably dating back no more than 30,000 years.

How, aside from migrations, can we explain the geographic distribution of skin color? Natural selection provides an answer. In the tropics, with intense ultraviolet radiation from the sun, unprotected humans face the threat of severe sunburn, which can increase susceptibility to disease. This confers a selective *dis*advantage (i.e., less success in surviving and reproducing) on lighter-skinned people in the tropics (unless they stay indoors or use cultural products, like umbrellas or lotions, to screen sunlight). Sunburn also impairs the body's ability to perspire. This is a second reason why light skin color, given tropical heat, can diminish the human ability to live and work in equatorial climates. A third disadvantage of having light skin color in the tropics is that extreme exposure to ultraviolet radiation can produce skin cancer in humans (Blum 1961). However, skin cancer is not usually fatal, and when it is, reproduction has generally ended. This casts doubt on skin cancer as a natural selective agent because it doesn't lead to differential reproduction. A fourth disadvantage associated with having light skin color in the tropics is discussed below.

W. F. Loomis (1967) and others explain both light and dark skin color in terms of natural selective forces. Loomis focuses on the role of ultraviolet radiation in stimulating the manufacture of vitamin D by the human body. The unclothed body can syn-

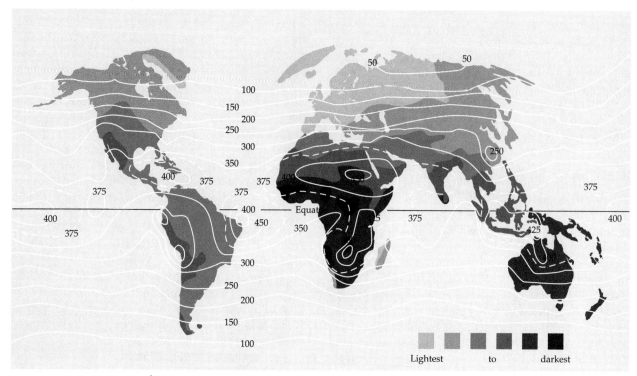

Figure 5.1 *The distribution of human skin color before* A.D. *1400. Also shown is the average amount of ultraviolet radiation in watt-seconds per square centimeter. (Figure from* Evolution and Human Origins *by B.J. Williams. Copyright © 1979 by B.J. Williams. Reprinted by permission of HarperCollins, Publishers, Inc.)*

thesize vitamin D directly from sunlight. However, in an overcast environment that is also cold enough for people to dress themselves for most of the year (like northern Europe, where light skin color evolved), clothing blocks the manufacture of vitamin D. A shortage of vitamin D interferes with the absorption of calcium in the intestines, and a nutritional disease known as **rickets** may develop. Rickets causes softening and deformation of the bones. In women, deformation of the pelvic bones can interfere with childbirth. There has been selection against dark skin in northern areas because melanin screens out ultraviolet radiation. During northern winters, light skin color maximizes the absorption of ultraviolet radiation by the few parts of the body that are exposed to direct sunlight. If the diet lacks vitamin D, reduced melanin is thus selectively favored.

Considering vitamin D production, light skin is advantageous in the cloudy north, but disadvantageous in the sun-lit tropics. Loomis has suggested that in the tropics, dark skin color protects the body against an *overproduction* of vitamin D by screening out ultraviolet radiation. Too much of this vitamin can lead to a potentially fatal condition (**hypervitaminosis D**) in which calcium deposits build up in the body's soft tissues and the kidneys may eventually fail. Gallstones, joint problems, and circulation problems are other symptoms of hypervitaminosis D.

This discussion of skin color shows that common ancestry isn't the only reason for biological similarities. Natural selection has made a major contribution to this expression of human diversity.

STRATIFICATION AND "INTELLIGENCE"

We see that scientists have shifted from racial *classification* to the *explanation* of human biological diversity. Race is no longer considered a valid biolog-

Before the sixteenth century, almost all the very dark-skinned populations of the world lived in the tropics, as does this Samburu woman from Kenya.

The northward trend toward lighter skin color continues around the Mediterranean into Europe. Very light skin color, illustrated in this photo, maximizes absorption of ultraviolet radiation by those few parts of the body exposed to direct sunlight during northern winters. This helps prevent rickets.

ical concept. Race has meaning only in social, cultural, and political terms. Over the centuries groups with power have used racial ideology to justify, explain, and preserve their privileged social positions. Dominant groups have declared minorities to be *innately*, that is, biologically, inferior. Racial ideas are used to suggest that social inferiority and presumed shortcomings (in intelligence, ability, character, or attractiveness) are immutable and passed across the generations. This ideology defends stratification as inevitable, enduring, and "natural"—based in biology rather than society. Thus the Nazis argued for the superiority of the "Aryan race," and European colonialists asserted the "white man's burden." South Africa institutionalized *apartheid*. Again and again, to justify exploitation of minorities and native peoples, those in control have proclaimed the innate inferiority of the oppressed. In the United States the supposed superiority of whites was once standard segregationist doctrine. Belief in the biologically based inferiority

of Native Americans has been an argument for their slaughter, confinement, and neglect.

However, anthropologists know that most of the behavioral variation among contemporary human groups rests on culture rather than biology. The cultural similarities revealed through thousands of ethnographic studies leave no doubt that capacities for cultural evolution are equal in all human populations. There is also excellent evidence that within any **stratified** (class-based) society, differences in performance between economic, social, and ethnic groups reflect different experiences and opportunities rather than genetic makeup. (Stratified societies are those with marked differences in wealth, prestige, and power between social classes.)

Stratification, political domination, prejudice, and ignorance continue to exist. They propagate the mistaken belief that misfortune and poverty result from lack of ability. Occasionally doctrines of innate superiority are even set forth by scientists, who, after all, tend to come from the favored stratum of

CULTURE, BIOLOGY, AND SPORTS

Culture constantly molds human biology. Culture promotes certain activities, discourages others, and sets standards of physical well-being and attractiveness. Sports activity, which is influenced by culture, helps build phenotype. American girls are encouraged to pursue—and they therefore do well in—competitive track and field, swimming, and diving. Brazilian girls, in contrast, haven't fared nearly as well in international athletic competition. Why are girls encouraged to become athletes in some nations but discouraged from physical activities in others? Why don't Brazilian women, and Latin women generally, do better in athletics?

Cultural standards of attractiveness affect athletic activities. Americans run or swim not just to compete but to keep trim and fit. Brazil's beauty standards accept more fat,

Years of swimming sculpt a distinctive physique—an enlarged upper torso, massive neck, powerful shoulders, and back. The countries that produce the most successful female swimmers are the United States, Germany, and the former Soviet Union, where this phenotype is not as stigmatized for women as it is in Latin countries.

society. Among recent examples, the best known is Jensenism, named for the educational psychologist Arthur Jensen (Jensen 1969; Herrnstein 1971), its leading proponent. Jensenism is a highly questionable interpretation of the observation that African-Americans, on average, perform less well on intelligence tests than Euro-Americans do. Jensenism asserts that blacks are hereditarily incapable of performing as well as whites do.

Environmental explanations for test scores are much more convincing than are the genetic tenets of Jensenism. An environmental explanation does not deny that some people may be smarter than others. In any society, for many reasons, genetic and environmental, the talents of individuals vary. An environmental explanation does deny, however, that these differences can be generalized to whole groups. Even when talking about individual intelligence, however, we have to decide which of several abilities is an accurate measure of intelligence.

Psychologists have devised several kinds of tests to measure intelligence, but there are problems with all of them. Early intelligence tests demanded skill in manipulating words. Such tests do not accurately measure learning ability for several reasons. For example, individuals who have learned two languages as children—bilinguals—don't do as well, on average, on verbal intelligence tests as do people who have learned a single language. It would be absurd to suppose that children who master two languages have inferior intelligence. One explanation seems to be that because bilinguals have vocabularies, concepts, and verbal skills in both languages, their ability to manipulate either one suffers a bit. Still, this is offset by the advantage of being fluent in two languages.

Most tests are written by educated people in Europe and North America. They reflect the experi-

especially in female buttocks and hips. Brazilian men have had some international success in swimming and running, but Brazil rarely sends female swimmers or runners to the Olympics. One reason Brazilian women avoid competitive swimming in particular is that sport's effects on phenotype. Years of swimming sculpt a distinctive physique—an enlarged upper torso, a massive neck, and powerful shoulders and back. Successful female swimmers tend to be big, strong, and bulky. The countries that produce them include the United States, Canada, Germany, and the former Soviet Union, where this phenotype isn't as stigmatized as it is in Latin countries. Swimmers develop hard bodies, but Brazilian culture says that women should be soft, with big hips and buttocks, not big shoulders.

Cultural factors also help explain why blacks excel in certain sports and whites in others. In North American schools, parks, sandlots, and city playgrounds, African-Americans have access to baseball diamonds, basketball courts, football fields, and tracks. However, because of restricted economic opportunities, many black families can't afford to buy hockey gear or ski equipment, take ski vacations, pay for tennis lessons, or belong to clubs with tennis courts and pools. In the United States mainly light-skinned boys (often in private schools) play soccer, the most popular sport in the world. In Brazil, however, soccer is the national pastime of all males—black and white, rich and poor. There is wide public access. Brazilians play soccer on the beach and in streets, squares, parks, and playgrounds. Many of Brazil's best soccer players, including the world-famous Pelé, have dark skins. When blacks have opportunities to do well in soccer, tennis, or any other sport, they are physically capable of doing as well as whites.

Why does the United States have so many black football and basketball players and so few black swimmers and hockey players? The answer lies mainly in cultural factors, such as variable access and social stratification. Many Brazilians practice soccer, hoping to play for money for a professional club. Similarly, American blacks are aware that certain sports have provided career opportunities for African-Americans. They start developing skills in those sports in childhood. The better they do, the more likely they are to persist, and the pattern continues. Countering a claim made by TV sports commentator Jimmy the Greek Snyder a few years ago, culture—specifically differential access to sports resources—has more to do with sports success than does "race."

ences of the people who devise them. It is not surprising that middle- and upper-class children do better because they are more likely to share the test makers' educational background and standards. Numerous studies have shown that performance on Scholastic Achievement Tests (SATs) can be improved by coaching and preparation. Parents who can afford $500 for an SAT preparation course enhance their kids' chances of getting high scores. Standardized college entrance exams are similar to IQ tests in that they purportedly measure intellectual aptitude. They may do this, but they also measure type and quality of high school education, linguistic and cultural background, and parental wealth. No test is free of class, ethnic, and cultural biases.

Tests invariably measure particular learning histories, not the potential for learning. They use middle-class performance as a standard for determining

No test is a pure measure of "native" intelligence—free of class, ethnic, and cultural biases. Standardized college entrance exams are similar to IQ tests in that they measure type and quality of high-school education, linguistic and cultural background, and parental wealth. An elite education, such as is available at this expensive private secondary school, produces higher average test scores.

what should be known at a given chronological age. Furthermore, tests are usually administered by middle-class white people who give instructions in a dialect or language that may not be totally familiar to the child being tested. Test performance improves when the subcultural, socioeconomic, and linguistic backgrounds of subjects and test personnel are similar (Watson 1972).

Recognizing the difficulties in devising a culture-free test, psychologists have developed several nonverbal tests, hoping to find an objective measure that is not bound to a single culture. In one such test, individuals score higher by adding body parts to a stick figure. In a maze test, subjects trace their way out of various mazes. The score increases with the speed of completion. Other tests also base scores on speed, for example, in fitting geometric objects into appropriately shaped holes. All these tests are culture-bound because American culture emphasizes speed and competition whereas most nonindustrial cultures do not.

Examples of cultural biases in intelligence testing abound. Biases affect performance by people in other cultures and by different groups within the same culture, such as Native Americans in the United States. Many Native Americans have grown up on reservations or under conditions of urban or rural poverty. They have suffered social, economic, political, and cultural discrimination. In one study, Native Americans scored the lowest (a mean of 81, compared with a standard of 100) of any minority group in the United States (Klineberg 1951). But when the environment offers opportunities similar to those available to middle-class Americans, test performance tends to equalize. Consider the Osage Indians, on whose reservation oil was discovered. Profiting from oil sales, the Osage did not experience the stresses of poverty. They developed a good school system, and their average IQ was 104. Here the relationship between test performance and environment is particularly clear. The Osage did not settle on the reservation because they knew that oil was there. There is no reason to believe that these people were innately more intelligent than were Indians on different reservations. They were just luckier.

Similar relationships between social, economic, and educational environment and test performance show up in comparisons of American blacks and whites. At the beginning of World War I, intelligence tests were given to approximately 1 million American army recruits. Blacks from some northern states had higher average scores than did whites from some southern states. This was caused by the fact that early in this century northern blacks got a better public education than did many southern whites. Thus, their superior performance is not surprising. On the other hand, southern whites did better than southern blacks. This is also expectable, given the unequal school systems then open to whites and blacks in the South.

Some people tried to get around the environmental explanation for the superior performance of northern blacks over southern whites by suggesting selective migration—smarter blacks had moved north. However, it was possible to test this hypothesis, which turned out to be false. If smarter blacks had moved north, their superior intelligence should have been obvious in their school records while they were still living in the South. It was not. Furthermore, studies in New York, Washington, and Philadelphia showed that as length of residence increased, test scores also rose.

Studies of identical twins raised apart also illustrate the impact of environment on identical heredity. In a study of nineteen pairs of twins, IQ scores varied directly with years in school. The average difference in IQ was only 1.5 points for the eight twin pairs with the same amount of schooling. It was 10 points for the eleven pairs with an average of five years' difference. One subject, with fourteen years more education than his twin, scored 24 points higher (Bronfenbrenner 1975).

These and similar studies provide overwhelming evidence that test performance measures education and social, economic, and cultural background rather than genetically determined intelligence. During the past 500 years Europeans and their descendants extended their political and economic control over most of the world. They colonized and occupied environments that they reached in their ships and conquered with their weapons. Most people in the most powerful contemporary nations—located in North America, Europe, and Asia—have light skin color. Some people in these currently powerful countries may incorrectly assert and believe that their world position has resulted from innate biological superiority. However, all contemporary human populations seem to have comparable learning abilities.

We are living in and interpreting the world at a

particular time. In the past there were far different associations between centers of power and human physical characteristics. When Europeans were barbarians, advanced civilizations thrived in the Middle East. When Europe was in the Dark Ages, there were civilizations in West Africa, on the East African coast, in Mexico, and in Asia. Before the Indus-trial Revolution, the ancestors of many white Europeans and Americans were living much more like precolonial Africans than like current members of the American middle class. Their average performance on twentieth-century IQ tests would have been abominable.

SUMMARY

An ethnic group assumed (by a particular culture) to have a biological basis is called a *race*. Race, like ethnicity in general, is a cultural category rather than a biological reality. That is, ethnic groups, including "races," derive from contrasts perceived and perpetuated in particular societies, rather than from scientific classifications based on common genes. In the United States "racial" labels like "white" and "black" designate social races—categories defined by American culture. Given the lack of a precise distinction between race and ethnicity, it is better to use the "ethnic group" instead of "race" to describe any such social group.

In American culture, one acquires his or her racial identity at birth, as an ascribed status, but American racial classification, governed by the rule of hypodescent, is based neither on phenotype nor genetics. Children of mixed unions are automatically classified with the minority-group parent.

Japan is not the uniform society that many imagine. Ten percent of the Japanese population consists of minorities: Ainu, Okinawans, outcast *burakumin*, children of mixed marriages, and immigrant nationalities, especially Koreans. Racial attitudes in Japan illustrate "intrinsic racism"—the belief that a perceived racial difference is a sufficient reason to value one person less than another. The valued group is majority ("pure") Japanese, who are believed to share "the same blood." Majority Japanese define themselves by opposition to others, whether minority groups in their own nation or outsiders—anyone who is "not us." Assimilation is discouraged; residential segregation and taboos on "interracial" marriage work to keep minorities "in their place." Japanese culture regards certain ethnic groups as having a biological basis, when there is no evidence that they do. The *burakumin*, for example, are physically and genetically indistinguishable from other Japanese but still face discrimination as a social race.

Racial classification in Brazil shows that the exclusionary American and Japanese systems are not inevitable.

Brazil shares a history of slavery with the United States, but it lacks the hypodescent rule. One illustration of the absence of hypodescent is the fact that (unlike the United States) full siblings may belong to different races if they are phenotypically different. Nor does Brazil have racial aversion of the sort found in Japan. Brazilians recognize more than 500 races. Brazilian racial identity is more of an achieved status; it can change during a person's lifetime, reflecting phenotypical changes. It also varies depending on who is doing the classifying. But given the correlation between poverty and dark skin, the class structure affects Brazilian racial classification, so that someone who has light skin and is poor will be perceived and classified as darker than a comparably colored person who is rich.

Historically, scientists have approached the study of human biological diversity from two main directions: racial classification, an approach that has been rejected, and the current explanatory approach. It is not possible at this time to define races biologically. Because of a range of problems involved in classifying humans into racial categories, contemporary biologists focus on specific biological differences and try to explain them. Skin color and other biological similarities between geographically separate groups may reflect—rather than common ancestry—similar but independent evolution in response to similar natural selective forces.

Some people assert that there are genetically determined differences in the learning abilities of "races," classes, and ethnic groups. However, environmental variables (particularly educational, economic, and social background) provide much better explanations for performance on intelligence tests by such groups. Intelligence tests reflect the cultural biases and life experiences of the people who develop and administer them. All tests are to some extent culture-bound. Equalized environmental opportunities show up in test scores.

GLOSSARY

descent: Rule assigning social identity on the basis of some aspect of one's ancestry.

hypervitaminosis D: Condition caused by an excess of vitamin D; calcium deposits build up in the body's soft tissues and the kidneys may fail; symptoms include gallstones, joint problems, and circulation problems; may affect unprotected light-skinned individuals in the tropics.

hypodescent: Rule that automatically places the children of a union or mating between members of different socioeconomic groups in the less-privileged group.

melanin: Substance manufactured in specialized cells in the lower layers of the epidermis (outer skin layer); melanin cells in dark skin produce more melanin than do those in light skin.

natural selection: Originally formulated by Charles Darwin and Alfred Russell Wallace, the process by which nature selects the forms most fit to survive and reproduce in a given environment—such as the tropics.

phenotype: An organism's evident traits, its "manifest biology"—anatomy and physiology.

Polynesia: Triangle of South Pacific islands formed by Hawaii to the north, Easter Island to the east, and New Zealand to the southwest.

rickets: Nutritional disease caused by a shortage of vitamin D; interferes with the absorption of calcium and causes softening and deformation of the bones.

social race: A group assumed to have a biological basis but actually perceived and defined in a social context—by a particular culture rather than by scientific criteria.

stratified: Class-structured; stratified societies have marked differences in wealth, prestige, and power between social classes.

tropics: Geographic belt extending about 23 degrees north and south of the equator, between the Tropic of Cancer (north) and the Tropic of Capricorn (south).

STUDY QUESTIONS

1. How do "races" differ from other kinds of ethnic groups?
2. Are races based on biology or culture?
3. Should categories like "African-American," "Anglo-American," and "Asian-American" be called "ethnic groups" or "races"? Why?
4. What is the hypodescent rule, and how does it affect American racial classification?
5. How may governments influence racial classification and discrimination?
6. How is race culturally constructed in Japan? What are the main physical differences between majority Japanese, on the one hand, and *burakumin* and Koreans in Japan, on the other?
7. What does it mean to say that the system of social race in Japan is based on opposition, intrinsic racism, aversion, and discrimination?
8. What kind of racial classification system operates in the community where you grew up or now live? Does it differ from the racial classification system described for American culture in this chapter?
9. What is the difference between race and skin color in contemporary American culture? Are the social identities of Americans and discrimination against some Americans based on one or both of these attributes?
10. What are the main contrasts between race in Brazil, the United States, and Japan?
11. If you had to devise an ideal system of "race relations," would it be more like the American, the Japanese, or the Brazilian system? Why?
12. Why is *race* a discredited term in biology? What has replaced it?
13. What are the main problems with racial classification based on phenotype?
14. What explanations have been proposed for the distribution of light and dark skin color?
15. What factors help us understand different average scores on "intelligence" tests by members of different stratified groups?
16. What is Jensenism, and what arguments and evidence may be offered for rejecting it?

SUGGESTED ADDITIONAL READING

AOKI, MICHIKO Y., AND MARGARET B. DARDESS, EDS.
1981   *As the Japanese See It: Past and Present.* Honolulu: The University Press of Hawaii. Personal accounts of Japanese culture, including experiences of discrimination.

CROSBY, A.W., JR.
1972   *The Columbian Exchange: Biological and Cultural Consequences of 1492.* Westport, CT: Greenwood Press. Disease, migration, slavery, and other consequences of the age of discovery.

DE VOS GEORGE A., AND HIROSHI WAGATSUMA
1966   *Japan's Invisible Race: Caste in Culture and Personality.* Berkeley: University of California Press. Considers many aspects of the *burakumin* (and other minorities) and their place in Japanese society and culture, including psychological factors.

DEGLER, C.
1970   *Neither Black or White: Slavery and Race Relations in Brazil and the United States.* New York: Macmillan. The main contrasts between Brazilian and American race relations and the historic, economic, and demographic reasons for them.

GOLDBERG, D.T., ED.
1990   *Anatomy of Racism.* Minneapolis: University of Minnesota Press. Recent collection of articles on race and racism.

HARRIS, M.
1964   *Patterns of Race in the Americas.* New York: Walker. Reasons for different racial and ethnic relations in North and South America and the Caribbean.

MONTAGU, A., ED.
1975   *Race and IQ.* New York: Oxford University Press. Scientists from several disciplines review and counter neoracist reasoning.

NELSON, H., AND R. JURMAIN
1991   *Introduction to Physical Anthropology.* 5th ed. St. Paul: West Publishing. This basic text discusses aspects of human biological diversity.

WEISS, M.L., AND A.E. MANN
1992   *Human Biology and Behavior: An Anthropological Perspective.* 6th ed. Glenview, IL: Scott, Foresman. Basic biological anthropology textbook; includes discussions of evolutionary principles, genetics, and human variability.

CHAPTER 6

EVOLUTION, GENETICS, AND BIOLOGICAL ADAPTATION

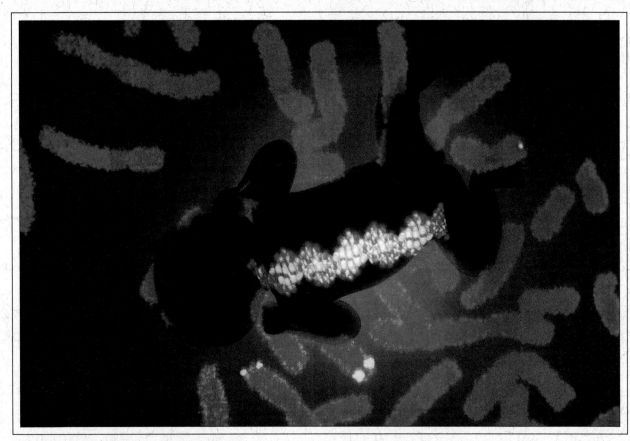

Humans have uniquely varied ways—cultural and biological—of adapting to environmental stresses. Chapter 3 considered adaptive (and maladaptive) aspects of *culture.* As individuals, we manipulate our artifacts and behavior in response to environmental conditions. We turn up thermostats or travel to Florida in the winter. We turn on fire hydrants, swim, or ride in air-conditioned cars from New York City to Maine to escape the summer's heat. Although such reliance on culture (artifacts) has increased during human evolution, people haven't stopped adapting biologically. As in other species, human *populations* adapt genetically in response to natural selection, and *individuals* react physiologically to stresses. Thus when we work in the midday sun, sweating occurs spontaneously, cooling the skin and reducing the temperature of subsurface blood vessels.

Chapter 5 considered issues involving human biological diversity—especially its cultural construction. Chapter 5 also stressed scientists' rejection of the discredited idea of race in favor of *explanation.* Instead of attempting to pigeonhole humanity into artificial categories assumed to share common ancestry, the focus has shifted toward explaining specific aspects of human variation. We saw that biological similarities (e.g., skin color) do not necessarily reflect common ancestry, as racial classification assumed. Similarities may also arise through the operation of natural selection and other mechanisms of evolution which affect biological (phenotypical and genetic) features of human populations. We are ready now for a more detailed look at principles of genetics and evolution, including natural selection, which determine human biological adaptation, variation, and change.

CREATIONISM, CATASTROPHISM, AND EVOLUTION

During the eighteenth century, many scholars became interested in human biology, human origins, biological diversity, and our position within the classification of plants and animals. At that time the commonly accepted explanation for the origin of species came from Genesis: God had created all life during six days of Creation. According to **creationism,** biological similarities and differences originated at the Creation. Characteristics of life forms are immutable; they cannot change. Through calculations based on genealogies in the Bible, the biblical scholars James Ussher and John Lightfoot even managed to trace the Creation to a very specific date—October 23, 4004 B.C. at 9 A.M.

Carolus Linnaeus (1707–1778), who accepted the biblical account of Creation, developed the first comprehensive taxonomy for living plants and animals. He grouped life forms on the basis of similarities and differences in their physical characteristics. He used traits such as the presence of a backbone to distinguish vertebrates from invertebrates and the presence of mammary glands to distinguish mammals from categories such as birds. Linnaeus viewed the differences between life forms as structural details in the Creator's orderly plan. Biological similarities and differences had been established at the Creation and did not reflect different degrees of genetic relationship.

Although Linnaeus's basic classification is still used by scientists, most now see an evolutionary basis for taxonomy. The animals included within a category are assumed to be more closely related to one another than they are to animals outside that category. In other words, classificatory similarities rest on common ancestry.

An increasing number of fossil discoveries during the eighteenth and nineteenth centuries raised doubts about creationism. Fossils showed that different kinds of life had once existed. If all life had originated at the same time, why weren't ancient species still around. Why weren't contemporary plants and animals found in the fossil record? A modified explanation combining creationism with **catastrophism** replaced the original doctrine. In this view fires, floods, and other catastrophes, including the biblical flood involving Noah's ark, had destroyed ancient species. After each destructive event, God had created again, leading to contemporary species. How did the catastrophists explain certain clear similarities between fossils and modern animals? They argued that some ancient species had managed to survive in isolated areas. For example, after the biblical flood, Noah's two of each kind spread throughout the world.

The alternative to creationism and catastrophism was **transformism,** also called **evolution.** Transformists believed that species arose from others through a long and gradual process of transformation, or descent with modification. Charles Darwin

According to creationism all life originated during the six days of creation described in the Bible. Catastrophism proposed that fires and floods, including the biblical deluge involving Noah's ark (depicted in this painting by the American artist Edward Hicks), destroyed certain species. But some ancient species managed to survive. According to catastrophism, after the biblical flood, Noah's two of each kind spread throughout the world.

became the best known of the transformists. However, he was influenced by earlier scholars, including his own grandfather. Erasmus Darwin, in a book called *Zoonomia* published in 1794, had proclaimed the common ancestry of all animal species.

Charles Darwin was also influenced by Sir Charles Lyell, the father of geology. During Darwin's famous voyage to South America aboard the *Beagle,* he read Lyell's influential *Principles of Geology* (1837/1969), which exposed him to Lyell's principle of **uniformitarianism.** Uniformitarianism states that the present is the key to the past. Explanations for past events should be sought in the long-term operation of ordinary forces that continue to work today. Thus, natural forces (rainfall, soil deposition, earthquakes, and volcanic action) have gradually built geological features such as mountain ranges. The earth's physical structure has been transformed gradually through the operation of natural forces over millions of years.

Uniformitarianism was a necessary building block for evolutionary theory. It cast serious doubt on the belief that the world was only 6,000 years old. It would take much longer for such ordinary forces as rain and wind to produce major geological fea-

tures. The longer time span also allowed enough time for the biological changes that fossil discoveries were revealing. Darwin applied uniformitarianism—long-term transformation through natural forces—to living things. Like other transformists, he argued that all life forms are ultimately related. In contrast to proponents of divine creation, Darwin argued that the number of species is not immutable. It has increased with time (although it is now decreasing as a result of human destruction of natural habitats).

Darwin offered *natural selection* as a single principle that could explain the origin of species, biological diversity, and similarities among related life forms. His major contribution was not the theory of evolution, as most people believe, but the idea that natural selection explains evolutionary change. However, natural selection was not Darwin's unique discovery. Working independently, naturalist Alfred Russel Wallace reached a similar conclusion. In a joint paper read to London's Linnaean Society in 1858, Darwin and Wallace made their discovery public. Darwin's book *On the Origin of Species* (1859/1958) offered fuller documentation but created great controversy.

Natural selection is the gradual process by which nature selects the forms most fit to survive and reproduce in a given environment. For natural selection to operate on a particular population, there must be variety within that population, as there always is. Natural selection operates when there is competition for **strategic resources** (those necessary for life), such as food and space, between members of the population. Organisms whose attributes render them most fit to survive and reproduce in their environment do so in greater numbers than do others. Over the years, the less fit organisms gradually die out and the favored types survive.

This process continues as long as the relationship between the population and its environment remains the same. However, if emigration or some change in the environment occurs, natural selection will begin to select types that are favored in the new environment. This selection will continue until an equilibrium is reached. Environmental change or emigration may then occur again. Through such a gradual, branching process, involving adaptation to thousands of environments, natural selection has produced the diverse plants and animals found in the world today.

GENETICS: THE BASIS OF BIOLOGICAL VARIATION

Darwin recognized that for natural selection to operate, there must be variety in the population undergoing selection. Documenting and explaining human variation is a major concern of modern biological anthropology. Genetics, a science that emerged after Darwin, helps us understand the causes of biological variation. We now know that DNA (deoxyribonucleic acid) molecules make up genes and chromosomes, which are the basic hereditary units. Biochemical changes (mutations) in DNA provide the variety on which natural selection operates. Genetic and chromosomal **recombination** produces additional variety; through bisexual reproduction, it leads to new arrangements of the hereditary units received from each parent.

Mendelian genetics is the study of the ways in which chromosomes transmit genes across the generations. **Biochemical genetics** examines structure, function, and changes in genetic materials. **Population genetics** investigates natural selection and other causes of genetic variation, maintenance, and change in breeding populations. To understand change and variation, we must be familiar with some basic terms.

Heredity Is Particulate

In 1856, in a monastery garden, the Austrian monk Gregor Mendel began a series of experiments that were to reveal basic principles of genetics. Mendel studied the inheritance of seven contrasting traits in pea plants. For each trait there were only two forms. For example, plants were either tall (6 to 7 feet) or short (9 to 18 inches), with no intermediate forms. Similarly, seeds were either smooth or wrinkled, and pea color was either yellow or green.

Mendel discovered that heredity is determined by discrete particles. Although traits could disappear in one generation, they reemerged in their original form in subsequent generations. For example, Mendel crossbred pure strains of tall and short plants. Their offspring were all tall. This was the first descending, or first filial, generation, designated F_1. Mendel then interbred the plants of the F_1 generation to produce a generation of grandchildren, the F_2 generation (Figure 6.1). In this generation, short plants reappeared; among thousands of plants in the F_2 generation, there was approximately one short plant for every three tall ones.

From similar results with the other six traits, Mendel concluded that although a **dominant** form could mask the other form in **hybrid,** or mixed, individuals, the dominated trait—the **recessive**—wasn't destroyed; it wasn't even changed. Recessive traits would reappear in unaltered form in subsequent generations because genetic traits were inherited as discrete units.

These basic genetic units that Mendel described are called **chromosomes.** Chromosomes are arranged in matching (homologous) pairs. Humans have forty-six chromosomes, arranged in twenty-three pairs, one in each pair from the father and the other from the mother.

For simplicity, a chromosome may be pictured as a surface (see Figure 6.2) with several positions, to each of which we assign a lowercase letter. Each position is a **gene,** or genetic locus (plural, *loci*). Each genetic locus determines, wholly or partially, a particular biological trait, such as whether one's blood is A, B, or O. When there is a biochemical difference

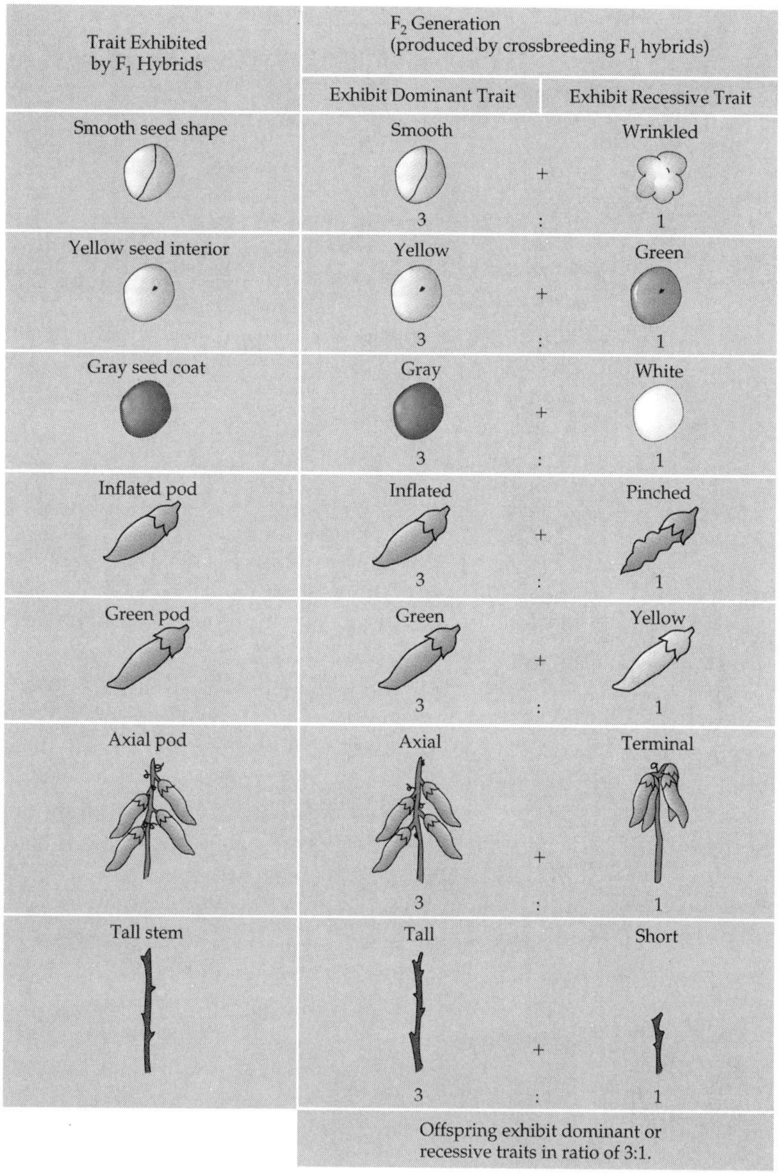

Trait Exhibited by F₁ Hybrids	F₂ Generation (produced by crossbreeding F₁ hybrids)	
	Exhibit Dominant Trait	Exhibit Recessive Trait
Smooth seed shape	Smooth + 3	Wrinkled : 1
Yellow seed interior	Yellow + 3	Green : 1
Gray seed coat	Gray + 3	White : 1
Inflated pod	Inflated + 3	Pinched : 1
Green pod	Green + 3	Yellow : 1
Axial pod	Axial + 3	Terminal : 1
Tall stem	Tall + 3	Short : 1
	Offspring exhibit dominant or recessive traits in ratio of 3:1.	

Figure 6.1 *Mendel's second set of experiments with pea plants. Dominant colors are shown unless otherwise indicated.*

at a given locus, we say that the chromosome pair has different genes, or alleles. **Alleles** (for example, b^1 and b^2 in Figure 6.2) are biochemically different forms that occur at a particular genetic locus. In humans, A, B, AB, and O blood result from different combinations of alleles at a certain locus in one of the chromosome pairs.

In Mendel's experiments, the seven contrasting traits were determined by genes located on seven different pairs of chromosomes. The gene for height occurred in one of the seven pairs. When Mendel crossbred pure tall and pure short plants to produce his F_1 generation, each of the offspring received an allele for tallness (T) from one parent and one for shortness (t) from the other. These offspring were mixed, or **heterozygous,** with respect to height; each had two dissimilar alleles at that genetic locus. Their parents, in contrast, had been **homozygous,** possessing two identical alleles at that locus.

In the next generation (F_2), after the mixed plants were interbred, short plants reappeared in the ratio of one short to three talls. Knowing that shorts only

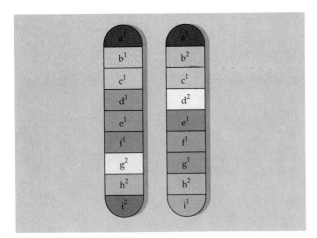

Figure 6.2 *A normal chromosome pair. (Letters indicate genes; superscripts indicate alleles.)*

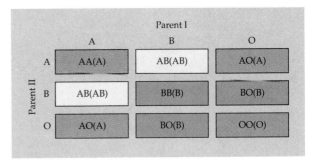

Figure 6.3 *Determinants of phenotypes (blood groups) in the ABO system. (The four phenotypes—A, B, AB, and O—are indicated in parentheses.)*

produced shorts, Mendel could assume that they were genetically pure. Another fourth of the F_2 plants produced only talls. The remaining half, like the F_1 generation, were heterozygous; when interbred, they produced three talls for each short.

Dominance produces a distinction between **genotype,** or hereditary makeup, and *phenotype,* or actual physical characteristics. There were three genotypes—TT, Tt, and tt—but only two phenotypes—tall and short. Because of dominance, the heterozygous plants were just as tall as genetically pure tall ones.

How do Mendel's discoveries apply to humans? Although some of our genetic traits follow Mendelian laws, with only two forms—dominant and recessive—other traits are determined differently. For instance, three alleles determine whether blood type is A, B, or O. People with two alleles for type O have that blood type. However, if they received a gene for either A or B from one parent and one for O from the other, they will have blood type A or B. In other words, A and B are both dominant over O. A and B are said to be *codominant.* If people inherit a gene for A from one parent and one for B from the other, they will have type AB blood, which is chemically different from the other varieties, A, B, and O.

These three alleles produce four phenotypes—A, B, AB, and O—and six different genotypes—OO, AO, BO, AA, BB, and AB (Figure 6.3). There are fewer phenotypes than genotypes because O is recessive to both A and B.

Independent Assortment and Recombination

No less important than Mendel's discovery of dominance and particulate heredity is his law of **independent assortment.** Through additional experiments, Mendel demonstrated that traits are inherited independently of one another. For example, he bred pure round yellow peas with pure wrinkled green ones. All the F_1 generation peas were round and yellow, the dominant forms. When Mendel interbred the F_1 generation to produce the F_2, four phenotypes turned up. Round greens and wrinkled yellows had been added to the original round yellows and wrinkled greens.

Independent assortment and recombination of genetic traits provide one of the principal ways by which variety is produced in any population. Recombination is important in biological evolution because it creates new types on which natural selection can operate.

BIOCHEMICAL, OR MOLECULAR, GENETICS

If the same genetic traits appear in predictable ratios from generation to generation, how can evolution take place? Since Mendel's time, geneticists have learned about **mutations,** or changes in the DNA molecules of which genes and chromosomes are built. Mendel demonstrated that variety is produced by genetic recombination. Mutation, however, is even more important as a source of new biochemical forms on which natural selection may operate.

DNA does several things basic to life. DNA can copy itself, forming new cells, replacing old ones, and producing the sex cells, or **gametes,** that make new generations. DNA's chemical structure also guides the body's production of proteins—enzymes, antigens, antibodies, hormones, and hundreds of others.

The DNA molecule is a double helix (Crick 1962/ 1968; Watson 1970). Imagine it as a small rubber ladder that you can twist into a spiral. Its sides are held together by chemical bonds between four bases: thymine (T), adenine (A), cytosine (C), and guanine (G). DNA's duplication leads to ordinary cell division, as shown in Figure 6.4.

In protein building, another molecule, RNA, carries DNA's message from the cell's nucleus to its

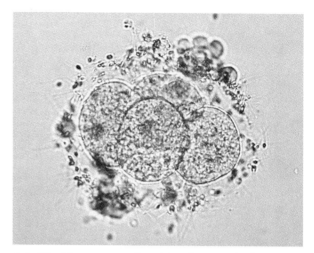

A fertilized human ovum (zygote) undergoes mitosis— ordinary cell division. Shown here, two cells have split to form four identical cells. The zygote grows rapidly through mitosis, as DNA molecules copy themselves; cell division continues as the organism grows.

Figure 6.4 *A double-stranded DNA molecule "unzips," and a new strand forms on each of the old ones, producing two molecules, and eventually two cells, each identical to the first.*

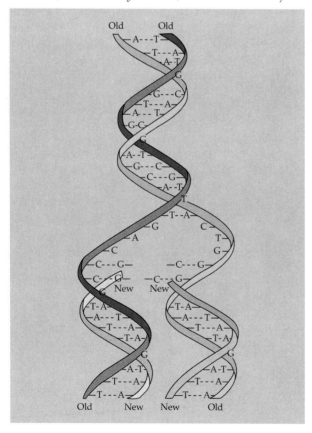

cytoplasm (outer area). The structure of RNA, with paired bases, matches that of DNA. This permits RNA to carry a message from DNA in the cell nucleus to guide the construction of proteins in the cytoplasm. A protein, which is a chain of amino acids, is constructed by "reading" a length of RNA. RNA's bases are read as three-letter "words," called **triplets**—for example, AAG. (Because DNA and RNA have four bases, which can occur anywhere in the "word," there are $4 \times 4 \times 4 = 64$ possible triplets.) Each triplet "calls" a particular amino acid, although there is some redundancy; for example, AAA and AAG both call for the amino acid lysine. A protein is made as amino acids are assembled in proper sequence.

Thus proteins are built following instructions sent by DNA, with RNA's assistance. In this way, DNA, the basic *hereditary* material, also initiates and guides the construction of hundreds of proteins necessary for bodily growth, maintenance, and repair.

Cell Division

An organism develops from a fertilized egg, or **zygote,** created by the union of two sex cells, one from each parent. The zygote grows rapidly through **mitosis,** or ordinary cell division, as DNA molecules copy themselves, creating two identical cells out of one; cell division continues as the organism grows.

The special process by which sex cells are produced is called **meiosis.** In contrast to ordinary cell division, in which two cells emerge from one, in meiosis four cells are produced from one. Each contains half the genetic material of the original cell. In human meiosis, four cells, each with twenty-three individual chromosomes, are produced from an original cell with twenty-three pairs.

With fertilization of egg by sperm, the father's twenty-three chromosomes join the mother's twenty-three to re-create the pairs in every generation. However, the chromosomes sort independently, so that a child's genotype is a random combination of the DNA of its four grandparents. It is conceivable that one grandparent will contribute very little to the grandchild's heredity.

Crossing Over

Independent assortment of chromosomes is a major source of variety, because the parents' genotypes can be assorted in 2^{23}, or more than 8 million, different ways. Another source of variety is **crossing over.** Before fertilization, early in meiosis, as a sperm or egg is being formed, paired chromosomes temporarily intertwine as they duplicate themselves. As they do this, they often exchange lengths of their DNA (Figure 6.5). Crossovers are the sites where homologous chromosomes have exchanged segments by breakage and recombination.

Because of crossing over, each new chromosome is partially different from either member of the original pair. As a person produces sex cells, replacing, say, part of a chromosome one has received from one's mother with a corresponding section of the homologous chromosome from one's father, crossing over partially contradicts Mendel's law of independent assortment and makes a new combination of genetic material available to the offspring. Because crossing over can occur with any chromosome pair, it is an important source of variety.

Mutation

Mutations are the most important source of variety on which natural selection operates. The simplest mutation results from substitution of just one base in a triplet by another. If such a mutation occurs in a sex cell that joins with another in a fertilized egg, the new organism will carry the mutation in every cell. As DNA directs protein building, a protein different from that produced by the nonmutant parent *may* be produced in the child. The child's protein building will differ from the parent's only if the new

Figure 6.5 *Crossing over. In the first phase of meiosis, homologous chromosomes intertwine as they duplicate themselves. As they do this, they often exchange lengths of their DNA, as shown here. This is known as crossing over. Note that the lower lengths of the original pair now differ. Each chromosome is therefore chemically different from either member of the original pair.*

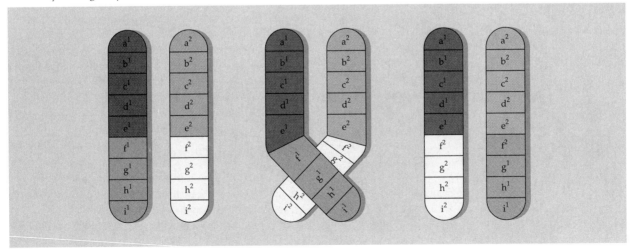

base codes for a different amino acid. Because the same amino acid can be coded by more than one triplet, a base-substitution mutation doesn't always produce a different protein. However, the abnormal protein associated with the hereditary disease sickle-cell anemia is caused by just such a difference in a single base between normal individuals and those afflicted with the disease.

Mutations occur in about 5 percent of sex cells, with the rate varying from gene to gene. Many geneticists believe that most mutations are neutral, conferring neither advantage nor disadvantage. Others argue that most mutations are harmful and will be weeded out because they deviate from types that have been selected over the generations. However, if the selective forces affecting a population change, mutations in its gene pool may acquire an adaptive advantage they lacked in the old environment.

POPULATION GENETICS AND MECHANISMS OF GENETIC EVOLUTION

Population genetics studies stable and changing populations in which most breeding normally takes place. The term **gene pool** refers to all the alleles and genotypes within a breeding population—the "pool" of genetic material available. When population geneticists use the term *evolution*, they have a more specific definition in mind than the one given earlier ("descent with modification over the generations"). For geneticists, **genetic evolution** is defined as change in gene frequency, that is, in the frequency of alleles in a breeding population from generation to generation. Any factor that contributes to such a change can be considered a mechanism of genetic evolution. Those mechanisms include natural selection, mutation, random genetic drift, and interbreeding and gene flow.

Natural Selection: Genotype and Phenotype

Natural selection is still the best explanation for evolution, but Charles Darwin's contribution must be placed in the context of more recent discoveries. Essential to understanding evolution through natural selection is the distinction between genotype and phenotype. Genotype refers to the *hereditary* factors that control the organism's form (anatomy) and function (physiology). Phenotype—actual anatomy and physiology—develops through a long-term interaction between genotype and environment. Because of dominance, individuals with different genotypes may have identical phenotypes (like Mendel's tall pea plants), and natural selection can operate only on phenotype. The processes that produce phenotype are varied and complex, and it is often difficult to disentangle the relative contributions of genotype and environment.

Phenotype includes outward physical appearance as well as internal organs, tissues, cells, and their constituents. Phenotype also encompasses physiological processes and systems. Many biological reactions to food, disease, heat, cold, sunlight, and other environmental factors are not automatic, genetically programmed responses but the product of years of exposure to particular environmental stresses. Human biology is not set inflexibly at birth but has considerable **plasticity;** that is, it is changeable, being affected by the environmental forces, such as diet and altitude, we experience as we grow up.

Natural Selection and Genetic Evolution

Heredity and environment combine to produce phenotype, and certain phenotypes do better in particular environments than other phenotypes do. However, because favored phenotypical traits can be produced by different genotypes, the process of perfecting the fit between organism and environment is gradual. Because natural selection works only on genes that are expressed phenotypically, **maladaptive**—that is, harmful—recessive alleles can be removed only when they are expressed in homozygous form. Heterozygous individuals carry the maladaptive recessive, but its effects are masked by the favored dominant.

After several generations of selection favoring a particular allele, gene frequencies will change. Thereafter, those traits that have proved to be the most **adaptive** (favored by natural selection) in that environment will be selected again and again from generation to generation. Given such **directional selection,** or long-term selection of the same trait(s), maladaptive recessive alleles will be removed—up to the point at which mutations from the dominant to the recessive allele balance the number of reces-

Phenotype reflects the interaction of genetic potential and environment. Shown here are identical twins—genetically the same—raised in different environments. The girl on the left was raised in Puerto Rico, the one on the right in the continental United States.

sives eliminated by natural selection. In this way, selection can operate as a force that maintains rather than changes the favored allele's frequency in the gene pool.

Directional selection will continue as long as environmental forces remain the same. However, if the environment changes or if part of the population colonizes a new environment, new selective forces start operating, favoring different phenotypes in the new environment. Selection continues until a new equilibrium is reached, and there is directional selection until another environmental change or emigration takes place. Over millions of years, such a process of successive adaptation to contrasting environments has led to biological modification and branching and to the tremendous array of plant and animal forms found in the world today.

It's important to remember that natural selection operates *only* on traits that are present in a population. A favorable mutation *may* occur, but a population doesn't normally come up with a new genotype or phenotype just because one is needed. Many species have become extinct because they weren't sufficiently varied to adapt to environmental shifts.

There are also differences in the amount of environmental stress that organisms' genetic potential enables them to tolerate. Some species are adapted to a narrow range of environments and are endangered by environmental fluctuation. Others—*Homo sapiens* among them—tolerate much more environmental variation because their genetic potential permits many adaptive possibilities. Humans adapt rapidly to changing conditions by modifying both biological responses and learned behavior. Humans don't have to delay adaptation until a favorable mutation appears.

Polymorphisms

We have seen that natural selection can reduce variety in a population through directional selection—by favoring one allele or trait over another. Selective forces can also work to preserve variety by favoring a **balanced polymorphism,** in which the frequencies of two or more alleles of a gene remain constant from generation to generation. This may be because the phenotypes they produce are neutral, or equally favored, or equally opposed, by selective forces. Sometimes a particular selective force favors (or opposes) one allele while a different but equally effective force favors (or opposes) the other allele.

In one example of a balanced polymorphism, the two alleles are called Hb^A and Hb^S. They affect the production of human hemoglobin, which makes up about 90 percent of the protein in red blood cells. Hemoglobin carries oxygen from the lungs to the rest of the body via the circulatory system.

The allele that produces the normal hemoglobin molecule is Hb^A. A variant allele, Hb^S, yields a different hemoglobin. Individuals who are homozy-

The red blood cells—some sickled, some normal (round)—of a sickle-cell carrier (an Hb^A-Hb^S heterozygote). Hb^S homozygotes suffer from sickle-cell anemia, in which the red blood cells are shaped like crescents or sickles and increase the heart's burden by clogging the small blood vessels. Heterozygotes have enough sickling hemoglobin to protect them against malaria and sufficient normal hemoglobin to fend off the anemia.

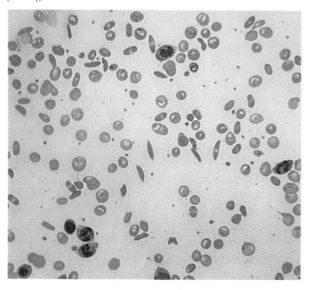

gous for Hb^S suffer from **sickle-cell anemia,** a usually fatal anemia, in which the red blood cells are shaped like crescents or sickles. This impairs the blood's ability to store oxygen and increases the heart's burden by clogging the small blood vessels.

Given the fatal disease associated with the Hb^S homozygote, geneticists were surprised to discover that certain populations in Africa, India, and the Mediterranean had very high frequencies of Hb^S (Figure 6.6). In some West African populations the frequency of Hb^S is around 20 percent. Researchers eventually discovered that both Hb^A and Hb^S are maintained because selective forces in those environments favor the heterozygote over either homozygote. This is one of the most thoroughly studied examples of natural selection working among contemporary human populations.

Initially, scientists wondered why, if most Hb^S homozygotes died before they reached reproductive age, the harmful allele hadn't been eliminated from the population. Why was its frequency so high? The answer turned out to lie in the heterozygote's greater fitness. Only people who were homozygous for Hb^S died from sickle-cell anemia. Heterozygotes suffered very mild anemia, if any. On the other hand, although people homozygous for Hb^A did not suffer from anemia, they were much more susceptible than were Hb^S homozygotes and heterozygotes to malaria—a killer disease that continues to plague *Homo sapiens* in the tropics.

The heterozygote, with one sickle-cell allele and one normal one, was the fittest phenotype for a malarial environment. Heterozygotes have enough abnormal hemoglobin, in which malaria parasites can't thrive, to protect them against malaria and enough normal hemoglobin to prevent severe sickle-cell anemia. The Hb^S allele therefore has been maintained in these populations because heterozygotes survived and reproduced in greater numbers than did people with any other phenotype.

The sickle-cell allele spread in the tropics as a result of certain economic and cultural changes—specifically, a shift from hunting and gathering to farming (Livingstone 1958). Many societies in West Africa adopted a form of cultivation known as **slash and burn.** With this system, trees were cut down and burned to provide ashes for fertilizing the soil. After the land was farmed for one or two years, yields began to drop, and farmers chose another plot to slash and burn.

GENES AND DISEASE

According to a report by the World Health Organization (*New York Times*, March 28, 1990) tropical diseases now affect 10 percent of the world population. Malaria, the most widespread of these, afflicts about 270 million people. Schistosomiasis, a waterborne parasitic disease, affects 200 million. Another 90 million people have filariasis, which causes elephantiasis—lymphatic obstruction leading to the enlargement of body parts, particularly the legs and scrotum.

The number of malaria cases is increasing. Brazil, for example, had 560,000 cases in 1988 versus 100,000 in 1977 (*New York Times* 1990). Contributing to this rise is the increasing resistance of parasites to the drugs (such as chloroquine) commonly used to treat malaria. However, hundreds of millions of people are genetically resistant. Sickle-cell hemoglobin (see the text) is the best known of the genetic antimalarials (Diamond 1989).

Microbes have been major selective agents for humans, particularly before the arrival of modern medicine. Some people are genetically more susceptible to certain diseases than are others, and the distribution of human blood types continues to change in response to natural selection.

After food production emerged around 10,000 years ago, infectious diseases posed a mounting risk and eventually became the foremost cause of human mortality. Food production favors infection for several reasons. Cultivation sustains larger, denser populations and a more sedentary life style than does hunting and gathering. People live closer to each other and to their own wastes, making it easier for microbes to survive and to find hosts. Domesticated animals also transmit diseases to people.

Until 1977, when the last case of smallpox was reported, smallpox had been a major threat to humans and a determinant of blood group frequencies (Diamond 1990). The smallpox virus is a mutation from one of the pox viruses that plague such domesticated animals as cows, sheep, goats, horses, and pigs. Smallpox appeared in human beings after people and animals started living together.

Smallpox epidemics have played important roles in world history, often killing one-fourth to one-half of the affected populations. Smallpox contributed to Sparta's defeat of Athens in 430 B.C. and to the decline of the Roman empire after A.D. 160.

Born in the Old World, the smallpox virus entered the Americas with the Spanish conquistadors around 1507. It helped the Spanish conquer the Aztecs and the Incas, who lacked antibodies and had populations large enough to sustain a smallpox epidemic. The Indians were both decimated and demoralized by a disease that appeared to affect them but not the Europeans.

The ABO blood groups have figured in human resistance to smallpox. Blood is typed according to the protein and sugar compounds on the surface of the red blood cells. Different substances (compounds) distinguish between type A and type B blood. Type A cells trigger the production of antibodies in B blood, so that A cells clot in B blood. The different substances work like chemical passwords; they help us distinguish our own cells from invading cells, including microbes, we ought to destroy. The surfaces of some microbes have substances similar to ABO blood group substances. We don't produce antibodies to substances

---

Slash-and-burn cultivation created breeding areas for *Anopheles* mosquitoes, which carry the malarial parasites and transmit them to people. Farming eroded and hardened the topsoil, increasing rain runoff to pools of stagnant water. The destruction of the forest promoted an increase in malarial mosquitoes, which bred more effectively in water exposed to the sun than in shaded areas. Rare in the forest, mosquitoes became common in the new environment.

Simultaneously, the new economy produced more food than did the old one, and this fueled human population increase. Villages became larger and closer together; human population density increased, providing more hosts for parasites. In this changed environment, the sickle-cell allele began to play an adaptive role.

The example of the sickle-cell allele demonstrates the **relativity** of evolution through natural selection: Adaptation and fitness are in relation to specific environments, and traits are not adaptive or maladaptive for all times and places. Even apparently maladaptive alleles can be selected if heterozygotes have a selective advantage. Moreover, as the envi-

similar to those on our own blood cells. We can think of this as a clever evolutionary trick by the microbes to deceive their hosts, because we don't normally develop antibodies against our own biochemistry.

People with A or AB blood are more susceptible to smallpox than are people with type B or type O. Presumably this is because a substance on the smallpox virus mimics the type A substance, permitting the virus to slip by the defenses of the type A individual. By contrast, type B and type O individuals produce antibodies against smallpox because they recognize it as a foreign substance.

The relationship between type A blood and susceptibility to smallpox was first suggested by the low frequencies of the A allele in areas of India and Africa where smallpox had been endemic. A comparative study done in rural India in 1965–66, during a virulent smallpox epidemic, did much to confirm this relationship. Drs. F. Vogel and M. R. Chakravartti analyzed blood samples from smallpox victims and their uninfected siblings (Diamond 1990). The researchers found 415 infected children, none ever vaccinated against smallpox. All but 8 of the infected children had an uninfected (also unvaccinated) sibling.

The results of the study were clear: Susceptibility to smallpox varied with ABO type. Of the 415 infected children, 261 had the A allele; 154 lacked it. Among their 407 uninfected siblings, the ratio was reversed. Only 80 had the A allele; 327 lacked it. The researchers calculated that a type A or type AB person had a seven times greater chance of getting smallpox than did an O or B person.

In most human populations the O allele is more common than A and B combined. A is most common in Europe; B frequencies are highest in Asia. Since smallpox was once widespread in the Old World, we might wonder why natural selection didn't eliminate the A allele entirely. The answer appears to be this: other diseases spared type A people and penalized those with other blood groups.

For example, type O people seem to be especially susceptible to bubonic plague—the "Black Death" that killed a third of the population of medieval Europe. Type O people are also more likely to get cholera, which has killed as many people in India as smallpox has. On the other hand, blood group O may increase resistance to syphilis. The ravages of that venereal disease, which probably originated in the New World, may explain the very high frequency of type O blood among the natives of Central and South America. The distribution of human blood groups appears to represent a compromise among the selective effects of many diseases.

In the case of diseases for which there are no effective drugs, genetic resistance maintains its significance. There is probably genetic variation in susceptibility to AIDS, for example. We know that people exposed to the AIDS virus vary in their risk of becoming infected and in the rate at which the disease progresses. AIDS is widespread in many African nations (and in the United States, France, and Brazil). In certain world areas the AIDS-related mortality rate could eventually (let us hope it does not) rival that of past epidemics of smallpox and plague. If so, AIDS could cause large shifts in human gene frequencies—again illustrating that natural selection is a continuing reality.

ronment changes, favored phenotypes and genes can change. In malaria-free environments, normal-hemoglobin homozygotes reproduce more effectively than heterozygotes do. With no malaria, the frequency of Hb^S declines, because Hb^S homozygotes can't compete in survival and reproduction with the other types. This has happened in areas of West Africa where malaria has been eradicated through drainage programs and insecticides. Selection against Hb^S has also occurred in the United States among Americans descended from West Africans (Diamond 1989).

Mutations and Variety

We have seen that mutations are a major source of genetically transmitted variety, raw material on which natural selection can work. (Crossing over, independent assortment, and chromosomal recombination are other sources.) Chemical alterations in genes may provide a population with entirely new phenotypes, which may offer some selective advantage. Variants produced through mutation can be especially significant if there is a change in selective forces. They may prove to have an advantage they

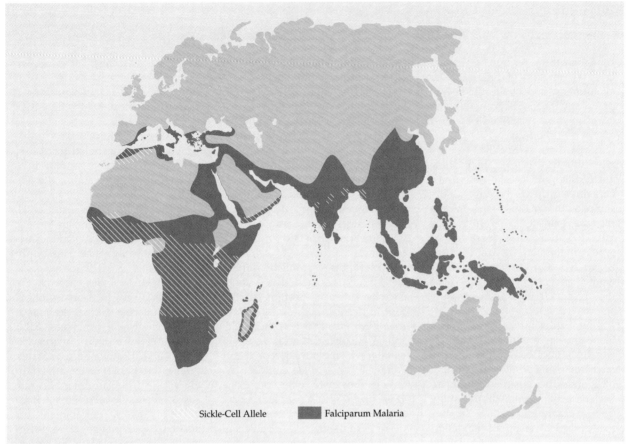

Figure 6.6 *Distribution of sickle-cell allele and falciparum malaria in the Old World.*
(Adapted from Human Evolution: An Introduction to the New Physical
Anthropology *by Joseph B. Birdsell. Copyright © 1975, 1981 by HarperCollins,
Publishers, Inc. Reprinted by permission of the publisher.)*

lacked in the old environment. The spread of Hb^S
offers one example.

Random Genetic Drift

A third mechanism of genetic evolution (along with
natural selection and mutation) is **random genetic
drift**—a change in gene frequency that results not
from natural selection but from chance. Since random genetic drift is most common in small populations, it has probably been important in human
evolution, because humans have lived in small
groups during much of our history. In a small population, alleles are likely to be lost by chance.

To understand why, compare the sorting of alleles to a game involving a bag of twelve marbles,
six red and six blue. In step 1 you draw six marbles

from the bag. Statistically, your chances of drawing
three reds and three blues are less than those of getting four of one color and two of the other. Step 2
is to fill a new bag with twelve marbles on the basis
of the ratio of marbles you drew in step 1. Assume
that you drew four reds and two blues: the new bag
will have eight red marbles and four blue ones. Step
3 is to draw six marbles from the new bag. Your
chances of drawing blues in step 3 is lower than it
was in step 1, and the probability of drawing all reds
increases. If you do draw all reds, the next bag (step
4) will have only red marbles.

This game is analogous to random genetic drift
operating over the generations. The blue marbles
were lost purely by chance. Alleles, too, can be lost
by chance rather than because of a disadvantage
they confer. Lost alleles can reappear in a gene pool
only through mutation.

Interbreeding and Gene Flow

A fourth cause of change in allele frequency is **gene flow,** the exchange of genetic material between populations of the same species. Gene flow, like mutation, works in conjunction with natural selection by providing variety on which selection can work. Gene flow may consist of direct interbreeding between formerly separated populations of the same species (for example, Europeans, Africans, and Native Americans in the United States), or it may be indirect and gradual.

Consider the following hypothetical case. In a certain part of the world live six local populations of a certain species. P_1 is the westernmost of these populations. P_2, which interbreeds with P_1, is located 50 miles to the east. P_2 also interbreeds with P_3, located 50 miles east of P_2. Assume that each population interbreeds with, and only with, the adjacent populations. P_6 is located 250 miles from P_1 and does not directly interbreed with P_1, but it is tied to P_1 through the chain of interbreeding that ultimately links all six populations.

Assume further that some allele exists in P_1 that isn't particularly advantageous in its environment. Because of gene flow, this allele may be passed on to P_2, by it to P_3, and so on, until it eventually reaches P_6. In P_6 or along the way, the allele may encounter an environment in which it does have a selective advantage. If this should happen, it may serve, like a new mutation, as raw material on which natural selection can operate (Figure 6.7).

Alleles are spread through gene flow even when selection is not operating on the allele. In the long run, natural selection works on the variety within a population, whatever its source—mutation, drift, or gene flow. Selection and gene flow have worked together to spread the Hb^S (sickle-cell) allele in Central Africa. Frequencies of Hb^S in Africa reflect not only the intensity of malaria but also the length of time gene flow has been going on (Livingstone 1969).

Gene flow is important in the study of the origin of species. A **species** may be defined as a population whose members can interbreed to produce offspring that can live and reproduce. A species must be able to reproduce itself through time. Gene flow tends to prevent **speciation**—the formation of new species—unless subgroups of the same species are separated for a sufficient length of time.

When gene flow is interrupted and genetically isolated subgroups are maintained, new species may arise. Imagine that an environmental barrier arises between P_3 and P_4, so that they no longer interbreed. If over time, as a result of isolation, P_1, P_2, and P_3 become incapable of interbreeding with the other three populations, speciation will have occurred.

DIVERSITY THROUGH ADAPTATION

This section considers several examples of human biological diversity that reflect adaptation to specific environmental stresses, such as disease, diet, tem-

Figure 6.7 *Gene flow between local populations. P_1–P_6 are six local populations of the same species. Each interbreeds (=) only with its neighbor(s). Although members of P_6 never interbreed with P_1, P_6 and P_1 are linked through gene flow. Genetic material that originates in P_1 eventually will reach P_6, and vice versa, as it is passed from one neighboring population to the next. Because they share genetic material in this way, P_1–P_6 remain members of the same species. In many species, local populations distributed throughout a larger territory than the 250 miles depicted here are linked through gene flow.*

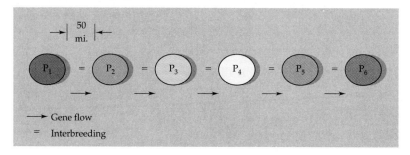

IN THE NEWS: BAD NEWS BORNE

Given the growing knowledge about genetically transmitted diseases, people with a family history of such a disease can be counseled about their chances and their children's chances of being affected. New genetic traits and tests are discovered almost every day.

This news item describes testing involving Huntington's disease, a disorder caused by a dominant allele ("bad gene") on chromosome 4. Huntington's disease, a fatal condition marked by mental and physical degeneration, usually develops in adults after age 30. This item describes a study of people with a family history of the disease who chose, or did not choose, to be tested for the allele in question. The study, done at the University of British Columbia in Canada, concluded that certainty was generally preferable to uncertainty, even when people learned they would develop the disease.

BOSTON — A study released today helps clear up a dilemma of genetic testing: Are people who are at risk of a terrible and untreatable disease better off knowing whether or not they will get it?

The answer, it seems, is yes. Even when the news is bad, knowing is better than uncertainty, researchers said.

An inherited disorder called Huntington's disease gave researchers a real-life example to test. When people have a parent with this fatal, incurable disease, they have a 50-50 chance of getting it themselves in middle age.

In 1986, a test was developed that reveals whether people have the bad gene that causes the illness. While people can learn with almost complete certainty whether they will get it, nothing can be done to stop the disease.

Some experts have argued that learning the truth is likely to be so devastating that those who inherit the bad gene are better off not knowing.

In today's *New England Journal of Medicine*, researchers from the University of British Columbia described the first major study of how people cope with the news.

The researchers studied 135 people who either sought testing or decided not to take it. One year after getting results, those who learned they were free of the disease felt much better off. Psychological tests showed they were less anxious, less depressed and more satisfied with their lives.

Those who got bad news initially felt slightly worse. But after a year, their outlooks were also considerably better than before they took the test.

"Living with Huntington's disease is a major burden," said Dr. Michael R. Hayden, a co-author of the study. "Modification of risk, irrespective of the direction, can improve the quality of life."

Nevertheless, Hayden said the researchers were surprised to find that people felt less anxious after learning that they were destined to get the inherited disease.

"We are all different," wrote Catherine V. Hayes, president of the Huntington's Disease Society of America. "But for most of us, an answer helps by eliminating the daily worrying and by allowing time for planning."

In an accompanying editorial, Hayes described her own happiness upon taking the test and finding out she did not have the Huntington's gene.

About five in 100,000 people develop Huntington's disease. Symptoms usually begin slowly between ages 30 and 50, and victims suffer relentless mental and physical degeneration until they die 10 or 15 years later.

In the study, anxiety levels of those who chose not to take the test remained relatively high and even worsened a bit as time passed.

About 10 percent of those who learned their fates suffered serious emotional difficulties, regardless of what they found.

Among those who discovered they would not die of Huntington's disease, some grew depressed because the news did not change their lives as much as they expected.

Others had undergone sterilization so they would not pass the disease to another generation. They grew despondent upon realizing this was unnecessary.

Hayden said one man was dispirited after learning that his wife would not get Huntington's. He had already taken early retirement so he could tend to her when she got sick.

Source: Daniel Q. Haney, "Bad News Borne," *Ann Arbor News,* November 12, 1992, p. A4.

perature, humidity, and altitude. There is abundant evidence for human genetic adaptation and thus evolution (change in allele frequency) through natural selection working in specific environments. One example is the adaptive value of the Hb^S heterozygote and its spread in malarial environments. Adaptation and evolution proceed in specific environments. There is no generally or ideally adaptive allele and no perfect phenotype. Nor can an allele be assumed to be maladaptive for all times and all places. Even Hb^S, which produces a lethal anemia, has a selective advantage in the heterozygous form in malarial environments.

Furthermore, alleles that were once maladaptive may lose their selective disadvantage if the environment shifts. Colorblindness (disadvantageous for hunters and forest dwellers) and genetic diabetes are examples. Today's environment contains medical techniques that allow people with such conditions to live fairly normal lives. Formerly maladaptive alleles have thus become neutral with respect to selection. The number of known human genetic characteristics now exceeds 5,000 (compared with just 1,487 in 1966—McKusick 1966 and 1990). New genetic traits are being discovered almost every day. Scientists are working on a map of the human genome—all our genes and chromosomes. Most studies so far have focused on genetic abnormalities, because of their medical and treatment implications. Given current knowledge about genetically transmitted diseases, people with a family history of such a disease can be counseled about their children's chances of being affected. Many currently incurable hereditary illnesses are destined to become neutral traits in tomorrow's medical environment.

Blood Factors

In Chapter 5 we considered the role of natural selection in producing adaptive skin color variation between human populations. Selection also affects blood factors. Adaptation to environmental factors, particularly infectious diseases, seems to have influenced the distribution of human blood groups, such as the ABO system. Blood groups are based on surface features of red blood cells and shouldn't be confused with hemoglobins, enzymes, and other proteins *within* the red blood cell. In the ABO blood group system, different surface molecules distinguish between type A and type B blood cells.

ABO typing is important because when type A cells are introduced into type B blood, they clot. Clotting is a result of anti-A antibodies present in type B serum; type A cells have an antigen that triggers the production of antibodies in type B serum. An **antigen** is a chemical substance that triggers the production of an **antibody**—a defending biochemical agent that reacts by attacking a foreign substance. In this case, recognition of a foreign antigen triggers the production of antibodies, which cause clotting in the blood.

Type O cells have neither the type B nor the type A antigen; they don't trigger antibody production or clot when mixed with A, B, and AB serum. People with type O blood therefore are universal donors. On the other hand, neither A cells nor B cells clot when transfused into the blood of an AB recipient. The biochemistry of the recipient recognizes both antigens (from its own blood) and produces antibodies to neither. Thus type AB individuals are universal recipients. Type O serum, which recognizes neither the A nor the B antigen, produces antibodies

The number of known human genes exceeds 5,000, with new traits being discovered almost every day. Scientists are working on a map of the human genome—all our genes and chromosomes. This photo shows one way of examining the base-pair sequence or chemical blueprint of lengths of DNA. Ultraviolet light reveals fragments of radioactively tagged DNA sorted by size.

to both. Thus people with type O blood can receive transfusions only from other type O donors.

There is evidence that infectious diseases have been selective agents affecting ABO allele frequencies (see box "Genes and Disease"). Individuals with type A and type AB blood, for example, are more susceptible to smallpox than type B and type O people are. Presumably this reflects a similarity between an antigen on the smallpox virus and an antigen carried by type A blood cells. The smallpox virus "fools" its host, which "thinks" the invader is one of its own type A blood cells.

We know that A and B antigens are similar in structure to antigens found on many disease microorganisms. Type A and type AB individuals have trouble producing antibodies against smallpox because such antibodies would also act against their own type A antigen and therefore their own blood cells. Type B and type O individuals, by contrast, can produce antibodies against smallpox without attacking their own red blood cells.

Associations between ABO blood type and noninfectious disorders have also been noted. Type O individuals are most susceptible to duodenal and gastric ulcers. Type A individuals seem most prone to stomach and cervical cancer and ovarian tumors. However, since these noninfectious disorders tend to occur after reproduction has ended, their relevance to adaptation and evolution through natural selection is doubtful.

Facial Features

Selection also affects facial features. For instance, long noses seem to be adaptive in arid areas (Brace 1964; Weiner 1954), because membranes and blood vessels inside the nose moisten the air as it is breathed in. Long noses are also adaptive in cold environments, because blood vessels warm the air as it is breathed in. This nose form distances the brain, which is sensitive to bitter cold, from raw outer air. These were adaptive biological features for humans who lived in cold climates before the invention of central heating.

The association between nose form and temperature is recognized as **Thomson's nose rule** (Thomson and Buxton 1923), which shows up statistically. In plotting the geographic distribution of nose length among human populations, the average nose does tend to be longer in areas with lower mean annual temperatures.

Other facial features also illustrate adaptation to selective forces. Among contemporary humans, average tooth size is largest among Native Australian hunters and gatherers, for whom large teeth had an adaptive advantage, given a diet based on foods with a considerable amount of sand and grit. People with small teeth—if false teeth and sand-free foods are unavailable—can't feed themselves as effectively as people with more massive dentition can.

Size and Body Build

Certain body builds have adaptive advantages for particular environments. A relationship between body weight and temperature is summarized in **Bergmann's rule:** The smaller of two bodies similar in shape has more surface area per unit of weight and therefore dissipates heat more efficiently. (Heat loss occurs on the body's surface—the skin perspires.) Indeed, average size does tend to increase in cold areas and decrease in hot ones because big bodies hold heat better than small ones do. To be more precise, in a large sample of native populations, average adult male weight increased by 0.66 pounds (0.3 kilogram) for every 1 degree Fahrenheit fall in mean annual temperature (Roberts 1953; Steegman 1975). The "pygmies" and the San, who live in hot climates and weigh only 90 pounds on the average, illustrate this relationship in reverse.

Body shape differences also reflect adaptation to temperature through natural selection. The relationship between temperature and body shape in animals and birds was first recognized in 1877 by the zoologist J. A. Allen. **Allen's rule** states that the relative size of protruding body parts—ears, tails, bills, fingers, toes, limbs, and so on—increases with temperature. Among humans, slender bodies with long digits and limbs are adaptively advantageous in tropical climates because they increase body surface relative to mass and allow for more efficient heat dissipation. Among the cold-adapted Eskimos, the opposite phenotype is found—short limbs and stocky bodies—to conserve heat. Cold area populations tend to have larger chests and shorter arms than do people from warm areas (Roberts 1953).

This discussion of adaptive relationships between temperature and body size and shape illustrates that natural selection may achieve the same effect in different ways. East African Nilotes, who live in a hot area, have tall, linear bodies with elongated ex-

Like East Africa Nilotes generally, this Nuer herder from the Sudan has a tall linear body with elongated extremities (note his fingers). Such proportioning increases the surface area relative to mass and thus dissipates heat (Allen's rule). The reduction of body size may achieve the same result (Bergmann's rule).

Allen's rule, cold area populations tend to have relatively larger chests and shorter arms than do people from warm areas. Among the cold-adapted Eskimos (like this woman of Nunivak Island, Alaska) short limbs and stocky bodies help conserve heat.

tremities that increase surface area relative to mass and thus maximize heat dissipation (illustrating Allen's rule). Among the "pygmies" the reduction of body size achieves the same result (illustrating Bergmann's rule). Similarly, the large bodies of northern Europeans and the compact stockiness of the Eskimos serve the same function of heat conservation.

Lactose Intolerance

Many biological traits that illustrate human adaptation are not under simple genetic control. Genetic determination of such traits may be likely but unconfirmed, or several genes may interact to influence the trait in question. Sometimes there is a ge-

netic component, but the trait also responds to stresses encountered during growth. We speak of **phenotypical adaptation** when adaptive changes occur during the individual's lifetime. Phenotypical adaptation is made possible by biological plasticity—our ability to change in response to the environments we encounter as we grow.

For example, genes and phenotypical adaptation work together to produce a biochemical difference between human groups: the ability to digest large amounts of milk—an adaptive advantage when other foods are scarce and milk is available, as it is in dairying societies. All milk, whatever its source, contains a complex sugar called **lactose.** The digestion of milk depends on an enzyme called **lactase,** which works in the small intestine. Among all mammals except humans and some of their pets, lactase production ceases after weaning, so that these animals can no longer digest milk.

Lactase production and the ability to tolerate milk vary between populations. About 90 percent of northern Europeans and their descendants are lactose tolerant; they can digest several glasses of milk with no difficulty. Similarly, about 80 percent of two African populations, the Tutsi of Rwanda and Burundi in East Africa and the Fulani of Nigeria in West Africa, produce lactase and digest milk easily. Both these groups are herders. However, such nonherders as the Yoruba and Igbo in Nigeria, the Ganda in Uganda, the Japanese and other Asians, Eskimos, South American Indians, and many Israelis cannot digest lactose (Kretchmer 1972/ 1975).

However, the variable human ability to digest milk seems to be a difference of degree rather than of kind. Some populations can tolerate very little or no milk, but others are able to metabolize much greater quantities. Studies show that people who move from no-milk or low-milk diets to high-milk diets increase their lactose tolerance; this suggests some phenotypical adaptation. We can conclude that no simple genetic trait accounts for the ability to digest milk. Lactose tolerance appears to be one of many aspects of human biology governed both by genes and by phenotypical adaptation to environmental conditions.

Physiological Adaptation to Altitude

We have seen that biological similarities may be due to common ancestry or to genetic adaptation to natural selective forces working on populations that live in similar environments. Human biological traits, including lactose tolerance and high altitude adaptation—to be considered next, may also develop during an individual lifetime, through physiological response to environmental stress. Human biology is inherently plastic, changing constantly, even without genetic variation.

We see this very clearly when we consider human adaptation to high altitudes. Approximately 25 million people live at altitudes above 6,000 feet (1,800 meters). Half as many live in mountainous country more than 12,000 feet (3,700 meters) high. Such high-altitude populations as the Quechua-speaking natives of the Peruvian Andes and the Sherpas of the Himalayas have developed genetic, physiolog-

ical, and sociocultural ways of adapting to such environmental stresses as cold, aridity, and oxygen deprivation.

Although the amount of oxygen remains constant from sea level to the high Andes, the difficulty of extracting it increases. This is because barometric pressure decreases with altitude, so that molecules of air, including oxygen, are farther apart. In popular language, "the air is thinner." Lowlanders who visit Mexico City, Cuzco (Peru), or certain Colorado towns may experience symptoms of **hypoxia** (oxygen deprivation), also known as "mountain sickness." The symptoms include shortness of breath, fatigue, rapid pulse, difficult sleep, headaches, nausea, vomiting, and visual disturbance. These symptoms worsen with increasing altitude. Many of them actually illustrate short-term physiological adaptation to hypoxia—aimed at increasing the supply and pressure of oxygen in the body.

The body tries to meet its oxygen needs by speeding up the blood flow. During the first week at a high altitude, the pulse rate may rise from 70 to 105 beats per minute. In the second week, it will start to decline. Other adaptive responses to hypoxia will take place later. However, people who migrate from the lowlands as adults will never tolerate high altitude as well as do people who have undergone long-term hypoxia adaptation, by living at a high altitude during childhood.

Anyone raised in the highlands will develop a more efficient respiratory system for extracting oxygen from thin air. The typical "barrel chest" of such people is the outward sign of many internal adaptations. Relative to body weight, lung capacity is larger. Larger lungs have a greater surface area and more capillaries. This aids the transport of oxygen to the bloodstream and then to the tissues. Through such long-term changes, highland natives are able to live and work more effectively than are lowlanders who move to a hypoxic environment as adults.

Although some of the biological means of adapting to high altitudes may be genetic, many of the most important changes rest on biological plasticity and take place during growth and development (Baker 1978; Baker and Weiner, eds. 1966; Frisancho 1975). Lowlanders raised in the highlands achieve the same lung capacity, work capacity, and breathing rate as highland natives. Adaptation to hypoxia again illustrates biological plasticity and phenotypical adaptation to the environment during the individual lifetime.

In this section we have looked at ways in which humans adapt biologically to environmental stresses, and the effects of that adaptation on human biological diversity. As in Chapter 5 we see again that modern biological anthropology seeks to *explain* specific aspects of human biological variation. The explanatory framework encompasses the same mechanisms—selection, drift, gene flow, migration, interbreeding, and plasticity—that govern adaptation, variation, and evolution among other life forms.

SUMMARY

Since the eighteenth century, natural scientists have proposed classifications of life forms. Scientific taxonomy can be traced to Carolus Linnaeus, who viewed differences and similarities among organisms as part of God's orderly plan rather than as evidence for evolution or common ancestry. Influenced by earlier transformists, Charles Darwin and Alfred Russel Wallace proposed that natural selection could explain the origin of species, biological diversity, and similarities among related life forms. Darwin recognized that for natural selection to work, there must be variety within the population undergoing selection.

Through breeding experiments with garden peas in 1856, Gregor Mendel discovered that genetic traits are transmitted as discrete units—now known to be chromosomes—which occur in homologous pairs. Alleles, some dominant, some recessive, are the chemically different variants that occur at a given genetic locus. Mendel also formulated the law of independent assortment, observing that each of the seven traits he studied in peas was inherited independently of all the others. Independent assortment of chromosomes and their recombination in all mathematically possible forms provide some of the variety essential to natural selection.

However, the major source of variety is not genetic recombination but mutation, a chemical change in the DNA molecules of which genes are made. DNA is basic to all life. By copying itself in mitosis and meiosis, DNA replaces cells within the living organism and produces the sex cells that create new generations. DNA's structure also guides the body's assembly of amino acids to build proteins. In addition to recombination and mutation, crossing over during meiosis also produces the variety on which natural selection operates.

Population genetics studies gene frequencies within stable and changing populations. Natural selection is the most important mechanism of evolutionary change—genetic or otherwise. Others are mutation, random genetic drift, and interbreeding and gene flow. The specificity and relativity of natural selection have been stressed. The adaptive value of particular alleles and phenotypes depends on the specific environment. Natural selection can operate only on the phenotypical material actually present in a population. Given environmental change, nature selects traits already present in the population. If variety is insufficient to permit adaptation to the environmental change, extinction is likely. New types don't appear just because they are needed.

One well-documented case of natural selection at work in contemporary human populations is that of the sickle-cell allele. In homozygous form, the sickle-cell allele, Hb^S, produces abnormal hemoglobin that clogs the small blood vessels and impairs the blood's capacity to store oxygen. This leads to an illness known as *sickle-cell anemia*, which is usually fatal. Nevertheless, high frequencies of Hb^S were found in West Africa. The distribution of Hb^S has been linked to that of malaria. Individuals homozygous for normal hemoglobin are susceptible to malaria and die in great numbers. Individuals homozygous for the sickle-cell allele die from anemia. However, heterozygotes suffer only from mild anemia and are resistant to malaria. In a malarial environment, the heterozygote has the selective advantage, which explains why an apparently maladaptive allele is preserved in the population.

In the long run, other mechanisms of genetic evolution (such as drift, interbreeding, gene flow) operate along with natural selection. Random genetic drift operates most obviously in small populations, where pure chance can most easily change allele frequencies. Gene flow and interbreeding keep subgroups of the same species genetically connected and thus impede speciation.

There are links between genetically determined traits, such as hemoglobins, and natural selective forces, such as malaria. Selection through differential resistance to infectious diseases has influenced the distribution of human blood groups. Selection has also operated on facial features and body size and shape. Phenotypical adaptation, based on biological plasticity, refers to adaptive changes that occur in the individual lifetime, in response to the environments the organism encounters as it grows. Selective forces, genetic adaptation, stresses during growth, and biological plasticity contribute to such complex traits as lactose tolerance and hypoxia adaptation. Biological similarities between geographically distant populations may reflect similar but independent genetic changes or similar physiological responses to similar stresses during growth rather than common ancestry.

GLOSSARY

adaptive: Favored by natural selection in a particular environment.

allele: A biochemical difference at a particular genetic locus.

Allen's rule: Rule stating that the relative size of protruding body parts (such as ears, tails, bills, fingers, toes, and limbs) tends to increase in warmer climates.

antibody: A defending protein that reacts by attacking a foreign substance; see *antigen*.

antigen: A chemical substance that triggers the production of an antibody.

balanced polymorphism: Two or more forms, such as alleles of the same gene, maintaining a constant frequency from generation to generation.

Bergmann's rule: Rule stating that the smaller of two bodies similar in shape has more surface area per unit of weight and can therefore dissipate heat more efficiently; hence large bodies tend to be found in colder areas, and small bodies in warmer ones.

biochemical genetics: Field that studies structure, function, and changes in genetic material.

catastrophism: View that extinct species were destroyed by fires, floods, and other catastrophes. After each destructive event, God created again, leading to contemporary species.

chromosomes: Basic genetic units, occurring in matching (homologous) pairs; lengths of DNA made up of multiple genetic loci.

creationism: Explanation for the origin of species given in Genesis: God created the species during the original six days of Creation.

crossing over: During meiosis, the process by which homologous chromosomes intertwine and exchange segments of their DNA.

cytoplasm: The outer area of the cell rather than the nucleus.

directional selection: Long-term selection of the same trait(s); may go on as long as environmental forces remain the same.

dominant: Allele that masks another allele in a heterozygote.

evolution: See *transformism*.

gametes: The sex cells: eggs (ova) and sperms.

gene, or genetic locus (plural, *loci*): Area in a chromosome pair that determines, wholly or partially, a particular biological trait, such as whether one's blood type is A, B, or O.

gene flow: Exchange of genetic material between populations of the same species through direct or indirect interbreeding.

gene pool: All the alleles and genotypes within a breeding population—the "pool" of genetic material available.

genetic evolution: Change in gene frequency within a breeding population.

genotype: An organism's hereditary makeup.

heterozygous: Having dissimilar alleles at a given genetic locus.

homozygous: Possessing identical alleles at a particular genetic locus.

hybrid: Mixed.

hypoxia: A body's oxygen deprivation; the difficulty of extracting oxygen from the air increases with altitude because barometric pressure decreases and molecules of air are farther apart.

independent assortment, Mendel's law of: Chromosomes are inherited independently of one another.

lactase: See *lactose*.

lactose: A complex sugar in milk; its digestion requires an enzyme called *lactase* in the small intestine. Among most mammals, lactase production ceases after weaning, and the ability to digest milk is lost.

maladaptive: Harmful; selected against; conferring a disadvantage with respect to survival and reproduction.

meiosis: Special process by which sex cells are produced; four cells are produced from one, each with half the genetic material of the original cell.

Mendelian genetics: Studies ways in which chromosomes transmit genes across the generations.

mitosis: Ordinary cell division; DNA molecules copy themselves, creating two identical cells out of one.

mutation: Change in the DNA molecules of which genes and chromosomes are built.

phenotypical adaptation: Adaptive biological changes that occur during the individual's lifetime, made possible by biological plasticity.

plasticity: The ability to change; notion that biology is affected by environmental forces, such as diet and altitude, experienced during growth.

population genetics: Field that studies causes of genetic variation, maintenance, and change in breeding populations.

random genetic drift: Change in gene frequency that results not from natural selection but from chance; most common in small populations.

recessive: Genetic trait masked by a dominant trait.

recombination: Following independent assortment of chromosomes, new arrangements of hereditary units produced through bisexual reproduction.

relativity: Of evolution through natural selection; adaptation and fitness are in relation to specific environments, and traits are not adaptive or maladaptive for all times and places.

sickle-cell anemia: Usually fatal disease in which the red blood cells are shaped like crescents or sickles and increase the heart's burden by clogging the small blood vessels.

slash and burn: Farming system in which trees are cut down and burned to provide ashes for fertilizing the soil.

speciation: Formation of new species; occurs when subgroups of the same species are separated for a sufficient length of time.

species: Population whose members can interbreed to produce offspring that can live and reproduce.

strategic resources: Those necessary for life, such as food and space.

Thomson's nose rule: Rule stating that the average nose tends to be longer in areas with lower mean annual temperatures; based on the geographic distribution of nose length among human populations.

transformism: Also called *evolution*; belief that species arose from others through a long and gradual process of transformation, or descent with modification.

triplet: Sequence of three DNA or RNA bases; codes for particular amino acids.

uniformitarianism: Belief that explanations for past events should be sought in ordinary forces that continue to work today.

zygote: Fertilized egg, created by the union of two sex cells, one from each parent.

STUDY QUESTIONS

1. What is the relationship between creationism and transformism?
2. What is the relationship between catastrophism and uniformitarianism?
3. What is natural selection, and why is it such an important scientific principle?
4. What are the sources of biological variation?
5. Why were Mendel's experiments with garden peas so significant?
6. What is DNA, and why is it significant?
7. What is the difference between genotype and phenotype? On which does natural selection work, and why?
8. Why is *Homo sapiens* so adaptable?
9. How does the case of the sickle-cell allele (Hb^S) illustrate the relationship between cultural change and biological evolution?
10. What are the causes of genetic evolution? Which retards speciation?
11. What is meant by the relativity of evolution?
12. What explanations have been proposed for ABO blood groups?
13. What explanations have been proposed for the distribution of human body sizes and shapes?
14. What are the rules of Allen, Bergmann, and Thomson?
15. What biological traits characterize people who grow to adulthood in high altitudes? How do they compare with traits of lowlanders who move to high altitudes at different stages of growth and development?
16. In addition to hypoxia adaptation, what is another example of a biological trait that depends on physiological adaptation?

SUGGESTED ADDITIONAL READING

BAKER, P.T.
    1978   *The Biology of High Altitude Peoples.* New York: Cambridge University Press. Influence of the environment on human biology at high altitudes.
BODMER, W.F., AND L.L. CAVALLI-SFORZA
    1976   *Genetics, Evolution, and Man.* San Francisco: Freeman. Basic reference book on genetics, especially human genetics.

CAVALLI-SFORZA, L.L.
    1977   *Elements of Human Genetics.* 2nd ed. Menlo Park, CA: W. A. Benjamin. Readable introduction to genetics.
CROSBY, A.W.
    1986   *Ecological Imperialism: The Biological Expansion of Europe.* New York: Cambridge University Press. How European-derived and Old World diseases affected the rest of the world.

DOBZHANSKY, T., F.J. AYALA, G.L. STEBBINS, AND J.W. VALENTINE
1977 *Evolution*. San Francisco: Freeman. Indispensable, comprehensive introduction to biological evolution.

EISELEY, L.
1961 *Darwin's Century*. Garden City, NY: Doubleday, Anchor Books. Discussion of Lyell, Darwin, Wallace, and other major contributors to natural selection and transformation.

FRISANCHO, A.R.
1981 *Human Adaptation: A Functional Interpretation*. Ann Arbor, MI: University of Michigan Press. Influence of the environment on phenotype, particularly during growth and development; a basic text.

FUTUYMA, D.J.
1983 *Science on Trial*. New York: Pantheon. The case of evolution versus creationism—favoring the former.

HARTL, D.
1989 *Principles of Population Genetics*. 2nd ed. Sunderland, MA: Sinaeur. Detailed text on population genetics.

JOLLY, C., AND R. WHITE
1994 *Physical Anthropology and Archeology*. 5th ed. New York: McGraw-Hill. Basic text in biological anthropology and archeology; discusses evolutionary principles, genetics, and human variability.

MORAN, E.F.
1982 *Human Adaptability: An Introduction to Ecological Anthropology*. Boulder, CO: Westview. Surveys cultural and biological dimensions of ecological approaches in anthropology.

NELSON, H., AND R. JURMAIN
1991 *Introduction to Physical Anthropology*. 5th ed. St. Paul, MN: West. Basic text in biological anthropology.

ROBERTS, D.F.
1986 *Genetic Variation and Its Maintenance: With Particular Reference to Tropical Populations*. New York: Cambridge University Press. Evidence for human genetic evolution, with a focus on tropical populations.

WEISS, M.L., AND A.E. MANN
1992 *Human Biology and Behavior: An Anthropological Perspective*. 6th ed. Glenview, IL: Scott, Foresman. A basic textbook of biological anthropology.

CHAPTER 7

THE PRIMATES

Primatology—the study of fossil and living apes, monkeys, and prosimians, including their behavior and social life—has grown substantially since the 1950s. Following the ethnographer's example, primatologists began to study their subjects in natural settings rather than in zoos. Field studies have corrected many misleading impressions about primates derived from observations in zoos.

The study of nonhuman primates is fascinating in itself, but it also helps anthropologists make inferences about the early social organization of **hominids** (members of the zoological family that includes fossil and living humans) and untangle issues of human nature and the origin of culture. Of particular relevance to humans are two kinds of primates:

1. Those whose ecological adaptations are similar to our own: **terrestrial** monkeys and apes, that is, primates that live on the ground rather than in the trees
2. Those which are most closely related to us: the great apes, specifically chimpanzees and gorillas

TAXONOMY AND THE PRIMATE ORDER

Similarities between humans and apes are obvious in anatomy, brain structure, genetics, and biochemistry. These resemblances are recognized in zoological **taxonomy**—the assignment of organisms to categories (*taxa*; singular, *taxon*) according to phylogenetic relationship and structural resemblance. Humans and apes belong to the same superfamily, **Hominoidea (hominoids)**. Monkeys are placed in two others (Ceboidea and Cercopithecoidea). This means that humans and apes are more closely related to each other than either is to monkeys.

Many structural similarities between organisms reflect their common **phylogeny**—their genetic relatedness based on common ancestry. In other words, organisms share features they have inherited from the same ancestor.

Similarities between humans and apes are obvious in brain structure, genetics, biochemistry, and anatomy. These resemblances are recognized in zoological taxonomy, with humans and apes assigned to the same superfamily, Hominoidea. The apes are also highly intelligent. Compare the hairy reasoner on the left with the late Harry Reasoner on the right.

Similar species belong to the same **genus** (plural, *genera*).

Similar genera make up the same **family.**

Similar families constitute the same **superfamily.**

Similar superfamilies form the same **suborder.**

Similar suborders belong to the same **order.**

Similar orders make up the same **class.**

Similar classes constitute the same **kingdom.**

The highest taxonomic division is the kingdom. At that level animals are distinguished from plants. The lowest-level taxa are species and subspecies. A *species* is a group of organisms whose members can mate and give birth to *viable* (capable of living) and *fertile* (capable of reproducing) offspring whose own offspring are viable and fertile. *Speciation* (the formation of a new species) occurs when groups that once belonged to the same species can no longer interbreed. After a sufficiently long period of reproductive isolation, two closely related species assigned to the same genus will have evolved out of one.

At the lowest level of taxonomy, a species may have subspecies. These are its more or less, but not yet totally, isolated subgroups. Subspecies can exist in time and space. For example, the Neandertals, who lived between 130,000 and 35,000 years ago, are often assigned not to a separate species but merely to a different subspecies of *Homo sapiens.* Just one subspecies of *Homo sapiens* survives today.

The similarities used to assign organisms to the same taxon are called **homologies,** similarities they have jointly inherited from a common ancestor. Table 7.1 summarizes the place of humans in zoological taxonomy. Table 7.2 shows our degree of relatedness to other primates. We see in Table 7.1 that we are mammals, members of the class Mammalia. This is a major subdivision of the kingdom Animalia. Mammals share certain traits, including mammary glands, that set them apart from other taxa, such as birds, reptiles, amphibians, and insects. Mammalian homologies indicate that all mammals share more recent common ancestry with each other than they do with any bird, reptile, or insect.

At a lower taxonomic level, humans belong to the order Primates. The carnivores (dogs, cats, foxes, wolves, badgers, weasels) form another mammalian order, as do rodents (rats, mice, beavers, squirrels). Primates share structural and biochemical homologies that distinguish them from other mammals. These resemblances were inherited from their common early primate ancestors after those early primates became reproductively isolated from the ancestors of other mammals.

Table 7.1 *The Place of Humans* (Homo sapiens) *in Zoological Taxonomy. Thus* Homo sapiens *is an Animal, Chordate, Vertebrate, Mammal, Primate, Anthropoid, Catarrhine, Hominoid, and Hominid. (Table 7.2 Shows the Taxonomic Placement of the Other Primates.)*

Taxon	Scientific (Latin) Name	Common (English) Name
Kingdom	Animalia	Animals
Phylum	Chordata	Chordates
Subphylum	Vertebrata	Vertebrates
Class	Mammalia	Mammals
Infraclass	Eutheria	Eutherians
Order	Primates	Primates
Suborder	Anthropoidea	Anthropoids
Infraorder	Catarrhini	Catarrhines
Superfamily	Hominoidea	Hominoids
Family	Hominidae	Hominids
Genus	Homo	Humans
Species	Homo sapiens	Recent humans
Subspecies	Homo sapiens sapiens	Anatomically modern humans

Table 7.2 *Taxonomic Classification of the Primates. Humans (See Also Table 7.1)*
Belong to the Superfamily Hominoidea (Hominoids) Along With the Apes.

Suborder
  Infraorder
    Superfamily
      Family
        Subfamily
		Number
		of Species

Prosimii	Prosimians	
Lemuriformes		22
Daubentonioidea		
Daubentoniidae	Aye-aye	1
Lemuroidea		
Cheirogaleidae	Mouse lemurs, dwarf lemurs, and forked lemur	7
Indriidae	Indri, sifakas, and woolly lemur	4
Lemuridae	Lemurs	7
Lepilemuridae	Gentle lemurs and sportive lemurs	3
Lorisiformes		13
Lorisidae		
Galaginae	Bushbabies	8
Lorisinae	Lorises	5
Tarsiiformes		3
Tarsiidae	Tarsiers	3
Anthropoidea	Monkeys and apes	
Platyrrhini	New World monkeys	47
Ceboidea		
Callimiconidae	Goeldi's marmoset	1
Callitrichidae	Tamarins and marmosets	15
Cebidae		
Alouattinae	Howler monkeys	6
Atelinae	Spider monkeys and woolly monkeys	7
Cebinae	Capuchins and squirrel monkeys	6
Pitheciinae	Owl monkeys, titi monkeys, uakaris, and sakis	12
Catarrhini	Old World monkeys and apes	81
Cercopithecoidea		
Cercopithecidae		
Cercopithecinae	Macaques, guenons, baboons, patas monkeys, and mangabeys	41
Colobinae	Colobines	27
Hominoidea		
Hylobatidae	Gibbons, Siamangs	9
Pongidae	Great apes (orangutans, gorillas, and chimpanzees)	4
Hominidae	Humans	1

Dorothy L. Cheney, Robert M. Seyfarth, Barbara B. Smuts, and Richard W. Wrangham,
"The Study of Primate Societies," in *Primate Societies*, ed. by Barbara B. Smuts, Dorothy
L. Cheney, Robert M. Seyfarth, Richard W. Wrangham, and Thomas T. Struhsaker. Copy-
right by The University of Chicago Press, 1987.

HOMOLOGIES AND ANALOGIES

In theory, groups are assigned to the same higher-level taxon by homologies. For example, there are many homologies between ape and human DNA and biochemistry that confirm our common ancestry and lead to our joint classification as hominoids.

However, common ancestry is not the only reason for similarities between species. Similar traits can also arise if species experience similar selective forces to which they respond or adapt in similar ways. We call such similarities **analogies.** The process by which analogies are produced is known as **convergent evolution.** Fish and porpoises share many analogies resulting from convergent evolution to life in the water. Like fish, porpoises, which are mammals, have fins. They are also hairless and streamlined for efficient locomotion. Analogies between birds and bats (wings, small size, light bones) illustrate convergent evolution to flying.

In theory, only homologies should be used in taxonomy. In practice, there is sometimes doubt about whether resemblances are homologies or analogies, and analogies influence classification. For example, consider the Hominoidea. Most scientists have no doubt that humans, gorillas, and chimpanzees are more closely related to each other than any of the three is to orangutans, which are Asiatic apes (Ciochon 1983). Because humans, chimps, and gorillas share a more recent ancestor with each other than they do with orangs, they should be assigned to a taxon distinct from the taxon that includes orangutans. Accordingly, some scientists assign gorillas and chimps, along with humans, to the **Hominidae** family. Other scientists assign chimps and gorillas to the family Panidae (from the chimpanzee genus name *Pan*). This leaves the orangutan (genus *Pongo*) as the only member of the pongid family and humans as the only members of the Hominidae. However, many more taxonomists still assign orangs, chimps, and gorillas to the family Pongidae on the basis of their structural analogies. Table 7.2 follows this traditional classification of the great apes as pongids. Here analogy has *improperly* influenced zoological classification.

PRIMATE TENDENCIES

No single feature distinguishes the primates from other orders. Primates are varied because they have adapted to diverse ecological niches. Some primates are active during the day; others at night. Some eat insects; others, fruits; others, shoots, leaves, and bulk vegetation; and others, seeds or roots. Still others are omnivorous. Some primates live on the ground, others live in trees, and there are intermediate adaptations. However, because the earliest primates were tree dwellers, modern primates share homologies reflecting their common **arboreal** heritage.

Many trends in primate evolution are best exemplified by monkeys, apes, and humans. These

primates constitute the suborder **Anthropoidea.** The other primate suborder, Prosimii, includes lemurs, loris, and tarsiers. These **prosimians** are more distant relatives of humans than are monkeys and apes. The primate trends—most developed in the anthropoids—can be summarized briefly. Together they constitute the anthropoid heritage that humans share with monkeys and apes.

1. Grasping. Primates have five-digited feet and hands which are well suited for grasping. Certain features of hands and feet that were originally adaptive for arboreal life have been transmitted to contemporary primates. Flexible hands and feet that could encircle branches were important features in the early primates' arboreal life. Thumb opposability and the resulting **precision grip** (between index finger and thumb), which is essential to tool manufacture, might have been favored by the inclusion of insects in the early primate diet. Manual dexterity makes it easier to catch insects attracted to abundant

Primates have five-digited feet and hands, well-suited for grasping. Flexible hands and feet that could encircle branches were important features in the early primates' arboreal life. In adapting to bipedal (two-footed) locomotion, hominids eliminated most of the foot's grasping ability—illustrated here by the orangutan.

arboreal flowers and fruits. Humans and many other primates have **opposable thumbs:** The thumb can touch all the other fingers. Many primates also have grasping feet, and some have opposable big toes. However, in adapting to **bipedal** (two-footed) locomotion, hominids eliminated most of the foot's grasping ability.

2. Smell to Sight. Several anatomic changes reflect the shift from smell to sight as the primates' most important means of obtaining information. Monkeys, apes, and humans have excellent **stereoscopic** (ability to see in depth) and color vision. The portion of the brain devoted to vision expanded, while the area concerned with smell shrank.

3. Nose to Hand. Sensations of touch, conveyed by tactile organs, also provide information. The tactile skin on a dog's or cat's nose transmits information. Cats' tactile hairs, or whiskers, also serve this function. In primates, however, the main touch organ is the hand, specifically the sensitive pads of the "fingerprint" region.

4. Brain Complexity. The proportion of brain tissue concerned with memory, thought, and association has increased in primates. The primate ratio of brain size to body size exceeds that of most mammals.

5. Parental Investment. Most primates give birth to a single offspring rather than a litter. Because of this, growing primates receive more attention and have more learning opportunities than do other mammals. Learned behavior is an important part of primate adaptation.

6. Sociality. Most primates are social animals that live with others of their species. The need for longer and more attentive care of offspring places a selective value on support by a social group.

PROSIMIANS

We have seen that the primate order includes two suborders—prosimians and anthropoids. The early history of the primates is limited to prosimianlike animals known through the fossil record. Around 30 million years ago, these early primates were driven from their niches by the ancestors of contemporary anthropoids. Some prosimians survived in Africa and Asia by adapting to nocturnal life. In so doing, they avoided competition with Old World

monkeys, which are active during the day. Prosimians (lemurs) on the island of Madagascar had no anthropoid competitors until human colonization 2,000 years ago.

Lemurs

Unimpeded until recently by higher primates, the Malagasy (of Madagascar) lemurs have had several—perhaps 40—million years to undergo an adaptive radiation—a population explosion and adaptation to a variety of specialized ecological niches—on the world's fourth-largest island. The variety encountered among Malagasy lemurs is extraordinary. In their behavior and biology, the thirteen genera and more than twenty species of lemur show adaptations to an array of environments. Their diets and time of activity differ. Some lemurs eat fruits, eggs, and insects; others are more omnivorous. Some are nocturnal; others are active during the day. Some are completely arboreal; others spend some time in the trees and some on the ground. One large terrestrial form, *Megaladapis,* became extinct 300 years ago. *Megaladapis* weighed about 100 pounds.

Tarsiers

From the fossil record, we know that 50 million years ago some twenty-five genera of tarsiers lived in North America and Europe, which were much warmer then than they are now. Only one genus of tarsier survives today, in insular Southeast Asia, Indonesia, and the Philippines. The tarsiers that survived were able to do so because they adapted to nocturnal life and thus avoided competition with monkeys for the same ecological niche.

PRIMATE TRENDS: ANTHROPOID TRAITS

All anthropoids share resemblances that can be considered trends in primate evolution in the sense that these traits are fully developed neither among the fossils of prosimianlike primates that lived prior to 30 million years ago nor among contemporary prosimians. These trends enabled anthropoids to displace prosimians from niches in which the latter once thrived. Some of these trends can be discerned in prosimians, but they are *fully expressed* only in monkeys, apes, and humans.

All anthropoids have overlapping fields of vision, permitting them to see things in depth. With reduction of the snout, anthropoid eyes are placed forward in the skull and look directly ahead. The fields of vision of our eyes overlap, whereas dogs and cats perceive double images. Depth perception, impossible without overlapping visual fields, proved adaptive in the trees, where early anthropoids lived. Tree-dwelling primates that could judge distance better because of depth perception survived and reproduced in greater numbers than did those which couldn't.

The abilities to see in depth and in color probably developed together, and both helped early anthropoids interpret their arboreal world. Superior vision made it easier to distinguish edible insects, fruits, berries, and leaves. Furthermore, having color and depth vision makes it easier to groom—to remove burrs, insects, and other small objects from other primates' hair.

Visual and tactile changes have been interrelated. Anthropoids have neither tactile muzzle skin nor "cat's whiskers." Instead, fingers are the main touch organs. The ends of the fingers and toes are sensitive tactile pads. Forward placement of the eyes and depth vision permit anthropoids to pick up small objects, hold them in front of their eyes, and appraise them. The human ability to thread a needle is a result of an intricate interplay of hands and eyes that took millions of years to achieve. Opposable thumb and precision grip confer a tremendous advantage in examining and manipulating objects and are crucial to one of the major human adaptive capacities—tool manufacture. Among monkeys, thumb opposability is indispensable for feeding and grooming.

Another anthropoid evolutionary trend is increased size of the **cranium** (skull) to accommodate a larger brain. The brain/body size ratio is greater among anthropoids than it is among prosimians. Even more important, the brain's outer layer—concerned with memory, association, and integration—is relatively larger. Anthropoids store an array of visual images in their memories, which permits them to learn more. The ability to learn from experience and from other group members is a major

reason for the success of the anthropoids compared to most other mammals.

MONKEYS

The anthropoids are divided into two infraorders, **platyrrhines** (New World monkeys) and **catarrhines** (Old World monkeys, apes, and humans). The catarrhines (sharp-nosed) and platyrrhines (flat-nosed) take their names from Latin terms that describe the placement of their nostrils (Figure 7.1). Old World monkeys, apes, and humans are all catarrhines; they are more closely related to one another than they are to New World monkeys. In anthropoid evolution, the platyrrhines were reproductively isolated from the catarrhines before the latter diverged into the Old World monkeys, apes, and humans. This is why New World monkeys are assigned to a separate infraorder.

All New World monkeys and many Old World monkeys are arboreal. Whether in the trees or on the ground, however, monkeys move differently from apes and humans. Their arms and legs move parallel to one another as dogs' legs do. This contrasts with the tendency toward **orthograde posture,** the straight and upright posture of apes and humans. Unlike apes, which have longer arms than legs, and humans, who have longer legs than arms, monkeys have arms and legs of about the same length. Most monkeys also have tails, which help them maintain balance in the trees.

New World Monkeys

New World monkeys, universally arboreal, are confined to the forests of Central and South America. There are interesting parallels between New World monkeys and some arboreal primates of the Old World. These analogies have developed as a result of adaptation to similar environments. Like the gibbon, a small Asiatic ape, some New World monkeys have developed **brachiation**—under-the-branch swinging. Most monkeys run and jump from branch to branch, but gibbons and some New World monkeys swing through the trees, using their hands as hooks. Hand over hand they move from branch to branch, propelled onward by the thrust of their bodies.

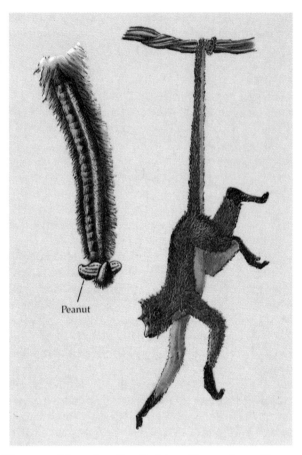

Figure 7.2 *The prehensile tail of the spider monkey, a New World monkey.*

Figure 7.1 *Nostril structure of catarrhines and platyrrhines. Above: narrow septum and "sharp nose" of a guenon, a catarrhine (Old World monkey). Below: broad septum and "flat nose" of Humboldt's woolly monkey, a platyrrhine (New World monkey).*

However, anatomic differences between Old and New World anthropoids are obvious. Many New World monkeys have **prehensile,** or grasping, tails (Figure 7.2). Sometimes the prehensile tail has tactile skin, which permits it to work like a hand, for instance, in conveying food to the mouth. Old World monkeys, however, have developed their own characteristic anatomic specialization for arboreal life. They have **ischial callosities,** rough patches of skin on the buttocks, adapted to sitting on hard rocky ground and rough branches. If the primate you see

in the zoo has ischial callosities, it's either an Old World monkey or a gibbon. If it has a prehensile tail, it's a New World monkey.

Old World Monkeys

Unlike the New World monkeys, the Old World monkeys include terrestrial (e.g., baboons and macaques) as well as arboreal species. Certain trends differentiate arboreal and terrestrial primates. Arboreal primates tend to be smaller because smaller animals have access to a greater variety of foods in trees and shrubs, where the most abundant foods are located at the ends of branches. Low weight is adaptive for end-of-branch feeding. Arboreal monkeys and gibbons, typically lithe and agile, escape from the few predators in their environment—snakes and monkey-eating eagles—through alert-

In a series of exposures, a gibbon is shown brachiating. Gibbons share this mode of arboreal locomotion with siamangs and certain New World monkeys.

ness and speed. Large size, by contrast, is advantageous for terrestrial primates in dealing with predators, which are more numerous on the ground.

Another contrast between arboreal and terrestrial primates is in **sexual dimorphism**—marked differences in male and female anatomy and temperament. Sexual dimorphism tends to be more marked in terrestrial than in arboreal species. Baboon and macaque males are much larger and fiercer than are females of the same species. However, it is often hard to tell, without close inspection, the sex of an arboreal monkey or gibbon.

Of the terrestrial monkeys, the baboons of Africa and the (mainly Asiatic) macaques have been the subjects of many studies. Terrestrial monkeys have developed specializations in anatomy, psychology, and social behavior that enable them to cope with terrestrial life. Baboon troops are protected by their adult males, whose anatomies, temperaments, and willingness to undertake team action deter predators, including leopards and cheetahs. Adult male baboons are fierce-looking animals that can weigh 100 pounds (45 kilograms). They display their long, projecting canines to intimidate predators and when confronting other baboons. Faced with a predator, a male baboon can also puff up his ample mane of shoulder hair, so that the would-be aggressor perceives the baboon as larger than he actually is.

Longitudinal, or long-term, studies have clarified our understanding of male and female dominance hierarchies among terrestrial monkeys. Before long-term research on the same troop was done, prima-tologists had assumed that male dominance relationships were more enduring than female rank orders. However, studies (Sade 1972) show that, near the time of puberty, baboon and macaque males typically leave their home troop for another. Because males move in and out, females form the stable core of the terrestrial monkey troop, and female dominance relationships are more stable than male hierarchies among those monkeys (Hinde 1983). By contrast, among chimpanzees and gorillas, females are more likely to emigrate and seek mates outside their natal social groups (Wrangham 1980; Van Schaik and Van Hooff 1983; Rodseth et al. 1991).

THE HOMINOIDS

Old World monkeys have their own separate superfamily (Cercopithecoidea), while humans and apes together compose the hominoid superfamily (Hominoidea). Traditionally, the hominoids are subdivided into three families—one human (Hominidae) and two ape (Pongidae and Hylobatidae). Humans are placed in the hominid family. The great apes (gorillas, chimpanzees, and orangutans) are assigned to the **pongid** family. The other ape family is the hylobatids, which includes the gibbons and siamangs of Southeast Asia and Indonesia.

In size, shape, and biochemistry, hominids and pongids are more similar to each other than either group is to the hylobatids. Furthermore, various comparisons of the biochemistry of humans and African apes—gorillas and chimpanzees—show that those apes are almost as similar to us as they are to each other. This suggests that chimps and gorillas are not much more closely related to each other than either is to us (Goodman et al. 1983; Sibley and Ahlquist 1984; Kluge 1983). Regardless of when our ancestors did diverge, millions of years of separation and adaptation to different environments have produced obvious differences between apes and humans.

APES

All contemporary apes live in forests and woodlands. Gibbons are completely arboreal, but the heavier gorillas, chimpanzees, and adult male orangutans spend considerable time on the ground. Nevertheless, ape anatomy reveals present or past adaptation to arboreal life (Figure 7.3). Gorillas and chimps use the long arms they have inherited from their more arboreal ancestors for life on the ground. Their terrestrial locomotion is known as **knuckle-walking.** In it, long arms and callused knuckles support the trunk as the apes amble around leaning forward.

Gibbons

The gibbon family—the hylobatids—gets its name from one of its two genera, *Hylobates*. There are nine species of gibbons and siamangs, a slightly larger but closely related arboreal ape. **Gibbons** are widespread in the forests of Southeast Asia, especially in Malaysia. Smallest of the apes, male and female gibbons have about the same average height (3 feet, or 1 meter) and weight (12 to 25 pounds, or 5 to 10 kilograms). Gibbons spend most of their time just below the forest canopy (treetops). For efficient brachiation, gibbons have evolved long arms and fingers, with short thumbs. Slenderly built, gibbons are the most agile apes. Unlike knuckle-walkers, they use their long arms for balance when they occasionally walk erect on the ground or along a branch. Gibbons, the preeminent arboreal specialists among the apes, subsist on a fruit diet. Gibbons and siamangs live in **primary groups,** which are composed of a permanently bonded male and female and their preadolescent offspring. Gibbon evolutionary success is confirmed by their numbers and range.

Figure 7.3 *The limb ratio of the highly arboreal gibbon and of terrestrial* Homo. *Note elongated gibbon arms and human legs, illustrating adaptation to brachiation and upright bipedalism, respectively.*

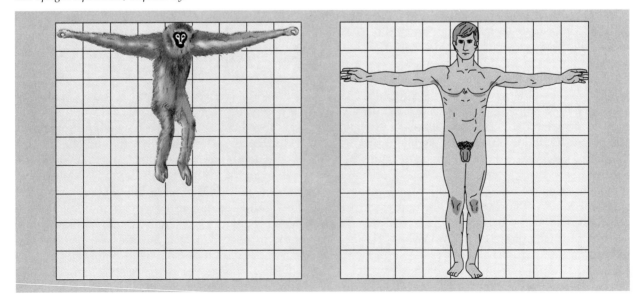

Hundreds of thousands of gibbons span a wide area of Southeast Asia.

Orangutans

The single orangutan species belongs to the genus *Pongo*. This Asiatic great ape's range once extended into China, but contemporary orangs are confined to two Indonesian islands. Sexual dimorphism is marked, with the adult male weighing more than twice as much as the female. The orangutan male, like his human counterpart, is intermediate in size between chimps and gorillas. Some orang males exceed 200 pounds (90 kilograms). With only half the gorilla's bulk, male orangs can be more arboreal, although they typically climb, rather than swing through, the trees. The smaller size of females and young permits them to spend more time in trees. Because orangutans live in jungles and feed in trees, they are especially difficult to study. However, field reports about orangutans in their natural setting (MacKinnon 1974) have clarified their behavior and social organization. Orangs tend to be solitary animals. Their tightest social units consist of females and preadolescent young. Males forage alone.

Gorillas

The single gorilla species *Gorilla gorilla* lives in equatorial Central Africa (Uganda, Rwanda, and Zaire). Full-grown wild males may weigh 400 pounds (180 kilograms) and stand 6 feet tall (183 centimeters). Like most terrestrial primates, gorillas show marked sexual dimorphism. The average adult female weighs half as much as the male.

Contemporary gorillas spend just 20 percent of their time in the trees. After all, it's cumbersome for an adult male gorilla to move his bulk about in a tree. When gorillas sleep in trees, they build nests, which are usually no more than 10 feet (3 meters)

The apes occupy an array of ecological niches in Africa and Asia, but all rely to some extent on forested areas. Gorillas, chimpanzees, and male orangutans spend most of their time on the ground. Most of the gorilla's day is spent feeding—on ground plants, leaves, bark, fruits, and other vegetation. Shown here are members of a mountain gorilla troop with primatologist Dian Fossey.

off the ground, in contrast to the nests of chimps and female orangs, which may be 100 feet (30 meters) above the ground.

Most of the gorilla's day is spent feeding. Gorillas move through jungle undergrowth eating ground plants, leaves, bark, fruits, and other vegetation. Like most primates, gorillas live in social groups. The troop is a common unit of primate social organization, consisting of multiple males and females and their offspring. Although troops with up to thirty gorillas have been observed, most gorillas live in groups of from ten to twenty. Gorilla troops tend to have fairly stable memberships, with little shifting between troops (Fossey 1983). The troop is headed by a silver-back male, so designated because of the strip of white hair that extends down his back. This is the physical sign of full maturity among male gorillas. The silver-back is usually the only breeding male in the troop, which is why gorilla troops are sometimes called "one-male groups." However, a few younger, subordinate males may also adhere to such a one-male group (Schaller 1963; Harcourt et al. 1981).

Chimpanzees

Chimpanzees belong to the genus *Pan*, which has two species—*Pan troglodytes* (the common chimpanzee) and *Pan paniscus* (the Bonobo or "pygmy" chimpanzee) (Susman 1987). Like humans, chimpanzees are closely related to the gorilla, although there are some obvious differences. Like gorillas, chimps live in tropical Africa, but they range over a larger area and more varied environments than gorillas do (Figure 7.4). Chimpanzees live mainly in tropical rain forests but also in woodlands and mixed forest-woodland-grassland areas, such as the Gombe Stream National Park, Tanzania, where Jane Goodall (1986) and other researchers began to study them in 1960.

There are dietary differences between chimps and gorillas. Gorillas consume large quantities of green bulk vegetation, but chimps, like orangutans and gibbons, prefer fruits. Chimps are actually omnivorous, adding animal protein to their diet by capturing small mammals, birds' eggs, and insects.

Chimps are lighter and more arboreal than gorillas are. The adult male's weight—between 100 and 200 pounds (45 to 90 kilograms)—is about a third that of the male gorilla. There is much less sexual

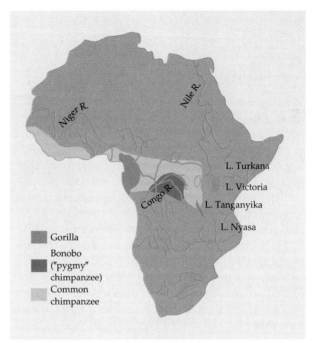

Figure 7.4 *Chimpanzees and gorillas are primarily rain forest dwellers. However, some chimpanzee populations live in woodland environments. This map shows the ranges of the three species of African apes. (From Jolly and Plog 1986, p. 115.)*

dimorphism among chimps than among gorillas. Females average 88 percent of the average male weight. This is similar to the ratio of sexual dimorphism in *Homo sapiens*.

Several scientists have studied wild chimps, and we know more about the full range of their behavior and social organization than we do about the other apes. The long-term research of Goodall and others at Gombe provides especially useful information. Approximately 150 chimpanzees range over Gombe's 30 square miles (80 square kilometers). Goodall (1986) has described communities of about fifty chimps, all of which know one another and from time to time interact. Communities regularly split up into smaller groups: a mother and her offspring; a few males; males, females, and young; and occasionally solitary animals. Chimpanzee communities are semiclosed. The social networks of males are more closed than are those of females, which are more likely to migrate and mate outside their natural group than males are (Wrangham 1987).

ENDANGERED PRIMATES

More than half of all plant and animal species live in tropical forests, which are disappearing rapidly, at a rate of 10 to 20 million hectares per year (the size of the state of New York). This is a serious problem because many people depend on these forests for their livelihood. Deforestation also entails the loss of biological diversity as the natural habitats of many species disappear.

Deforestation poses a special risk for the primates, because 90 percent of the 190 living primate species live in tropical forests—in Africa, Asia, South America, and Central America. If current trends continue, about 35 percent of all nonhuman primates, the most conspicuous mammals in the tropical forests, will become extinct within a decade (Mittermeier 1982).

As the earth's human population swells, the populations of nonhuman primates are shrinking. According to the Convention on International Trade in Endangered Species (ratified in 1973), all nonhuman primates are now endangered or soon to be endangered. The apes (gibbons, gorillas, orangutans, and chimps) are in the "most endangered" category. Gorillas, which once ranged widely in the forested mountains of East Africa, are now limited to a small area near the borders of Rwanda, Zaire, and Uganda. Other severely threatened species include the golden lion tamarin monkey of southeastern Brazil, the cotton-top tamarin of Colombia, the lion-tailed macaque of southern India, the woolly monkeys of Amazonia, and the orangutan of Southeast Asia.

Although the destruction of their natural habitats is the main reason the primates are disappearing, it is not the only reason. Another threat is human hunting of primates for food. In Amazonia, West Africa, and Central Africa, primates are a major source of food, and people kill thousands of monkeys each year. Human hunting is less of a threat to primates in Asia. In India Hindus avoid monkey meat because the monkey is sacred, while Moslems avoid it because monkeys are considered unclean and not fit for human consumption.

People also hunt primates for their skins and pelts; poachers sell their body parts as trophies and ornaments. Africans use the skins of black-and-white colobus monkeys for cloaks and headdresses, and American and European tourists buy coats and rugs made from colobus pelts. In Amazonia ocelot and jaguar hunters shoot woolly monkeys and spider monkeys to bait the traps they set for the cats.

Poachers pose the greatest threat to the mountain gorillas, of which there may be as few as 200 left in the wild (Fossey 1981, 1983). The poachers shoot the apes with high-powered rifles, then decapitate them and cut off their hands. They sell gorilla heads as trophies and turn their hands into grotesque ashtrays. Traps and snares set for antelope and buffalo also endanger gorillas, which sometimes get caught in the traps. Even if they manage to free themselves, they often die from infected wounds. The sad fate (murder and decapitation) of Dian Fossey's favorite gorilla, Digit, is familiar to those who have seen the 1988 film *Gorillas in the Mist*, the story of Fossey, her work with mountain gorillas, and her efforts to save them.

Chimpanzees are also vulnerable to poachers. One famous chimp, Lucy, raised by an American family and taught to use sign language, met a grim fate when she was taken to Africa to live in the wild. In 1986, soon after she had adjusted to an island colony of chimps in the Gambia, Lucy's mutilated corpse was discovered—minus skin, hair, hands, and feet. "We can only speculate that Lucy was killed—probably shot—and skinned. Because of her confidence with humans, she was always the first to confront newcomers to the island. She might have surprised an armed intruder, with fatal consequences" (Carter 1988, p. 47).

Primates are also killed when they are agricultural pests. In some areas of Africa and Asia baboons and macaques raid the crops people depend on for subsistence. Between 1947 and 1962 the government of Sierra Leone held annual drives to rid farm areas of monkeys, and between 15,000 and 20,000 primates perished each year.

A final reason for the demise of the primates is the capture of animals for lab use or pets. Although this threat is minor compared with deforestation and the hunting of primates for food, it does pose a serious risk to certain endangered species in heavy demand. One of the species most hurt by this trade is the chimpanzee, which has been widely used in biomedical research. One especially destructive way of capturing young primates is to shoot the mother and take her clinging infant.

When chimps meet, they greet one another with gestures, facial expressions, and calls, and they hoot to maintain contact during their daily rounds. Like other terrestrial primates, chimps exhibit dominance relationships through attacks and displacement. Some adult females outrank younger adult males, although males tend to dominate, and females do not display strong dominance relationships among themselves. Males occasionally cooperate in hunting parties.

SIMILARITIES BETWEEN HUMANS AND OTHER PRIMATES

There is a large gap between primate society and fully developed human culture. However, studies of primates in varied circumstances have revealed more similarities than were once imagined. Scholars used to contend that learned (versus instinctive) behavior separates humans from other animals. We know now that monkeys and apes also rely extensively on learning. Differences between humans and other primates are quantitative rather than qualitative: They are differences in *degree* rather than in kind. For example, chimpanzees make tools for specific tasks, but human reliance on tools is much greater.

Adaptive Flexibility Through Learning

Common to monkeys, apes, and humans is the fact that behavior and social organization aren't rigidly programmed by the genes. All anthropoids learn throughout their lives. In several cases, an entire troop has learned from the experiences of some of its members. In one group of Japanese macaques, a three-year-old female developed the habit of washing dirt off sweet potatoes before she ate them. First her mother, then her age peers, and finally the entire troop started washing sweet potatoes, too. The direction of learning was reversed when members of another macaque troop learned to eat wheat. Dominant males first tried the new food; within four hours the practice had spread throughout the troop. Changes in learned behavior seem to spread more quickly from the top down than from the bottom up.

For monkeys as for people, the ability to learn, to profit from experience, confers a tremendous adaptive advantage, permitting them to avoid fatal mistakes. Faced with environmental change, primates don't have to wait for a genetic or physiological response, since learned behavior and social patterns can be modified. Thus behavioral flexibility facilitates adaptation to diverse environments, although this occurs to a lesser degree than it does in humans.

Tools

Anthropologists used to distinguish humans from other animals as tool users, and there is no doubt that *Homo* does employ tools more than any other animal does. However, tool use also turns up among several nonhuman species. For example, in the Galápagos Islands off western South America there is a "woodpecker finch" that selects twigs to dig out insects and grubs from tree bark. Sea otters use rocks to break open mollusks, which are important in their diet. Beavers are famous for dam construction.

When it became obvious that people weren't the only tool users, anthropologists started contending that only humans manufacture tools with foresight, that is, with a specific purpose in mind. Chimpanzees show that this, too, is debatable. The research of many primatologists, particularly Jane Goodall (1986), has increased our knowledge of chimp behavior in natural settings. In 1960 Goodall began observing chimps in Gombe Stream National Park in Tanzania, East Africa. More than any other primate, chimps share the human capacity for deliberate tool manufacture, although in chimps the capacity remains rudimentary. Nevertheless, wild chimps regularly make tools. To get water from places their mouths can't reach, thirsty chimps pick leaves, chew and crumple them, and then dip them into the water. Thus, with a specific purpose in mind, they devise primitive "sponges."

More impressive is "termiting." Chimps make tools to probe termite hills. They choose twigs, which they modify by removing leaves and peeling off bark to expose the sticky surface beneath. They carry the twigs to termite hills, dig holes with their fingers, and insert the twigs. Finally they pull out the twigs and dine on termites that were attracted to the sticky surface.

Termiting isn't as easy as it might seem. Learning to termite takes time, and many Gombe chimps never master it. Twigs with certain characteristics

Learned behavior among wild chimps includes rudimentary tool making. Here, a chimpanzee uses a specially prepared twig to "fish" for termites.

must be chosen. Furthermore, once the twig is in the termite hill and the chimp judges that termites are crawling on its surface, the chimp must quickly flip the twig as it pulls it out so that the termites are on top. Otherwise they fall off as the twig comes out of the hole. This is an elaborate skill that neither all chimps nor human observers have been able to master.

Chimps have other abilities essential to culture. When they are trained by humans, their manipulatory skills flower, as anyone who has ever seen a movie, circus, or zoo chimp knows. Wild chimps aim and throw objects. The gorilla, our other nearest relative, lacks the chimp's proclivity for tool making. However, gorillas do build nests, and they throw branches, grass, vines, and other objects. Hominids have considerably elaborated the capacity to aim and throw, which is a likely homology passed down from the common ancestor of humans and apes. Without it we would have never developed projectile technology, weaponry, and baseball.

Communication Systems

Only humans speak. No other animal has anything approaching the complexity of language. However, evidence is accumulating that linguistic ability is also a quantitative rather than qualitative difference between humans and other primates, especially gorillas and chimps. The natural communication systems of other primates—their **call systems**—which

are composed of sounds that vary in intensity and duration, are much more complex than used to be supposed. Goodall (1968a) identified twenty-five distinct calls used by Gombe chimps. Each had a distinct meaning and was used only in particular situations. Calls are much less flexible than language because they are automatic and can't be combined. When primates encounter food and danger simultaneously, they can make only one call. They can't combine the calls for food and danger into a single utterance, indicating that both are present. If by chance they did so, others would probably not understand the message. At some point in hominid evolution, however, our ancestors began to combine calls and understand the combinations. The number of calls also expanded, eventually becoming too great to be transmitted even partly through the genes. Hominid communication came to rely almost totally on learning.

Although wild primates use call systems, the vocal tract of apes is not suitable for speech. Until the 1960s attempts to teach spoken language to apes suggested that they lack linguistic abilities. In the 1950s a couple raised a chimpanzee, Viki, as a member of their family and systematically tried to teach her to speak. However, Viki learned only four words ("mama," "papa," "up," and "cup").

More recent experiments have shown that apes can learn to use, if not speak, true language (Miles 1983). Several apes have learned to converse with people through means other than speech. One such

The male chimpanzee, Dar, 13 years old in this photo by Roger Fouts, makes the sign for "smile." Dar, Washoe, and other Ameslan-using chimps are now at Central Washington State University in Ellensburg.

communication system is American Sign Language, or **Ameslan,** which is widely used by deaf and mute Americans. Ameslan employs a limited number of basic gesture units that are analogous to sounds in spoken language. These units combine to form words and larger units of meaning.

The first chimpanzee to learn Ameslan was Washoe, a female. Captured in West Africa, Washoe was acquired by R. Allen Gardner and Beatrice Gardner, scientists at the University of Nevada in Reno, in 1966, when she was a year old. Four years later she moved to Norman, Oklahoma, to a converted farm that had become the Institute for Primate Studies. Washoe's experiences in Reno revolutionized the discussion of the language-learning abilities of apes. Washoe lived in a trailer and heard no spoken language. The researchers always used Ameslan to communicate with each other in her presence. The chimp gradually acquired a vocabulary of 132 signs representing English words (Gardner, Gardner, and Van Cantfort 1989). At the age of two, Washoe began to combine as many as five signs into rudimentary sentences such as "you, me, go out, hurry."

The second chimp to learn Ameslan was Lucy, Washoe's junior by one year. Lucy died, or was murdered by poachers, in 1986, after having been carefully introduced to "the wild" in Africa in 1979 (Carter 1988). From her second day of life until her move to Africa, Lucy lived with a family in Norman, Oklahoma. Roger Fouts, a researcher from the nearby Institute for Primate Studies, came two days a week to test and improve Lucy's knowledge of Ameslan. During the rest of the week Lucy used Ameslan to converse with her foster parents. After acquiring language, Washoe and Lucy expressed several human traits: swearing, joking, telling lies, and trying to teach language to others.

When irritated, Washoe has called her monkey neighbors at the institute "dirty monkeys." Lucy insulted her "dirty cat." On arrival at Lucy's place, Fouts once found a pile of excrement on the floor. When he asked the chimp what it was, she replied "dirty, dirty," her expression for feces. Asked whose "dirty, dirty" it was, Lucy named Fouts's coworker, Sue. When Fouts refused to believe her about Sue, the chimp blamed the excrement on Fouts himself.

Cultural transmission of a communication system through learning is a fundamental attribute of language. Both Washoe and Lucy have tried to teach Ameslan to other animals, including their own offspring. Washoe has taught gestures to other institute chimps, including her son Sequoia, who died in infancy (Fouts, Fouts, and Van Cantfort 1989). There have been other cases of cultural transmission of Ameslan from chimp to chimp.

Because of their size and strength as adults, gorillas are less likely subjects than chimps for such experiments. Lean adult male gorillas in the wild weigh 400 pounds (180 kilograms), and full-grown females can easily reach 250 pounds (110 kilograms). Because of this, psychologist Penny Patterson's work with gorillas at Stanford University seems more daring than the chimp experiments. Patterson raised her now full-grown female gorilla, Koko, in a trailer next to a Stanford museum. Koko's vocabulary surpasses that of any chimp. She regularly employs 400 Ameslan signs and has used about 700 at least once.

Koko and the chimps also show that apes share still another linguistic ability with humans—**productivity**. Speakers routinely use the rules of their language to produce entirely new expressions that are comprehensible to other native speakers. I can, for example, create "baboonlet" to refer to a baboon infant. I do this by analogy with English words in which the suffix *-let* designates the young of a species. Anyone who speaks English immediately understands the meaning of my new word. Koko,

(Cartoon by Sidney Harris)

Washoe, and Lucy have shown that apes also use language productively. Lucy used gestures she already knew to create "drinkfruit" for watermelon. Washoe, seeing a swan for the first time, coined "waterbird." Koko, who knew the gestures for "finger" and "bracelet," formed "finger bracelet" when she was given a ring.

Chimps and gorillas have at least a rudimentary capacity for language. They may never have invented a meaningful gesture system in the wild. However, given such a system, they show many humanlike abilities in learning and using it. Of course, language use by apes is a product of human intervention and teaching. The experiments mentioned here do not suggest that apes can invent language (nor are human children ever faced with that task). However, young apes have managed to learn the basics of gestural language. They can employ it productively and creatively, although not with the sophistication of human Ameslan users.

Apes, like humans, may also try to teach their language to others. Lucy, not fully realizing the difference between primate hands and feline paws, once tried to mold her pet cat's paw into Ameslan signs. Koko has taught gestures to Michael, a male gorilla six years her junior.

Apes also have the capacity for linguistic **displacement.** Absent in call systems, this is a key ingredient in language. Each call is tied to an environmental stimulus such as food. Calls are uttered only when that stimulus is present. Displacement permits humans to talk about things that are not present. We don't have to see the objects before we say the words. Human conversations are not bounded by place. We can discuss the past and future, share our experiences with others, and benefit from theirs.

Patterson has described several examples of Koko's capacity for displacement (Patterson 1978). The gorilla once expressed sorrow about having bitten Penny three days earlier. Koko has used the sign "later" to postpone doing things she doesn't want to do. Thus, she can reconstruct events, including emotional states. She imagines the future and uses language to express her thoughts.

Certain scholars still doubt the linguistic abilities of chimps and gorillas (Terrace 1979; Sebeok and Umiker-Sebeok 1980). These people contend that Koko and the chimps are comparable to trained circus animals and don't really have linguistic ability. However, in defense of Patterson and the other researchers, whose findings are impressive (Hill 1978; Van Cantfort and Rimpau 1982), only one of their critics has worked with an ape. This was Herbert Terrace, whose experience teaching a chimp sign language lacked the continuity and personal involvement that have contributed so much to Patterson's success with Koko.

No one denies the huge difference between human language and gorilla signs. There is a major gap between the ability to write a book or say a prayer and the few hundred gestures employed by a well-trained chimp. Apes aren't people, but they aren't just animals either. Let Koko express it: When asked by a reporter whether she was a person or an animal, Koko chose neither. Instead, she signed "fine animal gorilla" (Patterson 1978).

The capacity to remember and combine linguistic expressions is latent in the apes (Miles 1983). In hominid evolution the same ability flowered into language. Language did not appear miraculously at a certain moment in human history. It developed over hundreds of thousands of years, as our ancestors' call systems were gradually transformed. Language offered a tremendous adaptive advantage to *Homo.* Along with technology, language is a basic part of our cultural, nonbodily, or **extrasomatic,** means of adaptation. Language permits the information stored by a human society to exceed by far that of any nonhuman group. Language is a uniquely effective vehicle for learning. Because we can speak of things we have never experienced, we can anticipate responses before we encounter the stimuli. Adaptation can occur more rapidly in *Homo* than in the other primates because our adaptive means are more flexible. Humans routinely rely on biological, social, and cultural means of adaptation.

Predation and Hunting

Like tool making and language, hunting has been cited as a distinctive human activity that is not shared with our ape relatives. Again, however, primate research shows that what was previously thought to be a difference of kind is a difference of degree.

The diets of other terrestrial primates are not exclusively vegetarian, as was once thought. Baboons kill and eat young antelopes, and researchers have observed hunting by chimpanzees. Geza Teleki (1973) has provided a detailed report based on twelve months of observing predation among chimps at Tanzania's Gombe Stream National Park. He recorded thirty cases of chimpanzee hunting, twelve of which led to a kill. About a hundred kills were recorded during a decade of research by Goodall (1968*b*) and her associates at Gombe.

Generally, chimps simply lunged at and seized their prey, but they also did more complex hunting. Groups of five or six sometimes patiently stalked a prey animal. Stalking was silent; vocalization oc-

curred only when they seized the prey. Nor did the chimps use gestures to coordinate the hunt. After seizing an infant baboon, the hunter would bite or wring the baboon's neck or bash its head against the ground or a tree. Occasionally, young baboons were ripped apart when two chimps seized them simultaneously. For a few moments after the kill, chimps that had not taken part in the hunt could grab part of the carcass. Once this initial division occurred, however, meat sharing became more intricate. Chimps used a variety of gestures to request meat from their fellows. The hunters granted the requests about one-third of the time. Chimpanzee hunting is predominantly a male activity; insect eating is more common in females (McGrew 1979).

Predation, Aggression, and Resources

The potential for predation may be generalized in monkeys and apes, but its expression seems to depend on the environment. Hunting by chimpanzees might have developed in response to changes in their environment. Humans have been encroaching on their natural habitat.

Goodall specifically linked chimpanzee predation to human encroachment. The Gombe chimps are divided into a northern group and a smaller group of southerners. Parties from the north have invaded southern territory and killed southern chimps. Infant victims were partially eaten by the assailants (Goodall 1986). John MacKinnon's research (1974)

In Kenya this olive baboon munches on a baby Thompson's gazelle. Like chimpanzees, baboons occasionally hunt small animals and eat their meat.

among orangutans on the Indonesian islands of Borneo (Kalimantan) and Sumatra shows that orangutans have also suffered as a result of human encroachment, particularly farming and timbering. On Borneo, in response to nearby human activities, orangs have developed a pattern of extreme sexual antagonism which may further endanger their survival. During MacKinnon's field work, Bornean orangs rarely had sex. Their limited sexual encounters were always brief rapes, often with screaming infants clinging to their mothers throughout the ordeal.

As MacKinnon did his field work, logging operations were forcing orangs whose territory was destroyed into his research area, swelling the population it had to support. The response to this sudden overpopulation was a drastic decline in the local orang birth rate. Primates respond in various ways to encroachment and population pressure. A change in sexual relationships that reduces the birth rate is one way of easing population pressure on resources.

We see that primate behavior is not rigidly determined by the genes. It is plastic (flexible), capable of varying widely as environmental forces change. Among humans, too, aggression increases when resources are threatened or scarce. What we know about other primates makes it reasonable to assume that early hominids were neither uniformly aggressive nor consistently meek. Their aggression and predation reflected environmental variation.

DIFFERENCES BETWEEN HUMANS AND OTHER PRIMATES

The preceding sections emphasized similarities between humans and other primates. The differences discussed so far have been of degree rather than kind. Thus *Homo* has elaborated substantially on certain tendencies shared with the apes. A unique concentration and combination of characteristics makes humans distinct. However, the early hominid savanna niche also selected certain traits that are not so obviously foreshadowed by the apes.

Sharing, Cooperation, and Division of Labor

Early humans lived in small social groups called bands, with economies based on hunting and gathering. Some band-organized societies survived into

the modern world, and ethnographers have studied them. From those studies we can say that in such groups the strongest and most aggressive members do not dominate, as they do in a troop of terrestrial monkeys. Sharing and curbing of aggression are as basic to technologically simple humans as dominance and threats are to baboons.

Monkeys fend for themselves in the quest for food. However, among human foragers, men generally hunt and women gather. People bring resources back to the camp and share them. The most successful hunters are expected to be generous. Everyone shares the meat from a large animal. Older people who did not engage in the food quest receive food from younger adults. Nourished and protected by younger band members, elders live past the reproductive age. They receive special respect for their age and knowledge. The amount of information stored in a human band is far greater than that in any other primate society. Sharing, cooperation, and language are intrinsic to information storage.

Among all primates except *Homo*, most food comes from individual foraging, usually for vegetation. The rarity of meat eating and the concentration on vegetation are fundamental differences between apes and humans. Through millions of years of adaptation to an omnivorous diet, hominids have come to rely on hunting, meat eating, food sharing, and cooperative behavior. These are universal features in human adaptive strategies.

Mating, Exogamy, and Kinship

Another difference between humans and other primates concerns mating. Among baboons and chimpanzees, sexual intercourse occurs when females "go into heat" or enter **estrus,** a period of sexual receptivity. Estrus is signaled by swelling and coloration of the vaginal skin. Receptive females form temporary bonds with males. Among humans, sexual activity occurs throughout the year. Related to this more constant sexuality, all human societies have some form of marriage. Marriage gives mating a reliable basis and grants to each spouse special, though not always exclusive, sexual rights in the other.

Marriage creates another major contrast between human and nonhumans: exogamy and kinship systems. Most cultures have rules of exogamy requiring marriage outside one's kin or local group. Coupled with the recognition of kinship, exogamy confers adaptive advantages. It creates ties between the spouses' groups of origin. Their children have relatives, and therefore allies, in two kin groups rather than just one. The key point here is that ties of affection and mutual support between members of different local groups are absent among primates other than *Homo*. There is a tendency among primates to disperse at adolescence. Among chimps and gorillas, females tend to migrate, seeking mates in other groups. Both male and female gibbons leave home when they become sexually mature. Once they find mates and establish their own territories, ties with their native groups cease. Long-term studies of terrestrial monkeys reveal that males leave the troop at puberty, eventually finding places elsewhere. The troop's core members are females. They sometimes form **uterine** groups made up of mothers, sisters, daughters, and sons that have not yet emigrated. This dispersal of males reduces the incidence of incestuous matings. Females mate with males born elsewhere, which join the troop at adolescence. Although kin ties are maintained between female monkeys, no close lifelong links are preserved through males.

Humans choose mates from outside the native group (the family), and at least one spouse moves. However, *humans maintain lifelong ties with sons and daughters*. The systems of kinship and marriage that preserve these links provide a major contrast between humans and other primates.

SOCIOBIOLOGY AND INCLUSIVE FITNESS

According to evolutionary theory, when the environment changes, natural selection starts to modify the *population's* pool of genetic material. Natural selection has another key feature: the differential reproductive success of *individuals* within the population. **Sociobiology** is the study of the evolutionary basis of social behavior. Sociobiology assumes that the innate psychological traits that are typical of any species are the product of a long history of differential reproductive success (that is, natural selection). In other words, the biological traits evident in contemporary organisms have been transmitted across the generations because those traits enabled

their ancestors to survive and reproduce more effectively than their competition. Natural selection entails competition between **conspecifics** (individual members of the same species) to maximize their reproductive fitness—their genetic contribution to future generations. **Individual fitness** is measured by the number of direct descendants an individual has. Illustrating a primate strategy that may enhance individual fitness are cases in which male monkeys kill infants after entering a new troop. Destroying the offspring of other males, they clear a place for their own progeny (Hausfater and Hrdy 1984).

Besides competition, one's genetic contribution to future generations can also be maximized by cooperation, sharing, and other apparently unselfish behavior. This is because of **inclusive fitness**—reproductive success measured by the representation of genes one shares with other, related individuals. By sacrificing for their relatives—even if this means limiting their own direct reproduction—individuals may actually increase their genetic contributions (their shared genes) to the future. Inclusive fitness helps us understand why a female might invest in her sister's offspring, or why a male might risk his life to defend his brothers. If self-sacrifice perpetuates more of their genes than direct reproduction does, it makes sense in sociobiological terms. The following cases show how inclusive fitness theory can help us understand aspects of primate behavior and social organization.

Sex, Aggression, and Parenting

Maternal care always makes sense in terms of inclusive fitness because females know that their offspring are their own. However, it's harder for males to be sure about paternity. Inclusive fitness theory predicts that males will invest most in offspring when they are surest the offspring are theirs. Gibbons, for example, have strict male-female pair bonding, which makes it likely that the offspring are those of both members of the pair. Here we would expect males to offer care and protection to their young, and they do. However, when a male can't be sure about paternity, it may be more rational—in terms of maximizing fitness—to invest in a sister's child than a mate's because that niece or nephew definitely shares some of that male's genes.

For years anthropologists have speculated that

human pair bonding and, eventually, monogamy originated for economic reasons. All foraging populations divide labor by gender (women usually gather and men hunt). Because of this, some anthropologists have assumed that hominids started pairing to ensure that women got meat and men had access to gathered products. Pair bonding also increases the chance that the husband is the father of the wife's children. This justifies greater paternal investment.

Barbara Smuts's detailed study (1985) of long-lasting male-female "friendship" bonds among Kenyan baboons suggests that human pair bonding might have developed much earlier—by analogy with baboons. Among baboons, male-female bonds are useful for females, infants, and males. Females and infants need the protection provided by adult males' much larger size. Infants run to their mother's male friends when threatened.

One way for a male to win a place in a new troop is to find a friendly female as a sponsor. Friendship often leads to mating and thus helps maximize the male's fitness because his friend's future infants are likely to be his own. However, males also bolster friendships by protecting infants born before their arrival. Baboon friendships have benefits and costs. Rivals sometimes attack another male's female friend.

Another primate study has also shed light on mating and parenting patterns. Charles Janson (1986) studied two closely related but contrasting species of monkeys—brown- and white-fronted capuchin monkeys—in the forests of Amazonian Peru. The brown monkeys are bigger and live in smaller groups dominated by one male. They inhabit smaller trees and lower branches and eat tougher fruits. The dominant male has preferential access to food and to females. He gets the females not through competition with other males but because females seek him out and refuse to mate with anyone else. He is very aggressive with other males but tolerant and protective toward infants, which are likely to be his own. Only that dominant male defends the troop against threats from eagles or other monkeys. Subdominant males run away. According to inclusive fitness theory, they don't help out because they have a minimal genetic stake in the outcome.

White-fronted monkey males are much less aggressive with members of their own troops than are dominant brown-fronted males. However, they aren't as attentive to infants. Dominance is less marked among these monkeys. White males cooperate to defend the troop against eagles—or to displace brown monkeys when they wish to feed in the same tree. White males compete for females, but all males get to mate. Here, male cooperation to benefit the entire troop makes sense from the perspective of inclusive fitness: All the troop's infants may be any individual male's offspring.

These primate studies suggest that pair bonds and other stable social links between hominid males and females might have preceded the hunter-gatherer division of labor. Human pair bonding might have originated for social, protective, and reproductive reasons rather than economic ones.

White-fronted capuchin monkeys range from the forests of Amazonian Peru to Costa Rica, shown here. White-fronted capuchin males compete for females, but all males get to mate. Thus male cooperation to defend the troop makes sense from the inclusive fitness perspective because all the troop's infants have a chance to be the offspring of any one of its males.

SUMMARY

Humans, apes, monkeys, and prosimians all belong to the primate zoological order. This order is subdivided into suborders, superfamilies, families, genera, species, and subspecies. In general, organisms included within any subdivision, or taxon, of a zoological taxonomy are assumed to share more recent common ancestry with one another than they do with organisms in other taxa. They are therefore assumed to share more homologies, reflected in their appearance, structure, physiology, biochemistry, and genetic makeup. The fact that it is sometimes difficult to distinguish homologies, which reflect common ancestry, from analogies, which reflect convergent evolution, can create disagreement about taxonomic categories.

Primate trends, most obvious among the anthropoids, include changes in vision, smell, touch, grasping, brain complexity, parental investment, and social organization. Prosimians, members of the older primate suborder, were displaced from niches their ancestors once occupied by anthropoids, which were evolving around 30 million years ago. Some prosimians survived by adapting to nocturnal life. Lemurs survived on the geographically isolated island of Madagascar.

Anthropoids include humans, apes, and monkeys of the Old World and New World. All share certain traits—fully developed primate trends. Vision has developed at the expense of smell. All the anthropoids have depth and color vision. In prosimians, a large snout projects between the eyes and interferes with depth perception. Other anthropoid traits include a shift in tactile areas from the muzzle skin and whiskers to the fingers.

Anthropoids have adapted to a wide array of environments. All New World monkeys are arboreal. Old World monkeys include the terrestrial baboons and macaques of Africa and Asia, respectively, as well as arboreal species. Apes are traditionally classified in two families, hylobatids (gibbons and siamangs) and pongids (orangutans, gorillas, and chimpanzees).

Gibbons and siamangs, widespread in Southeast Asian forests, are slight, completely arboreal animals whose mode of locomotion is brachiation. Sexual dimorphism, slight among gibbons, is marked among orangutans, which are confined to two Indonesian islands. Female and young orangs are more arboreal than males are. Sexually dimorphic gorillas, the most terrestrial apes, are vegetarians confined to equatorial Africa. Two species of chimpanzees live in the forests and woodlands of tropical Africa; they are less sexually dimorphic, more numerous, and more omnivorous than gorillas. Terrestrial monkeys (baboons and macaques) live in troops and survive through a variety of anatomic, behavioral, and social means of adaptation. Baboon males, the troop's main protectors, are twice as large as females. The troop is tightly knit; internal conflict is minimized, and the troop presents a united front to outsiders.

Differences between humans and other primates have often been stressed, but their many similarities have been ignored. Recent research shows that similarities are extensive and that many differences are quantitative rather than qualitative. A unique concentration and combination of ingredients makes humans distinct.

Some of our most important adaptive traits are foreshadowed in other primates, particularly the African apes. Primate behavior and social organization aren't rigidly programmed by the genes. Monkeys rely extensively on learning and demonstrate subcultural variation. Chimpanzees make tools for several purposes. Thus learning ability, the basis of culture, is an adaptive advantage of many nonhuman primates.

Although wild primates have only call systems, chimpanzees and gorillas can understand and manipulate nonverbal symbols based on language. Primates emit calls only in the presence of particular environmental stimuli. Calls cannot be combined when different stimuli are present simultaneously. At some point in hominid evolution our ancestors became capable of displaced speech. Other contrasts between language and call systems include productivity and cultural transmission. Over time, our ancestral call systems developed into true language. Call systems grew too complicated for genetic transmission and began to rely on learning.

Primates other than humans sometimes hunt cooperatively. Chimps, which are more omnivorous than once was thought, occasionally hunt and share meat. Hunting and the killing of chimp by chimp, like sexual antagonism among orangutans, reflect pressure on strategic resources, especially human encroachment on their natural habitat. Chimps, baboons, and orangs, like humans, are flexible animals that increase or reduce their aggression as environmental conditions warrant. Primate social organization varies with environment.

Although most contrasts are of degree rather than kind, important differences between humans and other primates remain. Aggression and dominance are characteristic of terrestrial monkeys, whereas sharing and cooperation are equally significant among primitive human populations. Connected with sharing is the traditional division of subsistence labor by age and gender.

Other primates avoid incest through dispersal at adolescence. However, only humans have systems of kinship and marriage that permit us to maintain lifelong ties with relatives in different local groups.

From the perspective of sociobiology, individuals within a population strive to maximize their genetic contribution to future generations. Maternal care makes sense from an inclusive fitness perspective because females can be sure that their offspring are their own. Because it's harder for males to be sure about paternity, inclusive fitness theory predicts that they will invest most in offspring when they are surest that the offspring are theirs. The idea of inclusive fitness, based on the fact that individuals share their DNA with relatives, is also used to explain individual self-sacrifice and altruism as well as human pair bonding.

GLOSSARY

Ameslan: American Sign Language, a medium of communication for deaf and mute apes and humans.

analogies: Similarities arising as a result of similar selective forces; traits produced by convergent evolution.

Anthropoidea: One of two suborders of primates; includes monkeys, apes, and humans.

arboreal: Tree-dwelling.

bipedal: Two-footed.

brachiation: Under-the-branch swinging; characteristic of gibbons, siamangs, and some New World monkeys.

call systems: Systems of communication among nonhuman primates, composed of a limited number of sounds that vary in intensity and duration. Tied to environmental stimuli.

catarrhine: Sharp-nosed; anthropoid infraorder that includes Old World monkeys, apes, and humans.

class, zoological: Division of a kingdom; composed of related orders.

conspecifics: Individual members of the same species.

convergent evolution: Independent operation of similar selective forces; process by which analogies are produced.

cranium: Skull.

cultural transmission: A basic feature of language; transmission through learning.

displacement: A basic feature of language; the ability to speak of things and events that are not present.

estrus: Period of maximum sexual receptivity in female baboons and other primates, signaled by vaginal area swelling and coloration.

extrasomatic: Nonbodily; pertaining to culture, including language, tools, and other cultural means of adaptation.

family, zoological: Group of similar genera.

genus (plural, *genera*): Group of similar species.

gibbons: The smallest apes, natives of Asia; arboreal and territorial.

hominid: Zoological family that includes fossil and living humans.

Hominidae: Zoological superfamily that includes fossil and living humans; according to some taxonomists, also includes the African apes.

hominoid: Superfamily including humans and apes.

Hominoidea: Zoological superfamily that includes fossil and contemporary apes and humans.

homologies: Traits that organisms have jointly inherited from their common ancestor.

inclusive fitness: Reproductive success measured by the representation of genes one shares with other, related individuals.

individual fitness: Reproductive success measured by the number of direct descendants an individual has.

ischial callosities: Rough patches of skin of gibbons and Old World monkeys on the buttocks, adapted to sitting on hard rocky ground and rough branches.

kingdom, zoological: Group of related classes.

knuckle-walking: A form of terrestrial locomotion in which long arms and callused knuckles support the trunk; the ape ambles around leaning forward.

longitudinal: Long-term; refers to a study carried out over many years.

opposable thumb: A thumb that can touch all the other fingers.

order, zoological: Division of a zoological class; a group of related suborders, such as the primates.

orthograde posture: Straight and upright; the posture among apes and humans.

phylogeny: Genetic relatedness based on common ancestry.

platyrrhine: Flat-nosed; anthropoid infraorder that includes the New World monkeys.

pongid: Zoological family that includes the great apes.

precision grip: Grip between index finger and opposable thumb.

prehensile: Grasping, as in the tail of New World monkeys.

primary groups: Primate groups composed of a permanently bonded male and female and their preadolescent offspring.

primatology: The study of fossil and living apes, monkeys, and prosimians, including their behavior and social life.

productivity: A basic feature of language; the ability to use the rules of one's language to create new expressions comprehensible to other native speakers.

prosimians: The primate suborder that includes lemurs, loris, and tarsiers.

sexual dimorphism: Marked differences in male and female anatomy and temperament.

sociobiology: The study of the evolutionary basis of social behavior.

stereoscopic vision: Ability to see in depth.

suborder: Group of closely related superfamilies.

superfamily: Group of closely related zoological families.

taxonomy: Classification scheme; assignment to categories (*taxa*; singular, *taxon*).

terrestrial: Ground-dwelling.

uterine: Primate groups made up of mothers, sisters, daughters, and sons that have not emigrated.

STUDY QUESTIONS

1. What is the difference between phylogeny and taxonomy?
2. What is the difference between homologies and analogies?
3. Why isn't zoological taxonomy always based on homologies?
4. What major adaptive traits characterize the anthropoid primates?
5. What are the main differences between gorilla and chimpanzee social organization?
6. What is the evidence that nonhuman primates rely on learning as a means of adaptation?
7. How do tools distinguish between humans and other animals?
8. What are the features of primate call systems?
9. What attributes are basic to language? Does language use by apes show these characteristics?
10. Explain this statement: "Apes aren't people, but they aren't just animals either."
11. How might the use of Ameslan by apes affect interpretations of human evolution?
12. What environmental conditions might trigger predatory behavior among chimpanzees?
13. What causes sexual antagonism among orangs?
14. What behavioral differences distinguish humans from other primates?
15. Why is it significant that among primates, only hominids maintain ties of affection and mutual support between different local groups?
16. How does inclusive fitness theory help us understand differences between female and male parental investment strategies?

SUGGESTED ADDITIONAL READING

BARASH, D. P.
   1977   *Sociobiology and Behavior.* Amsterdam: Elsevier. Basics of sociobiology.
FEDIGAN, L. M.
   1982   *Primate Paradigms: Sex Roles and Social Bonds.* Montreal: Eden Press. Focuses on sex roles in primate social organization.
FOSSEY, D.
   1983   *Gorillas in the Mist.* Boston: Houghton Mifflin. Social organization of the mountain gorilla; basis of the popular film.
GOODALL, J.
   1986   *The Chimpanzees of Gombe: Patterns of Behavior.* Cambridge, MA: Belknap Press of Harvard University Press. Results of decades of research on primate behavior in Tanzania.
   1988   *In the Shadow of Man.* rev. ed. Boston: Houghton Mifflin. Popular account of the author's life among the chimps.

GRAY, J. P.
   1985   *Primate Sociobiology.* New Haven, CT: HRAF Press. A comparative study of parental investment and inclusive fitness in primate society.
HAMBURG, D. A., AND E. R. McCOWN, EDS.
   1979   *The Great Apes.* Menlo Park, CA: Benjamin Cummings. Collection of twenty-two papers based on field studies of chimps, gorillas, and orangutans. Excellent data and detailed bibliography.
HILL, J. H.
   1978   Apes and Language. *Annual Review of Anthropology* 7: 89–112. Thorough review of Ameslan and other language use by chimps and gorillas.
HINDE, R. A.
   1983   *Primate Social Relationships: An Integrated Approach.* Sunderland, MA: Sinaeur Associates.

Theoretical implications of aspects of social life among various primates.

JOLLY, A.
1985   *The Evolution of Primate Behavior.* 2nd ed. New York: Macmillan. Good introduction.

MAYR, E.
1970   *Animal Species and Evolution.* Cambridge, MA: Harvard University Press. Good discussion of evolutionary principles, speciation, and taxonomy.

MITTERMEIER, R. A., AND M. J. POLTKIN, EDS.
1982   *Primates and the Tropical Forest.* Washington, DC: World Wildlife Fund. Well-illustrated introduction to many primate species.

MOWAT, F.
1987   *Woman in the Mists: The Story of Dian Fossey and the Mountain Gorillas of Africa.* New York: Warner Books. Account of the well-known primatologist whose story was told in the film *Gorillas in the Mist.*

NAPIER, J. R. AND P. H.
1985   *The Natural History of Primates.* Cambridge, MA: The MIT Press. Readable and well-illustrated introduction to the primates.

REYNOLDS, V.
1971   *The Apes.* New York: Harper Colophon. Readable introduction to our nearest relatives.

SEBEOK, T. A., AND J. UMIKER-SEBEOK, EDS.
1980   *Speaking of Apes: A Critical Anthology of Two-Way Communication with Man.* New York: Plenum. Articles disputing the linguistic abilities of Ameslan-using primates.

SMALL, M., ED.
1984   *Female Primates: Studies by Women Primatologists.* New York: Liss. Differences in female strategies in various primate groups.

SMUTS, B. B.
1985   *Sex and Friendship in Baboons.* New York: Aldine. Pair bonding, mutual support, and parental investment in baboon social organization, with implications for early human evolution.

SZALAY, F. S., AND E. DELSON.
1980   *Evolutionary History of the Primates.* New York: Academic Press. Presents fossil evidence for primate evolution.

CHAPTER 8

EARLY HOMINIDS

Recent discoveries of fossils and tools have increased and revised our knowledge of early human evolution. Some of the most significant finds come from East Africa—Ethiopia, Kenya, and Tanzania. Speculation about these finds abounds. For one thing, they come from different places and may be the remains of individuals who lived thousands of years apart. Furthermore, geological processes operating over thousands or millions of years inevitably distort fossil remains.

The study of the processes—biological and geological—by which dead animals become fossils is called **taphonomy,** from the Greek *taphos,* which means "tomb." The fossil record does not present a representative sample of the species that have lived on earth. Some body parts and species are better represented than others, for a variety of reasons (Jolly and White 1994). Hard parts, like bones and teeth, preserve better than soft parts, like flesh and skin. The chances of fossilization increase when remains are buried in a newly forming sediment, such as silt, gravel, or sand. Good places for bones to be buried in sediments include swamps, floodplains, river deltas, lakes, and caves. The species that inhabit such areas have a better chance to be preserved than do animals that live in other habitats. Fossilization is favored in geologically active areas of rapid sedimentation, where ash from volcanoes or rock fragments eroding from rising highlands are accumulating in rift valleys or lake basins. Once remains do get buried, chemical conditions must also be right for fossilization to occur. If the sediment is too acid, even bone and teeth will dissolve.

The fossils available for study comprise a very small sample of all the animals that have ever lived. This sample is biased, with some areas and times much better represented than others are. Conditions favoring fossilization open special "time windows" for certain places and times, like western Kenya from 18 to 14 **m.y.a.**—million years ago. Because western Kenya was geologically active then, it has a substantial fossil record. Between 12 and 8 m.y.a., the area was quieter geologically, and there are few fossils. Similarly, after 8 m.y.a. a time window opens in the Rift Valley area of eastern Kenya. The East African highlands were rising, volcanoes were active, and many lake basins were forming and filling with sediments. This time window extends through the present and includes many hominid fossils. Compared with East Africa, West Africa was more stable geologically and has few time windows (Jolly and White 1994).

The conditions under which fossils are found also influence the fossil record. For example, fossils are more likely to be uncovered through erosion in arid than in wet areas because sparse vegetation allows wind and rain to scour the landscape and uncover fossils. The fossil record has been accumulating longer and is more extensive in Europe than in Africa because civil engineering projects and fossil hunting have been going on longer in Europe than in Africa. A map showing where fossils have been found does not indicate the true range of ancient animals. Such a map tells us more about ancient geological activity, modern erosion, or recent human activity—such as paleontological research or road building. In considering the hominid fossil record, we shall see that different areas provide more abundant fossil evidence for different time periods. This doesn't necessarily mean that hominids were not living elsewhere at the same time. For example, the fact that the earliest hominid fossils come from eastern Africa does not mean that comparable hominids did not also live in southern, central, or western Africa.

The following discussion of human evolution must therefore be tentative and speculative because the fossil record "is woefully limited and spotty. That is why each significant find sets off a new spate of speculations—and often a new barrage of attacks on some previously dug and stoutly held trenches" (Fisher 1988a, p. 23). Much is subject to change as knowledge increases. Before considering our fossil ancestors, however, we need to review some of the techniques used to establish when they lived.

DATING THE PAST

Anthropology and **paleontology,** the study of ancient life through the fossil record, share an interest in establishing a time frame, or **chronology,** for primate and human evolution. Scientists use several techniques to date fossils. These methods offer different degrees of precision and are applicable to different periods of the past.

Many dating methods are based on the geological study of **stratigraphy,** the science that examines the ways in which earth sediments accumulate in demarcated layers known as *strata* (singular, *stratum*).

Geological stratification in the Grand Canyon. Stratigraphic sequences permit anthropologists and paleontologists to establish relative dates of artifacts as well as of fossils. Normally, materials preserved in lower levels were deposited before those in upper levels.

In an undisturbed sequence of strata, age increases with depth. Soil that erodes from a hillside into a valley covers, and is younger than, the soil that was deposited there previously. Changing environmental forces, such as lava flows and the alternation of dry land and sea, cause different materials to be deposited, enabling scientists to distinguish between strata.

The remains of life forms deposited on the earth's surface may be covered and preserved as fossils. Remains of animals and plants that lived at the same time are normally found in the same strata. On the basis of fossils found in stratigraphic sequences, the history of vertebrate life has been divided into three main eras. The **Paleozoic** was the era of ancient life—fishes, amphibians, and primitive reptiles. The **Mesozoic** was the era of middle life—reptiles, including the dinosaurs. The **Cenozoic** is the era of recent life—birds and mammals. Each era is divided into periods, and the periods are divided into epochs.

Anthropologists are concerned with the Cenozoic era, which includes two periods—Tertiary and Quaternary. Each of these periods is subdivided into epochs. The Tertiary had five epochs—Paleocene, Eocene, Oligocene, Miocene, and Pliocene. The Quaternary includes just two epochs—Pleistocene and Holocene, or Recent. Figure 8.1 gives the approximate dates of these epochs. Sediments from the Paleocene epoch (65 to 54 m.y.a.) have yielded fossil remains of diverse small mammals, some possibly ancestral to the primates. Prosimianlike fossils abound in strata dating from the Eocene (54 to 36 m.y.a.). The first definitely anthropoid fossils date to the Oligocene (36 to 23 m.y.a.). Hominoids became widespread during the Miocene (23 to 5 m.y.a.), and hominids first appeared in the Pliocene (5 to 2 m.y.a.) (Table 8.1).

For the study of hominid evolution the Pliocene, Pleistocene (2 m.y.a. to 10,000 B.P.), and Recent (10,000 B.P. to the present) are most important. Until the end of the Pliocene, there may have been just one hominid genus, *Australopithecus*, which lived in sub-Saharan Africa. By the start of the Pleistocene, some form of *Australopithecus* had evolved into *Homo*. The **Pleistocene** is traditionally and correctly considered the epoch of human life. The subdivisions of the Pleistocene are the Lower Pleistocene (2 to 1 m.y.a.), the Middle Pleistocene (1 m.y.a. to 130,000 B.P.), and the Upper Pleistocene (130,000 to 10,000 B.P.). These subdivisions refer to the placement of strata containing, respectively, older, intermediate, and younger fossils. The Lower Pleistocene extends from the start of the Pleistocene to the ad-

Periods	Epochs	Climate and life forms
Quaternary	Pleistocene, Recent 2 m.y.a.	Climatic fluctuations, glaciation; *A. boisei*; *Homo*
Tertiary	Pliocene 5	*A. afarensis*; *A. africanus*; *A. robustus*
	Miocene 23	Cooler and drier grasslands spread in middle latitudes; Africa collides with Eurasia (16 m.y.a.); Proconsulids Dryopiths Ramapiths *Afropithecus*
	Oligocene 36	Cooler and drier in the north; Anthropoids in Africa (Fayum); separation of Catarrhines and Platyrrhines; separation of Hylobatids from Pongids and Hominids
	Eocene 54	Warm tropical climates widespread; modern orders of mammals appear; prosimianlike primates
	Paleocene 65	First major mammal radiation
Cretaceous		Last dinosaurs; early placental mammals
	135	

Figure 8.1 *The geological time scale of primate evolution, based on stratigraphy. Periods are subdivided into epochs.*

vent of the ice ages in the Northern Hemisphere around 1 m.y.a.

Each subdivision of the Pleistocene is roughly associated with a particular group of hominids. Late *Australopithecus* and early *Homo* lived during the Lower Pleistocene. *Homo erectus* spanned most of the Middle Pleistocene. *Homo sapiens* appeared late in the Middle Pleistocene and was the sole hominid of the Upper Pleistocene. We consider the hominids of the Middle and Upper Pleistocene in the following chapter.

During the latter million years of the Pleistocene there were several ice ages, or **glacials,** major advances of continental ice sheets in Europe and North America. These periods were separated by **interglacials,** extended warmer periods between the major glacials. (Scientists used to think there were four main glacial advances, but the picture has grown more complex.) With each advance, the world climate cooled and continental ice sheets—massive glaciers—covered the northern parts of Europe and North America. Climates that are temperate today were arctic during the glacials. During the interglacials, the climate warmed up and the **tundra**—the cold, treeless plain—retreated north with the ice sheets. Forests returned to areas, such as southwestern France, which had had tundra vegetation. The ice sheets advanced and receded several times during the last glacial, the **Würm** (75,000 to 12,000 B.P.). Brief periods of relative warmth during the Würm (and other glacials) are called **interstadials,** in contrast to the longer interglacials. Hominid fossils found in association with animals known to occur in cold or warm climates, respectively, permit us to date them to glacial or interglacial (or interstadial) periods.

Techniques of Dating Fossils

When fossils can be placed within a stratigraphic sequence, scientists know their dates relative to other fossils. (Such a determination is called *relative dating.*) When hominid fossils are found in a stratum, the associated geological features (such as frost patterning) and remains of particular plants and animals offer clues about the climate at the time of deposition.

Besides stratigraphic associations, another technique of relative dating is fluorine absorption analysis. Bones fossilizing in the same ground for the

Table 8.1 *Dates and Geographic Distribution of the Major Hominoid and Hominid Fossil Groups*

Fossil Group	Dates, m.y.a.	Known Distribution
Hominoids		
Proconsulids	23–16	Africa
Dryopiths	16–8	East Africa, Europe
Ramapiths (Sivapiths)	15–7.5	Asia, Europe
Afropithecus	18–16	East Africa
Hominids		
Australopithecines		
A. afarensis	3.8–3.0	East Africa (Laetoli, Hadar)
Robusts	2.6–1.2	East and South Africa
A. robustus	2.6?–2.0?	South Africa
A. boisei	2.6?–1.2	East Africa
Graciles		
A. africanus	3.0–2.5?	South Africa
Homo		
H. habilis	2.0?–1.6?	East Africa
H. erectus	1.6?–0.3	Africa, Asia, Europe?
Homo sapiens	0.3–present	
Archaic *H. sapiens*	0.3–0.035 (300,000–35,000)	Africa, Asia, Europe
H. sapiens neanderthalensis	0.13–0.035 (130,000–35,000)	Europe, Middle East
H. sapiens sapiens	0.1?–present (100,000–present)	Worldwide (after 25,000 B.P.)

same length of time absorb the same proportion of fluorine from the local ground water. Fluorine analysis uncovered a famous hoax involving "Piltdown man," once considered an unusual and perplexing human ancestor (Winslow and Meyer 1983). The Piltdown "find," from England, turned out to be the jaw of a young orangutan attached to a *H. sapiens* skull. Fluorine analysis showed the association to be false. The skull had much more fluorine than the jaw—impossible if they had come from the same individual and had been deposited in the same place at the same time. Someone had fabricated Piltdown man in an attempt to muddle the interpretation of the fossil record. (The attempt was partially successful—it did fool some scientists.)

Fossils can also be dated more precisely (*absolute dating*) through the use of several methods. For example, the ^{14}C, or carbon-14, technique is used to date organic remains. This is a **radiometric** technique (so called because it measures radioactive decay). ^{14}C is an unstable radioactive isotope of normal carbon, ^{12}C. Cosmic radiation entering the earth's atmosphere produces neutrons, which react with nitrogen to produce ^{14}C. Plants take in ^{14}C which mixes with ^{12}C as they absorb carbon dioxide. ^{14}C moves up the food chain as animals eat plants and as predators eat other animals.

With death, absorption of ^{14}C stops, and this unstable isotope starts to break down into nitrogen (^{14}N). It takes 5,730 years for half the ^{14}C to change to nitrogen; this is the half-life of ^{14}C. After another 5,730 years only one-quarter of the original ^{14}C will remain. After yet another 5,730 years only one-eighth will be left. By measuring the ratio of ^{14}C to ^{12}C in organic material, scientists can determine a fossil's date of death or the date of an ancient campfire. However, because the half-life of ^{14}C is short, this dating technique is less dependable, although it has still been used, for specimens older than 40,000 years. Thus ^{14}C dating is most useful for recent human evolution.

Fortunately, other radiometric dating techniques are available for earlier periods. One of the most widely used is the potassium-argon (K/A) technique. ^{40}K is a radioactive isotope of potassium that breaks down into argon 40, a gas. The half-life of ^{40}K is far longer than that of ^{14}C—1.3 *billion* years. With this method, the *older* the specimen, the more reliable the dating. Furthermore, whereas ^{14}C dating can be done only on organic remains, K/A dating can be used only for inorganic substances—minerals.

^{40}K in rocks gradually breaks down into argon 40. That gas is trapped in the rock until the rock is intensely heated (as with volcanic activity), at which point it may escape. When the rock cools, the breakdown of potassium into argon resumes. Dating is done by reheating the rock and measuring the escaping gas.

In Africa's Great Rift Valley, which runs down eastern Africa and in which early hominid fossils abound, past volcanic activity permits K/A dating. In studies of strata containing hominid fossils, scientists find out how much argon has accumulated in rocks since they were last heated. They then determine, using the standard ^{40}K deterioration rate, the date of that heating. Considering volcanic rocks at the top of a stratum with hominid remains, scientists establish that the hominid fossils are *older than*, say, 1.8 million years. By dating the volcanic rocks below the fossil remains, they determine that the fossils are *younger than*, say, 2 million years. Thus the age of the fossils and of associated material is set at between 2 million and 1.8 million years.

Not all early human remains can be dated by the K/A technique. Many fossils were found before the advent of modern stratigraphy, and we often can't determine their original stratigraphic placement. Furthermore, fossils aren't always discovered in vocanic layers. Like ^{14}C dating, the K/A technique applies to a limited period of the fossil record. Because the half-life of ^{40}K is so long, the technique cannot be used with materials less than 500,000 years old.

Another radiometric dating technique can be used to cross-check K/A dates, again by using minerals surrounding the fossils. This method measures *fission tracks* produced during the decay of radioactive uranium (^{238}U) into lead. Because the half-life of ^{238}U is 4.5 *billion* years, this technique is most useful for dating very early events, such as the origin of the earth. None of these methods is very useful for materials between 40,000 and 500,000 years old.

Two other radiometric techniques, **thermoluminescence (TL)** and **electron spin resonance (ESR)**, can be used to date more recent fossils, filling in the gap between ^{14}C (up to 40,000 B.P.) and ^{40}K (more than 500,000 B.P.). Both TL and ESR measure the electrons that are constantly being trapped in rocks and minerals (Shreeve 1992). Once a date is obtained for a rock found associated with a fossil, the date can also be applied to that fossil.

How do TL and ESR work? Radioactivity, in the rock itself and in the surrounding soil and atmosphere, constantly bombards the atoms in the rock, knocking electrons out of their orbits. Most electrons soon return "home," to their normal positions, but some become trapped in impurities or flaws in the mineral structure. Electrons stay in these traps until the rock is heated. Then the trap opens, and the electrons return to their normal position. As they escape, they release energy in the form of light—a photon for each electron. This light (luminescence) can be measured to provide a date.

TL can be used as a dating technique because the radioactivity that bombards a rock is fairly constant. Electrons become trapped at a fairly steady rate through time. When grains of the rock are heated to a high enough temperature, all the traps release their captive electrons at once, causing a burst of light, the intensity of which is measured with a device called a *photo multiplier*. This measurement indicates how much time has passed since the rock was last heated. Once a rock is heated sufficiently, its "clock" is set back to zero. That is, all its electrons have returned to their normal positions.

TL can be used on flints and other minerals that ancient humans happened to kick into their hearths or camp fires. When a piece of stone was heated in that way, its internal electron clock was set back to zero. When the rock cooled, the electron-trapping process resumed. TL has been used to date fossils of hominids that lived between 60,000 and 100,000 m.y.a. in the Middle East.

ESR doesn't use heat; it counts trapped electrons while they rest in their traps. A magnetic field is used to make the captive electrons "resonate," that is, to flip around and spin in an opposite direction. As they flip, each electron absorbs energy from a microwave field that is also applied to the sample. This energy loss can be measured, and it is a direct count of the number of electrons caught in the traps. ESR works especially well on tooth enamel. It can be used to date samples between 1,000 and 2 million years old, such as animal teeth in layers that contain human bones or artifacts. Both TL and ESR must be used carefully because radiation rates can vary, thus affecting the rate at which electrons get trapped. ESR works best in dry areas (such as the Middle East) because drier teeth absorb radioactivity at a more predictable rate than wet teeth do. Another new radiometric technique is uranium series dating, which measures the steady decay of uranium into various daughter elements inside anything formed from carbonates (limestone and cave stalactites, for example) (Shreeve 1992).

THE EMERGENCE OF THE HOMINOIDS

The ancestors of humans diverged from those of the great apes during the Miocene epoch. The evolutionary line leading to orangutans probably split off from the one leading to humans, chimps, and gorillas around 16 m.y.a. The split between humans and the African apes came much later. Drawing on the genus names *Homo, Gorilla,* and *Pan* (chimpanzee), I have coined the term **Hogopans** to refer to the ancestral population of Miocene hominoids that eventually split three ways to give rise to humans, gorillas, and chimps. Hogopans, in short, is my name for the common ancestors of humans and the African apes.

No more than 10 m.y.a. (and probably between 8 and 5 m.y.a.) the Hogopans split into three groups (Fisher 1988*a*). This split involved niche divergence, geographic separation, and reproductive isolation leading to speciation. Ancestral gorillas eventually occupied forested zones of the mountains and lowlands of equatorial Africa. They developed a diet based on leaves, shoots, and bulk vegetation. Chimps evolved into frugivores (fruit eaters) in the forests and woodlands of Central Africa. Ancestral hominids spent more time in the open grasslands, or savannas, of eastern and southern Africa.

Where are the fossils of the Hogopans? Miocene deposits in Africa, Asia, and Europe have yielded an abundance of hominoid fossils. Some of these may have evolved into modern apes and humans, but others became extinct. Hogopan identity remains a mystery. Do Hogopan fossils remain to be found? Perhaps they have been found already but haven't been generally recognized as Hogopans. (Much of the Miocene hominoid fossil record is under revision.)

Russell Ciochon (1983) distinguished between two major groups of Miocene hominoids, which he called "dryopiths" and "ramapiths." Arthur Fisher (1988*a*) makes a similar distinction but calls them "dryopithecines" and "ramapithecines." The **dryopiths** (16 to 8 m.y.a.) consisted of many species that lived in forests and were mainly arboreal. These apes evolved in Africa but expanded into Europe after 16 m.y.a. In the early Miocene a large body of water, the Tethys Sea—an enlarged Mediterranean—had separated Africa from Europe and Asia. Geological activity, continental drift, and a drier climate created a land bridge through Arabia around 16 m.y.a. (Jolly and White 1994). This allowed fauna from Africa to enter Eurasia, and vice versa. Hominoids that had evolved in Africa during the early Miocene were among the animals that spread to Eurasia. The dryopiths thrived in the subtropical woodlands of western Europe from 15 to 8 m.y.a.

The dryopiths had a lower-teeth cusp pattern (called the *dryopithecine pattern*) that distinguishes the hominoids from the Old World monkeys. The molars of Old World monkeys have only four cusps, or bumps, arranged in two parallel rows with a deep groove between them. By contrast, hominoid lower molars often have five cusps, separated by valleys, which form a contour resembling the letter Y.

The hominoids originated in Africa. The ancestors of the dryopiths probably belonged to the early Miocene **Proconsulid** group (23 to 16 m.y.a.), of which many species are known, the first having been discovered by Mary Leakey in 1948. Some Proconsulids were as large as chimps; others, as small as arboreal monkeys. The Proconsulids combined features of apes and monkeys. Their long bodies and short limbs recall the Old World monkeys, but the Proconsulids had apelike teeth (projecting, piercing, slashing canines and small molars). Canine sexual dimorphism was marked, and males might have weighed twice as much as females.

THE RAMAPITHS

Like the European dryopiths, the **ramapiths** (also known as *sivapiths*) were late Miocene hominoids (15 to 7.5 m.y.a.). The ramapiths also descend from an African ancestor and spread into Eurasia (mainly Asia) over the Arabian land bridge after 16 m.y.a. The habitat of the ramapiths wasn't mainly the forest but more open country, such as woodland, bush, grassland, and forest fringe. The oldest firmly dated ramapiths (at least 13 m.y.a.) are from the Siwalik Hills of Pakistan (foothills of the Himalayas), where ramapiths survived through 7.5 m.y.a. (Nelson and Jurmain 1991). Other fossils identified as ramapiths (illustrating a range of differently sized species) have been found in northern Greece, Hungary, Turkey, and southern China.

The first ramapith fossil, a portion of upper jaw and teeth discovered in the 1930s, was assigned to the genus *Ramapithecus.* It came from the Siwalik Hills, where excavations have by now produced the remains of more than fifty individuals. The genus name *Sivapithecus* is now preferred for those Siwalik apes, but "ramapith" has survived as a label for the entire group. Considering all sites, the ramapith fossil record consists mostly of thick-enameled teeth, rugged jaw bones, and some partial crania (skulls). Ramapith is now applied to a geographically widespread group with different genera, including *Sivapithecus* and *Gigantopithecus.*

The ramapiths were once thought to have played a central role in human evolution. Many anthropologists viewed them as the first true hominids and direct human ancestors. This opinion was based mainly on the teeth, particularly the molars. The ramapiths had sturdy jaws and teeth suitable for crunching resistant seeds, fruits, and nuts. Their molars were covered with a thick layer of enamel. This dentition seemed to suggest adaptation to a savanna niche comparable to that in which early hominids evolved. In the early hominids, such as the australopithecines (see below), large molar teeth are an adaptation to the tough, coarse, fibrous vegetation of the savanna. Such a diet requires thorough rotary chewing (up, down, and side to side) (Jolly 1970; Wolpoff 1980a). Large back teeth with thick enamel hold up against the wear and tear associated with such a diet.

The molars of the ramapiths were thick, but their canines and premolars were slashing, cutting, piercing tools, with marked sexual dimorphism. Such a mixed dentition—large and thick-enameled molars plus sharp canines and premolars—does not support the contention that the ramapiths lived in the savanna. In fact, most remains of ramapiths are associated with other fossils that suggest a mixture of forest, grassland, and woodland habitats.

The paleoanthropologists who stressed the similarities between the molars of ramapiths and those of early hominids were mistaken. The early hominids known as "australopithecines" did have large, thickly enameled molars, but so do orangutans. In-

deed, the Pakistani remains that were originally considered likely hominid ancestors have turned out to be much more similar to modern orangs, which also have molars with thick enamel. Rather than being a hominid, that ramapith (*Sivapithecus*) was probably ancestral to the orangutan.

The ramapiths ranged widely in space, time, and body size. They underwent an adaptive radiation that produced an array of hominoids of different sizes and characteristics. Some species might have averaged only 25 pounds (12 kilograms), whereas one species might have been as big as the gorilla. That species was *Gigantopithecus,* whose dentition suggests a diet of coarse foods. *Gigantopithecus* molars were huge, with thick enamel. The canines, though projecting, were worn down as they would be if the diet demanded side-to-side chewing and grinding. *Gigantopithecus* fossils from India date to 7 m.y.a., but this large ape may have survived in China until 500,000 B.P.

Some anthropologists have proposed *Gigantopithecus* as a possible hominid ancestor. However, the dentition of *Gigantopithecus* was merely hominid*like,* exemplifying convergent evolution rather than a close phylogeny. We now know that very definite hominids (the australopithecines) with few specific resemblances to *Gigantopithecus* lived in East Africa by 4 m.y.a. The earliest hominids were thus contemporaries rather than descendants of *Gigantopithecus.* The resemblances between *Gigantopithecus* and hominids must therefore be analogies, not homologies. That is, the dental similarities developed independently (exemplifying convergent evolution) among two separate hominoid groups experiencing similar dietary stresses, one (*Australopithecus*) in Africa, one (*Gigantopithecus*) in Asia.

There is another powerful reason to exclude *Gigantopithecus* (and any other Asian ape) from our ancestry. If we are to explain the many genetic and biochemical similarities between humans and the African apes, we must seek an African ancestor. One recently discovered possibility is **Afropithecus**, a large Miocene hominoid from northern Kenya, dated to 18 to 16 m.y.a. (Leakey, Leakey, and Walker 1988). The *Afropithecus* remains consist of skull, jaw, and **postcranial** (below the head) fragments. *Afropithecus* seems to have been a slow-moving arboreal ape, with robust projecting canines (similar to those of modern African apes) and large premolars. The *Afropithecus* evidence is still being interpreted, but it may find a position on the ancestral line leading to humans and the African apes. Except for *Afropithecus*, the fossil evidence for Miocene Hogopans is scant. There is, however, an abundant fossil record for the australopithecines, which had evolved in East Africa by 4 m.y.a.

THE VARIED AUSTRALOPITHECINES

Although we still don't know the exact identity of our Miocene ancestors, we do know that they evolved into a varied group of Pliocene-Pleistocene hominids known as the **australopithecines.** This term reflects their former classification as members of a distinct subfamily, the Australopithecinae. Today the distinction between the australopithecines and later hominids is made on the genus level. The australopithecines are assigned to the genus *Australopithecus (A.)*; later humans, to *Homo (H.)*.

In the scheme followed here, *Australopithecus* had four species: *A. afarensis* (4? to 3 m.y.a.), *A. africanus* (3? to 2.5? m.y.a.), *A. robustus* (2.6? to 2? m.y.a.), and *A. boisei* (2.6? to 1.2 m.y.a.). *A. afarensis*, which is clearly the earliest species, is probably ancestral to all the rest and to *Homo*, which appeared (as *H. habilis*) around 2 m.y.a. Early *Homo* then coexisted for about 800,000 years with *A. boisei*, which became extinct around 1.2 m.y.a. Thereafter *H. erectus*, our direct ancestors—creators of complex tools, cooperative hunters and gatherers—multiplied, expanded, and eventually colonized the world.

The dates given for each species are approximate and somewhat arbitrary because an organism is not a member of one species one day and a member of another species the next day. Furthermore, accurate dating may be lacking. This is particularly true for the South African australopithecines (*A. africanus* and *A. robustus*), which were discovered in a nonvolcanic area and cannot be radiometrically dated. The hominid fossils from the volcanic regions of East Africa (*A. afarensis*, *A. boisei*, *H. habilis*, and *H. erectus*) usually have radiometric dates.

Australopithecus afarensis

Fossils of the earliest definite hominids, members of our own zoological family and distinct from ancestral gorillas and chimps, were first assigned to *A. afarensis* by D. C. Johanson and T. D. White

"Lucy," a member of A. afarensis, *is shown here (upside down) with her discoverer, Dr. Donald Johanson. Lucy, who lived around 3 m.y.a., is one of the Hadar finds (from the Afar region of Ethiopia), which include remains of between thirty-five and sixty-five individuals.*

(1979). This early hominid species includes fossils found at two sites, Laetoli in northern Tanzania and Hadar in the Afar region of Ethiopia (Figure 8.2). Laetoli is earlier (3.8 to 3.6 m.y.a.). The Hadar fossils probably date to between 3.3 and 3.0 m.y.a. Possibly older hominid remains (teeth and jaw fragments) have been found at other sites, mainly in Kenya.

On the basis of the current evidence, *A. afarensis* lived between about 4 and 3 m.y.a. Research directed by Mary Leakey was responsible for the Laetoli finds. The Hadar discoveries resulted from an international expedition directed by D. C. Johanson and M. Taieb. The two sites have yielded significant samples of early hominid fossils. There are two dozen specimens from Laetoli, and the Hadar finds include the remains of between thirty-five and sixty-five individuals. The Laetoli remains are mainly teeth and jaw fragments, along with some very in-

IN THE NEWS: A POSSIBLE "MISSING LINK"

The term "missing link" survives from an old theological belief in "The Great Chain of Being." Monkeys, apes, and humans were viewed as closely linked in a chain of forms leading to Heaven. Humans, created in God's image, were seen as too special to be directly linked to the apes, so there arose a belief in a missing link, a form of life intermediate between apes and humans. From an evolutionary perspective, the term would be synonymous with the Hogopans, the most recent common ancestors of human and the African apes.

This news item describes a 1991 find, a mandible (jawbone) with teeth from a Miocene hominoid, dated to 13 million years B.P. This date is probably too early for the last Hogopans, but *Otavipithecus* may be a descendant of *Afropithecus* (18 to 16 m.y.a.), and have a place in Hogopan ancestry. This news item illustrates variant interpretations of the fossil record and alternative lines of evidence used to reconstruct hominid ancestry.

Ever since Darwin postulated a close relationship between humans and apes, scientists have found little more than false leads and true frustration in their search for the common ancestor, some "missing link" species that immediately preceded the evolutionary split giving rise to chimpanzees, gorillas and humans.

Where it counts, the period from 14 million to 4 million years ago, the fossil record is a virtual blank, a terra incognita on the map of prehuman antiquity. No one knows whether the split occurred as early as 10 million years ago or as recently as 5 million. No one has yet uncovered pre-split fossils that promise a ready resolution of the mystery.

But paleoanthropologists, who can find encouragement in the merest scraps of bone, think they may soon be able to tease some important evolutionary clues out of assorted ape-like fossil specimens that have turned up in recent years in Africa, Europe and southern Asia.

The discovery last summer of a 13-million-year-old fragment of a lower jaw has inspired a more concerted examination of these enigmatic creatures. These animals, remotely resembling Old World monkeys without tails, lived in the middle of the Miocene geological period, which extended from 24 million to 5 million years ago, and belonged to the superfamily of hominoids, which includes humans, apes and their many ancestors.

Scientists are not suggesting the jawbone represents the long-sought missing link or is necessarily part of any direct ancestral line leading to apes and humans. They concede that their task will not be easy, with only some teeth and a few bones to go on—nothing close to a full skeleton.

Dr. Glenn C. Conroy of Washington University Medical School, St. Louis, holds the jaw of Otavipithecus namibiensis, *the 13-million-year-old hominoid described in this article. From the left, the busts are of a young gorilla, a Neandertal, and a modern human.*

"It's almost like trying to identify a creature emerging from the shadows," said Dr. David Pilbeam, a paleontologist at Harvard University. "First, all you see are teeth, little else. That's about where we are, but the teeth are telling us there's a lot of diversity among these species at any given time."

The newly discovered jawbone, found in Namibia in southern Africa by a team of American and French scientists, was described in the current issue of the journal Nature as belonging to a previously unknown species of hominoids. The specimen has been named Otavipithecus namibiensis, or Otavi ape, for the Otavi Mountains where the fossil was plucked out of mine tailings.

Dr. Glenn C. Conroy, a professor of anatomy and anthropology at the Washington University Medical School in St. Louis and leader of the discovery team, said the limited evidence indicated that Otavipithecus did not closely resemble any of the other Miocene hominoids.

Otavipithecus is the first of these fossil species to be discovered south of the Equator, providing further evidence that they were more abundant, widespread and diversified than had been thought. This opens up a vast new area of Africa in which to search for these hominoid remains.

Dr. Martin Pickford, an experienced fossil hunter at the National Museum of Natural History in Paris, found the pale yellow jaw encrusted in rock. It was days before he or others in the expedition knew what they had. They soaked the rock in strong vinegar, which slowly dissolved the limestone and revealed the shape and details of a right lower jaw and three perfectly intact molars, two premolars and a root socket for a large canine tooth.

The age of the fossil was estimated on the basis of well-dated bones of small mammals found in the same rocks. From the size of the jaw, the scientists said the creature probably weighed 30 to 45 pounds. Using chimpanzee maturation as a guide, they said the teeth revealed that at the time of death the Otavipithecus was a young adult about 10 years old. The shape and wear of the teeth show that the animal fed on leaves, berries, seeds, flowers and other soft foods.

Not all scientists accept Dr. Conroy's assessment that the specimen is sufficiently unique to warrant being classified as not only a new fossil species, but a new genus as well. A genus is a more inclusive category of closely related species.

Dr. Peter Andrews, a paleontologist at the Natural History Museum in London, wrote in Nature that the jaw bears several similarities to the older hominoid Afropithecus. "More detailed examination may support the generic distinction," he said, "but on the evidence published here it would not appear to be justified."

Dr. Brenda Benefit, a paleontologist at Southern Illinois University in Carbondale who has examined the jawbone, disagreed. She noted several differences in anatomical detail between Afropithecus and Otavipithecus, concluding that they were not the same but that the first could have been ancestral to the other.

But Dr. Benefit, like others, emphasized that more fossils of Otavipithecus, including a cranium and limb bones, would be needed to determine whether it is somehow a distant ancestor of apes and humans, or simply some evolutionary dead end.

Recent studies by molecular biologists, comparing genetic material among living apes and humans, suggest that the branching of the two groups occurred 5 million to 8 million years ago. Some paleontologists suspect it was earlier, possibly 10 million years ago.

After the split, the earliest members of the line leading to humans were the australopithecines, the first of which show up in the fossil record about four million years ago. The "Lucy" specimen from Ethiopia, known formally as Australopithecus afarensis, is widely regarded as the common ancestor of all subsequent australopithecine apes, a line that became extinct about one million years ago, and the Homo genus that evolved into modern humans.

The earliest known australopithecines had already adopted bipedalism and were beginning to evolve larger brains, critical transformations that occurred back in the Miocene period at a time and for reasons still unknown.

The jawbone of Otavipithecus may clarify the issue and nudge paleontologists closer to finding the missing link between the Miocene hominoids and modern apes and humans. Or it could throw the field into even more confusion.

Source: John Noble Wilford, "Jawbone Offers Clues in Search for 'Missing Link,'" *The New York Times,* March 17, 1992, C1, C10.

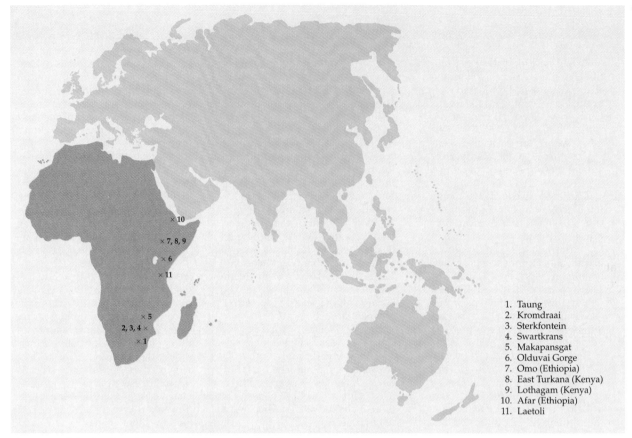

Figure 8.2 *Distribution of australopithecine and* H. habilis *fossil sites. These early hominid sites are confined to Africa. There are two clusters of sites, in South and East Africa.* A. afarensis, A. boisei, *and* H. habilis *fossils come from the East African sites. Specimens of* A. africanus *and* A. robustus *come from the South African sites.*

formative fossilized footprints. The Hadar sample includes skull fragments and postcranial material, most notably 40 percent of the complete skeleton of a tiny hominid female, dubbed "Lucy," who lived around 3 m.y.a.

Although the fossils at Laetoli and Afar were deposited perhaps half a million years apart, their many resemblances explain their placement in the same species. These finds prompted a reinterpretation of the early hominid fossil record. *A. afarensis* was clearly a hominid. However, it was also so similar in many ways to chimps and gorillas that our common ancestry with the African apes must be very recent, certainly no more than 10 m.y.a. Hominids are much closer to the apes than the previously known fossil record had suggested. Studies of the learning abilities and biochemistry of chimps and

gorillas have taught a valuable lesson about homologies that the fossil record is now confirming.

The *A. afarensis* finds make this clear. The many apelike features are surprising in definite hominids that lived as recently as 3 m.y.a. For example, the canines and premolars of *A. afarensis* had not yet been incorporated into the rotary chewing-grinding complex of the later australopithecines, whose diet was based on coarse savanna vegetation. *A. afarensis* canines are sharp and project beyond the other teeth. The lower premolar is pointed and projecting to sharpen the upper canine. It has one long cusp and one tiny bump that just hints at the bicuspid premolar that had not yet developed in hominid evolution. The first premolar had not yet been functionally incorporated into the **posterior** (back) dentition, as in the later australopithecines.

Although the molars of *A. afarensis* were smaller than those of the later australopithecines, there is evidence that powerful chewing associated with savanna vegetation was entering the *A. afarensis* feeding pattern. When the coarse, gritty, fibrous vegetation of grasslands and semidesert enters the diet, the back teeth change to accommodate heavy chewing stresses. Massive back teeth, jaws, and supporting cranial structures suggest that the diet demanded extensive grinding and powerful crushing. *A. afarensis* molars are large. The lower jaw (mandible) is thick and is buttressed with a bony ridge behind the front teeth. The cheekbones are large and flare out to the side for the attachment of powerful chewing muscles.

The skull of *A. afarensis* also contrasts with that of later hominids. The brain case is very small, with cranial capacities barely surpassing those of chimpanzees (about 400 cubic centimeters). However, the brain/body size ratio was probably larger. The form of the *A. afarensis* skull is like that of the chimpanzee.

Below the neck, however—particularly in regard to locomotion—*A. afarensis* was unquestionably human. The earliest evidence of striding bipedalism comes from Laetoli, where volcanic ash covered a trail of footprints of two or three hominids walking to a water hole. These prints leave no doubt that a small striding biped lived in Tanzania by 3.5 m.y.a. The structure of the pelvic, hip, leg, and foot bones also confirms that upright bipedalism was *A. afarensis*'s mode of locomotion.

A. afarensis still contrasts in many ways with later hominids. Sexual dimorphism is particularly obvious. Canine sexual dimorphism was less extreme in *A. afarensis* than it is in modern apes. However, the male-female contrast in jaw size in *A. afarensis* was more marked than in the orangutan. There was a similar contrast in body size. *A. afarensis* females stood between 3.5 and 4 feet (100 and 120 centimeters) tall; males might have reached 5 feet (152 centimeters). Wolpoff (1980*a*) estimates that *A. afarensis* males might have weighed twice as much as females.

However, Lucy and her kind were far from dainty. Her muscle-engraved bones are much more robust than ours. With only rudimentary tools and weapons, early hominids needed powerful and resistant bones and muscles. Lucy's arms are longer relative to her legs than are those of later hominids.

An ancient trail of hominid footprints fossilized in volcanic ash. Mary Leakey found this 70-meter trail at Laetoli, Tanzania, in 1978. It dates from 3.6 m.y.a. and confirms that A. afarensis *was a striding biped.*

Here again her proportions are more apelike than ours are. This offers further proof of our close phylogeny with the apes. Although Lucy neither brachiated nor knuckle-walked, she was probably a much better climber than modern people are.

The *A. afarensis* fossils show that between 4 and 3 m.y.a., our ancestors had a mixture of apelike and hominid features. Canines, premolars, and skulls were much more apelike than most scholars had imagined would exist in such a recent ancestor. On the other hand, the molars, chewing apparatus, and cheekbones foreshadowed later trends, and the pelvic and limb bones were indisputably hominid (Figure 8.3). *A. afarensis* was building the hominid pattern from the ground up.

Hominids walk with a striding gait that consists of alternating swing and stance phases for each leg and foot. As one leg is pushed off by the big toe and goes into the swing phase, the heel of the other leg is touching the ground and entering the stance phase. Quadrupedal locomotors such as Old World monkeys are always supported by two limbs.

Bipeds, by contrast, are supported by one limb at a time.

The pelvis, the lower spine, the hip joint, and the thigh bone (femur, plural *femora*) change in accordance with the stresses of bipedal locomotion. Australopithecine pelvises are much more similar (although far from identical) to *Homo*'s than to apes' and show adaptation to bipedalism (Figure 8.4). The blades of the australopithecine pelvis (iliac blades) are shorter and broader than those of the ape, and the sacrum, which anchors the pelvis's two side bones, is larger, as in *Homo*. With bipedalism the pelvis forms a sort of basket that balances the

Figure 8.3 *Comparison of* Homo sapiens *and* Pan troglodytes *(the common chimp): (a) skeleton of chimpanzee in bipedal position; (b) skeleton of modern human; (c) chimpanzee and human "bisected" and drawn to the same trunk length for comparison of limb proportions. The contrast in leg length is largely responsible for the proportional difference between humans and apes.*

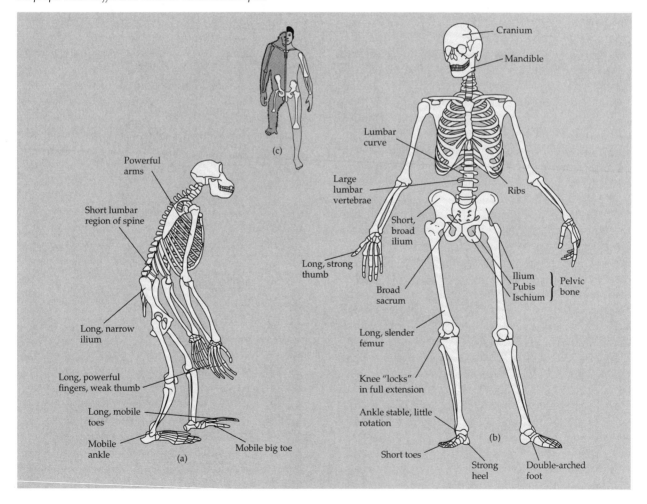

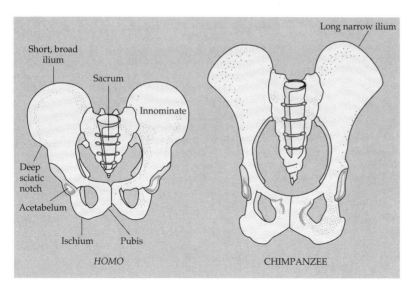

Figure 8.4 *A comparison of human and chimpanzee pelvises. The human pelvis has been modified to meet the demands of upright bipedalism. The blades (ilia; singular,* **ilium***) of the human pelvis are shorter and broader than those of the ape. The sacrum, which anchors the side bones, is wider. The australopithecine pelvis is far more similar to that of* Homo *than to that of the chimpanzee, as we would expect in an upright biped.*

weight of the trunk, supports this weight with less stress, and transmits it to the legs and feet. Fossilized spinal bones (vertebrae) show that the australopithecine spine also had the lower spine (lumbar) curve characteristic of *Homo*. This curvature helps transmit the weight of the upper body to the pelvis and the legs. Placement of the **foramen magnum** (the ''big hole'' through which the spinal cord joins the brain) farther forward in *Australopithecus* and *Homo* than in the ape also represents an adaptation to upright bipedalism (Figure 8.5).

In apes, the thigh bone extends straight down from the hip to the knees. In *Australopithecus* and *Homo*, however, the thigh bone angles into the hip, permitting the space between the knees to be narrower than the pelvis during walking. The pelvises of the australopithecines were similar but not identical to those of *Homo*. The most significant contrast is the more restricted birth canal in the australopithecines (Tague and Lovejoy 1986). Expansion of the birth canal is a trend in hominid evolution.

The width of the birth canal is related to the size of the skull and brain. *A. afarensis* had a small cranial capacity, and even in later australopithecines average brain size did not exceed 600 cubic centimeters. Undoubtedly the australopithecine skull grew after birth to accommodate a growing brain, as it does (much more) in *Homo*. However, the brains of the australopithecines expanded less than ours do. In the australopithecines the cranial sutures (the lines where the bones of the skull eventually come to-

gether) fused earlier in life relative to the eruption of the molars.

There is evidence from their patterns of molar eruption (Mann 1975) that australopithecine children, like our own, had a slower maturation rate than do the apes. Young australopithecines must have depended on their parents and kin for nurturance and protection. Those years of childhood dependency would have provided time for observation, teaching, and learning. This may provide indirect evidence for a rudimentary cultural life.

Gracile and Robust Australopithecines

The fossils assigned to *A. africanus* and *A. robustus* were discovered in South Africa. The anatomist Raymond Dart coined *Australopithecus africanus* in 1924 to describe the first fossil representative of this species, the skull of a juvenile that was discovered accidentally in a quarry at Taung, South Africa. Radiometric dates are lacking for this nonvolcanic region, but the fossil hominids found at the five main South African sites appear (from stratigraphy) to have lived between 3 and 2 m.y.a.

There were two groups of South African australopithecines—**gracile** (*A. africanus*) and **robust** (*A. robustus*). These terms are opposites. The graciles had slightly larger back teeth and a larger body than did *A. afarensis*, but they were smaller and slighter than the robusts. There were also robust australopithecines in East Africa, which I have assigned to

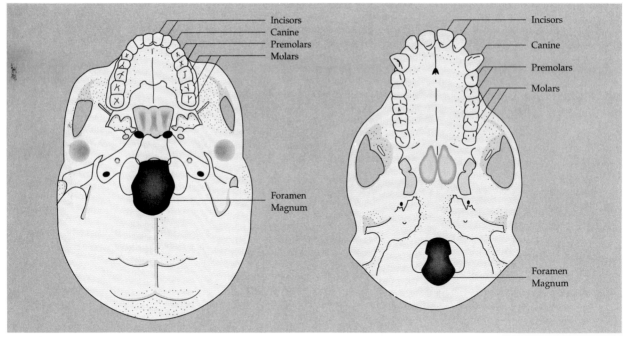

Figure 8.5 *A comparison of the skull and dentition (upper jaw) of* Homo *and the chimpanzee. The foramen magnum, through which the spinal cord joins the brain, is located farther forward in* Homo *than in the ape. This permits the head to balance atop the spine with upright bipedalism. The molars and premolars of the ape form parallel rows. Human teeth, by contrast, are arranged in rounded, parabolic form. Also note the contrast between the projecting canines of the ape and the reduced canines of the human. Canine reduction has been an important trend in hominid evolution.*

Hominid fossil skull of A. africanus, *a gracile australopithecine. The fossils assigned to* A. africanus *and* A. robustus *were discovered in South Africa and probably lived between 3 and 2 m.y.a.*

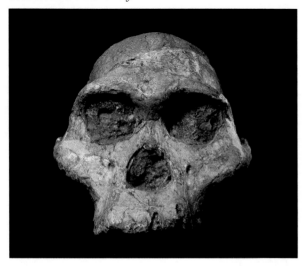

A. boisei. However, some scholars consider *A. robustus* and *A. boisei* to be regional variants of just one species, which some call *boisei* and others call *robustus.*

The relationship between the graciles and the robusts has been debated for generations but has not been resolved. Graciles and robusts probably descend from *A. afarensis* or from a South African version of *A. afarensis* that has not been found. Some scholars have argued that the graciles lived before (3 to 2.5 m.y.a.) and were ancestral to the robusts (2.5 to 2 m.y.a.). Others contend that the graciles and the robusts were separate species that overlapped in time. (Classifying them as members of different species implies that they were reproductively isolated from each other in time or space.) Other paleoanthropologists view the gracile and robust australopithecines as different ends of a continuum of variation in a single **polytypic species**—one with considerable phenotypic variation.

The trend toward enlarged back teeth, chewing muscles, and facial buttressing, which is already noticeable in *A. afarensis*, continues in the South African australopithecines. However, the canines are reduced and the premolars are fully bicuspid. Dental form and function changed as dietary needs shifted from cutting and slashing to chewing and grinding. The mainstay of the australopithecine diet was the vegetation of the savanna.

At times these early hominids might have hunted small and slow-moving game. Archeological analyses (Read-Martin and Read 1975) of animal remains at australopithecine camps suggest that these hominids scavenged, bringing home parts of kills made by large cats and other carnivores. The camp sites of early hominids in East Africa include the remains of small animals and scavenged parts of carnivores' kills. However, the ability to hunt large animals was an achievement of *Homo* and is discussed below.

The skulls, jaws, and teeth of the australopithecines leave no doubt that their diet was mainly vegetarian. Natural selection modifies the teeth to conform to the stresses associated with a particular diet. Massive back teeth, jaws, and associated facial and cranial structures reveal an australopithecine diet that required extensive grinding and powerful crushing.

In the South African australopithecines both deciduous ("baby") and permanent molars and premolars are massive and have multiple cusps. The later australopithecines had bigger back teeth than did the earlier ones. However, this evolutionary trend ended with early *Homo,* who had much smaller back teeth, reflecting a dietary change that will be described later.

Contrasts with *Homo* in regard to the front teeth are less obvious but are still of interest because of what they tell us about sexual dimorphism. *A. africanus*'s canines were more pointed, with larger roots, than *Homo*'s, although they were only 75 percent the size of those of *A. afarensis*. Despite this canine reduction, there was just as much canine sexual dimorphism in *A. africanus* as there was in *A. afarensis* (Wolpoff 1980a). Sexual dimorphism in general was much more pronounced among earlier hominids than among *H. sapiens. A. africanus* females were about 4 feet (120 centimeters), and males 5 feet (150 centimeters), tall. With massive musculature, the average male probably weighed 150

pounds (70 kilograms), compared with the female's 85 pounds (40 kilograms) (Wolpoff 1980a). (That 57 percent dimorphism contrasts with today's average female/male weight ratio of about 88 percent.)

Teeth, jaw, face, and skull changed to fit a diet based on tough, gritty, fibrous grasslands vegetation. A massive face housed large upper teeth and provided a base for the attachment of powerful chewing muscles. Australopithecine cheekbones were elongated and were massive structures (Figure 8.6) that anchored large chewing muscles running up the jaw. Another set of chewing muscles extended from the back of the jaw to the sides of the skull.

In the more robust australopithecines (*A. robustus* in South Africa and *A. boisei* in East Africa) these muscles were strong enough to produce a **sagittal crest,** a bony ridge on the top of the skull. Such a crest forms as the bone grows. It develops from the pull of the chewing muscles as they meet at the midline of the cranium.

Overall robustness, especially in the chewing apparatus, increased through time among the South African australopithecines. This trend was even more striking in *A. boisei*, in East Africa. The later australopithecines had greater overall size, larger skulls, bigger back teeth, thicker faces, more prominent crests, and more rugged muscle markings on the skeleton. By contrast, the front teeth stayed the same size.

Brain size (measured as cranial capacity) increased only slightly between *A. afarensis* and *A. africanus*. There is only a 20 percent difference between graciles (450 cubic centimeters) and robusts (550 cubic centimeters) (Wolpoff 1980a). These figures can be compared with an average cranial capacity of about 1,350 cubic centimeters in *H. sapiens.* The modern range goes from less than 1,000 cubic centimeters to more than 2,000 cubic centimeters in normal adults. Gorilla brains average around 500 cubic centimeters, about the same as australopithecine brains, but the body weight is much greater.

Casts of the inside of a skull (endocranial casts) provide information about the brain's size, proportions, and shape and the areas devoted to particular functions—such as motor activities, speech, memory, sensory integration, and vision. The brain organization of *A. africanus* was essentially human (Holloway 1974/1975). Australopithecine endocranial casts are more human than apelike, as we

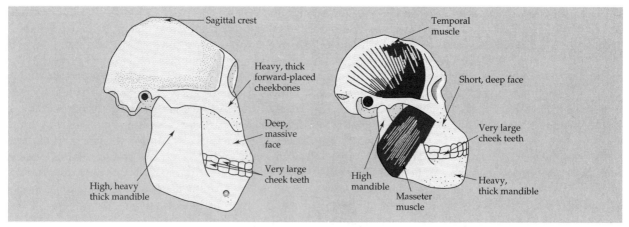

Figure 8.6 *Skulls of robust (left) and gracile (right) australopithecines, showing chewing muscles—temporals and masseters. Flaring cheek arches and, in some robusts, a sagittal crest supported this massive musculature. The early hominid diet—coarse, gritty vegetation of the savanna—demanded such structures. These features were most pronounced in* A. boisei.

would expect in an organism that relied more on learning, memory, and intellectual association.

Given the tool-making and language-learning abilities of the apes, there is no reason to doubt that the australopithecines relied on rudimentary cultural means of adaptation. Animal bones that are sharpened and scratched, as they might have been if used for digging, were found at one South African australopithecine site. The earliest known stone tools come from East Africa, with radiometric dates of 2 to 2.5 m.y.a. Additional evidence for early hominid tool use and manufacture is discussed below.

DIVERGENCE: AUSTRALOPITHECINES END, *HOMO* BEGINS

Sometime between 3 and 2 m.y.a. the ancestors of *Homo* split off and became reproductively isolated from the ancestors of the later australopithecines, such as *A. boisei,* which coexisted with *Homo* until around 1.2 m.y.a.

The first evidence for speciation is dental. The fossil sample of hominid teeth dated to 2 m.y.a. has two clearly different sizes of teeth. One set is huge, the largest molars and premolars in hominid evolution; these teeth belong to *A. boisei.* The other group of (smaller) teeth belonged to our ancestor, *H. habilis,* the first exemplar of the genus *Homo.*

By 1.6 m.y.a. the difference had become even more obvious. Two hominid groups occupied different ecological niches in Africa. One, *Homo*—by then *H. erectus*—had a larger brain and a reproportioned skull; it had increased the areas of the brain that regulate higher mental functions. These were our ancestors, hominids with greater capacities for culture than the australopithecines had. *H. erectus* hunted and gathered, made sophisticated tools, and eventually displaced its sole surviving cousin species, *A. boisei.*

A. boisei of East Africa, the hyperrobust australopithecines, had mammoth posterior teeth, which fit into a skull hardly bigger than those of the late robust australopithecines of South Africa. By the time of *H. erectus, A. boisei* females had bigger back teeth than did earlier australopithecine males. *A. boisei* became ever more specialized with respect to one part of the traditional australopithecine dietary pattern. *A. boisei* concentrated on coarse vegetation with a high grit content until it became extinct around 1.2 m.y.a.

The geographic separation and reproductive isolation that led to speciation between *A. boisei* and early *Homo* took time. And why, if two new *species* were forming, is one of them assigned to a new genus, *Homo?* This classification is done in retrospect, since we know that one species survived and evolved into a contemporary descendant whereas

Palates of Homo sapiens *(left) and* A. boisei *(right), late, hyperrobust australopithecine (L. S. B. Leakey's "Zinjanthropus" find). In comparing them, note the australopithecine's huge molars and premolars. This posterior dentition is an extreme adaptation to a diet based on coarse, gritty savanna vegetation. Note, too, that reduction in tooth size during human evolution applied to the back teeth much more than the front. The teeth of early* Homo (habilis *and* erectus) *were, however, still larger than contemporary humans'.*

the other one became extinct. Hindsight shows us their very different lifeways, which suggest their placement in different genera.

We still don't know why, how, and exactly when niche divergence took place. Scholars have defended many different models, or theoretical schemes, to interpret the early hominid fossil record (Figure 8.7). Because new finds have so often forced reappraisals, most scientists are willing to modify their interpretation when given new evidence.

The model of Johanson and White (1979), who coined the term *A. afarensis*, proposes that *A. afarensis* split into two groups. One group, the ancestors of *Homo*, became reproductively isolated from other hominids between 3 and 2 m.y.a. This group appeared as **H. habilis,** a term coined by L. S. B. and Mary Leakey for the first members of the genus *Homo* and the immediate ancestors of *H. erectus*. *H. habilis* lived between 2 m.y.a. and about 1.6 m.y.a., by which time it had evolved into *H. erectus*. Other members of *A. afarensis* evolved into the various kinds of australopithecines (*A. africanus, A. ro-*

bustus, and finally hyperrobust *A. boisei,* which became extinct). Wolpoff (1980*a*) proposed a simpler model in which the more gracile australopithecines gave rise to *Homo,* while the more robust forms evolved into *A. boisei.*

In summer 1985 Alan Walker, a paleontologist and professor of anatomy at Johns Hopkins University, made a particularly significant find near Lake Turkana in northern Kenya. Called the "black skull" because of the blue-black sheen it bore from the minerals surrounding it, the fossil displayed a "baffling combination of features" (Fisher 1988*a*). The jaw was apelike and the brain was small (as in *A. afarensis*), but there was a massive bony crest atop the skull (as in *A. boisei*). Walker and Richard Leakey (Walker's associate on the 1985 expedition) view the black skull (dated to 2.5 m.y.a.) as a very early hyperrobust *A. boisei,* 300,000 years older than the oldest *boisei* previously known. Others (e.g., Jolly and White 1994) assign the "black skull" to its own species, *A. aethiopicus.*

The black skull forced a reappraisal of the early

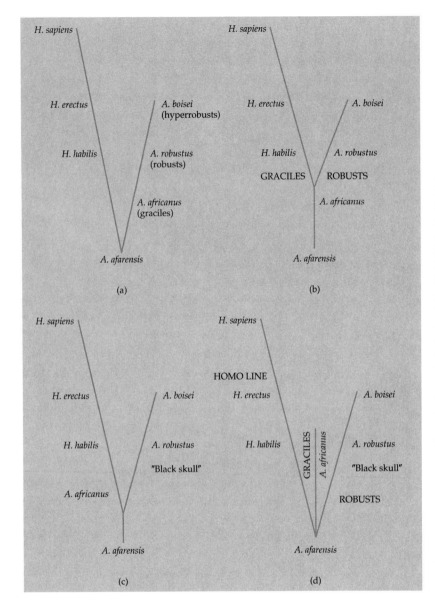

Figure 8.7 *Alternative models of early hominid phylogeny. Scheme (a) assumes an early split between australopithecines and* Homo. *Only* A. afarensis *is regarded as our ancestor. After the split between early* Homo *and* A. africanus, *the latter evolves into robust and then hyperrobust australopithecines.* Homo *evolves through* habilis *to* erectus *to* sapiens. *Scheme (b) views both* A. afarensis *and* A. africanus *as ancestral to* Homo. A. afarensis *evolves into* A. africanus. *There is a split between graciles (still classified as* A. africanus) *and robusts (*A. robustus). *Graciles evolve into* Homo. *Robusts evolve into* A. boisei. *Scheme (c), which takes the black skull into account, makes it ancestral to* A. robustus *and* A. boisei. *The more gracile* A. africanus *is assumed to be ancestral to* Homo. *Scheme (d) also takes the black skull into account.* A. afarensis *diverges into three groups: the ancestors of* Homo, *the ancestors of the robusts (including the black skull,* A. robustus, *and* A. boisei), *and the gracile australopithecines (*A. africanus). *The last two groups eventually became extinct.*

hominid fossil record. Its existence implies that the gracile australopithecines were contemporaries, rather than ancestors, of the robust australopithecines. Both probably descended from *A. afarensis.* The black skull shows that some of the anatomic features of the robust australopithecines (2.6 to 1.2 m.y.a.) didn't change very much during more than a million years. At the same time, there was an increase in brain size in the robust lineage.

How might the black skull fit into hominid phylogeny? One possibility is that it was ancestral to *A. robustus* and *A. boisei,* whereas the (more gracile)

A. africanus was ancestral to *Homo.* Another possibility is that *A. afarensis* diverged into three main groups: (1) the ancestors of *Homo,* (2) the ancestors of the robusts (including the black skull, *A. robustus,* and *A. boisei),* and (3) the gracile australopithecines (*A. africanus*). The last two groups eventually became extinct.

Regardless of when the divergence between *Homo* and the australopithecines took place, there is good fossil evidence that *Homo* and *A. boisei* coexisted in East Africa. *A. boisei* continued the australopithecine trend toward a powerful chewing apparatus with-

The "black skull," dated to 2.5 m.y.a., was discovered by Alan Walker in 1985 near Lake Turkana in northern Kenya. It gets its name from the blue-black sheen it acquired from the minerals surrounding it. The jaw is apelike and the brain is small (as in A. afarensis), but there is a massive bony crest atop the skull (as in A. boisei). The black skull shows that some of the anatomic features of the robust australopithecines (2.6 to 1.2 m.y.a.) didn't change very much during more than a million years.

example, the cranial capacity of one of the Turkana *erectus* skulls is 900 cubic centimeters, far above the *A. boisei* average.

Another important find was made in 1986 by Tim White of the University of California at Berkeley. OH62 (Olduvai Hominid 62) was the partial skeleton of a female *H. habilis* from Olduvai Bed I. This was the first find of a *H. habilis* skull with a significant amount of skeletal material. OH62, dating to 1.8 m.y.a., consists of parts of the skull, the right arm, and both legs.

This fossil was surprising because of its small size and apelike limb bones. Scientists had assumed that *H. habilis* would be taller than Lucy (*A. afarensis*), moving gradually in the direction of *H. erectus*, somewhere between Lucy's three feet and the five to six feet of *H. erectus*. However, not only was OH62 just as small as Lucy, its arms were longer and more apelike than expected, suggesting greater tree-climbing ability than later hominids had. *H. habilis* may still have sought occasional refuge in the trees.

out developing an increased cranial capacity, as *Homo* did. *A. boisei* seems to have lived in very arid areas, feeding on harder-to-chew vegetation than had any previous hominid. This diet would explain the hyperrobusts' huge back teeth, jaws, and associated areas of the face and skull.

There have been fossil finds of *H. habilis* (2.0 to 1.6 m.y.a.) in Tanzania and Kenya. The Leakeys coined the term *H. habilis* to describe very early members of our genus first found at Olduvai Gorge in Tanzania. Olduvai's oldest layer, Bed I, dated to 1.8 m.y.a., has yielded both small-brained *A. boisei* fossils and *H. habilis* skulls with cranial capacities between 600 and 700 cubic centimeters. A similarly dated skull found by Richard Leakey at East Turkana, Kenya (KNM-ER 1470), seems to be transitional between some kind of australopithecine and *H. habilis*. It combines a massive face and jaw with a cranial capacity between 750 and 800 cubic centimeters, well outside the australopithecine range of variation.

Also in deposits near Lake Turkana, Richard Leakey uncovered two *H. erectus* skulls dating to between 1.6 and 1.5 m.y.a. There is fossil evidence that *A. boisei* lived at the same time in the Turkana region. The anatomical contrast between early *H. erectus* and late *Australopithecus* is obvious. For

(Gary Larson)

Anthro horror films

IS EVOLUTION GRADUAL OR RAPID?

Does evolution occur gradually or in "punctuated equilibria"? Charles Darwin was a gradualist, maintaining that life forms arise from others in a gradual and orderly fashion. Small modifications accumulate over the generations and add up to major changes after millions of years. Gradualists cite intermediate fossils as evidence for their position, contending that there would be even more transitional forms if it weren't for gaps in the fossil record.

Advocates of the newer punctuated equilibrium model (see Eldredge 1985) believe that long periods of equilibrium, during which species change little, are interrupted (punctuated) by sudden changes—evolutionary jumps. One reason for leaps in the fossil record may be extinction followed by invasion by a closely related species. For example, a sea species may die out when a shallow body of water dries up, while a closely related species will survive in deeper waters. Later, when the sea reinvades the first locale, the protected species will extend its range to the first area. Another possibility is that when barriers are removed, a group may replace, rather than suc-

ceed, a related one because it has a trait that makes it adaptively superior in the environment they now share.

When a major environmental change occurs suddenly, one possibility is for the pace of evolution to increase. Another possibility is extinction. The earth has witnessed several mass extinctions—worldwide ecosystemic catastrophes that affect multiple species. The biggest one divided the era of "ancient life" (the Paleozoic) from the era of "middle life" (the Mesozoic). This mass extinction occurred 245 m.y.a., when 4.5 million of the earth's estimated 5 million species (mostly invertebrates) were wiped out. The second biggest extinction, which occurred 65 million years ago, destroyed the dinosaurs and many other Mesozoic species. One explanation for the extinction of the dinosaurs is that a massive, long-lasting cloud of gas and dust arose from the impact of a huge meteorite. The cloud blocked solar radiation and therefore photosynthesis, ultimately destroying most plants and the chain of animals that fed on them.

The hominid fossil record exem-

plifies both gradual and rapid change, confirming that evolution can be faster or slower depending on the rate of environmental change, the speed with which geographic barriers rise or fall, and the value of the group's adaptive response. Australopithecine teeth and skulls show some gradual transitions. For example, some of the fossils that are intermediate between *Australopithecus* and early *Homo* combine a larger brain (characteristic of *Homo*) with huge back teeth and supportive structures (characteristic of the australopithecines). However, there is no doubt that the pace of hominid evolution sped up around 1.8 m.y.a. This spurt resulted in the emergence (in just 200,000 years) of *H. erectus*. This was followed by a long period of relative stability. The probable key to the rapid emergence of *H. erectus* was a dramatic change in adaptive strategy: greater reliance on hunting through improved tools and other cultural means of adaptation. The new economy, tools, and phenotype arose and spread rapidly, then remained fairly stable for about 1 million years.

The small size and primitive proportions were unexpected because of what was known about early *H. erectus* in East Africa: By 1.6 m.y.a. *H. erectus* had already attained modern body shape and height. A young male *H. erectus* fossil (WT15,000) found at West Turkana in 1984 by Kimoya Kimeu, a collaborator of the Leakey family, has confirmed this. WT15,000 was a twelve-year-old male who had already reached 168 cm (5 feet 5 inches). He might have grown to 6 feet had he lived.

The sharp anatomic contrast between OH62 (1.8 m.y.a.) and early *H. erectus* (1.6 m.y.a.) suggests a marked acceleration in hominid evolution during

that 200,000-year period. This fossil evidence supports a punctuated equilibrium model of the early hominid fossil record (see box). In this view long periods of equilibrium, during which species change little, are interrupted (punctuated) by sudden changes—evolutionary jumps. Apparently hominids changed very little below the neck between Lucy (*A. afarensis*) and *H. habilis*. Then, between 1.8 and 1.6 m.y.a., a profound change—an evolutionary leap—took place. *H. erectus* looks much more human than *H. habilis* does.

Some of the notable contrasts between *Australopithecus* and *Homo* skulls are associated with changes in dentition. The back teeth of *H. erectus* are smaller and the front teeth relatively larger than australopithecine teeth. The front teeth of *H. erectus* were used to pull, twist, and grip. A massive ridge over the eyebrows provided protection against the forces exerted in these activities.

As hunting became more important to *H. erectus* groups, encounters between hominids and large game animals increased. Individuals with stronger skulls had better-protected brains and better survival rates. Given the dangers associated with larger prey, certain areas thickened for better protection. The base of the skull expanded dramatically, with a ridge of spongy bone across the back, for the attachment of massive neck muscles. The frontal and parietal (side) areas of the skull also increased, indicating expansion in those key areas of the brain. Finally, cranial capacity expanded from between 450 and 550 cubic centimeters among the australopithecines to an average of 1,000 cubic centimeters, which is within the modern range of variation.

TOOLS

Homo's increasing hunting proficiency might have forced *A. boisei* into becoming an increasingly spe-cialized vegetarian. Tool making might have had something to do with the split. The simplest obviously manufactured tools were discovered in 1931 by L. S. B. and Mary Leakey at Olduvai Gorge. This site gave the tools their name—**Oldowan pebble tools**. The oldest tools from Olduvai, about 1.8 million years old, were found in Bed I, and Richard Leakey has found tools that old at East Turkana. Still older (2.5 to 2 m.y.a.) tools have been found in the Omo River Valley of Ethiopia and, more recently, in Zaire and Malawi.

Pebble tools (Figure 8.8) are pieces of stone about the size of a tennis ball. Flakes were struck off both sides to form a cutting edge. Stone is more durable than is bone, horn, or wood, so that early tools made of those materials are less likely to have survived. Early hominids probably also used tools they did not make, for example, naturally chipped or cracked rock cores or flakes. We can tell that early pebble tools were manufactured because their cutting edges are flaked on both sides, whereas rocks that are fractured by natural forces usually have flakes removed from just one side. Other evidence for manufacture is that some tools were made from rocks that were not locally available. They must have been brought to the site from elsewhere (Isaac 1978).

Figure 8.8 *Evolution in tool making. Finds at Olduvai and elsewhere show how pebble tools (the first tool at the left) gradually evolved into the Acheulian hand ax of* H. erectus. *This drawing begins with an Oldowan pebble tool and moves through crude hand axes to fully developed Acheulian tools. The oldest tools date back more than 2 m.y.a. With the split between* Homo (habilis, *then* erectus) *and* A. boisei, *stone-tool manufacture rapidly grew more sophisticated. The Acheulian techniques of* H. erectus *are described in the following chapter.*

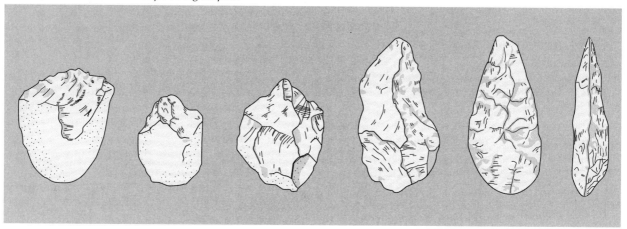

At the early hominid site of Koobi Fora, East Turkana, Kenya, the anthropologist John Shea demonstrates how H. habilis or H. erectus might have made early stone tools.

Scholars have debated the identity of the first tool makers, with some arguing for *Homo* and others arguing for the australopithecines. A recent *H. habilis* find, tentatively assigned the very early date of 2.4 m.y.a., places *Homo* near the origin of tool making. However, I suspect that the australopithecines could also have made crude tools. A series of anatomic features strongly suggest the existence of australopithecine culture. These include upright locomotion and evidence of a long period of infant and childhood dependency. Upright bipedalism would have permitted the use of tools and weapons against predators and competitors in an open grassland habitat. Bipedal locomotion also allowed early hominids to carry things, such as scavenged parts of carnivore kills. We know that primates have generalized abilities to adapt through learning. It would be amazing if the australopithecines, who are much more closely related to us than the apes are, did not have even greater cultural abilities than contemporary apes have.

However, tool making did get more sophisticated after *Homo* appeared. Significant changes in tools and camp sites took place during the 200,000-year evolutionary spurt between Bed I and lower Bed II at Olduvai. Out of the crude tools in Bed I evolved better-made and more varied tools. Edges were straighter, for example, and differences in form suggest functional differentiation—that is, the tools were being made and used for different jobs.

The efficiency of hunting also increased dramatically between 1.8 and 1.6 m.y.a. as *H. habilis*

evolved into *H. erectus.* Bed II Oldowan deposits, for example, contain bones from the whole skeletons of large game animals rather than only the bones that predators would have left. This means that *Homo* was hunting bigger game than previously and was no longer just scavenging the kills of large cats while hunting small and slow animals.

The more sophisticated tools aided in hunting and gathering. With the new tools *Homo* could obtain meat on a more regular basis and process seeds, tubers, nuts, and roots more efficiently. New tools that could batter, crush, and pulp coarse vegetation also reduced chewing demands. This technology made *Homo* competitive with the big-toothed *A. boisei* on the margins of the savanna.

H. erectus gradually increased its reliance on sociocultural adaptive means: hunting cooperatively, sharing the spoils of the hunt, controlling fire, and changing the techniques of food preparation—conceivably, though we can't say when, through cooking. With changes in the types of foods consumed, the burden on the chewing apparatus eased. The chewing muscles were less developed, and supporting structures such as the jaws and cranial crests were also reduced. With less chewing, jaws developed less, and so there was no place to put large teeth. Teeth form before they erupt and are in use. Since teeth are under stricter genetic control than jaw size and bone size are—that is, dietary stresses during growth affect jaws and bone but do not affect tooth size—natural selection began to operate against the genes that caused large teeth. In smaller jaws, large teeth now caused dental crowding, impaction, pain, sickness, fever, and sometimes death (there were no dentists).

Because of increasing reliance on hunting, tool making, and other cultural abilities, *H. erectus* eventually became the most efficient exploiter of the savanna niche. The last surviving members of *A. boisei* were forced into marginal niches. The relationship between *H. erectus* and *A. boisei* illustrates the ecological principle of **competitive exclusion**: If two similar species exploit the same ecological niche, any advantage on the part of one of them, even though minor, will eventually force the other from that niche.

Competitive exclusion may lead to niche divergence, as apparently happened with early *Homo* and the australopithecines, or it may lead to extinction. *A. boisei* eventually did become extinct, probably as *H. erectus*, becoming ever more adaptable to a variety of niches, extended its range even to the marginal environments in which *A. boisei* had managed to hold out.

Around 1 m.y.a. a single species of hominid, *H. erectus*, not only had rendered other hominid forms extinct but also was expanding the hominid range to Asia and Europe. An essentially human strategy of adaptation, incorporating hunting as a fundamental ingredient of a generalized foraging economy, had emerged. Despite regional variation, it was to be the basic economy for our genus until 10,000 years ago. We turn now to the fossils, tools, and life pattern of *H. erectus*.

SUMMARY

Anthropologists and paleontologists use stratigraphy and radiometric techniques to date fossils. Hominids have lived during the Pliocene (5 to 2 m.y.a.) and Pleistocene (2 m.y.a. to 10,000 B.P.) epochs. Carbon-14 (^{14}C) dating is most effective with fossils less than 40,000 years old. Potassium-argon (K/A) dating can be used for fossils older than 0.5 million years. ^{238}U can be used for even older fossils. ^{14}C dating is done on organic matter, whereas the K/A and ^{238}U dating techniques are used to analyze minerals that lie below and above fossils. TL and ESR can be used, respectively, to date rocks and teeth from the period between 40,000 and 500,000 B.P.

Anthropologists have yet to identify the fossils of the Hogopans, the common ancestors of humans, gorillas, and chimps. However, biochemical evidence strongly suggests that the Hogopans lived in Africa during the late Miocene.

The Miocene hominoids (dryopiths and ramapiths) evolved in Africa. After 16 m.y.a. they were able to spread into Eurasia. The dryopiths (16 to 8 m.y.a.) were arboreal and lived mainly in the forests of Europe. The ramapiths (15 to 7.5 m.y.a.) of Asia and Eastern Europe retained the slashing canines of earlier hominoids but had larger molars. The original Ramapithecus (now called *Sivapithecus*) find from the Siwalik Hills of Pakistan was once viewed as a likely hominid ancestor but is now considered ancestral to the orangutan. The dental similarities between *Gigantopithecus* and *Homo* are analogies rather than homologies. *Afropithecus*, a possible early Hogopan, lived in eastern Africa between 18 and 16 m.y.a.

The australopithecines had evolved by 4 m.y.a. The four species of *Australopithecus* were *A. afarensis* (4 to 3 m.y.a.), *A. africanus* (3 to 2.5 m.y.a.), *A. robustus* (2.6 to 2 m.y.a.), and *A. boisei* (2.6 to 1.2 m.y.a.). Early *Homo*, *H. habilis* (2 to 1.6 m.y.a.), evolved into *H. erectus* (1.6 m.y.a. to 300,000 B.P.). The earliest identifiable hominid remains come from Hadar, Ethiopia, and Laetoli, Tanzania. These fossils, classified as *A. afarensis*, suggest that the common ancestor of humans and the African apes lived more recently than had been thought. This conclusion was reached because *A. afarensis* had many primitive features, including slashing canines, elongated premolars, a small apelike skull, and marked sexual dimorphism. Still, *A. afarensis* was unquestionably a hominid. This is confirmed by its large molars and, most important, by skeletal evidence for upright bipedalism.

Remains of two groups, *A. africanus* (graciles) and *A. robustus* (robusts), were first found in South Africa. Both groups show the australopithecine trend toward a powerful chewing apparatus. They had large molars and premolars and large and robust faces, skulls, and muscle markings. All these features are more pronounced in the robusts than they are in the graciles. The basis of the australopithecine diet was savanna vegetation, but these early hominids also hunted small animals and scavenged the kills of predators.

By 2 m.y.a. there is ample evidence for two distinct hominid groups. One was *A. boisei*, the hyperrobust australopithecines, which eventually became extinct around 1.2 m.y.a. *A. boisei* became increasingly specialized, dependent on tough, coarse, gritty, fibrous savanna vegetation. The australopithecine trend toward dental, facial, and cranial robustness continued with *A. boisei*, but these structures were reduced as *H. habilis* rapidly evolved into *H. erectus*. *H. erectus* generalized the subsistence quest to the hunting of large animals to supplement the gathering of vegetation and scavenging. *H. erectus*, our ancestor, had smaller back teeth but larger front teeth and supporting structures, including a massive eyebrow ridge. Spongy bone at the rear of the skull and rugged bones offered protection when *H. erectus* hunted large animals.

Pebble tools dating to between 2.5 and 2 m.y.a. have been found in Ethiopia, Zaire, and Malawi. Scientists dis-agree about their maker, some arguing that only early *Homo* could have made them. The position taken here is that the australopithecines probably had a rudimentary capacity for culture and could have made pebble tools. However, cultural abilities developed exponentially with *Homo*'s appearance and evolution.

GLOSSARY

Afropithecus: Possible Hogopan, a Miocene ape dating to 18 to 16 m.y.a.; found in northern Kenya.

australopithecines: Varied group of Pliocene-Pleistocene hominids. The term is derived from their former classification as members of a distinct subfamily, the Australo-pithecinae; now they are distinguished from *Homo* only at the genus level.

Cenozoic: Era of recent life—birds and mammals.

chronology: Time frame, sequence.

competitive exclusion: Ecological principle that if two similar species exploit the same ecological niche, any advantage on the part of one of them, even though minor, will eventually force the other from that niche.

dryopiths: Miocene hominoids (16 to 8 m.y.a.); inhabited forests, primarily arboreal. Confined at first to Africa, they eventually expanded into Western Europe.

electron spin resonance (ESR): A radiometric dating technique that uses a magnetic field to "spin," and a microwave field to count, trapped electrons, particularly in teeth; ESR can be used for samples from 1,000 to 2 million years old and is most reliable for samples found in arid areas.

foramen magnum: "Big hole" through which the spinal cord joins the brain; located farther forward in *Austra-lopithecus* and *Homo* than in apes.

glacials: The four or five major advances of continental ice sheets in northern Europe and North America.

gracile: Opposite of robust.

Hogopans: The ancestral population of Miocene hominoids that eventually split three ways to give rise to humans, gorillas, and chimps; derived from the genus names *Homo*, *Gorilla*, and *Pan* (chimpanzee).

Homo habilis: Term coined by L. S. B. and Mary Leakey; immediate ancestor of *H. erectus*; lived from about 2 to 1.7 or 1.6 m.y.a.

interglacials: Extended warm periods between such major glacials as Riss and Würm.

interstadials: Brief warm periods during a glacial; not to be confused with the longer interglacials.

Mesozoic: Era of middle life—reptiles, including the dinosaurs.

m.y.a.: Million years ago.

Oldowan pebble tools: Earliest (2 to 2.5 m.y.a.) stone tools; first discovered in 1931 by L. S. B. and Mary Leakey at Olduvai Gorge.

paleontology: Study of ancient life through the fossil record.

Paleozoic: Era of ancient life—fishes, amphibians, and primitive reptiles.

Pleistocene: Epoch of *Homo*'s appearance and evolution; began 2 million years ago; divided into Lower, Middle, and Upper.

polytypic species: Species with considerable phenotypic variation.

postcranial: Below the head; the skeleton.

posterior: Back; for example, posterior or back denti-tion—premolars and molars.

proconsulids: Varied group of early Miocene hominoids (23 to 16 m.y.a.).

radiometric: Dating technique that measures radioactive decay.

ramapiths: Miocene hominoids (15 to 7.5 m.y.a.); of Asia and Eastern Europe; lived in more open country (woodland, bush, and savanna) than the dryopiths did.

robust: Strong, sturdy; said of skull, skeleton, muscle, and teeth; opposite of gracile.

sagittal crest: Bony ridge atop the skull that forms as bone grows; develops from the pull of chewing muscles as they meet at the midline of the cranium.

stratigraphy: Science that examines the ways in which earth sediments are deposited in demarcated layers known as *strata* (singular, *stratum*).

taphonomy: The study of the processes—biological and geological—by which dead animals become fossils; from the Greek *taphos*, which means "tomb."

thermoluminescence (TL): A radiometric dating technique based on heating a mineral sample, which then releases trapped electrons that have accumulated in that rock since it was last heated; the burst of light (luminescence) that occurs when the sample is heated is a measure of the trapped electrons and provides a date; TL can be used for materials less than 500,000 and more than 50,000 years old.

tundra: Cold, treeless plains.

Würm: The last glacial; began around 75,000 B.P. and ended between 17,000 and 12,000 B.P.

STUDY QUESTIONS

1. Why is paleoanthropology a speculative field?
2. What techniques do scientists use to determine the date of a fossil? To what time periods and kinds of materials do the different methods apply?
3. Who were the Hogopans, when and where did they live, and what is the fossil evidence for their existence?
4. What were the main groups of Miocene hominoids, and where did they live?
5. What anatomic characteristics distinguish the hominids from the apes?
6. How many species of australopithecines were there? Where and when did they live?
7. What are three different models for the phylogenetic relationships among the early hominids, from *Australopithecus* to *Homo*?
8. What were the two early species of *Homo*, and what were the main differences between them?
9. What evidence supports a punctuated equilibrium model of early hominid evolution?
10. What is the significance of the black skull?
11. What is the evidence for early hominid tool making? What are the reasons for thinking that the australopithecines could have made tools?
12. What factors led to the emergence of the genus *Homo*?

SUGGESTED ADDITIONAL READING

BRACE, C. L.
  1991 *The Stages of Human Evolution.* 4th ed. Englewood Cliffs, NJ: Prentice-Hall. Brief introduction to the hominid fossil record.

CAMPBELL, B. G.
  1988 *Humankin' Emerging.* 5th ed. Glenview, IL: Scott, Foresman. Well-illustrated survey of physical anthropology, particularly the fossil record.

CIOCHON, R. L., AND R. S. CORRUCCINI, EDS.
  1983 *New Interpretations of Ape and Human Ancestry.* New York: Plenum. Thirty articles, particularly useful on Miocene fossils.

COLE, S.
  1975 *Leakey's Luck: The Life of Louis Bazett Leakey, 1903–1972.* New York: Harcourt Brace Jovanovich. The personal and professional life of anthropology's greatest fossil finder, written by an archeologist.

FISHER, A.
  1988a The More Things Change. *Mosaic* 19(1): 22–33.
  1988b On the Emergence of Humanness. *Mosaic* 19(1): 34–45. Two readable special reports on recent discoveries and interpretations of human evolution.

JOHANSON, D. C., AND M. EDEY
  1981 *Lucy: The Origins of Humankind.* New York: Simon & Schuster. Popular account, written for a general audience, of Johanson's Ethiopian research that uncovered *A. afarensis.*

JOLLY, C., AND R. WHITE
  1994 New York: McGraw-Hill. Up-to-date text.

NELSON, H., AND R. JURMAIN
  1991 *Introduction to Physical Anthropology.* 5th ed. St. Paul, MN: West. This basic text in biological anthropology includes an extended discussion of primate and hominid evolution.

WASHBURN, S. L., AND R. MOORE
  1980 *Ape into Human: A Study of Human Evolution.* 2nd ed. Boston: Little, Brown. Revision of an engaging view of the fossil record.

WEISS, M. L., AND A. E. MANN
  1989 *Human Biology and Behavior: An Anthropological Perspective.* 5th ed. Glenview, IL: Scott, Foresman. Basic biological anthropology textbook includes discussion of the fossil record.

WOLPOFF, M. H.
  1980 *Paleoanthropology.* New York: McGraw-Hill. Excellent introduction to the hominid and prehominid fossil record.

CHAPTER 9

THE EMERGENCE OF MODERN HUMANS

iological and cultural advances enabled *Homo erectus* to exploit a new adaptive strategy—gathering *and* hunting. *H. erectus* pushed the hominid range beyond Africa—to Asia and ultimately to Europe. Small groups broke off from larger ones and moved a few miles away. They foraged new tracts of edible vegetation, carved out new hunting territories, and started harvesting the resources of the seashore as well as those of the savanna. Through population growth and dispersal *H. erectus* gradually spread and changed. By 500,000 years ago hominids were following an essentially human life style based on hunting and gathering. This basic pattern survived until recently in marginal areas of the world, although it is now fading rapidly.

This chapter covers a large span of human history. It begins more than 2 million years ago, with the transition from *Australopithecus* to *Homo*. It ends in the less distant past, when people physically similar to modern Western Europeans were painting artistic masterpieces on cave walls in France and Spain. We focus in this chapter on the biological and cultural changes that led from early *H. erectus*, through intermediate forms, to anatomically modern humans—*Homo sapiens sapiens*. Our subject matter here is that million-plus-year period of early human history, the era of hunting and gathering, before people started controlling the reproduction of plants and animals and living in villages, towns, and cities.

PALEOLITHIC TOOLS

Interrelated cultural and biological changes distinguish *H. erectus* from the australopithecines. The stone tool-making techniques that evolved out of the Oldowan, or pebble tool, tradition and lasted until about 15,000 years ago are described by the term **Paleolithic** (from Greek roots meaning "old" and "stone"). The Paleolithic, or Old Stone Age, has three divisions: Lower (early), Middle, and Upper (late). Each part is roughly associated with a particular stage in human evolution. The Lower Paleolithic is associated with *H. erectus*, the Middle Paleolithic with archaic *H. sapiens*, including the Neandertals of Western Europe and the Middle East, and the Upper Paleolithic with early members of our own subspecies, *H. sapiens sapiens*, anatomically modern humans.

The best stone tools are made from rocks such as flint that fracture sharply and in predictable ways when hammered. Quartz, quartzite, chert, and obsidian are also suitable. Each of the three main divisions of the Paleolithic had its typical **tool-making traditions**—coherent patterns of tool manufacture. The main Lower Paleolithic tool-making tradition was the **Acheulian**, named after the French village of St. Acheul, where it was first identified.

Like the earlier Oldowan tools, the characteristic Acheulian tool, the hand ax, consisted of a modified core of rock (Figure 8.8, p. 167). Flakes removed from the core when it was struck with a hammerstone were sometimes reworked to make smaller tools with finer cutting edges. Flakes became progressively more important later in human evolution, particularly in Middle and Upper Paleolithic tool making.

Acheulian tools were an advance over pebble tools in several ways. Early hominids had made simple tools by picking up pebbles the size of tennis balls and chipping off a few flakes from one end to form a rough and irregular edge. They used these pebble tools for a variety of purposes. The Acheulian technique involved chipping the core all over rather than at one end only. The core was converted from a round piece of rock into a flattish oval hand ax about 15 centimeters (6 inches) long. Its cutting edge was far superior to that of the pebble tool.

Hand axes were used to dig edible roots and other foods from the ground. Hunters made tools with a sharper cutting edge to skin and cut up their prey. Cleavers—core tools with a straight edge at one end—were used for heavy chopping and hacking at the sinews of larger animals. The Acheulian tradition illustrates trends in the evolution of technology: greater efficiency, manufacture of tools for specific tasks, and an increasingly complex technology. These trends became even more obvious with the advent of *H. sapiens*.

ADAPTIVE STRATEGIES OF *HOMO ERECTUS*

Interrelated changes in biology and culture have increased human adaptability—the capacity to live in and modify an ever wider range of environments. Acheulian tools helped *H. erectus* increase its range. Biological changes also increased hunting efficiency.

H. erectus had a rugged but essentially modern skeleton that permitted long-distance stalking and endurance during the hunt. There is archeological evidence of *H. erectus*'s success in hunting elephants, horses, rhinos, and giant baboons.

An increase in cranial capacity has been a trend in human evolution. The average *H. erectus* brain (about 1,000 cubic centimeters) doubled the australopithecine average. The capacities of *H. erectus* fossil skulls range from less than 800 to over 1,300 cubic centimeters, well above the *H. sapiens sapiens* minimum.

As noted earlier, larger skulls demand larger birth canals. However, the requirements of upright bipedalism impose limits on the expansion of the pelvic opening. If the opening is too large, the pelvis doesn't provide sufficient support for the trunk. Locomotion suffers, and posture problems appear. If, by contrast, the birth canal is too narrow, mother and child (without the modern option of Caesarian section) may die. Natural selection has struck a balance between the structural demands of upright posture and the tendency toward increased brain size—the birth of immature and dependent children whose brains and skulls grow dramatically after birth.

The interrelationship between immature birth, childhood dependency, and social nurturance applies with even greater force to *H. erectus* than it did to the australopithecines. During a long period of dependence, growth, and maturation, children can absorb the traditions and cultural directives of parents and other members of the group. Extended enculturation helps explain increasing complexity in tool manufacture and increasingly efficient coordination of hunting among *H. erectus*.

H. erectus had an essentially modern though very robust skeleton and a brain closer in size to *H. sapiens* than to *Australopithecus*. Still, several anatomic contrasts, particularly in the cranium, distinguish *H. erectus* from modern humans. Compared with moderns, *H. erectus* had a lower and more sloping forehead accentuated by a large brow ridge above the eyes. Skull bones were thicker, and, as noted, average cranial capacity was smaller. The braincase was lower and flatter than in *H. sapiens*, with spongy bone development at the lower rear of the skull. Seen from behind, the *H. erectus* skull has a broad-based angular shape that has been compared to a half-inflated football (Jolly and White 1994). The

H. erectus face, teeth, and jaws were larger than those in contemporary humans but smaller than those in *Australopithecus*. The front teeth were especially large, but molar size was well below the australopithecine average. Presumably, this reduction reflected changes in diet or food processing.

Taken together, the *H. erectus* skeleton and chewing apparatus provide biological evidence of a fuller commitment to hunting and gathering, which was *Homo*'s only adaptive strategy until plant cultivation and animal domestication emerged some 10,000 years ago. Archeologists have found and studied several sites of *H. erectus* activity, including cooperative hunting. At one of these sites, Terra Amata, overlooking Nice in southern France, archeologists have documented activities of late *H. erectus* (or possibly, early archaic *H. sapiens*) populations from around 300,000 years ago. Small bands of hunters and gatherers consisting of fifteen to twenty-five people made regular visits during the late spring and early summer to Terra Amata, a sandy cove on the coast of the Mediterranean (Figure 9.1).

Archeologists determined the season of occupation by examining fossilized human excrement, which contained pollen from flowers that are known to bloom in late spring. There is evidence for twenty-one such visits. Four groups camped on a sand bar, six on the beach, and eleven on a sand dune. Archeologists surmise that the eleven dune sites represent that number of annual visits by the same band (deLumley 1969/1976).

From a camp atop the dune, these people looked down on a river valley where animals were abundant. Bones found at Terra Amata show that their diet included red deer, young elephants, wild boars, wild mountain goats, an extinct variety of rhinoceros, and wild oxen. The Terra Amata people also hunted turtles and birds and collected oysters and mussels. Fish bones also were found at the site.

The arrangement of postholes shows that these people used saplings to support temporary huts. There were hearths—sunken pits and piled stone fireplaces—within the shelters. Stone chips inside the borders of the huts show that tools were made from locally available rocks and beach pebbles. Thus at Terra Amata, hundreds of thousands of years ago, people were already pursuing an essentially human life style, one that survived in certain coastal regions into the twentieth century.

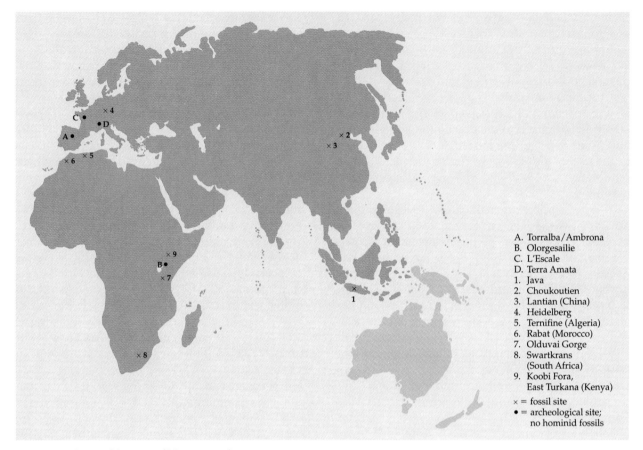

Figure 9.1 *Geographic range of* H. erectus *sites.*

The hearths at Terra Amata and other sites confirm that fire was part of the human adaptive kit by this time. Fire provided protection against cave bears and saber-toothed tigers. It permitted *H. erectus* to occupy cave sites, including Zhoukoudian, near Beijing in China, which has yielded the remains of more than forty specimens of *H. erectus*. Fire widened the range of climates open to human colonization. Its warmth enabled people to survive winter cold in temperate regions. Human control over fire offered other advantages, such as cooking, which breaks down vegetable fibers and tenderizes meat. Cooking kills parasites and makes meat more digestible, thus reducing strain on the chewing apparatus.

Fire can also be used in hunting. Two Spanish sites, Torralba and Ambrona, revealed that *H. erectus* (or, again, possibly early archaic *H. sapiens*) used fire in cooperative autumn hunts 300,000 years ago. Torralba and Ambrona stand atop two hillsides overlooking a broad valley 160 kilometers

(100 miles) northwest of Madrid. Ancient humans hunted there at a time when the climate was much colder than it is today. Although neither site has yielded human fossils, Acheulian tools were found in association with hunters' prey—deer, horses, a monkey, and birds.

Archeologists (Howell 1967) found evidence for ten different visits to the valley. In those ancient autumns, a species of elephant larger than the contemporary African variety traveled through this valley, going south to spend the winter in the warmer lowlands. At least two bands appear to have joined forces for an autumn hunt. Charcoal and carbon remains suggest the hunting strategy. After the elephants entered the valley, the hunters set fire to the grass behind them, driving their prey into swampy areas. Once the elephants were mired in the bogs, the hunters killed and butchered them, using stone tools, bone daggers, and wooden spears. This valley has yielded the remains of between forty and fifty elephants.

"*And what do you imagine will be the advantages of changing your name from Peking man to Beijing man?*"

Drawing by Handelman; © 1990 The New Yorker Magazine, Inc.

Ambrona and Torralba are open-air sites. Like Terra Amata, they were temporary, occupied only seasonally. Terra Amata was the site of generalized activity, including hunting, fishing, and collecting. Ambrona and Torralba were merely killing and butchering stations that were established when bands came together for a hunt. A similar temporary hunting site has been found at Olorgesailie in southwestern Kenya. There *H. erectus* brought stone tools made from raw materials 20 miles away to conduct a mass slaughter of an extinct giant baboon. Remains of sixty baboons show that this was a highly successful hunt. At China's Zhoukoudian cave, remains of wild sheep, horses, pigs, deer, and buffalo provide additional evidence of the varied prey of *H. erectus*.

Could language have been an additional advantage available to *H. erectus*? Archeological evidence confirms the cooperative hunting of large animals and the manufacture of complicated tools. These activities might have been too complex to have proceeded without some kind of language. Speech would have aided coordination, cooperation, and the learning of traditions, including tool making. Words, of course, aren't preserved until the advent of writing. However, given the potential for language-based communication—which even chimps and gorillas share with *H. sapiens*—and given brain size within the low *H. sapiens* range, it seems plausible to assume that *H. erectus* had rudimentary speech. For contrary views, see Binford (1981) and Fisher (1988*b*).

THE EVOLUTION AND EXPANSION OF *HOMO ERECTUS*

The archeological record of *H. erectus* activities can be combined with the fossil evidence to provide a more complete picture of our Lower Paleolithic ancestors. We now consider some of the fossil data in greater detail. The earliest *H. erectus* remains, found by Richard Leakey's team at East and West

Turkana, Kenya, and dated to around 1.6 m.y.a., were discussed in the preceding chapter.

Later *H. erectus* remains come from Upper Bed II at Olduvai. Those fossils, about a million years old, were associated with Acheulian tools. The time span of *H. erectus* in East Africa was long. *H. erectus* fossils have also been found in Bed IV at Olduvai, dating to 500,000 B.P.

In 1891, the Indonesian island of Java yielded the first *H. erectus* fossil find, popularly known as "Java man." Eugene Dubois, a Dutch army surgeon, had gone to Java to discover a transitional form between apes and humans. Of course, we now know that the transition to hominid had taken place much earlier than the *H. erectus* period and occurred in Africa. However, Dubois's good luck did lead him to the most ancient human fossils discovered at that time. Excavating near the village of Trinil, Dubois found parts of a *H. erectus* skull and a thigh bone. During the 1930s and 1940s excavations in Java uncovered additional remains.

The Indonesian *H. erectus* fossils probably date back about 700,000 years. Fragments of a skull and a lower jaw found in northern China at Lantien may be about the same age. Archeological evidence of human activity at l'Escale, France, possibly including the use of fire, may also come from the same period. However, actual fossil finds of *H. erectus* in Europe have more recent dates—500,000 years ago or less. Other *H. erectus* remains of uncertain date have been found in Algeria and Morocco in North Africa and in South Africa.

The largest group of *H. erectus* fossils was found in the Zhoukoudian cave in China. The Zhoukoudian ("Peking man") site, excavated during the 1930s and early 1940s, was a major find in the study of the human fossil record. Zhoukoudian yielded remains of tools, hearths, animal bones, and more than forty hominids, including five skulls. The analysis of these remains led to the conclusion that the Java and Zhoukoudian fossils were examples of the same broad stage of human evolution. Today they are commonly classified together as *H. erectus*.

The Zhoukoudian individuals lived more recently than did the Javanese *H. erectus*, between 500,000 and 350,000 years ago, when the climate in China was colder and moister than it is today. The inference about the climate has been made on the basis of the animal remains found with the human fossils. The people at Zhoukoudian ate venison, and

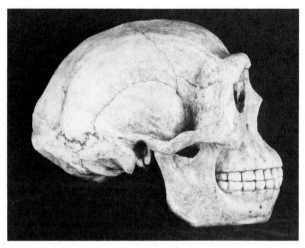

A reconstruction of one of the "Peking (now Beijing) Man" H. erectus *fossils from Zhoukoudian, China. Compared with moderns,* H. erectus *had a lower and more sloping forehead, accentuated by a large brow ridge above the eyes. Skull bones were thicker, and the braincase was lower and flatter than in* H. sapiens, *with spongy bone development at the lower rear of the skull.*

seed and plant remains suggest that they were both gatherers and hunters.

As mentioned before, probable *H. erectus* remains have been found in Europe, but their dates are uncertain. They are usually classified as late *H. erectus*, or transitional between *H. erectus* and early *H. sapiens*. For example, a jaw from a gravel pit at Mauer near Heidelberg, Germany, has been assigned a broad time span between 450,000 and 250,000 B.P. Nevertheless, although there is no sure fossil evidence that *H. erectus* reached Western Europe before 500,000 B.P., archeological evidence suggests the presence of hominids in Europe by 700,000 B.P. *H. erectus* therefore extended the hominid range from the tropics to the subtropical and temperate zones of Asia and Europe. Stone tools of a sort associated with *H. erectus* fossils are much more widespread than the fossils are. The combination of fossil and archeological evidence confirms the adaptability of *H. erectus*.

ARCHAIC *HOMO SAPIENS*

Africa, which was center stage during the australopithecine period, is joined by Asia and, later, Europe during the *H. erectus* and *H. sapiens* periods of hominid evolution. European fossils and tools have contributed disproportionately to our knowledge of early (archaic) *H. sapiens*. This doesn't mean that most *H. sapiens* evolved in Europe, that most early *H. sapiens* lived in Europe, or that comparable changes in biology and culture were not occurring elsewhere. Indeed, the fossil evidence suggests that parallel physical changes and cultural advances were proceeding in Africa and Asia (Wolpoff 1989, 1990). There were probably many more people in the tropics than in Europe during the ice ages. We merely *know more* about recent human evolution in Europe because archeology and physical anthropology—not human evolution—have been going on longer there than they have in Africa and Asia.

Recent discoveries, along with reinterpretation of the dating and the anatomic relevance of some earlier finds, are filling in the gap between *H. erectus* and archaic *H. sapiens*. **Archaic *H. sapiens*** (300,000 to 35,000 B.P.) encompasses the earliest members of our species, along with the **Neandertals** (*H. sapiens neanderthalensis*—130,000 to 35,000) of Europe and the Middle East and their Neandertal-like contemporaries in Africa and Asia. Brain size in archaic *H. sapiens* was within the modern human range. (The modern average is about 1350 cubic centimeters.) A rounding out of the braincase was associated with the increased brain size. As Jolly and White (1994) put it, evolution was pumping more brain into the *H. sapiens* cranium—like filling a football with air.

Archaic *H. sapiens* lived during the last part of the **Middle Pleistocene**—during the **Mindel** (second) glacial, the interglacial that followed it, and the following **Riss** (third) glacial. European Middle Pleistocene fossil hominids include Petralona, Bilzingsleben, and Vértesszöllös (all probable males) and Steinheim, Swanscombe, Arago, Biache, and La Chaise (probable females) (Wolpoff 1980*b*). Middle Pleistocene finds in Africa include Bodo and Saldanha (males) and Salé and Ndutu (females). Comparable Asian finds come from Java (the Solo group) and China (Changyang) (Figure 9.2). The Middle Pleistocene fossils of Europe tend to be anatomically intermediate between *H. erectus* and the Neandertals.

The distribution of the fossils and tools of archaic *H. sapiens* shows that *Homo's* tolerance of environmental diversity had increased. For example, the Neandertals and their immediate ancestors managed to survive extreme cold in Europe. Archaic *H. sapiens* occupied the Arago cave in southeastern France at a time when Europe was bitterly cold. The only Riss glacial site with facial material, Arago was excavated in 1971. It produced a partially intact skull, two jaw bones, and teeth from a dozen individuals. With an apparent date of about 200,000 B.P. the Arago fossils have features that seem transitional between *H. erectus* and the Neandertals.

Neandertals were first discovered in Western Europe. Remains of contemporaneous hominids with similar anatomical features (such as large faces and brow ridges) have been found elsewhere in the Old World, including Africa and Asia (Figure 9.3). The Kabwe skull from Zambia (130,000 B.P.) is an archaic *H. sapiens* with a Neandertal-like brow ridge. Archaic Chinese fossils with Neandertal-like features have been found at Maba and Dali. Neandertals have been found in Central Europe and the Middle East. For example, Neandertal fossils found at the Shanidar cave in northern Iraq date to around 60,000 B.P., as does a Neandertal skeleton found at Israel's Kebara cave (Shreeve 1992). At the Israeli site of Tabun on Mount Carmel, a Neandertal female skeleton was excavated in 1932. She was a contemporary of the Shanidar Neandertals, and her brow ridges, face, and teeth show typical Neandertal robustness.

THE NEANDERTALS

By 75,000 B.P., after an interglacial interlude, Western Europe's hominids (Neandertals, by then) again faced extreme cold as the Würm glacial began. To deal with this environment, they wore clothes, they made more elaborate tools than earlier humans had done, and they hunted reindeer, mammoths, and woolly rhinos.

The Neandertals were stocky, with large trunks relative to limb length—a phenotype that minimizes surface area and thus conserves heat. Another adaptation to extreme cold was the Neandertal face, which has been likened to a *H. erectus* face that has been pulled forward by the nose. This extension increased the distance between outside air and the arteries that carry blood to the brain and was adaptive in a cold climate. The brain is sensitive to temperature changes and must be kept warm. The massive nasal cavities of Neandertal fossils suggest long,

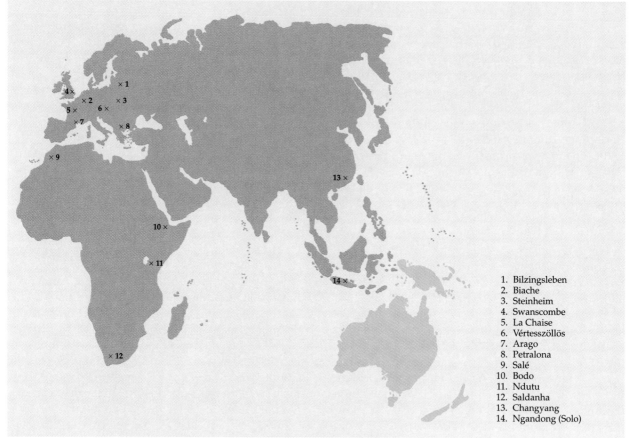

Figure 9.2 *Known distribution of archaic* H. sapiens *of the Middle Pleistocene. These fossil finds date from the Mindel (second) glacial, the interglacial that followed it, and the following Riss (third) glacial. European Middle Pleistocene fossils include Petralona, Bilzingsleben, and Vértesszöllös (all probable males) and Steinheim, Swanscombe, Arago, Biache, and La Chaise (probable females). Middle Pleistocene finds in Africa include Bodo and Saldanha (males) and Salé and Ndutu (females). Comparable Asian finds come from Java (the Solo group) and China (Changyang).*

1. Bilzingsleben
2. Biache
3. Steinheim
4. Swanscombe
5. La Chaise
6. Vértesszöllös
7. Arago
8. Petralona
9. Salé
10. Bodo
11. Ndutu
12. Saldanha
13. Changyang
14. Ngandong (Solo)

broad noses. This would expand the area for warming and moistening air.

Neandertal characteristics also include huge front teeth (the largest to appear in human evolution), broad faces and large brow ridges, and ruggedness of the skeleton and musculature. What activities were associated with these anatomic traits? Neandertal teeth probably did many jobs later done by tools (Brace 1991; Rak 1986; Smith 1990). The front teeth show heavy wear, suggesting that they were used for varied purposes, including chewing animal hides to make soft cold-weather clothing out of them. The massive Neandertal face showed the stresses of constantly using the front teeth for holding and pulling.

Comparison of early and later Neandertals shows a trend toward reduction of their robust features. Neandertal technology, a Middle Paleolithic tradition called **Mousterian**, improved considerably during the Würm glacial. Tools assumed many burdens formerly placed on the anatomy. For example, tools took over jobs once done by the front teeth. Through a still imperfectly understood mechanism, facial muscles and supporting structures developed less. Smaller front teeth—perhaps because of dental crowding—were favored. The projecting face reduced, as did the brow ridge, which had provided buttressing against the forces generated when the large front teeth were used for environmental manipulation.

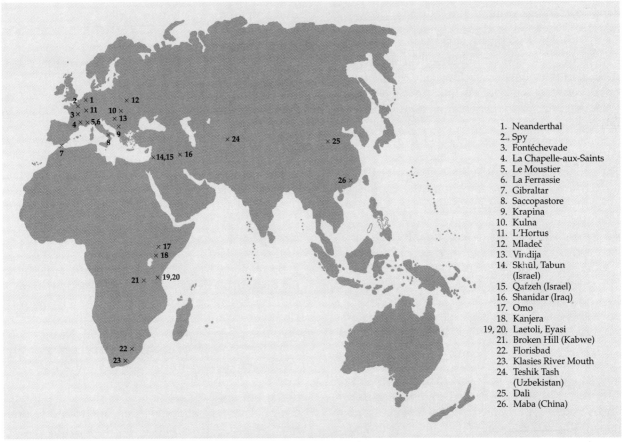

1. Neanderthal
2. Spy
3. Fontéchevade
4. La Chapelle-aux-Saints
5. Le Moustier
6. La Ferrassie
7. Gibraltar
8. Saccopastore
9. Krapina
10. Kulna
11. L'Hortus
12. Mladeč
13. Vindija
14. Skhūl, Tabun (Israel)
15. Qafzeh (Israel)
16. Shanidar (Iraq)
17. Omo
18. Kanjera
19, 20. Laetoli, Eyasi
21. Broken Hill (Kabwe)
22. Florisbad
23. Klasies River Mouth
24. Teshik Tash (Uzbekistan)
25. Dali
26. Maba (China)

Figure 9.3 *Known distribution of* H. sapiens *of the Upper Pleistocene—the Riss-Würm interglacial and the Würm glacial that followed it. This map locates fossil finds of the Neandertals* (H. sapiens neanderthalensis)—*mainly from Western Europe and the Middle East—and other (Neandertal-like) late archaic* H. sapiens. *Figure 9.3 also includes finds of anatomically modern humans—*H. sapiens sapiens—*for example, Skhūl, Qafzeh. Most of the fossils indicated in Figure 9.3 date to the period between 130,000 and 35,000 B.P. Paleoanthropologists continue to debate whether anatomically modern humans (AMHs) evolved in Africa, Asia, Europe, or the Middle East.*

THE NEANDERTALS IN RELATION TO ANATOMICALLY MODERN HUMANS (AMHs)

Scientists disagree about whether the Neandertals were ancestral to anatomically modern Western Europeans. The view disputing this ancestry proposes that *H. erectus* split into separate groups, one ancestral to the Neandertals and the other ancestral to *H. sapiens sapiens*—**anatomically modern humans (AMHs)** who appeared in Western Europe after 35,000 B.P. In different versions of this view, anatomically modern humans evolved in Africa,

Asia, Central Europe, or the Middle East and eventually colonized Western Europe, displacing the Neandertals there. In this interpretation, the Neandertals who lived in Western Europe during the Ice Age were too anatomically specialized to evolve into modern Europeans.

What were the contrasts between the Neandertals and AMHs? Like *H. erectus* before them, the Neandertals had heavy brow ridges; a braincase that was long, low, and flat; and a slanting forehead. Nevertheless, average Neandertal cranial capacity (more than 1,400 cubic centimeters) exceeded the modern average. Neandertal jaws were large, providing support for huge front teeth, and their faces were massive. The bones and skull were generally more rugged and had greater sexual dimorphism—particularly in the face and skull—than do those of AMHs. In some Western European fossils these contrasts between Neandertals and AMHs are accentuated—giving a stereotyped, or **classic Neandertal**, appearance.

Some scientists believe only the classic Neandertals were too different to be ancestors of AMHs. They contend that outside Western Europe the anatomic differences were fewer and the people who lived there were not really Neandertals but merely Neandertal-like in some respects. Actually, the European Neandertals were variable, and many lacked the "classic" constellation of features.

Doubt about the Neandertal ancestry of Western Europeans is partly due to the history of fossil discoveries. The first Neandertal remains were found in 1856 in a German valley called Neanderthal (*thal* is the old spelling for "valley" in German). Remember that the first *H. erectus* ("Java man") wasn't discovered until 1891. The inclusion of Java man in the human evolutionary tree was debated for decades after that. Nor was the first australopithecine skull, uncovered in 1924, immediately accepted as a hominid. Without these earlier hominids, which were

much more different from AMHs than the Neandertals were, the differences between Neandertals and moderns stood out and were emphasized.

One fossil contributed most to the scientific rejection of Neandertal ancestry (and to the popular stereotype of the slouching caveman). This was the complete human skeleton discovered in 1908 at La Chapelle-aux-Saints in southwestern France, in a layer containing the characteristic Mousterian tools made by Neandertals. This was the first Neandertal to be discovered with the whole skull, including the face, preserved.

The skeleton was given for study to the French paleontologist Marcellin Boule. His analysis of the fossil helped create the stereotype of Neandertals as brutes who had trouble walking upright. Boule argued that La Chapelle's brain, although larger than the modern average, was inferior to modern brains. Further, he suggested that the Neandertal head was slung forward like an ape's. To round out the primitive image, Boule proclaimed that the Neandertals were incapable of straightening their legs for fully erect locomotion. However, later fossil finds show that the La Chapelle fossil wasn't a typical Neandertal but an extreme one. Also, this much-publicized "classic" Neandertal turned out to be an aging man whose skeleton had been distorted by osteoarthritis.

Other Neandertal finds lack La Chapelle's combination of extreme features and are more acceptable ancestors for AMHs. For example, the remains of some twenty Neandertals found at Krapina in the former Yugoslavia (Smith 1984) are less different from the AMH than is the Neandertal stereotype. Other remains that are less extreme come from Spy in Belgium, La Moustier in southern France, Gibraltar, and Kulna and Vindija in Central and Eastern Europe (Smith 1982, 1984). It is now clear that European Neandertals were a variable population.

The scientists who regard the Neandertals as ancestral to AMHs (e.g., Brace 1991) base this opinion on anatomic and cultural similarities they detect between the Neandertals and later humans in the same area. They believe that the period between 50,000 and 35,000 B.P. provided enough time for the evolution of Neandertals into early European AMHs, such as "Cro-Magnon man"—a *H. sapiens sapiens* fossil found in southwestern France in 1868.

Advocates of the Neandertal ancestry of modern Europeans cite several fossils to support their view.

The skull of the classic Neandertal found in 1908 at La Chapelle-aux-Saints—the first Neandertal to be discovered with the whole skull, including the face, preserved. Later finds showed that La Chapelle wasn't a typical Neandertal but an extreme form. Furthermore, La Chapelle was an aging man with osteoarthritis.

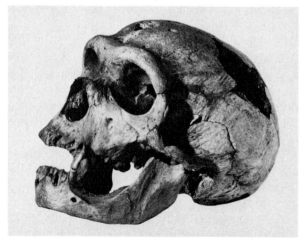

For example, the Central European site of Mladeč (31,000 to 33,000 B.P.) has yielded cranial remains of several hominids that combine Neandertal robustness with modern features. Wolpoff (1980a) also notes modern features in the late Neandertals found at l'Hortus in France and Vindija in Croatia.

Israel's Mount Carmel site of Skhūl, whose fossil hominids combine archaic and modern features, was formerly assigned the same date as Mladec (about 32,000 B.P.). Skhūl was once used to support the Neandertal ancestry of *H. sapiens sapiens*. Skhūl, which has yielded the remains of ten individuals of various ages and both sexes, seemed anatomically transitional between the Middle Eastern Neandertals (e.g., Shanidar, Tabun) and AMHs. Recently, however, most analyses have stressed the "modernness" of Skhūl compared with the female Neandertal from Tabun (also a Mount Carmel site—dating between 60,000 and 40,000 B.P.). Skhūl has been redated (by the ESR technique) to 100,000 B.P., and modern-looking skulls from Qafzeh, another Israeli site, have been dated (by the TL technique) to 92,000 B.P. If these dates are correct, the Skhūl and Qafzeh fossils cast serious doubt on the Neandertal ancestry of AMHs in Europe and the Middle East. The skulls from Skhūl (Figure 9.4) and Qafzeh have a modern, rather than a Neandertal, shape and are usually classified as AMHs. Their braincases are higher, shorter, and rounder than Neandertal skulls. There is a more filled-out forehead region, which rises more vertically above the brows. A marked chin is another modern feature. Still, these early AMHs do retain distinct brow ridges, though reduced from their archaic *H. sapiens* ancestor.

Dated to 100,000 and 92,000 B.P., Skhūl and Qafzeh suggest that archaic *H. sapiens* was evolving directly into AMH in the Middle East more than 50,000 years before the demise of the Western European Neandertals. Neandertals and AMHs overlapped in time, rather than being ancestor and descendant, and AMHs may have inhabited the Middle East before the Neandertals did. Ofer Bar-Yosef (1987) suggests that during the last (Würm) glacial period, which began around 75,000 B.P., Western European Neandertals spread east and south (and into the Middle East) as part of a general southward expansion of cold-adapted fauna. AMHs, in turn, followed warmer-climate fauna south into Africa, returning to the Middle East once the Würm ended.

Current interpretations of the fossil evidence and

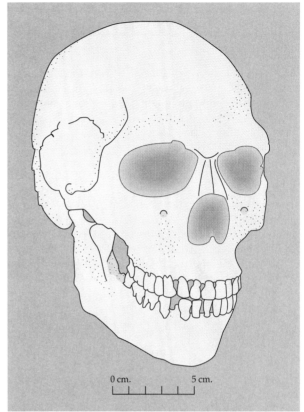

Figure 9.4 *Skhūl V, an anatomically modern human with some archaic features, recently redated to 100,000 B.P. This is one of several fossils found at Skhūl, Israel. Formerly dated to 32,000 B.P., this fossil group once seemed transitional between Neandertals and* H. sapiens sapiens.

dating seem to support the replacement hypothesis, which denies the Neandertal ancestry of AMHs in Western Europe and the Middle East. AMHs seem likely to have evolved from an archaic *H. sapiens* ancestor in the Middle East, Africa, or Asia, where most of the archaic *H. sapiens* fossils had flatter, less projecting faces than the Neandertals did. Eventually AMHs spread to other areas, including Western Europe, where they replaced, or interbred with, the Neandertals, whose robust traits eventually disappeared.

Certain anatomic changes, including facial reduction and declining robustness, may be linked to improved technology. Better tools did the holding, pulling, twisting, prying, and lifting once done by muscle, bone, and teeth. We shift focus now from anatomic changes to archeological evidence of in-

MITOCHONDRIAL EVE IN AN AFRICAN GARDEN OF EDEN

W. W. Howells (1976) distinguished between two schools of thought on how modern humans originated—the "Noah's ark" hypothesis and the "candelabra" hypothesis. The first is now usually called the "Garden of Eden" hypothesis. It posits that a small group of modern people arose recently in one place and then spread out and colonized the world. According to the alternative candelabra hypothesis, regional populations of *Homo* (such as those of Africa, Asia, and Europe) separated long ago and evolved independently into modern humans. Like the parallel lines of a candelabra, the Neandertals evolved into modern Europeans while the descendants of "Peking man" were evolving into the modern Chinese.

In 1987 a group of molecular geneticists at the University of California at Berkeley set forth the Garden of Eden hypothesis in its most modern form. Rebecca Cann, Mark Stoneking, and Allan C. Wilson (1987) analyzed placentas donated by 147 women in the United States, Papua–New Guinea, and Australia.

The women's ancestors represented the native populations of Africa, Europe, the Middle East, Asia, New Guinea, and Australia.

The researchers focused on mitochondrial DNA (mtDNA). This genetic material is found in the cytoplasm, not the nucleus, of cells. Ordinary DNA, which makes up the genes that determine most physical traits, is found in the nucleus and comes from both parents. However, only the mother contributes mitochondrial DNA (cloned from her own mtDNA) to the fertilized egg. The father plays no part in mtDNA transmission, just as the mother has nothing to do with the transmission of the Y chromosome, which comes from the father and determines the sex of the child. Because mtDNA is cloned, its genetic pattern is usually an exact replica of the mother's, except when mutations occur.

To establish a "genetic clock," the Berkeley researchers measured the variation in mtDNA in their 147 tissue samples. They cut each sample into segments to compare with the others. By estimating the number of

mutations that had taken place in each sample since its common origin with the 146 others, the researchers drew an evolutionary tree with the help of a computer.

That tree started in Africa and then branched in two. One group remained in Africa, while the other one split off, carrying its mtDNA to the rest of the world. The variation in mtDNA was greatest among Africans, suggesting that they had been evolving the longest. Some of the earliest dates for "modern" fossils also come from Africa. For example, a date of 92,000 B.P. has been obtained for a find that some consider *H. sapiens sapiens* from Jebel Qafzeh, Israel (Valladas et al. 1988) and the anatomically modern Skhūl fossils, also from Israel, have recently been dated to 100,000 B.P.

The Berkeley researchers concluded that everyone alive today descends from a woman (dubbed "Eve") who lived in sub-Saharan Africa around 200,000 years ago. Eve wasn't the only woman alive then, just the only one whose descendants have included a daughter in each

---

creasingly sophisticated technologies, which paved the way for a major change in human cultural adaptation 10,000 years ago: the origin of food production—plant cultivation and animal domestication.

EVOLUTION IN TECHNOLOGY

In archeology, as with recent hominid fossils, European evidence for the activities of early *H. sapiens sapiens* has contributed disproportionately. We know more about advances in stone-tool making in Europe because archeology—not human evolution—has been going on longer there than in Africa

and Asia. Technological changes were occurring elsewhere, but the European evidence is best known and thus will be the focus of this discussion. Early *H. sapiens sapiens* made tools in a variety of traditions, collectively known as **Upper Paleolithic** because of the tools' location in the upper, or more recent, layers of sedimentary deposits. Some cave deposits have Mousterian tools at lower levels and increasing numbers of Upper Paleolithic tools at higher levels.

Although the Neandertals are remembered more for their physiques than for their manufacturing abilities, their tool kits were sophisticated. Mousterian technology included at least fourteen categories of tools designed for different jobs. The Neandertals

generation through the present. Because mtDNA passes exclusively through females, mtDNA lines disappear whenever a woman has no children or has only sons. The details of the Eve theory suggest that her descendants left Africa no more than 135,000 years ago. They then colonized the rest of the world, replacing all other hominids.

Milford Wolpoff (1989, 1990) argues that the fossil evidence contradicts the theory of a recent Eve. The fossils show that certain physical features have persisted in particular regions for hundreds of thousands of years. For example, there are striking similarities between fossils dating back 750,000 to 500,000 years in Australasia (Indonesia and Australia), China, and Europe and the people who live in each of those regions today. One example is the facial similarity between modern Chinese people and the "vertical flat face" (Fenlason 1990) of *H. erectus* fossils found near Beijing. Another example is the "protruding face with large teeth and heavy brows," which is characteristic of both Indonesian *H. erectus* fossils and modern Native

Australians. A third example is the prevalence among both ancient and modern Europeans of "angular faces with large projecting noses." If Eve's descendants arrived later than these fossils and wiped out the previous inhabitants of China, Australasia, and Europe, these specific similarities between the fossils and the modern people of each region wouldn't exist.

After analyzing the fossil record, Wolpoff and Wu Xin Zhi of the Institute for Vertebrate Paleontology and Paleoanthropology in Beijing agreed that these unique regional features appeared (in *H. erectus*) long before the proposed migration of Eve's descendants. These distinctive anatomic features arose through the *founder effect* (random genetic drift). By chance, the ancient founders of each regional population happened to have either flat, protruding, or angular faces. After the founders settled each region, some of their unique physical features became common among their descendants.

Accepting parallel evolution from *H. erectus* to modern *H. sapiens* in each region (Africa, Europe, north-

ern Asia, and Australasia), Wolpoff modifies the candelabra hypothesis into a "trellis" theory. (The vertical slats of a trellis are parallel, but horizontal slats connect them.) As the regional populations evolved along their parallel lines, gene flow always connected them, so that they always belonged to the same species.

Wolpoff agrees that a mitochondrial Eve might have existed, but much earlier than the Berkeley researchers suggest. According to Wolpoff (1989), by changing just a few assumptions about the mutation rate of mtDNA, we can push Eve's birthday back hundreds of thousands of years. This would provide a good fit with fossil evidence extending back 750,000 years. Many anthropologists doubt that Eve could have been as recent as 200,000 B.P. However, most anthropologists would have no trouble at all accepting a *H. erectus* Eve. Our common African mother could easily have been a member of one of the first hominid groups to migrate out of Africa, between 1 m.y.a. and 750,000 B.P.

---

elaborated on a revolutionary technique of flake tool manufacture invented in southern Africa around 200,000 years ago, which spread widely throughout the Old World. Uniform flakes were chipped off a specially prepared core of rock. Additional work on the flakes produced such special-purpose tools as those shown in Figure 9.5. Scrapers were used to prepare animal hides for clothing. Special tools were designed for sawing, gouging, and piercing (Binford and Binford 1979).

The Upper Paleolithic traditions of early *H. sapiens sapiens* all emphasized **blade tools**. Blades were hammered off a prepared core, as in Mousterian technology, but a blade is longer than a flake—its length is more than twice its width. Blades were

chipped off cores 4 to 6 inches high by hitting a punch made of bone or antler with a hammerstone (Figure 9.6). Blades were then modified to produce a variety of special-purpose implements. Some were composite tools that were made by joining reworked blades to other materials.

The blade-core method was faster than the Mousterian and produced fifteen times as many cutting edges from the same amount of material. More efficient tool production might have been especially valued by people whose economy depended on cooperative hunting of mammoths, woolly rhinoceroses, bison, wild horses, bears, wild cattle, wild boars, and—principally—reindeer. It has been estimated that approximately 90 percent of the meat

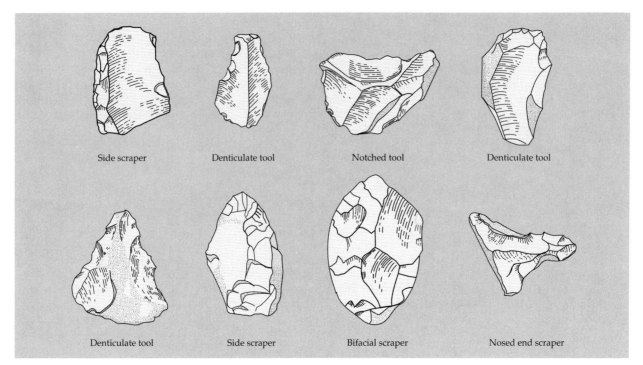

Side scraper   Denticulate tool   Notched tool   Denticulate tool

Denticulate tool   Side scraper   Bifacial scraper   Nosed end scraper

Figure 9.5 *Middle Paleolithic tools of the Mousterian tool-making tradition. The manufacture of diverse tool types for a variety of purposes confirms Neandertal sophistication.*

Figure 9.6 *Upper Paleolithic blade-tool making. Blades are flakes that are detached from a specially prepared core. A punch (usually a piece of bone or antler) and a hammerstone (not shown here) were used to knock the blade off the core.*

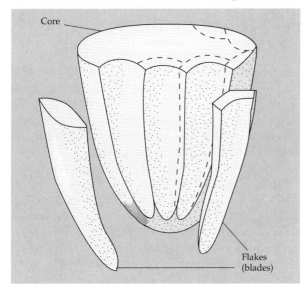

Core

Flakes (blades)

eaten by Western Europeans between 25,000 and 15,000 B.P. came from reindeer.

Trends observable throughout the entire archeological record also mark the changeover from the Mousterian to the Upper Paleolithic. First, the number of distinct tool types increased, reflecting functional specialization—the manufacture of special tools for particular jobs. A second trend was increasing standardization in tool manufacture. The form and inventory of tools reflect several factors: the jobs tools are intended to perform, the physical properties of the raw materials from which they are made, and distinctive cultural traditions about how to make tools. Furthermore, accidental or random factors also influenced tool forms and the proportions of particular tool types (Isaac 1972). However, Mousterian and Upper Paleolithic tools were more standardized than those of *H. erectus* were.

Other trends demonstrated by the fossil and archeological records include growth in *Homo*'s total population and geographic range and increasing local cultural diversity as people specialized in particular ecological niches and economic activities. Illustrating increasing economic diversity are the varied special-purpose tools made by Upper Paleolithic populations. Scrapers were used to hollow out wood and bone, scrape animal hides, and remove bark from trees. Burins, the first chisels, were used to make slots in bone and wood and to engrave designs on bone. Awls, which were drills with sharp points, were used to make holes in wood, bone, shell, and skin.

Upper Paleolithic bone tools have survived: knives, pins, needles with eyes, and fishhooks. The needles suggest that clothes sewn with thread—made from the sinews of animals—were being worn. Fishhooks and harpoons confirm an increased emphasis on fishing.

Another illustration of increasing diversity was that different Upper Paleolithic traditions could flourish in the same general area. For example, the **Aurignacian** and **Perigordian** traditions coexisted in Europe between 35,000 and 20,000 B.P. Perigordian tools are usually found in thin deposits and are scattered over large areas. Aurignacian tools are usually found in narrow valleys or near cliff walls, and layers are thick, suggesting long occupation of these sites (Sonneville-Bordes 1963). The Perigordian seems likely to have evolved in Western Europe out of Mousterian antecedents, but the Aurignacian seems to have originated elsewhere and diffused to Europe.

Different tool types may represent culturally distinct populations who made their tools differently because of different ancestral traditions. Archeological sites may also represent different activities carried out at different times of the year by a single population. Some sites, for example, are obviously butchering stations, where prehistoric people hunted, made their kills, and carved them up. Others are residential sites, where a wider range of activities was carried out. The major fossils, hominid types, and tool-making traditions found in the Old World through the Upper Paleolithic are summarized in Figure 9.7.

To sum up hominid evolutionary trends: With increasing technological differentiation, specialization, and efficiency, humans have become increasingly adaptable. Through heavy reliance on cultural means of adaptation, *Homo* has become (in numbers and range) the most successful primate by far. The

hominid range expanded significantly in Upper Paleolithic times with the colonization of two new continents—North America and South America—a story told in the chapter "The Origin and Spread of Food Production." (Australia was colonized by at least 40,000 B.P.)

GLACIAL RETREAT AND THE BROAD-SPECTRUM ECONOMY

The Würm glacial ended in Europe between 17,000 and 12,000 years ago, with the melting of the ice sheet in northern Europe (Scotland, Scandinavia, northern Germany, and Russia). As the ice retreated, the tundra and steppe vegetation grazed by reindeer and other large herbivores gradually moved north. Some humans moved north, too, following their prey.

Shrubs, forests, and more solitary animals appeared in southwestern Europe. With most of the big-game animals gone, Western Europeans were forced to use a greater variety of foods. To replace specialized economies based on big game, more generalized adaptations developed during the 5,000 years of glacial retreat.

Water flowed from melting glacial ice, and sea levels all over the world started rising. Today, off most coasts, there is a shallow-water zone called the **continental shelf**, over which the sea gradually deepens until the abrupt fall to deep water, which is known as the **continental slope**. During the ice ages, so much water was frozen in glaciers that most continental shelves were exposed. Dry land extended right up to the slope's edge. The waters immediately offshore were deep, cold, and dark. Few species of marine life thrived in this inhospitable environment.

How did people adapt to the postglacial environment in southwestern Europe? As seas rose, conditions more encouraging to marine life developed in the shallower, warmer offshore waters. The quantity and variety of edible species increased tremendously in waters over the shelf. Furthermore, because rivers now flowed more gently into the oceans, fish such as salmon could ascend European rivers to spawn. Flocks of birds that nested in seaside marshes migrated across Europe during the winter. Even inland Europeans could take advan-

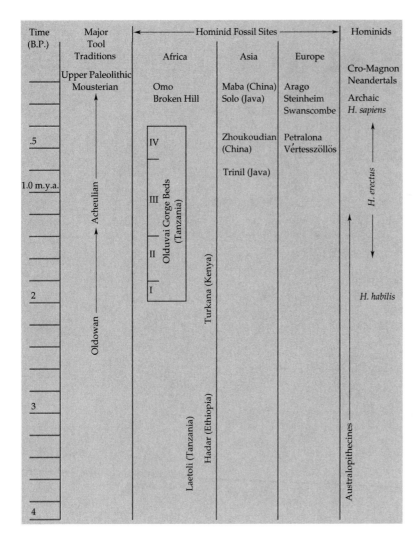

Figure 9.7 *Chronology of evolution in human biology and tool making over the past 4 million years. See the text for particular fossils found at the different sites.*

tage of new resources, such as migratory birds and springtime fish runs, which filled the rivers of southwestern France.

Although hunting remained important, southwestern European economies became less specialized. A wider range, or broader spectrum, of plant and animal life was being hunted, gathered, collected, caught, and fished. This was the beginning of what anthropologist Kent Flannery (1969) has called the **broad-spectrum revolution**—revolutionary because in the Middle East it led to food production—human control over the reproduction of plants and animals. In a mere 10,000 years—after more than a million years during which hominids had subsisted by foraging for natural resources— food production based on plant cultivation and an-

imal domestication replaced hunting and gathering in most areas.

CAVE ART

It isn't the tools or the skeletons of Upper Paleolithic people but their art that has made them most familiar to us. Most extraordinary are the cave paintings, the earliest of which dates back some 30,000 years. More than a hundred cave painting sites are known, mainly from a limited area of southwestern France and adjacent northeastern Spain. The most famous site is Lascaux, found in 1940 in southwestern France by a dog and his young human companions.

The paintings adorn limestone walls of true caves located deep in the earth. Over time, the paintings have been absorbed by the limestone and thus preserved. Prehistoric big-game hunters painted their prey: woolly mammoths, wild cattle and horses, deer and reindeer. The largest animal image is 18 feet long.

Most interpretations associate cave painting with magic and ritual surrounding the hunt. For example, because animals are sometimes depicted with spears in their bodies, the paintings might have been attempts to ensure success in hunting. Artists might have believed that by capturing the animal's image in paint and predicting the kill, they could influence the hunt's outcome.

Another interpretation sees cave painting as a magical human attempt to control animal reproduction. Something analogous was done by Native Australian (Australian aboriginal) hunters and gatherers, who held annual **ceremonies of increase** to honor and to promote, magically, the fertility of the plants and animals that shared their homeland. Australians believed that ceremonies were necessary to perpetuate the species on which humans de-

pended. Similarly, cave paintings might have been part of annual ceremonies of increase. Some of the animals in the cave murals are pregnant, and some are copulating. Did Upper Paleolithic people believe they could influence the sexual behavior or reproduction of their prey by drawing them? Or did they perhaps think that animals would return each year to the place where their souls had been captured pictorially?

Paintings often occur in clusters. In some caves as many as three paintings have been drawn over the original, yet next to these superimposed paintings stand blank walls never used for painting. It seems reasonable to speculate that an event in the outside world sometimes reinforced a painter's choice of a given spot. Perhaps there was an especially successful hunt soon after the painting had been done. Perhaps members of a social subdivision significant in Upper Paleolithic society customarily used a given area of wall for their drawings.

Cave paintings also might have been a kind of pictorial history. Perhaps Upper Paleolithic people were, through their drawings, reenacting the hunt after it took place, as hunters of the Kalahari Desert

According to one interpretation, Upper Paleolithic cave paintings represent a human attempt to control animal reproduction by magical means. Native Australian hunters and gatherers still do cave paintings. They also hold annual ceremonies of increase—to honor and to promote, magically, the fertility of the plants and animals that share their homeland. Dancers may either act out the exploits of mythological heroes or enact more recent, mundane events. Here natives of Australia's northern territory do a dance mimicking an emu hunt.

IN THE NEWS: NEW DISCOVERIES OF UPPER PALEOLITHIC CAVE PAINTINGS

Most Upper Paleolithic cave paintings have been found in a limited area of southwestern France and northern Spain. The important 1991 discovery described here comes from farther east, Mediterranean southern France near Marseille. Like other cave art sites, this one is isolated, in a remote cavern that could be reached by land 18,000 years ago, when the paintings were done. Here as elsewhere, Upper Paleolithic people (e.g., Cro-Magnons) painted their prey, but the hands and arms here are more novel. The birds mentioned in the news item were probably northern auks, rather than penguins.

France has limited tourists' access to such cave sites because human breathing harms the paintings. However, the polychrome majesty of the original Lascaux (now off-limits) has been meticulously reconstructed at Lascaux II, in southwestern France, which is well worth a visit.

A cave painting of a "penguin"—actually a northern auk—from the recently discovered underwater cave near Marseille, southern France.

Toulon, France.

French divers have discovered a partly flooded cave filled with prehistoric rock paintings and engravings, a great underground amphitheater studded with running horses, bison and deer as well as images of human hands believed to have been drawn some 18,000 years ago.

The cave lies deep inside a cliff on the edge of the Mediterranean. Its murals have surprised specialists because they include drawings of seals and penguins, the first images of such sea creatures ever 'found in Western Europe's prehistoric caves. Seals still exist here today but the penguins are an unusual souvenir from an era when much of Europe was under ice and

the Mediterranean was a chilly region with a climate more like today's Scandinavia.

Historians have compared the great parade of more than 100 animals to the paintings of Lascaux, in France's Dordogne, which is widely held to be the region's most beautiful collection of mural paintings of the Paleolithic era. They say that the newly found paintings are fewer, but possibly several thousand years older than those of Lascaux.

The ancient art gallery was discovered in a cove on Cap Morgiou, 7.5 miles southeast of Marseilles, a region of unspoiled inlets and cliffs and a favorite haunt of divers who like to explore its grottos and crevices.

Henri Cosquer, a diving instructor who often explored the

area, first saw the paintings in July 1991, when he and several friends entered an underwater hollow at a depth of 121 feet. Here the swimmers threaded through a narrow tunnel 574 feet long that steadily rose until it reached the first of two great caverns. As Mr. Cosquer later told it, he was astonished when a searchlight suddenly revealed the first image: the black outlines of a human hand.

Although a small team of divers photographed and explored the chambers last fall, researchers have taken almost a year to study their initial findings and to assure themselves through tests of charcoal and calcium deposits that the paintings and engravings are indeed from prehistoric times. They have published their first study in the latest issue of The Bulletin of the French Prehistoric Society, as well as in the journal Antiquity, but during new explorations of the cave this summer the researchers have found many more paintings and engravings than they cited in their report.

In September the French Government declared the cave a historic monument, pre-empting local plans already on the table to develop the cove there for tourism.

"It's a very important find, the first on the coast and the first in this region," said Philippe Grenier de Monner, a director of archeology at the Culture Ministry, noting that this will make an important change on the map of prehistoric mural art. Most of Europe's painted prehistoric caves are in southern France and northern Spain, but they are several hundred miles to the west. "We knew that people lived here in the Stone Age because we had found tools and remains," he said, "but we had never found their art work east of the Rhone."

The hunting people who decorated the great coastal cavern probably had an easy way to reach it because they lived in a different landscape. For one, the cave was dry. Geologists say that at the end of the last ice age, the shore of the Mediterranean was at least six miles to the south and the water level was probably 400 feet lower than it is today. The large stalagmites in the two adjoining chambers, according to researchers, are a sign that the caves were open to the air and probably had another access route.

The painted chamber was probably used as a temple for religious or magic rituals, researchers believe. "Most painted caves were not habitats but meeting places,"

said Mr. Grenier de Monner, "and these caves showed no signs of habitation."

Researchers said the art corresponded to at least two different periods, with the newer drawings superimposed on older work. The oldest, possibly dating as far back as 20,000 B.C., included more than 20 stenciled hands, which the Cro-Magnon people ostensibly drew by placing their hands on the wall and drawing their contours in charcoal. The hands are grouped together, as though they were intended as signatures.

Similar hands have been found in other caves in the Pyrenees and their presence here has rekindled the debate about their meaning. Some hands have forearms and wrists, and the majority have one or more shortened fingers. Specialists say it is unclear whether the fingers are mutilated or bent, but they agree that the shortened fingers point to a kind of code.

The gallery of beasts is made up of more than a hundred engraved and painted animals and birds, among them many horses, bisons, ibex and chamois that were known to be common in the region. Five bison are particularly expressive because they have their heads turned, showing both eyes, instead of the more common, flat profile found in prehistoric caves.

In the chamber, which is some 200 feet wide and 6 to 16 feet high, there are also a red deer, a feline, three penguins and 10 seals and several images that are thought to be megaceros. Penguin bones have been found in the past in the south of Spain and southern Italy, but no penguin images were ever found before along the Mediterranean.

In some parts of the cave, the animal paintings are drawn over the hands and over many small

and large engravings. This is one reason the cave explorers believe the animal paintings belong to a second and later period. The explorers have found sharp flint-stones in the cave, which they think may have been used to make the engravings. Paintings are almost all black, done in charcoal and oxide of manganese. The naturalistic scenes are crisscrossed with fingermarks and an array of signs and geometric designs, zig-zagged, straight and curved.

"Three-quarters of the cave is submerged in water," said Jean Courtin, an archeologist and senior researcher at the French National Center for Scientific Research who has led the exploration in the cave. After three weeks of dives this summer, Mr. Courtin said, he had concluded that the great cave once held many more paintings. "Many must have washed away in the salt water," he said in an interview. At the water level, some animals have half their bodies missing.

On the floor in dry parts of the cave, the researchers found two hearths. They also picked up charcoal from crevices and ledges, which they believe are from pinewood torches that the Stone Age visitors carried. Two of the pine species whose pollen was found in the cave no longer grow in this region, Mr. Courtin said.

Carbon dating of charcoal from the cave has set its age at 17,000 to 18,000 years. Tiny quantities of the pigment from the paintings are still being dated by nuclear physicists, Mr. Courtin said.

Source: Marlise Simons, "Stone Age Art Shows Penguins at Mediterranean," *The New York Times*, October 20, 1992, C1, C10.

in southern Africa still do today. Designs and markings on animal bones may indicate that Upper Paleolithic people had developed a calendar based on the phases of the moon (Marshack 1972). If this is so, it seems possible that late Stone Age hunters, who were certainly as intelligent as we are, would have been interested in recording important events in their lives.

There is reason to doubt that cave paintings were simply expressions of individual artistic temperament, that is, art for art's sake. Why would artists choose remote locales where few could appreciate their work? And why would artists obliterate someone else's work by painting over it?

Still another interpretation associates cave paintings with initiation rites. Examples of initiation rites—also called *rites of passage*—in our own society include fraternity hazing and the process by which a woman retreats from secular life and gradually becomes a Roman Catholic nun. Other examples are boot-camp training prior to full-fledged military service and training camp prior to a sports season.

Considering other cultures, some of the best-known initiation rites are associated with the quest for a guardian spirit in certain Native American (North American Indian) cultures. To be considered a man, an adolescent male had to withdraw temporarily from normal social life and go into the wilderness, where he sought contact with an animal spirit, which would become his personal guardian spirit. If mere seclusion didn't bring the desired spirit, the boy tried to reach a state of spiritual receptivity by fasting, taking drugs, or inflicting pain on himself. After the vision appeared, the young man returned home, told of his experience, and was reintegrated into his group with adult status. Dark and remote cave passages and interior caverns would be appropriate places for similar rites of passage (Pfeiffer 1985).

Associated with initiation rites in West Africa and northern Australia are so-called **bush schools**, which are located far from residential areas. Young people go there when they reach puberty, to be instructed by an older person in tribal lore—knowledge viewed as essential to adult status. On the floor of one European cavern, several small heel prints have been fossilized. Could this cave have been the site of an Upper Paleolithic bush school, a place where the young were instructed by specialists in tribal lore? Were there such specialists? Again, Upper Paleolithic cave paintings offer a hint. Humans are shown in about fifty cave paintings, usually in animal skins. Sometimes they seem to be dancing. It has been suggested that these were the shamans, the religious specialists, of Upper Paleolithic society.

Finally, the *late* Upper Paleolithic, when many of the most spectacular multicolored cave paintings were done and Paleolithic artistic techniques were perfected, coincides with the period of glacial retreat. An intensification of cave painting for any of the reasons connected with hunting magic could have been caused by concern about decreases in herds as the open lands of southwestern Europe were being replaced by forests.

THE MESOLITHIC

The broad-spectrum revolution in Europe includes the late Upper Paleolithic and the **Mesolithic**, which followed it. Again, because of the long history of European archeology, our knowledge of the Mesolithic (particularly in southwestern Europe and the British Isles) is extensive. According to the traditional typology that distinguishes between Old, Middle, and New Stone Ages, the Middle Stone Age, the Mesolithic, had a characteristic tool type—the **microlith** (Greek for "small stone"). Of interest to us is what an abundant inventory of small and delicately shaped stone tools can tell us about the total economy and way of life of the people who made them.

By 12,000 B.P. there were no longer subarctic animals in southwestern Europe. By 10,000 B.P. the glaciers had retreated to such a point that the range of hunting, gathering, and fishing populations in Europe extended to the formerly glaciated British Isles and Scandinavia. The reindeer herds had gradually retreated to the far north, with some human groups following (and ultimately domesticating) them. Europe around 10,000 B.P. was forest rather than treeless steppe and tundra. Europeans were exploiting a wider variety of resources and gearing their lives to the seasonal appearance of particular plants and animals.

People still hunted, but their prey were solitary forest animals, such as the roe deer, the wild ox, and the wild pig, rather than herd species. This led to new hunting techniques—solitary stalking and trapping, similar to more recent practices of many American Indian groups. The coasts and lakes of Europe and the Middle East were fished intensively. Some important Mesolithic sites are Scandinavian shell mounds—the garbage dumps of prehistoric oyster collectors. Microliths were used as fishhooks and in harpoons. Dugout canoes were used for fishing and travel. The process of preserving meat and fish by smoking and salting grew increasingly important. (Meat preservation had been less of a problem in a subarctic environment since winter snow and ice, often on the ground nine months of the year, offered convenient refrigeration.) The bow and arrow became essential for hunting water fowl in swamps and marshes. Dogs were domesticated, as retrievers, by Mesolithic people (Champion et al. 1984). Woodworking was important in the forested environment of northern and Western Europe. Tools used by Mesolithic carpenters appear in the archeological record: new kinds of axes, chisels, and gouges.

The decline of big-game hunting probably brought a change in the gender-based division of labor. Hunting and fishing, usually male tasks, tend to be more important in temperate areas than they are in warmer climates, particularly the tropics. In Europe, male dominance of big-game hunting gave way to more equal economic roles for the sexes. On the basis of what we know ethnographically about temperate zone foragers, although Mesolithic men still hunted and fished, women gathered wild plants, small animals, insects, and shellfish. Women probably contributed more to subsistence during the Mesolithic than they had during the Upper Paleolithic.

Big-game hunting and, thereafter, Mesolithic hunting and fishing were important in Europe, but other foraging strategies were used by prehistoric humans in Africa and Asia. Among contemporary foragers in the tropics, gathering is the dietary mainstay (Lee 1968/1974). Although herds of big-game animals were more abundant in the tropics in prehistory than they are today, gathering has probably always been at least as important as hunting for tropical foragers. When gathering contributes more to the diet than hunting does, women's economic labor is highly valued and social status discrimination based on gender is rudimentary (Draper 1975).

Generalized, broad-spectrum economies persisted about 5,000 years longer in Europe than in the Middle East. Whereas Middle Easterners had begun to cultivate plants and breed animals by 10,000 B.P., food production came to Western Europe only around 5000 B.P. (3000 B.C.) and to northern Europe 500 years later. We must therefore shift our focus to the Middle East, where the next cultural advance, the origin of food production, took place.

SUMMARY

The first members of the genus *Homo*, more adaptable than their australopithecine ancestors, extended the hominid range beyond Africa to Asia and Europe. Population increase and expansion of range were caused by interrelated biological and cultural changes. The Lower Paleolithic Acheulian tradition provided *H. erectus* with better tools. The new hominid economy was based on gathering *and* hunting.

H. erectus's average cranial capacity doubled the australopithecine average. Tool complexity and archeological evidence of cooperative hunting suggest a long period of enculturation and learning. *H. erectus* might have spoken primitive languages, which would have facilitated learning.

H. erectus's posterior teeth were no longer the powerful australopithecine crushers but were smaller and were used to chew a more generalized diet. Fire eventually allowed *H. erectus* to expand into cooler areas, to cook, and to live in caves. Fire was also used in hunting. Evidence of cooperative hunting and butchering of large mammals—for example, elephants and giant baboons—comes from Spain and Kenya. Terra Amata in southern France confirms a diversified foraging pattern, including an annual late spring trip to the beach, by a fire-wielding, hut-building *H. erectus* or early archaic *H. sapiens* band some 300,000 years ago.

From Kenya and Tanzania come *H. erectus* fossils more than 1 million years old. The oldest *H. erectus* skull comes from Kenya and is about 1.6 million years old. At Olduvai Gorge, Tanzania, geological strata spanning more than a million years demonstrate a transition from Oldowan tools to the Archeulian implements of *H. erectus*. *H. erectus* persisted for more than 1 million years, evolving into archaic *H. sapiens* by the Middle Pleistocene epoch, some 300,000 years ago.

The classic Neandertals who lived in Western Europe during the early part of the Würm glacial came under intensive scrutiny because they were among the first hominid fossils found. In the absence of representatives of the *Australopithecus* and *H. erectus* stages, the differences rather than the similarities between Neandertals and moderns were accentuated. Even today, many anthropologists think that classic Neandertals were too rugged and specialized to be the ancestors of Western Europeans. They seek that ancestry among other archaic *H. sapiens* from Africa, Asia, the Middle East, or Central Europe.

Those who contend that Neandertals and *H. sapiens sapiens* (moderns) have different ancestries point to anatomically modern human (AMH) fossil finds such as Skhūl (100,000 B.P.) and Qafzeh (92,000 B.P.) to support the contention that the Neandertals (130,000 to 35,000 B.P.) and AMHs were contemporaries, rather than ancestor and descendant.

The classic Neandertals adapted physically and culturally to bitter cold. Their tool kits were much more complex than those of preceding humans. Their front teeth were among the largest to appear in human evolution. The Neandertals manufactured Mousterian flake tools. *H. sapiens sapiens* made Upper Paleolithic blade tools. The changeover from Neandertal to modern appears to have occurred in Western Europe by 30,000 B.P.

The Upper Paleolithic culminates many trends in stone technology observable during the Old Stone Age: increasing reliance on technological means of adaptation, increasing diversity and functional specialization of tools, increasing efficiency of varied tool kits, and more efficient and standardized tool production.

As glacial ice melted in northern Europe, Western European foraging became more generalized, less focused on a single species—reindeer. With the rise in sea level that accompanied glacial retreat, coastal areas became favorable habitats for marine species and fish ascended European waters to spawn. Foraging patterns were generalized to include fish, fowl, and plant foods in addition to the diminishing herds of big game.

The beginning of the broad-spectrum economy in Europe coincided with an intensification of Upper Paleolithic cave art. On limestone cave walls, prehistoric hunters painted images of animals important in their lives. Explanations of cave paintings link them to hunting magic, ceremonies of increase, and initiation rites.

By 10,000 B.P., people were pursuing broad-spectrum economies in the British Isles and Scandinavia. Tool kits adapted to a forested environment included small, delicately shaped stone tools called microliths. The transitional period called the Mesolithic, or Middle Stone Age, had begun. The broad-spectrum revolution, based on a wide variety of dietary resources, began in the Middle East somewhat earlier than in Europe, culminating in the first food-producing economies around 10,000 B.P. Foraging strategies of adaptation persisted longer in Europe; food production was established in Western Europe only 5,000 years ago, in northern Europe 500 years later.

GLOSSARY

Acheulian: Derived from the French village of St. Acheul, where these tools were first identified; Lower Paleolithic tool tradition associated with *H. erectus*.

anatomically modern humans (AMHs): Including the Cro-Magnons of Europe (31,000 B.P.) and the older fossils from Skhūl (100,000) and Qafzeh (92,000); continue through the present; also known as *H. sapiens sapiens*.

archaic *Homo sapiens*: Early *H. sapiens*, consisting of the Neandertals of Europe and the Middle East, the Neandertal-like hominids of Africa and Asia, and the immediate ancestors of all these hominids; lived from about 300,000 to 35,000 B.P.

Aurignacian: Upper Paleolithic tradition, 35,000 to 20,000 B.P.; tools usually found in narrow valleys or near cliff walls, and thick layers suggest long occupation; may have diffused into Europe from elsewhere.

blade tool: The basic Upper Paleolithic tool type, hammered off a prepared core.

broad-spectrum revolution: Period beginning around 20,000 B.P. in the Middle East and 12,000 B.P. in Europe, during which a wider range, or broader spectrum, of plant and animal life was hunted, gathered, collected, caught, and fished; revolutionary because it led to food production.

bush school: Held in a location remote from residential areas; young people go there when they reach puberty to be instructed in knowledge viewed as essential to adult status.

ceremonies of increase: Rituals held to promote the fertility and reproduction of plants and animals.

classic Neandertals: Stereotypical Neandertals of Western Europe; considered by some scholars to be too specialized to have evolved into *H. sapiens sapiens*.

continental shelf: Offshore shallow-water zone over which the ocean gradually deepens until the abrupt fall to deep water, which is known as the *continental slope*.

continental slope: See *continental shelf.*

Homo sapiens sapiens: Anatomically modern humans.

Mesolithic: Middle Stone Age, whose characteristic tool type was the microlith; broad-spectrum economy.

microlith: Greek for "small stone"; characteristic Mesolithic tool.

Middle Pleistocene: The period from the Mindel glacial through the Riss-Würm interglacial.

Mindel: The second major glacial advance in Europe.

Mousterian: Middle Paleolithic tool-making tradition associated with Neandertals.

Neandertals: *H. sapiens neanderthalensis,* an archaic *H. sapiens* subspecies, lived in Europe and the Middle East between 130,000 and 35,000 B.P.

Paleolithic: Old Stone Age (from Greek roots meaning "old" and "stone"); divided into Lower (early), Middle, and Upper (late).

Perigordian: An Upper Paleolithic tradition that coexisted with the Aurignacian in Europe between 35,000 and 20,000 B.P. Perigordian tools are usually found in thin deposits and are scattered over large areas; evolved in Western Europe out of Mousterian antecedents.

Riss: The third major glacial advance in Europe.

traditions, in tool making: Coherent patterns of tool manufacture.

Upper Paleolithic: Blade tool-making traditions associated with early *H. sapiens sapiens;* named from their location in the upper, or more recent, layers of sedimentary deposits.

STUDY QUESTIONS

1. What were the main trends in the evolution of technology during the Paleolithic?
2. What was Acheulian tool manufacture, and what advantages did it give *H. erectus?*
3. How do the geographic distribution and ecological range (variety of environments occupied) of *H. erectus* compare with those of the australopithecines?
4. What anatomical characteristics distinguish *H. erectus?*
5. What do the sites of Terra Amata, Torralba, and Ambrona reveal about the life of *H. erectus?*
6. What are reasons for suspecting that *H. erectus* had language?
7. Why do paleontological and archeological data from

Europe dominate the period between 300,000 and 12,000 B.P.?
8. What is the evidence for and against the Neandertal ancestry of *H. sapiens sapiens?*
9. What is the significance of La Chapelle-aux-Saints?
10. What biological and cultural adaptations may be related to the distinctive features of the Neandertal jaw, face, and teeth?
11. What cultural adaptive changes accompanied glacial retreat at the end of the Pleistocene in Europe?
12. What explanations have been given for Upper Paleolithic cave painting?
13. What is a broad-spectrum economy, and how was it exemplified by the European Mesolithic?

SUGGESTED ADDITIONAL READING

CHAMPION, T., AND C. GAMBLE, EDS.
1984 *Prehistoric Europe.* New York: Academic Press. From the Mesolithic to the spread of food production into Europe.
DELSON, E., ED.
1985 *Ancestors: The Hard Evidence.* New York: Liss. Articles on the hominid fossil record.
FAGAN, B. M.
1988 *Archeology: A Brief Introduction.* 2nd ed. Glenview, IL: Scott, Foresman. How archeologists reconstruct the past.
1989 *People of the Earth: An Introduction to World Prehistory.* 6th ed. Glenview, IL: Scott, Foresman.

From the Paleolithic to the Neolithic around the world.
JOLLY, C. J., AND R. WHITE
1994 *Physical Anthropology and Archeology.* 5th ed. New York: McGraw-Hill. Basic text covering the hominid fossil record and archeology.
KLEIN, R. G.
1989 *The Human Career: Human Biological and Cultural Origins.* Chicago: University of Chicago Press. Comprehensive review of the fossil and archeological record.
NELSON, H., AND R. JURMAIN
1991 *Introduction to Physical Anthropology.* 5th ed. St.

Paul, MN: West. Another basic text providing detailed information on the most recent hominid fossil finds.

OAKLEY, K. P.
1976 *Man the Tool-Maker.* 6th ed. Chicago: University of Chicago Press. Brief introduction to tool making.

PFEIFFER, J. E.
1985 *The Emergence of Humankind.* 4th ed. New York: HarperCollins. Very readable account of hominid biological and cultural evolution through the origins of agriculture.

RIGHTMIRE, G. P.
1990 *The Evolution of* Homo erectus: *Comparative Anatomical Studies of an Extinct Human Species.* New York: Cambridge University Press. Thorough review of the fossil evidence for the *H. erectus* period of human evolution.

UCKO, P., AND A. ROSENFELD
1967 *Paleolithic Cave Art.* London: Weidenfeld and Nicolson. A survey, including finds and interpretations.

WEISS, M. L., AND A. E. MANN
1989 *Human Biology and Behavior: An Anthropological Perspective.* 5th ed. Glenview, IL: Scott, Foresman. Another comprehensive text with detailed information on the fossil record.

WENKE, R. J.
1990 *Patterns in Prehistory: Mankind's First Three Million Years.* 3rd ed. New York: Oxford University Press. Very thorough survey of fossil and archeological reconstruction of human evolution.

THE ORIGIN AND SPREAD OF FOOD PRODUCTION

For thousands of years after the appearance of anatomically modern humans, a basic foraging pattern that was as old as *H. erectus* persisted. However, a widespread intensification of resource use followed global warming and the retreat of the northern ice sheets after 15,000 B.P. Throughout the inhabited world, as the big-game supply diminished, foragers had to pursue new resources. Human attention shifted from large-bodied, slow reproducers (such as mammoths) to species like fish, mollusks, and rabbits that reproduce quickly and prolifically (Hayden 1981).

For example, David Lubell and his colleagues have reconstructed a pattern of intensive snail collecting at Kef Zoura, eastern Algeria. Dozens of sites in and around the Kef Zoura valley were occupied between 10,000 and 7,000 years ago by members of the Capsian culture. The **Capsians** were a Mesolithic people who based much of their subsistence on land snails, including the modern species the French call *escargot*. The Kef Zoura site has yielded millions of land snail shells. The Capsians were nomadic, continually shifting campsites after depleting the local snail supply. They also ate plant species, including various grasses, acorns, pine nuts, and pistachio nuts (Bower and Lubell 1988).

The Japanese site of Nittano (Akazawa 1980), on an inlet near Tokyo, offers additional evidence for the widespread importance of broad-spectrum foraging. Nittano was occupied several times between 6000 and 5000 B.P. by members of the **Jomon** culture, for which 30,000 sites are known in Japan. The Jomon people hunted deer, pigs, bears, and antelope, and also ate fish, shellfish, and plants. Jomon sites have yielded the remains of 300 species of shellfish and 180 species of edible plants (including berries, nuts, and tubers) (Akazawa and Aikens, eds. 1986).

Early experiments in food production illustrate another—and the most significant—form of intensified resource use. By 10,000 B.P., a major economic shift was underway in the Middle East (Turkey, Iraq, Iran, Syria, Jordan, and Israel). People started intervening in the reproductive cycles of some of the plants and animals their ancestors had foraged for generations. Middle Easterners eventually became the world's first farmers and herders (Moore 1985). No longer simply harvesting nature's bounty, they produced their own food and modified the biological characteristics of the plants and animals in their

diet. By 10,000 B.P., domesticated plants and animals were included within the broad spectrum of resources used by Middle Eastern populations. By 7500 B.P., most Middle Easterners were moving away from a broad-spectrum foraging pattern toward more specialized economies based on fewer species, which were domesticates.

Kent Flannery (1969) has proposed a series of eras during which the Middle Eastern transition to food production took place (Table 10.1). The era of seminomadic hunting and gathering (12,000 to 10,000 B.P.) encompasses the last stages of broad-spectrum foraging before the addition of domesticated plants and animals. Next came the era of early dry farming and caprine domestication (10,000 to 7500 B.P.). **Dry farming** refers to rainfall-dependent cultivation, without irrigation. **Caprine** (from *capra*, Latin for "goat") refers to goats and sheep, which were domesticated during this era.

During the era of increasing specialization in food production (7500 to 5500 B.P.), new crops were added to the diet, along with more productive varieties of wheat and barley. Cattle and pigs were domesticated. By 5500 B.P., agriculture extended to the alluvial plain of the Tigris and Euphrates rivers (Figure 10.1), where early Mesopotamians lived in walled towns, some of which grew into cities. Metallurgy and the wheel were invented. After 2 million years of stone-tool making, *H. sapiens* was living in the Bronze Age.

The archeologist V. Gordon Childe (1951) used the term *Neolithic Revolution* to categorize the origin and impact of **food production**—plant cultivation and animal domestication. **Neolithic,** which means "New Stone Age," was coined to describe techniques of grinding and polishing stone tools. However, the main significance of the Neolithic was the new total economy rather than just the tool-making techniques. *Neolithic* now refers to the first cultural

Table 10.1 *Eras in the transition to food production in the Middle East*

Era	Dates (B.P.)
Seminomadic hunting and gathering (e.g., Natufians)	12,000–10,000
Early dry farming and caprine domestication	10,000–7500
Increasing specialization in food production	7500–5500
Origin of state (Sumer)	5500

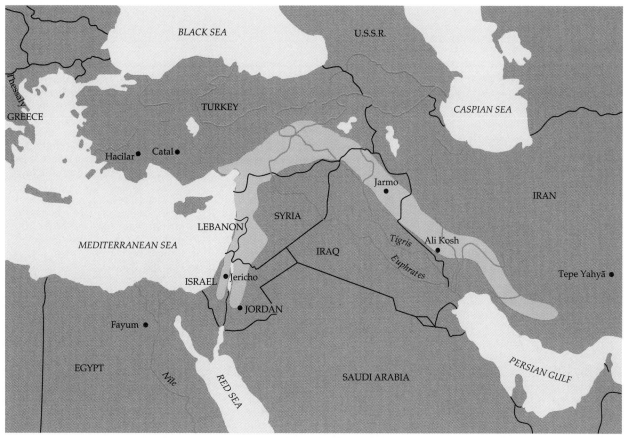

Figure 10.1 *The ancestors of wheat and barley grew wild in the Hilly Flanks (shaded).*
Food production emerged on the margins of that zone rather than within it. Food
production did not reach the alluvial lowlands near the Tigris and Euphrates rivers, where
Mesopotamian civilization arose around 5500 B.P., until irrigation was invented, much
later.

period in a given region in which the first signs of domestication are present. The Neolithic began around 10,000 B.P. in the Middle East, 8000 B.P. in South and Southeast Asia, 7000 B.P. in Africa and Eastern Europe, and 5000 B.P. in Western Europe and Mexico (Bogucki 1987, 1988). The Neolithic economy based on food production produced substantial alterations in human life styles. The pace of social and cultural change increased enormously.

THE ORIGIN OF FOOD PRODUCTION IN THE MIDDLE EAST

How and why did food production originate in the Middle East? To answer this question, we must recognize four important environmental zones. They are (from highest to lowest): high plateau (5,000 feet, or 1,500 meters), the Hilly Flanks, steppe (treeless plain), and the alluvial plain of the Tigris and Euphrates rivers (100 to 500 feet, or 30 to 150 meters). The **Hilly Flanks** is a woodland zone that flanks the rivers to the north (Figures 10.1 and 10.2).

It was once thought that food production began in oases in the alluvial plain, where Mesopotamian civilization arose later. (**Alluvial** describes rich, fertile soil deposited by rivers and streams.) Today, we know that although the world's first civilization (Mesopotamian) did indeed develop in this zone, irrigation, a late (7000 B.P.) invention, was necessary for food production in this very arid area. Plant cultivation and animal domestication started not in the arid river zone but in areas where rainfall was reliable.

Another doubtful theory, proposed by archeologist Robert J. Braidwood (1975), was that food pro-

IN THE NEWS: A MAN WHO LIVED 5,300 YEARS AGO

This item describes the 1991 discovery and subsequent identification of the glacially preserved "Iceman" as a Neolithic Alpine European who lived around 5300 B.P. The find is significant because of its age, its state of preservation, and its combination of a human cadaver with clothing and possessions, including stone and metal (copper) tools. The Iceman, who probably came from an Alpine farming village, was on an autumn hunting trip when he was killed and eventually frozen. The Neolithic, which began some 10,000 years ago in the Middle East, spread from Eastern to Western Europe between 7000 B.P. and 5000 B.P.

They call him the man in the ice. As scientists have come to realize since his frozen body emerged from a glacier in the Italian Alps last year, he is the nearest we may ever come to meeting a real person from the Stone Age.

The "Iceman," who scientists now know lived about 5,300 years ago, had been in the ice 1,000 years when the Egyptians built the pyramids at Giza, more than 3,000 years when Jesus was born. Yet he was found with a remarkable array of clothing, weapons and equipment, including some mysterious objects of types never seen before.

Some—including the man's fur hat, the oldest known in Europe—were found just last summer in a new expedition to the normally icebound site on the Austrian-Italian border.

Archaeologists are excited, because the man's body was found not in a grave, the usual source of ancient remains, but at a campsite he made during a sojourn in the mountains, and because snow and ice covered him and his things, preserving them almost perfectly.

His perishable belongings— items made of wood, leather, grass, and apparently even food and medicines—have come out of the ice virtually intact, providing scientists with the most intimate picture even seen of the daily life of a prehistoric man.

For example, his ax, which has a copper head, looks and feels as new and dangerous as on the fall day in about 3300 B.C., when the man leaned it against a rock before bedding down for his last night. It is among the oldest copper axes known and one of the best made, dating from the dawn of the use of metals.

Archaeologists know that fateful night was in the autumn, because frozen with him was a ripe blackthorn fruit, the plumlike berry also called sloe, which grows at lower altitudes and ripens in the fall.

The man's body is startlingly well preserved—by far the most lifelike from prehistoric times— and is being kept in a high-security freezer at the University of Innsbruck medical school.

The body was naturally freeze-dried and is in such good condition that pores in the skin look normal. Even his eyeballs can still be seen behind lids frozen open, and CT scans show the brain and other internal organs in place.

"We have never had a prehistoric discovery as complete as this," said Andreas Lippert, a University of Vienna archaeologist who led the expedition to the site last summer. The group found more than 400 objects, most of them parts of the man's clothing.

Yet several key questions remain. What was he doing so high in the mountains? How did he die? And, most intriguing to archaeologists, did he come from one of the known prehistoric cultures of the region, or does he represent something entirely new?

What is clear is that he lived during one of the more critical transitions in the development of human culture, when stone tools were beginning to give way to metal.

Farming, which began in the Middle East about 5,000 years earlier, had spread to much of Eurasia by 5,300 years ago. The man probably came from a village of farmers who raised wheat, barley and oats and herded sheep and goats.

The man in the ice was discovered Sept. 19, 1991, by Helmut and Erika Simon, a German couple hiking in the Alps. Near the 10,500-foot-high ridge that defines the Austrian-Italian border they were tramping over the snow and ice of a commonly used pass when they saw a human head and shoulders sticking out of the ice. The body was lying face down, its skin a tawny color and the head hairless. The Simons reported it to police in the Italian state of South Tirol.

The local Carabinieri, Italian police familiar with the common problem of retrieving bodies of modern climbers, insisted that this

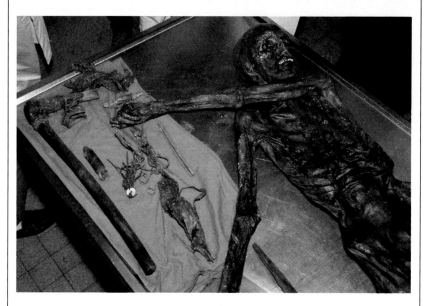

The "Iceman"—a glacially preserved Neolithic European who lived around 5300 B.P.—with his possessions.

time the site was in Austria and not their problem.

Two days later the Austrian police from north Tirol arrived with a helicopter and—not realizing the site's importance—used an air hammer to hack the body out of the ice. They accidentally cut into the man's hip, but his legs stayed stuck. Forensic officials spotted the copper-bladed ax on a nearby rock and, presuming foul play in the man's death, took it as "evidence."

Bad weather forced a temporary retreat. But word of the find encouraged curious hikers to trek to the body, and several tried to chop it free.

On Sept. 23, four days after the find, a forensic team from the University of Innsbruck helicoptered to the site, found that meltwater had refrozen around the body and began again to chop. When they pulled out the prone body, it was later realized, the man's penis remained embedded in the ice.

Workers also gathered up some pieces of fur and leather clothing, string, a leather bag and a flint dagger. A long stick, apparently a bow, was still partly embedded in ice, so workers broke off part and took that, too.

Hikers and skiers had been lost in the Alps many times, but they usually emerged a few decades later when the flow of the glaciers transported them to lower altitudes where they melted out. Moreover, these "young" bodies were usually horribly transformed by the ice, their flesh turned into misshapen blobs of "fat wax." This man in the ice, though dried and somewhat shriveled like a mummy, looked too good to be very old.

A team of glaciologists soon resolved the question with another visit to the site. They found that the body had lain at the bottom of a narrow ravine. Snow could have filled the 6-to-10-foot-deep crevice, but the resulting ice was trapped.

The glaciologists also found evidence to support the man's antiquity—his quiver, which contained 14 arrows, two of them fitted with flint arrowheads, hardly the choice of any bowman who lived since the Iron Age swept Eurasia more than 3,000 years ago.

And the glaciologists explained why the body had only just emerged. Earlier in 1991 great storms had blown dust from North Africa into the Alps, darkening the snow cover. The dust absorbed solar heat, causing more than the usual amount of snow to melt during the summer of 1991, exposing the body.

Source: Boyce Rensberger, "A Man Who Lived 5,300 Years Ago," *The Washington Post,* November 26, 1992, E1.

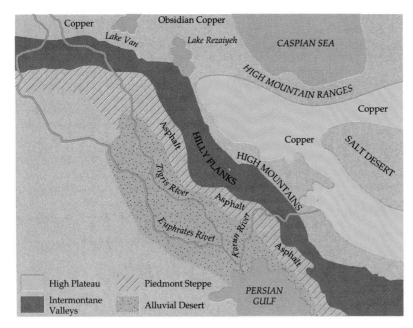

Figure 10.2 *The ecology of food production: the vertical economy of the Middle East. Geographically close but ecologically different environments were linked during the emergence of food production by seasonal movements and trade patterns of broad-spectrum foragers. Domestication emerged as plants were removed from the zones where they grew wild—intermontane valleys (the Hilly Flanks)—into adjacent zones where selective pressures were different and humans themselves became agents of selection.*

duction began in the Hilly Flanks. Wheat and barley, the earliest domesticated grain plants, still grow wild there. Braidwood believed that cultivation would have begun in the zone where food plants grew in nature. In 1948, Braidwood's team started excavations at Jarmo, an early food-producing village inhabited between 9000 and 8500 B.P., located in the Hilly Flanks. We now know, however, that there were food-producing villages earlier than Jarmo, in zones adjacent to the Hilly Flanks. One example is Ali Kosh, a village in the foothills (piedmont steppe) of the Zagros mountains. By 9000 B.P. the people of Ali Kosh were herding goats, intensively collecting various wild plants, and harvesting wheat during the late winter and early spring (Hole, Flannery, and Neely 1969).

Climate change played a role in the origin of food production. The end of the Ice Age brought greater regional and local variation in climatic conditions. Lewis Binford (1968) proposed that in certain areas of the Middle East (such as the Hilly Flanks), local environments were so rich in resources that people could adopt **sedentism**—sedentary (settled) life in villages. Binford's prime example is the widespread Natufian culture (12,500 to 10,500 B.P.), based on broad-spectrum foraging. The **Natufians,** who subsisted on intensive wild cereal collecting and gazelle hunting, had year-round villages. They were able to

stay in the same place (early villages) because they could harvest nearby wild cereals for 6 months.

Henry (1989) documented a climate change just before the Natufian period—toward warmer, more humid conditions. This led to an expansion in the altitude range of wild wheat and barley, enlarging the potential foraging area in space and time—allowing a longer harvest season. Wheat and barley ripened in the spring at low altitudes, in the summer at middle altitudes, and in the fall at high altitudes. The Natufians built their villages in locations from which they could most easily harvest the wild plants in all three zones.

This favorable foraging pattern was threatened by a second climate change—to much drier conditions—around 11,000 B.P. Many of the habitats of the wild cereals dried up, and the optimal zone for foraging shrank. Large Natufian villages were now restricted to areas with permanent water. As population continued to grow, some Natufians attempted to maintain productivity by transferring wild cereals to these well-watered areas, where they started cultivating.

To explain the origin of food production (and economic change in general), many scholars now assume that the people most likely to adopt a new subsistence strategy are those who are having trouble following the subsistence practices that are common to their group (Binford 1968; Flannery 1973; Wenke 1990). Thus, ancient Middle Easterners who lived outside the zone where wild foods were most abundant (and especially after the climate got drier) would be the most likely to experiment—leading to new subsistence strategies. Recent archeological finds support the hypothesis that domestication began in *marginal areas* rather than in the optimal zones, such as the Hilly Flanks, where traditional foods were most abundant.

Even today, wild wheat grows so densely in the Hilly Flanks that one person working just an hour with Neolithic technology can easily harvest a kilogram of wheat (Harlan and Zohary 1966). People would have had no reason to invent cultivation when wild grain was ample to feed them. Wild wheat ripens rapidly and can be harvested over a three-week period. According to Flannery, a family of experienced plant collectors could in that three weeks harvest enough cereal—2,200 pounds (1,000 kilograms) of it—to feed themselves for the entire year. However, after harvesting all that wheat, they would need a place to put it. They wouldn't be able to continue a totally nomadic existence because they would need to stay close to this basic dietary resource.

Now we see why sedentary village life *preceded* a full-fledged food-producing economy in the Middle East. The Natufians and other Hilly Flanks foragers had no choice but to build villages near the densest stands of wild grains. They needed a permanent place to put their grain. Furthermore, animals—sheep and goats—came to graze on the stubble that remained after people had harvested the grain. This also favored sedentary life; basic plants and animals were available in the same area. Hilly Flanks foragers built houses, dug storage pits for grain, and made ovens to roast it.

Many Natufian settlements were occupied year round and show permanent architectural features and evidence for the processing and storage of wild cereals. One such site is Abu Hureyra, Syria, which was initially occupied by Natufians around 11,000 to 10,500 B.P. Then it was abandoned—to be reoccupied later by food producers, between 9500 and 8000 B.P. From the Natufian period, Abu Hureyra has yielded the remains of grinding stones, wild plants (including wheat, barley, and rye), and 50,000 gazelle bones, which represent 80 percent of all the bones recovered at the site (Jolly and White 1994).

Before domestication, the favored Hilly Flanks zone had the densest populations. Eventually, excess population started spilling over into adjacent areas. Emigrants from the Hilly Flanks at first tried to maintain a broad-spectrum economy in these marginal zones, where wild plants and animals were less abundant. Eventually, however, population pressure on more limited resources forced them to become the first food producers (Binford 1968; Flannery 1969). *Early cultivation began as an attempt to copy, in a less favorable environment, the dense stands of wheat and barley that grew wild in the Hilly Flanks.*

The Middle East and other world areas where food production originated are regions of **vertical economy.** (Other examples include Peru and **Mesoamerica**—Middle America, including Mexico, Guatemala, and Belize.) A vertical economy exploits environmental zones that, although close together in space, contrast with one another in altitude, rainfall, overall climate, and vegetation (Figure 10.2). This close juxtaposition of varied environments allowed broad-spectrum foragers to use different resources in different seasons.

Early seminomadic foragers followed game as it moved from zone to zone. The steppe region, for example, which had rain rather than snow during the winter, provided winter pasture for game animals 12,000 years ago. (Indeed, it is still used for winter grazing by herders today.) When winter ended, the steppe dried up. Game moved up to the Hilly Flanks and plateau country as the snow melted, and pasture land became available at higher elevations. Foragers gathered as they climbed, harvesting wild grains that ripened later at higher altitudes. Sheep and goats followed the stubble in the wheat and barley fields after the people had harvested the grain.

The four Middle Eastern environmental zones shown in Figure 10.2 were also tied together through trade. Certain resources were confined to specific zones. Asphalt, used as an adhesive in the manufacture of sickles, came from the steppe. Copper and turquoise sources were located in the high plateau. Contrasting environments were therefore linked in two ways: by foragers' seasonal migration and by trade.

A pattern of movement of people, animals, and products between zones—plus population increase supported by highly productive broad-spectrum foraging—was a precondition for the emergence of

As the transition to food production began, between 12,000 and 10,000 years ago, ancient Middle Easterners were broad-spectrum foragers who moved, in accordance with the availability of plants and animals, between lower and higher zones in a vertical economy. With domestication, this pattern evolved into nomadic herding economies. Here Jordanian herders follow their flocks in hillside grazing.

food production. Trading and traveling between zones, people removed grains from the zone where they grew wild and carried the grains into environments where selective pressures were different. Mutations and genetic recombinations leading to new kinds of wheat and barley appeared and survived in the new environments. Some of the new varieties were better adapted to the steppe and, eventually, the alluvial plain than the wild forms had been. Selective pressures also changed because people became agents of selection.

Genetic Changes and Domestication

What are some of the differences between wild and domesticated plants? The seeds of domesticated cereals, and sometimes the entire plant, are larger. Compared with wild plants, crops produce a higher yield per unit of area. Domesticated plants also lose their natural seed dispersal mechanisms. Cultivated beans, for example, have pods that hold together, rather than shattering as they do in the wild. Domesticated cereals have tougher connective tissue holding the seedpods to the stem.

Grains of wheat, barley, and other cereals occur in bunches at the end of a stalk (Figure 10.3). The grains are attached to the stalk by an **axis.** In wild cereals this axis is brittle. Sections of the axis break off one by one, and a seed attached to each section falls to the ground. This is how wild cereals spread their seeds and propagate their species. But a brittle

axis is a problem for people. Imagine the annoyance experienced by broad-spectrum foragers as they tried to harvest wild wheat, only to have the grain fall off or be blown away.

In very dry weather, wild wheat and barley ripen—their axes totally disintegrating—in just three days (Flannery 1973). The brittle axis must have been even more irritating to people who planted the seeds and waited for the harvest. But fortunately, certain stalks of wild wheat and barley happened to have tough axes. These were the ones whose seeds people saved to plant the following year.

Another problem with wild cereals is that the edible portion is enclosed in a tough husk. This husk was too tough to remove with a pounding stone. Foragers had to roast the grain to make the husk brittle enough to come off. However, some wild plants happened to have genes for brittle husks. Humans chose the seeds of these plants (which would have germinated prematurely in nature) because they could be more effectively prepared for eating.

People also started selecting certain features in animals (Ucko and Dimbleby, eds. 1969). Some time after sheep were domesticated, advantageous new phenotypes arose. Wild sheep aren't woolly; wool coats were products of domestication. Although it's hard to imagine, a wool coat offers protection against extreme heat. Skin temperatures of sheep living in very hot areas are much lower than temperatures on the surface of their wool. Woolly

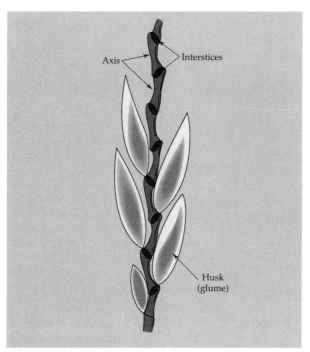

Figure 10.3 *A head of wheat or barley. The central stalk, or axis, is divided by interstices where, in the wild, the axis comes apart as its parts fall off one by one. These interstices are tough and don't come apart in domesticated grains. In wild wheat and barley, husks, in which the edible grain develops, are hard. In domestic plants, they are brittle, permitting easy access to the grain.*

sheep, but not their wild ancestors, could survive in hot, dry alluvial lowlands. Wool had an additional advantage: its use for clothing.

What are some of the differences between wild and domesticated animals? Unlike plant size, which increases with domestication, animal size tends to decrease—perhaps because smaller animals are easier to control. Middle Eastern sites document changes in the horns of domesticated goats. This change may have been genetically linked to some other desirable trait that has left no skeletal evidence behind.

Food Production and the State

The shift from broad-spectrum foraging to food production was gradual. The knowledge of how to grow crops and breed livestock didn't immediately convert Middle Easterners into full-time farmers and herders. Domesticated plants and animals be-

gan as minor parts of a broad-spectrum economy. Foraging for fruits, nuts, grasses, grains, snails, and insects continued.

Over time Middle Eastern economies grew more specialized, geared more exclusively toward crops and herds. The former marginal zones became centers of the new economy and of population increase and emigration. Some of the increasing population spilled back into the Hilly Flanks, where people finally had to intensify their own production by cultivating. Domesticated crops could now provide a bigger harvest than could the grains that grew wild there. In the Hilly Flanks, too, farming replaced foraging as the economic mainstay.

Farming colonies spread down into drier areas. By 7000 B.P. simple irrigation systems had developed, tapping springs in the foothills. By 6000 B.P. more complex irrigation techniques made agriculture possible in the arid lowlands of southern Mesopotamia. In the alluvial plain of the Tigris and Euphrates rivers, a new economy based on irrigation and trade fueled the growth of an entirely new form of society. This was the state, based on central government, extreme contrasts of wealth, and social classes.

We now understand why the first farmers lived neither in the alluvial lowlands, where Mesopotamian civilization had developed by 5500 B.P., nor in the Hilly Flanks woodlands, where wild plants and animals abounded. Food production began in marginal zones, such as the steppe, as people experimented at reproducing, artificially, the dense grain stands that grew wild in the Hilly Flanks. As seeds were taken to new environments, new phenotypes were favored by a combination of natural conditions and human selection. The spread of cereal grains outside their natural habitats was part of a system of migration and trade between zones, which had developed in the Middle East during the broad-spectrum period. Food production also owed its origin to the need to intensify production to feed an increasing human population—the legacy of thousands of years of productive foraging.

During the rise of Middle Eastern food production, the center of population growth had shifted from the zone where grains grew wild (Hilly Flanks) to adjacent areas (steppe) where grains were first domesticated. By 6000 B.P. population was increasing most rapidly in the alluvial plain of southern Mesopotamia. This growing population sup-

Simple irrigation systems were supplementing dry farming in the Middle East by 7000 B.P. By 6000 B.P. complex irrigation techniques made intensive agriculture possible in the arid lowlands of southern Mesopotamia. Irrigation and trade spurred the growth of the state, based on central government, extreme contrasts of wealth, and social classes.

ported itself through irrigation and intensive river valley agriculture. By 5500 B.P. towns had grown into cities. The earliest city-states were Sumer (southern Iraq) and Elam (southwestern Iran), with their capitals at Uruk and Susa, respectively.

Literacy and temples played key roles in the Mesopotamian economy. For the historic period after 5600 B.P., when writing was invented, there are temple records of economic activities. Although states can exist without writing, it facilitates the flow and storage of information. We know that Mesopotamian priests held political posts and managed herding, farming, manufacture, and trade. Temple officials allocated fodder and pasture land for cattle and donkeys, which were used as plow and cart animals. Centralized plowing came under temple direction, and irrigation grew in scale.

Political control grew as the economy diversified. There were centrally managed systems of trade, manufacture, and grain storage. Temples collected and distributed meat, dairy products, clothing, crops, fish, tools, and trade items. Potters, metal workers, weavers, sculptors, and other artisans perfected their crafts.

Intensive agriculture supported a spurt in population and an increase in urban sites. By 4800 B.P. Uruk, the largest early Mesopotamian city, had a population of 50,000. As irrigation and the population expanded, communities came into conflict over water, and people sought protection in fortified cities (Adams 1981). Cities defended themselves when neighbors or invaders threatened.

Between 5000 and 4500 B.P., secular authority replaced temple rule. With conflict and militarism, the office of military coordinator developed into kingship. This change shows up architecturally in palaces and royal tombs. The palace raised armies, supplying them with armor, chariots, and metal armaments.

Agricultural intensification made it possible for the number of people supported by a given area of land to increase. Population pressure on scarce irrigated fields helped create a class-structured society. Land became scarce private property. No longer part of a kin group's estate, land could be bought and sold, as can be seen in the records of sales of lots and fields between 5000 and 4500 B.P. Some people amassed large estates, and their wealth set them off from ordinary farmers. Eventually these landlords entered the urban elite, while sharecroppers and serfs toiled in the fields. Mesopotamia had a well-defined class structure by 4500 B.P., with complex stratification into nobles, commoners, and slaves.

THE EMERGENCE OF FOOD PRODUCTION IN OTHER OLD WORLD AREAS

Compared with the Middle East, less is known about prehistoric food-producing societies in other parts of the Old World—sub-Saharan Africa (Clark and Brandt 1984), South and Southeast Asia, and

China. Partly this reflects the poorer preservation of archeological remains in hot, moist habitats. Mostly it reflects the need for additional archeological research in these areas. From Pakistan's Indus River Valley, where ancient cities emerged slightly later than did the first Mesopotamian city-states, recent research confirms the early domestication of goats, sheep, cattle, wheat, and barley—by 8000 B.P. (Meadow, ed. 1991).

China and Southeast Asia were also among the first regions of the world to develop farming. The first plants to be domesticated were millet and rice (Jolly and White 1994). Millet is a tall, coarse cereal grass still grown in northern China. This grain, which today feeds a third of the world's population, is used in the United States mainly as bird seed. By 7000 B.P. foxtail millet supported early farming communities in northern China. Its cultivation paved the way for widespread village life and eventually for Shang dynasty civilization between 3600 and 3100 B.P. The northern Chinese had also domesticated dogs, pigs, and possibly cattle, goats, and sheep by 7000 B.P. (K. C. Chang 1977).

Spirit Cave in northwestern Thailand has yielded the earliest plant remains from Southeast Asia (Gorman 1969). Between about 9200 and about 8600 B.P. the people at Spirit Cave relied on wild nuts, bottle gourds, water chestnuts, black pepper, and cucumbers. Although there is no evidence that these plants were domesticated, their association at the same site indicates a diverse diet and a broad-spectrum pattern that could have led to food production (see *In the News*).

There is speculation that rice may have first been domesticated in Southeast Asia, as early as 8800 B.P. However, the earliest domesticated rice found so far comes from the 7,000-year-old site Hemudu, on Lake Dongting in southern China. The people of Hemudu used both wild and domesticated rice, along with domesticated water buffalo, dogs, and pigs. They also hunted wild game (Jolly and White 1994).

At Nok Nok Tha in central Thailand, pottery made more than 5,000 years ago has imprints of husks and grains of domesticated rice (Solheim 1972/1976). Animal bones show that the people of Nok Nok Tha also had humped zebu cattle similar to those of contemporary India. Rice might have been cultivated at about the same time in the Indus River Valley of Pakistan and adjacent western India.

Let us turn now to archeological sequences in the Americas.

THE FIRST AMERICAN FARMERS

Homo did not, of course, originate in the New World. Never have fossils of Neandertals or earlier hominids been found in North or South America (Fagan 1987; Irving 1985). The settlement of the New World was one of the major achievements of *H. sapiens sapiens*. This colonization continued the trends toward expansion of numbers and range that have marked human evolution generally.

Millet, being harvested here on a Chinese plateau, was grown in the Hwang-Ho (Yellow River) Valley of northern China by 7000 B.P. This grain supported early farming communities in northern China and paved the way for Shang dynasty civilization between 3600 and 3100 B.P.

IN THE NEWS: NEW EVIDENCE OF EARLY FOOD PRODUCTION IN AFRICA

Plant cultivation began in the Middle East (the Levant) around 10,000 years ago, after a 2,000 year period of intensive collecting of the wild ancestors of wheat and barley. This item describes new evidence for similar intensive collecting around 8000 B.P. in southern Egypt near Sudan. Like Middle Easterners, and just 2,000 years later, these African foragers were paving the way for food production by harvesting a broad spectrum of grains, the ancestors of millet and sorghum. We know from other world areas that cultivation soon follows this kind of intensive collecting. The find described here thus suggests an early date (perhaps 6000 B.P.) and an independent invention of food production in interior Africa. Later, wheat and barley diffused into Africa from the Middle East, providing additional caloric staples.

Archeologists digging in the Sahara Desert of southern Egypt have found 8,000-year-old seeds of sorghum and millet, indicating that the domestication of these important African food crops occurred much earlier than previously thought.

The discovery, reported in the current issue of the journal Nature, provides some of the first direct evidence for the early history of agriculture in a major region other than the Levant or pre-Columbian America. The findings surprised experts because they had assumed that these plants were first domesticated in the African savanna to the south, presumably well after the introduction of cultivated barley and wheat in lower Egypt about 6,400 years ago.

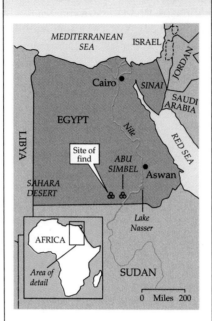

The seeds were found charred and buried in the ruins of a prehistoric settlement 60 miles west of Abu Simbel, on the Nile River near the Sudanese border. The variety of more than 40 different plant seeds showed that vegetation in that region then must have been more abundant than it is now.

The excavations were conducted over the last two years by a team of American and Polish archeologists led by Dr. Fred Wendorf, a professor of archeology at Southern Methodist University in Dallas.

Dr. Jack R. Harlan, a retired agronomist from the University of Illinois and an expert on sorghum who advised the archeologists, cautioned that there was still no evidence to support a conclusion that sorghum had been domesticated at this time, though the wild plants were apparently being regularly harvested. But he agreed that the findings indicated the domestication of these crops must

have come several thousand years earlier than thought. Previous evidence had dated the domestication of sorghum in Africa at about 1000 B.C.

In their report, Dr. Wendorf and his associates wrote: "The evidence for the intensive use of sorghum and millets some 8,000 years ago indicates that such use first occurred much earlier than previously thought, and took place in what is today a rainless desert. It is a short step from intensive use of wild plants, to planting and protecting these plants, and thus to the genetic changes involved in domestication."

In fact, the archeologists said, infrared analysis of the lipids, or fats, in the sorghum grains revealed that they were closer genetically to modern cultivated plants than to wild ones. In other respects, however, the seeds appeared to be entirely wild, scientists said.

Archeologists generally place the beginning of agriculture at about 10,000 years ago in the regions of present-day Turkey, Syria and Iraq. Cereal grains began to be harvested intensively there even earlier, about 12,000 years ago. But it was 2,000 years more before there was evidence of domestic varieties of peas, lentils, barley and emmer wheat.

Since there is no evidence that these Levantine plants were introduced into Egypt until 6,400 years ago, Dr. Wendorf's team noted, the new findings suggest that Africans began domesticating plants independently of outside influences.

Source: John Noble Wilford, "Clues to Food Crops Are Found in Africa," *The New York Times,* October 27, 1992, C2.

America's First Immigrants

The original settlers of the New World were Northeast Asians, ancestors of American Indians. They entered North America via the Bering land bridge, **Beringia,** which connected North America and Siberia several times during the ice ages. Beringia, which today lies under the Bering Sea, was a dry land area several hundred miles wide, exposed during the glacial advances (Figure 10.4).

Living in Beringia perhaps 25,000 years ago, the ancestors of Native Americans didn't realize they were embarking on the colonization of a new continent. They were merely big-game hunters who, over the generations, moved gradually eastward as they spread their camps and followed their prey —woolly mammoths and other tundra-adapted herbivores.

This was truly a "new world" to its early colonists, as it would be to the European voyagers who rediscovered it thousands of years later. Its natural resources, particularly its big game, had never before been exploited by humans. Early bands followed the game south and eventually entered the North American heartland. Although ice sheets covered Canada then, colonization gradually penetrated the United States. Successive generations of hunters followed game through unglaciated corridors, breaks in the continental ice sheets.

In North America's rolling grasslands, early American Indians, **Paleoindians,** hunted horses, camels, bison, elephants, mammoths, and giant sloths. The **Clovis tradition**—a sophisticated stone technology based on a projectile point that was fastened to the end of a hunting spear (Figure 10.5)— flourished between 12,000 and 11,000 B.P. in the Central Plains, on their western margins, and over a large area of the eastern United States.

Adaptive Radiation of Foragers and the Foundations of Food Production

The abundance of big game supported a human population explosion. Bands of foragers gradually spread throughout North and South America. As they moved, these early Americans modified their

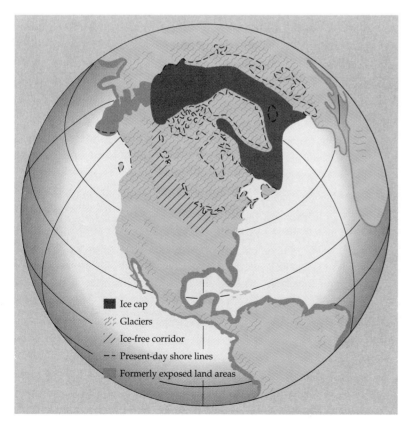

Figure 10.4 *The ancestors of Native Americans entered North America, probably no more than 25,000 years ago, as migrants from Asia. Following big-game herds across Beringia, an immense stretch of land exposed during the ice ages, they had no way of knowing they were entering a New World. Over the generations, the population grew, hunting bands split up, and colonists reached the Great Plains of North America. They thrived there 12,000 years ago as big-game hunters.*

Ice cap
Glaciers
Ice-free corridor
Present-day shore lines
Formerly exposed land areas

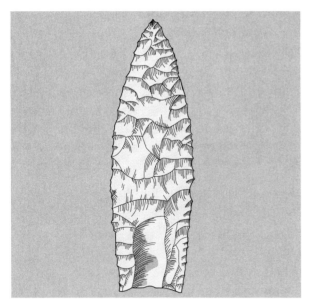

Figure 10.5 *A Clovis spear point, which was fastened to spears used by Paleoindians of the North American plains and other areas between 12,000 and 11,000 B.P.*

sociocultural means of adaptation to cope with the great diversity of environments.

Thousands of years later, the advent of food production and, subsequently, of civilizations based on agriculture and trade in Mexico and Peru produced the second and third population explosions in the New World. New World food production emerged 3,000 to 4,000 years later than in the Middle East, as did the first New World civilizations.

The most significant contrast between Old and New World food production involved animal domestication, which was much more important in the Old World than in the New World. The animals that had been hunted during the early American big-game tradition either became extinct before people could domesticate them or were not domesticable. The largest animal ever domesticated in the New World (in Peru) was the llama. Early Peruvians and Bolivians ate llama meat and used that animal as a beast of burden (Flannery, Marcus, and Reynolds 1989). They bred the llama's relative, the alpaca, for its wool. Early farmers in the Andes mountains also used animal manure to fertilize their fields. (Human feces was used similarly by farmers in the Mexican highlands.) Peruvians added animal protein to their diet by raising and eating guinea pigs and ducks.

The turkey was domesticated in Mesoamerica and in the southwestern United States. Lowland South Americans domesticated the Muscovy duck. The dog is the only animal that was domesticated throughout the New World. Since cattle, sheep, and goats were absent in the areas where food production arose, neither herding nor the kinds of relationships that developed between herders and farmers in many parts of Europe, Asia, and Africa emerged in the precolonial Americas. The New World crops were different, although staples as nutritious as those of the Old World were domesticated from native wild plants.

Three **caloric staples,** major sources of carbohydrates, were domesticated by Native American farmers. **Maize,** or corn, domesticated in highland Mexico, became the caloric staple in Mesoamerica,

The largest animal domesticated in the New World was the llama. Early Peruvians and Bolivians ate llama meat, harnessed llamas as beasts of burden, and used its manure to fertilize their fields. These llamas are grazing in Machu Picchu, Peru.

Central America, and, eventually, coastal Peru. The other two were root crops: white ("Irish") potatoes, first domesticated in the Andes, and **manioc,** or cassava, a tuber first cultivated in the South American lowlands. Other crops, often combined with foraging, added variety to New World diets and made them nutritious. Beans and squash, for instance, provided essential proteins, vitamins, and minerals.

Early Food Production in the Mexican Highlands

Long before Mexican highlanders developed food production, they hunted as part of a pattern of broad-spectrum foraging. Mammoth remains dated to 11,000 B.P. have been found along with projectile points in the basin that surrounds Mexico City. Small animals were more important than big game, as were the grains, pods, fruits, and leaves of wild plants.

The Valley of Oaxaca

In the **Valley of Oaxaca,** in the southern highlands of Mexico (Flannery, ed. 1986), between 10,000 and 4000 B.P., foragers concentrated on five groups of plants and animals, although they certainly used others. Three categories of wild plants were especially significant. The first was the maguey, or century plant, which is available year-round. The maguey's heart is edible only after twenty-four to seventy-two hours of roasting. In some areas foragers had little else to eat between October and May. Certain cactuses provided tender edible leaves throughout the year and fruits in the late spring. The third plant group consisted of tree pods, including mesquite. Mesquite, like maize, grows best in the rich alluvial soil of valley floors and river flood plains. Mesquite trees produced edible pods during the summer, the rainy season, between June and September.

Two animal species, the white-tailed deer and the cottontail rabbit, were additional subsistence resources in the southern Mexican highlands between 10,000 and 4000 B.P. Deer were available throughout the year, although they were especially easy to hunt in fall and winter, their breeding season, when herds were larger than at other times. Cottontail rabbits were available year-round for trapping.

On the basis of archeological evidence from caves and open sites in and around the Valley of Oaxaca,

Flannery reconstructed the seasonal economy and social organization of foragers between 10,000 and 4000 B.P. Those foragers modified their social organization seasonally to meet their dietary needs. From May to September they assembled in **macrobands** to harvest seasonally available plants. Cactus fruits appeared in the spring. Since summer rains would reduce the fruits to mush and since birds, bats, and rodents competed for them, cactus collection required hard work by large groups of people. The edible pods of the mesquite, available in June, also required intensive gathering.

In the dry season the macrobands broke up into **microbands,** small family groups of foragers. Dry-season campsites lack the food variety of summer ones. The highest percentage of deer bones are found in dry-season camps, which also contain abundant remains of the plants that were available year-round, such as maguey and cactus leaves.

Hunting stopped when more varied plant resources became available. Although the white-tailed deer was available year-round, it wasn't hunted during the summer period of intensive collecting. Summer foragers obtained meat protein by using smaller animals, especially the cottontail rabbit, which could be trapped; trap setting and inspection demanded little time.

Wild Grasses

Early Oaxacan foragers focused on the five groups of plants and animals just discussed. Of much less importance at first were such wild grasses as **teocentli,** or *teosinte*, the apparent wild ancestor of maize, which was harvested in October. However, between 7000 and 4000 B.P. a series of genetic changes took place in some of the Mesoamerican wild plants. Teocentli-maize, for example, underwent a series of genetic changes like those described for Middle Eastern wheat and barley. These alterations made it increasingly profitable to collect wild maize and eventually to plant maize. These changes included increases in the number of kernels per cob, cob size, and the number of cobs per stalk (Flannery 1973).

Maize Domestication

Undoubtedly, some of the mutations necessary for domesticated maize had occurred in wild teocentli before people started growing it. However, since teocentli was well adapted to its natural niche, the mutations offered no advantage and didn't spread. Once people began to harvest wild maize intensively, however, they became selective agents. As foragers wandered during the year, they carried teocentli to environments different from its natural one.

Furthermore, as people harvested teocentli, they took back to camp a greater proportion of plants with tough axes and stalks. These were the plants most likely to hold together during harvesting and least likely to disintegrate on the way back home. This variety of teocentli depended on humans for its survival, since it lacked the natural means of dispersal—a brittle axis or stalk. If humans chose plants with tough axes inadvertently, their selection of plants with soft husks must have been intentional. Their selection of corn ears with larger cobs, more kernels per cob, and more cobs per plant was also intentional.

Eventually, people started planting maize in the alluvial soils of valley floors. This was the zone in which foragers had traditionally congregated in macrobands for the annual summer harvest of mesquite pods. Sometime between 7000 and 4000 B.P. a variety of maize was developed that provided more food than the mesquite pods did. Once that happened, people started cutting down mesquite trees and replacing them with corn fields.

The old summer pattern of macroband formation was accentuated by maize cultivation. Like the traditional mesquite harvest, corn cultivation occurred during the summer rainy season. Waiting for the corn to ripen, people could remain in valley macrobands, feeding themselves by trapping and foraging in the immediate vicinity.

The addition of food production to the economy triggered a population explosion and adaptive radiation throughout Mesoamerica. Yet again, changes were gradual. In the Middle East, thousands of years intervened between the first experiments in domestication and the appearance of the state. The same was true in Mesoamerica (Figure 10.6).

Time	Economy	Demography-settlement pattern
A.D. 700–A.D. 1540	Becomes specialized point in interregional trade network	Continuation of trends
A.D. 200–A.D. 700	Full-time irrigation agriculturalists	Increasing population; large ceremonial centers; cities
2900 B.P–1800 B.P. (A.D. 200)	Interregional trade; broad spectrum continues, but crops yield more	Settlements differentiated by size and function; some ceremonial centers
3500 B.P.–2900 B.P.	Shift toward cultivation continues; varied crops; still broad-spectrum foraging	Small villages; part of population still disperses seasonally
4300 B.P.–3500 B.P.	Cultivation increasingly important	Increasing sedentism
5400 B.P.–4300 B.P.	Cultivation of hybrid corn and common beans; 70% of diet still from foraging	Settlements on river terraces
7200 B.P–5400 B.P.	Incipient cultivation	Macrobands larger, stay together longer
9200 B.P.–7200 B.P.	Foraging of deer, cottontail rabbits; plant collection increasingly important	Seasonal; rainy season macrobands
12,000 B.P.–9200 B.P.	Foraging of wild plants, horses, antelope	

Figure 10.6 *Cultural evolution in the Valley of Tehuacan. Archeological research led by R. S. MacNeish documented the gradual emergence of food production and related changes in settlement pattern, population size and density, and sociopolitical and religious organization in Mexico's Valley of Tehuacan over a 12,000-year period. Note that once people began cultivating some crops around 7,200 years ago, foraging was not suddenly abandoned but remained important for more than 5,000 years thereafter.*

The Early Village Farming Community

Eventually, food production led to what is often called the *early village farming community*—permanent villages occupied year-round and sustained by plant cultivation. Note that *sedentary life came before food production in the Old World but after it in the New World.* The earliest permanent settlements in Mesoamerica developed for different reasons in two areas, around 3500 B.P. The first villages appeared in the humid lowlands of the Pacific Coast of Mexico and Guatemala and the Gulf Coast of Mexico. The economy combined maize cultivation in rich soils with foraging of natural resources available in a variety of distinct but closely packed microenvironments.

Early Highland Villages

The village farming community also developed at an early date in certain favored highland areas. However, the areas where this was possible were limited by frost and dryness. Some areas were too arid to grow much corn until complex irrigation systems were developed around 2000 B.P. In the Valley of Mexico, where Mexico City now stands and where the great cities of Teotihuacan and Tenochtitlan, the Aztec capital, eventually developed, winter frosts at first limited cultivation. Not until maize varieties with a shorter growing season were developed after 2500 B.P. did village farming spread widely in the Valley of Mexico.

However, in the highland Valley of Oaxaca, far south of the Valley of Mexico, winter frosts were absent and simple irrigation permitted the establishment of early permanent villages based on maize agriculture. Water close to the surface allowed early farmers to dig wells right in their corn fields. Using pots, they dipped water out of these wells and poured it on their growing plants, a technique known as **pot irrigation.** The earliest year-round Mesoamerican farming depended on reliable rainfall, pot irrigation, or access to humid river bottomlands.

Early Lowland Villages

Maize reached the coastal lowlands of Mesoamerica by 3500 B.P. Its cultivation was adopted by lowlanders who, like their highland cousins, had previously been broad-spectrum foragers. There were, however, significant differences between highland and lowland foraging systems.

Early highland hunters and gatherers ranged over a large territory in accordance with the movement and seasonal availability of plants and animals. In the moister lowlands, by contrast, resources were concentrated in smaller areas, where different microenvironments, each with different resources, were available. Coastal foragers didn't have to travel as far to have an adequate diet. Once they started growing maize, lowland foragers could stay closer to home cultivating maize and foraging the nearest microenvironments. Because of these favorable conditions, the early village farming community was established in the lowlands long before it developed in most of the highlands (Coe and Flannery 1964). The highland exception, as we have seen, was Oaxaca.

From Early Village Farming to the State

More widespread maize cultivation led to further genetic changes, greater yields, higher human populations, and more intensive farming. Pressures to intensify cultivation helped improve early water-control systems, such as well and canal irrigation. New varieties of fast-growing maize eventually appeared and made farming more productive in the Valley of Mexico and in other highland areas. Increasing population and irrigation spread maize throughout the highlands.

This gradual transformation of broad-spectrum foraging into intensive cultivation laid the foundation for the emergence of the state in Mesoamerica—some 3,000 years later than in the Middle East (Table 10.2). Evidence of what archeologists call the **elite level,** indicating differential access to resources (found in chiefdoms and states), appears around 3500 B.P. An early example comes from Mexico's Gulf Coast, where between 3200 and 2500 B.P. the **Olmecs** (a chiefdom) built several ritual centers. Large earthen mounds, presumably dedicated to religion, document the ability of Olmec elites to marshal labor. The Olmecs also sculpted massive stone heads, which may be representations of their chiefs.

By 2500 B.P. Olmec culture had dimmed, but the elite level was spreading throughout Mesoamerica. By 1 A.D. (2000 B.P.) the highlands, particularly the Valley of Mexico, where Mexico City now stands, moved to center stage in the Mesoamerican transformation. It was in the Valley of Mexico that the

POP PREHISTORY

The study of prehistory has spawned popular-culture creations, including books, TV programs, cartoons, and movies. In these fictional works the anthropologists usually don't bear much resemblance to their real-life counterparts. Unlike Indiana Jones, normal and reputable archeologists don't have nonstop adventures—fighting Nazis, lashing whips, or rescuing antiquities. The archeologist's profession isn't a matter of raiding lost arks or going on crusades but of reconstructing lifeways through painstaking analysis of fragmentary, mundane, otherwise valueless material remains.

Much of the popular nonfiction dealing with prehistory is also suspect. Through books and the mass media, we have been exposed to the ideas of popular writers like Thor Heyerdahl and Erich van Daniken. Heyerdahl, a well-known diffusionist, believes that developments in one world area are usually based on ideas borrowed from another.

Van Daniken carries diffusionism one step further, proposing that major human achievements have been borrowed from beings from space who have visited us at various periods of our past. Heyerdahl and van Daniken seem to share (with some science-fiction writers) a certain contempt for human inventiveness and originality. They take the position that major changes in ancient human life styles were the results of outside instruction or interference rather than achievements of the natives of the places where the changes took place.

In *The Ra Expeditions* (Heyerdahl 1971), for example, world traveler and adventurer Heyerdahl argued that his voyage in a papyrus boat from the Mediterranean to the Caribbean demonstrates that ancient Egyptians could have navigated to the New World. (The boat was modeled on an ancient Egyptian vessel, but Heyerdahl and his crew took along such modern conveniences as a radio and canned goods.) Heyer-

dahl maintained that given the possibility of ancient transatlantic voyages, Old World people could have influenced the emergence of civilization in the Americas.

What is the scientific evaluation of Heyerdahl's contention? Even if Old World ancients had reached the New World, they couldn't have done much to propel Native Americans toward civilization because the New World wasn't yet ready for food production and the state. When Egypt became a major power capable of sending scouts across the seas, some 5,000 years ago, Mexicans were broad-spectrum foragers who had barely begun to cultivate corn. The gradual nature of the Mesoamerican transition from foraging to food production is clearly demonstrated by archeological sequences in such sites as Oaxaca, Tehuacan (Figure 10.6), and the Valley of Mexico. Had foreign inputs been important, they would have shown up in the material remains that constitute the archeological record.

---

city and state of **Teotihuacan** flourished between 1900 and 1300 B.P. (A.D. 100 and A.D. 700). The **Aztec** state, which lasted until the Spanish conquest in 1520, arose in the valley around 1325.

State Formation in the Valley of Mexico

The Valley of Mexico (Figure 10.7) is a large basin surrounded by mountains. A lake covered much of the valley in prehistoric times. The valley had rich volcanic soils, but rainfall wasn't always reliable. The north, where Teotihuacan grew up, was colder and drier than the south. Frosts there limited farming until quick-growing varieties of maize were developed.

Until 2500 B.P., population was sparse, as food production was developing. Most people lived in

the warmer and wetter southern area, where rainfall made cultivation possible. After 2500 B.P., new maize varieties and small-scale irrigation were associated with population increase. The population began to spread north.

By A.D. 1 Teotihuacan was a town of 10,000 people. It administered a territory of a few thousand square kilometers and, within these boundaries, perhaps 50,000 people (Parsons 1974). Teotihuacan's growth reflected its agricultural potential. Perpetual springs permitted large-scale irrigation of a large alluvial plain. Rural villages supplied food for a growing urban population.

A clear **settlement hierarchy** had emerged. This is a ranked series of communities that differ in size, function, and building types. The settlements at the top of the hierarchy were political and religious cen-

Beginning some 2,000 years ago, civilizations fully comparable to those of Mesopotamia and Egypt began to rise and fall in the Mexican highlands. This occurred more than 1,000 years after the height of ancient Egyptian influence, between 3600 and 3400 B.P. Had Egypt or any other ancient Old World civilization contributed to the rise or fall of Mesoamerican civilization, we would expect this influence to have been exerted during Egypt's heyday as an ancient power—not 1,500 years later.

There is abundant archeological evidence for the gradual, evolutionary emergence of food production and civilization in the Middle East, in Mesoamerica, and in Peru. This evidence effectively counters the diffusionist theories about how and why human achievements, including farming and civilization, began. Popular theories to the contrary, changes, advances, and setbacks in ancient American social life were the products of the ideas and activities of Native Americans themselves.

There are certain problems, to be sure, in explaining why Mesoamerican civilizations rose and fell. Archeologists are still unraveling the causes of the collapse around A.D. 900 of the Mayan culture of Mexico and Guatemala. However, there is simply no valid evidence for Old World interference before the European Age of Discovery, which began late in the fifteenth century. (There is, however, abundant archeological evidence for this recent, historically known contact between Europeans and Native Americans.)

The archeological record also casts doubt on contentions that the advances of earthlings came with extraterrestrial help, as Erich van Daniken argued in his book *Chariots of the Gods* (1971). Abundant, well-analyzed archeological data from the Middle East, Mesoamerica, and Peru tell a clear story. Plant and animal domestication, civilization, and city life were not brilliant discoveries, inventions, or secrets that humans needed to borrow from extraterrestrials. They were long-term, gradual proc-

esses, developments with down-to-earth causes and effects. They required thousands of years of orderly change, not some chance meeting in the high Andes between an ancient Inca chief and a beneficent Johnny Appleseed from Aldeberan.

This is not to deny, by the way, that intelligent life and civilizations at a variety of technological levels—some more, some less advanced than earth—may exist throughout the galaxy or even that extraterrestrials may have occasionally ventured into this relatively isolated outer spiral arm of the Milky Way galaxy and even visited earth itself. However, even if extraterrestrials have been on earth, archeological evidence suggests that their starship commanders observed a prime directive of noninterference in the affairs of less advanced planets. There is no scientifically valid evidence for the rapid kind of changes that sustained extraterrestrial intervention would have produced.

---

ters; those at the bottom were rural villages. Such a three-level settlement hierarchy (capital city, smaller urban centers, and rural villages) provides evidence of state organization (Wright and Johnson 1975). Along with state organization went large-scale irrigation, status differentiation, and complex architecture.

Teotihuacan became a macrostate or empire between A.D. 100 and A.D. 700. By A.D. 500, its population had reached 130,000. Farmers were one of its diverse specialized groups, along with artisans, merchants, and political, religious, and military personnel.

After A.D. 700 Teotihuacan declined in size and power. By A.D. 900 its population had shrunk to 30,000. Between 900 and 1200, the Toltec period, the population scattered as small cities and towns

sprang up throughout the valley. People also left the Valley of Mexico to live in larger cities—like Tula, the Toltec capital—on its edge.

Population increase (including immigration by the ancestors of the Aztecs) and urban growth returned to the Valley of Mexico between 1200 and 1520. During the Aztec period (1325 to 1520) there were several cities, the largest of which—Tenochtitlan, the capital—may have surpassed Teotihuacan at its height. A dozen towns had between 10,000 and 15,000 people. Fueling this population growth was intensification of agriculture, particularly in the southern part of the valley, where the drainage of lake bottoms and swamps added new cultivable land (Parsons 1976). Another factor in the renaissance of the Valley of Mexico was trade. Local manufacturing created products for a series of markets. The major towns and markets were concentrated on the lake shores, with easy access to canoe traffic. The Aztec capital stood on an island in the lake. Aztec society and the origin of the state are examined further in the chapter "Chiefdoms and Nonindustrial States."

COSTS AND BENEFITS OF FOOD PRODUCTION

Food production brought advantages and disadvantages. The advantages included many discoveries and inventions. People learned to spin and weave, to make pottery, bricks, and arched masonry, and to smelt and cast metals. They developed increasingly intricate trade systems. By 5500 B.P. Middle Easterners were living in vibrant cities with markets, streets, temples, and palaces. They created sculpture, mural art, writing systems, weights, measures, mathematics, and new forms of political and social organization (Jolly and White 1994).

Because it increased economic production and led to new social, scientific, and creative forms, food production is often considered an evolutionary advance. But the new economy also brought hardships. One was that food producers typically work harder than foragers do—and for a less adequate diet. Diets based on crops and dairy products tend to be less varied, nutritious, and healthful than foragers' diet, which are usually higher in proteins and lower in fats and carbohydrates. With the shift to food production, the physical well-being of the population often declines. Communicable diseases, protein deficiency, and dental caries increase, while average stature tends to decrease (Cohen and Armelagos eds. 1984.) By contrast, most foragers are, compared with farmers and herders, relatively disease-free, stress-free, and well-nourished. Other disadvantages accompanied food production and the state. Social inequality increased, as elaborate systems of social stratification replaced the egalitarianism of the past. Slavery was invented. Poverty, crime, war, and human sacrifice became widespread, and the rate at which human beings degraded their environments increased. Progress is much too optimistic a word to describe the evolution of society. The costs of cultural evolution often outweigh the benefits.

Table 10.2 *The rise of food production and the state in Mesoamerica*

Period	Date (B.P.)	Area/Sites	Settlement Types	Ranking/Stratification System
Earliest domestication	5000	Tehuacan Oaxaca	Seminomadic bands	Egalitarian
Early food production	4000–3500	Oaxaca Pacific Coast Gulf Coast	Village farming community	Ranking
Preclassic (Formative)	3500–1750	Olmec Oaxaca	Ceremonial centers Writing (by end)	Ranking, chiefdoms Stratification (by end)
Classic	1750–1150	Teotihuacan Oaxaca Maya	Cities Trade, crafts expand	Stratification, states
Postclassic	1150–500 (A.D. 900–1200) (A.D. 1325–1520)	Toltec Aztec	Cities, social unrest Increased militarism More secular rule Expanded trade	State Empire Empire
Conquest (Cortez)	1520 A.D.	Mexico	Colony of Spain	Spanish domination; world system

The developments discussed in the section on Mesoamerica, from early corn domestication at Tehuacan to the fall of the Aztec state, are organized here according to period names. Elite-level societies (beginning with the Olmecs, through the Spanish conquest of the Aztecs) are described as Preclassic (Olmecs and Oaxaca), Classic (Oaxaca continues, along with Teotihuacan and the Maya area), and Postclassic (Toltecs and Aztecs).

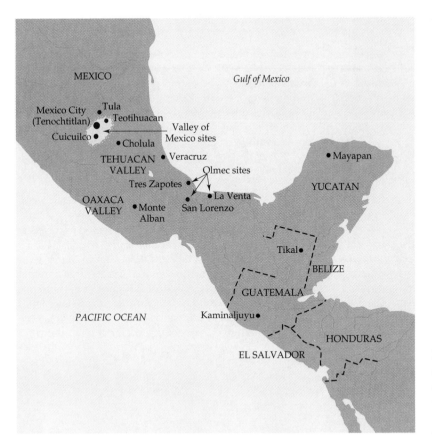

Figure 10.7 *Major sites in the emergence of food production and the state in Mesoamerica. (From* Physical Anthropology and Archeology, *4th Edition, by C. J. Jolly and F. Plog, McGraw-Hill Publishing Co., p. 115.)*

A view of Teotihuacan from the Pyramid of the Moon. The Pyramid of the Sun, Teotihuacan's largest structure, is shown in the upper part of the photo. Note the city's broad avenue (to the right) and the surrounding mountains. At its height around A.D. *500, Teotihuacan was larger than imperial Rome.*

SUMMARY

A widespread intensification of resource use followed global warming and the retreat of the northern ice sheets after 15,000 B.P. As big game diminished, foragers had to pursue new resources. Experiments in food production were the most significant form of intensified resource use. By 10,000 B.P., domesticated plants and animals were included in the broad spectrum of resources used by Middle Eastern populations. By 7500 B.P., most Middle Easterners were moving away from broad-spectrum foraging toward more specialized economies based on fewer species, which were domesticates. *Neolithic* refers to the first cultural period in a given region in which the first signs of domestication are present.

Robert Braidwood proposed that the first experiments in food production took place north of the Tigris and Euphrates rivers, in the Hilly Flanks zone where the ancestors of wheat and barley grow wild. Others questioned this assumption because stands of wild wheat and barley there were dense enough to provide adequate diets for ancient Middle Easterners like the Natufians and to encourage sedentary life before food production. There would have been no incentive to intensify production through cultivation. Binford, Flannery, and Henry view the origin of food production in the context of increasing population, climate changes, and a vertical economy.

By 12,000 B.P., Middle Easterners were broad-spectrum foragers who migrated seasonally in pursuit of game and collected wild plant foods as they ripened at different altitudes. Through migration and trade, people removed grains from the Hilly Flanks zone, where they grew wild, to adjacent areas, where selective pressures were different. Humans became agents of selection, preferring plants with certain attributes. Excess population gradually spilled over from the optimal zone—the Hilly Flanks—into adjacent areas like the piedmont steppe. In these marginal zones people began to cultivate plants, trying to duplicate the dense wild stands of their natural habitat. Sheep and goats fed on the stubble of the wild plants. Animal domestication occurred as people started selecting certain animal features and behavior and influencing the reproduction of goats, sheep, cattle, and pigs. Gradually, food production spread back into the Hilly Flanks and—later, with irrigation—down into Mesopotamia's alluvial desert, where the first cities, states, and civilizations had developed by 5500 B.P.

Food production also emerged in sub-Saharan Africa, South and Southeast Asia, and China. There was early domestication of goats, sheep, cattle, wheat, and barley—by 8000 B.P.—in Pakistan's Indus Valley. Millet was domesticated by 7000 B.P. in northern China, and rice by the same date in southern China.

A convergent transition from broad-spectrum foraging to food production took place thousands of years later in the New World. Humans first entered the New World no more than 25,000 years ago. They didn't realize they were colonizing a "new world" as they hunted herds of tundra-adapted herbivores across Beringia, which linked Siberia and North America. Early humans followed abundant big game, gradually penetrating the interior of North America. Adapting to different environments, Native Americans developed a variety of cultures. Some continued to rely on big game; others reoriented their subsistence toward wild plants and smaller animals and became broad-spectrum foragers.

Wild plants were eventually domesticated in the New World. The most important domesticates were maize, Irish potatoes, and manioc. The llama of the central Andes, used as a beast of burden and for its meat, was the largest animal domesticated in the New World. Stockbreeding traditions analogous to those of the Old World were missing in precolonial America, and economic similarities between the hemispheres must be sought in foraging and farming.

The first New World food-producing economies developed in Mesoamerica. At Oaxaca, in the southern highlands of Mexico, maize and other domesticated plants were gradually added to a broad-spectrum economy between 7000 and 4000 B.P. Genetic changes analogous to those that affected wheat and barley gradually occurred, as a result of selection by humans, in maize. New varieties spread throughout the highlands and lowlands of Mesoamerica. The first permanent villages—early farming communities supported by cultivation—arose in the lowlands and in a few frost-free areas of the highlands where people could cultivate productively by using simple irrigation techniques. As population grew, new varieties of maize and new techniques of cultivation appeared. In the Valley of Mexico, frost-resistant maize made year-round village life possible and paved the way for the emergence of civilization and city life at Teotihuacan (A.D. 100 to A.D. 700) and Tenochtitlan, the Aztec capital (1325 to 1520).

In both the Middle East and Mexico, food production gradually evolved out of hunting and gathering as humans incorporated early domesticates into the broad spectrum of resources they relied on for subsistence. In both hemispheres, wild grains were removed from their natural environments and subjected to new selective pressures, including humans. In both hemispheres, food production eventually led to the appearance of early village farming communities and differentiation of village types, paving the way for the emergence of the state.

Food production brought advantages and disadvantages. The advantages included discoveries and inventions. The disadvantages included harder work, poorer health, crime, war, and social inequality.

GLOSSARY

alluvial: Pertaining to rich, fertile soil deposited by rivers and streams.

axis: Plant part that attaches the grains to the stalk; brittle in wild grains, tough in domesticated ones.

Aztec: Last independent state in the Valley of Mexico; capital was Tenochtitlan. Thrived between A.D. 1325 and the Spanish conquest in 1520.

Beringia: Area now under the Bering Sea; a dry land mass several hundred miles wide, exposed during the glacial advances.

caloric staple: Major source of dietary carbohydrates—such as wheat, rice, or maize.

caprine: From *capra,* Latin for "goat"; refers to goats and sheep.

Capsians: Mesolithic North African foragers who based much of their subsistence on land snails.

Clovis tradition: Stone technology based on a projectile point that was fastened to the end of a hunting spear; flourished between 12,000 and 11,000 B.P. in North America.

dry farming: Cultivation that is rainfall-dependent, without irrigation.

elite level: Archeological term for evidence of differential access to strategic resources; found in chiefdoms and states.

food production: Human control over the reproduction of plants and animals.

Hilly Flanks: Woodland zone that flanks the Tigris and Euphrates rivers to the north; zone of wild wheat and barley and of sedentism (settled, nonmigratory life) preceding food production.

Jomon: Widespread (30,000 sites known) Japanese Mesolithic culture, dated to 6000 to 5000 B.P.; hunted deer, pigs, bear, and antelope, and also ate fish, shellfish, and plants.

macroband: Assembly of foraging bands for intensive collecting or cooperative hunting.

maize: Corn; domesticated in highland Mexico.

manioc: Cassava; a tuber domesticated in the South American lowlands.

Mesoamerica: Middle America, including Mexico, Guatemala, and Belize.

microband: Small family group of foragers.

Natufians: Widespread Middle Eastern culture, dated to between 12,500 and 10,500 B.P.; subsisted on intensive wild cereal collecting and gazelle hunting and had year-round villages.

Neolithic: "New Stone Age," coined to describe techniques of grinding and polishing stone tools; the first cultural period in a region in which the first signs of domestication are present.

Oaxaca, Valley of: Southern Mexican valley that was an early area of food production and state formation.

Olmec: Elite-level society on Mexico's Gulf Coast, 3200 to 2500 B.P.

Paleoindians: Early North American Indians who hunted horses, camels, bison, elephants, mammoths, and giant sloths.

pot irrigation: Simple irrigation technique used in Oaxaca; by means of pots, water close to the surface is dipped and poured on plants.

sedentism: Settled (sedentary) life; preceded food production in the Old World and followed it in the New World.

settlement hierarchy: A ranked series of communities differing in size, function, and type of building; a three-level settlement hierarchy indicates state organization.

teocentli: Or *teosinte,* a wild grass; apparent ancestor of maize.

Teotihuacan: A.D. 100 to 700, first state in the Valley of Mexico and earliest major Mesoamerican empire.

vertical economy: Economy based on environmental zones that, although close together in space, contrast in altitude, rainfall, overall climate, and vegetation.

STUDY QUESTIONS

1. What explanations have anthropologists offered for the origin of food production? Compare the theories of Braidwood with those of Binford, Flannery, and Henry.
2. What ecological (environmental and demographic) conditions contributed to the origin of food production in the Middle East?
3. What is meant by *a broad-spectrum transition to food production?*
4. What were the adaptive eras in the transition to food production in the Middle East?
5. What are caloric staples? What were four such staples in the Old World (where, specifically?), and

what were three staples in the New World (where, specifically?)?

6. What evidence supports the statement that transitions to food production were gradual and evolutionary?

7. How did prehistoric cultural adaptation in Oaxaca change through time, and what were its ecological correlates?

8. How did microbands and macrobands function as cultural adaptations in prehistoric Oaxaca? How was maize cultivation added to the preexisting pattern of social organization in Oaxaca?

9. What were the main parallels in the transition to food production in the Old World and the New World?

10. What were the main differences between the Old World and the New World in the rise of the Neolithic economy?

11. What were common features of state formation in Mesopotamia and Mesoamerica? What were the main differences?

12. What are the costs and benefits of food production and the state?

SUGGESTED ADDITIONAL READING

ADAMS, R. M.
1981 *Heartland of Cities*. Chicago: Aldine. State formation in Mesopotamia, by an acknowledged expert.

BLANTON, R. E., S. A. KOWALEWSKI, G. FEINMAN, AND J. APPEL
1981 *Ancient Mesoamerica*. New York: Cambridge University Press. Overview of a center of food production and the state.

CHANG, K. C.
1977 *The Archaeology of Ancient China*. New Haven: Yale University Press. The growth of Chinese civilization.

CLARK, J. D., AND S. A. BRANDT
1984 *From Hunters to Farmers: The Causes and Consequences of Food Production in Africa*. Berkeley: University of California Press. Transitions to food production in Africa.

COHEN, M. N., AND G. J. ARMELAGOS, EDS.
1984 *Paleopathology at the Origins of Agriculture*. London: Academic Press. Some of the negative consequences of food production for human health.

CONNAH, G.
1987 *African Civilizations*. New York: Cambridge University Press. The archeological evidence for African state formation.

HARRIS, N. M., AND HILLMAN, G.
1989 *Foraging and Farming: The Evolution of Plant Exploitation*. London: Unwin Hyman. Forty-five papers, covering all parts of the world, examine shifts from foraging to food production.

HENRY, D.
1989 *From Foraging to Agriculture: The Levant at the End of the Ice Age*. Philadelphia: University of Pennsylvania Press. Excellent synthesis of the Middle Eastern Neolithic and explanations for the origin of food production there.

SAGGS, H.
1989 *Civilization before Greece and Rome*. New Haven: Yale University Press. Overview of the earliest states.

TAINTER, J.
1987 *The Collapse of Complex Societies*. New York: Cambridge University Press. Why states fail.

WENKE, R.
1990 *Patterns in Prehistory*, 3rd ed. New York: Oxford University Press. Rise of food production and the state throughout the world; useful text.

CHAPTER 11

CULTURAL CHANGE AND ADAPTATION

Ethnic and cultural diversity survive, even thrive, in an increasingly interconnected world. Cultures and communities are being incorporated, at an accelerating rate, into larger systems. An important impetus to the formation of regional social systems, and eventually of nation-states, was the origin of **food production**—plant cultivation and animal domestication. By 10,000 years ago, people in the Middle East were intervening in the reproduction of plants and animals. Those ancient Middle Easterners, pioneers in food production, added new, domesticated foods (wheat and barley, sheep and goats) to their diet. For hundreds of thousands of years before then, people had relied on wild foods, nature's bounty. Humans had always supported themselves by **foraging**—hunting and gathering.

This chapter examines some of the implications of food production and compares cultivators and herders with foragers (hunter-gatherers). First, however, a brief review of previous human evolution will be helpful. Between 2 million and 4 million years ago strong-toothed *australopithecine* hominids lived off the tough, gritty vegetation of the African savanna. Some of the australopithecines evolved into our own genus, *Homo*, around 2 million years ago. Greater reliance on hunting, made possible by anatomical and cultural changes, was a primary cause of this evolution.

All modern humans belong to *Homo sapiens*, the species that first colonized Australia, the Pacific islands, and North and South America (the New World). The previous species, *Homo erectus*—whose earliest fossil remains, in East Africa, date back 1.6 million years—spread into tropical and subtropical Asia, eventually to reach temperate Europe. *Homo erectus* had more than a million years to perfect the foraging mode of existence.

Fossils assigned to (archaic) *Homo sapiens* date back 300,000 years. The anatomically modern subspecies *Homo sapiens sapiens*, which includes all contemporary humans, goes back perhaps 100,000 years. *Homo sapiens sapiens*, including the "Cro-Magnons" who lived in France around 30,000 years ago, continued to rely on foraging. This remained the sole human economic strategy until food production emerged in the Middle East around 10,000 years ago. A parallel and comparable emergence took place in **Mesoamerica** (Mexico, Guatemala, Belize) somewhat later. In both areas people added domesticates to wild foods. Wheat and barley were the main Middle Eastern crops. Corn (maize), cassava (manioc), and potatoes were the staples of the New World.

Food production led to major changes in human life, as the pace of cultural transformation increased enormously. This chapter provides a framework for understanding human adaptive strategies and cul-

Peruvian women work in a high-altitude field near Lake Titicaca. The "Irish" potato—originally domesticated in the Andes and still important in Peruvian subsistence—was one of the caloric staples of the pre-Columbian New World.

tural change. Remember that humans adapt through both biological traits and learned behavior patterns (aspects of culture), which help them cope with problems posed by their environments. Once a viable and stable relationship with the environment is established, that relationship tends to persist until something—internal or external—causes the environment to change.

Facing environmental change, humans experiment with new coping mechanisms. The possession of both cultural and biological means of adaptation doesn't free us from nature, nor does culture guarantee that humans can or will adapt to new circumstances. Reliance on culture merely allows *Homo sapiens* to cope with change more flexibly than other species do. Still, if the environmental change is too severe or the adaptive potential of the group too limited or inflexible, extinction rather than adaptation may result.

EVOLUTION

Anthropologists have considered both general and specific dimensions of human evolution. **General evolution** describes the principal changes, biological and cultural, that have occurred, over thousands of years, in the genus *Homo*. General evolution involves long-term trends—major changes across a sweep of time. Ethnologists and archeologists have determined these trends by considering human populations from many times and places. Specific evolution, by contrast, involves particular populations. It describes their long-term adaptation and changes within particular environments—a valley in Mexico, a plain in Iran, the Nile delta, or Australia, for example.

General Evolution

Trends in the evolution of the stone tools used by our foraging ancestors illustrate general evolution. Thus, during hominid evolution:

1. Reliance on tools has increased.
2. Tools have become more numerous.
3. Tools have become diversified and functionally differentiated; they are designed for more specialized tasks.

Here are some other trends. During hominid evolution, reliance on culture has increased. The number of people and the range of human activities have expanded. Methods by which humans control energy have become more complex, if not always more efficient. Fire, an energy source first tamed by *Homo erectus*, permitted adaptation to new environments, and cooking allowed hominids to eat more types of foods. Plants, through photosynthesis, capture solar energy and transform it into carbohydrates. Some animals eat plants, and higher up the food chain, some eat other animals. When people gather plants or hunt animals, they use some of this stored solar energy to keep themselves alive. Then, when humans shift from foraging to food production, growing crops and managing animal reproduction, they concentrate and control these and other forms of nonhuman energy. There are many ways of controlling energy sources: harnessing an ox to a plow, using the wind to sail boats, using rivers to run industrial plants, and employing natural gas or solar radiation for heat.

The Main Trends of General Evolution

Enlarging our frame of reference from humans to the history of life itself, certain general evolutionary trends are also apparent. They are the following:

1. Parts and subparts have increased.
2. Parts and subparts have become functionally specialized.
3. More effective coordinating mechanisms—means of regulation and integration—have evolved.
4. Population size and **adaptability** (range of environments occupied) have expanded.

First, parts and subparts have increased. Multicelled organisms evolved from early plants and animals that had only one cell. Social evolution shows a similar trend toward an increase in parts. Early hominids lived in small bands (groups of fewer than 100 people that often split up seasonally). These bands belonged to no larger group. Each band was structurally like any other, just as one amoeba resembles another. By the time of *Homo erectus*, however, larger social units (macrobands) formed seasonally as their parts (microbands) came together to hunt. The number of human groups, the size of

Anthropologist Nadine Peacock studies Efe "pygmies" in Zaire's Ituri forest. The Efe have a foraging economy and live in small mobile groups called bands. The number of human groups, the size of each, and their reliance on others has steadily increased during human evolution.

each, and their reliance on others have increased steadily during human evolution.

Functional specialization is a second trend. In simple one-celled organisms, a single structure has many functions or jobs. More complex organisms have several systems, each with a special function. Our bodies, for example, have reproductive, circulatory, and excretory systems, among others. In cultural evolution the trend toward specialization shows up in the appearance of separate economic, political, and religious spheres in more complex societies. The special-purpose institutions found in nation-states, for example, include military, judiciary, and administrative systems.

The third trend involves regulation, coordination, and integration. We can compare the integrative role of a central government (in a nation-state) to that of the nervous system, which coordinates bodily parts and systems.

The fourth trend is toward increasing population size and adaptability—greater tolerance of environmental diversity. Over billions of years life forms have proliferated and diversified. More sophisticated adaptive means have enabled life to spread (radiate) into a wider range of environments. This process of population increase and adaptation to varied environments is called **adaptive radiation**. Human reproductive success shows up in population growth, particularly during the past 10,000 years. *Homo*'s widening environmental and geographic range illustrates increasing adaptability.

These trends accelerated with the origin and spread of food production and, later, of the nation-state. Although village life preceded food production in certain areas where natural resources were abundant and concentrated, the domestication of plants and animals permitted widespread sedentary life. **Sedentism** describes a nonmobile existence in permanent settlements. Food production supported larger populations and allowed humans to expand their range.

Leslie White and the Evolution of Culture

Leslie White was a major and controversial figure in mid-twentieth-century American anthropology. Concerned with general evolution, White (1959) examined major developments in culture from early foragers through the fall of Rome. He described the transition from "primitive" society, which relied almost exclusively on human energy, to the more complex societies that emerged with food production. White applied his grand-movement view of evolution to historical developments from foraging through food production to civilization (nation-states and empires), as revealed by archeology.

He applied the same evolutionary perspective to contemporary cultures. This led him to regard twentieth-century foragers and simple cultivators as kinds of "living fossils," similar in their economies, social structures, and political institutions to ancient foragers and the earliest cultivators, respectively. (See the box, "The Great Forager Debate," for a critique of such an approach.) White and other evolutionists have used ethnography to complement archeology: Living societies with economies like those of ancient groups suggest inferences about correlated cultural features.

Technological determinism dominated White's theories. He claimed that culture advanced through refinements in tool making, especially advances that permitted greater energy capture. Improved tools and new economic practices had social implications. For example, agriculture led to many social, political, and legal changes, including notions of property and distinctions in wealth, class, and power. White compared past and present cultures, using such terms as *primitive* or *simple* versus *complex* or *civilized* to describe them. However, he did not mean these labels to imply moral progress; on the contrary, *he believed that simpler social systems are better social environments for humans than are civilizations.*

Unilinear Evolution

In the nineteenth century many social scientists, including Lewis Henry Morgan (1877/1963) and Auguste Comte (1880), believed in a process of unilinear evolution. Morgan described the development of society from "savagery" through "barbarism" to "civilization." Comte saw social evolution as based on increasing order and progress. **Unilinear evolution** assumes that all cultures tend to evolve in the same order through a set sequence of stages. Any society at a "higher" (more complex) stage must have passed through all the "lower" ones. We know now that cultural change is not unilinear. Societies may develop the same traits in different order. Cultures may even "devolve" (move to a less complex condition or a less productive economy— for example, from food production to foraging).

Specific, Multilinear, and Convergent Evolution

A study of **specific evolution** examines changes (adaptive processes—see below) in a particular environment. It focuses on the major changes in a spe-

cific culture, rather than in human society generally. Once several such studies have been done (usually by archeological anthropologists), the specific evolutionary sequences from different parts of the world can be compared. Such comparison (e.g., of ancient Peru, Mexico, the Middle East, India, and China) can reveal generalized features and causes of culture change. Julian Steward, the best-known such comparativist, applied the term *multilinear evolution* to the cultural developments he compared (Steward 1955). *Multi-* means "many." **Multilinear evolution** refers to the fact that cultures have followed many different lines of development. Any one of those lines or sequences considered individually is a case of specific evolution.

Steward chose a middle ground between studies of general and specific cultural evolution. He concentrated on cases in which unrelated populations had followed convergent paths. **Convergent evolution** refers to the development of similar traits, institutions, or behavior patterns by separate groups as a result of adaptation to similar environments. Given long-term adaptation by different cultures to similar environments, the same institutions tend to develop, in the same order. Steward, an influential advocate of the position that scientific laws govern human behavior and culture change, sought to explain convergent cultural evolution. He contributed to anthropological theory by showing that parallel cultural changes have occurred repeatedly and independently in different places.

Steward also contributed to cultural **typology** (the grouping of cultures into types). One type he defined was the **irrigation state.** According to Steward, the emergence of civilization in five arid areas (Mesopotamia, Egypt, Peru, China, and Mesoamerica) exemplified a single **developmental type** (a category based on convergent evolution and environmental similarity). There had been different developmental types in nonarid areas (e.g., tropical rain forests).

STRATEGIES OF ADAPTATION

John Bennett (1969) has divided the concept of cultural adaptation into two parts. First, **adaptive strategies** are patterns formed by the many separate adjustments that individuals make to obtain and use resources and to solve immediate problems in a par-

THE GREAT FORAGER DEBATE

How representative are modern hunter-gatherers of Paleolithic (Stone Age) peoples, all of whom were foragers? G. P. Murdock (1934) described living hunter-gatherers as "our primitive contemporaries." This label gave an image of foragers as living fossils—frozen, primitive, unchanging social forms that had managed to hang on in remote areas (like the Hollywood natives on King Kong's island).

Later, many anthropologists followed the prolific ethnographer Richard Lee (1984) in using the San ("Bushmen") of the Kalahari Desert of southern Africa to represent the hunting-gathering way of life. But critics increasingly wonder about how much modern foragers can tell us about the economic and social relations that characterized humanity before food production. Modern foragers, after all, live in nation-states and an increasingly interlinked world. For generations, the pygmies of Zaire have traded with their neighbors who are cultivators. They exchange forest products (e.g., honey and meat) for crops (e.g., bananas and manioc). The San have been influenced by Bantu speakers for 2,000 years and by Europeans for centuries. All foragers now trade with food producers, and most rely on governments and missionaries for at

least part of what they consume. The Aché of Paraguay get food from missionaries, grow crops, and have domesticated animals (Hawkes et al. 1982; Hill et al. 1987). They spend only a third of their subsistence time foraging.

A debate is now raging in hunter-gatherer studies between "traditionalists" (e.g., Richard Lee) and "revisionists" (e.g., Edwin Wilmsen). Reconsideration of the status of contemporary foragers is related to the reaction against the ethnographic present discussed in the box in Chapter 2. Anthropologists have rejected the old tendency to depict societies as uniform and frozen in time and space. Attempts to capture the ethnographic present often ignored internal variation, change, and the influence of the world system.

The debate over foragers has focused on the San, whom the traditionalists view as autonomous foragers with a cultural identity different from that of their neighbors who are herders and cultivators (Lee 1979; Silberbauer 1981; Tanaka 1980). These scholars depict most San as egalitarian band-organized people who until recently were nomadic or seminomadic. Traditionalists recognize contact between the San and food producers, but they don't think this contact has destroyed San culture.

The revisionists claim the San tell us little about the ancient world in which all humans were foragers. They argue that the San have been linked to food producers for generations, and that this contact has changed the basis of their culture. For Edwin Wilmsen (1989) the San are far from being isolated survivors of a pristine era. They are a rural underclass in a larger political and economic system dominated by Europeans and Bantu food producers. Many San now tend cattle for wealthier Bantu, rather than foraging independently. Wilmsen also argues that many San descend from herders who were pushed into the desert by poverty or oppression.

The isolation and autonomy of foragers have also been questioned for African pygmies (Bailey et al. 1989) and for foragers in the Philippines (Headland and Reid 1989). The Mikea of southwest Madagascar may have moved into their remote forest habitat to escape the nearby Sakalava state. Eventually the Mikea became an economically specialized group of hunter-gatherers on the fringes of that state. The Tasaday of the Philippines maintain ties with food producers and probably descend from cultivating ancestors. This is true despite the initial "Lost Tribe" media accounts. The reports

---

ticular society. Second, **adaptive processes** are long-term (*specific evolutionary*) changes resulting from the repeated use of such strategies in a particular locale. People are usually conscious of their adaptive strategies but often do not discern adaptive processes, which are detected by observers and analysts, such as the archeologist or the historically oriented ethnologist.

Yehudi Cohen (1974) used *adaptive strategy* to describe a group's system of economic production. He argued that the most important reason for similarities between two (or more) unrelated cultures is their possession of a similar adaptive strategy. Similar economic causes, in other words, produce similar cultural effects. For example, there are striking similarities among most cultures that have a forag-

that followed the "discovery" of the Tasaday portrayed them as survivors of the Stone Age, hermetically sealed in a pristine world all their own. Many scholars now question the authenticity of the Tasaday as a separate cultural group (Headland, ed. 1992).

The debate about foragers raises a larger question: Why do ethnographic accounts and interpretations vary? The reasons include variation in space and time in the society, and different assumptions by ethnographers. Susan Kent (1992) notes a tendency to stereotype foragers, to treat them as all alike. Foragers used to be stereotyped as isolated, primitive survivors of the Stone Age. A new stereotype sees them as culturally deprived people forced by states, colonialism, or world events into marginal environments. This view is probably more accurate, although often exaggerated. All modern foragers have links with external systems, including food producers and nation-states. Because of this they differ substantially from Paleolithic hunter-gatherers.

Challenging both stereotypes, Kent (1992) stresses variation among foragers. She focuses on diversity in time and space among the San. The traditionalist-revisionist debate, suggests Kent, is largely based on failure to recognize the extent of diversity among the San. Researchers on both sides may be correct, depending on the group of San being described and the time period of the research.

San economic adaptations range from hunting and gathering to fishing, farming, herding, and wage work. Solway and Lee (1990) describe environmental degradation caused by herding and population increase. These factors are depleting game and forcing more and more San to give up foraging. Even traditionalists recognize that all San are being drawn inexorably into the modern world system. (Many of us remember the Coke bottle that fell from the sky into a San band in the movie *The Gods Must be Crazy*—a film filled with many stereotypes.)

The nature of San life has changed appreciably since the 1950s and 1960s, when a series of anthropologists from Harvard University, including Richard Lee, embarked on a systematic study of life in the Kalahari. Lee and others have documented many of the changes in various publications. Such longitudinal research monitors variation in time, while field work in many San areas has revealed variation in space. One of the most important contrasts is between settled (sedentary) and nomadic groups (Kent and Vierich 1989). Sedentism is increasing, but some San groups (along rivers) have been sedentary, or have traded with outsiders, for generations. Others, including Lee's Dobe !Kung San and Kent's Kutse San, have been more cut off and have retained more of the hunter-gatherer lifestyle.

Modern foragers are not Stone Age relics, living fossils, lost tribes, or noble savages. Still, to the extent that foraging is the basis of subsistence, modern hunter-gatherers can illustrate links between a foraging economy and other aspects of culture. For example, San groups that are still mobile, or that were so until recently, emphasize social, political, and gender equality. Social relations that stress kinship, reciprocity, and sharing work well in an economy with limited resources and few people. The nomadic pursuit of wild plants and animals tends to discourage permanent settlements, accumulation of wealth, and status distinctions. People have to share meat when they get it; otherwise it rots. Kent (1992) suggests that by studying diversity among the San, we can better understand foraging and how it is influenced by sedentism and other factors. Such study will enhance our knowledge of past, present, and future small-scale societies.

ing strategy. Cohen developed a useful typology of cultures based on correlations between economies and social features. His typology includes six adaptive strategies: foraging, horticulture, agriculture, pastoralism, mercantilism (trade), and industrialism. I examine the last two strategies in the chapter "The World System, Industrialism, and Stratification." I focus on the first four here.

FORAGING

Until 10,000 years ago all humans were foragers. However, environmental specifics created contrasts between foraging populations. Some were big game hunters; others hunted and collected a wider range of animals and plants. Nevertheless, ancient foraging economies shared one essential feature: People relied on nature for food and other necessities.

Domestication (initially of sheep and goats) and cultivation (of wheat and barley) began 10,000 to 12,000 years ago in the Middle East. Cultivation (of different crops, such as maize, manioc, and potatoes) came 3,000 to 4,000 years later in the Western Hemisphere. In both hemispheres the new economy spread rapidly. Most foragers eventually turned to food production. Today almost all foragers have at least some dependence on food production or food producers (Kent 1992).

The foraging way of life held on (and sometimes *re*emerged) in a few areas. In most of those places, foraging should be described as "recent" rather than "contemporary." All modern foragers live in nation-states, depend to some extent on government assistance, and have contacts with food-producing neighbors, missionaries, and other outsiders. We should not view contemporary foragers as isolated or pristine survivors of the Stone Age. Modern foragers are late-twentieth-century people who are influenced by regional forces (e.g., trade and war), national and international policies, and political and economic events in the world system (see the box).

Although foraging is on the wane, the outlines of Africa's two broad belts of recent foraging remain evident. One is the Kalahari Desert of southern Africa. This is the home of the **San** ("Bushmen"), who include the **!Kung.** (The exclamation point stands for a distinctive sound made in their language, a click.) Richard Lee (Lee 1984; Lee and DeVore 1977) and many other anthropologists (see box) have spent years studying the San. I shall draw on their findings throughout this book. The other main African foraging area is the equatorial forest of central and eastern Africa, home of the Mbuti and other "pygmies" (Turnbull 1965; Bailey et al. 1989).

People still do subsistence foraging in certain remote forests in Madagascar, Southeast Asia, Malaysia, the Philippines, and on certain islands off the Indian coast. Some of the best-known recent foragers are the aborigines of Australia. Those Native Australians lived on their island continent for more than 40,000 years without developing food production.

The Western Hemisphere also had recent foragers. The Eskimos, or Inuit, of Alaska and Canada are well-known hunters. These (and other) northern foragers now use modern technology, including ri-

All modern foragers live in nation-states, depend to some extent on government assistance, and have contact with outsiders. Contemporary hunter-gatherers are not isolated or pristine survivors of the Stone Age. Modern foragers—such as this rifle-wielding Australian hunter—are influenced by regional forces, national and international policies, and political and economic events in the world system.

fles and snowmobiles, in their subsistence activities (Pelto 1973). The native populations of California, Oregon, Washington, and British Columbia were all foragers, as were those of inland subarctic Canada and the Great Lakes. For many Native Americans fishing, hunting, and gathering remain important subsistence (and sometimes commercial) activities.

Coastal foragers also lived near the southern tip of South America, in Patagonia. On the grassy plains of Argentina, southern Brazil, Uruguay, and Paraguay, there were other hunters-gatherers. The contemporary Aché of Paraguay are usually called "hunter-gatherers" even though they get just a third of their livelihood from foraging. The Aché also grow crops, have domesticated animals, and live in or near mission posts, where they receive food from missionaries (Hawkes et al. 1982; Hill et al. 1987).

Throughout the world, foraging survived mainly in environments that posed major obstacles to food production. (Some foragers took refuge in such areas after the rise of food production, the state, colonialism, or the modern world system.) The difficulties of cultivating at the North Pole are obvious. In southern Africa the Dobe !Kung San area studied by Richard Lee is surrounded by a waterless belt 70 to 200 kilometers in depth. The Dobe area is hard to reach even today, and there is no archeological evidence of occupation of this area by food producers before the twentieth century (Solway and Lee 1990, p. 115). However, environmental limits to other adaptive strategies aren't the only reason foragers survived. Their niches have one thing in common—their marginality. Their environments haven't been of immediate interest to groups with other adaptive strategies.

I should note, too, that foraging held on in a few areas that could be cultivated, even after contact with cultivators. Those tenacious foragers did not become food producers because they were supporting themselves adequately by hunting and gathering. As the modern world system spreads, the number of foragers continues to decline. (I consider issues of the cultural survival of foragers and other groups in later chapters, especially the chapter "Cultural Exchange and Survival.")

Correlates of Foraging

Typologies, such as Cohen's adaptive strategies, are useful because they suggest **correlations**—that is, associations or covariation between two or more variables. (Correlated variables are factors that are linked and interrelated, such as food intake and weight, such that when one increases or decreases, the other tends to change, too.) Ethnographic studies in hundreds of cultures have revealed many correlations between the economy and social life. Associated (correlated) with each adaptive strategy is a bundle of particular cultural features. Correlations, however, are rarely perfect. Some foragers lack cultural features usually associated with foraging, and some of those features are found in groups with other adaptive strategies.

What, then, are the usual correlates of foraging? People who subsist by hunting, gathering, and fishing often live in band-organized societies. Their basic social unit, the **band,** is a small group of fewer than a hundred people, all related by kinship or marriage. Band size varies between cultures and often from one season to the next in a given culture. In some foraging societies, band size stays about the same year-round. In others, the band splits up for part of the year. Families leave to gather resources that are better exploited by just a few people. Later, they regroup for cooperative work and ceremonies. Several examples of seasonal splits and recongregation are known from archeology and ethnography. In southern Africa, some San aggregate around water holes in the dry season and split up in the wet season, whereas other bands disperse in the dry season (Barnard 1979; Kent 1992). This reflects environmental variation. San who lack permanent water must disperse and forage widely for moisture-filled plants.

One typical characteristic of the foraging life is mobility. In many San groups, as among the Mbuti of Zaire, people shift band membership several times in a lifetime. One may be born, for example, in a band where one's mother has kin. Later, one's family may move to a band where the father has relatives. Because bands are exogamous, one's parents come from two different bands, and one's grandparents may come from four. People may affiliate with any band to which they have kinship or marriage links. A couple may live in, or shift between, the husband's and the wife's band.

One may also affiliate with a band through **fictive kinship**—personal relationships modeled on kinship, such as that between godparents and godchildren. San, for example, have a limited number of personal names. People with the same name have a special relationship; they treat each other like siblings. San expect the same hospitality in bands where they have **namesakes** as they do in a band in which a real sibling lives. Namesakes share a strong identity. They call everyone in a namesake's band by the kin terms the namesake uses. Those people reply as if they were addressing a real relative. Kinship, marriage, and fictive kinship permit San to join several bands, and nomadic (constantly on-the-move) foragers do change bands often. Band membership can therefore change tremendously from year to year.

All human societies have some kind of division of labor based on gender. Among foragers, men typ-

Table 11.1 *Among foragers, animals (including fish) generally give a better yield (measured in kilocalories per hour spent searching for and processing them) than do vegetable foods (nuts, berries, fruits). This is illustrated by data from three foraging societies in different parts of the world.*

Food Item	Yield in Kilocalories per Hour's Work*
Anbarra (coastal northern Australia)†	
Fish (speared)	14,000
Wallaby	12,500
Cycad nut	1,300
Wild yams	1,170
Shellfish	1,000
Aché (Paraguay)‡	
Collared peccary	65,000
Armadillo	5,909
Oranges	5,071
Birds	4,769
Honey	3,266
Palm fruit	946
Palm fiber and heart	810
Canada (boreal forest)§	
Moose and caribou	95,600–8,200
Hare	8,260
Net fishing	34,000–1,790
Blueberries	650

*Labor costs include rate at which resource is encountered, pursuit time, preparation time (e.g., butchering an animal, winnowing and grinding seeds, cracking nuts.)
†Jones 1980, p. 137.
‡Hawkes, Hill, and O'Connell 1982, Table 3.
§Winterhalder 1981, pp. 82–83.
Source: Layton, Foley, and Williams 1991.

ically hunt and fish while women gather and collect, but the specific nature of the work varies among cultures. Sometimes women's work contributes most to the diet. Sometimes male hunting and fishing predominate. Among foragers in tropical and semitropical areas, gathering tends to contribute more to the diet than hunting and fishing do—even though the labor costs of gathering tend to be much higher than those of hunting and fishing (Table 11.1).

Quantitative data on production and consumption gathered by Richard Lee among the !Kung San helped correct widespread misconceptions about foragers (Lee 1968/1974). First, Lee showed that gathering—not hunting—was the mainstay of their diet. Second, he found that foragers' work, rather

than being a constant struggle against starvation, was less time-consuming than, and could support at least as many dependents as, the average American's job.

Lee also gathered quantitative data on consumption. Rather than being marginal, the !Kung diet turned out to be as nutritious as that enjoyed by middle-class Americans. !Kung food output was found to exceed their minimum daily requirements (1,965 calories and 60 grams of protein per person per day, given their size and level of activity) by 165 calories and 33 grams of protein. The !Kung, working only two or three days per week on the average, could even have increased production a bit. They could have obtained more calories and protein without danger of degrading their environment. They did not do so simply because there was no need to work harder.

All foragers make social distinctions based on age. Often old people receive great respect as guardians of myths, legends, stories, and traditions. Younger people value the elders' special knowledge of ritual and practical matters. Most foraging societies are *egalitarian*. This means that contrasts in status are minor and are based on age and gender.

When considering issues of "human nature," we should not forget that the egalitarian band was a basic form of human social life for most of our history. Food production has existed less than 1 percent of the time *Homo* has spent on earth. However, it has produced huge social differences. We now consider the main economic features of food-producing strategies.

CULTIVATION

The three adaptive strategies based on food production in nonindustrial societies are horticulture, agriculture, and pastoralism. In non-Western cultures, as in the United States and Canada, people carry out a variety of economic activities. Each adaptive strategy refers to the main economic activity. Pastoralists (herders), for example, consume milk, butter, blood, and meat from their animals as mainstays of their diet. However, they also add grain to the diet by doing some cultivating or by trading with neighbors. Food producers may also hunt or gather to supplement a diet based on domesticated species.

Horticulture

Horticulture and agriculture are two types of cultivation found in nonindustrial societies. Both differ from the farming systems of industrial nations like the United States and Canada, which use large land areas, machinery, and petrochemicals. **Horticulture** makes intensive use of *none* of the factors of production: land, labor, capital, and machinery. Horticulturalists use simple tools such as hoes and digging sticks to grow their crops. Their fields are not permanent property and lie fallow for varying lengths of time.

Horticulture is also known as **slash-and-burn** cultivation. Each year horticulturalists clear land by cutting down (slashing) and burning forest or bush or by setting fire to the grass covering the plot. The ashes remain to fertilize the soil. Crops are then sown, tended, and harvested. Use of the plot is not continuous. Often it is cultivated for only a year. This depends, however, on soil fertility and weeds, which compete with cultivated plants for nutrients.

When horticulturalists abandon a plot because of soil exhaustion or a thick weed cover, they clear another piece of land, and the original plot reverts to forest. After several years of fallowing (the duration varies in different societies), the cultivator returns to farm the original plot again. Because the relationship between people and land is not permanent,

horticulture is also called *shifting cultivation*. Shifting cultivation does not mean that whole villages must move when plots are abandoned. Horticulture can support large permanent villages. Among the Kuikuru of the South American tropical forest, for example, one village of 150 people remained in the same place for ninety years (Carneiro 1956). Kuikuru houses are large and well made. Because the work involved in building them is great, the Kuikuru would rather walk farther to their fields than construct a new village. They shift their plots rather than their settlements. On the other hand, horticulturalists in the montaña (Andean foothills) of Peru live in small villages of about thirty people (Carneiro 1961/1968). Their houses are small and simple. After a few years in one place, these people build new villages near virgin land. Because their houses are so simple, they prefer rebuilding to walking even a half mile to their fields.

Agriculture

Agriculture is cultivation that requires more labor than horticulture does, because it uses land intensively and continuously. The greater labor demands associated with agriculture reflect its common use of domesticated animals, irrigation, or terracing.

In slash-and-burn cultivation horticulturalists clear land by cutting down (slashing) and burning forest or bush. The ashes remain to fertilize the soil.

Domesticated Animals

Many agriculturalists use animals as means of production—for transport, as cultivating machines, and for their manure. For example, the Betsileo of central Madagascar incorporate cattle into their agricultural economy based on rice production (Kottak 1980). First the Betsileo sow rice in nursery beds. Then, once the seedlings are big enough, women transplant them into flooded rice fields. Before transplanting, the men till and flood the fields. They bring cattle to trample the prepared fields just before transplanting. Young men yell at and beat the cattle, striving to drive them into a frenzy so that they will trample the fields properly. Trampling breaks up clumps of earth and mixes irrigation water with soil to form a smooth mud into which women transplant seedlings. Like many other agriculturalists, the Betsileo collect manure from their animals, using it to fertilize their plots, thus increasing the yield.

Irrigation

While horticulturalists must await the rainy season, agriculturalists can schedule their planting in advance, because they control water. The Betsileo irrigate their fields with canals from rivers, streams, springs, and ponds. Irrigation makes it possible to cultivate a plot year after year. Irrigation enriches the soil because the irrigated field is a unique ecosystem with several species of plants and animals, many of them minute organisms, whose wastes fertilize the land.

An irrigated field is a capital investment that usually increases in value. It takes time for a field to start yielding; it reaches full productivity only after several years of cultivation. The Betsileo, like other irrigators, have farmed the same fields for generations. In some agricultural areas, including the Middle East, however, salts carried in the irrigation water can make fields unusable after fifty or sixty years.

Terracing

Terracing is another agricultural technique the Betsileo have mastered. Central Madagascar has small valleys separated by steep hillsides. Because the population is dense, people need to farm the hills. However, if they simply planted on the steep hillsides, fertile soil and crops would be washed away during the rainy season. To prevent this, the Betsileo, like the rice-farming Ifugao of the Philippines, cut into the hillside and build stage after stage of terraced fields rising above the valley floor. Springs

Agriculturalists use domesticated animals as means of production, for transport, as cultivating machines, and for their manure. Here a woman and water buffalo plow a rice field in Yangshuo, China.

In some areas of Irian Jaya, Indonesia (which is on the island of New Guinea), labor-intensive cultivation in valleys involves the construction of long drainage ditches. Here, members of the Dani tribe use their bare hands and feet to maintain such a canal.

located above the terraces supply their irrigation water. The labor necessary to build and maintain a system of terraces is great. Terrace walls crumble each year and must be partially rebuilt. The canals that bring water down through the terraces also demand attention.

Costs and Benefits of Agriculture

Agriculture requires human labor to build and maintain irrigation systems and terraces. People must feed, water, and care for their animals. Given sufficient labor input and management, agricultural land can yield one or two crops annually for years or even generations. An agricultural field does not necessarily produce a higher single-year yield than does a horticultural plot. The first crop grown by horticulturalists on long-idle land may be larger than that from an agricultural plot of the same size. Furthermore, because agriculturalists work harder than horticulturalists do, agriculture's yield relative to labor is also lower. Agriculture's main advantage is that the long-term yield per area is far greater and more dependable. Because a single field sustains its owners year after year, there is no need to maintain a reserve of uncultivated land as horticulturalists

do. This is why agricultural societies are more densely populated than are horticultural ones.

The Cultivation Continuum

Because nonindustrial economies can have features of both horticulture and agriculture, it is useful to discuss cultivators as being arranged along a **cultivation continuum**. Horticultural systems stand at one end—the "low-labor, shifting-plot" end. Agriculturalists are at the other—the "labor-intensive, permanent-plot"—end.

We speak of a continuum because there are today intermediate economies, combining horticultural and agricultural features—more intensive than annually shifting horticulture but less intensive than agriculture. These recall the intermediate economies revealed by archeological sequences leading from horticulture to agriculture in the Middle East, Mexico, and other areas of early food production. Unlike nonintensive horticulturalists, who farm a plot just once before fallowing it, the South American Kuikuru grow two or three crops of **manioc**, or cassava—an edible tuber—before abandoning their plots. Cultivation is even more intense in certain densely populated areas of Papua–New Guinea,

Agriculture requires more labor than horticulture does and uses land intensively and continuously. Labor demands associated with agriculture reflect its use of domesticated animals, irrigation, and terracing. The Ifugao of the Philippines are famous for their terraced rice fields.

where plots are planted for two or three years, allowed to rest for three to five, and then recultivated. After several of these cycles the plots are abandoned for a longer fallow period. Such a pattern is called **sectorial fallowing** (Wolf 1966). Besides Papua–New Guinea, such systems occur in places as distant as West Africa and highland Mexico. Sectorial fallowing is associated with denser populations than is simple horticulture. The simpler system is the norm in tropical forests, where weed invasion and delicate soils prevent more intensive cultivation.

The key difference between horticulture and agriculture is that horticulture always uses a fallow period whereas agriculture does not. The earliest cultivators in the Middle East and Mexico were rain-fall-dependent horticulturalists. Until recently, horticulture was the main form of cultivation in several areas, including parts of Africa, Southeast Asia, Indonesia, the Philippines, the Pacific islands, Mexico, Central America, and the South American tropical forest.

Implications of Intensification

The range of environments open to human use widens as people increase their control over nature. Agricultural populations exist in many areas that are too arid for nonirrigators or too hilly for non-terracers. Many ancient civilizations in arid lands arose on an agricultural base. Increasing labor intensity and permanent land use have major demographic, social, and political consequences. These consequences illustrate general evolutionary trends, as discussed earlier.

Because of their permanent fields, intensive cultivators are sedentary. People live in larger and more permanent communities located closer to other settlements. Growth in population size and density increases contact between individuals and groups. There is more need to regulate interpersonal relations, including conflicts of interest. Economies that support more people usually require more coordination in the use of land, labor, and other resources.

Agriculture poses many regulatory problems—which central governments have often arisen to solve. Most agriculturalists live in **states** (nation-states)—complex sociopolitical systems that administer a territory and populace with substantial contrasts in occupation, wealth, prestige, and power. In such societies, cultivators play their role as one part of a differentiated, functionally specialized, and tightly integrated sociopolitical system. The social and political implications of food production and intensification are examined more fully in the chapters "Bands and Tribes" and "Chiefdoms and Nonindustrial States."

PASTORALISM

Pastoralists live in North Africa, the Middle East, Europe, Asia, and sub-Saharan Africa. These herders are people whose activities focus on such domesticated animals as cattle, sheep, goats, camels, and yak. East African pastoralists, like many others, live in symbiosis with their herds. (**Symbiosis** is an obligatory interaction between groups—here humans and animals—that is beneficial to each.) Herders attempt to protect their animals and ensure their reproduction in return for food and other products, like leather. Herds provide dairy products and meat. East Africans also consume cooked cattle blood. Animals are killed at ceremonies, which occur throughout the year, and so beef is available regularly.

People use livestock in a variety of ways. Natives of North America's Great Plains, for example, didn't eat, but only rode, their horses. (Europeans reintroduced horses to the Western Hemisphere; the native American horse had become extinct thousands of years earlier.) For Plains Indians horses served as "tools of the trade," means of production used to hunt buffalo, a main target of their economies. So the Plains Indians were not true pastoralists but *hunters* who used horses—as many agriculturalists use animals—as means of production.

Unlike the use of animals merely as productive machines, pastoralists typically make direct use of their herds for food. They consume their meat, blood, and milk, from which they make yogurt, butter, and cheese. Although some pastoralists rely on their herds more completely than others do, it is impossible to base subsistence solely on animals. Most pastoralists therefore supplement their diet by hunting, gathering, fishing, cultivating, or trading.

To get crops, pastoralists either trade with cultivators or do some cultivating or gathering themselves. Since their beginning, herding and cultivation have often been interdependent. Nineteenth-century anthropologists, lacking today's knowledge, speculated about whether cultivation or animal domestication came first. We now know that pastoralism and cultivation emerged and spread together in the Old World as interrelated parts of a pattern of increasing human intervention in nature.

Unlike foraging and cultivation, which existed throughout the world before the Industrial Revolution, pastoralism was almost totally confined to the Old World. Before European conquest, the only pastoralists in the Americas lived in the Peruvian Andes. They used their llamas and alpacas for food and in agriculture and transport. Much more recently, Navajo of the southwestern United States de-veloped a pastoral economy based on sheep, which were brought to North America by Europeans. The populous Navajo are now the major pastoral population in the western hemisphere.

Two patterns of movement occur with pastoralism: nomadism and transhumance. Both are based on the fact that herds must move to use pasture available in particular places in different seasons. In **pastoral nomadism**, the entire group—women, men, and children—moves with the animals throughout the year. With **transhumance**, only part of the group follows the herds while the rest remain in home villages. During their annual trek, nomads trade for crops and other products with more sedentary people. Transhumants don't have to trade for crops. Because only part of the population accompanies the herds, transhumants can maintain year-round villages and grow their own crops. Another name for groups that divide their subsistence between agriculture and pastoralism is *agro-pastoralists*. **Agro-pastoralism** is a common form of economic adaptation in the Himalayas (being found among such peoples as the Tamang, Sherpas, and Gurungs) and in the Andes.

The Jie of Uganda, a transhumant population of some 18,000 people (Gulliver 1955), have a home territory about 105 kilometers (65 miles) long by 40 kilometers (25 miles) wide. Because the western area has year-round water, the Jie have their villages there and grow crops using horticultural techniques. When the rainy season begins, grass appears in eastern pastures, and the men take the herds there. Later they move west of the villages, where pasture remains after the east is dry. Having exhausted the western pastures, they return to the villages to spend the rest of the year in the best-watered area of all. While younger men are accompanying the herds, women, older men, and children stay home.

Europe's Alps also have people who live by transhumance. The annual movement to spring and summer pastures at higher elevations is familiar to anyone who has read the children's book *Heidi*. Transhumance and nomadism once again illustrate a continuum: the proportion of the population accompanying the herds, the time spent in any one place, and the amount of labor devoted to other activities are all matters of "more or less" rather than absolute contrasts.

IN THE NEWS: DINKALAND, WHERE CATTLE ARE TREATED LIKE EQUALS

Like other East African herders, the Dinka, a populous Nilotic tribe in southern Sudan, live in symbiosis with their cattle. They make varied use of their milk, blood, meat, skin, and waste products. This item describes one man's success in protecting his herd against the warfare that still rages in southern Sudan. The Sudan People's Liberation Front, whose rebellion against that nation's Islamic central government has faltered since 1990, when this item appeared, has enlisted many Dinka fighters. War and disease have ravaged the Nilotic homeland, where rinderpest epidemics have decimated cattle herds several times in the past. As is reported here, pastoralists like the Dinka are eager participants in cattle vaccination campaigns.

Bor, the Sudan—To visit the cattle camp of Chief Alier Ayen, a Dinka tribesman, in the gray dawn of the southern Sudan is to see a gathering resembling ghosts.

Many of the men and boys, tall and thin, have coated their naked bodies and faces in the white ashes of cow dung, a centuries-old protection against flies and mosquitoes. Their cows adorned with

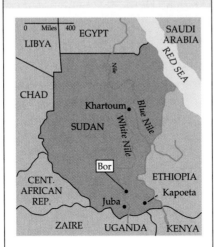

high lyre-shaped horns are dusted in the same powder. The ground is scattered with the pale cinders of campfires.

The orange hair of the young adult men stands out against the whiteness. Coiffed into the shape of snug skullcaps their naturally black hair has been colored by repeated washings in cow urine and blanching by the sun.

The Dinka, the dominant tribe in the southern Sudan, regard cattle as sacred, approximating human beings in value. They live in symbiosis with their cows, sleeping outdoors in the same camp with them and using the cow's

milk, blood, skin and waste as vital resources for survival. In the cool dawn air, Awar, a boy of about 12, rested his body covered only in ash, on a cow skin by the fire he had spent the night by.

The seven-year-old Sudanese civil war has sharply reduced both the human and cow population in the southern Sudan. It has forced many Dinka, bereft of their prized cattle, to flee to refugee camps in neighboring Ethiopia, to the Arab north or to the southern town of Juba.

Lucky and perhaps wily, Dinka like Chief Alier have escaped the war with their cattle herds mostly intact. In April 1988, Bor was the scene of fighting between forces of the northern Government and the rebel group known as the Sudan People's Liberation Front. . . .

"I was always hiding my cows from the war," said the Chief, who supported his thin body, bent with age, with a chin-level walking stick. "In the dry season, I escaped to islands in the Nile. In the wet season, I took my cattle into the forest. Now I am happy there is no war."

This is the beginning of the wet season in the southern Sudan, and Chief Alier had brought his cattle in from the Nile. They are now

SUMMARY

General evolution refers to long-term trends in human evolution, including the consequences of food production. *Specific evolution* refers to particular human populations adapting to changing environments. Julian Steward compared cases of specific evolution to discover cross-cultural regularities, instances of convergent cultural evolution. Leslie White described the general evolution of culture. He believed that technological changes, particularly new ways of harnessing nonhuman energy, caused social and political evolution.

Yehudi Cohen's six adaptive strategies are foraging (hunting and gathering), horticulture, agriculture, pastoralism, mercantilism (trade), and industrialism. Foraging was the only human strategy until food production (cultivation and animal domestication) appeared around 10,000 years ago. Food production eventually replaced foraging in most areas. Almost all modern foragers have at least some dependence on food production or food producers.

Among most foragers, the band is a basic social unit. Often band members split up seasonally into microbands or families. Kinship, marriage, and other arrangements

based in a large circular clearing in the bush, a 45-minute vehicle ride from Bor. Within the camp's main circle are smaller circles—known as djinn by the Dinka—marked by pegs for each cow. One of Chief Alier's herdsmen was proud to note there were 21 djinn in the camp.

The proximity of the Chief's cows to Bor meant that a team of Sudanese veterinarians and paramedics, led by Adrián Pintos, an Argentine veterinarian of the United Nations Children's Fund, could inoculate the cattle against the deadly cattle virus rinderpest.

After the battle of Bor, the adult cows in Mr. Alier's 1,000-strong herd—a large herd for one man— were vaccinated last year for the first time in five years. Because the war forced cattle to be kept in confined areas where disease could easily spread and Government vaccination ended in 1983, untold numbers of cattle—no one will hazard a guess how many—are believed to have died in the southern Sudan.

In all, Unicef estimates that it vaccinated 95,000 cattle in Bor last year and 100,000 in Kapoeta, a rebel town to the southeast. This year, the Unicef team was back to inject Chief Alier's young cows.

As unchanged as the traditions

The Dinka of southern Sudan live in symbiosis with their cattle, using their milk, blood, meat, skin, and waste products. This boy is polishing the horns of one member of his family herd.

of the Dinka remain, the veterinarians say the people are sophisticated and knowledgeable about the need for immunization against rinderpest, which once it infects a herd is liable to kill 95 percent of

the cows, Dr. Pintos said.

Once the inoculations were finished, the cows would be released to pasture, a regular procedure every morning at 10 A.M. About half the 40 or so people would go out with the cattle to protect them against hyena and the other half would stay behind to rest, the Chief said.

"The bigger people go with the bigger cows and the smaller boys with the small cows," he said. "The cattle and our people are friends."

The Chief pointed to two young men with orange hair who were his sons. He has three daughters. "They do not look after the cows, they milk them," he said.

The Dinka rely on the cows' milk, not the meat, for sustenance. "Only if we have hunger and there is no milk will we kill a bull to eat," the Chief said. "When I kill a bull, it is not only for my family but everyone. Since God gave me cows, I will give to everyone."

At the end of May, he killed one bull. "We had no milk," he said.

Source: Jane Perlez, "Dinkaland, Where Cattle Are Treated Like Equals," *The New York Times,* July 18, 1990, A4.

---

link band members. Foragers assign tasks by gender and age. Men usually hunt and fish, and women gather. Old people guard traditions.

Cultivation is often combined with other adaptive strategies, such as pastoralism or foraging. Horticulture and agriculture stand at different ends of a continuum based on labor intensity and continuity of land use. Horticulture does not use land or labor intensively. Horticulturalists cultivate a plot for one or two years and then abandon it. Further along the continuum, horticulture becomes more intensive, but there is always a fallow period. Horticulturalists can shift plots while living in permanent villages. The first cultivating economies were horticultural. Horticulture still occurs in many areas of both hemispheres.

Agriculturalists farm the same plot of land continuously and use labor intensively. They use one or more of the following practices: irrigation, terracing, domesticated animals as means of production, and manuring. Because of permanent land use, agricultural populations are denser than are those associated with other adaptive strategies. Agriculturalists often have complex regulatory systems, including state organization.

The mixed nature of the pastoral strategy is evident. Nomadic pastoralists trade with cultivators. Transhumants grow their own crops. Part of the transhumant population cultivates while another part takes the herds to pasture. Except for some Peruvians and the Navajo, who are recent herders, the New World lacks native pastoralists.

GLOSSARY

adaptability: Tolerance of environmental diversity; the ability to cope with a range of environments.

adaptive processes: Long-term (specific evolutionary) changes resulting from repeated use of adaptive strategies (in Bennett's sense) in a particular locale.

adaptive radiation: Process of population increase and adaptation to varied environments.

adaptive strategies: Patterns formed by the many separate adjustments individuals make to obtain and use resources and solve immediate problems; in Cohen's sixfold typology of cultures, foraging, horticulture, agriculture, pastoralism, mercantilism (trade), and industrialism.

agriculture: Nonindustrial system of plant cultivation characterized by continuous and intensive use of land and labor.

agro-pastoralism: Subsistence economy based on both agriculture and (transhumant) pastoralism; the most common form of economic adaptation in the Himalayas.

band: Basic unit of social organization among foragers. A band includes fewer than a hundred people; it often splits up seasonally.

convergent evolution: Development of similar traits, institutions, or behavior patterns as a result of adaptation to similar environments.

correlation: An association between two or more variables such that when one changes (varies), the other(s) also change(s) (covaries); for example, temperature and sweating.

cultivation continuum: A continuum based on the comparative study of nonindustrial cultivating societies in which labor intensity increases and fallowing decreases.

developmental type: Category based on convergent evolution and environmental similarity; includes societies in ecologically similar areas that evolved in an analogous fashion.

fictive kinship: Personal relationships modeled on kinship, such as that between godparents and godchildren.

food production: Plant cultivation and animal domestication.

foraging: Hunting and gathering.

general evolution: Study of major changes, biological and cultural, in *Homo*; abstracted from a variety of times, places, and populations.

horticulture: Nonindustrial system of plant cultivation in which plots lie fallow for varying lengths of time.

irrigation state: Nonindustrial state, for example, ancient Mesopotamia, Egypt, Peru, China, and Mesoamerica, based on irrigation in an arid area; one of Julian Steward's development types.

!Kung: Group of San (Bushmen) foragers of southern Africa; the exclamation point indicates a click sound in the San language.

manioc: Cassava, a tuber abundant in South American tropical forests. Along with maize and white potatoes, it is one of the three major caloric staples of the aboriginal New World.

Mesoamerica: Middle America—Mexico, Guatemala, and Belize.

multilinear evolution: Study of the evolution of human society "along its many lines" through examination of specific evolutionary sequences; associated with Julian Steward.

namesakes: People who share the same name; a form of fictive kinship among the San, who have a limited number of personal names.

nomadism, pastoral: Movement throughout the year by the whole pastoral group (men, women, and children) with their animals. More generally, such constant movement in pursuit of strategic resources.

pastoralists: People who use a food-producing strategy of adaptation based on care of herds of domesticated animals.

San: Foragers of southern Africa, also known as Bushmen; speakers of San languages.

sectorial fallowing: Intensive horticulture; plots are cultivated for two to three years, then fallowed for three to five, with a longer rest after several of these shorter cycles.

sedentism: Sedentary life; remaining in one place; a sedentary village is one in which people remain together year-round and for several years.

slash and burn: Form of horticulture in which the forest cover of a plot is cut down and burned before planting to allow the ashes to fertilize the soil.

specific evolution: Studies of changes in relationships between specific populations and their environments.

state (nation-state): Complex sociopolitical system that administers a territory and populace with substantial contrasts in occupation, wealth, prestige, and power.

symbiosis: An obligatory interaction between groups that is beneficial to each.

transhumance: One of two variants of pastoralism; part of the population moves seasonally with the herds while the other part remains in home villages.

typology: A system of classification of cultures into types.

unilinear evolution: The view that all cultures have evolved in the same order through a set sequence of stages.

STUDY QUESTIONS

1. How do general and specific evolution differ?
2. What is the relationship between specific, convergent, and multilinear evolution?
3. What are the four main general evolutionary trends?
4. What was Leslie White's view of cultural evolution?
5. What are Cohen's four nonindustrial strategies of adaptation? What are the main characteristics of each?
6. How do social ties facilitate individual mobility between bands?
7. What are the main differences and similarities between modern and ancient foragers?
8. What are the main differences between horticulture and agriculture?
9. What are the advantages and disadvantages of irrigation?
10. What is the difference between nomadism and transhumance?

SUGGESTED ADDITIONAL READING

BOSERUP, E.
 1965   *The Conditions of Agricultural Growth*. Chicago: Aldine. Influential book linking population increase, agricultural intensity, and level of sociopolitical development.

BOYD, R., AND P. J. RICHERSON
 1985   *Culture and the Evolutionary Process*. Chicago: University of Chicago Press. Social evolution within the larger context of human evolution and recent evolutionary theory.

COHEN, Y., ED.
 1974   *Man in Adaptation: The Cultural Present*. 2nd ed. Chicago: Aldine. Sets forth Cohen's typology of strategies of adaptation and uses it to organize interesting essays on cultural anthropology.

INGOLD, T., D. RICHES, AND J. WOODBURN
 1991   *Hunters and Gatherers*. New York: Berg (St. Martin's). Volume I examines history, evolution, and social change among foragers. Volume II looks at their property, ideology, and power relations. These broad regional surveys illuminate current issues and debates.

JOHNSON, A. W., AND T. EARLE
 1987   *The Evolution of Human Societies: From Foraging Group to Agrarian State*. Stanford, CA: Stanford University Press. Up-to-date synthesis of findings on human cultural evolution.

LEE, R. B.
 1984   *The Dobe !Kung*. Fort Worth: Harcourt, Brace, Jovanovich. Account of well-known San foragers, by one of their principal ethnographers.

LEE, R. B., AND I. DEVORE, EDS.
 1977   *Kalahari Hunter-Gatherers: Studies of the !Kung San and Their Neighbors*. Cambridge, MA: Harvard University Press. Long-term interdisciplinary study.

SAHLINS, M. D., AND E. R. SERVICE
 1960   *Evolution and Culture*. Ann Arbor: University of Michigan Press. Application of evolutionary principles to cultural anthropological data a century after Darwin.

WHITE, L. A.
 1965   *The Evolution of Culture: The Development of Civilization to the Fall of Rome*. New York: McGraw-Hill. Classic sketch of human cultural evolution and diversity.

WILMSEN, E.
 1989   *Land Filled with Flies: A Political Economy of the Kalahari*. Chicago: University of Chicago Press. A revisionist view of the San, in the context of colonialism and the world system.

C H A P T E R   1 2

BANDS AND TRIBES

Several years ago anthropologist Elman Service (1962) listed four types, or levels, of social and political organization: band, tribe, chiefdom, and state. *Bands,* as we have seen, are small kin-based groups found among foragers. **Tribes,** which are associated with nonintensive food production (horticulture and pastoralism), have villages and/or descent groups but lack a government (centralized rule) and social classes (socioeconomic stratification). In a tribe, there is no reliable means of enforcing political decisions. The **chiefdom,** a form of sociopolitical organization that is intermediate between the tribe and the state, is kin-based, but it has differential access to resources and a permanent political structure. The **state** is a form of sociopolitical organization based on central government and socioeconomic stratification.

Many anthropologists have criticized Service's typology as being too simple. However, it does offer a handy set of labels for highlighting cross-cultural similarities and differences in social and political organization. Accordingly, most anthropologists use the classification occasionally. Service's four types reflect the general evolutionary trends discussed in the last chapter. To restate those trends, as we move from band to tribe to chiefdom to state:

1. Parts and subparts increase.
2. Parts and subparts become more functionally specialized.
3. More effective coordinating mechanisms (means of regulation and integration) appear.
4. Population size increases, along with the range or scale of the sociopolitical system (from local to regional to national).

Parts and subparts proliferate as villages and descent groups are added to families and kin-based bands. Functional specialization increases as political, economic, and religious figures and institutions appear. Regulatory systems expand from local (band or village) to regional to national (the state) levels as the population grows and political control strengthens.

POLITICS

Anthropologists and political scientists share an interest in political organization, but the anthropological approach is global and comparative. Anthropological data reveal substantial variations in power, authority, and legal systems in different cultures. (*Power* is the ability to exercise one's will over others; *authority* is the socially approved use of power.) In bands and tribes, the political order, or **polity,** is not a separate entity but is submerged in the total social order. It is difficult to characterize an act or event as political rather than merely social.

Recognizing that political organization is sometimes just an aspect of social organization, Morton Fried offered this definition:

> Political organization comprises those portions of social organization that specifically relate to the individuals or groups that manage the affairs of *public policy* or seek to control the appointment or activities of those individuals or groups. (Fried 1967, pp. 20–21, emphasis added)

This definition certainly fits contemporary North America. Under "individuals or groups that manage the affairs of public policy" come federal, state (provincial), and local (municipal) governments. Those who "seek to control . . . appointment or activities" include such interest groups as political parties, unions, corporations, consumers, activists, action committees, and religious groups.

Fried's definition is much less applicable to bands and tribes, where it is often difficult to detect any "public policy." For this reason, I prefer to speak of *socio*political organization in discussing cross-cultural similarities and differences in the **regulation** or management of interrelationships among groups and their representatives. In a general sense regulation is the process that ensures that variables stay within their normal ranges, corrects deviations from the norm, and thus maintains a system's integrity. In the case of political regulation this includes such things as the settling of conflicts between individuals and groups and methods of decision making within the group. The study of political regulation draws our attention to questions about who performs these tasks (are there formal leaders?) and how they are managed.

TYPES AND TRENDS

Ethnographic and archeological studies in hundreds of places have revealed many correlations between economy and social and political organization. Band, tribe, chiefdom, and state are categories or types in a system of **sociopolitical typology.** These types are correlated with the adaptive strategies (**economic typology**) discussed in the last chapter. Thus, foragers (an economic type) tend to have band organization (a sociopolitical type). Similarly, many horticulturalists and pastoralists live in tribal societies (or, more simply, tribes). The economies of chiefdoms tend to be based on intensive horticulture or agriculture, but some pastoralists also participate in chiefdoms. Nonindustrial states usually have an agricultural base.

Food producers tend to have larger, denser populations and more complex economies than do foragers. These features create new regulatory problems, which give rise to more complex relationships and linkages. Many sociopolitical trends reflect the increased regulatory demands associated with food production. Archeologists have studied these trends through time, and cultural anthropologists have observed them among contemporary groups.

This chapter and the next one examine societies that differ in their adaptive strategies and levels of sociopolitical complexity. A common set of questions will be considered for different types of societies. What kinds of social groups do they have? How do people affiliate with those groups? How do the groups link up with larger ones? How do the groups represent themselves to each other? How are their internal and external relations regulated? This chapter focuses on bands and tribes, and the following chapter deals with chiefdoms and states.

FORAGING BANDS

The groups that are significant in a given society tend to reflect that society's sociopolitical type and adaptive strategy. For example, in most foraging societies only two kinds of groups are significant: the nuclear family and the band. Unlike sedentary villages (which appear in tribal societies), bands are impermanent. They form seasonally as component nuclear families assemble. The particular combination of families in a band may vary from year to year.

In such settings the main social building blocks (linking principles) are the personal relationships of individuals. For example, marriage and kinship create ties between members of different bands. Because one's parents and grandparents come from different bands, a person has relatives in several of these groups. Trade and visiting also link local groups, as does fictive kinship, such as the San namesake system described in the last chapter. Similarly, Eskimo men traditionally had trade partners, whom they treated almost like brothers, in different bands. The natives of Australia had an institution known as the "section system" that had similar linking functions.

In a foraging band, there is very little differential authority and no differential power, although particular talents lead to special respect. For example, someone can sing or dance well, is an especially good storyteller, or can go into a trance and communicate with spirits. Band leaders are leaders in name only. They are first among equals. Sometimes they give advice or make decisions, but they have no means of enforcing their decisions.

Although foragers lack formal **law** in the sense of a legal code that includes trial and enforcement, they do have methods of social control and dispute settlement. The absence of law does not mean total anarchy. The aboriginal Eskimos (Hoebel 1954, 1968), or Inuit, as they are called in Canada, provide a good example of methods of settling disputes in stateless societies. As described by E. A. Hoebel (1954) in a study of Eskimo conflict resolution, a sparse population of some 20,000 Eskimos spanned 9,500 kilometers (6,000 miles) of the Arctic region. The most significant Eskimo social groups were the nuclear family and the band. Personal relationships linked the families and bands. Some bands had headmen. There were also shamans (part-time religious specialists). However, these positions conferred little power on those who occupied them.

Unlike tropical foraging societies, in which gathering—usually a female task—is more important, hunting and fishing by men were the primary Eskimo subsistence activities. The diverse and abundant plant foods available in warmer areas were absent in the Arctic. Traveling on land and sea in a bitter environment, Eskimo men faced more dangers than women did. The traditional male role took its toll in lives. Adult women would have outnumbered men substantially without occasional female **infanticide** (killing of a baby), which Eskimo culture permitted.

As is true of most foragers, the most significant social groups among the Eskimos (or Inuit, as they are called in Canada) were the nuclear family and the band. This historic photo shows a family group of eleven Eskimo men, women, and children in Port Clarence, Alaska.

Despite this crude (and to us unthinkable) means of population regulation, there were still more adult women than men. This permitted some men to have two or three wives. The ability to support more than one wife conferred a certain amount of prestige, but it also encouraged envy. (*Prestige* is esteem, respect, or approval for culturally valued acts or qualities.) If a man seemed to be taking additional wives just to enhance his reputation, a rival was likely to steal one of them. Most disputes were between men and originated over women, caused by wife stealing or adultery. If a man discovered that his wife had been having sexual relations without his permission, he considered himself wronged.

Although public opinion would not let the husband ignore the matter, he had several options. He could try to kill the wife stealer. However, if he succeeded, one of his rival's kinsmen would surely try to kill him in retaliation. One dispute could escalate into several deaths as relatives avenged a succession of murders. No government existed to intervene and stop such a **blood feud** (a feud between families). However, one could also challenge a rival to a song battle. In a public setting, contestants made up insulting songs about each other. At the end of the

match, the audience judged one of them the winner. However, if a man whose wife had been stolen won, there was no guarantee she would return. Often she would decide to stay with her abductor.

Several acts of killing that are crimes in contemporary North America were not considered criminal by the Eskimos. Infanticide has already been mentioned. Furthermore, people who felt that, because of age or infirmity, they were no longer useful might kill themselves or ask others to kill them. Old people or invalids who wished to die would ask a close relative, such as a son, to end their lives. It was necessary to ask a close relative in order to ensure that the kin of the deceased did not take revenge on the killer.

Thefts are common in state-organized societies, which have marked property differentials. However, thefts were not a problem for the Eskimos—or for most foragers. Each Eskimo had access to the resources needed to sustain life. Every man could hunt, fish, and make the tools necessary for subsistence. Every woman could obtain the implements and materials needed to make clothing, prepare food, and do domestic work. Eskimos could even hunt and fish in territories of other local groups.

There was no notion of private ownership of territory or animals.

To describe certain property notions of people who live in societies without state organization, Elman Service (1966) coined the term **personalty** (note the spelling). Personalty refers to items other than strategic resources that are indelibly associated with a specific person. These items include things such as arrows, a tobacco pouch, clothing, and personal ornaments. The term points to the personal relationship between such items and their owner. Personalty is so tied to specific people that theft is inconceivable (think of your toothbrush). The "grave goods" that are often found in archeological sites dating to the period before food production probably represent personalty. These items were not passed on to heirs. Their association with the deceased was too definite.

One of the most basic Eskimo beliefs was that "all natural resources are free or common goods" (Hoebel 1968). Band-organized societies usually lack differential access to strategic resources. The only private property is personalty. If people want something from someone else, they ask for it, and it is usually given.

TRIBAL CULTIVATORS

Tribes usually have a horticultural or pastoral economy and are organized by village life and/or descent-group membership. Socioeconomic stratification (i.e., a class structure) and centralized rule are absent. Many tribes have small-scale warfare, often in the form of intervillage raiding. Tribes have more effective regulatory mechanisms than do foragers, but tribalists have no sure means of enforcing political decisions. The main regulatory officials are village heads, "big men," descent-group leaders, village councils, and leaders of pantribal associations. All these figures and groups have limited authority.

Like foragers, horticulturalists tend to be egalitarian, although some have marked gender stratification—an unequal distribution of resources, power, prestige, and personal freedom between men and women. Horticultural villages are usually small, with low population density and open access to strategic resources. Age, gender, and personal traits determine how much respect people receive and how much support they get from others. Egalitari-

anism diminishes, however, as village size and population density increase. Horticultural villages usually have headmen—rarely, if ever, headwomen.

Descent-Group Organization

Kin-based bands are basic social units among foragers. An analogous group among food producers is the **descent group.** A descent group is a permanent social unit whose members claim common ancestry. The group endures even though its membership changes as members are born and die, move in and move out. Often, descent-group membership is determined at birth and is lifelong.

Descent groups frequently are exogamous (members must seek their mates from other descent groups). Two common rules serve to admit certain people as descent-group members while excluding others. With a rule of **matrilineal descent,** people join the mother's group automatically at birth and stay members throughout life. Matrilineal descent groups therefore include only the children of the group's women. With **patrilineal descent,** people automatically have lifetime membership in the father's group. The children of all the men join the group, but the children of the women are excluded. Matrilineal and patrilineal descent are types of **unilineal descent.** This means that the descent rule uses *one line* only, either the male or the female (Figures 12.1 and 12.2). Patrilineal descent is much more common than is matrilineal descent. In a sample of 564 societies (Murdock 1957), about three times as many were found to be patrilineal (247 to 84).

Descent groups may be **lineages** or **clans.** Common to both is the belief that members descend from the same **apical ancestor.** This person stands at the apex, or top, of the common genealogy. How do lineages and clans differ? A lineage uses **demonstrated descent.** Members can recite the names of their forebears in each generation from the apical ancestor through the present. (This doesn't mean that their recitations are accurate, only that lineage members think they are.) Clans use **stipulated descent.** Clan members merely say they descend from the apical ancestor. They don't try to trace the actual genealogical links between themselves and that ancestor.

Some societies have both lineages and clans. In this case, clans have more members and cover a larger geographical area than lineages do. Some-

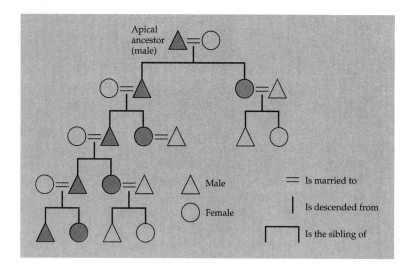

Figure 12.1 *A patrilineage five generations deep. Lineages are based on demonstrated descent from an apical ancestor. With patrilineal descent children of men (blue) are included as descent-group members. Children of women are excluded; they belong to their father's patrilineage. Also notice lineage exogamy.*

times a clan's apical ancestor is not a human at all but an animal or plant (called a **totem**). Whether human or not, the ancestor symbolizes the social unity and identity of the members, distinguishing them from other groups.

A tribal society normally contains several descent groups. Any one of them may be confined to a single village, but they usually span more than one village. Any branch of a descent group that lives in one place is a **local descent group.** Two or more local branches of different descent groups may live in the same village. Descent groups in the same village or different villages establish alliances through frequent intermarriage.

The Village Headman

The Yanomami (Chagnon 1992) are Native Americans who live in southern Venezuela and adjacent Brazil. Their tribal society has about 20,000 people living in 200 to 250 widely scattered villages, each with a population between 40 and 250. The Yanomami are horticulturalists who also hunt and gather. Their staple crops are bananas and plantains (a bananalike crop). There are more significant social groups among the Yanomami than exist in a foraging society. The Yanomami have nuclear families, villages, and descent groups. Their descent groups are patrilineal and exogamous. They span more than one village. However, local branches of two different descent groups may live in the same village and intermarry.

As in many village-based tribal societies, the only leadership position among the Yanomami is that of **village head** (always a man). His authority, like that of the foraging band leader, is severely limited. If a headman wants something done, he must lead by example and persuasion. The headman lacks the right to issue orders. He can only persuade, harangue, and try to influence public opinion. For example, if he wants people to clean up the central plaza in preparation for a feast, he must start sweep-

Figure 12.2 *A matrilineage five generations deep. Matrilineages are based on demonstrated descent from a female ancestor. Only the children of women (red) belong to the matrilineage. The children of men are excluded; they belong to their mother's matrilineage.*

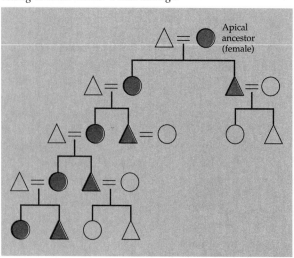

ing it himself, hoping that his covillagers will take the hint and relieve him.

When conflict erupts, the headman may be called on as a mediator who listens to both sides. He will give an opinion and advice. If a disputant is unsatisfied, the headman can do nothing. He has no power to back his decisions and no way to impose punishments. Like the band leader, he is first among equals.

A Yanomami village headman must also lead in generosity. Because he must be more generous than any other villager, he cultivates more land. His garden provides much of the food consumed when his village holds a feast for another village. The headman represents the village in its dealings with outsiders. Sometimes he visits other villages to invite people to a feast.

The way a person acts as headman depends on his personal traits and the number of supporters he can muster. One village headman, Kaobawa, intervened in a dispute between a husband and wife and kept him from killing her (Chagnon 1992). He also guaranteed safety to a delegation from a village with which a covillager of his wanted to start a war. Kaobawa was a particularly effective headman. He had demonstrated his fierceness in battle, but he also knew how to use diplomacy to avoid offending other villagers. No one in the village had a better personality for the headmanship. Nor (because Kaobawa had many brothers) did anyone have more supporters. Among the Yanomami, when a group is dissatisfied with a village headman, its members can leave and found a new village; this is done from time to time.

Village Raiding

Yanomami society, with its many villages and descent groups, is more complex than a band-organized society. The Yanomami also face more regulatory problems. A headman can sometimes prevent a specific violent act, but there is no government to maintain order. In fact, intervillage raiding in which men are killed and women are captured has been a feature of some areas of Yanomami territory, particularly those studied by Chagnon (1992).

Traditional Yanomami intratribal warfare is similar to, but more extreme than, raiding in other tribal societies. Chagnon describes male supremacy as a central theme in Yanomami culture. Gender stratification is so extreme that we may speak of a *male supremacist complex,* in which males are valued more than females and women are deprived of prestige, power, and personal freedom. The Yanomami prefer sons to daughters, especially as firstborn children. If the firstborn is a girl, she may be killed, but boys are allowed to live. Females also die in warfare, and there are more male than female Yanomami (449 to 391 in seven villages that Chagnon studied). Furthermore, although there are too few women to provide even one wife for each man, 25 percent of the men are polygynous—they have multiple mates. The scarcity of women is one reason men go on fighting. They want to capture additional women, as wives. Figure 12.3 summarizes the way in which the pattern of Yanomami warfare perpetuates itself.

There is very lively debate among anthropologists about the nature and causes of intervillage raiding among the Yanomami (Albert 1989; Chagnon 1988, 1992; Ferguson 1989a, b, and c; Heider 1988; Lizot 1985; Ramos 1987). However, we must also stress that the Yanomami are not isolated from outside events (although there are still uncontacted villages). The Yanomami live in two nation-states, Venezuela and Brazil, and external warfare waged by Brazilian ranchers and miners has increasingly threatened them (*Cultural Survival Quarterly* 1989; Chagnon 1992). During the recent Brazilian gold rush (1987–1991), one Yanomami died each day, on

Figure 12.3 *Continued selection for warfare among the Yanomami.*

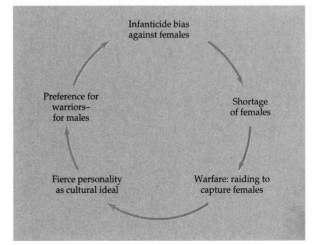

average, from external attacks (including biological warfare—introduced diseases to which the Indians lack resistance). By 1991 there were some 40,000 Brazilian miners in the Yanomami homeland. Some Indians were killed outright. The miners introduced new diseases, and the swollen population ensured that old diseases became epidemic. In 1991 a commission of the American Anthropological Association reported on the plight of the Yanomami (*Anthropology Newsletter*, September 1991). Brazilian Yanomami were dying at a rate of 10 percent annually, and their fertility rate had dropped to zero. Since then, both the Brazilian and the Venezuelan governments have intervened to protect the Yanomami. The former Brazilian president, Fernando Collor, declared a huge Yanomami territory off-limits to outsiders. Unfortunately, by mid-1992 local politicians, miners, and ranchers were increasingly evading the ban. These external attacks pose a much more serious threat to Yanomami survival than does traditional intervillage raiding.

Tribal Warfare

In a cross-cultural study of tribal warfare, Divale and Harris (1976) used the **Human Relations Area Files (HRAF),** a voluminous archive housed in New Haven, Connecticut, but available on microfiche in most college and university libraries. The HRAF is

assembled from ethnographic reports and historical accounts of more than 300 cultures. Divale and Harris define warfare as

> all organized forms of intergroup homicide involving combat teams of two or more persons, including feuding and raiding. (1976, p. 521)

Divale and Harris located 112 societies with good information on warfare. In 49 percent of them, warfare was going on at the time of the report. In 30 percent, it had stopped between five and twenty-five years earlier. In the remaining 21 percent, war had ceased more than twenty-five years before the report.

Divale and Harris argue that warfare acts to curb population growth among tribal cultivators. This is not mainly because of combat deaths but because tribal warfare can affect reproduction indirectly, by inculcating cultural values that lead to overt or covert female infanticide. In warring tribes, newborn females are more likely to be killed than male babies are. Female infanticide isn't always direct. There is also preferential treatment of boys and neglect of girls, leading to girls' deaths. In any population, the lower the proportion of females who survive to reproductive age, the lower the rate of population growth.

In aboriginal times, no state intervened to curb intervillage warfare among the tribal Asmat of West Irian, Indonesia, shown here with their war canoes.

According to Divale and Harris, tribal warfare creates a preference for warriors, and thus for boys over girls. This preference promotes female infanticide. In the societies in their study where warfare was still going on, the ratio of males to females in the junior age group (fourteen years and under) was 127:100. In those in which warfare had stopped, junior sex ratios approached that of our own society (106:100). Divale and Harris argue that in nonindustrial societies men do the fighting because, on the average, they are taller and heavier than women are. Size confers an advantage in combat with handheld, muscle-powered weapons. Note that the military significance of physical size and strength declines in industrial societies. A few North American women with rifles or even handguns could easily best a party of tribal raiders.

When warfare is frequent, a male supremacist complex often pervades the culture. Men control access to resources and labor. Patrilineal descent rules, residence customs, and marital privileges emphasize and maintain male solidarity. The most successful warriors have multiple wives. This polygyny intensifies any shortage of females that may already exist and stimulates additional fighting—to capture women.

Divale and Harris view the expansion of tribal warfare as one consequence of the emergence and spread of food production, which increased the rate of population growth. To understand why, we must consider the relationship between diet and fertility. Foragers tend to have a diet that is high in protein and low in fats and carbohydrates. The diet of cultivators is just the opposite. Diet affects the ratio of body fat to total weight, and foragers have less fat than food producers do. The physical results of diet affect fertility in two ways. First, the high-fat diets associated with food production promote earlier puberty and lengthen the childbearing period. Second, high-fat diets make women more likely to get pregnant, even when they are nursing.

Foragers, with their low body fat, can delay conception by nursing their babies for years. Lactation (milk production) keeps body fat down and disrupts normal ovulation, so sexual intercourse is less likely to result in a new pregnancy. However, because prolonged lactation is only partially effective as contraception, infanticide also occurs among foragers.

The high-fat and high-carbohydrate diet of culti-vators reduces the effectiveness of lactation as contraception. In cultivating societies, nursing women often get pregnant, and other practices arise to limit population growth. For example, there may be a **postpartum taboo:** Women must avoid sexual intercourse for a culturally determined period after giving birth.

Abortion, although practiced in some cultures—for example, among certain tropical forest groups in South America—is not very common because it often kills the pregnant woman along with the fetus. Divale and Harris contend that without effective contraception and abortion, the most widespread custom that serves to limit population growth among tribal cultivators is female infanticide, which intensifies with warfare and the male supremacist complex. Females are valued less than males are, and this makes it psychologically easier for members of such groups (often the mothers) to kill female babies. Reliable contraception, based on recent inventions, permits more humane population limitation.

Village Councils

Whatever the reasons for increased population density and the presence of larger villages in an area, these demographic changes pose new regulatory problems. As the number of people living together increases, the potential for interpersonal conflict grows. Nigeria has villages of more than 1,000 people in areas where population densities exceed 200 people per square mile (about 75 people per square kilometer). In Amazonia, native horticulture has supported villages with 1,400 people (Carneiro 1961/1968). When village population exceeds 1,000, there may be a dozen descent groups in a village instead of just one or two.

In large villages, not only are there many interpersonal relationships requiring regulation, but there are intergroup relations as well. In societies with a well-developed descent-group structure, a person's allegiance is mainly to the descent group and only secondarily to the village and tribe. People must take the side of their group in any dispute with another descent group residing in the same village.

If disorder is not to reign in such larger-scale cultivating societies, political leaders must arbitrate disputes. Large villages have more effective heads than the Yanomami have. The specific activities and

MURDER, LIFE, AND PERSONHOOD

Americans have different opinions about when life begins and when one person can take it from another. So do different cultures. Although American law defines infanticide as murder, it has been widespread in non-Western cultures. One of the keenest moral dilemmas that some anthropologists face in the field is how to deal with infanticide. Understandably, ethnographers have trouble standing by while their hosts carry out a custom that to us is considered murder. Fortunately, I have never seen overt infanticide, nor did the villagers I studied in Brazil and Madagascar practice it. However, other anthropologists have seen babies put to death, usually because the culture being studied considered it immoral or unethical to let certain kinds of infants survive. Many cultures, for example, required that one or both twins be killed. They viewed twin births as inhuman; only animals, they say, should have multiple births.

In cultures with infanticide, *parents* (usually the mother) sometimes kill their own progeny. Powerful moral and religious rules and standards compel such an intrinsically difficult act. Natives believe that the survival of unusual children or those born under exceptional, dubious, or culturally inappropriate circumstances poses a threat to the entire group. Letting both twins live, for instance, might damage the survival chances of either twin because of scarce resources, including mother's milk. (A side effect of killing *both* twins is to remove genes that lead to twinning from the population.)

Among the Tapirapé Indians of Brazil, couples could raise two children of one sex, three in all. Tapirapé culture banned parents from raising more, because additional mouths would siphon resources needed by other families. The Tapirapé considered it selfish and immoral to try to keep a surplus baby. The death of the infant, who was not defined as human, was considered morally necessary for other members of the group to survive.

Among the world's cultures, infanticide may be overt or covert. When there is another small child or many children in the family, if a baby is not killed at birth, it is often neglected until it dies. This is covert infanticide. If the baby survives, the mother may change her strategy and begin to invest more in its care, particularly if it shows culturally valued characteristics (Scheper-Hughes 1987, 1992).

Most cultures that practice overt infanticide justify it by excluding newborn babies from their definition of human life. They do not consider baby killing to be murder. When does humanity begin? In the United States, the question was answered judicially in 1973. In its *Roe* v. *Wade* decision, the U.S. Supreme Court divided the genesis of human life into three parts. During the first trimester of pregnancy, a woman may seek abortion on demand. In the second trimester, abortions may be obtained in specified circumstances. During the third trimester, abortions are normally prohibited because the fetus may be able to survive independently. That judicial decision suggested that human life begins with the third trimester.

The ancestors of the Betsileo of Madagascar, whom I studied in 1966–1967, practiced occasional infanticide. Their culture did not define it as murder, because in the Betsileo view it takes several years for a child to become fully human. Parental and social investment gradually increases as the child survives and matures.

Even today, although infanticide has ended, the Betsileo do not define a baby as fully human. When a baby is born, an astrologer calculates its lifetime horoscope. Formerly, when the horoscope was unlucky or seemed to threaten the parents or the group, the infant could be subjected to a death ordeal. It was placed at the entrance to the cattle corral, where it was likely to be trampled by livestock returning in the evening. If it survived, it was assumed to have positive qualities that offset its apparent negative destiny.

Although infanticide has ended, the process by which a Betsileo child grows into a human being (the acquisition of personhood) is still gradual. During the first two years of its life, people call the baby such derogatory names as "little dog," "slave," and "pile of feces." By devaluing the child in this way, the Betsileo think they are increasing its chances for survival. They are trying to divert ancestral spirits who might want to seize the child for the spirit world. The American anthropologist, whom a different culture has trained to say, "Oh, how cute," must repress the urge to compliment a baby and produce an insult instead. If a Betsileo baby dies during its first two years, it is buried in the rice fields. Until adolescence, it can be buried in the children's tomb. Only in adolescence does it acquire full personhood and the right to a place in the ancestral tomb, which has tremendous cultural significance in Betsileo culture.

manner of selection of the head (usually a man) vary, but the task of regulator is demanding. Heads may direct military actions or hunting expeditions. They may reallocate land if, because of different rates of population increase, some descent groups have grown too big for their estates while others are still too small to make full use of their own.

In smaller-scale societies a person's position depends on age, gender, and personality traits. When societies have descent groups, however, another basis for status develops—descent-group leadership. In villages with multiple descent groups, each descent group has a head. All the heads together may form a council of advisers or elders to work with the village head. In cooperation, they make up the local power structure. The council backs the village head's authority and ensures that decisions are carried out by the descent groups the members represent.

The village head must obtain council support for decisions applying to the entire village. Sometimes, however, it is difficult to reach agreement, since decisions that are good for the community at large may harm the interests of a particular descent group. Decisions usually are not enforced through physical means. If the head of one descent group refuses to cooperate, persuasion and public opinion are used. If people refuse to follow the advice of their elders, they may be asked to leave the village. However, in tribes, as in bands, community opinion and persuasion are usually sufficient.

Despite their enlarged powers, the descent-group leaders and the village head must still be generous. Their wealth and life styles are not noticeably superior to those of their fellow villagers. They are only part-time political specialists. They are also subsistence farmers. If they control more land and larger and more productive households, they must give more feasts and support more dependents.

The manner of choosing the village head varies from one tribal society to another. Sometimes the headship rotates among descent groups. In other cultures the office is confined to one descent group, perhaps the largest, but the incumbent relies on the support and approval of representatives of the others. Finally, the choice of the village head may be associated with religion. Heads may be chosen because of supernatural powers. Their abilities may be a result of training, or people may believe they are inherited or come from divine revelation.

The "big man" is an important regulator of regional events. He persuades people to organize feasts, which distribute pork and wealth. Shown here is such a regional event, drawing on several villages, in Papua–New Guinea. Big men owe their status to their individual personalities rather than to inherited wealth or position.

The "Big Man"

In many areas of the South Pacific, particularly the Melanesian Islands and Papua–New Guirea, native cultures have a kind of political leader that we call the **big man.** The big man (almost always a male) is an elaborate version of the village head, but there is one very significant difference. The village head's leadership is within one village; the big man has supporters in several villages. He is therefore a more effective (but still limited) regulator of *regional* political organization. Here we see the trend toward expansion in the scale of sociopolitical regulation— from village to region.

The Kapauku Papuans live in Irian Jaya, Indonesia (which is on the island of New Guinea). Anthropologist Leopold Pospisil (1963) studied the Kapauku (45,000 people), who grow crops (with the sweet potato as their staple) and raise pigs. Their economy is too complex to be described as simple horticulture. Beyond the household, the only political figure among the Kapauku is the big man, known as a *tonowi*. A *tonowi* achieves his status through hard work, amassing wealth in the form of pigs and other native riches. Characteristics that can distinguish a big man from his fellows include wealth, generosity, eloquence, physical fitness, bravery, and supernatural powers. Notice that big men are what they are because they have certain personalities, not because they have inherited their wealth or position.

Any man who is determined enough can become a big man, because people create their own wealth through hard work and good judgment. Wealth depends on successful pig breeding and trading. As a man's pig herd and prestige grow, he attracts supporters. He sponsors ceremonial pig feasts in which pigs are slaughtered and their meat is distributed to guests.

The big man has some advantages that the Yanomami village headman lacks. His wealth exceeds that of his fellows. His primary supporters, in recognition of past favors and anticipation of future rewards, recognize him as a leader and accept his decisions as binding. He is an important regulator of regional events in Kapauku life. He helps determine the dates for feasts and markets. He persuades people to sponsor feasts, which distribute pork and wealth. He regulates intervillage contacts by sponsoring dance expeditions. He initiates economic projects that require the cooperation of a regional community.

The Kapauku big man again exemplifies a generalization about leadership in tribal societies: If people achieve wealth and widespread respect and support, they must be generous. The big man works hard not to hoard wealth but to be able to *give away* the fruits of his labor, to convert wealth into prestige and gratitude. If a big man is stingy, he loses his supporters, and his reputation plummets. The Kapauku take even more extreme measures against big men who hoard. Selfish and greedy rich men may be murdered by their fellows.

Political figures such as the big man emerge as regulators both of demographic growth and of economic complexity. Kapauku cultivation uses varied techniques for specific kinds of land. Labor-intensive cultivation in valleys involves mutual aid in turning the soil before planting. The digging of long drainage ditches is even more complex. Kapauku plant cultivation supports a larger and denser population than does the simpler horticulture of the Yanomami. Kapauku society could not survive in its present form without collective cultivation and political regulation of the more complex economic tasks.

Segmentary Lineage Organization

The big man is a *temporary* regional regulator. Big men can mobilize supporters in several villages to pool produce and labor on specific occasions. Another temporary form of regional political organization in tribal society is **segmentary lineage organization (SLO)**. This means that the descent-group structure (usually patrilineal) has several levels—nested segments—that are like dolls nesting inside other dolls or boxes placed within boxes (Figure 12.4). The largest segments are maximal lineages, segments of which are known as major lineages. Major lineages are divided up into minor lineages. Minor lineages in turn are segmented into minimal lineages, whose common ancestor lived fairly recently—no more than four generations ago. The larger segments have spread throughout a region, but members of the minimal lineage occupy the same village. New minimal lineages develop when people move away and establish new settlements. Over time, minimal lineages grow into minor ones, minor into major ones, and major into maximal ones.

Segmentary lineage organization exists in broad outline in many cultures, such as the traditional societies of North Africa and the Middle East, including prestate Arabs and biblical Jews. However, the classic examples of SLO are two African groups, the Tiv of Nigeria and the Nuer of the Sudan (Sahlins 1961). Segmentary lineage structure organized more than 1 million Tiv, who believe that they all share the same remote ancestor, a man named Tiv who settled in their homeland many generations ago. They trace the line of descent leading from Tiv to the present, listing his male descendants in each generation.

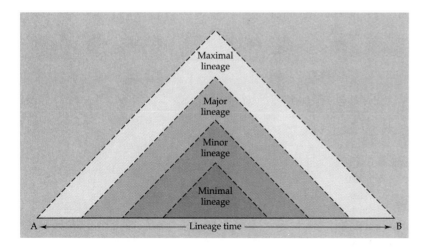

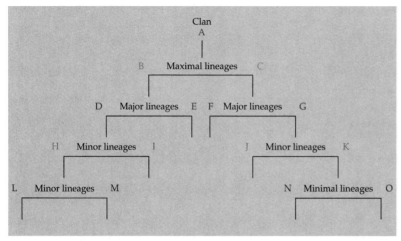

Figure 12.4 *Two views of segmentary lineage organization. (Reprinted by permission from E. E. Evans-Pritchard,* The Nuer: A Description of the Modes of Livelihood and Political Institutions of a Nilotic People *[Oxford: Clarendon Press, 1940].)*

(top) *Minimal lineages nest within minor lineages, which nest within major lineages, which nest within maximal lineages, which may in turn belong to a clan, as in the bottom figure. Common ancestry is most recent in the minimal lineage.*

(bottom) *Clan A is segmented into* maximal lineages *B and C. These have divided into* major lineages *D, E, F, and G. At the next level down,* minor lineages *H, I, J, and K are segments of major lineages D and G. L, M, N, and O are* minimal lineages *that are segments of H and K. For simplification, the minor lineages of E and F and the minimal lineages of I and J aren't shown.*

Although the Nuer cannot demonstrate patrilineal descent that far back, they believe that they have a common ancestry separate from that of their neighbors. One of several **Nilotic populations** (populations that inhabit the Upper Nile region of eastern Africa), the Nuer (Evans-Pritchard 1940), numbering more than 200,000, live in Sudan. Cattle pastoralism is fundamental to their mixed economy, which also includes horticulture. The Nuer have many institutions that are typical of tribal societies, including patrilineal descent groups arranged into a segmentary structure. Their political organization is based on descent rules and genealogical reckoning.

Brothers are very close in segmentary societies, especially when the father is alive. He manages their joint property and stops them from quarreling too much. He also arranges their marriages. When he

dies, the brothers usually keep on living in the same village, but one may take his share of the herds and start a settlement of his own. However, his brothers are still his closest allies. He will live as close as he can to them. Even if the brothers all stay in the same village, some of the grandchildren will move away in search of new pastures. However, each will try to remain as close to the home village as possible, settling nearest his brothers and nearer to his first cousins than to more distant relatives.

With SLO, the basic principle of solidarity is that the closer the descent-group relationship, the greater the mutual support. The more distant the shared ancestor, the greater the potential for hostility. This extends right up the genealogy; maximal lineages are more likely to fight each other than are major lineages.

Segmentary lineage organization seems to have

been advantageous for the Tiv and the Nuer, allowing them to expand at their neighbors' expense. This sociopolitical organization confers a feeling of tribal identity. It provides an orderly way to mobilize temporarily against other societies. When the need arises, the Nuer or the Tiv can easily present a common front against outsiders—people who claim different genealogical and ethnic identity (Sahlins 1961).

Segmentary descent also regulates disputes and their resolution. If a fight breaks out between men who share a living patrilineal ancestor, he intervenes to settle it. As head of the minimal descent group that includes the disputants, he backs his authority with the threat of banishment. However, when there is no common living ancestor, a blood feud may develop.

Disputes among the Nuer do not arise over land, which a person acquires as a member of a lineage. As a member of a minimal descent group, one has a right to its estate. A frequent cause of quarrels is adultery, and if a person injures or kills someone, a feud may develop. Conflicts also arise over divorce.

There is an alternative to a blood feud. The disputants may consult the leopard-skin man, so called because he customarily wears a leopard skin over his shoulders. Leopard-skin men conduct rituals, but their most important role is to mediate disputes. For instance, elders may ask a leopard-skin man to persuade a murder victim's kin to accept a certain number of cattle in recompense. While the mediator attempts to arrange a peaceful settlement, the murderer may take refuge in the leopard-skin man's village, which offers sanctuary until the mediator resolves the dispute or withdraws.

The leopard-skin man relies on persuasion and avoids blaming either side. He cannot enforce his decisions, but in theory he can use the threat of supernatural punishment. If one of the disputing groups is adamant, he may, in disgust, threaten to curse it. If, after seeking mediation, the disputants refuse to agree, the leopard-skin man may withdraw.

Negotiations involve the disputants, their elders, and other close kin. There is full and free discussion before a settlement is reached. The disputants may gradually come to accept the collective opinion of the mediator and the elders. However, although the peace-making abilities of the leopard-skin man are greater than anything found among the Yanomami

A leopard-skin man, mediator among the Nuer—tribal cattle herders and horticulturalists of the Sudan. The Nuer mediator has recourse only to supernatural sanctions when arbitrating descent-group feuds in this segmentary society.

and Eskimos, blood feuds still exist among the stateless Nuer.

With SLO, no one has a constant group of allies. One's allies change from one dispute to the next, depending on genealogical distance. Still, common descent does permit a temporary common front, as minimal lineages unite to form minor ones. Minor lineages form majors, and major lineages come together in a maximal lineage that, in the presence of an outside threat, unites all Nuer or Tiv society through its claim of common patrilineal descent.

Similarly, Arabs claim to demonstrate their segmentary descent patrilineally from the biblical Ishmael. There is an Arab adage, "I and my brother against my cousin [father's brother's son]. I, my brother, and my cousin against all other Arabs. I, my brother, my cousin, and all other Arabs against all the world" (Murphy and Kasdan 1959, p. 20).

Jews believe themselves to be descended from Isaac, half-brother of Ishmael. The Jews and Arabs share a common ancestor, Abraham, the father of both Ishmael and Isaac. In the modern world, of course, political mechanisms other than SLO, including national governments and regional alliances, work to determine relations between Arabs and Jews.

Pantribal Sodalities, Associations, and Age Grades

We have seen that events initiated by big men temporarily unite people from different villages. Segmentary lineage organization permits short-term mobilization of an entire society against an outside threat. There are many other kinds of sociopolitical linkages between local groups in a region. Clans, for example, often span several villages.

Kinship and descent provide important social linkages in tribal societies. Principles other than kinship also may link local groups. In a modern nation, a labor union, national sorority or fraternity, political party, or religious denomination may provide such a non-kin-based link. In tribes, nonkin groups called associations or **sodalities** may serve the same linking function. Often sodalities are based on common age or gender, with all-male sodalities more common than all-female ones.

Pantribal sodalities (those which extend across the whole tribe, spanning several villages) tend to be found in areas where two or more different cultures come into regular contact. They are especially likely to develop when there is warfare *between tribes* (as opposed to raiding between villages of the same tribe, as practiced by the Yanomami). Sodalities help organize the warfare that men wage against neighboring cultures. Since sodalities draw their members from different villages of the same tribe, they can mobilize men in many local groups for attack or retaliation against another tribe. Like SLO, pantribal sodalities have military value because they facilitate temporary regional mobilization. In particular, pantribal sodalities are common among pastoralists. One culture's sodality may organize raids to steal cattle or horses from another.

In the cross-cultural study of nonkin groups, we must distinguish between those which are confined to a single village and those which span several local groups. Only the latter, the *pantribal* groups, are important in general military mobilization and regional political organization. *Localized* men's houses and clubs, limited to particular villages, are found in many horticultural societies in tropical South America, Melanesia, and Papua–New Guinea. These groups may organize village activities and even intervillage raiding, but their political role is like that of village councils, and their leaders are similar to village heads. Their political scope is mainly local. The following discussion, which continues our examination of the growth in scale of re-

Some unigender groups (all male or all female) are confined to a single village. This is true of the Turkoman women's quarters in Central Asia shown here. Other unigender groups span several local groups. Only the latter, the pantribal groups, are important in regional political organization.

gional sociopolitical organization, concerns pantribal groups.

The best examples of pantribal sodalities come from the Central Plains of North America and from tropical Africa. During the eighteenth and nineteenth centuries, native populations of the Great Plains of the United States and Canada experienced a rapid growth of pantribal sodalities. This development reflected an economic change that followed the spread of horses, which had been brought to the New World by the Spanish, to the states between the Rocky Mountains and the Mississippi River. Many Plains Indian societies changed their adaptive strategies because of the horse. At first they had been foragers who hunted bison (buffalo) on foot. Later they adopted a mixed economy based on hunting, gathering, and horticulture. Finally they changed to a much more specialized economy based on horseback hunting of bison (eventually with rifles).

As the Plains tribes were undergoing these changes, other Indians also adopted horseback hunting and moved into the Plains. Attempting to occupy the same ecological niche, groups came into conflict. A pattern of warfare developed in which the members of one tribe raided another, usually for horses, as was portrayed in the movie *Dances with Wolves*. The new economy demanded that people follow the movement of the bison herds. During the winter, when the bison dispersed, a tribe fragmented into small bands and families. In the summer, as huge herds assembled on the Plains, members of the tribe reunited. They camped together for social, political, and religious activities, but mainly for communal bison hunting.

Only two activities in the new adaptive strategy demanded strong leadership: organizing and carrying out raids on enemy camps (to capture horses) and managing the summer bison hunt. All the Plains cultures developed pantribal sodalities, and leadership roles within them, to police the summer hunt. Leaders coordinated hunting efforts, making sure that people did not cause a stampede with an early shot or an ill-advised action. Leaders imposed severe penalties, including seizure of a culprit's wealth, for disobedience.

Some of the Plains sodalities were **age sets** of increasing rank. Each set included all the men—from that tribe's component bands—born during a certain time span. Each set had its distinctive dance, songs, possessions, and privileges. Members of each set had to pool their wealth to buy admission to the next higher level as they moved up the age hierarchy. Most Plains societies had pantribal warrior associations whose rituals celebrated militarism. As noted previously, the leaders of these associations organized bison hunting and raiding. They also arbitrated disputes during the summer, when large numbers of people came together.

Many of the tribes that adopted this Plains

Plains Indians were originally foragers who hunted bison (buffalo) on foot. Later they adopted a mixed economy based on hunting, gathering, and horticulture but then changed to a much more specialized economy based on hunting bison on horseback (eventually with rifles).

Among the pastoral Masai of Kenya, men born during the same four-year period were circumcised together and belonged to the same named group, an age set, throughout their lives. The sets moved through grades, of which the most important was the warrior grade. Two Masai age sets are shown here.

strategy of adaptation had once been foragers for whom hunting and gathering had been individual or small-group affairs. They had never come together previously as a single social unit. *Age and gender were available as social principles that could quickly and efficiently forge unrelated people into pantribal groups.* Other means of creating and intensifying tribal spirit also developed, for example, the fervent Sun Dance religion, which spread rapidly among the Plains groups as a summertime ceremony. Common participation in the Sun Dance ceremonies became a powerful forger of new tribal ethnic identities.

Raiding of one tribe by another, this time for cattle rather than horses, was also common in eastern and southeastern Africa, where pantribal sodalities, including age sets, also developed. Among the pastoral Masai of Kenya, men born during the same four-year period were circumcised together and belonged to the same named group, an age set, throughout their lives. The sets moved through grades, the most important of which was the warrior grade. Members of the set who wished to enter the warrior grade were at first discouraged by its current occupants, who eventually vacated the warrior grade and married. Members of a set felt a strong allegiance to one another and eventually had sexual rights to each other's wives. Masai women lacked comparable set organization, but they also passed through culturally recognized age grades:

initiate, married woman, and postmenopausal woman.

To understand the difference between an *age set* and an *age grade,* think of a college class, the Class of '96, for example, and its progress through the university. The age set would be the group of people constituting the Class of '96, while the first ("freshman"), sophomore, junior, and senior years would represent the age grades.

Not all cultures with age grades also have age sets. When there are no sets, men can enter or leave a particular grade individually or collectively, often by going through a predetermined ritual. The grades most commonly recognized in Africa are these:

1. Recently initiated youths
2. Warriors
3. One or more grades of mature men who play important roles in pantribal government
4. Elders, who may have special ritual responsibilities

In certain parts of West Africa and Central Africa, the pantribal sodalities are **secret societies,** made up exclusively of men or women. Like our college fraternities and sororities, these associations have secret initiation ceremonies. Among the Mende of Sierra Leone, men's and women's secret societies are very influential. The men's group, the Poro,

Political organization is well-developed among the Qashqai, who share their nomadic route and strategic resources with several other tribes. Here Qashqai nomads cross a river in Iran's Fars province.

trains boys in social conduct, ethics, and religion and supervises political and economic activities. Leadership roles in the Poro often overshadow village headship and play an important part in social control, dispute management, and tribal political regulation. Like descent, then, age, gender, and ritual can link members of different local groups into a single social collectivity in tribal society and thus create a sense of ethnic identity, of belonging to the same cultural tradition.

PASTORALISTS

Although many pastoralists live in tribes, a range of demographic and sociopolitical diversity occurs with pastoralism. A comparison of pastoralists shows that as regulatory problems increase, political hierarchies become more complex. Political organization becomes less personal, more formal, and less kinship-oriented. The pastoral strategy of adaptation does not dictate any particular political organization. A range of authority structures manage regulatory problems associated with specific environments. Many pastoralists (such as the Nuer and other East African herders) live in tribal societies. Others have powerful chiefs and live in nation-states. This reflects pastoralists' need to interact with other populations—a need that is less characteristic of the other adaptive strategies.

The scope of political authority among pastoralists expands considerably as regulatory problems increase in densely populated regions. Consider two Iranian pastoral nomadic tribes—the Basseri and the Qashqai (Salzman 1974). These groups followed a nomadic route more than 480 kilometers (300 miles) long. Starting each year from a plateau near the coast, they took their animals to grazing land 5,400 meters (17,000 feet) above sea level. These tribes shared this route with one another and with several other ethnic groups.

Use of the same pasture land at different times was carefully scheduled. Ethnic-group movements were tightly coordinated. Expressing this schedule is *il-rah*, a concept common to all Iranian nomads. A group's *il-rah* is its customary path in time and space. It is the schedule, different for each group, of when specific areas can be used in the annual trek.

Each tribe had its own leader, known as the *khan* or *il-khan*. The Basseri *khan*, because he dealt with a smaller population, faced fewer problems in coordinating its movements than did the leaders of the Qashqai. Correspondingly, his rights, privileges, duties, and authority were weaker. Nevertheless, his authority exceeded that of any political figure we have discussed so far. However, the *khan*'s authority still came from his personal traits rather than from his office. That is, the Basseri followed a particular *khan* not because of a political position he happened to fill but because of their personal allegiance and loyalty to him as a man. The *khan* relied on the support of the heads of the descent groups into which Basseri society was divided, following a rough segmentary lineage model.

In Qashqai society, however, allegiance shifts from the person to the office. The Qashqai had multiple levels of authority and more powerful *khans*. Managing 400,000 people required a complex hierarchy. Heading it was the *il-khan*, helped by a deputy, under whom were the heads of constituent tribes, under each of whom were descent-group heads.

A case illustrates just how developed the Qashqai authority structure was. A hailstorm prevented some nomads from joining the annual migration at the appointed time. Although everyone recognized that they were not responsible for their delay, the *il-khan* assigned them less favorable grazing land, for that year only, in place of their usual pasture. The tardy herders and other Qashqai considered the judgment fair and didn't question it. Thus Qashqai authorities regulated the annual migration. They also adjudicated disputes between people, tribes, and descent groups.

These Iranian cases illustrate the fact that pastoralism is often just one among many specialized economic activities within complex nation-states and regional systems. As part of a larger whole, pastoral tribes are constantly pitted against other ethnic groups. In these nations, the state becomes a final authority, a higher-level regulator that attempts to limit conflict between ethnic groups. State organization arose not just to manage agricultural economies but also to regulate the activities of ethnic groups within expanding social and economic systems. We turn in the next chapter to chiefdoms and states.

SUMMARY

Anthropologists may use a sociopolitical typology of bands, tribes, chiefdoms, and states along with an economic typology based on adaptive strategy. Through these classification schemes we can compare the scale and effectiveness of social linkages and political regulation and of variations in power, authority, and legal systems cross-culturally. There are important cross-cultural contrasts in the kinds of groups that are significant, determinants of leadership, reasons for disputes, and means for resolving them.

Illustrating trends in the evolution of sociopolitical complexity, parts and subparts proliferate as villages and descent groups are added to families and bands. Functional specialization increases as political, economic, and religious figures and institutions appear. Regulatory systems expand from local (band or village) to regional to national (the state) levels as the population grows and political control strengthens.

Foragers usually have egalitarian societies, with bands and families as characteristic groups. Personal networks link individuals, families, and bands. There is little differential power. Band leaders are first among equals and have no means of enforcing decisions. Disputes rarely arise over strategic resources, because the resources are available to everyone. Among the Eskimos, used in this chapter to exemplify sociopolitical regulation among foragers, disputes traditionally originated in adultery or wife stealing. Aggrieved individuals might kill offenders, but this could trigger a blood feud. Although no government existed to halt blood feuds, there were certain customary means of resolving disputes.

The descent group is a basic kin group in tribal societies. Unlike families, descent groups have perpetuity—they last for generations. There are several types of descent groups. Lineages are based on demonstrated descent; clans, on stipulated descent. Patrilineal and matrilineal descent are unilineal descent rules.

Political authority increases as population size and density and the scale of regulatory problems grow. Egalitarianism diminishes as village size increases. With more people, there are more interpersonal relationships to regulate. Increasingly complex economies pose further regulatory problems.

Horticultural villages generally have heads with limited authority. The heads lead by example and persuasion and have no sure means of enforcing their decisions. The Yanomami are tribal horticulturalists. Their sociopolitical organization has more varied groups than does the foraging society. There are villages and patrilineal descent groups. Authority is more developed than it is among foragers. However, village heads, the main Yanomami political figures, have no sure power. The Yanomami also illustrate a pattern of warfare that is widespread among tribal cultivators. Warfare produces a male supremacist complex, which leads to female infanticide.

Other tribal societies have councils of elders or descent-group heads who deliberate and make decisions about village affairs. Their authority varies with the scale of regulatory problems. Big men are temporary regional regulators. Their influence extends beyond the village; they mobilize the labor of supporters in several villages. Big men have prestige, commanding the loyalty of many, but they must be generous. Sponsorship of feasts leaves them with little wealth but with a reputation for generosity, which must be maintained if the big man is to retain his influence.

Another form of temporary regional sociopolitical organization is segmentary lineage organization (SLO). The Nuer, tribal pastoralists of the Upper Nile, have SLO, as do the horticultural Tiv of Nigeria. The closest allies of the Tiv and the Nuer are their patrilineal relatives. The term *segmentary* describes the organization of descent groups into segments at different genealogical levels. Nuer belong to minimal lineages, which are residential units. Groups of minimal lineages constitute minor lineages, and groups of minor lineages make up major lineages. Groups of major lineages make up maximal lineages, and groups of maximal lineages make up clans. Although Nuer clans do not trace descent from the same ancestor, they believe that they share a common ethnic origin separate from that of their neighbors.

Among populations with segmentary descent organization, alliance is relative, depending on genealogical distance. Social solidarity is proportional to the closeness of patrilineal ancestry and geographical proximity. The Nuer have disputes over murder, injuries, and adultery.

People support the disputant with whom they share the closest ancestor. Despite mediators, there is no sure way of halting feuds. Disputes can mobilize the entire segmentary lineage—that is, the entire society—against outsiders.

Age and gender are obvious social variables that, like SLO, can be used in regional political integration. The Plains cultures of native North America developed pantribal sodalities during the eighteenth and nineteenth centuries as they changed from generalized foraging and horticulture to horseback hunting of bison. Men's associations organized raiding parties and communal hunting and maintained order in the summer camp.

Religion can also bolster ethnic identity among local groups who assemble for the same ceremonies. This was true in the Sun Dance religion of the Plains and in the initiation ceremonies of African age sets, grades, and secret societies. Pantribal sodalities, often emphasizing the warrior grade, develop in areas where people from different cultures come into contact, particularly when there is intertribal raiding for domesticated animals.

Differential authority relationships among pastoralists reflect population size and density, interethnic relationships, and pressure on resources. Regulatory problems increase and political organization is well-developed among the Basseri and especially the Qashqai of Iran. Each group shares its nomadic route and its strategic resources with several others.

GLOSSARY

age set: Group uniting all men or women born during a certain time span; this group controls property and often has political and military functions.

apical ancestor: In a descent group, the individual who stands at the apex, or top, of the common genealogy.

big man: Figure often found among tribal horticulturalists and pastoralists. The big man occupies no office but creates his reputation through entrepreneurship and generosity to others. Neither his wealth nor his position passes to his heirs.

blood feud: Feud between families, usually in a nonstate society.

chiefdom: Form of sociopolitical organization intermediate between the tribe and the state; kin-based with differential access to resources and a permanent political structure.

clan: Unilineal descent group based on stipulated descent.

demonstrated descent: Basis of the lineage; descent-group members cite the names of their forebears in each generation from the apical ancestor through the present.

descent group: A permanent social unit whose members claim common ancestry; fundamental to tribal society.

economic typology: Classification of societies based on their adaptive strategies, for example, foraging, horticulture, pastoralism, agriculture.

head, village: A local leader in a tribal society who has limited authority, leads by example and persuasion, and must be generous.

Human Relations Area Files (HRAF): Voluminous archive assembled from ethnographic reports and historical accounts of more than 300 cultures.

infanticide: Killing a baby; a form of population control in some societies.

lactation: Milk production.

law: A legal code, including trial and enforcement; characteristic of state-organized societies.

lineage: Unilineal descent group based on demonstrated descent.

local descent group: All the members of a particular descent group who live in the same place, such as the same village.

matrilineal descent: Unilineal descent rule in which people join the mother's group automatically at birth and stay members throughout life.

Nilotic populations: Populations, including the Nuer, that inhabit the Upper Nile region of eastern Africa.

pantribal sodality: A non-kin-based group that exists throughout a tribe, spanning several villages.

patrilineal descent: Unilineal descent rule in which people join the father's group automatically at birth and stay members throughout life.

personalty: Items other than strategic resources that are indelibly associated with a particular person; contrasts with property.

polity: The political order.

postpartum taboo: Prohibition of sexual relations for a culturally determined period after childbirth.

regulation: Management of variables within a system of related and interacting variables. Regulation assures that variables stay within their normal ranges, corrects deviations from the norm, and thus maintains the system's integrity.

secret societies: Sodalities, usually all-male or all-female, with secret initiation ceremonies.

segmentary lineage organization (SLO): Political organization based on descent, usually patrilineal, with multiple descent segments that form at different genealogical levels and function in different contexts.

sociopolitical typology: Classification scheme based on the scale and complexity of social organization and the effectiveness of political regulation; includes band, tribe, chiefdom, and state.

sodality: See *pantribal sodality*.

state: Sociopolitical organization based on central government and socioeconomic stratification—a division of society into classes.

stipulated descent: Basis of the clan; members merely say they descend from their apical ancestor; they don't trace the actual genealogical links between themselves and that ancestor.

totem: An animal or plant apical ancestor of a clan.

tribe: Form of sociopolitical organization usually based on horticulture or pastoralism. Socioeconomic stratification and centralized rule are absent in tribes, and there is no means of enforcing political decisions.

typology, economic: See *economic typology*.

typology, sociopolitical: See *sociopolitical typology*.

unilineal descent: Matrilineal or patrilineal descent.

STUDY QUESTIONS

1. What is the rationale for using the term *sociopolitical organization* rather than *political organization*?
2. How is the sociopolitical typology discussed in this chapter related to the previously discussed economic typology based on adaptive strategy?
3. How would you characterize the usual sociopolitical organization of foragers?
4. How does comparative sociopolitical organization illustrate the four general evolutionary trends?
5. What are the main types of descent groups, and how do they differ?
6. What is the significance of Yanomami warfare?
7. How do the political roles of village head and big man differ?
8. What is segmentary lineage organization (SLO), and how does it work politically? How is it similar to a big man system?
9. What are sodalities, and how do they work politically? How are they similar to SLO?
10. What conclusions can be drawn from this chapter about the relationship between population density and political hierarchy?
11. List the local, regional, temporary, and permanent forms of sociopolitical organization discussed in this chapter.

SUGGESTED ADDITIONAL READING

CHAGNON, N.
  1992 *Yanomamö*, 4th ed. Fort Worth: Harcourt, Brace, Jovanovich. Most recent revision of a classic account of the Yanomami, including their social organization, politics, warfare, cultural change, and the crisis they now confront.

EDER, JAMES
  1987 *On the Road to Tribal Extinction: Depopulation, Deculturation, and Adaptive Well-Being among the Batak of the Philippines*. Berkeley: University of California Press. Cultural devastation among hunter-gatherers in the Philippines.

FERGUSON, B., AND N. L. WHITEHEAD
    1991   *War in the Tribal Zone: Expanding States and Indigenous Warfare.* Santa Fe: School of American Research Press. The effects of colonialism and the world system on native warfare.
HARRIS, M.
    1989   *Our Kind: Who We Are, Where We Came From, Where We Are Going.* New York: Harper & Row. Popular anthropology; origins of humans, culture, and major sociopolitical institutions.
INGOLD, T., D. RICHES, AND J. WOODBURN
    1991   *Hunters and Gatherers.* New York: Berg (St. Martin's). Volume I examines history, evolution, and social change among foragers. Volume II looks at their property, ideology, and power relations. These broad regional surveys illuminate current issues and debates.

LIZOT, J.
    1985   *Tales of the Yanomami: Daily Life in the Venezuelan Forest.* New York: Cambridge University Press. Account of the Yanomami by a French anthropologist who has spent about two decades in the field with them.
ROBERTS, S.
    1979   *Order and Dispute: An Introduction to Legal Anthropology.* New York: Penguin Books. Social control in Africa and New Guinea.
SCHEPER-HUGHES, NANCY
    1992   *Death without Weeping: The Violence of Everyday Life in Brazil.* Berkeley: University of California Press. Reproductive strategies and mother-love in the context of poverty in northeastern Brazil.

C H A P T E R 1 3

CHIEFDOMS AND NONINDUSTRIAL STATES

263

Having looked at bands and tribes, we turn to more complex forms of sociopolitical organization—chiefdoms and states. The first states (or *civilizations*, a near synonym) emerged in the Old World about 5,500 years ago. The first chiefdoms developed perhaps a thousand years earlier, but few survive today. The chiefdom was a transitional form of sociopolitical organization that emerged during the evolution of tribes into states. State formation began in Mesopotamia (currently Iran and Iraq) and then occurred in Egypt, the Indus Valley of Pakistan and India, and northern China. A few thousand years later states also arose in two parts of the Western Hemisphere—Mesoamerica (Mexico, Guatemala, Belize) and the central Andes (Peru and Bolivia). Early states are known as **archaic**, or nonindustrial, **states**, in contrast to modern industrial nation-states. Robert Carneiro defines the state as

> an autonomous political unit encompassing many communities within its territory, having a centralized government with the power to collect taxes, draft men for work or war, and decree and enforce laws. (Carneiro 1970, p. 733)

The chiefdom and the state, like many categories used by social scientists, are **ideal types.** That is, they are labels that make social contrasts seem more definite than they really are. In reality there is a continuum from tribe to chiefdom to state. Some societies have many attributes of chiefdoms but retain tribal features. Some advanced chiefdoms have many attributes of archaic states and thus are difficult to assign to either category. We see this when our sample of societies in time and space is large enough. Recognizing this "continuous change" (Johnson and Earle 1987), some anthropologists speak of "complex chiefdoms" (Earle 1987), which are almost states.

POLITICAL AND ECONOMIC SYSTEMS IN CHIEFDOMS

As we shall see later in this chapter (for Peru and Buganda), archaic state formation has often gone through a chiefdom phase. However, state formation remained incomplete and only chiefdoms emerged in several areas, including the circum-Caribbean (e.g., Caribbean islands, Panama, Colombia), lowland Amazonia, what is now the southeastern United States, and Polynesia. Chiefdoms created the megalithic cultures of Europe, such as the one that built Stonehenge. Indeed, between the emergence and spread of food production and the expansion of the Roman empire, much of Europe was organized at the chiefdom level, to which it reverted after the fall of Rome. The foundations of historic Europe (and thus of the modern world system) emerged as some of those chiefdoms developed into states during the Dark Ages (Johnson and Earle 1987).

Chiefdoms created the megalithic cultures of Europe, such as the one that built Stonehenge—shown here. Between the emergence and spread of food production and the expansion of the Roman empire, much of Europe was organized at the chiefdom level, to which it reverted after the fall of Rome.

Much of our ethnographic knowledge about chiefdoms comes from Polynesia, where they were common at the time of European exploration. In chiefdoms, social relations are regulated by kinship, marriage, descent, age, generation, and gender—just as they are in bands and tribes. This is a fundamental difference between chiefdoms and states. States bring nonrelatives together and oblige them all to pledge allegiance to a government.

Table 13.1 lists some of the main contrasts between bands, tribes, chiefdoms, and states. You may want to refer to it as you read the following discussion. Unlike bands and tribes, chiefdoms are characterized by *permanent political regulation* of the territory they administer, which includes thousands of people living in many villages and/or hamlets. Regulation is carried out by the chief and his or her assistants, who occupy political offices. An **office** is a permanent position, which must be refilled when it is vacated by death or retirement. Because offices are systematically refilled, the structure of a chiefdom endures across the generations, ensuring permanent political regulation.

In the Polynesian chiefdoms, the chiefs were full-time political specialists in charge of regulating production, distribution, and consumption. Polynesian chiefs relied on religion to buttress their authority. They regulated production by commanding or pro-

Chiefdoms were common in Polynesia at the time of European exploration. Some "complex" chiefdoms, such as ancient Hawaii, had many attributes of archaic states. Monument building begins in chiefdoms, where "ceremonies of place" are associated with the creation of a "sacred landscape" through temples and sculptures, such as the Hawaiian statues shown here.

Table 13.1 *Sociopolitical types and their correlates. This table summarizes typical features of bands and tribes, as discussed in the last chapter, and chiefdoms and states, as discussed in this chapter. For example, band-organized societies have foraging as their adaptive strategy. They usually have egalitarian ranking systems, sometimes with gender stratification. Social identity, rights, and obligations are based on kinship and marriage. The scope of political structure and regulation is limited.*

Archaic states, by contrast, have agricultural economies and differential access to resources based on stratification. Social identity has a territorial rather than a kin basis. That is, political rights and responsibilities depend mainly on living in a government unit (e.g., a nation, state, province, or township), rather than belonging to a kin-based group. States have permanent political structures and regulate large regions.

Sociopolitical Type	Most Common Adaptive Strategy	Ranking/Stratification	Kin/Nonkin Basis	Political Scale
Band	Foraging	Egalitarian/gender	Kinship/marriage	Limited
Tribe	Horticulture/pastoralism	Prestige/gender	Kinship/marriage/descent	Temporary Regional
Chiefdom	Intensive cultivation	Differential access/ranked	Kinship/marriage/ descent/seniority	Permanent Regional
State				
Archaic	Agriculture	Differential access/ stratification	Territorial/government	Permanent Regional
Industrial	Industrialism	Class system	Territorial/government	Permanent Regional

hibiting (using religious taboos) the cultivation of certain lands and crops. Chiefs also regulated distribution and consumption. At certain seasons— often on a ritualized occasion such as a first-fruit ceremony—people would offer part of their harvest to the chief through his or her representatives. Products moved up the hierarchy, eventually reaching the chief. Conversely, illustrating obligatory sharing with kin, chiefs sponsored feasts at which they gave back much of what they had received.

Such a flow of resources to and then from a central office is known as *chiefly redistribution.* Redistribution offers economic advantages. If different areas specialized in particular crops, goods, or services, chiefly redistribution made those products available to the whole society. Chiefly redistribution also played a role in risk management. It stimulated production beyond the immediate subsistence level and provided a central storehouse for goods that might become scarce at times of famine. Chiefdoms and archaic states had similar economies, often based on intensive cultivation, and both administered systems of regional trade or exchange. (Earle [1987, 1991] reviews the economic foundations of chiefdoms.) The more limited scale of political and economic regulation in chiefdoms tended to be short-lived, developing rapidly into a central government, one of the defining features of the state.

SOCIAL STATUS IN CHIEFDOMS

Social status in chiefdoms was based on seniority of descent. Because rank, power, prestige, and resources came through kinship and descent, Polynesian chiefs kept extremely long genealogies. Some chiefs (without writing) managed to trace their ancestry back fifty generations. All the people in the chiefdom were thought to be related to each other. Presumably, all were descended from a group of founding ancestors.

The chief (usually a man) had to demonstrate seniority in descent. Degrees of seniority were calculated so intricately on some islands that there were as many ranks as people. For example, the third son would rank below the second, who in turn would rank below the first. The children of an eldest brother, however, would all rank above the children of the next brother, whose children would in turn outrank those of younger brothers. However, even the lowest-ranking person in a chiefdom was still the chief's relative. In such a kin-based context, everyone, even a chief, had to share with his or her relatives.

Because everyone had a slightly different status, it was difficult to draw a line between elites and common people. Although other chiefdoms calculated seniority differently and had shorter genealo-

Social status in chiefdoms is based on seniority of descent. In the modern world system, seniority may still confer prestige, but the differences in wealth and power between chiefs and their juniors are often minor. Shown here is a contemporary chief (center) in the Marquesas Islands, Polynesia.

gies than did those in Polynesia, the concern for genealogy and seniority and the absence of sharp gaps between elites and commoners are features of all chiefdoms.

STATUS SYSTEMS IN CHIEFDOMS AND STATES

The status systems of chiefdoms and states are similar in that both are based on **differential access** to resources. This means that some men and women had privileged access to power, prestige, and wealth. They controlled strategic resources such as land, water, and other means of production. Earle characterizes chiefs as "an incipient aristocracy with advantages in wealth and lifestyle" (1987, p. 290). Nevertheless, differential access in chiefdoms was still very much tied to kinship. The people with privileged access were generally chiefs and their nearest relatives and assistants.

Compared with chiefdoms, archaic states drew a much firmer line between elites and masses, distinguishing at least between nobles and commoners. Kinship ties did not extend from the nobles to the commoners because of *stratum endogamy*—marriage within one's own group. Commoners married commoners; elites married elites. Such a division of society into socioeconomic strata contrasts strongly with the status systems of bands and tribes, which are based on prestige, not resources. The prestige differentials that do exist in bands reflect special qualities, talents, and abilities. Good hunters get respect from their fellows as long as they are generous. So does a skilled curer, dancer, storyteller—or anyone else with a talent or skill that others appreciate.

In tribes, some prestige goes to descent-group leaders, to village heads, and especially to the big man, a regional figure who commands the loyalty and labor of others. However, all these figures must be generous. If they accumulate more resources—i.e., property or food—than others in the village, they must share them with the others. Since strategic resources are available to everyone, social classes based on the possession of unequal amounts of resources can never exist.

In many tribes, particularly those with patrilineal descent, men have much greater prestige and power than women do. The gender contrast in rights diminishes in chiefdoms, where prestige and access to resources are based on seniority of descent, so that some women are senior to some men. Unlike big men, chiefs are exempt from ordinary work and have rights and privileges that are unavailable to the masses. However, like big men, they still return much of the wealth they take in.

The status system in chiefdoms, although based on differential access, differed from the status system in states because the privileged few were always relatives and assistants of the chief. However, this type of status system didn't last very long. Chiefs would start acting like kings and try to erode the kinship basis of the chiefdom. In Madagascar they would do this by demoting their more distant relatives to commoner status and banning marriage between nobles and commoners (Kottak 1980). Such moves, *if accepted by the society*, created separate social strata—*unrelated* groups that differ in their access to wealth, prestige, and power. (A **stratum** is one of two or more groups that contrast in regard to social status and access to strategic resources. Each stratum includes people of both sexes and all ages.) The creation of separate social strata is called **stratification**, and its emergence signified the transition from chiefdom to state. *The presence and acceptance of stratification is one of the key distinguishing features of a state.*

The influential sociologist Max Weber (1922) defined three related dimensions of social stratification: (1) Economic status, or **wealth,** encompasses all a person's material assets, including income, land, and other types of property (Schaefer and Lamm 1992). (2) **Power,** the ability to exercise one's will over others—to do what one wants—is the basis of political status. (3) **Prestige**—the basis of social status—refers to esteem, respect, or approval for acts, deeds, or qualities considered exemplary. Prestige, or "cultural capital" (Bourdieu 1984), provides people with a sense of worth and respect, which they may often convert into economic advantage (Table 13.2).

Table 13.2 *Max Weber's three dimensions of stratification*

wealth	→	economic status
power	→	political status
prestige	→	social status

These Weberian dimensions of stratification are present to varying degrees in chiefdoms. However, chiefdoms lack the sharp division into classes that characterizes states. Wealth, power, and prestige in chiefdoms are all tied to kinship factors.

Historically, the emergence of differential access, the chiefdom, stratification, and the state was a gradual process. In some societies, evolution was slowed by temporary collapses of developing political machinery, as happened in Europe after the Roman collapse. Because of this, anthropologists must sometimes decide arbitrarily whether a particular society with political regulation and differential access should be called a chiefdom or a state.

In archaic states—for the first time in human evolution—there were contrasts in wealth, power, and prestige between entire groups (social strata) of men and women. Each stratum included people of both sexes and all ages. The **superordinate** (the higher or elite) stratum had privileged access to wealth, power, and other valued resources. Access to resources by members of the **subordinate** (lower or underprivileged) stratum was limited by the privileged group.

Socioeconomic stratification continues as a defining feature of all states, archaic or industrial. The elites control a significant part of the means of production, for example, land, herds, water, capital, farms, or factories. Those born at the bottom of the hierarchy have reduced chances of social mobility. Because of elite ownership rights, ordinary people lack free access to resources. Only in states do the elites get to keep their differential wealth. Unlike big men and chiefs, they don't have to give it back to the people whose labor has built and increased it.

STATUS AND ROLE

Before discussing the state, we pause to note that **status** has two meanings in social science. One (as in Weber's discussion of social status) is close to the definition of *prestige* and refers to social ranking. Thus, someone (such as a chief) may have more (or higher) social status than someone else does. The other meaning, examined in the chapter on ethnicity and ethnic relations, is neutral. Here a status is simply a position in a social structure—any position that determines where someone fits within society (Light, Keller, and Calhoun 1994). Such social sta-

tuses include mother, father, son, daughter, club or team member, Republican, Baptist, accountant, farm worker, herder, hunter, and—in our own society—thousands of others (Figure 13.1).

Among the multiple statuses we occupy, particular ones dominate in particular settings, such as son or daughter at home and student in the classroom. Moving through life, we leave some statuses behind (e.g., high school senior) and enter others (e.g., first-year college student). When we vacate one status or die, we leave those positions, and others fill them. The occupant changes while the status endures as part of the social structure.

Some statuses are **ascribed:** people have little or no choice about occupying them. Gender is normally an ascribed status, although some cultures permit gender changes. Age is another ascribed status. In unilineal societies, descent-group membership is ascribed. People automatically belong to the father's descent group in a patrilineal society and to the mother's in a matrilineal one. In chiefdoms and states, many contrasts in wealth, prestige, and

Figure 13.1 *Social statuses. The person in this figure— "ego," or "I"—occupies many social statuses. The green circles indicate ascribed statuses; the orange circles represent achieved statuses.*

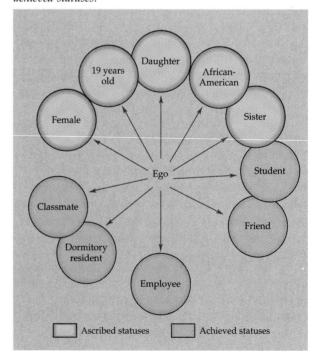

Elizabeth II, Queen (left), and Margaret Thatcher, former Prime Minister (right), of Great Britain. Elizabeth gained office through ascription—a formal rule of succession—whereas Thatcher achieved her status by her election as a member of Parliament and as head of Britain's Conservative party. While Elizabeth will remain ruler until her death or abdication, prime ministers come and go, depending on which party has a majority in Parliament. However, both women belong to the elite—the rich, famous, privileged, and powerful—and both occupy offices that survive even though their occupants change.

power are ascribed. In chiefdoms they are ascribed by genealogy and seniority. In states some people are born into rich or noble families while others are born into poverty. In archaic states the paramount ruling status known as king or queen was usually ascribed, as was the status of chief in chiefdoms.

Achieved statuses, in contrast, aren't automatic but come through traits, talents, actions, efforts, activities, and accomplishments. Achieved statuses in bands include healer, dancer, and storyteller. In tribes, people may become leaders through work, generosity, charisma, and particular skills. Achieved statuses in tribes include polygynist, warrior, magician, trading partner, and trance specialist, among hundreds of others. *The number of social statuses increases with (and can be used as a rough measure of) social complexity.* More complex societies offer more choices; the number of achieved statuses in particular increases. In the modern world we choose

to marry or not and have children or not, so that even our statuses as spouse or parent are achieved. People in traditional societies have less choice about marriage and parenthood.

The distinction between ascribed status and achieved status isn't always clear-cut. For example, although we choose our colleges (from those to which we apply and are accepted) and our jobs (from those we seek out and are offered), family background influences our success. Despite the North American value of individual achievement (including the possibility of rising from "rags to riches"), it is easier for offspring of the middle and upper classes to succeed than it is for people born in poverty.

Each status has an associated **role**—a set of expected (culturally "proper") behaviors, attitudes, rights, and obligations. Through enculturation, we come to expect certain behavior to characterize certain statuses. Cultures develop images of how a "good" or "proper" boss, teacher, mother, or coach acts. For example, "fatherly" behavior might be defined as affectionate, nurturing, and supportive. In some societies, the status of son-in-law entails strict avoidance of the mother-in-law—to the point of leaping off the road if she approaches. In other cultures, the son-in-law role is to treat the mother-in-law like his own mother (or, in still other cultures, like his wife). Cultures may define a girl's younger brother as a pal, a pest, or someone who is socially distant and to be avoided.

Anthropologist Ralph Linton (1936) drew a distinction between status and role by saying that people *occupy* a status but *play* a role. A status is a position in the social structure, but a role involves thought and action. People differ in how well they play the roles that go with the various statuses they occupy. There are disruptive students, sinful ministers, and lousy bosses. A man may be a skilled craftsman but an inattentive father.

STATES

Although multiple statuses and roles exist in all societies, they are more numerous, complex, and specialized in states than they are in bands, tribes, and chiefdoms. Illustrating general evolutionary trends, certain statuses, systems, and subsystems with specialized functions are found in all states. They include the following:

1. *Population control:* fixing of boundaries, establishment of citizenship categories, and the taking of a census
2. *Judiciary:* laws, legal procedure, and judges
3. *Enforcement:* permanent military and police forces
4. *Fiscal:* taxation

In archaic states, these subsystems were integrated by a ruling system or government composed of civil, military, and religious officials (Fried 1960).

Population Control

To know whom they govern, all states conduct censuses. States demarcate boundaries that separate them from other societies. Customs agents, immi-

gration officers, navies, and coast guards patrol frontiers, regulating passage from one state to another. Even nonindustrial states have boundary-maintenance forces. In Buganda, an archaic state on the shores of Lake Victoria in Uganda, the king rewarded military officers with estates in outlying provinces. They became his guardians against foreign intrusion.

States also control population through administrative subdivision: provinces, districts, "states," counties, subcounties, and parishes. Lower-level officials manage the populations and territories of the subdivisions.

In nonstates, people work and relax with their relatives, in-laws, fictive kin, and age mates—people with whom they have a personal relationship. Such a personal social life existed throughout most of human history, but food production spelled its eventual decline. After millions of years of human evolution, it took a mere 4,000 years for the population increase and regulatory problems spawned by food production to lead from tribe to chiefdom to state. With state organization, kinship's pervasive role diminished. Descent groups may continue as kin groups within archaic states, but their importance in political organization declines, and their exclusive control over their members ends.

States—archaic and modern—foster geographic mobility and resettlement, severing long-standing ties between people, land, and kin. Population displacements have increased in the modern world. War, famine, and job seeking across national boundaries churn up migratory currents. People in states come to identify themselves by new statuses, both ascribed and achieved, including ethnic background, place of birth or residence, occupation, party, religion, and team or club affiliation, rather than as members of a descent group or extended family.

States also manage their populations by granting different rights and obligations to (making status distinctions between) citizens and noncitizens. Distinctions among citizens are also common. Many archaic states granted different rights to nobles, commoners, and slaves. Unequal rights within state-organized societies persist in today's world, very obviously in South Africa. In recent American history, before the Emancipation Proclamation, there were different laws for slaves and free people. In European colonies, separate courts judged cases

Unequal rights in state-organized societies persist in today's world. Under South Africa's apartheid system, blacks, whites, and Asians have had their own separate (and unequal) neighborhoods, schools, laws, and punishments. There has been both social and legal resistance to the weakening of apartheid.

involving only natives and those which involved Europeans. In contemporary America, a military code of justice and court system continue to coexist alongside the civil judiciary.

Judiciary

States have *laws* based on precedent and legislative proclamations. Without writing, laws may be preserved in oral tradition, with justices, elders, and other specialists responsible for remembering them. Oral traditions as repositories of legal wisdom have continued in some nations with writing, such as Great Britain. Laws regulate relations between individuals and groups.

Crimes are violations of the legal code, with specified types of punishment. However, a given act, such as killing someone, may be legally defined in different ways (e.g., as manslaughter, justifiable homicide, or first-degree murder). Furthermore, even in contemporary North America, where justice is supposed to be "blind" to social distinctions, the poor are prosecuted more often and more severely than are the rich.

To handle disputes and crimes, all states have courts and judges. Precolonial African states had subcounty, county, and district courts, plus a high court formed by the king or queen and his or her advisers. Most states allow appeals to higher courts, although people are encouraged to solve problems locally.

A striking contrast between states and nonstates is intervention in family affairs. In states, aspects of parenting and marriage enter the domain of public law. Governments step in to halt blood feuds and regulate previously private disputes. States attempt to curb *internal* conflict, but they aren't always successful. About 85 percent of the world's armed conflicts since 1945 have begun within states—in efforts to overthrow a ruling regime or as disputes over tribal, religious, and ethnic minority issues. Only 15 percent have been fights across national borders (Barnaby 1985).

People in modern nations no longer fight for spouses and cattle but for political, economic, religious, and ideological reasons. Nations battle over philosophies of government—to subdue "the infidel," to "halt the spread of communism," or to undermine "capitalist imperialism." Rebellion, resistance, repression, terrorism, and warfare continue. Indeed, recent states have perpetrated some of history's bloodiest deeds.

Enforcement

All states have agents to enforce judicial decisions. Confinement requires jailers, and a death penalty calls for executioners. Agents of the state collect fines and confiscate property. These officials wield power that is much more effective than the curse of the Nuer leopard-skin man.

A major concern of government is to defend hierarchy, property, and the power of the law. The government suppresses internal disorder (with police) and guards the nation against external threats (with the military). As a relatively new form of sociopolitical organization, states have competed successfully with less complex societies throughout the world. Military organization helps states subdue neighboring nonstates, but this is not the only reason for the spread of state organization. Although states impose hardships, they also offer advantages. Most obviously, they provide protection from outsiders and preserve internal order. They curb the feuding that has plagued tribes such as the Yanomami and the Nuer. By promoting internal peace, states enhance production. Their economies support massive, dense populations, which supply armies and colonists to promote expansion.

Fiscal

A financial or **fiscal** subsystem is needed in states to support rulers, nobles, officials, judges, military personnel, and thousands of other specialists. As in the chiefdom, the state intervenes in production, distribution, and consumption. The state may decree that a certain area will produce certain things or forbid certain activities in particular places. Although, like chiefdoms, states also have redistribution (through taxation), generosity and sharing are played down. A smaller proportion of what comes in flows back to the people.

In nonstates, people customarily share with relatives, but residents of states face added obligations to bureaucrats and officials. Citizens must turn over a substantial portion of what they produce to the state. Of the resources that the state collects, it reallocates part for the general good and uses another part (often larger) for the elite.

The state does not bring more freedom or leisure to the common people, who usually work harder than do the people in nonstates. They may be called on to build monumental public works. Some of these projects, such as dams and irrigation systems, may be economically necessary. However, people also build temples, palaces, and tombs for the elites.

Monument building began in chiefdoms, where "ceremonies of place" were associated with the creation of a "sacred landscape" through constructions such as (stone) henges of Europe, the mounds of the southeastern United States, and the temples of Hawaii (Earle 1987, 1991). Like chiefs, state officials may use religion to buttress their authority. Archeology shows that temples abounded in early states. Even in mature states, rulers may link themselves to godhood through divine right or claim to be deities or their earthly representatives. Rulers convoke peons or slaves to build magnificent castles or tombs, cementing the ruler's place in history or status in the afterlife. Monumental architecture survives as an enduring reminder of the exalted prestige of priests and kings.

Markets and trade are usually under at least some state control, with officials overseeing distribution and exchange, standardizing weights and measures, and collecting taxes on goods passing into or through the state. States also set standards for artisans, manufacturers, and members of other professions.

Taxes support government and the ruling class, which is clearly separated from the common people in regard to activities, privileges, rights, and obligations. Elites take no part in subsistence activities. Taxes also support the many specialists—administrators, tax collectors, judges, lawmakers, generals, scholars, and priests. As the state matures, the segment of the population freed from direct concern with subsistence grows.

The elites of archaic states revel in the consumption of **sumptuary goods**—jewelry, exotic food and drink, and stylish clothing reserved for, or affordable only by, the rich. Peasants' diets suffer as they struggle to meet government demands. Commoners perish in territorial wars that have little relevance to their own needs.

THE ORIGIN OF THE STATE

Why were people willing to give up so many of the freedoms, pleasures, and personal bonds that their ancestors had enjoyed throughout human history? The answer is that people didn't choose but were *forced* to accept state organization. Because state for-

RIDDLES OF ANCIENT CIVILIZATIONS

Anthropologist Marvin Harris (1978) uses a theoretical approach called *cultural materialism* to answer questions raised by the rise and fall of archaic states. Cultural materialism begins with the assumption that cultures are influenced by material conditions: physical resources, plants and animals, relationships (such as trade and war) with other groups, and systems of production and reproduction. According to Harris, history's prime movers have been continually repeated economic cycles. Population pressure promotes intensification of production; eventually this depletes the environment; renewed population pressure then leads to new systems of production.

For example, Harris has cast a materialist eye on the Maya of Mexico's Yucatán peninsula and adjacent Guatemala. For years archeologists have wondered how, between A.D. 300 and 900, the Maya supported state organization with an economy seemingly based only on nonintensive slash-and-burn cultivation. How did they feed dense urban populations? How did they build and maintain impressive ceremonial centers? For some scholars, the mysterious Maya seem to contradict the tendency for archaic states to have dense populations and a sedentary agricultural economy.

However, Harris showed that the Mayas' economy was more productive than was once thought. For instance, high-yield breadnut trees could have provided 80 percent of the calories in their diet. Aerial photographs taken during the rainy season revealed a previously undetected pattern of canals. This suggests that the Maya, like most ancient state builders, did some irrigated farming.

Nonetheless, the Maya material base really was poorer than that of other states. It is not surprising, then, that Maya civilization collapsed around A.D. 900 and that nothing comparable reappeared in the depleted area, where slash-and-burn cultivation now supports a sparse population. In contrast to the Mexican highlands, where successive cycles of agricultural intensification supported the rise, fall, and reappearance of state organization (Teotihuacan, Toltecs, and Aztecs), the Maya state rose just once and fell forever.

Harris's views have been criticized as mechanical and simpleminded, but they are almost always intriguing. One of the most controversial is his interpretation of Aztec religion. When the emperor Montezuma II showed Cortés and his men around Tenochtitlan, the Aztec capital, the Spaniards were struck not just by the city's bustling population and imposing architecture but by bloodstains on the pyramids. Atop those imposing structures, priests regularly cut out the hearts of prisoners of war to slake the blood cravings of the Aztec gods.

Why were these gods so bloodthirsty, and why did the Aztecs sacrifice so many people? It isn't enough, says Harris, to explain Aztec sacrifice in terms of religious motives. We need to know why Aztec religion differed from other state religions and to explain a key difference: Aztec victims weren't just sacrificed—they were cannibalized.

Many Old World state religions sacrificed animals to the gods and distributed their meat to humans, but all those societies tabooed cannibalism. In Aztec sacrifice, "all edible parts were used in a manner strictly comparable to the consumption of the flesh of domesticated animals" (Harris 1978, p. 164). The ultimate fate of many victims was to be stewed with tomatoes and chili peppers in Tenochtitlan's residential compounds.

According to Harris, ancient Mexico's distinctive material conditions provide the solution to the puzzle. Ecological conditions in the Valley of Mexico made it possible to support population growth by intensifying agriculture. However, in contrast to all Old World civilizations—and to Peru's Incas, who feasted on sacrificial llamas and guinea pigs rather than people—ancient Mexico lacked domesticated animals that could be used to increase the food supply. Old World societies and the Incas had sheep, goats, cattle, camels, or llamas; the Aztecs had only dogs and turkeys.

The Aztecs, faced with these material conditions, presided over the only major ancient state that didn't ban cannibalism. Harris believes that the Aztecs developed a taste for human flesh because their diet was meat-poor. Dense populations, especially urban ones, are subject to food crises. Disastrous famines occasionally plagued the Aztecs, and their legends recall times when ancestors had to eat snakes, vermin (Coe 1962), and algae skimmed from the lake. Aztec sacrifice thus had both a religious purpose and a material result—distribution of animal protein to the urban population. According to Harris, lack of domesticated animals and the dietary needs of a dense population were the conditions responsible for Aztec sacrifice and cannibalism. For an opposing view, see the review of Harris's book by Sahlins (1978).

mation may take centuries, people experiencing the process at any time rarely perceive the significance of the long-term changes. Later generations find themselves dependent on government institutions that took generations to develop.

The state develops to handle regulatory problems encountered as the population grows and/or the economy increases in scale and diversity. Anthropologists and historians have identified the causes of state formation and have reconstructed the rise of several states. Many factors always contribute to state formation, with the effects of one magnifying those of the others. Although some contributing factors appear again and again, no single one is always present. In other words, state formation has generalized rather than universal causes.

Hydraulic Systems

One suggested cause of state formation is the need to regulate **hydraulic** (water-based) agricultural economies (Wittfogel 1957). States have emerged in certain arid areas to manage systems of irrigation, drainage, and flood control. Nevertheless, hydraulic agriculture is neither a sufficient nor a necessary condition for the rise of the state. That is, many societies with irrigation never developed state structure, and many states developed without hydraulic systems.

However, hydraulic agriculture does have certain implications for state formation. Water control increases production in arid lands. Irrigated agriculture fuels population growth because of its labor demands and its ability to feed more people. This in turn leads to enlargement of the system. The expanding hydraulic system supports larger and denser concentrations of people. Interpersonal problems increase, and conflicts over access to water and irrigated land become more frequent. Political systems may arise to regulate interpersonal relations and the means of production.

Larger hydraulic works can sustain towns and cities and become essential to their subsistence. Given such urban dependence, regulators protect the economy by mobilizing crews to maintain and repair the hydraulic system. These life-and-death functions enhance the authority of state officials. Thus, growth in hydraulic systems is often, but not always, associated with state formation.

Ecological Diversity

Some anthropologists have suggested that states tend to arise in areas of ecological diversity in order to regulate the production and exchange of products between zones. What about this theory? Although ecological diversity and interzonal regulation do strengthen state organization, such diversity is neither necessary nor sufficient to cause state formation. Diversity is a matter of scale, and state formation has occurred in places without much environmental diversity—the Nile Valley, for example. Furthermore, in many areas with environmental diversity, no indigenous states developed. Finally, diversity is as much a result as a cause of state formation. As states grow, they create diversity, promoting regional and local specialization in the production, manufacture, and supply of goods and services.

Long-Distance Trade Routes

Another theory is that states develop at strategic locations in regional trade networks. These sites include points of supply or exchange, such as crossroads of caravan routes, and places (e.g., mountain passes and river narrows) situated so as to threaten or halt trade between centers. Like ecological diversity, features of regional trade can certainly contribute to state formation. Here again, however, the cause is generalized but neither necessary nor sufficient. Although long-distance trade has been important in the evolution of many states and does eventually develop in all states, it can follow rather than precede state formation. Furthermore, long-distance trade also occurs in tribal societies, such as those of Papua–New Guinea, where no states developed.

Population Growth, Warfare, and Environmental Circumscription

Anthropologist Robert Carneiro (1970) proposed a theory that incorporates three factors working together instead of a single cause of state formation. (We call a theory involving multiple factors or variables a **multivariate** theory.) Wherever and whenever *environmental circumscription* (or *resource concentration*), *increasing population*, and *warfare* exist, says Carneiro, state formation will begin. Environmental circumscription may be physical or social. Physically circumscribed environments include small islands and, in arid areas, river plains, oases, and valleys with streams. Social circumscription exists when neighboring societies block expansion, emigration, or access to resources. When strategic resources are concentrated in limited areas—even when no obstacles to migration exist—the effects are similar to those of circumscription.

Coastal Peru, one of the world's most arid areas, illustrates the interaction of environmental circumscription, warfare, and population increase. Early cultivation was limited to valleys with springs. Each valley was circumscribed by the Andes mountains to the east, the Pacific Ocean to the west, and desert to the north and south. The transition from foraging to food production triggered population increase in these valleys (Figure 13.2). In each valley, villages got bigger. Colonists split off from the old villages and founded new ones. Rivalries and raiding developed between villages in the same valley. As villages proliferated and the valley population grew, a scarcity of land developed.

Population pressure and land shortages were developing in all the valleys. Because the valleys were circumscribed, when one village conquered another, the losers had to submit to the winners—they had nowhere else to go. Conquered villagers could keep their land only if they agreed to pay tribute to their conquerors. To do this, they had to intensify production, using new techniques to produce more food. By working harder, they managed to pay tribute while meeting their subsistence needs. Villagers brought new areas under cultivation by means of irrigation and terracing.

Those early Peruvians didn't work harder because they chose to. They were *forced* to pay tribute, accept political domination, and intensify production by factors beyond their control. Once established, all these trends accelerated. Population grew, warfare intensified, and villages were eventually united in chiefdoms. The first states developed when one chiefdom in a valley conquered the others (Carneiro 1987). Eventually, different valleys began to fight, and the winners brought the losers into growing empires. States expanded from the coast to the highlands. By the sixteenth century, from their capital, Cuzco, in the high Andes, the Incas ruled one of the major empires of the tropics.

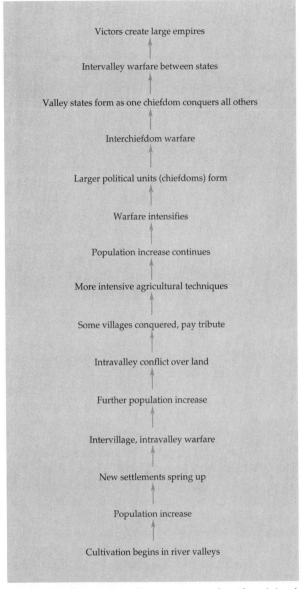

Figure 13.2 *Carneiro's multivariate approach to the origin of the state as applied to coastal Peru. In this very arid area, food production developed in narrow river valleys where water for cultivation was available (resource concentration). With cultivation, the population increased. Population pressure on land led to warfare, and some villages conquered others. Physical circumscription (an arid area) meant that the losers had no way to escape. The process accelerated as the population grew and as warfare and cultivation intensified. Chiefdoms, states, and empires eventually developed.*

Carneiro's theory is very useful, but again, the association between population density and state organization is generalized rather than universal. States do tend to have large and dense populations (Stevenson 1968). However, population increase and warfare within a circumscribed environment were insufficient to trigger state formation in highland Papua–New Guinea. Certain valleys there are socially or physically circumscribed and have population densities similar to those of many states. Warfare was also present, but no states emerged. Again we are dealing with an important theory that explains many but not all cases of state formation.

States arose in different areas for many reasons. In each case, interacting causes (often comparable ones) magnified each other's effects. To explain any instance of state formation, we must search for the specific changes in access to resources and in regulation that fostered stratification and state machinery.

CONVERGENCE IN STATE FORMATION

One of the first anthropologists to demonstrate **convergence** (parallel development without contact or mutual influence) in state formation was Julian Steward (1949). He did this by comparing five areas: Mesopotamia, Egypt, northern China, Peru, and Mexico. These were all arid places where irrigation, flood control, and other hydraulic techniques became significant. What impressed Steward was not so much that the final product—the state—was the same but that in all five areas social, religious, and military patterns and institutions had developed similarly and in the same order. Although these developments occurred 3,000 to 4,000 years later in the New World, in both hemispheres foraging was succeeded by food production, which set off a series of changes that led eventually to the formation of states.

The process began with communities based on food production, which supported growing population density. At first, irrigation systems (necessary for food production in these arid areas) were simple. They were managed by individual cultivators, kin groups, and communities. Eventually, however, some people were allowed to withdraw from subsistence to become chiefs and managers. Differences

in wealth, prestige, and power appeared as chiefdoms emerged. Craft specialists made varied goods, including sumptuary goods for the elite, marking a contrast in life style between chiefs, their nearest relatives and assistants, and the common people.

As chiefdoms evolved into early states, religion continued to bolster managerial authority. Temples and pyramids were built in new ceremonial centers. Priests emerged who combined ritual, political, and economic functions. They coordinated manufacturing, exchange, and irrigation. As states grew, militarism increased. Powerful states arose as others were conquered or collapsed. Towns multiplied, and major cities appeared. Agricultural techniques became more intensive to sustain a growing population and a larger group engaged in nonsubsistence activities. Hydraulic systems were enlarged.

Although political authority was still buttressed by religion, stronger rule with a more secular basis developed, along with growing militarism. Conflicts grew more frequent as states collided. States conquered others and became empires. Local, regional, and long-distance trade expanded with improved means of transportation. The scale of architecture continued to increase, and art and manufactured items—many destined for consumption by elites—were produced. Eventually, manufacturing became more standardized, oriented toward mass production and consumption.

Stratification also grew more complex. As an illustration of stratification in a mature archaic state, consider the Aztecs of sixteenth-century Mexico, as described in Spanish documents. Heading the Aztec state was the monarch; the last one, conquered by the Spanish, was named Montezuma. He was surrounded by an elaborate court—the palace elite. Immediately below him were princes and nobles.

Next came the commoners, internally divided into groups based on occupation and urban versus rural residence. City dwellers ranked highest among the commoners. They included warriors, merchants, and artisans such as goldsmiths, stone workers, and feather workers. The lowest of the commoners were peasants, agriculturists who lived in villages.

Below the Aztec commoners were three oppressed groups: serfs attached to estates, slaves who had been criminals or debtors, and slaves who had been prisoners of war (Sanders and Price 1968). Soldiers, merchants, and artisans paid tribute to the

Social stratification, monumental architecture, urbanization, and a lively market system characterized Aztec culture, which thrived in the valley of Mexico between A.D. 1325 and 1520. Tenochtitlan, the Aztec capital, is depicted in this mural by the renowned Mexican artist Diego Rivera.

state in the form of military service, taxes, and manufactures, respectively. Those below them paid in produce and public labor. Aztec serfs and slaves, of course, bore heavier burdens.

ETHNOHISTORY

Archeologists have documented many cases of early state formation. Cultural anthropologists have also studied state formation through historical, ethnohistorical, and ethnographic data. For example, this has been done in Africa, where there were diverse precolonial sociopolitical types and environmental adaptations. Some of the most complex and tightly organized preindustrial states, including Buganda in the Great Lakes area of East Africa, developed in the African tropics.

Ethnohistory encompasses oral and written accounts of a culture's past by insiders and outsiders. Written historical records about precolonial Africa are rich compared with those of the precolonial New World. Centuries of accounts by Arab, European, and Chinese merchants, travelers, explorers, and missionaries are available. Also, even when there are no written records, African states preserved detailed oral traditions, one of whose main concerns was tracing genealogies.

However, there are certain risks in using oral traditions (a culture's accounts of its own past) to re-

construct history. In any society, present realities affect memories. History is often fictionalized in various ways and for various reasons. Nevertheless, oral traditions often contain useful historical data. Reconstructions and hypotheses based on oral traditions often can be tested later by archeologists. And cross-cultural regularities known from better-documented sequences can be used to judge the probability of oral traditions. Such an approach has been used in reconstructing the evolution of the state in Buganda (Kottak 1972).

STATE FORMATION IN BUGANDA

The former kingdom of Buganda, northwest of Lake Victoria, is now a province of the nation of Uganda. When the English travelers John Speke and Richard Francis Burton, searching for the source of the Nile, visited Buganda in 1862, it was the most populous and powerful state in this area (Figure 13.3). Because rainfall was heavy and was evenly distributed throughout the year, the Ganda (people of Buganda) were able to grow many varieties of bananas and the closely related **plantains.** These crops are perennial and highly productive and have many advantages as subsistence crops.

Unlike grains, they are not harvested all at once but are picked during the year as needed. Once planted, banana and plantain trees can yield for up

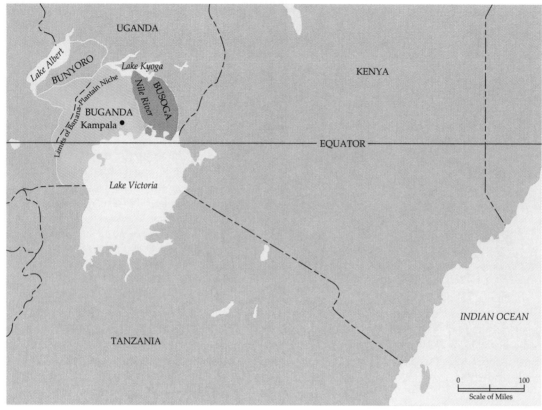

Figure 13.3 *Map of precolonial Buganda. Borders fluctuated but increased through militarism as Buganda extended its influence north, east, and west.*

For centuries the Ganda of Buganda have grown several varieties of bananas and closely related plantains. Banana trees yield for up to forty years. Unlike grains, bananas are not harvested all at once but can be picked during the year as needed. These crops provide a high caloric yield for a remarkably low labor investment.

to forty years. Like irrigated cereals, such as wheat and barley in the ancient Middle East, Buganda's plantains and bananas were concentrated and reliable sources of calories. They could support a dense sedentary population.

In sharp contrast to irrigated agriculture, however, labor investment in bananas was very low. The low labor requirements of subsistence farming meant that women could maintain the subsistence economy while men's labor was put to work for higher-level authorities. Men were withdrawn from cultivation to take part in public works, the army, and manufacturing.

Nutrition required that bananas and plantains be supplemented with other foods, particularly protein sources. This promoted a varied economy and interregional trade, which influenced state formation. The Ganda hunted, fished, and kept sheep, goats, cattle, poultry, and buffalo. Near Lake Victoria, fish were an important part of the diet. (Regulation of the inland trade of fish and other lake products was one way in which the government controlled areas distant from the capital.)

All states promote economic specialization, so that some people withdraw from subsistence and work as artisans and administrators, among other specialized jobs. Buganda had an even more obvious specialization based on gender. It is very unusual in states with cultivation-based economies for men to be freed totally from subsistence activities. The low labor requirements of plantains and bananas permitted this in Buganda.

Men were able to be full-time soldiers. They could specialize in crafts or trade. They could build canoes for the navy. They could work on the roads, bridges, and public works that extended the transportation network and facilitated Buganda's military advance at its neighbors' expense.

How did Buganda develop, and what can this process tell us about state formation in general? As in other cases of state formation, Buganda's rise can ultimately be traced to the emergence of food production. Plant cultivation, accompanied by iron tools, spread rapidly in eastern Africa during the first centuries A.D. The emergence of plantain and banana cultivation near the lakes did not replace foraging. It merely added a secure source of calories to hunting, fishing, and gathering, which continued alongside cultivation. The early tribal Ganda, with their iron tools, plantains, and bananas, were free to

expand until they were blocked by neighboring groups or reached the natural limits of the banana and plantain niche. In other words, they could expand until they encountered factors that led to their social or physical circumscription, to recall Carneiro's theory of state formation.

The population increased and spread; new villages were built farther from Lake Victoria. To maintain a diversified diet that included fish, inland people traded with lakeshore communities. A basis for the ranking of descent groups arose through their differential population growth—some got to

Figure 13.4 *The process of state formation in Buganda. Several variables interacted throughout the sequence. Permanent cultivation based on plantains and bananas enabled men to be diverted to military operations. This favored Buganda's military success, conquest of its neighbors, and further expansion. Expansion and conquest continued to add new areas, contributing to ecological diversity and interregional trade.*

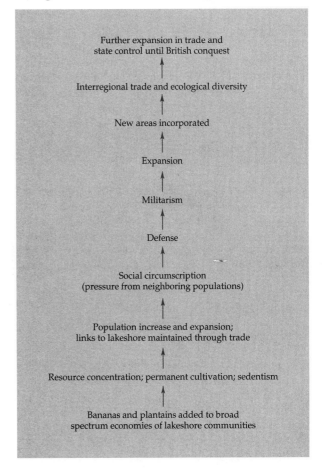

Further expansion in trade and state control until British conquest

↑

Interregional trade and ecological diversity

↑

New areas incorporated

↑

Expansion

↑

Militarism

↑

Defense

↑

Social circumscription
(pressure from neighboring populations)

↑

Population increase and expansion;
links to lakeshore maintained through trade

↑

Resource concentration; permanent cultivation; sedentism

↑

Bananas and plantains added to broad
spectrum economies of lakeshore communities

be larger and more widespread than did others. Given warfare, which was present in Buganda by the year 1600, the larger descent groups had more members in more places and thus more widespread support. Buganda had reached the chiefdom level.

The largest descent groups gained power. They managed the regional economy that was developing. They administered the sociopolitical system that was evolving from chiefdom into state. By the nineteenth century, when Buganda was at its height, the regulation of ecological diversity and interregional trade had become a major concern of state officials.

Plantain-banana subsistence favored Buganda's domination of its region, as did its position near water transport and lakeshore trade. Eventually the army became a powerful offensive force, extending Buganda's boundaries by encroaching on its neighbors. We see then that, as in other cases of state formation, several factors contributed to the process in Buganda. Population increase, warfare, environmental circumscription, ecological diversity, trade, and permanent cultivation (but not irrigation) were all important (Figure 13.4).

SUMMARY

The first states emerged in the Old World, in Mesopotamia, about 5,500 years ago. The first chiefdoms had developed a thousand years earlier, but few survive today. States also arose in two parts of the Western Hemisphere—Mesoamerica and the central Andes. The state is an autonomous political unit encompassing many communities; its central government has the power to collect taxes, draft people for work or war, and decree and enforce laws. The state is defined as a form of sociopolitical organization based on central government and socioeconomic stratification—a division of society into classes. Early states are known as archaic, or nonindustrial, states, in contrast to modern industrial nation-states.

The chiefdom is a form of sociopolitical organization intermediate and transitional between tribes and states. Like states and unlike tribes, chiefdoms are characterized by permanent regional regulation and differential access to strategic resources, but chiefdoms lack stratification. Unlike states but like bands and tribes, chiefdoms are organized by kinship, descent, and marriage.

State formation remained incomplete, and only chiefdoms emerged in several areas, including the circum-Caribbean, lowland Amazonia, the southeastern United States, and Polynesia. Between the rise of food production and the Roman empire, much of Europe was organized at the chiefdom level, to which it reverted after Rome's collapse. Much of our ethnographic knowledge of chiefdoms comes from Polynesia, where they were common at the time of European exploration. Although other chiefdoms calculated seniority differently and had shorter genealogies, the concern for genealogy and seniority and the absence of sharp gaps between elites and commoners are features of all chiefdoms. Chiefdoms have redistribution, a flow of resources to and then from a central office.

The sociologist Max Weber defined three related dimensions of social stratification: wealth, power, and prestige. In archaic states—for the first time in human evolution—contrasts in wealth, power, and prestige between entire groups (social strata) of men and women came into being. A socioeconomic stratum includes people of both sexes and all ages. The superordinate—higher or elite—stratum enjoys privileged access to wealth, power, and other valued resources. The lower stratum is subordinate. Its members' access to resources is limited by the privileged group.

Status has two meanings. One is close to the definition of prestige and refers to social ranking. The other is neutral: a status is simply a position in a social structure. Some statuses are ascribed; others are achieved. The number of social statuses increases with (and is a measure of) social complexity. Each status has an associated role—a set of expected (culturally "proper") behaviors, attitudes, rights, and obligations. A status is a position in the social structure, but a role involves thought and action. People occupy a status but play a role.

Illustrating general evolutionary trends, certain systems and subsystems with specialized functions are found in all states. They include population control, judiciary, enforcement, and fiscal. In archaic states, these subsystems were integrated by a ruling system or government composed of civil, military, and religious officials. To know whom they govern, all states conduct censuses and demarcate boundaries. States have laws based on precedent and legislative proclamations. To handle disputes and crimes, all states have courts and judges. Governments intervene to preserve internal peace, halt blood feuds, and regulate previously private disputes. All states have agents to enforce judicial decisions.

The major concern of government is to defend hierarchy, property, and the power of the law. The government suppresses internal disorder (with the police) and defends the nation against external threats (with the military). As a relatively new form of sociopolitical organization, states have competed successfully with less complex societies throughout the world.

A financial or fiscal subsystem is necessary to support rulers, nobles, officials, judges, military personnel, and other specialists. The state does not bring more freedom or leisure to the common people, who usually work harder than people do in nonstates.

People did not choose but were forced to accept state organization. Complex political organization develops to handle regulatory problems as the population grows and the economy increases in scale and diversity. Anthropologists and historians have reconstructed evolutionary sequences leading to formation of the state in several areas. Many factors always contribute to this process, with the effects of one magnifying those of the others. Although some contributing factors appear again and again, no single one is always present. The most important contributing factors are hydraulic (water-based) agricultural economies, ecological diversity, long-distance trade, population growth, warfare, and environmental circumscrip-

tion. Coastal Peru, one of the world's most arid areas, illustrates the interaction of environmental circumscription, warfare, and population increase.

Archeologists have documented many cases of early state formation. Cultural anthropologists have also studied state formation through historical, ethnohistorical, and ethnographic data. Such an approach has been used in reconstructing the evolution of the state in Buganda.

In Buganda, plantain-banana cultivation supported population growth; permitted the release of male labor for military service, trade, and other special functions; and thus paved the way for state formation. Trade, warfare, and differential descent-group growth led to contrasts in wealth and power. Both Buganda and coastal Peru illustrate the effects of warfare, population increase, environmental circumscription, and resource concentration. In all cases of state formation, there are several contributing factors. Population increase, warfare, environmental circumscription, ecological diversity, trade, and permanent cultivation are some of the most important ones.

GLOSSARY

achieved status: Position that people occupy through their own efforts, activities, and accomplishments, for example, big man.

archaic state: Nonindustrial state.

ascribed status: Position occupied without choice by an individual, for example, gender and age.

convergence: Parallel development without contact or mutual influence.

differential access: Unequal access to resources; basic attribute of chiefdoms and states. Superordinates have favored access to such resources, while the access of subordinates is limited by superordinates.

ethnohistory: Oral and written accounts of a culture's past by insiders and outsiders.

fiscal: Pertaining to finances and taxation.

hydraulic systems: Systems of water management, including irrigation, drainage, and flood control. Often associated with agricultural societies in arid and river environments.

ideal types: Labels that make contrasts seem more extreme than they really are (e.g., big and little). Instead of discrete categories, there is a continuum from one type to the next.

multivariate: Involving multiple factors or variables.

office: Permanent political position.

plantain: Bananalike staple of the Yanomami and Ganda.

power: The ability to exercise one's will over others—to do what one wants; the basis of political status.

prestige: Esteem, respect, or approval for acts, deeds, or qualities considered exemplary.

role: A set of expected (culturally "proper") behaviors, attitudes, rights, and obligations attached to a particular status.

status: A position within a social structure; alternatively, differential social ranking.

stratification: Characteristic of a system with socioeconomic strata; see *stratum*.

stratum: One of two or more groups that contrast in regard to social status and access to strategic resources. Each stratum includes people of both sexes and all ages.

subordinate: The lower, or underprivileged, group in a stratified system.

sumptuary goods: Items whose consumption is limited to the elite.

superordinate: The upper, or privileged, group in a stratified system.

wealth: All a person's material assets, including income, land, and other types of property; the basis of economic status.

STUDY QUESTIONS

1. What are the similarities and differences between chiefdoms and tribes?
2. What are the similarities and differences between chiefdoms and states?
3. What is redistribution, and what are its economic advantages? How does it differ from taxation?
4. What is the difference between the two meanings of *status*? Give examples of each.
5. What is the difference between ascribed status and achieved status? Give three examples of each.
6. What is the difference between status and role? Give examples of each.
7. What are the four special-purpose subsystems found in all states? How do they illustrate the four general evolutionary principles?
8. What is the relationship between state organization, conflicts, and warfare?
9. What are the advantages and disadvantages of the state from the citizen's perspective? Why have people been willing to sacrifice personal freedom to live in states?
10. How have anthropologists attempted to explain state formation? Which do you think is the best explanation, and why?
11. What is ethnohistory, and why do anthropologists study it?
12. What were the common variables in state formation in Peru and Buganda? What were the main differences?

SUGGESTED ADDITIONAL READING

COHEN, R., AND E. R. SERVICE, EDS.
　1978　*Origins of the State: The Anthropology of Political Evolution.* Philadelphia: Institute for the Study of Human Issues. Several articles on state formation in many areas.

DRENNAN, R. D., AND C. A. URIBE, EDS.
　1987　*Chiefdoms in the Americas.* Landon, MD: University Press of America. Chiefdoms in the precolonial Western Hemisphere.

EARLE, T.
　1987　Chiefdoms in Archaeological and Ethnohistorical Perspective. *Annual Review of Anthropology* 16: 279–308. Comprehensive review of early and recent chiefdoms worldwide; includes economy, stratification, and ideology.

EARLE, T.
　1991　*Chiefdoms: Power, Economy, and Ideology.* New York: Cambridge University Press. Ten case studies illustrate the dynamics of chiefdoms as political institutions.

FLANNERY, K. V.
　1972　The Cultural Evolution of Civilizations. *Annual Review of Ecology and Systematics* 3: 399–426. Survey of theories of state origins.

FOX, J. W.
　1987　*Maya Postclassic State Formation.* Cambridge: Cambridge University Press. The role of the "segmentary state" among the Mayas.

FRIEDMAN, J., AND M. J. ROWLANDS, EDS.
　1978　*The Evolution of Social Systems.* Pittsburgh, PA: University of Pittsburgh Press. Twenty studies of social change, including the rise of the state.

JOHNSON, A. W., AND T. EARLE, EDS.
　1987　*The Evolution of Human Society: From Forager Group to Agrarian State.* Stanford, CA: Stanford University Press. Recent comprehensive look at sociocultural evolution.

JONES, G., AND R. KRAUTZ
　1981　*The Transition to Statehood in the New World.* Cambridge: Cambridge University Press. Processes of state formation, including chiefdoms, in the Americas.

KIRSCH, P. V.
　1984　*The Evolution of the Polynesian Chiefdoms.* Cambridge: Cambridge University Press. Diversity and sociopolitical complexity in native Oceania.

KOTTAK, C. P.
　1980　*The Past in the Present: History, Ecology, and Cultural Variation in Highland Madagascar.* Ann Arbor: University of Michigan Press. Examines the process of state formation using ethnohistorical and ethnographic data and relates this historical process to contemporary cultural variation.

PFFEIFER, J.
1977   *The Emergence of Society.* New York: McGraw-Hill. A journalist with considerable anthropological expertise surveys the implications of food production and the rise of complex societies throughout the world.

READE, J.
1991   *Mesopotamia.* Cambridge, MA: Harvard University Press. The origin of irrigation, writing, and mathematics; surveys the world's first civilization from prehistoric times to the rise of Babylon.

SERVICE, E. R.
1975   *Origins of the State and Civilization: The Process of Cultural Evolution.* New York: W. W. Norton. State formation accessed through several case studies.

STEPONAITIS, V.
1986   Prehistoric Archaeology in the Southeastern United States. *Annual Review of Anthropology* 15: 363–404. Overview of the archeology of an area of chiefdoms.

THE WORLD SYSTEM, INDUSTRIALISM, AND STRATIFICATION

Although field work in small communities is anthropology's hallmark, isolated groups are impossible to find today. Truly isolated cultures probably have never existed. For thousands of years, human groups have been in contact with one another. Local societies have always participated in a larger system, which today has global dimensions. We call it the *modern world system,* by which we mean a world in which nations are economically and politically interdependent.

City, nation, and world increasingly invade local communities. Today, if anthropologists want to study a fairly isolated society, they must journey to the highlands of Papua–New Guinea or the tropical forests of South America. Even in those places they will probably encounter missionaries or prospectors. In contemporary Australia sheep owned by people who speak English graze where totemic ceremonies once were held. Farther in the outback some descendants of those totemites work in a movie crew making *Crocodile Dundee IV.* A Hilton hotel stands in the capital of faraway Madagascar, and a paved highway now has an exit for Arembepe, the Brazilian fishing village I have been studying since 1962. My son and I have a bet about when the first McDonald's will open there. When and how did the modern world system begin?

THE EMERGENCE OF THE WORLD SYSTEM

As Europeans took to ships, developing a transoceanic trade-oriented economy, people throughout the world entered Europe's sphere of influence. The origins of the European Age of Discovery, which was well under way by 1400, can be traced back to the Crusades, which began in 1096. The Crusades were Christian military expeditions undertaken between the eleventh and fourteenth centuries to recapture the Holy Land (particularly the city of Jerusalem) from the Moslems. Rising European powers (particularly Italian city-states) used the Crusades to establish and extend trade routes.

Marco Polo journeyed to China between 1271 and 1295, and in 1352 the Arab geographer Muhammad ibn-Batuta explored the Sahara desert. In the fifteenth century Europe established regular contact with Asia, Africa, and eventually the Americas. During the early years of exploration Europeans visited Asia and Africa as transient sailors, traders, missionaries, and officials sent to govern small outposts. Contact with Asia led to a trade relationship in which Europeans imported highly refined cottons and porcelains from India and China.

Trade was also established with the New World

The pace of social change is accelerating within the modern world system, based on international capitalism. This Malaysian woman pumps gasoline produced from Middle Eastern petroleum by a multinational organization (Shell) based in the Netherlands.

(the Caribbean and the Americas). Christopher Columbus's first voyage from Spain to the Bahamas and the Caribbean in 1492 was soon followed by additional voyages. These journeys opened the way for a major exchange of people, resources, diseases, and ideas, as the Old and New Worlds were forever linked (Crosby 1972, 1986; Viola and Margolis 1991). Led by Spain and Portugal, Europeans extracted silver and gold, conquered the natives (taking some as slaves), and colonized their lands.

Previously in Europe as throughout the world, rural people had produced mainly for their own needs, growing their own food and making clothing, furniture, and tools from local products. Production beyond immediate needs was undertaken to pay taxes and purchase trade items such as salt and iron. In the preindustrial cities of Europe craftspeople worked in their own shops, using simple tools to make hardware, cloth, jewelry, silverware, guns, cannon, and ammunition. As late as 1650 the English diet, like diets in most of the world today, was based on locally grown starches (Mintz 1985). However, in the 200 years that followed, the English became extraordinary consumers of imported goods. One of the earliest and most popular of those goods was sugar (Mintz 1985).

By 1650 England's nobility and wealthy classes were habitual sugar eaters. After 1650 sugar began to change from a luxury into a necessity, as tobacco had done a century earlier. By 1750 even the poorest English farm woman took sugar in her tea. The English consumed sugar in the form of rum and with coffee, chocolate, and especially tea.

Sugar was originally domesticated in Papua–New Guinea and was first processed in India. Reaching Europe via the Middle East and the eastern Mediterranean, it was carried to the New World by Columbus (Mintz 1985). The climate of Brazil and the Caribbean proved ideal for growing sugarcane, and Europeans built plantations there to supply the growing demand for sugar. This led to the development in the seventeenth century of a plantation economy based on a single cash crop—a system known as **monocrop production**.

The demand for sugar and the emergence of a sugar supply geared to an international market spurred the development of one of the most inhumane—and profitable—trade systems in the preindustrial world—the slave trade. Two triangles of trade involving sugar and slaves arose in the sev-

enteenth century and matured in the eighteenth. In the first triangle, English manufactured goods were sold to Africa, African slaves were sold to the Americas, and American tropical commodities (especially sugar) were sold to England and its neighbors. (**Commodities** are articles of trade, products with commercial value.) In the second triangle, New England rum was shipped to Africa, slaves were sent from Africa to the Caribbean, and molasses (from sugar) was shipped to New England to make rum. In the eighteenth century an increased English demand for raw cotton led to the rapid settlement of what is now the southeastern United States and the emergence of monocrop production there. This was another instance of a plantation economy based on slave labor.

In the Americas the labor of African slaves created wealth, which returned mostly to Europe. Products grown by slaves were consumed in Europe. The Caribbean and Brazil supplied Europe with spices, beverages (coffee and chocolate), dyes, sugar, and rum (Mintz 1985). The United States supplied cotton and additional rum.

Like sugar, cotton was a key trade item that spurred the development of the world system and industrialization. Cotton cloth, which initially was imported from India, became increasingly fashionable in England after 1690. Cotton's popularity grew steadily during the eighteenth century. The English cotton industry began to thrive when Parliament banned the importation of Indian cotton. Some of the cotton spun in England found its way back to the Americas to clothe slaves on English plantations in the Caribbean (Mintz 1985).

The increasing dominance of international trade led to the **capitalist world economy** (Wallerstein 1982)—a single world system committed to production for sale or exchange, with the object of maximizing profits rather than supplying domestic needs. The defining attribute of capitalism is *economic orientation to the world market for profit*.

The world system and the relations between the countries within that system are shaped by the world economy. World-system theory can be traced to the French social historian Fernand Braudel. In his three-volume work *Civilization and Capitalism, 15th–18th Century* (1981, 1982, 1984), Braudel argues that society consists of parts assembled into an interrelated system. Societies are subsystems of bigger systems, with the world system as the largest.

The key claim of world-system theory is that an identifiable social system extends beyond individual states and nations. That system is formed by a set of economic and political relations that has characterized much of the globe since the sixteenth century, when the Old World established regular contact with the New World.

According to Wallerstein (1982), the nations within the world system occupy three different positions: core, periphery, and semiperiphery. There is a geographic center or **core**, the dominant position in the world system, which consists of the strongest and most powerful nations, with advanced systems of production. In core nations, "the complexity of economic activities and the level of capital accumulation is the greatest" (Thompson 1983, p. 12). Core countries specialize in producing the most "advanced" goods, using the most sophisticated technologies and mechanized means of production. The core produces capital-intensive high-technology goods and exports some of them to the periphery and semiperiphery.

Semiperiphery and **periphery** nations, which roughly correspond to what is usually called the Third World, have less power, wealth, and influence. The semiperiphery is intermediate between the core and the periphery. Contemporary nations of the semiperiphery are industrialized. Like core nations, they export both industrial goods and commodities, but they lack the power and economic dominance of core nations. Thus Brazil, a semiperiphery nation, exports automobiles to Nigeria and auto engines, orange juice extract, and coffee to the United States.

Economic activities in the periphery are less mechanized and use human labor more intensively than do those in the semiperiphery. The periphery produces raw materials and agricultural commodities for export to the core and the semiperiphery. However, in the modern world, industrialization is invading even peripheral nations. Although the weakest structural position in the world system, the periphery is an essential part of the world economy. Peripheral nations exist to serve the interests of the core (see the box "Spirit Possession in Malaysian Factories" in this chapter). The relationship between the core and the periphery is fundamentally exploitative. Trade and other forms of economic relations between core and periphery benefit capitalists in the

core at the expense of the periphery (Shannon 1989).

Usually, at a given time, one state dominates the core, but dominance shifts over time. The northern Italian city-states dominated world trade in the fourteenth century. Holland dominated in the seventeenth, England after 1750, and the United States after 1900. In 1560 (Figure 14.1) the core of the world system was in western Europe (England, France, the Netherlands, Portugal, and Spain). The northern Italian city-states, which had once been more powerful, had joined the semiperiphery. Northeastern Europe and particularly Latin America formed the periphery. Many societies (particularly in Oceania and in the interior of Africa and Asia) were still beyond the periphery. They had not yet joined the world capitalist economy and were still self-sufficient, producing and consuming their own goods. Today there are virtually no societies beyond the periphery. The former Soviet bloc ("Second World") nations, traditionally shielded from the world capitalist economy, now belong to the semiperiphery or periphery.

INDUSTRIALIZATION

By the eighteenth century the stage had been set for the **Industrial Revolution**—the historical transformation (in Europe, after 1750) of "traditional" into "modern" societies through industrialization of the economy. Industrialization required capital for investment. The established system of transoceanic trade and commerce, controlled by a small group of merchants and mercantile companies, supplied this capital from the enormous profits it generated. Wealthy people sought investment opportunities and eventually found them in machines and engines to drive machines. Industrialization increased production in both farming and manufacturing, as capital and scientific innovation fueled invention.

European industrialization developed from (and eventually replaced) the **domestic system** (or home handicraft system) of manufacture. In this system, an organizer-entrepreneur supplied raw materials to workers in their homes and collected finished products from them. The entrepreneur, whose sphere of operations might span several villages, owned the materials, paid for the work, and arranged the marketing.

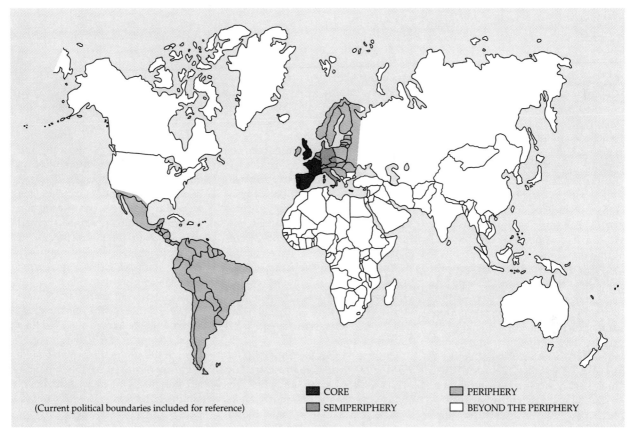

Figure 14.1 *The world system in 1560. (Reprinted by permission of Westview Press from* An Introduction to the World-System Perspective *by Thomas Richard Shannon. Copyright Westview Press 1989, Boulder, Colorado.)*

Causes of the Industrial Revolution

The Industrial Revolution began in the cotton products, iron, and pottery trades, whose growing markets were very attractive to capitalists with money to risk. The manufacture of cotton, iron, and earthenware could be broken down into simple routine motions that machines could perform. Factories could produce cheap staple goods.

Industrialization began in industries that produced *goods that were widely used already*. This illustrates **Romer's rule**—a generalization about evolutionary processes, biological or cultural, originally proposed by the paleontologist Alfred S. Romer (1960). The key is that an innovation that evolves to maintain an existing system can play a major role in changing that system. Romer used the rule to explain the evolution of land-dwelling vertebrates

from fish. The ancestors of land vertebrates were animals that lived in pools of water that dried up seasonally. Fins gradually evolved into legs, not to permit vertebrates to live full-time on the land but to enable them to get back to the water when particular pools dried up. In other words, an innovation (legs) that proved essential to land life originated to maintain life in the water.

We can apply Romer's rule to many major changes in human adaptive strategies. One example is the transition to food production in the Middle East. The "first farmers" did not start cultivating in order to become cultivators but to maintain the basis of their traditional foraging economy. Population increase forced foragers into a marginal zone that lacked the bountiful wild fields of wheat and barley of their nearby homeland. They began sowing seeds (cultivating) in the marginal zone in order to create

SPIRIT POSSESSION IN MALAYSIAN FACTORIES

Successive waves of integration into the world system have washed Malaysia, a former British colony. The Malays have witnessed sea trade, conquest, the influx of British and Chinese capital, and immigration from China and India. For centuries Malaysia has been part of the world system, but the immediate effects of industrialization are recent. The Malaysian government has promoted export-oriented industry to bring rural Malays into the capitalist system. This has been done in response to rural discontent over poverty and landlessness as some 10,000 families per year are pushed off the land. Since 1970 transnational companies have been installing labor-intensive manufacturing operations in rural Malaysia. Between 1970 and 1980 agriculture's contribution to the national labor force fell from 53 to 41 percent as manufacturing jobs proliferated.

The industrialization of Malaysia is part of a global strategy. To escape mounting labor costs in the core, corporations headquartered in Japan, Western Europe, and the United States have been moving labor-intensive factories to the periphery. Malaysia now has hundreds of Japanese and American subsidiaries, which mainly produce garments, foodstuffs, and electronics components. In electronics plants in rural Malaysia, thousands of young women from peasant families now assemble microchips and microcomponents for transistors and capacitors. Aihwa Ong (1987) did a study of electronics assembly workers in an area where 85 percent of the workers were young unmarried females from nearby villages.

Ong found that factory discipline and social relations contrast strongly with traditional community life. Previously, agricultural cycles and daily Islamic prayers, rather than production quotas and work shifts, had framed the rural economy and social life. Villagers had planned and done their own work, without bosses. In factories, however, village women had to cope with a rigid work routine and constant supervision by men.

Factory relations of production featured a hierarchy, pay scale, and division of labor based on ethnicity and gender. Japanese men filled top management, while Chinese men were the engineers and production supervisors. Malay men also worked as supervisors of the factory work force, which consisted of nonunion female semiskilled workers from poor Malay peasant families.

The Japanese firms in rural Malaysia were paternalistic. Managers assured village parents that they would care for their daughters as though they were their own. Unlike the American firms, the Japanese subsidiaries worked hard at maintaining good relations with rural elders. Management gave money for village events, visited workers' home communities, and invited parents to the plant for receptions. In

---

artificial fields like the natural ones in which they once had gathered. As often happens in cultural evolution, the actions of those ancient Middle Easterners had unintended consequences. The process they set in motion led to full-fledged food production, as their descendants eventually developed new varieties of wheat and barley that outyielded the wild forms.

Similarly, the Industrial Revolution led to a dramatic increase in production. Manufacturing moved from home to factory, where machinery replaced handwork. Agrarian societies evolved into industrial ones. Industrialization fueled urban growth and created a new kind of city, with factories crowded together in places where coal and labor were cheap.

Revolution is not the right term to describe either food production or industrialism, because both were long-term processes that began in order to maintain rather than to change. Romer's lesson is that evolution (biological or cultural) tends to occur in small increments. Gradually changing systems make adaptations to maintain themselves as they change. The rule also applies to conscious economic changes: People usually want to *change just enough to maintain what they have*. Motives to modify behavior arise within a particular culture and reflect the small concerns and demands of daily life, such as improved crop yields and increased profit (assuming that the profit motive has been established in that culture).

Romer's rule helps us understand why the Industrial Revolution began in England rather than France. The French were able to maintain the form of their manufacturing system (even as they were changing their *political* system through the French Revolution and Napoleon). With a late eighteenth-century population at least twice that of Great Brit-

return, village elders accorded high status to the Japanese managers. The elders colluded with the managers to urge young women to accept and stay with factory work.

The discipline, diligence, and obedience that factories value is learned in local schools, where uniforms help prepare girls for the factory dress code. Peasant women wear loose, flowing tunics, sarongs, and sandals, but factory workers must don tight overalls and heavy rubber gloves, in which they feel constrained and controlled.

Assembling electronics components requires precise, concentrated labor. Demanding, exhausting, depleting, and dehumanizing, labor in these factories illustrates the separation of intellectual and manual activity that Marx considered the defining feature of industrial work. One woman said about her bosses, "They exhaust us very much, as if they do not think that we too are human beings" (Ong 1987, p. 202). Nor does factory work bring women a sub-

stantial financial reward, given low wages, job uncertainty, and family claims on wages. Young women typically work just a few years. Production quotas, three daily shifts, overtime, and surveillance take their toll in mental and physical exhaustion.

One response to factory discipline and relations of production is spirit possession, which Ong interprets as an unconscious protest against labor discipline and male control of the industrial setting. Sometimes possession takes the form of mass hysteria. Spirits have simultaneously invaded as many as 120 factory workers. Weretigers (the Malay equivalent of the werewolf) arrive to avenge the construction of a factory on aboriginal burial grounds. Disturbed earth and grave spirits swarm on the shop floor. First the women see the spirits; then their bodies are invaded. The women become violent and scream abuses. Vengeful weretigers send the women into sobbing, laughing, and shrieking fits. To deal with possession, factories employ local medicine

men, who sacrifice chickens and goats to fend off the spirits. This solution works only some of the time; possession still goes on. Factory women continue to act as vehicles to express the anger of avenging ghosts and their own frustrations.

Ong argues that spirit possession expresses anguish caused by and resistance to capitalist relations of production. However, she also notes that by engaging in this form of rebellion, factory women avoid a direct confrontation with the source of their distress. Ong concludes that spirit possession, while expressing repressed resentment, doesn't do much to modify factory conditions. (Unionization would do more.) Spirit possession may even help maintain the current conditions of inequality and dehumanization by operating as a safety valve for accumulated tensions.

ain, France could simply expand its domestic system of production by drawing in new homes. Thus the French could increase production without innovating—they could enlarge the existing system rather than adopt a new one. However, to meet mounting demand for staples—at home and in the colonies—England had to industrialize.

Anthropologist Marvin Harris (1978) contends that history's prime movers are economic cycles of intensification, depletion, and innovation. Population pressure leads to intensified production, but this eventually depletes the environment. Renewed pressure (resulting from depleted resources) spurs innovative solutions in production systems. This process seems to apply (at least partially) to the Industrial Revolution in England.

Accompanying English industrialization was agrarian intensification stimulated by population pressure and demand for food. The English population was increasing faster than the food supply was. In response, the eighteenth-century enclosure movement created more efficient farming, as more easily cultivated compact private holdings replaced common pastures and fields. Experiments with root crop rotation and shifts between pastureland and farmland also enhanced productivity. Inventions bolstered both farming and industry. Fewer farmers were able to feed a growing manufacturing work force.

Britain's population doubled during the eighteenth century (particularly after 1750) and did so again between 1800 and 1850. This demographic explosion fueled consumption, but British entrepreneurs couldn't meet increased demand with traditional production methods. This spurred experimentation, innovation, and rapid technological change. English industrialization also rested on the accumulation of capital from land and overseas

The Caribbean sugar plantations of the seventeenth century shared many features with, and may have served as models for, industrial factories, which developed a century later. On sugar plantations as in factories, workers were organized into crews, shifts, and gangs, and punctuality and discipline were stressed in the coordinated operations. Shown here is a contemporary sugar cane harvest in Trinidad.

trade. This capital had been growing through saving, and banking stimulated the industrial market economy. By 1800 factory-based mechanization was rapidly replacing Britain's domestic system.

According to Sidney Mintz (1985), Caribbean sugar plantations played a key role in the emergence of industrialism. Mintz makes the unorthodox suggestion that industrialism was invented in the Third World rather than in Europe. Specifically, he traces industrialization back to the Caribbean sugar plantations of the seventeenth century. Those enterprises shared many features with, and thus might have served as models for, the industrial factories that developed a century later. The plantations, where cane was grown and chemically transformed into sugar, were a synthesis of field and factory unlike anything known in Europe during the seventeenth century. Sugar plantations were like factories because they had specialization by job and skill level. They maintained a division of labor by age, gender, and condition (slave, free, or indentured worker). As in factories, workers were organized into crews, shifts, and gangs, and punctuality and discipline were stressed in the coordinated operations.

As we saw in the discussion of theories of state formation in the last chapter, multivariate approaches are more convincing than single-factor explanations of major socioeconomic changes. Just as

several factors contributed to state formation, several also propelled industrialization. English industrialization could draw on national advantages in natural resources. Great Britain was rich in coal and iron ore and had navigable waterways and easily negotiated coasts. It was a seafaring island nation located at the crossroads of international trade. These features gave Britain a favored position for importing raw materials and exporting manufactured goods.

Another factor in England's industrial ascendancy was the fact that much of its eighteenth-century colonial empire was occupied by English settler families who looked to the mother country as they tried to replicate European civilization in the New World. These colonies bought large quantities of English staples. By contrast, the French New World colonies had fewer French settlers. Neither Caribbean slaves, who worked on the sugar plantations, nor French Canadian and Indian trappers, who provided furs, formed a particularly lucrative market for French manufactures.

It has also been argued that particular cultural values and religion contributed to industrialization. Thus, many members of the emerging English middle class were Protestant nonconformists. Their beliefs and values encouraged industry, thrift, the dissemination of new knowledge, inventiveness, and willingness to accept change (Weber 1904/1949).

STRATIFICATION

The worldwide effects of the Industrial Revolution continue today, extending our familiar general evolutionary trends: proliferation, specialization, integration, and expansion. Thus parts and subparts have proliferated with the emergence of new social categories and occupations. Functional differentiation and specialization have increased. For example, each European nation promoted differentiation within its trade zone and specialization in its colonies in order to supply particular commodities. Integration and system scale increased as new areas entered the world capitalist economy and colonialism engulfed the globe. The growth rate of world population also increased. The Industrial Revolution produced another quantum leap in the rate of cultural evolutionary change, which had previously accelerated with food production and again with state formation.

How does social stratification in the industrial world system compare with that in archaic states, as examined in the preceding chapter? The hereditary rulers and elites of archaic states and ancient empires, like the feudal nobility that ruled Europe before 1500, viewed the state as their property (conferred by gods, tradition, or war) to control and do with as they pleased (Shannon 1989). The most basic distinction in archaic states was between those who controlled the state machinery and those who did not. But in the world system of the industrial era, the main differentiating factor became ownership of the means of production.

Marx and Weber on Stratification

Karl Marx and Max Weber focused on the stratification systems associated with industrialization. The socioeconomic effects of industrialization were mixed. English national income tripled between 1700 and 1815 and increased thirty times more by 1939. Standards of comfort rose, but prosperity was uneven. At first, factory workers got wages higher than those available in the domestic system. Later, owners started recruiting labor in places where living standards were low and labor (including that of women and children) was cheap.

Social ills increased with the growth of factory towns and industrial cities, with conditions like those Charles Dickens described in *Hard Times*. Filth and smoke polluted nineteenth-century cities. Housing was crowded and unsanitary, with insufficient water and sewage disposal facilities and rising disease and death rates. This was the world of Ebenezer Scrooge, Bob Cratchit, Tiny Tim—and Karl Marx.

From his observations in England and his analysis of nineteenth-century industrial capitalism, Marx (Marx and Engels 1848/1976) saw socioeconomic stratification as a sharp and simple division between two opposed classes: the bourgeoisie (capitalists) and the proletariat (propertyless workers). The bourgeoisie traced its origins to overseas ventures and the world capitalist economy, which had transformed the social structure of northwestern Europe, creating a wealthy commercial class.

Industrialization shifted production from farms and cottages to mills and factories, where mechanical power was available and where workers could be assembled to operate heavy machinery. The **bourgeoisie** were the owners of the factories, mines, large farms, and other means of production. The **working class**, or proletariat, was made up of people who had to sell their labor to survive. With the decline of subsistence production and with the rise of urban migration and the possibility of unemployment, the bourgeoisie came to stand between workers and the means of production.

Industrialization hastened the process of **proletarianization**—the separation of workers from the means of production. The bourgeoisie also came to dominate the means of communication, the schools, and other key institutions. Marx viewed the nation-state as an instrument of oppression and religion as a method of diverting and controlling the masses.

Faulting Marx for an overly simple and exclusively economic view of stratification, Weber (1922) defined the three related dimensions of social stratification examined in the preceding chapter: wealth (economic status), power (political status), and prestige (social status). Having one of the three doesn't entail having the others. Band societies have slight contrasts in prestige and power but none in wealth; lottery winners gain wealth but usually not prestige. Although, as Weber showed, wealth, power, and prestige are separate components of social ranking, they do tend to be correlated.

Class consciousness (recognition of collective interests and personal identification with one's economic group) was a vital part of Marx's view of

Social ills increased with the growth of factory towns and industrial cities. This drawing depicts nineteenth-century air pollution in England's "Black Country" (Wolverhampton)—a coal- and iron-producing district covered with manufacturing towns, mines, blasting furnaces, and forges.

class. He saw bourgeoisie and proletariat as socioeconomic divisions with radically opposed interests. Marx viewed classes as powerful collective forces that could mobilize human energies to influence the course of history. Finding strength through common experience, workers would develop organizations to protect their interests and increase their share of industrial profits.

And so they did. During the nineteenth century trade unions and socialist parties emerged to express a rising anticapitalist spirit. The concerns of the English labor movement were to remove young children from factories and limit the hours during which women and children could work. The profile of stratification in industrial core nations gradually became clear: Capitalists controlled production, but labor was organizing to improve wages and working conditions. By 1900 many governments had factory legislation and social-welfare programs. Mass living standards in core nations rose as population grew.

The modern capitalist world system maintains the distinction between those who own the means of production and those who don't. The class division into capitalists and propertyless workers is now worldwide. Nevertheless, modern stratification systems aren't simple and dichotomous. They include (particularly in core and semiperiphery nations) a growing middle class of skilled and professional workers. Gerhard Lenski (1966) argues that social equality tends to increase in advanced industrial societies as the masses acquire and use political power and get economic benefits. In his scheme, the shift of political power to the masses reflects the growth of the middle class, which reduces the polarization between owning and working classes. The proliferation of intermediate occupations creates opportunities for social mobility, and the stratification system grows more complex (Giddens 1973).

Weber believed that social identities based on ethnicity, religion, race, nationality, and other attributes could take priority over class (social identity based on economic status). In addition to class contrasts, the modern world system is cross-cut by status groups, such as ethnic and religious groups and nations (Shannon 1989). Class conflicts tend to occur within nations, and nationalism has prevented global class solidarity, particularly of proletarians.

Although the capitalist class dominates politically in most countries, the leaders of core nations have found it to be in their interest to allow proletarians to organize and make demands. Growing wealth has made it easier for core nations to become less authoritarian and to grant higher wages (Hopkins and Wallerstein 1982). However, the improvement in core workers' living standards wouldn't have occurred without the world system. The added surplus that comes from the periphery allows core capitalists to maintain their profits while satisfying the demands of core workers. In the periphery, wages and living standards are much lower. A system of intense labor exploitation is maintained at low levels of compensation. Thus the current *world stratification system* features a substantial contrast between both capitalists and workers in core nations and workers on the periphery.

In times of economic stagnation in the core, class conflict intensifies as workers and capitalists compete to increase their share of declining national wealth. The conflict ends with some income redistribution to workers and the middle class. Once workers have more to spend, market demand increases, triggering renewed economic expansion. Workers in core nations benefit from economic expansion, but increased demand fuels the process of proletarianization in the periphery (Shannon 1989).

With the expansion of the world capitalist economy, people on the periphery have been removed from the land by large landowners and multinational agribusiness interests. One result is increased poverty, including food shortages. Displaced people can't earn enough to buy the food they can no longer grow. The effects of the world economy can also create peripheral regions within core nations, such as areas of the rural South in the United States (see the box "The American Periphery" in this chapter).

Bangladesh illustrates some of the causes of Third World poverty and food shortages. Climate, soils, and water availability in Bangladesh are favorable for productive agriculture. Indeed, before the arrival of the British in the eighteenth century, Bangladesh (then called Bengal) had a prosperous local cotton industry. There was some stratification, but peasants had enough land to provide an adequate

diet. Land was neither privately owned nor part of the market economy. Under colonialism, the British forced the Bengalis to grow cash crops for export and converted land into a commodity that could be bought and sold.

Increased stratification was a result of colonialism and tighter linkage with the world capitalist economy. The peasantry of Bangladesh gradually lost its land. A study done in 1977 (Bodley 1985) showed that a small group of wealthy people owned most of the land. One-third of the households owned no land at all. Poverty was expressed in food shortages. Many landless people worked as sharecroppers, with landowners claiming at least half the crop. The peasants were underpaid for their crops and overcharged for the commodities they needed. Local landowners (capitalists of the periphery) also monopolized international development aid and even emergency food aid.

Open and Closed Class Systems

Inequalities, which are built into the structure of state organization, tend to persist across the generations. The extent to which they do or don't is a measure of the openness of the stratification system, the ease of social mobility it permits. Within the world capitalist economy, stratification has taken many forms, including caste, slavery, and class systems.

Caste systems are closed, hereditary systems of stratification that are often dictated by religion. Hierarchical social status is ascribed at birth, so that people are locked into their parents' social position. Caste lines are clearly defined, and legal and religious sanctions are applied against those who seek to cross them.

The world's best-known caste system is associated with Hinduism in traditional India, Pakistan, and Sri Lanka. As described by Gargan (1992), caste-based stratification remains important in modern India. In a national population of 850 million people, an estimated 5 million adults and 10 million children are bonded laborers. These people live in complete servitude, working to repay real or imagined debts. Most of them are untouchables, impoverished and powerless people at the bottom of the caste hierarchy. Some families have been bonded for generations; people are born into servitude because their parents or grandparents were

THE AMERICAN PERIPHERY

In a comparative study of two counties at opposite ends of Tennessee, Thomas Collins (1989) reviews the effects of industrialization on poverty and unemployment. Hill County, with an Appalachian white population, is on the Cumberland Plateau in eastern Tennessee. Delta County, predominantly African-American, is 60 miles from Memphis in western Tennessee's lower Mississippi region. Both counties once had economies based on agriculture and timber, but jobs in those sectors declined sharply with the advent of mechanization. Both counties have unemployment rates more than twice that of Tennessee as a whole. More than a third of the people in each county live below the poverty level. Such poverty pockets represent a slice of the world periphery within modern America. Given very restricted job opportunities, the best-educated local youths have migrated to northern cities for three generations.

To increase jobs, local officials and business leaders have tried to attract industries from outside. Their efforts exemplify a more general rural southern strategy, which began during the 1950s, of courting industry by advertising "a good business climate"—which means low rents, cheap utilities, and a nonunion labor pool. However, few firms are attracted to an impoverished and poorly educated work force. All the industries that have come to such areas have very limited market power and a narrow profit margin. Such firms survive by offering low wages and minimal benefits, with frequent layoffs. These industries tend to emphasize traditional female skills such as sewing and mostly attract women.

The garment industry, which is highly mobile, is Hill County's main employer. The knowledge that a garment plant can be moved to another site very rapidly tends to reduce employee demands. Management can be as arbitrary and authoritarian as it wishes. The unemployment rate and low educational level ensure that many women will accept sewing jobs for a bit more than the minimum wage.

In neither county has new industry brought many jobs for men, who have a higher unemployment rate than do women (as do blacks, compared with whites). Collins found that many men in Hill County had never been permanently employed; they had just done temporary jobs, always for cash.

The effects of industrialization in Delta County have been similar. That county's recruitment efforts have also drawn only marginal industries. The largest is a bicycle seat and toy manufacturer, which employs 60 percent women. Three other large plants, which make clothing and auto seat covers, employ 95 percent women. Egg production was once significant in Delta County but folded when the market for eggs fell in response to rising national concern over the effects of cholesterol.

In both counties the men, ignored

---

sold previously. Bonded workers toil unpaid in stone quarries, brick kilns, and rice paddies.

Once indentured, it is difficult to escape. Bonded labor is against Indian law, but it persists despite court rulings and efforts to stop it. Social workers obtain court orders to release bonded workers, but local officials and police often ignore them. Agents for quarries and kilns continue to entice untouchables into bonded labor with deceptive promises. Others enter bondage seeking to repay loans that can never be fully repaid. Thus the caste system, which is described more fully in the chapter on marriage, continues to form a highly restrictive system of social and economic stratification in India.

Another castelike system, **apartheid,** existed until recently in South Africa. In that legally maintained hierarchy, blacks, whites, and Asians had their own separate (and unequal) neighborhoods, schools, laws, and punishments.

In **slavery** people are treated as property. In the Atlantic slave trade millions of human beings were treated as commodities. The plantation systems of the Caribbean, the southeastern United States, and Brazil were based on forced slave labor. Slaves were like proletarians in that they lacked control over the means of production, but proletarians have some control over where they work, how much they work, for whom they work, and what they do with their wages. Slaves, in contrast, have nothing to sell—not even their own labor (Mintz 1985). Slavery is the most extreme and coercive form of legalized inequality.

Vertical mobility is an upward or downward change in a person's social status. A truly **open class**

by industrialization, maintain an informal economy. They sell and trade used goods through personal networks. They take casual jobs, such as operating farm equipment on a daily or seasonal basis. Collins found that maintaining an automobile was the most important and prestigious contribution these men made to their families. Neither county has public transportation; Hill County even lacks school buses. Families need cars to get women to work and kids to school. Men who keep an old car running longest get special respect.

Reduced opportunities for men to do well at work—to which American culture attributes great importance—lead to a feeling of lowered self-worth, which is expressed in physical violence. The rate of domestic violence in Hill County exceeds the state average. Spousal abuse arises from men's demands to control women's paychecks. (Men regard the cash they earn themselves as their own, to spend on male activities.)

One important difference between the two counties involves unionization. In Delta County, organizers have waged campaigns for unionization. There is just one unionized plant in Delta County now, but recent campaigns in two other factories failed in close votes. Attitudes toward workers' rights in Tennessee correlate with race. Rural southern whites usually don't vote for unions when they have a chance to do so, whereas African-Americans are more likely to challenge management about pay and work rules. Local blacks view their work situation in terms of black against white rather than from a position of working-class solidarity. They are attracted to unions because they see only whites in managerial positions and resent differential advancement of white factory workers. One manager told Collins that "once the work force of a plant becomes more than one-third black, you can expect to have union representation within a year" (Collins 1989, p. 10). Responding to the probability of unionization, canny core capitalists from Japan don't build plants in the primarily African-American counties of the lower Mississippi. The state's Japanese factories cluster in eastern and central Tennessee.

Poverty pockets of the rural South (and other regions) represent a slice of the world periphery within modern America. Through mechanization, industrialization, and other changes promoted by larger systems, local people have been deprived of land and jobs. After years of industrial development, a third of the people of Hill and Delta counties remain below the poverty level. Emigration of educated and talented locals continues as opportunities shrink. Collins concludes that rural poverty won't be reduced by attracting additional peripheral industries because these firms lack the market power to improve wages and benefits. Different development schemes are needed for these counties and the rural South generally.

system would facilitate mobility, with individual achievement and personal merit determining social rank. Hierarchical social statuses would be achieved on the basis of people's efforts. Ascribed statuses (family background, ethnicity, gender, religion) would be less important. Open class systems would have blurred class lines and a wide range of status positions.

Compared with archaic states and contemporary peripheral and semiperipheral nations, core industrial nations tend to have more open class systems. Under industrialism, wealth is based to some extent on **income**—earnings from wages and salaries. Economists contrast such a *return on labor* with interest, dividends, and rent, which are *returns on property* or capital.

Even in advanced industrial nations, stratification is more marked in wealth than it is in income. Thus in 1985 the bottom fifth of American households got 4.6 percent of total national income, compared with 43.5 percent for the top fifth. However, if we consider wealth rather than income, the contrast is much more extreme: One percent of American families hold one-third of the nation's wealth (Light, Keller, and Calhoun 1994).

INDUSTRIAL AND NONINDUSTRIAL SOCIETIES IN THE WORLD SYSTEM TODAY

World-system theory stresses the existence of a global culture. It emphasizes historical contacts and linkages between local people and international

In India's caste system, most untouchables are impoverished and powerless people at the bottom of the caste hierarchy. Untouchables are assigned menial tasks, which include janitorial duties and other ''unclean'' activities, like piling up cow cakes—cattle dung, used as a cooking fuel.

Plantation systems in the New World were based on forced slave labor. Proletarians, such as these ''white slaves of England,'' also lacked control over the means of production, but they did have some control over where and for whom they worked.

forces. The major forces influencing cultural inter-action during the past 500 years have been commercial expansion and industrial capitalism (Wolf 1982; Wallerstein 1982). As state formation had done previously, industrialization accelerated local participation in larger networks. According to Bodley (1985), perpetual expansion (whether in population or consumption) is the distinguishing feature of industrial economic systems. Unlike bands and tribes, which are small, self-sufficient, subsistence-based systems, industrial economies are large, highly specialized systems in which local areas don't consume the products they produce and in which market exchanges occur with profit as the primary motive (Bodley 1985).

There is a *world* economy because the first loyalty of capitalism is to itself rather than to any community, region, or nation. Because capitalists do not freely subordinate their profit-seeking goals to national interests, most countries have erected protective barriers designed to protect their own products from foreign competition. In world-system theory, **mercantilism** refers to the system of tariffs, trade laws, and other barriers designed to protect national products and industries from (often cheaper) foreign competition.

The twentieth-century world economy and the nations within it have witnessed cycles of expansion, overproduction, falling demand, and depression. Industrial capitalism depends on distant markets, which can expand rapidly and contract unpredictably. Colonization, international competition, and the diffusion of fads and fashions have fueled industrial expansion. However, massive unemployment may follow when distant wars or fads run their course.

During the nineteenth century, industrialization spread beyond England. Belgium became the first nation in continental Europe to industrialize—in the 1820s—on the strength of its iron and coal resources. France followed in the 1830s, as did Germany (Prussia) in the 1840s. By the middle of the nineteenth century the United States had joined the roster of industrializing nations.

After 1870 European business began a concerted search for more secure markets in Asia, Africa, and other less-developed areas. This process, which led to European imperialism in Africa, Asia, and Oceania, was aided by improved transportation, which brought huge new areas within easy reach. Europeans also colonized vast areas of previously unsettled or sparsely settled lands in the interior of North and South America and Australia. The new colonies purchased masses of goods from the industrial centers and shipped back wheat, cotton, wool, mutton, beef, and leather. Thus began the second phase of colonialism (the first had been in the New World after Columbus) as European nations competed for colonies between 1875 and 1914, a process that helped cause World War I.

Manufacturing has been declining in the United States but not internationally. Continuing to place capital above national loyalty, North American (and Western European and Japanese) businesses pursue their search for markets, profits, and cheap labor abroad. These women employed by a toy factory on the Mexican side of the U.S.-Mexico border are willing to work for lower wages than American workers would accept. Because capitalists do not freely subordinate their profit-seeking goals to national interests, most countries have erected protective barriers designed to protect their own products from foreign competition.

By 1900 the United States had become a core nation within the world system (Figure 14.2). It had overtaken Great Britain in iron, coal, and cotton production. With its older plants and equipment, Britain faced increased international competition. England began to lag behind Germany (in chemicals) and the United States (in electric and automobile industries).

Industrialization spread to many other nations in a process that continues today (Table 14.1). In a few decades (1868–1900) Japan changed from a medieval handicraft country to an industrial one, joining the semiperiphery by 1900 and moving to the core between 1945 and 1970. Italy and the Netherlands industrialized by 1914. Russian industrialization had begun somewhat earlier. However, World War I and the 1917 Bolshevik Revolution halted industrialization, which resumed in the 1930s—no longer as a response to market forces but as planned economic development by the Soviet state. The basis of Soviet industrialization was state investment in plants, machinery, and heavy industrial goods—with restricted consumerism. In the 1950s China also embarked on planned industrial development, seeking to accomplish in a decade what had taken Britain a century.

Twentieth-century industrialization has added hundreds of new industries and millions of new jobs. Its early hallmarks were mass production and the assembly line. Jobs in offices and stores also increased, and more young women began to do wage work. Production increased, often beyond immediate demand, and this spurred strategies such as advertising to sell everything that industry could churn out. Mass production gave rise to a culture of overconsumption, which valued acquisitiveness and conspicuous consumption.

Bodley defines overconsumption as "consump-

Figure 14.2 *The world system in 1900. (Reprinted by permission of Westview Press from* An Introduction to the World-System Perspective *by Thomas Richard Shannon. Copyright Westview Press 1989, Boulder, Colorado.)*

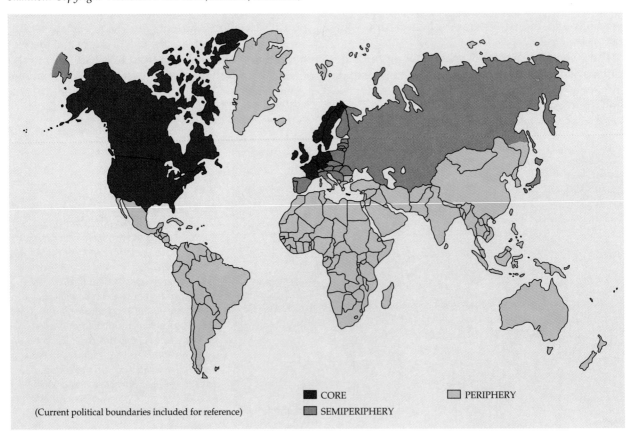

(Current political boundaries included for reference)

CORE SEMIPERIPHERY PERIPHERY

Table 14.1 *Ascent and decline of nations within the world system*

Periphery to Semiperiphery	Semiperiphery to Core	Core to Semiperiphery
United States (1800–1860)	United States (1860–1900)	Spain (1620–1700)
Japan (1868–1900)	Japan (1945–1970)	
Taiwan (1949–1980)	Germany (1870–1900)	
S. Korea (1953–1980)		

Source: Reprinted by permission of Westview Press from *An Introduction to the World-System Perspective* by Thomas Richard Shannon. Copyright Westview Press 1989, Boulder, Colorado.

tion in a given area that exceeds the rates at which natural resources are produced by natural processes, to such an extent that the long-run stability of the culture involved is threatened" (1985, p. 39). Industrialization entailed a shift from reliance on renewable resources to the use of fossil fuels. Fossil fuel energy, stored over millions of years, is being rapidly depleted to support a previously unknown and probably unsustainable level of consumption (Bodley 1985). Table 14.2 compares energy consumption in various types of cultures. Americans are the world's foremost consumers of nonrenewable resources. Since becoming a core nation in 1900, the United States has tripled its per capita energy use while increasing its total energy consumption thirtyfold.

The Effects of Industrialization on the World System

How has industrialization affected the Third World—Latin America, Africa, the Pacific, and the less-developed parts of Asia? One effect is the destruction of indigenous economies, ecologies, and populations. Two centuries ago, as industrialization was developing, 50 million people still lived beyond

Table 14.2 *Energy consumption in various contexts*

Type of Society	Daily Kilocalories per Person
Bands and tribes	4,000–12,000
Preindustrial states	26,000 (maximum)
Early industrial states	70,000
Americans in 1970	230,000
Americans in 1990	275,000

Source: From John H. Bodley, *Anthropology and Contemporary Human Problems*, 1985. Reprinted by permission of Mayfield Publishing.

the periphery in politically independent bands, tribes, and chiefdoms. Occupying vast areas, those nonstate societies, although not totally isolated, were only marginally affected by nation-states and the world capitalist economy. Bands, tribes, and chiefdoms controlled half the globe and 20 percent of its population in 1800 (Bodley, ed. 1988). Industrialization then tipped the balance in favor of states. The war of conquest between states and tribes, under way for 6,000 years, continues in just a few remote places today. In the rest of the world, states now govern.

Industrialization is "a global process that has destroyed or transformed all previous cultural adaptations and has given humanity the power not only to bring about its own extinction as a species, but also to speed the extinction of many other species and to alter biological and geological processes as well" (Bodley 1985, p. 4). The negative effects of an expanding industrial world system include genocide, ethnocide, and ecocide. **Genocide** is the physical destruction of ethnic groups by murder, warfare, and introduced diseases. When ethnic groups survive but lose or severely modify their ancestral cultures, we speak of **ethnocide**. The term for the destruction of local ecosystems is **ecocide**.

As industrial states have conquered, annexed, and "developed" nonstates, there has been genocide on a grand scale. Bodley (1988) estimates that an average of 250,000 indigenous people perished annually between 1800 and 1950. Foreign diseases (to which natives had no resistance), warfare, slavery, land grabbing, and other forms of dispossession and impoverishment contributed to this genocide.

In the South Pacific, the population of the Solomon Islands, which had numbered at least 500 before contact, fell to 100 soon after 1900 as forty-six villages were reduced to three. Depopulation plagued Melanesia to such an extent that colonial authorities worried about maintaining the native labor force (Bodley, ed. 1988). By 1800 the world capitalist economy had penetrated Alaska, where, during the nineteenth century, the fur trade, the commercial use of sea animals and salmon, and the gold rush combined to undermine the traditional resource base. Indigenous bands, tribes, and chiefdoms from Alaska down the North Pacific Coast suffered impoverishment, disease, and depopulation. (The following chapter considers some of the economic and cultural effects of this process there.)

After initial contact and conquest, many native groups, having been incorporated as ethnic minorities within nation-states, recouped their population. Many indigenous peoples survive and maintain their ethnic identity despite having lost their ancestral cultures to varying degrees (partial ethnocide).

During the nineteenth century, with the abolition of slavery in the Caribbean and the Americas, many of the plantation economies that had been based on slavery became monocrop economies using free but poorly paid labor. After World War II many Asian, African, and Oceanian colonies gained political independence. Often, however, their economic dependence on the industrial world continued. Peripheral and semiperipheral nations continue to specialize in cash crops, raw materials, and unskilled and semiskilled labor.

The American economy has recently shifted from heavy-goods manufacture toward a high-tech economy based on information processing and the provision of specialized services. The term *postindustrial* has been coined to describe this economic transformation. However, this term seems inappropriate, because industrialization certainly continues today in a world economy in which the United States is a full participant. Manufacturing is declining in the United States but not internationally. Continuing to place capital above national loyalty, American (and Western European and Japanese) businesses pursue their search for markets, profits, and cheap labor abroad. Thus industrialization continues, and the world system goes on evolving.

The notion of a constant human struggle to tame nature—missing in bands and tribes but a hallmark of industrialism—promotes increasing exploitation of the earth's finite store of natural resources. Industrialism, seemingly a cultural evolutionary advance, may eventually prove disastrous because of the ecological destruction left in its wake. Indigenous cultures have been devastated along with their environments as resources within their territories have been exploited for industrial growth.

Today's world contains some 200 million people who are members of conquered tribes or of still autonomous tribal nations, of which, however, only a handful survive. Compare this with 75 million people living in perhaps 150,000 independent bands and tribes 10,000 years ago at the dawn of food production (Bodley 1988). Many descendants of tribespeople live on as culturally distinct colonized peo-

The notion of a constant struggle to tame nature is a hallmark of industrialism and promotes increasing exploitation of the earth's finite store of natural resources. Industrialism, seemingly a cultural evolutionary advance, may eventually prove disastrous because of the ecological destruction left in its wake. This 1989 photo illustrates the ecocide that has been caused by gold prospectors—using poisonous mercury—in Brazilian rivers.

ples, many of whom aspire to autonomy. As the original inhabitants of their territories, they are called **indigenous peoples.** They become *peasants* when their dependency and integration within states are complete and they remain on the land. When they move to urban areas, they are often called **ethnic minorities.** Bodley (1988) argues that indigenous peoples have consistently resisted integration within nation-states because such integration—usually into the impoverished classes—is likely to lead to a decline in their quality of life.

Many contemporary nations are repeating—at an accelerated rate—the process of resource depletion that occurred in Europe and the United States during the Industrial Revolution. Fortunately, however, today's world has some environmental watchdogs that were absent during the first centuries of the Industrial Revolution. Given national and international cooperation and sanctions, the modern world may benefit from the lessons of the past.

Although the more isolated societies that represent anthropology's traditional concern are disappearing, the subject matter open to anthropology is actually expanding. This book examines the many ways in which people modify their customs and behavior in adapting to environmental change. Alterations in the wider environments of human groups—that is, in their relationship with foreigners—represent changes to which people must adapt. Furthermore, although the pressure to change may come from the outside, people are not always the helpless prey of social processes beyond their control. They should be seen as potential or actual participants, rather than mere victims, in a process of change generated by larger forces. Not only are today's international safeguards more effective than were those of 1800, there is often local mobilization against threats from larger-scale systems (see the chapter "Cultural Exchange and Survival").

SUMMARY

Local societies increasingly participate in wider systems—regional, national, and global. Columbus's voyages opened the way for a major and continuing exchange between the Old and New Worlds. The first plantation economies based on a single cash crop (most notably sugar) appeared in the seventeenth century. The plantations of Brazil and the Caribbean spurred the development of two triangles of trade involving sugar and slaves. In the eighteenth century a monocrop economy based on slave labor also emerged in the cotton plantations of the southeastern United States. Cotton was another key trade item that spurred the development of the world system and industrialization.

The capitalist world economy is based on production for sale, with the goal of maximizing profits. The capitalist world economy has political and economic specialization based on three positions. Core, semiperiphery, and periphery have existed within the world system since the sixteenth century, although the particular countries filling these niches have changed.

The Industrial Revolution—the historical transformation of "traditional" into "modern" societies through industrialization of the economy—began around 1760. Transoceanic trade and commerce supplied capital for industrial investment.

Industrialization developed from the domestic system of manufacture, and increased production in farming and manufacturing. Industrialization began in industries that

produced goods that were widely used already. This illustrates Romer's rule: an innovation that evolves to maintain an existing system can play a major role in changing that system. The Industrial Revolution started in England rather than France because French industry could grow through expansion of the domestic system. England, with fewer people, had to industrialize. A demographic explosion fueled consumption and demand.

The Caribbean sugar plantation played a key role in the emergence of industrialism. Sugar plantations of the seventeenth century might have served as models for the industrial factories that developed a century later. Just as several factors contributed to state formation, several also propelled industrialization.

The worldwide effects of industrialism continue today, extending the general evolutionary trends of proliferation, specialization, integration, and expansion. The most basic distinction in archaic states was between those who controlled the state machinery and those who did not. In the world system, particularly after industrialization, the main differentiating factor became ownership of the means of production. Marx saw socioeconomic stratification as a sharp and simple division between the bourgeoisie (capitalists) and the proletariat (propertyless workers). Industrialization hastened the separation of workers from the means of production. Class consciousness was a vital part of Marx's view of class. Weber, on the other hand, believed that social identity based on ethnicity, religion, race, or nationality could take priority over class.

The modern capitalist world system maintains the distinction between those who own the means of production and those who don't, but the division is now worldwide. Modern stratification systems also include a middle class of skilled and professional workers.

In addition to class contrasts, the modern world system is cross-cut by status groups, of which nations are the most important. Class conflicts tend to occur within nations, and nationalism has prevented global class solidarity. The added surplus from the periphery allows core capitalists to maintain their profits while satisfying the demands of core workers. World stratification features a substantial contrast between capitalists and workers in core nations and workers on the periphery. With the expansion of world capitalism, Third World peoples have been removed from the land by large landowners and multinational agribusiness interests.

The extent to which inequalities persist across the generations is a measure of the openness of the stratification system, the ease of social mobility it permits. Within the world capitalist economy, stratification has taken many forms, including caste, slavery, and class systems. Caste systems are closed, hereditary systems of stratification, often dictated by religion. In slavery, the most extreme and coercive form of legalized inequality, people are treated as property. Core industrial nations tend to have the most open class systems.

The major forces influencing cultural interaction during the past 500 years have been commercial expansion and industrial capitalism. Perpetual expansion is a distinguishing feature of industrial economic systems. The first loyalty of capitalism is to itself rather than to any community, region, or nation. Mercantilism refers to the system of tariffs, trade laws, and other barriers designed to protect national products and industries from foreign competition.

During the first half of the nineteenth century, industrialization spread to Belgium, France, Germany, and the United States. After 1870 businesses began a concerted search for more secure markets. This process led to European imperialism in Africa, Asia, and Oceania. Europeans also colonized vast areas of previously unsettled or sparsely settled lands in the interior of North and South America and Australia. This was the second phase of colonialism. The first had occurred in the New World after Columbus.

By 1900 the United States had become a core nation within the world system. Industrialization spread to many other countries, including Japan, Italy, the Netherlands, Russia, and China, in a process that continues today. Mass production gave rise to a culture of overconsumption, which valued acquisitiveness and conspicuous consumption. Industrialization shifted reliance from renewable resources to fossil fuels.

One effect of industrialization is the destruction of indigenous economies, ecologies, and populations. Two centuries ago, 50 million people still lived in politically independent bands, tribes, and chiefdoms, which controlled half the globe and 20 percent of its population. Industrialization tipped the balance in favor of states. The negative effects of the industrial world system include genocide, ethnocide, and ecocide. The specialization and peripheralization promoted by world capitalism and colonialism are basic to much of the poverty in the world today. Many former colonies remain economic satellites.

The American economy has recently shifted from manufacture toward information processing and services. The term *postindustrial,* sometimes used to describe this change, is inappropriate because industrialization continues today in a world economy in which the United States is a full participant.

The more isolated societies that represent anthropology's traditional concern are disappearing, but the subject matter open to anthropology is expanding. Alterations in the wider environments of human groups—that is, in their relationships with foreigners—represent changes to which people must adapt.

GLOSSARY

apartheid: Castelike system in South Africa; blacks, whites, and Asians have separate (and unequal) neighborhoods, schools, laws, and punishments.

bourgeoisie: One of Marx's opposed classes; owners of the means of production (factories, mines, large farms, and other sources of subsistence).

capitalist world economy: The single world system, which emerged in the sixteenth century, committed to production for sale, with the object of maximizing profits rather than supplying domestic needs.

caste system: Closed, hereditary system of stratification, often dictated by religion; hierarchical social status is ascribed at birth, so that people are locked into their parents' social position.

class consciousness: Recognition of collective interests and personal identification with one's economic group (particularly the proletariat); basic to Marx's view of class.

commodities: Articles of trade, products with commercial value.

core: Dominant structural position in the world system; consists of the strongest and most powerful states with advanced systems of production.

domestic system (of manufacture): Also known as "home handicraft production"; preindustrial manufacturing system in which organizer-entrepreneurs supplied raw materials to people who worked at home and collected finished products from them.

ecocide: Destruction of local ecosystems.

ethnic minorities: Indigenous peoples who have moved to urban areas.

ethnocide: Process in which ethnic groups survive but lose or severely modify their ancestral cultures.

genocide: Physical destruction of ethnic groups by murder, warfare, and introduced diseases.

income: Earnings from wages and salaries.

indigenous peoples: The original inhabitants of particular territories; often descendants of tribespeople who live on as culturally distinct colonized peoples, many of whom aspire to autonomy.

Industrial Revolution: The historical transformation (in Europe, after 1750) of "traditional" into "modern" societies through industrialization of the economy.

mercantilism: System of tariffs, trade laws, and other barriers designed to protect national products and industries from (often cheaper) foreign competition.

monocrop production: System of production, often on plantations, based on the cultivation of a single cash crop.

open class system: Stratification system that facilitates social mobility, with individual achievement and personal merit determining social rank.

periphery: Weakest structural position in the world system.

proletarianization: Separation of workers from the means of production through industrialism.

Romer's rule: Evolutionary rule stating that an innovation that evolves to maintain an existing system can play a major role in changing that system.

semiperiphery: Structural position in the world system intermediate between core and periphery.

slavery: The most extreme and coercive form of legalized inequality; people are treated as property.

vertical mobility: Upward or downward change in a person's social status.

working class: Or proletariat; those who must sell their labor to survive; the antithesis of the bourgeoisie in Marx's class analysis.

STUDY QUESTIONS

1. What is the world-system perspective, and why is it important in anthropology?
2. What were the two triangles of trade involving sugar and slaves?
3. How did the Caribbean sugar plantation play a key role in the emergence of world capitalism and industrialism?
4. What was the Age of Discovery, and how did it contribute to the Industrial Revolution?
5. What is the capitalist world economy? When did it originate, and what are its features?
6. What is the defining feature of capitalism? Why does capitalism require a world economy?
7. What are core, semiperiphery, and periphery? What is their relationship to world capitalism?
8. How do the worldwide effects of industrialism illustrate the general evolutionary trends of proliferation, specialization, integration, and expansion?
9. What was the Industrial Revolution, and how did it differ from previous life in villages, towns, and cities?
10. Why might the Industrial "Revolution" be better viewed in an evolutionary context?
11. What is Romer's rule, and how does it apply to food production and the Industrial Revolution?
12. Why did the Industrial Revolution begin in the cotton, iron, and pottery trades?
13. Why did the Industrial Revolution begin in England rather than France?
14. How did population growth and the accumulation of capital contribute to the Industrial Revolution?
15. How did proletarianization change human work?
16. How did the views of Marx and Weber on stratification differ?
17. What are the differences between open and closed class systems?
18. How is the world stratification system related to structural positions within the world capitalist economy?
19. What have been the major forces influencing cultural interaction during the past 500 years?
20. What was the second phase of colonialism, and what caused it?
21. How does industrialization destroy indigenous economies, ecologies, and populations?
22. What is mercantilism, and what is its relationship to capitalism?
23. What is *postindustrialism*, and why is this a problematic term?

SUGGESTED ADDITIONAL READING

BRAUDEL, F.

1973 *Capitalism and Material Life: 1400–1800.* London: Weidenfeld and Nicolson. The role of the masses in the history of capitalism.

1977 *Afterthoughts on Material Civilization and Capitalism.* Baltimore: Johns Hopkins University Press. Reflections on the history of industrial capitalism.

1982 *Civilization and Capitalism 15th–18th Century. Volume II: The Wheels of Commerce.* New York: HarperCollins. On the history of capitalism and the role of trade from precapitalist mercantilism to the present.

1984 *Civilization and Capitalism 15th–18th Century. Volume III: The Perspective of the World.* New York: HarperCollins. On the emergence of the world capitalist economy; case histories of European countries and various areas of the rest of the world.

CROSBY, A. W., JR.

1972 *The Columbian Exchange: Biological and Cultural Consequences of 1492.* Westport, CT: Greenwood Press. Describes how Columbus's voyages opened the way for a major exchange of people, resources, and ideas as the Old and New Worlds were forever joined together.

1986 *Ecological Imperialism: The Biological Expansion of Europe 900–1900.* Cambridge: Cambridge University Press. The spread of diseases, foods, people, and ecological devastation, as the world system took shape.

MINTZ, S.

1985 *Sweetness and Power: The Place of Sugar in Modern History.* New York: Viking Penguin. The place of sugar in the formation of the modern world system.

ROSEBERRY, W.

1988 Political Economy. *Annual Review of Anthropology* 17: 161–185. Reviews works on industrialization, political economy, local and regional social history, and world-system studies.

VIOLA, H. J., AND C. MARGOLIS

1991 *Seeds of Change: Five Hundred Years since Columbus, a Quincentennial Commemoration.* Washington, D.C.: Smithsonian Institution Press. People, plants, animals, and customs mingle between the Old World and the New—based on a Smithsonian exhibition.

WALLERSTEIN, I.

1974 *The Modern World-System: Capitalist Agriculture and the Origins of the European World-Economy in the Sixteenth Century.* New York: Academic Press. The origins of the capitalist world economy; a classic work.

1980 *The Modern World-System II: Mercantilism and the Consolidation of the European World-Economy, 1600–1750.* New York: Academic Press. Further development of the world system and the underpinnings of industrialization.

WOLF, E. R.

1982 *Europe and the People without History.* Berkeley: University of California Press. An anthropologist examines the effects of European expansion on tribal peoples and sets forth a world-system approach to anthropology.

CHAPTER 15

ECONOMIC SYSTEMS

Economic anthropology looks at economics in a comparative perspective. A population's **economy** is its system of production, distribution, and consumption of resources. *Economics* is the study of such systems. **Comparative economics** examines these systems in different societies. It is in this last area that anthropologists have contributed most. Economists concentrate on modern nations and capitalist systems. It has remained for anthropologists to broaden economics by gathering data on nonindustrial economies.

Economic anthropologists are concerned with two questions:

1. How are production, distribution, and consumption organized in different societies? This question focuses on *systems* of human behavior and their organization.
2. What motivates people in different cultures to produce, distribute or exchange, and consume? Here the focus is not on systems of behavior but on the *individuals* who participate in those systems.

Anthropologists view both economic systems and motivations in a cross-cultural perspective. Motivation is a concern of psychologists, but it has also been, implicitly or explicitly, a concern of economists and anthropologists. American economists assume that producers and distributors make decisions rationally using the *profit motive,* as do consumers when they shop around for the best value. However, anthropologists know that the motives of people in one culture are not necessarily the same as those of people in another. We compare the motivations, beliefs, and values that influence personality formation and cause individuals to behave differently in different cultures.

ECONOMIZING AND MAXIMIZATION

Although anthropologists know that the profit motive is not universal, the assumption that individuals try to maximize profits is basic to the capitalist world economy and to Western economic theory. In fact, the subject matter of economics is often defined as **economizing,** or the rational allocation of scarce means (or resources) to alternative ends (or uses). What does that mean? Classical economic theory assumes that our wants are infinite and that our resources are limited. Since means are always scarce, people have to make choices. They must decide how they will use their scarce resources—their time, labor, money, and capital. Western economists assume that when confronted with alternatives, people tend to choose the one that maximizes profit. This is assumed to be the most rational (reasonable) choice.

The idea that individuals maximize profits was a basic assumption of the classical economists of the nineteenth century and one that is held by many contemporary economists. However, certain economists now recognize that individuals in Western cultures, as in others, may be motivated by many other goals. Depending on the society and the situation, people may try to maximize profit, wealth, prestige, pleasure, comfort, or social harmony. Individuals may want to realize their personal or family ambitions or those of another group to which they belong.

Alternative Ends

To what uses do people in various societies put their scarce resources? Throughout the world, people devote some of their time and energy to building up a **subsistence fund** (Wolf 1966). In other words, they have to work to eat, to replace the calories they use in their daily activity. People must also invest in a **replacement fund.** They must maintain their technology and other items essential to production. If a hoe or plow breaks, they must repair or replace it. They must also obtain and replace items that are essential not to production but to everyday life, such as clothing and shelter.

People everywhere also have to invest in a **social fund.** They have to help their friends, relatives, in-laws, and, especially in states, unrelated neighbors. It is useful to distinguish between a social fund and a **ceremonial fund.** The latter term refers to expenditures on ceremonies or rituals. To prepare a festival honoring one's ancestors, for example, requires time and the outlay of wealth.

Citizens of states must also allocate scarce resources to a **rent fund.** We think of rent as payment for the use of property. However, *rent fund* has a wider meaning. It refers to resources that people must render to an individual or agency that is superior politically or economically. Tenant farmers and sharecroppers, for example, either pay rent or give some of their produce to their landlords, as peasants did under feudalism.

Peasants are small-scale agriculturalists who live in states with rent fund obligations. They produce to feed themselves and to sell. All peasants have two things in common:

1. They live in state-organized societies.
2. They produce food without the elaborate technology—chemical fertilizers, tractors, airplanes to spray crops, and so on—of modern farming or agribusiness.

In addition to paying rent to landlords, peasants must satisfy government obligations, paying taxes in the form of money, produce, or labor. The rent fund is not simply an *additional* obligation for peasants. Often it becomes their foremost and unavoidable duty. Sometimes, to meet the obligation to pay rent, their own diets suffer. The demands of social superiors may divert resources from subsistence, replacement, social, and ceremonial funds.

Social and ceremonial funds assume new functions in states. Many states use ceremonies as occasions to collect fees. In the Merina kingdom of Madagascar, circumcision, which once had been just a ritual and social event, became a device for collecting taxes and carrying out a census. In prestate times circumcision had been a small-scale ritual uniting the boy, other members of his household, and his close relatives on his mother's and father's sides. It affirmed kinship between the boy, usually a member of his father's group, and his maternal relatives. As the Merina state developed, however, the king made circumcision a concern of the state. Every seventh year, boys were circumcised. Their sponsors, similar to godparents, had to pay a set fee (a single coin) to state officials. The coins collected were tallied to get a census of the boys born during the cycle.

Motivations vary from society to society, and people often lack freedom of choice in allocating their resources. Because of obligations to pay rent, peasants may allocate their scarce means toward ends that are not their own but those of state officials. Thus, even in societies where there is a profit motive, people are often prevented from rationally maximizing self-interest by factors beyond their control.

PRODUCTION

Strategies of adaptation, as discussed in the chapter "Cultural Change and Adaptation," are based on the system (mode) of production that predominates in a particular society. Production varies somewhat within any adaptive strategy, depending on the environment. Thus the social organization of the foraging mode of production—for example, individual hunters or teams—depends on whether the game is a solitary or a herd animal. Gathering is usually more individualistic than hunting. People may fish alone or in crews.

Organization in Nonindustrial Populations

Although some kind of division of economic labor related to age and gender is a cultural universal, the specific tasks assigned to each sex and to people of different ages vary. Some horticulturalists assign a major productive role to women; others make men's work primary. Similarly, among pastoralists men generally tend large animals, but in some cultures women do the milking. Jobs accomplished through teamwork in some cultivating societies are done by smaller groups or individuals working over a longer period of time in others.

Among the Betsileo of Madagascar there are two stages of teamwork in rice cultivation: transplanting and harvesting. Team size varies with the size of the field. Both transplanting and harvesting feature a traditional division of labor by age and gender which is well known to all Betsileo and is repeated across the generations. The first job in transplanting is the trampling of a flooded field by young men driving cattle in order to mix earth and water. Once the tramplers leave the field, older men arrive. With their spades they break up the clumps that the cattle missed. Meanwhile, the owner and other adults uproot rice seedlings and bring them to the field. Women plant the seedlings.

At harvest time, four or five months later, young men cut the rice off the stalks. Young women carry it to a clearing above the field. Older women arrange and stack it. The oldest men and women then stand on the stack, stomping and compacting it. Three days later, young men thresh the rice, beating the stalks against a rock to remove the grain. Older men then attack the stalks with sticks to make sure all the grains have fallen off.

Most of the other tasks in Betsileo rice cultivation

The cultivation of rice, one of the world's most important food crops, often features a division of task by age and gender. Women often transplant; men often thresh. These young women are transplanting rice seedlings in Sulawesi, Indonesia, and these men are threshing rice, to separate the grains from the stem, in Bangladesh.

are done by owners and their immediate families. Men maintain and repair the irrigation and drainage systems and the earth walls that separate one plot from the next. Men also till with spade or plow. All members of the household help weed the rice field.

In any culture, the organization of production may change over time. The Betsileo no longer use teams to maintain the irrigation network. Each man cleans the sections of the canals that irrigate and drain his own field. Irrigation ditches start at stone dams built across the shallow parts of rivers. Canals that run for miles irrigate the fields of as many as thirty people. These systems were originally constructed and repaired by work parties organized by political officials. Now, however, they are individually maintained without teamwork and political regulation.

SCARCITY AND THE BETSILEO

From October 1966 through December 1967 my wife and I lived among the Betsileo people of Madagascar, studying their economy and social life (Kottak 1980). Soon after our arrival we met two well-educated schoolteachers who were interested in our research. The woman's father was a congressman who became a cabinet minister during our stay. Our schoolteacher friends told us that their family came from a historically important and typical Betsileo village called Ivato, which they invited us to visit with them.

We had traveled to many other villages, where we were often displeased with our reception. As we drove up, children would run away screaming. Women would hurry inside. Men would retreat to doorways, where they lurked bashfully. Eventually someone would summon the courage to ask what we wanted. This behavior expressed the Betsileos' great fear of the *mpakafo*. Believed to cut out and devour his victim's heart and liver, the *mpakafo* is the Malagasy vampire. These cannibals are said to have fair skin and to be very tall. Because I have light skin and stand six feet four inches tall, I was a natural suspect. The fact that such creatures were not known to travel with their wives helped convince the Betsileo that I wasn't really a *mpakafo*.

When we visited Ivato, we found that its people were different. They were friendly and hospitable. Our very first day there we did a brief census and found out who lived in which households. We learned people's names and relationships to our schoolteacher friends and to each other. We met an excellent informant who knew all about the local history. In a few afternoons I learned much more than I had in the other villages in several sessions.

Ivatans were willing to talk because I had powerful sponsors, village natives who had made it in the outside world, people the Ivatans knew would protect them. The schoolteachers vouched for us, but even more significant was the cabinet minister, who was like a grandfather and benefactor to everyone in town. The Ivatans had no reason to fear me because their most influential native son had asked them to answer my questions.

Once we moved to Ivato, the elders established a pattern of visiting us every evening. They came to talk, attracted by the inquisitive foreigners but also by the wine, cigarettes, and food we offered. I asked questions about their customs and beliefs. I eventually developed interview schedules about various subjects, including rice production. I mimeographed these forms to use in Ivato and in two other villages I was studying less intensively. Never have I interviewed as easily as I did in Ivato. So enthusiastic were the Ivatans about my questions that even people from neighboring villages came to join the study. Since these people know nothing about social scientists' techniques, I couldn't discourage them by saying that they weren't in my sample. Instead, I agreed to visit each village, where I filled out the interview schedule in just one house. Then I told the other villagers that the household head had done such a good job of teaching me about their village I wouldn't need to ask questions in the other households.

As our stay drew to an end, the elders of Ivato began to lament, saying, "We'll miss you. When you leave, there won't be any more cigarettes, any more wine, or any more questions." They wondered what it would be like for us back in the United States. Ivatans had heard of American plans to send a man to the moon. Did I think it would succeed? They knew that I had an automobile and that I regularly purchased things, including the wine, cigarettes, and food I shared with them. I could afford to buy products they would never have. They commented, "When you go back to your country, you'll need a lot of money for things like cars, clothes, and food. We don't need to buy those things. We make almost everything we use. We don't need as much money as you, because we produce for ourselves."

The Betsileo are not unusual among people whom anthropologists have studied. Strange as it may seem to an American consumer, who may believe that he or she can never have enough money, some rice farmers actually believe that *they have all they need*. The lesson from the Betsileo is that scarcity, which economists view as universal, is variable. Although shortages do arise in nonindustrial societies, the concept of scarcity (insufficient means) is much less developed in stable subsistence-oriented societies than in societies characterized by industrialism, particularly as consumerism increases.

Means of Production

In nonindustrial societies there is a more intimate relationship between the worker and the means of production than there is in industrial nations. **Means, or factors, of production** include land, labor, technology, and capital.

Territory

Among foragers, ties between people and land are less permanent than they are among food producers. Although many bands have territories, the boundaries are not usually marked, and there is no way they can be enforced. The hunter's stake in an animal that is being stalked or has been hit with a poisoned arrow is more important than where the animal finally dies. A person acquires the right to use a band's territory by being born in the band or by joining it through a tie of kinship, marriage, or fictive kinship. In Botswana in southern Africa, !Kung San women, whose work provides over half the food, habitually use specific tracts of berry-bearing trees. However, when a woman changes bands, she immediately acquires a new gathering area.

Among food producers, rights to the means of production also come through kinship and marriage. Descent groups are common among nonindustrial food producers, and those who descend from the founder share the group's territory and re-

sources. If the adaptive strategy is horticulture, the estate includes garden and fallow land for shifting cultivation. As members of a descent group, pastoralists have access to animals to start their own herds, to grazing land, to garden land, and to other means of production.

In states, the means of production are unequally distributed. Stratification implies the existence of rent. Among the Betsileo, however, even after two centuries of life in nation-states, descent still plays a role in allocating land, although that role has weakened considerably. Today land is held in common by people with the same grandfather. The Betsileo have the legal right to end the condominium (joint holding) at any time and register their share of the rice field as private property, which may be sold. However, the Betsileo discourage the sale of rice fields to outsiders. If people wish to sell a field and still have good relations with their kin, they must sell it to a fellow descent-group member.

Labor, Technology, Technical Knowledge, and Specialization

Like land, labor is a means of production. In nonindustrial societies, access to both land and labor comes through social links such as kinship, marriage, and descent. Mutual aid in production is merely one aspect of ongoing social relationships that are expressed on many other occasions.

Manufacturing is often linked to age and gender. Men may make pottery and women, baskets (like these Malaysians)— or vice versa. In traditional societies most people of a particular age and gender share the technical knowledge associated with that age and gender. Thus, if married women customarily make baskets, most married women know how to make baskets.

Nonindustrial societies contrast with industrial nations in regard to another means of production—technology. In bands and tribes manufacturing is often linked to age and gender. Women may weave and men may make pottery or vice versa. Most people of a particular age and gender share the technical knowledge associated with that age and gender. If married women customarily make baskets, most married women know how to make baskets. Neither technology nor technical knowledge is as specialized as it is in states.

However, some tribal societies do promote specialization. Among the Yanomami of Venezuela and Brazil, for instance, certain villages manufacture clay pots and others make hammocks. They don't specialize, as one might suppose, because certain raw materials happen to be available near particular villages. Clay suitable for pots is widely available. Everyone knows how to make pots, but not everybody does so. Craft specialization reflects the social and political environment rather than the natural environment. Such specialization promotes trade, which is the first step in creating an alliance with enemy villages (Chagnon 1983/1992). Specialization contributes to keeping the peace, although it has not prevented intervillage warfare.

Among the Trobriand Islanders of the South Pacific, Malinowski (1922/1961) found that only two out of several villages manufactured certain ceremonial items that were important in a regional exchange network called the kula ring. As among the Yanomami, this specialization was unrelated to the location of raw materials. We don't know why this specialization began, but we do know that it persisted within the kula ring, which allied several communities and islands in a common trade network.

Alienation and Impersonality in Industrial Economies

What are the most significant contrasts between industrial and nonindustrial economies? When factory workers produce for sale and for the employer's profit rather than for their own use, they may be alienated from the items they make. Such alienation means they do not feel strong pride in or personal identification with their products. In nonindustrial societies people see their work through from start to finish and have a sense of accomplishment in the product.

In nonindustrial societies the economic relation-

In nonindustrial communities people usually see their work through from start to finish and have a sense of accomplishment. By contrast, assembly-line workers may be alienated from production—feeling no strong pride in or personal identification with their products. Compare this Dai woman weaving a fishing net in China's Yunnan province with these Japanese line workers sorting out substandard oranges.

ship between coworkers is just one aspect of a more general social relationship. They aren't just coworkers but kin, in-laws, or celebrants in the same ritual. In industrial nations, people don't usually work with relatives and neighbors. If coworkers are friends, the personal relationship usually develops during their common employment rather than being based on a previous association.

Thus, industrial workers have impersonal relationships with their products, coworkers, and employers. People sell their labor for cash. They don't give it to members of their personal networks as readily or as often as they do in tribes. In bands, tribes, and chiefdoms people work for their relatives toward family or community goals. The goals of the factory owner, by contrast, usually differ from those of workers and consumers.

In industrial nations the economic domain stands apart from ordinary social life. In nonindustrial societies, however, the relations of production, distribution, and consumption are *social relations with economic aspects*. The economy is not a separate entity but is *embedded* in the society.

DISTRIBUTION, EXCHANGE

Besides studying production cross-culturally, economic anthropologists investigate exchange or distribution systems. The economist Karl Polanyi (1957) stimulated the comparative study of exchange, and several anthropologists followed his lead. To study exchange cross-culturally, Polanyi defined three principles orienting exchanges: the **market principle, redistribution,** and **reciprocity.** These principles can all be present in the same society, but in that case they govern different kinds of transactions. In any society, one of them usually dominates. The principle of exchange that dominates is the one that allocates the means of production. Roughly speaking, the market principle dominates in states, particularly industrial states. Redistribution is the main exchange principle of chiefdoms, and reciprocity dominates in band and tribal societies.

The Market Principle

In nonsocialist industrial nations, as in the world capitalist economy, the market principle dominates.

Thus, in the United States it governs the distribution of the means of production—land, labor, natural resources, technology, and capital. "Market exchange refers to the organizational process of purchase and sale at money price" (Dalton 1967). With market exchange, items are bought and sold with an eye to maximizing profit, and value is determined by the **law of supply and demand** (things cost more the scarcer they are and the more people want them).

Bargaining is characteristic of market-principle exchanges. The buyer and seller strive to maximize—to get their "money's worth." Bargaining doesn't require that the buyer and seller meet. Consumers bargain whenever they shop around or use advertisements in their decision making.

Redistribution

Redistribution is the dominant exchange principle in chiefdoms and some nonindustrial states and in states with managed economies. Redistribution operates when goods, services, or their equivalent move from the local level to a center. In states, the center is often a capital or a regional collection point. In chiefdoms, it may be a storehouse near the chief's residence. Products move through a hierarchy of officials for storage at the center. Along the way officials and their dependents consume some of them, but the exchange principle here is *re*distribution. The flow of goods eventually reverses direction— out from the center, down through the hierarchy, and back to the common people.

Reciprocity

Reciprocity is exchange between social equals, who are normally related by kinship, marriage, or another close personal tie. Because it occurs between social equals, it is dominant in the more egalitarian societies—among foragers, cultivators, and pastoralists living in bands and tribes. There are three degrees of reciprocity: generalized, balanced, and negative (Sahlins 1968, 1972; Service 1966). These may be imagined as areas on a continuum defined by these questions:

1. How closely related are the parties to the exchange?
2. How quickly are gifts reciprocated?

Generalized reciprocity, the purest form of reciprocity, is characteristic of exchanges between closely related people. In **balanced reciprocity,** social distance increases, as does the need to reciprocate. In **negative reciprocity,** social distance is greatest and reciprocation is most urgent.

With generalized reciprocity, someone gives to another person and expects nothing concrete or immediate in return. Such exchanges (including parental gift giving in contemporary North America) are not primarily economic transactions but expressions of personal relationships. Most parents don't keep accounts of every penny they spend on their children. They merely hope that the children will respect their culture's customs involving love, honor, loyalty, and other obligations to parents.

Among foragers, generalized reciprocity tends to govern exchanges. People routinely share with other band members (Bird-David 1992; Kent 1992). A study of the !Kung San found that 40 percent of the population contributed little to the food supply (Lee 1974). Children, teenagers, and people over sixty depended on other people for their food. Despite the high proportion of dependents, the average worker hunted or gathered less than half as much (twelve to nineteen hours a week) as the average American works. Nonetheless, there was always food because different people worked on different days.

So strong is the ethic of reciprocal sharing that most foragers lack an expression for "thank you." To offer thanks would be impolite because it would imply that a particular act of sharing, which is the keystone of egalitarian society, was unusual. Among the Semai, foragers of central Malaysia (Dentan 1979), to express gratitude would suggest surprise at the hunter's generosity or success (Harris 1974).

Balanced reciprocity applies to exchanges between people who are more distantly related than are members of the same band or household. In a tribal society, for example, a man presents a gift to someone in another village. The recipient may be a cousin, a trading partner, or a brother's fictive kinsman. The giver expects something in return. This may not come immediately, but the social relationship will be strained if there is no reciprocation.

Foragers and members of tribes also have negative reciprocity, which applies to people on the fringes of their social systems. To people who live in a world of close personal relations, exchanges with outsiders are full of ambiguity and distrust. Exchange is one way of establishing friendly relations with outsiders, but when trade begins, the relationship is still tentative. The initial exchange is as close to being purely economic as anything that ever happens in tribal society. People want something back immediately, and just as in market economies,

Sharing the fruits of production, which is the keystone of egalitarian societies, has also been a goal of socialist nations, such as China. These workers in Yunnan province strive for an equal distribution of meat.

they try to get the best possible immediate return for their investment.

One example of negative reciprocity is silent trade or barter between the Mbuti "pygmy" foragers of the African equatorial forest and neighboring horticultural villagers. There is no personal contact during the exchange. A Mbuti hunter leaves game, honey, or another forest product at a customary site. Villagers collect it and leave crops in exchange. The parties can bargain silently. If one feels that the return is insufficient, he or she simply leaves it at the trading site. If the other party wants to continue trade, it will be increased.

As people exchange with more and more distantly related individuals, they move along the continuum from generalized toward negative reciprocity. However, because the differences are of degree rather than kind, exchange relationships may shift as personal relationships change. A good example, which also illustrates the role of exchange in establishing alliances, comes from the Yanomami. Two hostile villages may initiate an alliance by beginning reciprocal exchange. The first step is an exchange of products in which each of the villages specializes. The next step is the exchange of food and hospitality, with each village inviting the other to a feast.

Exchanges have now moved from negative reciprocity, in which hostility, fear, distrust, immediate return, and equivalence are characteristic, toward balanced reciprocity, in which gifts may be returned later. Mutual feasting doesn't guarantee that an alliance between villages will last, but it is a closer relationship than is one based on intervillage trade of arrows, pots, and hammocks.

The final stage in establishing an alliance between two Yanomami villages is intermarriage. Many Yanomami marriages result from an arrangement called *sister exchange*. If two men have unmarried sisters, each man marries the other's sister. The notion of equivalence operates here: a sister is given "in exchange for" a wife. Once the marriages take place, the brother-in-law relationship becomes one of generalized reciprocity, because a close personal relationship has been established.

However, Yanomami villages can fall out of alliance the way modern North Americans fall out of love. Villages may split and stop exchanging spouses. They go on feasting for a while and still trade. Finally, one village may invite the other to a "treacherous feast" in which the hosts attack and try to kill their guests. With the alliance ended, there is no longer even negative reciprocity. Instead, there is open hostility and feuding (Chagnon 1992).

Coexistence of Modes of Exchange

In contemporary North America, the market principle governs the means of production and most exchanges, for example, those involving consumer goods. We also have redistribution, but it is not highly developed. Much of our tax money goes to support the government, but some of it comes back as social services, education, Medicare, and road building. We also have reciprocal exchanges. Generalized reciprocity characterizes the relationship between parents and children. However, even here the dominant market mentality surfaces in comments about the high cost of raising children and in the stereotypical statement of the disappointed parent: "We gave you everything money could buy."

Exchanges of gifts, cards, and invitations exemplify reciprocity, usually balanced. Everyone has heard remarks like "They invited us to their daughter's wedding, so when ours gets married, we'll have to invite them" and "They've been here for dinner three times and haven't invited us yet. I don't think we should ask them back until they do." Such precise balancing of reciprocity would be out of place in a foraging band, where resources are communal (common to all) and daily sharing based on generalized reciprocity is an essential ingredient of social life and survival.

It often takes time for Western ethnographers to get used to generalized reciprocity in the societies they study. For example, among the Betsileo (Kottak 1980) and Merina (Bloch 1971) of Madagascar, men routinely march up to covillagers and demand chewing tobacco. Kin are expected to share with one another. This test of kin loyalty, which none dares refuse, helps maintain village solidarity.

Once anthropologists are accepted within the community, they often find *their* possessions disappearing at an alarming rate. People are using up the ethnographer's resources just as they do with those of their own relatives. Anthropologists gradually learn that our culture's "stealing" is another's kin-based sharing. The ethnographer is simply being treated as part of community life. Of course, he or she must also devise a way of preserving necessary items for the remainder of the field stay.

MONEY AND SPHERES OF EXCHANGE

Money is of such overwhelming importance to us that it is difficult to conceive of its absence. However, it is not a cultural universal. Money has several different functions (Bohannan 1963). First, it may be a *means of exchange*. In contemporary North America it is the most common means of exchange. We don't give food to a bank teller and expect our accounts to be credited or give a cashier a dozen roses in exchange for a steak. We give money in exchange for food.

Second, money may function as a *standard of value*. Indeed, it is the main standard we use to evaluate what something is worth. A washing machine is worth $400, not 225 chickens or 4 pigs. Third, money functions as a *means of payment*. We pay money to the government, often not in exchange for anything but simply to fulfill an obligation, such as paying a parking ticket.

Because the currencies of modern nations serve all three functions, each is a **general-purpose money**. Any currency that doesn't serve all three functions is a **special-purpose money** (Bohannan 1963). In some societies a cow is a means of exchange but not a standard of value. To understand the difference between general-purpose and special-purpose money, we need to discuss multicentric exchange systems.

Many tribal societies have **multicentric exchange systems**, or systems which are organized into different categories or spheres. Bohannan (1955) found that the Tiv of Nigeria had such a system. They assigned relative value to exchanges and divided them into three spheres: subsistence, prestige, and marriage partners. The Tiv thought that items within a given sphere should be exchanged only for each other. The subsistence sphere included food, small livestock, and tools. The prestige sphere encompassed slaves, cattle, large bolts of white cloth, and metal bars. The third sphere included only one ''item''—marriage partners.

Although the number of spheres and the items they contain vary from society to society, multicentric economies are common in tribes and chiefdoms. How do they work? Exchanges for items in the same sphere are called **conveyances**, which are considered normal and appropriate. Tiv examples include yams for pots (subsistence conveyances) and cloth or brass rods for slaves (prestige conveyances). Like Yanomami men, who exchange sisters as marriage partners, Tiv men were found to control the marriage system. Tiv society had a system of wardship in which men tried to obtain female wards in order to arrange marriages for them. In return, the men received wives of their own.

Viewing conveyances as proper, the Tiv avoided exchanging higher-sphere for lower-sphere items. Occasionally, however, exchanges between different spheres, called **conversions**, did take place, for example, a brass rod for food. The people who managed to convert subsistence into prestige items were pleased, whereas those who had to do the contrary were shamed.

We can return now to the matter of money. Despite their multicentric economy, the Tiv had a general-purpose money consisting of metal bars. However, this general-purpose money worked in just one sphere—the prestige sphere. Contemporary nations, participating in an international economy, have eliminated spheres of exchange. General-purpose currencies regulate the entire modern exchange system.

POTLATCHING

Spheres of exchange are widespread because they are cultural mechanisms that help populations adapt to their environments. In societies without banks, the higher spheres serve some of the same functions that banks do in modern nations. In times of plenty, people convert subsistence surpluses into higher categories. In times of need, they reconvert the surpluses back into subsistence goods. In multicentric economies, as in our own, people save for a rainy day. However, the context of their saving is personal, and the situations in which deposits and withdrawals take place are social and ceremonial. Consider the following case.

One of the most famous cultural practices studied by ethnographers is the **potlatch**, which was widely practiced by tribes of the North Pacific Coast of North America, including the Tlingit, Salish and **Kwakiutl** of Washington and British Columbia. The potlatch, which some tribes still practice (sometimes as a memorial to the dead) (Kan 1986, 1989), was a festive event. Assisted by members of their communities, sponsors gave away food, blankets, pieces of copper, and other items. In return for this, they

Billy Frank, Jr., who has been called the Martin Luther King, Jr., of Native Americans, recently received the Albert Schweitzer Prize for Humanitarianism. Mr. Frank's efforts have been on behalf of his people, the Nisqually Indians of Washington state, whose traditional economy, based on salmon fishing, has been threatened by whites. Billy Frank's efforts helped produce the Boldt decision of 1974, granting the Nisqually half the salmon caught in the Puget Sound area. The Nisqually are one of the traditional potlatching tribes of the North Pacific coast. Their foraging economy, based on productive salmon fishing in Puget Sound area rivers, was threatened by competition with white fishermen and ecological damage from logging and dams.

Frank's Landing, Wash.—Turning off his car phone, Billy Frank Jr. pointed to a tree, a weathered skeleton in the bog of the Nisqually River delta. It was there, on Christmas morning 1854, that the Indians of southern Puget Sound gave up 2.2 million acres to the United States Government.

The treaty tree is dying, but the people who have lived near this river off and on for nearly 10,000 years are not. That, in itself, is a miracle of sorts to Mr. Frank.

"Hey, how about this," he said. "We're alive!" He clapped his hands and laughed. "They tried to make welders out of us and they tried to make barbers out of us, but the Indian people survived," he said.

He is 61 years old, a husband, the father of three sons, and he has a face that belongs on a woodcut. In this corner of Puget Sound it is as familiar as Mount Rainier, the volcano that holds glaciers from a thousand years of storms.

Last month, Mr. Frank, a Nisqually Indian who has spent at least as much time in jail as Columbus spent on his first voyage to the New World, was awarded the Albert Schweitzer Prize for Humanitarianism. Past winners include President Jimmy Carter, the former Surgeon General C. Everett Koop, and the author Norman Cousins. The prize, with $10,000, is given by the Alexander von Humboldt Foundation of New York and administered by Johns Hopkins University. The prize was a recognition of Mr. Frank's lifetime spent on the Nisqually River and in the courts trying to save the salmon and the Indians, whose fates are intertwined, a fight that still faces long odds.

"We've been in bad shape ever since Columbus landed," Mr. Frank said, tossing a twig into the swirl of the Nisqually. "But that's O.K. You can't go back. We must live in this modern world and do what we can to keep it livable."

Don't expect boilerplate Euro-bashing from Mr. Frank, who has been called the Martin Luther King of American Indians. Sure, he gets his licks in, pointing to Interstate 5, the eight-lane freeway that runs the length of the West Coast and through a favorite fishing spot. "An eagle used to live there, right where traffic is starting to back up now," he said.

But Mr. Frank long ago made peace with his bitterness. Give him a day when the sky is scrubbed clean and the cottonwoods are gold, and he's Robert Bly without the belly.

When a bunch of Really Important People get together in a conference room, you can always tell Mr. Frank, even from afar. Amid the governors and corporate executives, all tasseled loafers and silk ties, he's the one with the long pony tail, the gold salmon medallion, the open-necked shirt. And he's the one with the scars—nicks, cuts and slash marks—from a lifetime of being harassed by people who don't like Indians and from an all-season outdoor life.

On a recent day, he sat on the bank of the river in this Indian hamlet that carries his family name. Billy Frank's father, who lived to be 104, used to tell his son that when the salmon were gone, there would be no more Indians. Billy Frank was planning to eat turkey for Thanksgiving, like most Americans, but his mind was on salmon.

A good run of coho salmon was making its way up the Nisqually, a river born in the glaciers of Mount Rainier and bordered by the sprawl of nearly three million people in the Puget Sound area. There is a small Indian school here, where the dialect of the Nisqually is taught. It is likely that none of this—the salmon, the school, the relative prosperity of the 2,000 remaining Nisqually people—would have been possible without Billy Frank Jr.

"I never gave up," he said. "Getting beat up, my tires slashed, shot at, arrested, cursed, cussed, spit on. You name it, I still don't hate anyone."

One tribe in a sea of sorrow is nothing in the grand scheme of things. But what Mr. Frank has done, his admirers say, is to fuse outrage with hope. What's more, he has accomplishments that will outlive him.

When Mr. Frank looks out at the river, he sees the currents of history. Not just ghosts, but his own past. From the time he was 14 until he was 43, he was arrested more than 50 times on this river. In the later stages, celebrity protesters like Marlon Brando joined him. The crime was fishing.

Until about 130 years ago, the native people here could live for an entire year on the salmon they took in the fall runs. The stunning artwork of the Northwest Coast Indians has been attributed, in large part, to the amount of time they had on their hands because gathering food was so simple. As regular as the seasons, millions of salmon returned to the rivers of

Billy Frank, Jr., a recent recipient of the Albert Schweitzer Prize for Humanitarianism for his efforts on behalf of the Nisqually Indians of Washington state, whose salmon fishing has been threatened by whites.

the Northwest. When the Medicine Creek Treaty was signed in 1854, it guaranteed that the Indians would have the right to fish at all "the usual and accustomed grounds" of their ancestors.

Citing the treaty, Billy Frank and his father would paddle out on the river here at Frank's Landing. No sooner would they begin pulling in fish than the state game wardens would arrest them as poachers, for fishing out of season and without licenses. Mr. Frank tried to use the treaty as a defense. But it did not mean much until Mr. Frank, joined by members of other tribes, got into Federal Court. Three years of litigation produced the 1974 Boldt decision, giving the tribes the right to half of all the salmon caught in the Puget Sound area. It was one of the most far-reaching court decisions in the modern history of Indian relations.

Tribes that had all but disappeared, their members falling into the familiar traps of alcoholism and despair, were revitalized by the salmon decision. The mysterious fish that return to the waters of their hatching to spawn are as necessary to the existence of Northwest Indians as the air the people breathe, the Supreme Court wrote.

But random acts of violence by white fishermen who felt their livelihoods threatened by the court decision followed Mr. Frank

for nearly a decade after the Boldt decision.

"When I think of all the days I got beat up, I can remember what my dad said, that these people are trying to kill us," Mr. Frank said. "But we got through it. We did. We did!"

After a while, Mr. Frank pointed out that all the lawsuits in the world were not going to create more salmon. He won written promises from timber companies to stop logging near salmon streams. He got the state and Federal governments to agree to protect certain fish runs. He lobbied the United Nations to pass a resolution banning the huge drift nets that Asian fishermen use to drag the ocean indiscriminately for fish.

Today, as chairman of the Northwest Indian Fisheries Commission, Mr. Frank helps make many of the decisions that used to be made by the game wardens who arrested him. He counts senators, governors and corporate leaders among his friends. But for all his honors and friends in high places, he still sees himself as the outlaw of Frank's Landing.

He wants to use his visibility to remind the nation of a people who have long been virtually invisible. It's fine, he says, that movies like "Dances With Wolves" or "The Last of the Mohicans" are trying to balance Hollywood's stereotypical depiction of Indians, but that won't change public policy.

"Most of the tribes are so poor because they just don't have anything," he said. "An Indian needs his river, his mountain, wherever he prays, so when he comes back from wherever he's been, there's a place to go. At least I have a river I can sit by. A lot of Indians don't have a river."

The salmon, lifeblood of the Puget Sound Indians, are in trouble. Hydroelectric dams, which provide the West Coast with the cheapest electricity of any place in the country, have blocked countless fish runs and thus prevented the fish from spawning.

"When an electric light is turned on in Seattle, a salmon comes flying out," Mr. Frank said. "When a room is air-conditioned in Los Angeles, they're doing that on the back of the salmon."

He strolls down the river bank, near the school. A little girl runs up to Mr. Frank and hugs him. Then she runs to the shade of an ancient maple tree. A friend approaches, kidding him about cutting part of his steel-gray pony tail off, though it still falls well below his shoulders.

"See, I believe in dreams," Mr. Frank said. That's why I never get too mad for too long. This school, that was a dream. These salmon, this river, dreams. But here they are. How about that?"

Source: Timothy Egan, "Indians and Salmon: Making Nature Whole," *The New York Times*, November 26, 1992, B1.

Piling up blankets to burn in a Kwakiutl potlatch on Vancouver Island in British Columbia. As European trade goods poured in, some Kwakiutl hosts became so wealthy that they destroyed most of their property. They even burned down their houses in impressive displays of the conversion of wealth into prestige.

got prestige. To give a potlatch enhanced one's reputation. Prestige increased with the lavishness of the potlatch, the value of the goods given away in it.

Within the spreading world capitalist economy of the nineteenth century, the potlatching tribes, particularly the Kwakiutl, began to trade with Europeans (fur for blankets, for example), and their wealth increased as a result. Simultaneously, a huge proportion of the population died from previously unknown diseases brought by the Europeans. The increased wealth from trade flowed into a drastically reduced population. With many of the traditional sponsors dead, the Kwakiutl extended the right to give a potlatch to the entire population, and this stimulated intense competition for prestige. Given trade, increased wealth, and a decreased population, the Kwakiutl also started converting wealth into prestige by *destroying* wealth items such as blankets and pieces of copper (Vayda 1961/1968).

Both the Salish and the Kwakiutl had multicentric economies with a subsistence sphere and a wealth sphere. The third sphere, the highest one, contained a nonmaterial item—prestige. Included in the subsistence sphere were several foods. The potlatching tribes were hunters and gatherers, but compared with other foragers, they were more like food producers. They lived in sedentary tribes and chiefdoms rather than in bands. In contrast to most foragers, their environments were not marginal. They had access to a wide variety of land and sea resources. Their most important foods were salmon, herring, candlefish, berries, mountain goats, seals, and porpoises (Piddocke 1969).

There were some differences in the diets of the Salish and the Kwakiutl, and their wealth spheres also differed. Among the Salish, blankets, shell ornaments, hide shirts, and fine baskets were wealth items. The Kwakiutl wealth sphere included slaves, canoes, skins, blankets, and pieces of copper. Nevertheless, people in both societies could convert wealth into prestige by giving away (or destroying, among the Kwakiutl) wealth items at potlatches.

Scholars once regarded Kwakiutl potlatching as economically wasteful behavior, the result of an irrational drive for social status and prestige. They stressed the destructiveness of the Kwakiutl to support their contention that in some societies people strive irrationally to maximize prestige—even by destroying valuable resources.

However, a more recent interpretation views potlatching not as wasteful but as a useful cultural adaptive mechanism. This view not only helps us understand potlatching, it also has comparative value because it helps us understand similar feasts and multicentric economies throughout the world. This is the new interpretation: *Customs such as the potlatch are adaptations to alternating periods of local abundance and shortage.*

How did this work? The overall natural environment of the North Pacific Coast is favorable, but resources fluctuate from year to year and place to place. Salmon and herring aren't equally abundant every year in a given locality. One village can have a good year while another is experiencing a bad one. Later their fortunes reverse. In this context, the multicentric economies of the Kwakiutl and Salish had adaptive value, and the potlatch was not an irrational competitive display.

A village enjoying an especially good year had a surplus of subsistence items, which it could exchange for wealth, and wealth could be converted into prestige. Potlatches distributed food and wealth to other communities that needed it. In return, the sponsors and their villages got prestige. The decision to potlatch was determined by the health of the local economy. If there had been a subsistence surplus, and thus a buildup of wealth over several good years, the village could afford a potlatch to convert food and wealth into prestige.

The adaptive value of intercommunity feasting becomes clear when we consider what happened when a formerly prosperous village had a bad year. Its people started accepting invitations to potlatches in villages that were doing better. The tables were turned as the temporarily rich became temporarily poor and vice versa. The newly needy accepted food and wealth items. They were willing to receive rather than bestow gifts and thus to relinquish some of their stored-up prestige. Later, if the village's fortunes continued to decline, its people could exchange wealth items for food, for example, slaves for herring or canoes for cherries (Vayda 1961/1968). They hoped that their luck would eventually improve so that the process of converting up could resume.

Note that potlatching also impeded the development of socioeconomic stratification. Wealth relinquished or destroyed was converted into a nonmaterial item—prestige. Under capitalism we reinvest our profits (rather than burning our cash)

with the hope of making an additional profit. However, the potlatching tribes were content to destroy their surpluses rather than use them to widen the social distance between themselves and fellow tribe members.

Multicentric economies and regional systems of intervillage feasting can therefore have adaptive value. Similar to our banks, their wealth and prestige spheres are places where people can store surpluses. Multicentric economies also provide for communities in need. As fortunes fluctuate, food is converted into wealth and prestige, wealth is converted into prestige, prestige is converted back into wealth and food, and wealth is converted back into food.

The potlatch linked local groups along the North Pacific Coast into a regional alliance and exchange network. Potlatching and multicentric exchange had adaptive functions, regardless of the motivations of the individual participants. The anthropologists who stressed rivalry for prestige were not wrong. They were merely emphasizing motivations at the expense of an analysis of economic and ecological systems.

The use of feasts to enhance individual and community reputations and to redistribute wealth is not peculiar to the Kwakiutl and the Salish. Competitive but adaptive feasting is widely characteristic of tribal economies. Among foragers in marginal areas, resources are too meager to support feasting on such a level. Further along the evolutionary continuum, chiefdoms and states have more effective means of distributing resources among local groups.

SUMMARY

Economic anthropologists study systems of production, distribution, and consumption cross-culturally. Economics has been defined as the science of allocating scarce means to alternative ends. Western economists assume that the notion of scarcity is universal—which it isn't—and that in making choices, people strive to maximize personal profit. However, in nonindustrial societies, as in our own, people maximize values other than individual profit. Furthermore, people often lack free choice in allocating their resources.

In bands and tribes, people invest in subsistence, replacement, social, and ceremonial funds. States add a rent fund: People must share their output with government

officials and other social superiors. In states, the obligation to pay rent often becomes primary, and family subsistence may suffer.

Strategies of adaptation are actually systems of production. In nonindustrial societies, production is personal. The relations of production are aspects of continuous social relationships. One acquires rights to resources through membership in bands, descent groups, villages, and other social units, not impersonally through purchase and sale. Labor is also recruited through personal ties. Work is merely one aspect of social relationships that are expressed in a variety of social and ceremonial contexts.

Manufacturing specialization can exist in tribal societies, promoting trade and alliance between groups. In nonindustrial societies there is usually a personal relationship between producer and commodity, in contrast to the alienation of labor, product, and management in industrial economies.

Besides production, economic anthropologists study and compare exchange systems. The three principles of exchange are the market principle, redistribution, and reciprocity. The market principle, based on supply and demand and the profit motive, is dominant in states. Its characteristics are impersonal purchase and sale and bargaining. Redistribution is the characteristic exchange mode in chiefdoms, some nonindustrial states, and managed economies. Goods are collected at a central place, and some of them are eventually given back, or redistributed, to the people.

Reciprocity governs exchanges between social equals. It is the characteristic mode of exchange in bands and tribes. There are different degrees of reciprocity. With generalized reciprocity, there is no immediate expectation of return. With balanced reciprocity, which is character-

istic of exchanges between more distantly related people, donors expect their gifts to be returned, although not immediately. Exchanges on the fringes of the social system are governed by negative reciprocity. As with the market principle, there is concern about immediate return, as well as bargaining. Reciprocity, redistribution, and the market principle may coexist in a society, but the primary exchange mode is the one that allocates the means of production.

A general-purpose money is a standard of value, a means of exchange, and a means of payment. Special-purpose monies are currencies that don't serve all these functions. Multicentric exchange systems, which are common in tribal societies, are organized into ranked spheres of exchange (subsistence, wealth, and prestige). Multicentric economies have adaptive relevance: conversions of subsistence goods to wealth or prestige are ways of saving in tribal societies. Conversions to such nonmaterial items as prestige also impede the emergence of socioeconomic stratification.

GLOSSARY

balanced reciprocity: See *generalized reciprocity.*

ceremonial fund: Resources invested in ceremonial or ritual expenses or activity.

comparative economics: The study of economic systems in different societies.

conversion: Exchange between different spheres of a multicentric economy.

conveyance: Exchange within the same sphere of a multicentric economy.

economizing: The rational allocation of scarce means (or resources) to alternative ends (or uses); often considered the subject matter of economics.

economy: A population's system of production, distribution, and consumption of resources.

generalized reciprocity: Principle that characterizes exchanges between closely related individuals: As social distance increases, reciprocity becomes *balanced* and finally *negative.*

general-purpose money: Currency that functions as a means of exchange, a standard of value, and a means of payment.

Kwakiutl: A potlatching society on the North Pacific Coast of North America.

market principle: Profit-oriented principle of exchange that dominates in states, particularly industrial states. Goods and services are bought and sold, and values are determined by supply and demand.

means (or factors) of production: Land, labor, technology, and capital—major productive resources.

multicentric exchange system: Economy organized into different categories or spheres.

negative reciprocity: See *generalized reciprocity.*

peasant: Small-scale agriculturalist living in a state with rent fund obligations.

potlatch: Competitive feast among Indians on the North Pacific Coast of North America.

reciprocity: One of the three principles of exchange. Governs exchange between social equals; major exchange mode in band and tribal societies.

redistribution: Major exchange mode of chiefdoms, many archaic states, and some states with managed economies.

rent fund: Scarce resources that a social inferior is required to render to an individual or agency that is superior politically or economically.

replacement fund: Scarce resources invested in technology and other items essential to production.

social fund: Scarce resources invested to assist friends, relatives, in-laws, and neighbors.

special-purpose money: Currency that serves only one or two of the three functions associated with general-purpose money.

subsistence fund: Scarce resources invested to provide food in order to replace the calories expended in daily activity.

supply and demand, law of: Economic rule that things cost more the scarcer they are and the more people want them.

STUDY QUESTIONS

1. What do economists mean by *economizing?*
2. What are the main differences between the economies of bands and tribes and peasant economies?
3. What are some of the main contrasts between industrial and nonindustrial economies?
4. What are the main differences between reciprocity, redistribution, and the market principle?
5. What examples can you give from your own culture to illustrate each of these three types of exchange?
6. What are the main differences between the three degrees of reciprocity?
7. How are multicentric exchange systems adaptive?
8. What were the adaptive functions of the potlatch?

SUGGESTED ADDITIONAL READING

CLAMMER, J., ED.
1976 *The New Economic Anthropology.* New York: St. Martin's Press. Essays link economic anthropology to problems affecting Third World nations and to Marxist analysis.

GOODY, J.
1977 *Production and Reproduction: A Comparative Study of the Domestic Domain.* New York: Cambridge University Press. Relationships between agriculture, property transmission, and domestic relations in Africa, Asia, and Europe.

HARRIS, M.
1974 *Cows, Pigs, Wars, and Witches: The Riddles of Culture.* New York: Random House. Good discussion of different exchange systems.

INGOLD, T., D. RICHES, AND J. WOODBURN
1991 *Hunters and Gatherers,* v. 2. New York: Berg (St. Martin's). Considers economic and political issues among foragers, including their property, ideology, and power relations.

LECLAIR, E. E., AND H. K. SCHNEIDER, EDS.
1968 (orig. 1961). *Economic Anthropology: Readings in Theory and Analysis.* New York: Holt, Rinehart & Winston. Defines the "substantive" approach in economic anthropology and advocates the study of exchange systems in different societies.

MAUSS, M.
1954 (orig. 1925). *The Gift: Forms and Functions of Exchange in Archaic Societies.* New York: Free Press. Uses comparative data to emphasize the positive values of giving. Has influenced generations of anthropologists, especially French.

PLATTNER, S., ED.
1989 *Economic Anthropology.* Stanford, CA: Stanford University Press. Recent comprehensive text in economic anthropology, including original articles by twelve authors on bands, tribes, states, peasants, and industrial economies.

WOLF, E. R.
1966 *Peasants.* Englewood Cliffs, NJ: Prentice-Hall. Fascinating theoretical and comparative introduction to peasants.

C H A P T E R   1 6

KINSHIP AND DESCENT

The kinds of societies that anthropologists have traditionally studied have stimulated a strong interest in systems of kinship and marriage. Kinship—as vitally important in daily life in nonindustrial societies as work outside the home is in our own—has become an essential part of anthropology because of its importance to the people we study. We are ready to take a closer look at the systems of kinship and descent that have organized human life for much of our history. We consider actual kin groups, along with the more personal matter of how people think about kinship and classify their relatives.

KINSHIP GROUPS AND KINSHIP CALCULATION

Anthropologists study the kinship *groups* that are significant in a society as well as **kinship calculation**—the system by which people in a society reckon kin relationships. Ethnographers quickly recognize social divisions (groups) within any society they study. During field work, they learn about significant groups by observing their activities and composition. People often live in the same village or neighborhood or work, pray, or celebrate together because they are related in some way. To understand the social structure, an ethnographer must investigate such kin ties. For example, the most significant local groups may consist of descendants of the same grandfather. These people may live in neighboring houses, farm adjoining fields, and help each other in everyday tasks. Other groups, perhaps based on other kin links, get together less often.

To study kinship calculation, an ethnographer must first determine the word or words for different types of "relatives" used in a particular language and then ask questions such as, "Who are your relatives?" Kinship, like race and gender (discussed extensively in other chapters), is culturally constructed. This means that some biological kin are considered to be relatives whereas others are not. Through questioning, the ethnographer discovers the specific genealogical relationships between "relatives" and the person who has named them—the **ego.** By posing the same questions to several informants, the ethnographer learns about the extent and direction of kinship calculation in that society. The ethnographer also begins to understand the relationship between kinship calculation and kinship groups—how people use kinship to create and maintain personal ties and to join social groups. In several of the kinship charts that follow, the black square labeled "ego" (Latin for *I*) identifies the person whose kinship calculation is being examined.

Biological Kin Types and Kinship Calculation

At this point we may distinguish between **kin terms** (the words used for different relatives in a particular language) and **biological kin types.** We designate biological kin types with the letters and symbols shown in Figure 16.1. *Biological kin type* refers to an actual genealogical relationship (e.g., father's brother) as opposed to a kin term (e.g., *uncle*).

Kin terms reflect the social construction of kinship

Figure 16.1 *Kinship symbols and biological kin type notation.*

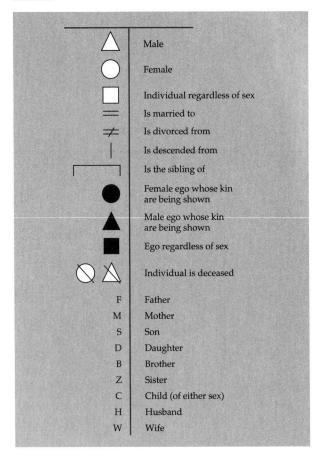

in a given culture. A kin term may (and usually does) lump together several genealogical relationships. In English, for instance, we use *father* primarily for one kin type—the genealogical father. However, *father* can be extended to an adoptive father or stepfather—and even to a priest. *Grandfather* includes mother's father and father's father. The term *cousin* lumps several kin types. Even the more specific *first cousin* includes mother's brother's son (MBS), mother's brother's daughter (MBD), mother's sister's son (MZS), mother's sister's daughter (MZD), father's brother's son (FBS), father's brother's daughter (FBD), father's sister's son (FZS), and father's sister's daughter (FZD). *First cousin* thus lumps together at least eight biological kin types.

Uncle encompasses mother's and father's brothers, and *aunt* includes mother's and father's sisters. We also use *uncle* and *aunt* for the spouses of our "blood" aunts and uncles. We use the same term for mother's brother and father's brother because we perceive them as being the same sort of relative. Calling them *uncles*, we distinguish between them and another kin type, F, whom we call *Father, Dad,* or *Pop*. In many societies, however, it is common to call a father and a father's brother by the same term. Later we'll see why.

In the United States and Canada, the *nuclear family* (a kin group composed of parents and children residing together) continues to be the most important group based on kinship. This is true despite an increased incidence of single parenthood, divorce, and remarriage. The nuclear family's relative isolation from other kin groups in modern nations reflects geographical mobility within an industrial economy with sale of labor for cash. (The nuclear family is also the most important kin group in many foraging societies for reasons that will be discussed later.)

It's reasonable for North Americans to distinguish between relatives who belong to their nuclear families and those who don't. We are more likely to grow up with our parents than with our aunts or uncles. We tend to see our parents more often than we see our uncles and aunts, who may live in different towns and cities. We often inherit from our parents, but our cousins have first claim to inherit from our aunts and uncles. If our marriage is stable, we see our children daily as long as they remain at home. They are our heirs. We feel closer to them than to our nieces and nephews.

American kinship calculation and kin terminology reflect these social features. Thus the term *uncle* distinguishes between the kin types MB and FB on the one hand and the kin type F on the other. However, this term also lumps kin types together. We use the same term for MB and FB, two different kin types. We do this because American kinship calculation is **bilateral**—traced equally through males and females, for example, father and mother. Both kinds of uncle are brothers of one of our parents. We think of both as roughly the same kind of relative.

"No," you may object, "I'm closer to my mother's brother than to my father's brother." That may be. However, in a representative sample of American students, we would find a split, with some favoring one side and some favoring the other. We'd actually expect a bit of **matrilateral skewing**—a preference for relatives on the mother's side. This occurs because—for many reasons—when contemporary children are raised by just one parent, it's more likely to be the mother than the father. Thus, in the United States in 1990, 21.6 percent of all children lived in fatherless homes versus 3.1 percent residing in motherless homes and 72.5 percent living with both parents (*The World Almanac and Book of Facts* 1992, p. 944).

Bilateral kinship means that people tend to perceive kin links through males and females as being similar or equivalent. This bilaterality is expressed in interaction with, living with or near, and rights to inherit from relatives. We don't usually inherit from uncles, but if we do, there's about as much chance that we'll inherit from the father's brother as from the mother's brother. We don't usually live with either aunt, but if we do, the chances are about the same that it will be the father's sister as the mother's sister.

KIN GROUPS

The nuclear family is one kind of kin group that is widespread in human societies. Other kin groups include extended families and descent groups— lineages and clans. *Descent groups,* which are composed of people claiming common ancestry, are basic units in the social organization of nonindustrial food producers.

There are important differences between nuclear

families and descent groups. A descent group is *permanent*; a nuclear family lasts only as long as the parents and children remain together. Descent-group membership often is ascribed at birth (by a rule of patrilineal or matrilineal descent, as discussed in the chapter "Bands and Tribes") and lifelong. In contrast, most people belong to at least two nuclear families at different times in their lives. They are born into a family consisting of their parents and siblings. When they reach adulthood, they may marry and establish a nuclear family that includes the spouse and eventually the children. Since most societies permit divorce, some people establish more than one family through marriage.

Anthropologists distinguish between the **family of orientation** (the family in which one is born and grows up) and the **family of procreation** (formed when one marries and has children). From the individual's point of view, the critical relationships are with parents and siblings in the family of orientation and with spouse and children in the family of procreation.

Defining Marriage

Marriage (discussed more fully in the next chapter) is often the basis of a new nuclear family. No definition of marriage is broad enough to apply easily to all societies. A commonly quoted definition comes from *Notes and Queries in Anthropology:*

Marriage is a union between a man and a woman such that the children born to the woman are recognized as legitimate offspring of both partners. (Royal Anthropological Institute 1951, p. 111)

This definition may describe marriage in contemporary North America, but it isn't universally valid for several reasons. For example, some nations recognize homosexual marriages. Also, in many societies marriages unite more than two spouses. Here we speak of *plural marriages,* as when a woman weds a group of brothers—an arrangement called *fraternal polyandry* that is characteristic of certain Himalayan cultures. In certain societies (usually patrilineal), a woman may marry another woman, in a nonsexual union. This can happen in West Africa when a successful market woman (perhaps already married to a man) wants a wife of her own to take care of her home and children while she works outside (Amadiume 1987).

In the African Sudan a Nuer woman can marry a woman if her father has only daughters but no male heirs, who are necessary if his patrilineage is to survive. He may ask his daughter to stand as a son in order to take a bride. This is a symbolic and social relationship rather than a sexual one. Indeed, the woman who serves as a man may already be living in another village as a man's wife!

The Nuer woman doesn't live with her "wife," who has sex with a man or men until she becomes pregnant. What's important here is *social* rather than

Besides childrearing, several kinds of rights, obligations, and benefits (sexual, economic, property, and inheritance) may be allocated by forms of marriage. Here two gay men register their (marriage) partnership at San Francisco's city hall.

biological paternity; we see again how kinship is socially constructed. The bride's children are considered the legitimate offspring of her "husband," who is biologically a woman but socially a man, and the descent line continues.

The British anthropologist Edmund Leach (1955) despaired of ever arriving at a universal definition of marriage. Instead, he suggested that depending on the society, several different kinds of rights are allocated by institutions classified as marriage. These rights vary from one culture to another, and no single one is widespread enough to provide a basis for defining marriage.

According to Leach, marriage can do the following:

1. Establish the legal father of a woman's children and the legal mother of a man's
2. Give either or both spouses a monopoly in the sexuality of the other
3. Give either or both spouses rights to the labor of the other
4. Give either or both spouses rights over the other's property
5. Establish a joint fund of property—a partnership—for the benefit of the children
6. Establish a socially significant "relationship of affinity" between spouses and their relatives

This list highlights particular aspects of marriage in different cultural contexts. However, I believe that we need some definition—even a loose one—to identify an institution found in some form in all human societies. I suggest the following:

> **Marriage** is a socially approved relationship between a socially recognized male (the husband) and a socially recognized female (the wife) such that the children born to the wife are accepted as the offspring of both husband and wife. The husband may be the actual **genitor** (biological father) of the children or only the **pater** (socially recognized father).

THE NUCLEAR FAMILY

Because marriage is a cultural universal, necessary for the formation of a nuclear family, some anthropologists argue that the nuclear family itself is universal. G. P. Murdock (1949), for example, viewed the nuclear family as universal because, he argued, its component relationships (wife-husband and parent-child) fulfill four essential social functions: sexual, reproductive, economic, and educational. Unlike Murdock, most contemporary anthropologists recognize that nuclear family organization is widespread but not universal. In certain societies, the nuclear family is rare or nonexistent. In other cultures, the nuclear family has no special role in social life. Other social units—most notably descent groups and extended families—can assume most or all of the functions otherwise associated with the nuclear family. In other words, there are many alternatives to nuclear family organization.

Sex

Murdock argued that because the nuclear family includes the husband-wife relationship, it fulfills a sexual function. More accurately, it is marriage that has a sexual function—granting social approval to regular mating. (Many societies also permit premarital and extramarital sex.) Although marriage is a cultural universal, it doesn't always lead to the same kind of family organization.

Reproduction

Murdock viewed the nuclear family as necessary for a society's reproduction, but again, reproduction is better seen as a function of marriage, which legitimizes children and thus provides them with social rights. However, we may note certain exceptions.

In most societies, most adult men and women marry and become parents. However, in certain Caribbean island societies, many women head households with no permanently resident husband-father. We call these *matrifocal* families or households because the mother (*mater*) is the household head.

The Trans-Fly region of Papua–New Guinea is the homeland of several homosexual tribes. Here, although men must marry women, they prefer homosexual acts to heterosexual coitus with their wives. One of the Trans-Fly groups, the Etoro, are so disapproving of heterosexual intercourse that they prohibit it for more than 200 days annually (Kelly 1976). Men of the neighboring Marind-anim tribe (van Baal 1966) also prefer homosexuality, and their birth rate is so low that in order to reproduce

In certain Caribbean island societies, such as the Bahamas (shown here), many women head households with no permanently resident husband-father. These are called matrifocal *families because the mother is the household head.*

the population, villages must raid their neighbors. Many children who grow up to be Marind-anim have been captured in raids on other tribes rather than born into Marind-anim society.

Another exception to reproduction through marriage and the nuclear family is provided by the Nayars, who live on the Malabar Coast of southern India. Their kinship system is matrilineal (descent is traced only through females). Traditional Nayar marriages were mere formalities. Adolescent females went through a marriage ceremony with a man, after which the girl returned home, usually without having had sex with her husband. The man returned to his own household. Thereafter, Nayar women had many sexual partners. Children became members of the mother's household and kin group; they were not considered to be relatives of the biological father. Indeed, many Nayar children didn't even know who their father was. However, for children to be legitimate, a man, often neither the genitor nor the mother's original "husband," had to go through a ritual acknowledging paternity. Nayar society therefore reproduced itself biologically without the nuclear family.

Family Economics

The supposed universality of the nuclear family has also been attributed to an economic function related to the fact that all cultures have some kind of division of labor by gender. The nuclear family's eco-

nomic function is especially important in societies where it is a self-contained unit of production and consumption. However, the division of labor is often much more complex. Among the agricultural Betsileo of Madagascar, for example, traditional tasks are allocated by gender, age, and generation. Grandfathers have certain jobs, and adolescent boys and girls have others. In such agricultural settings, the nuclear family does not encompass in microcosm all the significant economic roles, as it may among foragers. Food-producing societies usually have larger kinship groups that bridge at least three generations.

Education

Education isn't the same thing as enculturation—the universal process by which children internalize their culture by learning how they are supposed to act. *Education* refers to the acquisition of more formal knowledge and normally occurs in a place called a *school*. Education exposes certain—not all—people in a society to a body of formal knowledge or lore. Studying education cross-culturally, we see that it is usually found in state-organized societies. Furthermore, education is a strategic resource to which there is differential access based on stratification. All nations have educational systems, but access to the full range of educational possibilities is always unequal.

There are exceptions to the correlation between

education and state-organized societies. Certain populations in West Africa, and even the Tiwi, foragers of northern Australia (Hart and Pilling 1960), traditionally had "bush" schools in the hinterland. Even here, however, there was differential access based on gender. Only Tiwi boys received formal instruction in tribal lore. By finishing bush school, Tiwi boys became men in a rite of passage from one social status to another.

It is clear that education is not normally a function of the nuclear family, as Murdock contended, but a function of a state or church institution. The nuclear family isn't even the exclusive enculturative agent. In modern societies it isn't just parents and siblings who transmit culture but friends, schoolmates, age peers, teachers, and neighbors.

The nuclear family's enculturative role is most prominent in societies that isolate the married couple and the nuclear family from other kin. In many cultures, however, grandparents, uncles, aunts, and other nonnuclear kin play important roles in childrearing. Among the Betsileo of Madagascar, for example, grandparents often spend more time with a child and have more to say about its upbringing than do its parents.

In summary, in cultures in which the nuclear family is the most important kin group, its sexual, reproductive, economic, and enculturative functions stand out. However, enculturation is never confined to the nuclear family, and in most societies economic activities are carried out by larger groups. In fact, in only two types of society does the nuclear family tend to be the most important kinship group: industrial nations and foraging societies. Why should such different economies have similar family organization?

Industrialism, Stratification, and Family Organization

For many Americans and Canadians, the nuclear family is the only well-defined kin group. Because family isolation arises from geographic mobility, which is associated with industrialism, a nuclear family focus is characteristic of many modern nations. Born into a family of orientation, North Americans leave home for work or college, and the break with parents is underway. Eventually most North Americans marry and start a family of procreation. Because less than 3 percent of the American popu-

In many cultures grandparents, uncles, aunts, and other nonnuclear kin play important roles in childrearing. Grandparents take an active role in child care in many parts of China. This extended family lives in China's Yunnan province.

lation now farms, most people aren't tied to the land. Selling our labor on the market, we often move to places where jobs are available.

Many married couples live hundreds of miles from their parents. Their jobs have determined where they live. Such a postmarital residence pattern is called **neolocality**: Married couples are expected to establish a new place of residence—a "home of their own." Among middle-class North Americans, neolocal residence is both a cultural preference and a statistical norm. Most middle-class Americans eventually establish households and nuclear families of their own.

Within stratified nations, value systems vary to some extent from class to class, and so does kinship. There are significant differences between middle-class, poorer, and richer North Americans. For example, in the lower class the incidence of **expanded family households** (those which include nonnuclear relatives) is greater than it is in the middle class. When an expanded family household includes three or more generations, it is an **extended family**. Another type of expanded family is the **collateral household**, which includes siblings and their spouses and children.

The higher proportion of expanded family households in certain North American ethnic groups and

Compared with middle-class whites, certain ethnic groups in the United States and Canada—especially Native Americans—have a larger proportion of expanded family households. This reflects a combination of cultural values and economic necessity. Finding it difficult to survive economically as nuclear families, relatives may pool their resources in an expanded family household. Here, in Arizona, Hopi Indians assemble in such a household to celebrate an infant-naming ceremony.

classes has been explained as an adaptation to poverty (Stack 1975). Unable to survive economically as nuclear family units, relatives band together in an expanded household and pool their resources.

Poverty causes kinship values and attitudes to diverge from middle-class norms. Thus, when North Americans raised in poverty achieve financial success, they often feel obligated to provide considerable financial help to less fortunate relatives. Upperclass households, living in bigger homes supported by greater wealth, may also diverge from the nuclear family norm. Upper-class households can afford to lodge and feed extended family kin, guests, and servants.

North American neolocality is therefore linked to both the geographical mobility and the distribution of wealth associated with industrialism. Neolocal residence tends to isolate the nuclear family, making it the best-defined kinship group. Figure 16.2 categorizes the relationship between these factors and household composition by class. The arrows show the direction of causality.

Recent Changes in North American Kinship Patterns

Although the nuclear family remains a cultural ideal for many Americans, Figure 16.3 shows that nuclear families accounted for just 25.9 percent of American households in 1991. *Nonnuclear family arrangements now outnumber the "traditional" American household by almost four to one.* Table 16.1, which compares American and Canadian households of the 1960s with households in those countries in the 1980s, demonstrates substantial change. There are several reasons for changing household composition. North Americans leave home to work, often in a different community. Women are increasingly joining men in the work force. This often removes them from the family of orientation while making it economically feasible to delay marriage. Furthermore, job demands compete with romantic attachments.

According to the U.S. Census Bureau, the average age at first marriage for American women rose from 20.2 years in 1955 to 23.9 years in 1990. The comparable figures for men were 22.6 and 26.1 (*World Almanac 1992*, p. 943). The U.S. divorce rate rose steeply during the 1970s and early 1980s, so that more than one-third of marriages now end in divorce. In 1960 there were 35 divorced Americans for

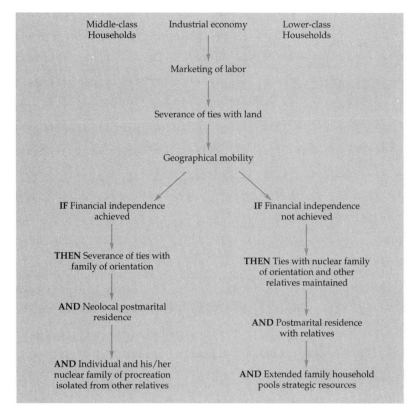

Figure 16.2 *The relationships among industrial economy, social class, and kinship-group organization.*

every 1,000 married people living with a spouse; by 1990 there were 142 (*World Almanac 1992*, p. 945). Single-parent families are increasing at a rapid rate. In 1960, 88 percent of American children lived with both parents, versus 72 percent in 1990 (*World Almanac 1992*, p. 944). The percentage of American children living in fatherless households rose from 8 percent in 1960 to 22 percent in 1990. The percentage living in motherless households increased from 1 percent in 1960 to 3 percent in 1990 (Table 16.2).

The cost of maintaining a middle-class life style forces men, women, and teenagers to work outside the home. Job demands compete with child care, which has become an expensive proposition in itself—it now costs more than $100,000 to raise an American child to age eighteen. In response, nuclear

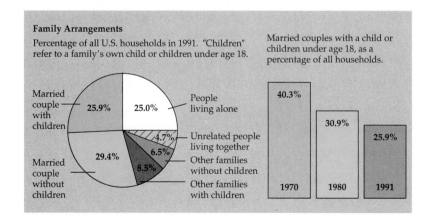

Figure 16.3 *a + b*
Source: The *New York Times*, August 23, 1992, p. 4-2.

Table 16.1 *Classification of North American households, United States (1960 and 1988) and Canada (1961 and 1986)*

	PERCENTAGE OF ALL HOUSEHOLDS			
	UNITED STATES		CANADA	
	1960	1988	1961	1986
Married with children	44	27	51	32
Married couple, no resident children	30	30	27	32
One adult	13	24	9	22
One parent and child(ren)	4	8	4	6
Other*	8	11	9	8

*Includes unrelated people living together, extended families, adult siblings, and so on.
Source: Statistical Abstract, 1991, p. 837.

families have shrunk, and more couples now raise one child than two children. "Beaver Cleaver" families, consisting of children, a working father, and a homemaker mother, now constitute less than 10 percent of all households.

The numbers in Table 16.1 suggest that life is growing increasingly lonely for many North Americans. The disappearance of extended families and descent groups reflects the mobility of industrialism. However, even nuclear families are breaking up. In the United States the unmarried population aged eighteen and over (single, widowed, and divorced) rose from 38 million in 1970 (28 percent of all adults) to 68 million in 1990 (38 percent of all adults) (*Statistical Abstract 1991*, p. 43). To be sure, contemporary Americans maintain social lives through work, friendship, sports, clubs, religion, and organized social activities. However, the isolation from kin that these figures suggest is unprecedented in human history. Because primates are intensely social animals, many observers of contemporary society see the decline of kinship as unfortunate and wonder how these trends are harming our mental health.

Table 16.2 *Percentage of American children residing with one or both parents, 1960 and 1990*

	1960	1990
Both parents present	88	72
No resident father	8	22
No resident mother	1	3
Other	3	3

Source: World Almanac 1992, p. 944.

Our changing household organization has been reflected in the mass media. During the 1950s and early 1960s such television sitcoms as *Ozzie and Harriet* and *Leave It to Beaver* portrayed "traditional" nuclear families. The incidence of **blended families** (kin units formed when parents remarry and bring their children into a new household) has risen, as represented in programs such as *The Brady Bunch*. Three-quarters of divorced Americans remarry (*Ann Arbor News* 1989). Television programs and other media presentations now routinely feature coresident "roommates," unmarried couples, "singles," single parents, unrelated retirees, hired male housekeepers, working mothers, and even "two dads." Changes in life styles are reflected by the media, which in turn help promote further modifications in our values concerning kinship, marriage, and living arrangements (Kottak 1990).

The entire range of kin attachments is narrower for North Americans, particularly those in the middle class, than it is for nonindustrial peoples. Although we recognize ties to grandparents, uncles, aunts, and cousins, we have less contact with, and depend less on, those relatives than people in other cultures do. We see this when we answer a few questions: Do we know exactly how we are related to all our cousins? How much do we know about our ancestors, such as their full names and where they lived? How many of the people with whom we associate regularly are our relatives?

Differences in the answers to these questions by people from industrial and those from nonindustrial societies confirm the declining importance of kinship in contemporary nations. Most of the people whom middle-class North Americans see every day

The Brady Bunch, *a blended family, was created not through divorce, as happens so frequently in the media and in "real life" today, but through the deaths of former spouses.*

Changes in modern social life are reflected by the media, which, in turn, help promote further change in values concerning kinship, marriage, and living arrangements. Current TV programs routinely feature "roommates," unmarried sexual partners, "singles," working mothers, single parents, unrelated retirees, hired male housekeepers, and even "two dads." Murphy Brown, a fictional working woman who became a single mother, was a prominent part of a debate about "family values" in the 1992 U.S. presidential election.

are either nonrelatives or members of the nuclear family. On the other hand, Stack's (1975) study of welfare-dependent families in a ghetto area of a midwestern city shows that sharing with nonnuclear relatives is an important strategy that the urban poor use to adapt to poverty. In this sense, lower-class kinship patterns in America are more like those of nonindustrial societies than are those of the middle class, as you will see below.

One of the most striking contrasts between the United States and Brazil, the two most populous nations of the Western Hemisphere, is in the meaning and role of the family. Contemporary North American adults usually define their families as consisting of their husbands or wives and their children. However, when Brazilians talk about their families, they mean their parents, siblings, aunts, uncles, grandparents, and cousins. Later they add their children, but rarely the husband or wife, who has his or her own family. The children are shared by the two families. Because middle-class Americans lack

an extended family support system, marriage assumes more importance. The husband-wife relationship is supposed to take precedence over either spouse's relationship with his or her own parents. This places a significant strain on North American marriages.

The cultural contrast runs even deeper. Family relationships themselves are more important in Brazil than they are in the United States. Living in a less mobile society, Brazilians stay in closer contact with their relatives, including members of the extended family. Residents of Rio de Janeiro and São Paulo, two of South America's largest cities, are reluctant to leave those urban centers to live away from fam-

IS THERE ANYTHING WRONG WITH THE BLACK FAMILY?

A social issue that receives frequent media attention is "the problem of the black family"—the problematic status of which, from the anthropologist's perspective, originates in the American cultural preference for marriage and the nuclear family. The apparent problem is that over 60 percent of the African-American babies born in the United States today are born to unmarried mothers. Furthermore, more than half (55 percent) of African-American households with children are classified as single-parent families (*World Almanac 1992*, p. 944).

We must first recognize the role of the state in creating "the problem of the black family." Welfare policies that deny Aid to Families with Dependent Children to households with able-bodied male residents have helped create the pattern of unwed mothers and female-headed households.

Just how serious are these problems, and what does the view of such families as constituting a problem tell us about American culture? For most Americans, the ideal family consists of a married couple and their children. American culture favors this kind of family and is biased against others. Even anthropologists sometimes fall into the trap, teaching a course entitled "Marriage and the Family" rather than the more neutral "Kinship and Social Organization."

A cross-cultural perspective makes it obvious (although American culture tends to deny it) that families can exist without a marital tie. Unmarried Brazilians, for example, easily perceive the ethnocentrism in the American viewpoint. Adult Brazilians certainly believe they have families (parents, siblings, aunts, nephews, cousins, etc.) even though they may lack a husband or wife.

Even in the United States, there

Although "Beaver Cleaver" families may be less common among African-Americans than among white Americans, blacks maintain very strong ties with their kin. African-American children tend to see their extended kin more often than their white middle-class compatriots do. Shown here, an African-American family reunion outside a Baptist church in Virginia.

can be families without marriage. Although many Americans don't realize it, strong kin relationships exist among African-Americans, as anthropologist Carol Stack (1975) showed in a classic field study of black family structure and kin relations in urban America. Stack demonstrated that although "Beaver Cleaver" families are less common among poverty-level blacks than among middle-class whites, blacks still maintain very strong ties with their kin. Even if fathers live elsewhere, children often know and visit their fathers and paternal kin. Furthermore, children see their extended kin—grandparents, uncles,

aunts, great-aunts and uncles, and cousins—more often than their white middle-class counterparts do.

Confirming Stack's findings are comprehensive statistical surveys done by the Institute of Social Research of the University of Michigan. This research has shown that families and churches are very important sources of emotional support and sustenance for African-Americans. Twenty percent of the black households surveyed were extended families. Sixty percent of the respondents saw, phoned, or wrote to relatives outside their own households at least once a week. Ninety-two percent had attended a church regularly since age eighteen (*Ann Arbor Observer* 1985). Indeed, compared with blacks, many American whites are more cut off from their kin, living alone or in nuclear family houses in suburban neighborhoods. Significantly, every one of the unmarried black teenage mothers shown in a *Today* show report of October 1984 was living not as an isolated young woman but with her own mother.

The most severe problems facing African-Americans today do not arise from black family structure but from the increasing social and economic polarization of American society. More than three times more African-American than white children are poor (*Statistical Abstract*, 1991, p. 462). On the average, black children spend more than five years of their lives in poverty, versus less than one year for white children (*Ann Arbor News* 1985). Contemporary urban African-Americans must also cope with other forms of social oppression, including drugs and disease. Welfare laws that make coresidence of adult men and women an economically irrational decision make coping even more difficult and fuel the "problem of the black family."

ily and friends. Brazilians find it hard to imagine, and unpleasant to live in, social worlds without relatives. Contrast this with a characteristic American theme—learning to live with strangers. We live with strangers more and more, even at home. The data in Figure 16.3 show that only 70 percent of American households were composed of family members in 1991, compared with 80 percent in 1980 and 89 percent in 1950 (*New York Times* 1992, August 23, p. 4-2; Barringer 1989).

The Nuclear Family among Foragers

Populations with foraging economies are far removed from industrial societies in terms of social complexity. Here again, however, the nuclear family is often the most significant kin group, although in no foraging culture is the nuclear family the only group based on kinship. The two basic social units of traditional foraging societies are the nuclear family and the band.

Unlike middle-class couples in industrial nations, foragers don't usually reside neolocally. Instead, they join a band in which either the husband or the wife has relatives. However, couples and families may move from one band to another several times. Although nuclear families are ultimately as impermanent among foragers as they are in any other society, they are usually more stable than bands are.

Many foraging societies lacked year-round band organization. The Native American Shoshone of the Great Basin in Utah and Nevada provide an example. The resources available to the Shoshone were so meager that for most of the year families traveled alone through the countryside hunting and gathering. In certain seasons families assembled to hunt cooperatively as a band; after a few months together they dispersed.

Industrial and foraging economies do have something in common. In neither type are people tied permanently to the land. The mobility and the emphasis on small, economically self-sufficient family units promote the nuclear family as a basic kin group in both types of societies.

TRIBAL SOCIAL ORGANIZATION

Lineages and Clans

We have seen that the nuclear family is important among foragers and in industrial nations. The anal-

ogous group among nonindustrial food producers is the descent group (described in the chapter "Bands and Tribes," where we distinguished between clans and lineages). In many societies, lineages are **corporate groups**. Like businesses in modern nations, corporate descent groups manage an *estate*, a pool of property and resources. Such an estate may include fields, an irrigation system, house sites, and herds. American culture teaches that people should acquire management positions through individual achievement rather than through kinship ties. We tend to disapprove of employees who hold their positions not because of special competence but because they happen to be the boss's son, daughter, or spouse. In contrast, rights in nonindustrial corporations, such as lineages and their estates, usually come through kinship and descent.

Another characteristic shared by industrial corporations and corporate descent groups is *perpetuity*. Descent groups, unlike nuclear families, are permanent and enduring units, with new members added in every generation. Members have access to the lineage estate. Unlike the nuclear family, the descent group lives on even though specific members die.

Unilineal Descent Groups and Unilocal Residence

Most cultures have a prevailing opinion about where couples should live after they marry. Neolocality, which is the rule for most middle-class Americans, is not very common outside modern North America, Western Europe, and the European-derived cultures of Latin America. Much more common is **virilocality** (*vir* in Latin means "husband"): Married couples live with the husband's relatives. Often virilocality is associated with patrilineal descent. This makes sense. If the children of males are to become descent-group members, with rights in the father's estate, it's a good idea to raise them on that estate. This can be done if a wife moves to her husband's village rather than vice versa.

A less common postmarital residence rule that often is associated with matrilineal descent is **uxorilocality** (*uxor* in Latin means "wife"): Married couples live with the wife's relatives. Together, virilocality and uxorilocality are known as **unilocal** rules of postmarital residence.

Flexibility in Descent-Group Organization

Some descent rules admit certain people as members while excluding others. A unilineal rule uses one line only, either the female or the male. Besides the unilineal rules, there is another descent rule called nonunilineal or **ambilineal** descent. As in any descent group, membership comes through descent from a common ancestor. However, ambilineal groups differ from unilineal groups in that they do not *automatically* exclude either the children of sons or those of daughters. People can choose the group they join (for example, that of their FF, FM, MF, or MM), change their descent-group membership, or belong to two or more groups at the same time. With unilineal descent, membership is automatic—with no choice permitted. People are born members of the father's group in a patrilineal society or of the mother's group in a matrilineal society. They stay members of that group for the rest of their lives.

Before 1950, descent groups were generally described simply as patrilineal or matrilineal. If the society tended toward patrilineality, the anthropologist classified it as patrilineal rather than ambilineal. The treatment of ambilineal descent as a separate category was a formal recognition that many descent systems are flexible—some more so than others.

Determinants of Kinship Systems

There is a definite relationship between ecological factors and principles of social organization, including kinship and descent. Thus, because foragers live off nature rather than controlling it, families move about during the year and throughout their lives. Industrialism also fosters nuclear family organization (and even more severe kinship disintegration), because ties with the land are cut and the economy rewards geographical mobility.

Descent-group organization is especially characteristic of populations whose economies are based on a stable relationship between people and estates. By admitting some people and excluding others, a descent rule regulates access to resources. But descent is a flexible cultural means of adaptation. If there are too many people for a given estate to support, descent rules may get stricter. If, by contrast, the population exploiting the estate starts to decline, descent rules may become more flexible.

However, the functions of descent and descent-group organization extend well beyond the context of population pressure on resources. In the discussion of segmentary lineage organization (in the chapter ''Bands and Tribes'') we saw that people may use common descent to create a regional political organization that allows them to unite and expand against other tribes.

KINSHIP TERMINOLOGY

People define kin relationships differently in different cultures, using different patterns of kinship terminology to refer to relatives. In any culture, kinship terminology is a classification system, a taxonomy or typology. However, it is not a system developed by anthropologists. Rather, it is a **native taxonomy**, developed over generations by the people who live in a particular society. A native classification system is based on how people perceive similarities and differences in the things being classified.

However, anthropologists have discovered that there are a limited number of ways in which people classify their kin. People who speak very different languages may use exactly the same system of kinship terminology. This section examines the four main ways of classifying kin on the parental generation: lineal, bifurcate merging, generational, and bifurcate collateral. We also consider the social correlates of these classification systems.

Several factors influence the way people interact with, perceive, and classify relatives. For example, do certain kinds of relatives customarily live together or apart? How far apart? What benefits do they derive from each other, and what are their obligations? Are they members of the same descent group or of different descent groups? With these questions in mind, let's examine systems of kinship terminology.

Kinship Terminology on the Parental Generation

Figure 16.4 applies to kin types on the generation above ego, the first ascending generation. The letters at the top identify six biological kin types. Numbers and colors indicate the manner of classification. Where the same number and color is shown below

	MB	MZ	M	F	FB	FZ
Lineal	3	4	1	2	3	4
Bifurcate merging	3	1	1	2	2	4
Generational	2	1	1	2	2	1
Bifurcate collateral	3	6	1	2	5	4

Figure 16.4 *Types of kinship classification on the first ascending generation.*

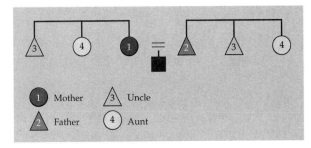

Figure 16.5 *Lineal kinship terminology.*

two biological kin types, the kin types are called by the same term.

Lineal Terminology

Our system of kinship classification is called the *lineal system* (Figure 16.5). The number 3 and the color green, which appear below the kin types FB and MB in Figures 16.4 and 16.5, stand for the term *uncle*, which we apply both to FB and to MB. **Lineal kinship terminology** is found in societies such as the United States and Canada, in which the nuclear family is the most important group based on kinship.

Lineal kinship terminology distinguishes lineal relatives from collateral relatives. A **lineal relative** is an ancestor or descendant, anyone on the direct line of descent that leads to and from ego (Figure 16.6). Thus, lineal relatives are one's parents, grandparents, great-grandparents, and other direct forebears. Lineal relatives also include children, grandchildren, and great-grandchildren.

Collateral relatives are all other biological kin types. They include siblings, nieces and nephews, aunts and uncles, and cousins (Figure 16.6). **Affinals** are relatives by marriage, whether of lineals (e.g., son's wife) or collaterals (sister's husband).

Bifurcate Merging Kinship Terminology

Bifurcate merging kinship terminology is the most common way of classifying kin types (Figure 16.7). People use this system in societies with unilineal descent rules and unilocal postmarital residence. When the society is both unilocal and unilineal, the logic of bifurcate merging terminology is fairly

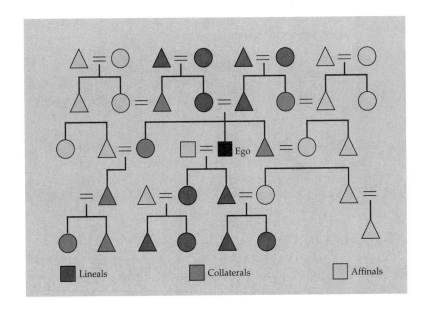

Figure 16.6 *The distinctions among lineals, collaterals, and affinals as perceived by ego.*

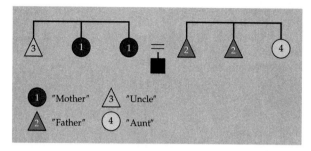

Figure 16.7 *Bifurcate merging kinship terminology.*

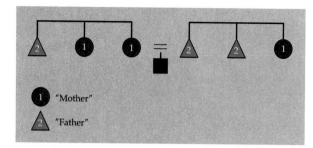

Figure 16.8 *Generational kinship terminology.*

clear. In a patrilineal society, for example, father and father's brother belong to the same descent group, gender, and generation. Since patrilineal societies usually have virilocal residence, the father and his brother live in the same local group. Because they share so many attributes that are socially relevant, ego regards them as social equivalents and calls them by the same kinship term—2. However, the mother's brother belongs to a different descent group, lives elsewhere, and has a different kin term—3.

What about mother and mother's sister in a patrilineal society? They belong to the same descent group, the same gender, and the same generation. Often they marry men from the same village and go to live there. These social similarities help explain the use of the same term—1—for both.

Similar observations apply to matrilineal societies. Consider a society with two matrilineal clans, the Ravens and the Wolves. Ego is a member of his mother's clan, the Raven clan. Ego's father is a member of the Wolf clan. His mother and her sister are female Ravens of the same generation. If there is uxorilocal residence, as there often is in matrilineal societies, they will live in the same village. Because they are so similar socially, ego calls them by the same kin term—1.

The father's sister, however, belongs to a different group, the Wolves, lives elsewhere, and has a different kin term—4. Ego's father and father's brother are male Wolves of the same generation. If they marry women of the same clan and live in the same village, this creates additional social similarities that reinforce this usage.

Generational Kinship Terminology

Like bifurcate merging kinship terminology, **generational kinship terminology** uses the same term for parents and their siblings, but the lumping is more complete (Figure 16.8). With generational terminology, there are only two terms for the parental generation. We may translate them as "father" and "mother," but more accurate translations would be "male member of the parental generation" and "female member of the parental generation."

Generational kinship terminology does not distinguish between the mother's and father's sides. It uses just one term for father, father's brother, and mother's brother. In matrilineal and patrilineal societies, these three kin types do not belong to the same descent group. Generational kinship terminology also uses a single term for mother, mother's sister, and father's sister. In a unilineal society, these three would never be members of the same group.

Nevertheless, generational terminology suggests closeness between ego and his or her aunts and uncles—much more closeness than exists between Americans and these kin types. We would therefore expect to find generational terminology in cultures in which kinship is much more important than it is in our own but in which there is no rigid distinction between the father's side and the mother's side.

It is no surprise, then, that generational kin terminology is typical of societies with ambilineal descent. In such contexts, descent-group membership is not automatic. People may choose the group they join, change their descent-group membership, or belong to two or more descent groups simultaneously. Generational terminology fits these conditions. The use of intimate kin terms allows people to maintain close personal relationships with all their relatives on the parental generation. People exhibit similar behavior toward aunts, uncles, and parents. Someday they will have to choose a descent group to join. Furthermore, in ambilineal societies, postmarital residence is usually **ambilocal**. This means that the married couple can live with either the husband's or the wife's group.

Significantly, generational terminology also characterizes certain foraging bands, including Kalahari groups and several native cultures of North America. Use of the same kinship terminology reflects certain similarities between foraging bands and ambilineal descent groups. In both societies, people have a choice about their kin-group affiliation. Foragers always live with kin, but they often shift band affiliation and so may be members of several different bands during their lifetimes. Just as in food-producing societies with ambilineal descent, generational kinship terminology among foragers helps maintain close personal relationships with several parental-generation relatives whom ego may eventually use as a point of entry into different groups.

Bifurcate Collateral Kinship Terminology

Of all the kinship classification systems, **bifurcate collateral terminology** is the most specific. It has separate terms for each of the six kin types on the parental generation (Figure 16.9). Bifurcate collateral terminology isn't as common as the other types. Most of the societies that use it are in North Africa and the Middle East, and many of them are off-shoots of the same ancestral group. They are also geographically close and have experienced many of the same historical events.

How can we explain bifurcate collateral terminology? Perhaps it arose accidentally in one society in this region and then diffused to others. Or perhaps bifurcate collateral terminology emerged in an ancient Middle Eastern society and now exists among descendant societies because of their common cultural heritage. Either explanation would be an example of a **historical explanation**. Similar customs often exist in different societies because those cultures have shared a period of common history or common sources of information.

Notice that the explanation being proposed for bifurcate collateral terminology is unlike the **functional explanations** that were offered for the other systems of kinship terminology. Functional explanations attempt to relate particular customs to other features of a society. Certain aspects of a culture are

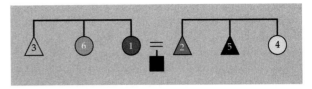

Figure 16.9 *Bifurcate collateral kinship terminology.*

so closely related that when one of them changes, the others inevitably change too. For lineal, bifurcate merging, and generational terminologies, the social correlates (as discussed above) are very clear. However, because we lack a satisfactory functional explanation for bifurcate collateral terminology, a historical explanation was proposed instead. This discussion has a more general aim: It helps illustrate the kinds of explanations that anthropologists have proposed or considered for many other aspects of culture.

Relevance of Kinship Terminology

Anthropologists have to pay attention to kinship terminology because kinship is vitally important in bands, tribes, and chiefdoms. We saw in earlier chapters that kinship and descent play basic roles in regulating both interpersonal relations and political organization in such cultures. Kinship terms provide useful information about social patterns. If two relatives are designated by the same term, we can assume that they are perceived as sharing socially significant attributes.

Nevertheless, cross-cultural studies have found that kinship *terminology* is one of the slowest-changing aspects of social organization. Land ownership, inheritance patterns, residence rules, and descent rules all change more easily and quickly than terminology does. As a result, many societies have kinship terminology that doesn't fit their other social patterns. If we find generational terminology in a society with virilocal residence and patrilineal descent, for example, we may conclude that kinship terminology has lagged behind changes in residence and descent. We expect that the kinship terminology will eventually become bifurcate merging.

SUMMARY

In non-Western, nonindustrial cultures, kinship is very important. In fact, kinship, descent, and marriage form the basis of social life and political organization. We must distinguish between kinship groups, whose composition and activities can be observed, and kinship calculation—the manner in which people identify and designate their relatives.

One widespread but nonuniversal kin group is the nuclear family, which consists of a married couple and their children. There are many functional alternatives to the nuclear family. These are social forms that assume functions that devolve on the nuclear family in other societies.

The nuclear family is most important in foraging and industrial societies. Food producers have kinship-based ties to estates, and other kinds of kinship and descent groups often overshadow the nuclear family.

In contemporary North America, the nuclear family is the characteristic kinship group for the middle class. Other kin groups assume somewhat greater importance in different social strata. Expanded households and sharing with extended family kin occur more frequently among disadvantaged minorities. The greater significance of expanded kinship in the lower class is an adaptation to poverty. It entails pooling of strategic resources by people with limited access to wealth and power. Today, however, even in the American middle class, nuclear family households are declining as single-person households and other domestic arrangements increase.

The descent group is the basic kin group among nonindustrial food producers. Unlike nuclear families, descent groups have perpetuity—they last for several generations. Descent-group members share and manage a common estate. Because of this, anthropologists have compared corporate descent groups to modern business corporation. Descent rules may be unilineal or ambilineal.

Unilineal (patrilineal and matrilineal) descent is associated with unilocal (respectively, virilocal and uxorilocal) postmarital residence rules.

Like many cultural features, descent rules help people adapt to their environments. Usually, these rules don't govern people's lives rigidly. The rules are often flexible. Ecological conditions help determine the types of kin groups that exist in a society and the extent to which people observe or depart from the rules.

Kinship terms, in contrast to biological kin types, are parts of native taxonomies. These are culturally specific ways of dividing up the world of kin relations on the basis of perceived differences and similarities. Although perceptions and classifications vary from culture to culture, comparative research has revealed a limited number of systems of kinship terminology. Because there are correlations between kinship terminology and other social practices, we can, with fair accuracy, predict kinship terminology from other aspects of culture.

Four basic classification systems, three of which are widely distributed throughout the world, categorize kin types on the parental generation. Many foraging and industrial societies have lineal terminology, which is correlated with nuclear family organization. Cultures with unilocal residence and unilineal descent tend to have bifurcate merging terminology. Generational terminology correlates with ambilineal descent and ambilocal residence. The more restricted bifurcate collateral terminology is concentrated among societies of the Middle East and North Africa. Its social functions and correlates are unclear. Kinship terminology changes more slowly than do patterns of inheritance, postmarital residence, and descent-group organization. Therefore, the correlation between kin terms and social structure is often incomplete.

GLOSSARY

affinals: Relatives by marriage, whether of lineals (e.g., son's wife) or collaterals (e.g., sister's husband).

ambilineal: Principle of descent that does not automatically exclude the children of either sons or daughters.

ambilocal: Postmarital residence pattern in which the couple may reside with either the husband's or the wife's group.

bifurcate collateral kinship terminology: Kinship terminology employing separate terms for M, F, MB, MZ, FB, and FZ.

bifurcate merging kinship terminology: Kinship terminology in which M and MZ are called by the same term, F and FB are called by the same term, and MB and FZ are called by different terms.

bilateral kinship calculation: A system in which kinship ties are calculated equally through both sexes: mother and father, sister and brother, daughter and son, and so on.

biological kin types: Actual genealogical relationships, designated by letters and symbols (e.g., FB), as opposed to the kin terms (e.g., *uncle*) used in a particular society.

blended family: Kin unit formed when parents remarry and bring their children into a new household.

collateral household: Type of expanded family household including siblings and their spouses and children.

collateral relative: A biological relative who is not a lineal.

corporate groups: Groups that exist in perpetuity and manage a common estate; include descent groups and modern corporations.

ego: Latin for *I*. In kinship charts, the point from which one views an egocentric genealogy.

expanded family household: Coresident group that can include siblings and their spouses and children (a *collateral* household) or three generations of kin and their spouses (an *extended family* household).

extended family: Expanded household including three or more generations.

family of orientation: Nuclear family in which one is born and grows up.

family of procreation: Nuclear family established when one marries and has children.

functional explanation: Explanation that establishes a correlation or interrelationship between social customs. When customs are functionally interrelated, if one changes, the others also change.

generational kinship terminology: Kinship terminology with only two terms for the parental generation, one designating M, MZ, and FZ and the other designating F, FB, and MB.

genitor: Biological father of a child.

historical explanation: Demonstration that a social institution or practice exists among different populations because they share a period of common history or have been exposed to common sources of information; includes diffusion.

kin terms: The words used for different relatives in a particular language, as opposed to actual genealogical relationships (*biological kin types*).

kinship calculation: The system by which people in a particular society reckon kin relationships.

lineal kinship terminology: Parental generation kin terminology with four terms: one for M, one for F, one for FB and MB, and one for MZ and FZ.

lineal relative: Any of ego's ancestors or descendants (e.g., parents, grandparents, children, grandchildren); on the direct line of descent that leads to and from ego.

marriage: Socially approved relationship between a socially recognized male (the husband) and a socially recognized female (the wife) such that the children born to the wife are accepted as the offspring of both husband and wife.

matrilateral skewing: A preference for relatives on the mother's side.

native taxonomy: Classification system invented and used by natives rather than anthropologists.

neolocality: Postmarital residence pattern in which a couple establishes a new place of residence rather than living with or near either set of parents.

pater: Socially recognized father of a child; not necessarily the genitor.

unilocal: Either virilocal or uxorilocal postmarital residence; requires that a married couple reside with the relatives of either the husband (*vir*) or the wife (*uxor*), depending on the society.

uxorilocality: Customary residence with the wife's relatives after marriage.

virilocality: Customary residence with the husband's relatives after marriage.

STUDY QUESTIONS

1. Why has kinship been so important in ethnographic studies?
2. What is the nuclear family, and why is it significant?
3. What is the difference between the family of orientation and the family of procreation?
4. What kinds of rights may marriage transmit?
5. What is the relationship between the nuclear family and marriage?
6. What four "essential" social functions have been attributed to the nuclear family, and what is the argument against this view?
7. What is the difference between education and enculturation?
8. How did Nayar society reproduce itself biologically without the nuclear family?
9. What three factors are linked with neolocal postmarital residence and household composition?
10. Nuclear families account for what percentage of North American households? What are the other household types?

11. How is the content of television programs related to changes in household organization in twentieth-century North America?
12. What is the key causal factor underlying the nuclear family's role in both foraging and industrial societies?
13. How is descent related to ecological adaptation?
14. What is lineal kinship terminology, and how is it related to American culture?
15. What types of explanations do anthropologists use for systems of kinship terminology?

SUGGESTED ADDITIONAL READING

AMADIUME, I.
1987 *Male Daughters, Female Husbands.* Atlantic Highlands, NJ: Zed. How women fill male roles, including husband, among the Igbo of Nigeria.

BUCHLER, I. R., AND H. A. SELBY
1968 *Kinship and Social Organization: An Introduction to Theory and Method.* New York: Macmillan. Introduction to comparative social organization; includes several chapters on interpretations of kinship classification systems.

COLLIER, J. F., AND S. J. YANAGISAKO, EDS.
1987 *Gender and Kinship: Essays toward a Unified Analysis.* Stanford, CA: Stanford University Press. Recent consideration of kinship in the context of gender issues.

GRABURN, N., ED.
1971 *Readings in Kinship and Social Structure.* New York: Harper & Row. Several important articles on kinship terminology.

MORGEN, S., ED.
1989 *Gender and Anthropology: Critical Reviews for Research and Teaching.* Washington, DC: American Anthropological Association. Reviews aspects of gender, kinship, marriage, and household organization in many areas and in a biosocial perspective.

NETTING, R. M. C., E. R. WILK, AND E. J. ARNOULD, EDS.
1984 *Households: Comparative and Historical Studies of the Domestic Group.* Berkeley: University of California Press. Excellent collection of articles on household research.

RADCLIFFE-BROWN, A. R.
1950 Introduction to *African Systems of Kinship and Marriage,* ed. A.R. Radcliffe-Brown and D. Forde, pp. 1–85. London: Oxford University Press. Classic introduction to kinship and classification systems.

SAHLINS, M. D.
1968 *Tribesmen.* Englewood Cliffs, NJ: Prentice-Hall. Kinship, descent, and marriage in tribal societies.

SERVICE, E. R.
1971 *Primitive Social Organization: An Evolutionary Perspective,* 2nd ed. New York: Random House. Includes a theoretical discussion, from a general evolutionary point of view, of kinship terms in bands, tribes, and chiefdoms.

STACEY, J.
1991 *Brave New Families: Stories of Domestic Upheaval in Late Twentieth Century America.* New York: Basic Books. Contemporary family life in the United States, based on fieldwork in California's Silicon Valley.

CHAPTER 17

MARRIAGE

In stateless societies a person's social world includes two main categories—friends and strangers. Strangers are potential or actual enemies. Marriage is one of the primary ways of converting strangers into friends, of creating and maintaining personal and political alliances. **Exogamy,** the practice of seeking a mate outside one's own group, has adaptive value because it links people into a wider social network that nurtures, helps, and protects them in times of need.

THE INCEST TABOO AND EXOGAMY

Incest refers to sexual relations with a close relative. All cultures have taboos against it. However, although the taboo is a cultural universal, cultures define incest differently. As an illustration, consider some implications of the distinction between two kinds of first cousins, cross cousins and parallel cousins.

The children of two brothers or two sisters are **parallel cousins.** The children of a brother and a sister are **cross cousins.** Your mother's sister's children and your father's brother's children are your parallel cousins. Your father's sister's children and your mother's brother's children are your cross cousins.

The American kin term *cousin* doesn't distinguish between cross and parallel cousins, but in many societies, especially those with unilineal descent, the distinction is essential. As an example, consider a community with only two descent groups. This ex-

emplifies what is known as **moiety** organization—from the French *moitié,* which means "half." Descent bifurcates the community so that everyone belongs to one half or the other. Some societies have patrilineal moieties; others have matrilineal moieties.

In Figures 17.1 and 17.2, notice that cross cousins are always members of the opposite moiety and parallel cousins always belong to your (ego's) own moiety. With patrilineal descent (Figure 17.1), people take the father's descent-group affiliation; in a matrilineal society (Figure 17.2), they take the mother's. You can see from these diagrams that your mother's sister's children (MZC) and your father's brother's children (FBC) belong to your group. Your cross cousins—that is, FZC and MBC—belong to the other moiety.

Parallel cousins therefore belong to the same generation and the same descent group as ego does, and they are like ego's brothers and sisters. They are called by the same kin terms as brother and sister are. Defined as close relatives, parallel cousins are tabooed as sex or marriage partners. They fall within the incest taboo, but cross cousins don't.

In societies with unilineal moieties, cross cousins belong to the opposite group. Sex with cross cousins isn't incestuous, because they aren't considered relatives. In fact, in many unilineal societies people must marry either a cross cousin or someone from the same descent group as a cross cousin. A unilineal descent rule ensures that the cross cousin's descent group is never one's own. With moiety exogamy, spouses must belong to different moieties.

Among the Yanomami of Venezuela and Brazil

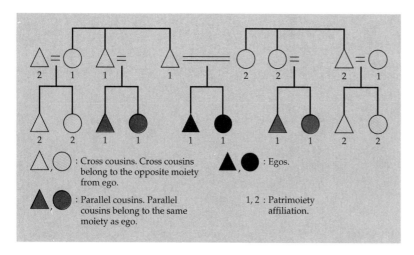

△, ◯ : Cross cousins. Cross cousins belong to the opposite moiety from ego.

▲, ● : Parallel cousins. Parallel cousins belong to the same moiety as ego.

▲ ● : Egos.

1, 2 : Patrimoiety affiliation.

Figure 17.1 *Parallel and cross cousins and patrilineal moiety organization.*

346

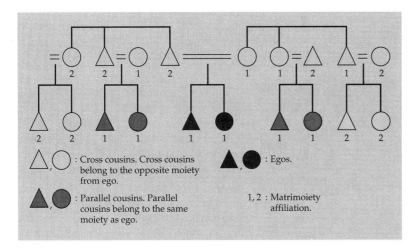

△, ○ : Cross cousins. Cross cousins belong to the opposite moiety from ego.

▲, ● : Parallel cousins. Parallel cousins belong to the same moiety as ego.

▲, ● : Egos.

1, 2 : Matrimoiety affiliation.

Figure 17.2 *Matrilineal moiety organization.*

(Chagnon 1983/1992), men anticipate eventual marriage to a cross cousin by calling her "wife." They call their male cross cousins "brother-in-law." Yanomami women call their male cross cousins "husband" and their female cross cousins "sister-in-law." Among the Yanomami, as in many societies with unilineal descent, sex with cross cousins is proper but sex with parallel cousins is considered incestuous.

A custom that is much rarer than cross-cousin marriage also illustrates that people define their kin, and thus incest, differently in different societies. When unilineal descent is very strongly developed, the parent who does not belong to one's own descent group isn't considered a relative. Thus, with strict patrilineality, the mother is not a relative but a kind of in-law who has married a member of ego's group—ego's father. With strict matrilineality, the father isn't a relative, because he belongs to a different descent group.

The Lakher of Southeast Asia are strictly patrilineal (Leach 1961). Using the male ego in Figure 17.3, let's suppose that ego's father and mother get divorced. Each remarries and has a daughter by a second marriage. A Lakher always belongs to his or her father's group, all the members of which (one's **agnates,** or patrikin) are considered too closely related to marry because they are members of the

Among the Yanomami of Venezuela and Brazil, sex with (and marriage to) cross cousins is proper, but sex with parallel cousins is considered incestuous. With unilineal descent, sex with cross cousins isn't incestuous because cross cousins never belong to ego's descent group.

same patrilineal descent group. Therefore, ego can't marry his father's daughter by the second marriage, just as in contemporary North America it's illegal for half-siblings to marry.

However, in contrast to our society, where all half-siblings are tabooed, the Lakher permit ego to marry his mother's daughter by a different father. She is not ego's relative because she belongs to her own father's descent group rather than ego's. The Lakher illustrate very well that definitions of relatives, and therefore of incest, vary from culture to culture.

We can extend these observations to strict matrilineal societies. If a man's parents divorce and his father remarries, ego may marry his paternal half-sister. By contrast, if his mother remarries and has a daughter, the daughter is considered ego's sister, and sex between them is taboo. Cultures therefore have different definitions of relationships that are biologically or genetically equivalent.

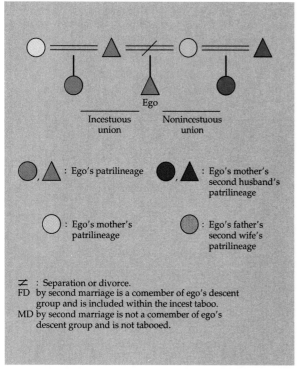

Figure 17.3 *Patrilineal descent-group identity and incest among the Lakher.*

EXPLANATIONS FOR THE INCEST TABOO

Instinctive Horror

There is no simple or universally accepted explanation for the fact that all cultures ban incest. Do primate studies offer any clues? Research with primates does show that adolescent males (among monkeys) or females (among apes) often move away from the group in which they were born (Rodseth et al. 1991). This emigration helps reduce the frequency of incestuous unions. The human avoidance of mating with close relatives may therefore express a generalized primate tendency.

One argument (Westermarck 1894; Hobhouse 1915; Lowie 1920/1961) is that the incest taboo is universal because incest horror is instinctive—*Homo sapiens* has a genetically programmed disgust toward incest. Because of this feeling, early humans banned it. However, cultural universality doesn't necessarily entail an instinctual basis. Fire making, for example, is a cultural universal, but it certainly is not an ability transmitted by the genes. Furthermore, if people really did have an instinctive horror of mating with blood relatives, a formal incest taboo would be unnecessary. No one would ever do it. However, as social workers, judges, psychiatrists, and psychologists know, incest isn't rare but happens all the time.

A final objection to the instinctive horror theory is that it can't explain why in some societies people can marry their cross cousins but not their parallel cousins. Nor does it tell us why the Lakher can marry their maternal, but not their paternal, half-siblings. No known instinct can distinguish between parallel and cross cousins.

The specific kin types included within the incest taboo—and the taboo itself—have a cultural rather than a biological basis. Even among nonhuman primates there is no evidence for an instinct against incest. Adolescent dispersal does not prevent—but merely limits the frequency of—incestuous unions. Among humans, cultural traditions determine the specific relatives with whom sex is considered incestuous. They also deal with people who violate prohibited relationships in different ways. Banishment, imprisonment, death, and threats of supernatural retaliation are some of the punishments imposed.

Biological Degeneration

Another theory is that the taboo emerged because early *Homo* noticed that abnormal offspring were born from incestuous unions (Morgan 1877/1963). To prevent this, our ancestors banned incest. The human stock produced after the taboo originated was so successful that it spread everywhere.

What is the evidence for this theory? Laboratory experiments with animals that reproduce faster than humans do (such as mice and fruit flies) have been used to investigate the effects of inbreeding: A decline in survival and fertility does accompany brother-sister mating across several generations. However, despite the potentially harmful biological results of systematic inbreeding, human marriage patterns are based on specific cultural beliefs rather than universal concerns about biological degeneration several generations in the future. Neither instinctive horror nor fear of biological degeneration explains the very widespread custom of marrying cross cousins. Nor can fears about degeneration explain why breeding with parallel cousins but not cross cousins is so often tabooed.

Marry Out or Die Out

One of the most accepted explanations for the incest taboo is that it arose in order to ensure exogamy, to force people to marry outside their kin groups (Tylor 1889; White 1959; Lévi-Strauss 1949/1969). In this view, the taboo originated early in human evolution because it was adaptively advantageous. Marrying a close relative, with whom one is already on peaceful terms, would be counterproductive. There is more to gain by extending peaceful relations to a wider network of groups.

This view emphasizes the role of marriage in creating and maintaining alliances. By forcing members to marry out, a group increases its allies. Marriage within the group, by contrast, would isolate that group and might ultimately lead to its extinction. Exogamy and the incest taboo that propels it help explain human adaptive success. Besides the sociopolitical function, exogamy also ensures genetic mixture between groups and thus maintains a successful human species.

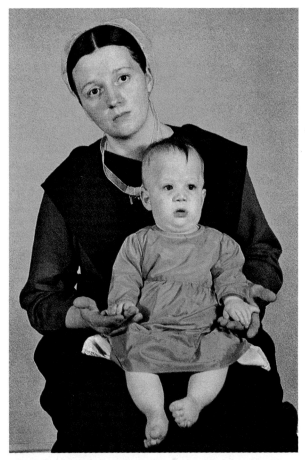

The Old Order Amish of Lancaster, Pennsylvania, have a high frequency of a gene that causes a combination of dwarfism and polydactylism (extra fingers). The Amish, who settled this area in the 1770s, have maintained a high incidence of endogamy. Despite the potentially harmful biological effects of systematic inbreeding, marriage preferences and prohibitions are based on specific cultural beliefs rather than universal concerns about future biological degeneration.

Cultural Continuity and Family Roles

Bronislaw Malinowski (1927) explained the incest taboo with reference to enculturation and the family. Malinowski believed in the generalized importance of nuclear family relationships. He saw the family as the setting in which the knowledge and feelings on which culture is based are transmitted. Cultural continuity across the generations requires feelings of family interdependence and respect.

Malinowski's interest in family sentiments and attachments reflected his reading of early twentieth-

In nonindustrial societies, marriage and exogamy play key roles in forming alliances between groups. One marries not just an individual but an entire kin group. Here a groom's sister mimics her brother's role as husband, dressing as a man and embracing "their" bride.

century psychologists, especially Sigmund Freud. Malinowski rejected the Freudian theory that children have strong sexual feelings before puberty. Instead, he argued that young children have different kinds of affectionate feelings. He believed that nonsexual affection between parents and prepubescent children is important. Malinowski thought that only at puberty do sexual urges develop. He argued that children entering puberty would naturally attempt to gratify their emerging sexual urges with the people who are already emotionally closest to them. They would therefore seek members of their nuclear family as sexual partners. To phrase it with a pun, "familiarity breeds attempt."

Malinowski argued that the incest taboo arose to displace and direct outward this universal temptation toward incestuous unions. If sexual urges were satisfied within the family, conflict would arise and halt the group's normal functioning. Fundamental social bonds—the child's relationships with its parents—would be destroyed, and cultural transmission could not continue. Thus, the incest taboo became a cultural universal to keep all this from happening.

Much of Malinowski's argument seems reasonable. As a child grows up, he or she learns that father, mother, brother, and sister have different and distinct roles (behavioral expectations and obligations) within the family. A boy's attempt to emulate his

father by having sex with his mother could destroy the role structure on which the family is based. However, Malinowski's interpretation is not so satisfactory when it comes to the taboo against sex between siblings.

A more complete and satisfactory explanation for the taboo combines several views. Thus, exogamy and its alliances do have adaptive value and biologically desirable results. Close relatives do provide enculturative models for role differentiation by age and gender. Incestuous gratification of sexual urges *would* threaten relationships among close relatives and create conflict. The universal combination of incest taboo plus exogamy therefore does all the following:

1. It establishes alliances and extends peaceful relations beyond the group.
2. It promotes genetic mixture.
3. It preserves family roles, guarding against socially destructive conflict.

ENDOGAMY

Exogamy pushes social organization outward, establishing and preserving alliances among groups. In contrast, rules of **endogamy** dictate mating or marriage within a group to which one belongs. Endogamic rules are less common but are still familiar to anthropologists. Indeed, most cultures *are* endogamous units, although they usually do not need a formal rule requiring people to marry someone from their own society. Members of the endogamic groups would never consider doing anything else.

Some societies have both exogamic and endogamic rules. However, these rules cannot apply to the same social unit. In stratified societies, for example, people are often expected to marry someone from the same social class. However, the classes, or strata, themselves may be divided into descent groups or other subdivisions, each of which may be an exogamous unit. Exogamy links groups together and merges their resources. However, endogamy keeps groups apart and prevents their resources from blending. Endogamic rules in stratified societies help maintain social, economic, and political distinctions and preserve differential access to culturally valued resources.

Caste

An extreme example of endogamy is India's caste system. Castes are stratified groups in which membership is ascribed at birth and is lifelong. Castes are usually endogamous groups, and the caste system has rules that automatically and unambiguously classify a person at birth. People have no choice about their caste affiliation. The main difference between castes and unilineal descent groups, which also automatically and unambiguously recruit members at birth, is that castes are stratified and endogamous.

Indian castes are grouped into five major categories, or *varna*. Each is ranked relative to the other four, and these categories extend throughout India. Each *varna* includes a large number of castes (*jati*), each of which includes people within a region who may intermarry. All the *jati* in a single *varna* in a given region are ranked, just as the *varna* themselves are ranked.

Occupational specialization often sets off one caste from another. A community may include castes of agricultural workers, merchants, artisans, priests, and sweepers. The untouchable *varna*, found throughout India, includes castes whose ancestry, ritual status, and occupations are considered so impure that higher-caste people consider even casual contact with untouchables to be defiling.

The belief that intercaste sexual unions lead to ritual impurity for the higher-caste partner is important in maintaining endogamy. A man who has sex with a lower-caste woman can restore his purity with a bath and a prayer. However, a woman who has intercourse with a man of a lower caste has no such recourse. Her defilement cannot be undone. Because the women have the babies, these differences protect the purity of the caste line, ensuring the pure ancestry of high-caste children. Although Indian castes are endogamous groups, many of them are internally subdivided into exogamous lineages. This means that Indians must marry a member of another descent group from the same caste.

A long history, an ideology that includes notions of ritual purity and contamination, and intricate occupational and economic distinctions buttress the Indian caste system. However, the principle of caste, without all these particular cultural features, is widely encountered in stratified societies. For example, the ethnic groups called black and white, which are known as "races" in the contemporary United States, have traditionally been castelike groups (see the chapter on the cultural construction of race).

Royal Incest

Royal incest is similar to caste endogamy. The best-known examples come from Inca Peru, ancient Egypt, and traditional Hawaii. Those cultures allowed royal brother-sister marriages. Privileged endogamy, a violation of the incest taboo that applied to commoners in those cultures, was a means of differentiating between rulers and subjects.

Manifest and Latent Functions

To understand why royalty did not observe the incest taboo, it is useful to distinguish between the manifest and latent functions of behavior. The **manifest function** of a custom refers to the reasons natives give for it. Its **latent function** is an effect the custom has on the society that the native people don't mention or may not even recognize.

Royal incest illustrates this distinction. Hawaiians and other Polynesians believed in an impersonal force called *mana*. Mana could exist in things or people, in the latter case marking them off from other people and making them divine. The Hawaiians believed that no one had as much mana as the ruler. Mana depended on genealogy. The person whose own mana was exceeded only by the king's was his sibling. The most appropriate wife for a king was his own full sister. Notice that brother-sister marriage also meant that royal heirs would be as manaful, or divine, as possible. The manifest function of royal incest in ancient Hawaii was part of that culture's beliefs about mana and divinity.

Royal incest also had latent functions—political repercussions. The ruler and his spouse had the same parents. Since mana was believed to be inherited, they were almost equally divine. When the king and his sister married, their children indisputably had the most mana in the land. No one could question their right to rule. However, if the king had taken a wife with less mana than his sister, his sister's children with someone else might eventually cause problems. Both sets of children could assert their divinity and right to rule. Royal sibling marriage therefore limited conflicts about succession because it reduced the number of people with claims to rule. Other kingdoms have solved this problem differently. Some succession rules, for instance, specify that only the oldest child (usually the son) of the reigning monarch can succeed; this custom is called **primogeniture.** Commonly, rulers have banished or killed claimants who rival the chosen heir.

Royal incest also had a latent economic function. If the king and his sister had rights to inherit the ancestral estate, their marriage to each other, again by limiting the number of heirs, kept it intact. Power often rests on wealth, and royal incest tended to ensure that royal wealth remained concentrated in the same line.

Patrilateral Parallel-Cousin Marriage

Functionally similar to royal incest is **patrilateral parallel-cousin marriage** (marriage of the children of brothers) among Islamic, or Moslem, societies of the Middle East and North Africa, particularly the Arabs. Arabs trace their descent patrilineally from Abraham's son Ishmael in the Bible. The Arabs' genealogy enhances their feelings of ethnic identity because they all belong to a huge patrilineage.

Arabs say that a man likes to marry his father's brother's daughter in order to keep property in the family. This manifest function originated as patrilineal Arabs adapted to the imposition of Islamic

inheritance laws. In contrast to patrilineality, in which only males inherit, Islam stipulates that daughters must share in their parents' estates. Patrilateral parallel-cousin marriage helps prevent fragmentation of estates that brothers have inherited from their parents.

EXOGAMY

We move now from endogamy, which isolates groups, back to exogamy, which forges them into social and political networks. In many tribal societies, rules of exogamy are rigid and very specific. For example, some cultures with strongly developed unilineal descent organization not only prohibit descent-group endogamy but also specify where people should seek their spouses.

Generalized Exchange

Directing his attention toward such societies, the renowned French anthropologist Claude Lévi-Strauss (1949/1969) analyzed the exogamic rules that give rise to what he calls *generalized exchange systems.* In societies with generalized exchange, there is an established marital relationship between descent groups. The men of B always marry women from A, and the women of B always marry men from C. Generalized exchange is associated with patrilineal descent and virilocal residence. Men stay put, and women marry out.

Virilocal residence always ensures that patrilineally related men stay together; uxorilocal residence does the same for women in a matrilineal society. Combined with virilocality, generalized exchange means that a patrilineage's men live together and that its women marry into the same village. This rule thus grants both men and women lifelong residence with members of their own descent groups. This can provide important psychological support for women who might otherwise have to leave their kinsmen and kinswomen behind and live with strangers in a husband's village. To be sure, women do live in the husband's village. However, that village is filled with women from their own descent group, including their sisters, paternal aunts, and brother's daughters.

MARRIAGE IN TRIBAL SOCIETIES

Outside of industrial societies, marriage is often more a relationship between groups than one between individuals. We think of marriage as an individual matter. Although the bride and groom usually seek their parents' approval, the final choice (to live together, to marry, to divorce) lies with the couple. The idea of romantic love symbolizes this individual relationship.

In nonindustrial societies, marriage is a group concern. People don't just take a spouse; they assume obligations to a group of in-laws. When residence is virilocal, for example, a woman must leave the community where she was born. Unless there is generalized exchange, she must leave most of her relatives behind. She faces the prospect of spending the rest of her life in her husband's village, with his relatives. She may even have to transfer her major allegiance from her own group to her husband's. If there are disputes between her group and her husband's, she may have to side with him.

Bridewealth

In societies with descent groups, people enter marriage not alone but with the help of the descent group. Descent-group members often have to contribute to **bridewealth,** a customary gift before, at, or after marriage from the husband and his kin to the wife and her kin. Another word for bridewealth is **brideprice,** but this term is inaccurate because people with the custom don't usually regard the exchange as a sale. They don't think of marriage as a commercial relationship between a man and an object that can be bought and sold.

Bridewealth compensates the bride's group for the loss of her companionship and labor. More important, it makes the children born to the woman full members of her husband's descent group. For this reason, the institution is also called **progeny price.** Rather than the woman herself, it is her children who are permanently transferred to the husband's group. Whatever we call it, such a transfer of wealth at marriage is common in patrilineal tribes. In matrilineal societies, children are members of the mother's group, and there is no reason to pay a progeny price.

Dowry is a marital exchange in which the wife's group provides substantial gifts to the husband's family. Dowry, best known from India, correlates with low female status. Women are perceived as burdens. When husbands and their families take a wife, they expect to be compensated for the added responsibility.

Bridewealth exists in many more cultures than dowry does, but the nature and quantity of transferred items differ. In many African societies, cattle constitute bridewealth, but the number of cattle given varies from society to society. *As the value of bridewealth increases, marriages become more stable.* Bridewealth is insurance against divorce.

Imagine a patrilineal society in which a marriage requires the transfer of about twenty-five cattle from the groom's descent group to the bride's. Michael, a member of descent group A, marries Sarah from group B. His relatives help him assemble the bridewealth. He gets the most help from his close agnates—his older brother, father, father's brother, and closest patrilineal cousins. His maternal grandfather or uncle also contributes on behalf of Michael's mother's group as a token of a continuing alliance established a generation earlier, when Michael's father and mother married.

Michael's marriage is the concern of his entire corporate lineage, especially his father or, if his father is dead, his older brother or father's brother. Some of the cattle are from the herds of Michael's descent group. Others have come in as bridewealth for the women of Michael's group, for example, his sister Jennifer and his paternal aunts.

The distribution of the cattle once they reach Sarah's group mirrors the manner in which they were assembled. Sarah's father, or her oldest brother if the father is dead, receives her bridewealth. He keeps most of the cattle to use as bridewealth for his sons' marriages. However, a share also goes to everyone who will be expected to help when Sarah's brothers marry.

When Sarah's brother David gets married, many of the cattle go to a third group—C, which is David's wife's group. Thereafter, they may serve as bridewealth to still other groups. Men constantly use their sisters' bridewealth cattle to acquire their own wives. In a decade, the cattle given when Michael married Sarah will have been exchanged widely.

In tribal societies, marriage entails an agreement between descent groups. Cultural traditions define specific roles for husband and wife. Everyone un-

Love and marriage, the song says, go together like a horse and carriage. But the link between love and marriage, like the horse-carriage combination, isn't a cultural universal. This news item describes a recent cross-cultural survey, published in the anthropological journal *Ethnology,* which found romantic ardor to be widespread, perhaps universal. Previously anthropologists had tended to ignore evidence for romantic love in other cultures, probably because arranged marriages were so common. Today, diffusion, mainly via the mass media, of Western ideas about the importance of love for marriage appears to be influencing marital decisions in other cultures.

Some influential Western social historians have argued that romance was a product of European medieval culture that spread only recently to other cultures. They dismissed romantic tales from other cultures as representing the behavior of just the elites. Under the sway of this view, Western anthropologists did not even look for romantic love among the peoples they studied. But they are now beginning to think that romantic love is universal.

The fact that it does not loom large in anthropology, they say, reflects the efforts most societies have made to quash the unruly inclination. In many countries, they suspect, what appears to be romance newly in bloom is rather the flowering of instincts that were always there, but held in check by tradition and custom. Romantic ardor has long been at odds with social institutions that knit peoples together in an orderly fashion: romantic choices rarely match the "proper" mates a family would select.

In that light, falling in love has been seen by many peoples throughout the world as a dangerous and subversive—though undeniably alluring—act, one

Romantic love may be muted or repressed by arranged marriages, which become political alliances between groups. Many cultures have arranged marriages between young children, as is shown in this wedding procession in Lombok, the Lesser Sunda Islands, Indonesia.

warned against in folk tale and legend. "For decades anthropologists and other scholars have assumed romantic love was unique to the modern West," said Dr. Leonard Plotnicov, an anthropologist at the University of Pittsburgh and editor of the journal Ethnology. "Anthropologists came across it in their field work, but they rarely mentioned it because it wasn't supposed to happen."

Anthropologists distinguish between romantic passion and plain lust, as well as other kinds of love, like that between companions or parents and children. By "romantic love," anthropologists mean an intense attraction and longing to be with the loved one.

"Why has something so central to our culture been so ignored by anthropology?" asked Dr. William Jankowiak, an anthropologist at the University of Nevada.

The reason, in the view of Dr. Jankowiak and others, is a scholarly bias throughout the social sciences that viewed romantic love as a luxury in human life, one that could be indulged only by people in Westernized cultures or among

the educated elites of other societies. For example it was assumed in societies where life is hard that romantic love has less chance to blossom, because higher economic standards and more leisure time create more opportunity for dalliance. That also contributed to the belief that romance was for the ruling class, not the peasants.

But, said Dr. Jankowiak, "There is romantic love in cultures around the world." Last year Dr. Jankowiak, with Dr. Edward Fischer, an anthropologist at Tulane University, published in Ethnology the first cross-cultural study, systematically comparing romantic love in many cultures.

In the survey of ethnographies from 166 cultures, they found what they considered clear evidence that romantic love was known in 147 of them—89 percent. And in the other 19 cultures, Dr. Jankowiak said, the absence of conclusive evidence seemed due more to anthropologists' oversight than to a lack of romance.

Some of the evidence came from tales about lovers, or folklore that offered love potions or other advice on making someone fall in love.

Another source was accounts by informants to anthropologists. For example, Nisa, a Kung woman among the Bushmen of the Kalahari, made a clear distinction between the affection she felt for her husband, and that she felt for her lovers, which was "passionate and exciting," though fleeting. Of these extramarital affairs, she said: "When two people come together their hearts are on fire and their passion is very great. After a while the fire cools and that's how it stays."

Much of the evidence for romantic love came from cautionary tales. For example, a famous story in China during the Song Dynasty (960–1279) was that of the Jade Goddess. Similar in its description of romantic love to the European tale of Tristan and Isolde, it recounts how a young man falls in love with a woman who has been committed by her family to marry someone else, but who returns his love. The couple elope, but end in desperate straits and finally return home, in disgrace.

Still, given cultures may channel romantic feelings in different ways. Romantic love, Dr. Jankowiak said, may be muted or repressed by cultural mores like marriages arranged by families while the betrothed are still children.

"The proportion of members of a community who experience romantic love may well depend on that culture's social organization," Dr. Jankowiak said.

In an editorial note to the cross-cultural survey of romantic love, Dr. Plotnicov wrote that, in retrospect, it was an oversight to ignore the topic in his own field work. "I wish I had thought of looking at this 30 years ago in Nigeria," he said. "But it wasn't part of our tool kit."

The traditional pattern of marriage among the people Dr. Plotnicov studied was for a man to ask his relatives to find him a wife. But, if they could afford the expense, men there could have more than one wife—allowing romance to enter the picture.

"It's often the third wife who is married for romantic reasons," said Dr. Plotnicov. "I remember one man who told me he first saw his third wife walking through the market and, as he put it, 'she took my life away.' He was passionately in love, and pursued her until she married him."

While finding that romantic love appears to be a human universal, Dr. Jankowiak allows that it is still an alien idea in many cultures that such infatuation has anything to do with the choice of a spouse.

"What's new in many cultures is the idea that romantic love should be the reason to marry someone," said Dr. Jankowiak. "Some cultures see being in love as a state to be pitied. One tribe in the mountains of Iran ridicules people who marry for love."

Of course, even in arranged marriages, partners may grow to feel romantic love for each other. For example, among villagers in the Kangra valley of northern India, "people's romantic longings and yearnings ideally would become focused on the person they're matched with by their families," said Dr. Kirin Narayan, an anthropologist at the University of Wisconsin.

But that has begun to change, Dr. Narayan is finding, under the influence of popular songs and movies. "In these villages the elders are worried that the younger men and women are getting a different idea of romantic love, one where you choose a partner yourself," said Dr. Narayan. "There are starting to be elopements, which are absolutely scandalous."

The same trend toward love matches, rather than arranged marriages, is being noted by anthropologists in many other cultures. Among aborigines in Australia's Outback, for example, marriages had for centuries been arranged when children were very young.

That pattern was disrupted earlier in this century by missionaries, who urged that marriage not occur until children reached adolescence. Dr. Victoria Burbank, an anthropologist at the University of California at Davis, said that in pre-missionary days, the average age of a girl at marriage was always before menarche, sometimes as young as 9 years. Today the average age at marriage is 17; girls are more independent by the time their parents try to arrange a marriage for them.

"More and more adolescent girls are breaking away from arranged marriages," said Dr. Burbank. "They prefer to go off into the bush for a 'date' with someone they like, get pregnant, and use that pregnancy to get parental approval for the match."

Even so, parents sometimes are adamant that the young people should not get married. They prefer, instead, that the girls follow the traditional pattern of having their mothers choose a husband for them.

"Traditionally among these people, you can't choose just any son-in-law," said Dr. Burbank. "Ideally, the mother wants to find a boy who is her maternal grandmother's brother's son, a pattern that insures partners are in the proper kin group."

Dr. Burbank added: "These groups have critical ritual functions. A marriage based on romantic love, which ignores what's a proper partner, undermines the system of kinship, ritual, and obligation."

Nevertheless, the rules for marriage are weakening. "In the grandmothers' generation, all marriages were arranged. Romantic love had no place, though there were a few stories of a young man and woman in love running off together. But in the group I studied, in only one recent case did the girl marry the man selected for her. All the rest are love matches."

A similar pattern is going on in the village in northern Morocco studied by Dr. Susan Davis, an anthropologist and consultant in Haverford, Pa. "When I first went there in 1965, marriage was a strictly utilitarian economic arrangement," she said. "Your parents arranged your marriage."

But with the arrival of television and cinema in the village, bringing Egyptian soap operas and American movies, ideas of romance spread. "It's still taboo for a girl to say to her parents, 'I love a certain boy and want to marry him,'" said Dr. Davis. "But what's new is that a girl now expects to have a veto over the mate her parents propose, and that her parents will eventually approve of someone she likes."

Source: Daniel Goleman, "Anthropology Goes Looking in All the Old Places," *The New York Times,* November 24, 1992, B1.

Gift-giving customs, including dowry and brideprice, are associated with marriage throughout the world. In the photo above, guests bring presents in baskets to a wedding in Wenjiang, China. In the more elaborate royal wedding photo below, plates of money are presented at the marriage of an Indian maharajah.

derstands that neither Sarah nor Michael should stray too far from the behavior expected of a married couple in that society. Sarah owes certain things to Michael's group and can expect certain things from him and his relatives, and vice versa.

Still, several problems may arise. Sarah may find that Michael is a poor husband. She may have trouble getting along with him or his relatives, with whom she resides virilocally. If she convinces her relatives that her complaints are justified and if the bridewealth is easy to repay, her group may return the cattle, and a divorce will take place.

However, marriages in such societies aren't usually so brittle. A woman's relatives generally try to persuade her to work things out with her husband. This is especially true if the bridewealth was substantial and has been distributed among many of Sarah's relatives or if most of it has been used to obtain a wife for her brother. We may generalize: The more difficult it is to reassemble the bridewealth, the more stable is marriage and the rarer is divorce.

If Sarah and Michael try to make their marriage succeed but fail to do so, both groups may conclude that the marriage can't last. Here it becomes especially obvious that tribal marriages are relationships between groups as well as between individuals. If Sarah has a younger sister or niece (her older brother's daughter, for example), the concerned parties may agree to Sarah's replacement by a kinswoman.

There is another possibility. When a woman divorces a man, he may sometimes claim her brother's wife. After all, Sarah's father might have used Michael's cattle to obtain a wife for his son (Sarah's brother) David. Thus, through his bridewealth cattle, Michael has a claim on David's wife. This practice existed among the Ba-Thonga of southeastern Africa.

However, incompatibility isn't the main problem that threatens marriage in societies with bridewealth. Infertility is a more important concern. If Sarah has no children, she and her group have not fulfilled their part of the marriage agreement. If the relationship is to endure, Sarah's group must furnish another woman, perhaps her younger sister, who can have children.

So important is fertility among the Betsileo of Madagascar that it is often only after a woman is pregnant that the marriage takes place and bridewealth is given. During a period of trial marriage, the woman lives in her husband's village. She may demonstrate her fertility by getting pregnant. She also learns whether she is compatible with her prospective husband and his relatives. If she gets pregnant and the couple doesn't want to marry, the child can join its mother's descent group, with full rights.

In societies with descent groups and bridewealth, every marriage entails an agreement between groups. An infertile woman's group must return the progeny price or provide a substitute childbearer. The original wife may choose to stay in her husband's village. Perhaps she will someday have a child. If she does stay on, her husband will have established a plural marriage.

Most nonindustrial food-producing societies, unlike most foraging societies and industrial nations, allow **plural marriages,** or **polygamy.** There are two varieties, one common and the other very rare. The more common variant is **polygyny,** in which a man has more than one wife. The rare variant is **polyandry,** in which a woman has more than one husband. If the infertile wife remains married to her husband after he has taken a substitute wife provided by her descent group, this is polygyny. I will discuss reasons for polygyny other than infertility shortly.

Durable Alliances

It is possible to exemplify the group-alliance nature of marriage in tribal societies by examining still another common practice—continuation of marital alliances when one spouse dies.

Sororate

What happens if Sarah dies young? Michael's group will ask Sarah's group for a substitute, often her sister. This custom is known as the **sororate** (Figure 17.4). If Sarah has no sister or if all her sisters are already married, another woman from her group may be available. Michael marries her, there is no need to return the bridewealth, and the alliance continues. The sororate exists in both matrilineal and patrilineal societies. In a matrilineal society with uxorilocal postmarital residence, a widower may remain with his wife's group by marrying her sister or another female member of her matrilineage (Figure 17.4).

Levirate and Other Arrangements

What happens if the husband dies? In many societies, the widow may marry his brother. This custom is known as the **levirate** (Figure 17.4). Like the sororate, it is a continuation marriage that maintains the alliance between descent groups, in this case by replacing the husband with another member of his group. The implications of the levirate vary with age.

Returning to Michael, Sarah, and company, what happens if Michael dies after Sarah has had children? When they married, it was understood that his group would provide a husband for Sarah. She fulfilled her part of the agreement by producing the children necessary to perpetuate Michael's descent group. When Michael dies, the levirate assigns one of his brothers to Sarah. If that brother already has a wife, he will now be polygynous. Michael's

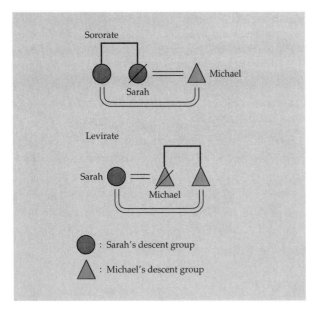

Figure 17.4 *Sororate and levirate.*

brother must accept Sarah and treat her as his wife. Depending on their ages, their marriage may or may not involve sex. A recent study found that in African societies the levirate, though widely permitted, rarely involves coresidence of the widow and her new husband. Furthermore, widows don't automatically marry the husband's brother just because they are allowed to. Often they prefer to make other arrangements (Potash 1986).

PLURAL MARRIAGES

In contemporary North America, where divorce is fairly easy and common, polygamy (marriage to more than one spouse at the same time) is against the law. Marriage in industrial nations joins individuals, and relationships between individuals can be severed more easily than can those between groups. As divorce grows more common, North Americans practice **serial monogamy:** Individuals have more than one spouse but never, legally, more than one at the same time. As stated earlier, the two forms of polygamy are polygyny and polyandry. Polyandry is practiced in only a few cultures, notably among Polynesia's Marquesas Islanders and among certain groups in Tibet, Nepal, and India. Polygyny is much more common.

Polygyny

We must distinguish between the social approval of plural marriage and its actual frequency in a particular society. Many cultures approve of a man's having more than one wife. However, even when polygyny is encouraged, most people are monogamous, and polygyny characterizes only a fraction of the marriages. Why?

One reason is equal sex ratios. In the United States, about 105 males are born for every 100 females. In adulthood the ratio of men to women equalizes, and eventually it reverses. The average North American woman outlives the average man. In many nonindustrial societies as well, a male-biased sex ratio among children also reverses in adulthood. This occurs because many cultures allocate the most dangerous tasks to men. They have to climb, hunt, make war, fish, sail, and travel, sometimes into alien territory. The Eskimos, who traditionally assigned dangerous jobs to men, practiced female infanticide. The practice of killing girl babies ensured that there were approximately equal numbers of adult Eskimo men and women.

There are demographic reasons why polygyny is more common than polyandry. Without female infanticide, if customary male tasks are more dangerous, more females survive into adulthood. Polygyny is the cultural response. The custom of men marrying later than women also promotes polygyny. Among Nigeria's Kanuri people (Cohen 1967), men get married between the ages of eighteen and thirty; women, between twelve and fourteen. The age difference between spouses means that there are more widows than widowers. Most of the widows remarry, some in polygynous unions. Among the Kanuri and in other polygynous societies, widows make up a large number of the women involved in plural marriages (Hart and Pilling 1960).

In many societies, including the Kanuri, the number of wives is a measure of a man's prestige and social position. The Kanuri live in expanded family households headed by men. The man's wives and unmarried children also live there. Because residence is virilocal, married sons and their wives and children (Figure 17.5) are also household members.

The household is the main productive unit. The more wives, the more workers. Increased productivity means more wealth. This wealth in turn at-

BRADY BUNCH NIRVANA

The first-year students I teach at the University of Michigan belong to a generation raised after the almost total diffusion of television into the American home. Most young Americans have never known a world without TV. The tube is as familiar as Mom or Dad. Indeed, considering how common divorce has become, TV sets outlast the father in many homes. One habit I began about ten years ago, taking advantage of my students' familiarity with television, is to demonstrate changes in American kinship and marriage patterns by contrasting the programs of the fifties with more recent ones. Four decades ago, the usual TV family was a nuclear family made up of father (who often knew best), homemaker mother, and children. Examples include *Father Knows Best, Ozzie and Harriet,* and *Leave It to Beaver.* These programs were appropriate for the 1950s market, but they are out of sync with today's social and economic realities. Only 16 million American women worked outside the home in 1950, compared with three times that number today. Today less than 7 percent of American households fit the former ideal: breadwinner father, homemaker mother, and two children.

Virtually all my students have seen reruns of the more recent family series *The Brady Bunch.* The social organization of *The Brady Bunch* provides an instructive contrast with 1950s programs, because it illustrates what we call *blended family organization.* A new (blended) family forms when a widow with three daughters marries a widower with three sons. Blended families have been increasing in American society because of

more frequent divorce and remarriage. During *The Brady Bunch*'s heyday, divorce remained controversial and could not give rise to a TV family. However, the first spouse's death may also lead to a blended family, as in *The Brady Bunch.*

The Brady husband-father was a successful architect. Even today, the average TV family tends to be more professional, successful, and rich than the average real-life family. The Bradys were wealthy enough to employ a housekeeper, Alice. Mirroring American culture when the program was produced, the wife's career was part-time and subsidiary. Women lucky enough to find wealthy husbands did not compete with other women—even professional housekeepers—in the work force. (It is noteworthy that when *The Bradys* was revived as a weekly series in 1990, Mrs. Brady had a full-time job.)

Students enjoy learning about anthropological techniques through culturally familiar examples. Each time I begin my kinship lecture, a few people in the class immediately recognize (from reruns) the nuclear families of the 1950s. However, as soon as I begin diagramming the Brady characters (without saying what I'm doing), students start shouting out their names: "Jan," "Bobby," "Greg," "Cindy," "Marsha," "Peter," "Mike," "Carol," "Alice." The response mounts. As the cast of characters nears completion, almost everyone has joined in. Whenever I give my kinship lecture, Anthropology 101 is guaranteed to resemble a revival meeting, as hundreds of TV-enculturated American natives shout out in unison names made almost as familiar as

their parents' through exposure to television reruns.

Furthermore, as the natives participate in this chant, based on common knowledge acquired by growing up in the post-1950s United States, there is an enthusiasm, a warm glow, that my course will not recapture until the next semester's rerun of my *Brady Bunch* lecture. My students seem to find *nirvana* (a feeling of religious ecstasy) through their collective remembrance of the Bradys and in the rituallike incantation of their names.

Some segments of our society stigmatize television as "trivial," yet the average American family owns 2.3 television sets (*World Almanac* 1992, p. 318). Given this massive penetration of the modern home (98 percent of all households), television's effects on our socialization and enculturation can hardly be trivial. Indeed, the common information and knowledge we acquire by watching the same TV programs is indisputably culture in the anthropological sense. Culture is collective, shared, meaningful. It is transmitted by conscious and unconscious learning experiences acquired by humans not through their genes but as a result of growing up in a particular society. Of the hundreds of culture bearers who have passed through the Anthropology 101 classroom over the past decade, many have been unable to recall the full names of their parents' first cousins. Some have forgotten their grandmother's maiden name. But most have absolutely no trouble identifying names and relationships in a family that exists only in television land.

In many societies polygyny is a measure of a man's prestige and social position. Shown here are a Masai chief, his two wives, and their children (in Kenya).

tracts additional wives. Wealth and wives bring greater prestige to the household and head. In many societies, the first wife requests a second wife to help with household chores. The second wife's status is lower than that of the first; they are senior and junior wives. The senior wife sometimes chooses the junior one from among her close kinswomen.

Among the Betsileo of Madagascar, the different wives always lived in different villages. A man's first and senior wife, called ''Big Wife,'' lived in the village where he cultivated his best rice field and

spent most of his time. However, the Betsileo inherit from several different ancestors and cultivate different areas. High-status men with several rice fields had households near each field. They spent most of their time with the senior wife but visited the others occasionally throughout the year.

Plural wives can also play important political roles in nonindustrial states. The king of the Merina, a society with more than 1 million people in the highlands of Madagascar, had palaces for each of his twelve wives in different provinces. He stayed

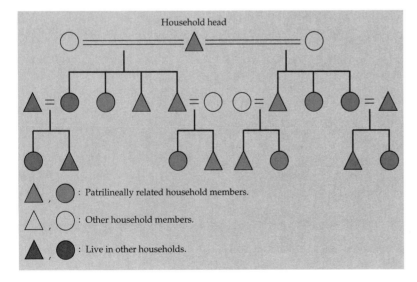

Figure 17.5 *A polygynous expanded Kanuri household.*

with them when he traveled through the kingdom. They were his local agents, overseeing and reporting on provincial matters. The king of Buganda, the major precolonial state of Uganda, took hundreds of wives, representing all the clans in his nation. Everyone in the kingdom became the king's in-law, and all the clans had a chance to provide the next ruler. This was a way of giving the common people a stake in the government.

These examples show that there is no single explanation for polygyny. Its context and function vary from society to society and even within the same society. Some men are polygynous because they have inherited a widow from a brother. Others have plural wives because they seek prestige or want to increase household productivity. Still others use marriage as a political tool or a means of economic advancement. Men and women with political and economic ambitions cultivate marital alliances that serve their aims. In many societies, including the Betsileo of Madagascar and the Igbo of Nigeria, women arrange the marriages.

Polyandry

Polyandry is very rare and is practiced under very specific conditions. Most of the world's polyandrous peoples live in South Asia—Tibet, Nepal, India, and Sri Lanka. India's polyandrous groups inhabit the lower ranges of the Himalayas, in northern India. They are known as Paharis, which means "people of the mountains." Gerald Berreman (1962, 1975) did a comparative study of two Pahari groups, one in the foothills of the western Himalayas and the other in the central foothills.

The western and central Paharis are historically and genetically related and speak dialects of the same language. Polyandry exists among the western, but not the central, Paharis. Because there are so many other cultural and social similarities between the western and central Paharis, including caste stratification and patrilineal clans, Berreman wondered why one group practiced polyandry and the other didn't.

Pahari marriage customs turned out to correlate with demographic contrasts. Sex ratios were different in the two areas. In the polyandrous west, there was a shortage of females (789 per 1,000 males). Although female infanticide was not documented in the area, neglect of girls (*covert* female infanticide) helped explain the shortage of women (Levine 1988). Western Pahari polyandry was always **fraternal**: Husbands were brothers. The oldest brother arranged the marriage, which made all the brothers legal husbands of the wife. Subsequently, they could marry additional women. All these women

Polyandry in northwest Nepal. The seated young woman is Terribal, age 15. She holds her youngest husband, age 5. To her left is another husband, age 12. Standing directly behind her is her third husband, age 9. The two older standing men are brothers who are married to the same woman, standing to the right. These are Terribal's "fathers" and mother.

were joint wives and sexual partners of the brothers. Children born to any wife called all the brothers "father."

Nevertheless, there was considerable variation in the actual marriage arrangements in western Pahari households (Berreman 1975). In one village only 9 percent of the households were polyandrous, 25 percent were polygynous, and 34 percent were monogamous. Variation in marriage type and household composition reflected household wealth, the age of the brothers, and divorce. Household composition went through a developmental cycle. For example, one group of three brothers took their first wife in 1910. In 1915 they added a second wife. This changed simple fraternal polyandry into a polyandrous-polygynous household. A few years later they added a third wife, and later they added a fourth. By a decade later, one of the brothers had died and two of the wives had divorced and remarried elsewhere. By 1955 the household had become monogamous, as only one husband and one wife survived.

This flexible marriage system was adaptive because it allowed the western Paharis to spread people and labor out over the land. The number of working adults in a western Pahari household was proportional to the amount of farmland it owned. Because women did as much agricultural work as men, given the same amount of land, two brothers might require and support three or four wives whereas three or four brothers might have only one or two. Plural marriages were uncommon in landless households, whose resources and labor needs were lowest. Landless people were more monogamous (43 percent) than were landowners (26 percent).

Among the nonpolyandrous central Paharis, by contrast, there were more women than men. Most (85 percent) marriages were monogamous. Only 15 percent were plural—polygynous. Despite the absence of formal polyandry here, it was customary for brothers to contribute to each other's bride-wealth, and they could have sex with each other's

wives. The major difference was that central Pahari children recognized only one father. However, because brothers had common sexual rights, socially recognized fathers were not necessarily the true genitors.

Polyandry in other parts of South Asia seems to be a cultural adaptation to mobility associated with customary male travel for trade, commerce, and military operations. Polyandry ensures that there is always a man at home. Fraternal polyandry is also an effective strategy when resources are scarce. Like poverty-level Americans, brothers with limited resources (in land) pool their resources in expanded (polyandrous) households. They take just one wife. Polyandry restricts the number of wives and heirs. Less competition among heirs means that land can be transmitted with minimal fragmentation.

The reasons for polyandry among the Marquesan Islanders of Polynesia were different. Marquesan polyandry was not fraternal. During the nineteenth century, intertribal raiding, warfare with European explorers, smallpox, and famine produced a substantial population decline (Otterbein 1963/1968). More women than men died. By 1900, the ratio was six males to five females. Polyandry, in a variety of forms, was the response.

The Marquesans developed four types of marriage. One was monogamy. Another was simple polyandry. A third type was the polygynous-polyandrous household. Here a woman and her husband moved in with a new husband (always a richer man) and his wife. All spouses had sexual rights to those of the opposite sex. In the final type—the composite household—unmarried men attached themselves to one of the other three types. These bachelors did not marry but were permissible sexual partners for the women in the household.

The Marquesan example is rare and highly unusual. Like marriage in South Asia, however, it illustrates that monogamy, polyandry, and polygyny can all coexist in the same culture as part of a flexible set of marriage rules with value for cultural adaptation.

SUMMARY

All societies have incest taboos. However, different cultures taboo different biological kin types. Among the explanations that have been offered for the taboo's univer-

sality are the following: (1) It codifies instinctive human horror of incest, (2) it results from concern about the biological degeneration that can follow from incestuous unions, (3) it has a selective advantage because it promotes exogamy and intergroup alliances, and (4) it is necessary to maintain family role structure and cultural continuity. The third and fourth explanations are the most useful. The taboo promotes exogamy, therefore increasing networks of friends and allies. Furthermore, sex between close relatives, especially parents and children, would create conflict that could impair sociocultural cohesion and continuity.

The main adaptive advantage of exogamy is the extension of social and political ties outward. This is confirmed by a consideration of endogamy—marriage within the group. Endogamic rules are common in stratified societies. One example is India, where castes are the endogamous units. However, castes are subdivided into exogamous descent groups. The same culture can therefore have both endogamic and exogamic rules. The U.S. ''racial'' system is structurally similar to the Indian caste system, although it lacks many of the specific cultural features.

Certain ancient kingdoms encouraged royal incest while condemning incest by commoners. The manifest functions of royal incest in ancient Hawaii were linked to the idea of mana. However, royal incest also served latent functions in the political and economic domains—limiting succession struggles and keeping royal wealth intact. Preferential marriage of brothers' children among Arabs is another example of endogamy.

Many tribal societies not only prohibit people from marrying within their own group but also rigidly dictate their choice of spouses. Generalized exchange exemplifies such marriage systems. Generalized exchange links exogamous descent groups in an established system of marital relationships. Women from group B always marry men from group C, men from group B always take wives from group A, and so on.

In societies with descent groups, marriages are relationships between groups as well as between spouses. With the custom of bridewealth, the groom and his relatives transmit wealth to the bride and her relatives. As the bridewealth's value increases, the divorce rate declines.

Bridewealth customs show that marriages among nonindustrial food producers create and maintain group alliances. So do the sororate, by which a man marries the sister of his deceased wife, and the levirate, by which a woman marries the brother of her deceased husband. Replacement marriages in cases of spousal incompatibility also confirm the importance of group alliances.

Many cultures permit plural marriages. The two kinds of polygamy are polygyny and polyandry. The former involves multiple wives; the latter, multiple husbands. Polygyny and polyandry are found in varied social and cultural contexts and occur for many reasons. Polygyny is much more common than is polyandry. There are demographic, economic, and ecological reasons for plural marriage systems.

GLOSSARY

agnates: Members of the same patrilineal descent group.

brideprice: See *progeny price.*

bridewealth: See *progeny price.*

cross cousins: Children of a brother and a sister.

dowry: A marital exchange in which the wife's group provides substantial gifts to the husband's family.

endogamy: Marriage between people of the same social group.

exogamy: Rule requiring people to marry outside their own group.

fraternal polyandry: Marriage of a group of brothers to the same woman or women.

incest: Sexual relations with a close relative.

latent function: A custom's underlying function, often unperceived by natives.

levirate: Custom by which a widow marries the brother of her deceased husband.

manifest function: The reasons that natives offer for a custom.

parallel cousins: Children of two brothers or two sisters.

patrilateral parallel-cousin marriage: Marriage of the children of brothers.

plural marriage: See *polygamy.*

polyandry: Variety of plural marriage in which a woman has more than one husband.

polygamy: Any marriage with more than two spouses.

polygyny: Variety of plural marriage in which a man has more than one wife.

primogeniture: Inheritance rule that makes the oldest child (usually the oldest son) the only heir.

progeny price: A gift from the husband and his kin to the wife and her kin before, at, or after marriage; legitimizes children born to the woman as members of the husband's descent group.

moiety: One of two descent groups in a given population; usually moieties intermarry.

serial monogamy: Marriage of a given individual to several spouses, but not at the same time.

sororate: Custom by which a widower marries the sister of the deceased wife.

STUDY QUESTIONS

1. What explanations have been offered for the universality of the incest taboo? Which do you prefer, and why?
2. What are the respective functions of endogamy and exogamy within the Indian caste system?
3. What aspect of contemporary American stratification most resembles the Indian caste system?
4. What were the manifest and latent functions of privileged royal incest?
5. What is generalized exchange, and what is its advantage for women?
6. What is bridewealth? What else is it called, and why?
7. What is the difference between sororate and levirate? What do they have in common?
8. What is the difference between polygyny and polyandry?
9. What are some of the reasons for polygyny?
10. What are some of the reasons for polyandry?
11. What general conclusions do you draw from the two chapters on kinship and marriage?

SUGGESTED ADDITIONAL READING

BOHANNAN, P., AND J. MIDDLETON, EDS.
  1968 *Marriage, Family, and Residence.* Garden City, NY: Natural History Press. Articles about marriage, incest, exogamy, and family and household organization.
COLLIER, J.F., ED.
  1988 *Marriage and Inequality in Classless Societies.* Stanford, CA: Stanford University Press. Marriage and issues of gender stratification in bands and tribes.
COMAROFF, J., ED.
  1980 *The Meaning of Marriage Payments.* New York: Academic Press. Economic, symbolic, and social organizational components of marital gifts in varied cultures.
FOX, R.
  1985 *Kinship and Marriage.* New York: Viking Penguin. Well-written survey of kinship and marriage systems and theories about them.
GOODY, J., AND S.T. TAMBIAH
  1973 *Bridewealth and Dowry.* Cambridge: Cambridge University Press. Marital exchanges in comparative perspective.
HENDRY, J.
  1981 *Marriage in Changing Japan.* London: Croom Helm. A thorough look at the institution of marriage in post– versus pre–World War II Japan.

LEACH, E.
  1985 *Social Anthropology.* New York: Oxford University Press. A well-known British anthropologist who studied the kinship and marriage systems of many peoples wrote this nontechnical survey of social anthropology and the anthropologists who have contributed to it.
LEVINE, N.
  1988 *The Dynamics of Polyandry: Kinship, Domesticity, and Population in the Tibetan Border.* Chicago: University of Chicago Press. Case study of fraternal polyandry and household organization in northwestern Nepal.
POTASH, B., ED.
  1986 *Widows in African Societies: Choices and Constraints.* Stanford, CA: Stanford University Press. Ten case studies giving widows' perspectives on African marriage systems.
WATSON, R. S., AND P. B. EBREY
  1991 *Marriage and Inequality in Chinese Society.* Berkeley: University of California Press. Essays examine marriage and gender inequalities in the context of the Chinese economy and politics.

CHAPTER 18

GENDER

Because anthropologists study biology, psychology, society, and culture, they are in a unique position to comment on nature (biological predispositions) and nurture (environment) as determinants of human behavior. Human attitudes, values, and behavior are limited not only by our genetic predispositions—which are difficult to identify—but also by our experiences during enculturation. Our attributes as adults are determined both by our genes and by our environment during growth and development.

Debate about the effects of nature and nurture proceeds today in scientific and public arenas. **Naturists** assume that some—they differ about how much—human behavior and social organization is biologically determined. **Nurturists, or environmentalists,** do not deny that some universal aspects of human behavior may have a genetic base. However, they find most attempts to link behavior to genes unconvincing. The basic environmentalist assumption is that human evolutionary success rests on flexibility, or the ability to adapt in various ways. Because human adaptation relies so strongly on cultural learning, we can change our behavior more readily than members of other species can.

The nature-nurture debate emerges in the discussion of human sex-gender roles and sexuality. Men and women differ genetically. Women have two X chromosomes, and men have an X and a Y. The father determines a baby's sex because only he has the Y chromosome to transmit. The mother always provides an X chromosome.

The chromosomal difference is expressed in hormonal and physiological contrasts. Humans are sexually dimorphic. **Sexual dimorphism** refers to marked differences in male and female biology besides the contrasts in breasts and genitals. Men and women differ not just in primary (genitalia and reproductive organs) and secondary (breasts, voice, hair distribution) sexual characteristics but in average weight, height, and strength.

Just how far, however, do these genetically and physiologically determined differences go? What effect do they have on the way men and women act and are treated in different cultures? On the environmentalist side, anthropologists have discovered substantial variability in the roles of men and women in different cultures. The anthropological position on sex-gender roles and biology may be stated as follows:

The biological nature of men and women [should be seen] not as a narrow enclosure limiting the human organism, but rather as a broad base upon which a variety of structures can be built. (Friedl 1975, p. 6)

Although in most cultures men tend to be somewhat more aggressive than women, many of the behavioral and attitudinal differences between the sexes emerge from culture rather than biology. *Sex* differences are biological, but *gender* encompasses all the traits that a culture assigns to and inculcates in males and females. "Gender," in other words, refers to the cultural construction of male and female characteristics (Rosaldo 1980b).

Given "rich and various constructions of gender" within the realm of cultural diversity, Susan Bourque and Kay Warren (1987) note that the same images of masculinity and feminity do not always apply. Margaret Mead did an early ethnographic study of variation in gender roles. Her book *Sex and Temperament in Three Primitive Societies* (1935/1950) was based on field work in three societies in Papua–New Guinea: Arapesh, Mundugumor, and Tchambuli. The extent of personality variation in men and women in these three societies on the same island amazed Mead. She found that Arapesh men and women acted as Americans have traditionally expected women to act—in a mild, parental, responsive way. Mundugumor men and women, in contrast, acted as she believed we expect men to act—fiercely and aggressively. Tchambuli men were "catty," wore curls, and went shopping, but Tchambuli women were energetic and managerial and placed less emphasis on personal adornment than did the men. [Drawing on their recent case study of the Tchambuli, whom they call the Chambri, Errington and Gewertz (1987), while recognizing gender malleability, have disputed the specifics of Mead's account.]

There is a growing field of feminist scholarship within anthropology (di Leonardo, ed. 1991; Nash and Safa 1986; Rosaldo 1980b; Strathern 1988), and in recent years ethnographers have been gathering systematic ethnographic data about gender in many cultural settings (Morgen, ed. 1989; Mukhopadhyay and Higgins 1988). We can see that gender roles vary with environment, economy, adaptive strategy, and level of social complexity. Before we examine the cross-cultural data, some definitions are in order.

Gender roles are the tasks and activities that a culture assigns to the sexes. Related to gender roles are **gender stereotypes,** which are oversimplified but strongly held ideas about the characteristics of males and females. **Gender stratification** describes an unequal distribution of rewards (socially valued resources, power, prestige, and personal freedom) between men and women, reflecting their different positions in a social hierarchy (Light, Keller, and Calhoun 1994). According to Ann Stoler (1977), the "economic determinants of female status" include freedom or autonomy (in disposing of one's labor and its fruits) and social power (control over the lives, labor, and produce of others).

In stateless societies, gender stratification is often more obvious in regard to prestige than it is in regard to wealth. In her study of the Ilongots of northern Luzon in the Philippines, Michelle Rosaldo (1980*a*) described gender differences related to the positive cultural value placed on adventure, travel, and knowledge of the external world. More often than women, Ilongot men, as headhunters, visited distant places. They acquired knowledge of the external world, amassed experiences there, and returned to express their knowledge, adventures, and feelings in public oratory. They received acclaim as a result. Ilongot women had inferior prestige because they lacked external experiences on which to base knowledge and dramatic expression. On the basis of Rosaldo's study and findings in other stateless societies, Ong (1989) argues that we must distinguish between prestige systems and actual power in a given society. High male prestige may not entail economic or political power held by men over their families.

GENDER ISSUES AMONG FORAGERS

Several studies have shown that economic roles affect gender stratification. In one cross-cultural study Peggy Sanday (1974) found that gender stratification decreased when men and women made roughly equal contributions to subsistence. She found that gender stratification was *greatest* when the women contributed either *much more* or *much less* than the men did.

This finding applied mainly to food producers, not to foragers. In foraging societies gender stratification was most marked when men contributed much *more* to the diet than women did. This was true among the Eskimo, Inuit, and other northern hunters and fishers. Among tropical and semitropical foragers, by contrast, gathering usually supplies more food than hunting and fishing do. Gathering is generally women's work; men usually hunt and fish. With gathering prominent, gender status tends to be more equal than it is when hunting and fishing are the main subsistence activities.

Gender status is also more equal when the domestic and public spheres aren't sharply separated. (**Domestic** means within or pertaining to the home.)

In foraging societies gender stratification is most marked when men contribute much more to the diet than women do—as has been true among the Eskimos, Inuit, and other northern hunters and fishers. These Alaskan Eskimos are preparing a bowhead whale for distribution and storage.

Strong differentiation between the home and the outside world is called the **domestic-public dichotomy** or the *private-public contrast*. The outside world can include politics, trade, warfare, or work. Often when domestic and public spheres are clearly separated, public activities have greater prestige than domestic ones do. This can promote gender stratification, because men are more likely to be active in the public domain than women are. Cross-culturally, women's activities tend to be closer to home than men's are. Thus, another reason hunter-gatherers have less gender stratification than food producers do is that the domestic-public dichotomy is more developed among food producers.

A division of labor linked to gender has been found in all cultures. However, the particular tasks assigned to men and women don't always reflect differences in strength and endurance. Food producers often assign the arduous tasks of carrying water and firewood and pounding grain to women. In 1967 in the Soviet Union women filled 47 percent of factory positions, including many unmechanized jobs requiring hard physical labor. Most Soviet sanitation workers, physicians, and nurses were women (Martin and Voorhies 1975). Many jobs that men do in some societies are done by women in others, and vice versa.

Certain roles are more sex-linked than others. Men are the usual hunters and warriors. Given such weapons as spears, knives, and bows, men make better fighters because they are bigger and stronger on the average than are women in the same population (Divale and Harris 1976). The male hunter-fighter role also reflects a tendency toward greater male mobility.

In foraging societies, women are either pregnant or lactating during most of their childbearing period. Late in pregnancy and after childbirth, carrying a baby limits a woman's movements, even her gathering. Given the effects of pregnancy and lactation on mobility, it is rarely feasible for women to be the primary hunters (Friedl 1975). Warfare, which also requires mobility, is not found in most foraging societies, nor is interregional trade well developed. Warfare and trade are two public arenas that contribute to status inequality of males and females among food producers.

The !Kung San illustrate the extent to which the activities and spheres of influence of men and women may overlap among foragers (Draper 1975). Traditional !Kung gender roles were interdependent. During gathering, women discovered information about game animals, which they passed on to the men. Men and women spent about the same amount of time away from camp, but neither worked more than three days a week. Between one-third and one-half of the band stayed home while the others worked.

The !Kung saw nothing wrong in doing the work of the other gender. Men often gathered food and collected water. A general sharing ethos dictated that men distribute meat and that women share the

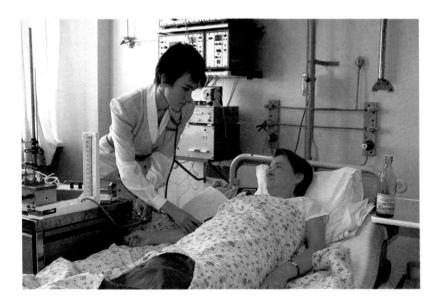

Many jobs that men do in some societies are done by women in others, and vice versa. In the Soviet Union most physicians, nurses, sanitation workers, and about half of all factory workers were women. Here an endocrinologist examines a patient in a state hospital in Riga, Latvia, formerly a Soviet Baltic state.

IN THE NEWS: MASAI GENDER ROLES

A gender-based division of labor has been found in all cultures, but the tasks assigned by gender don't necessarily reflect differences in strength or endurance. Many food producing societies, including the patrilineal, polygynous Masai pastoralists described here, assign heavy subsistence work to women, leaving the men free to be warrior-raiders. This article also describes increasing Masai poverty in the Ngorongoro crater area, where much of their traditional pasture land is now reserved for wild game and ecotourism.

Ngorongoro Conservation Area, Tanzania—Parimitoro Ole Kasiaro, a 35-year-old elder of the Masai tribe, recently married his third wife. Waiting in the wings is a fourth, a 10-year-old girl paid for with cattle by his father to her father before she was born.

With three underfed wives and three scrawny children, Mr. Kasiaro, whose cattle are dying of disease and who often confesses to being hungry himself, knows he cannot afford another wife. But Masai custom, which is paramount among the mud and dung houses here on the edge of the Serengeti Plain, dictates that he must in time marry again.

Mr. Kasiaro is proud of his Masai heritage, which anthropologists find remarkable for being so resilient to Western influences. But he admits to being troubled by some aspects of his society, especially its miserable treatment of women.

"Men in this community live as supervisors," he said, surveying a group of women sitting in the dirt. The women were resting after lugging containers of water from a stream as men stood by watching. "They leave the women to do all the everyday activities. It is not unusual to see a woman, even if she is pregnant, looking after cattle, sheep and goats, or taking donkeys to fetch cornmeal from the very distant shops."

Traditionally, Masai women performed the heavy work, leaving men free to be warriors, defending territory and raiding cattle. The warrior days are over, but rather than pitch in with the domestic chores, men typically spend their days drinking alcohol or playing bao, a popular board game. . . .

Mr. Kasiaro led an effort last year to help the women sell Masai jewelry to the tourists who drive past on their way to see the big game around the Ngorongoro Crater or the nearby Serengeti plain. But Mr. Kasiaro discovered that the women could not run a shop and lacked sufficient capital to buy the beads to make the elaborate necklaces the tourists want to buy.

"The men offered no capital for the women," he said. "The women had to sell their own necklaces to start."

After last year's rather poor beginning, Mr. Kasiaro is looking for a way to educate the women in running a small business. He believes that the income from the crafts will give the Masai women a new independence. And he sees another value in the project.

When men have money, he said, they often spend it on homemade liquor. "But when women get money," he continued, "they spend it on cornmeal for their children and helping the families."

Mr. Kasiaro's concern about the status of women has evolved slowly, and comes mainly, he suggested, from his better educational background, travels and reading.

Unlike most of the other men and women in the villages around Ngorongoro, Mr. Kasiaro attended school. As a member of the regional council he travels regularly to the regional capital of Arusha, 80 miles to the east, and has been to Dar-es-Salaam, the national capital, on several occasions. He recently accompanied a group of Masai dancers on a trip to Denmark, the first time he has been out of Africa.

A disproportional division of labor is by no means confined to Masai culture. The World Bank estimates that about 70 percent of the food crops in Africa are cultivated by women. Efforts by international organizations to improve the lot of the African woman have met with meager success, largely because many of the continent's national economies have weakened, putting women in even more vulnerable positions.

Such is the case among the estimated 300,000 Masai in Tanzania, particularly those living around the Ngorongoro crater, where much of the traditional rangeland for the all-important Masai cattle has been reserved for game and tourists. As a result, the Masai in the area are much poorer and have clung to their traditional ways to a greater degree than the estimated 200,000 Masai in southern Kenya.

Mr. Kasiaro said that the first to be affected by the rising poverty were the women, who must look after the malnourished and often sick children.

Source: Jane Perlez, "Woman's Work Is Never Done (Not by Masai Men)," *The New York Times*, December 2, 1991, p. A4.

fruits of gathering. Boys and girls of all ages played together. Fathers took an active role in raising children. Resources were adequate, and competition and aggression were discouraged. Exchangeability and interdependence of roles are adaptive in small groups.

Patricia Draper's field work among the !Kung is especially useful in showing the relationships between economy, gender roles, and stratification because she studied both foragers and a group of former foragers who had become sedentary. Just a few thousand !Kung continue their culture's traditional foraging pattern. Most are now sedentary, living near food producers or ranchers (see Kent 1992; Solway and Lee 1990; Wilmsen 1989).

Draper studied sedentary !Kung at Mahopa, a village where they herded, grew crops, worked for wages, and did a small amount of gathering. Their gender roles were becoming more rigidly defined. A domestic-public dichotomy was developing as men traveled farther than women did. With less gathering, women were confined more to the home. Boys could gain mobility through herding, but girls' movements were more limited. The equal and communal world of the bush was yielding to the social features of sedentary life. A differential ranking of men according to their herds, houses, and sons began to replace sharing. Males came to be seen as the most valuable producers.

If there is some degree of male dominance in every contemporary society, it may be because of changes such as those which have drawn the !Kung into wage work, market sales, and thus the world capitalist economy. A historical interplay between local, national, and international forces influences systems of gender stratification (Ong 1989). In traditional foraging cultures, however, egalitarianism extended to the relations between the sexes. The social spheres, activities, rights, and obligations of men and women overlapped. Foragers' kinship systems tend to be bilateral (calculated equally through males and females) rather than favoring either the mother's side or the father's side. Foragers may live with either the husband's or the wife's kin and often shift between one group and the other.

One last observation about foragers: It is among them that the public and private spheres are least separate, hierarchy is least marked, aggression and competition are most discouraged, and the rights, activities, and spheres of influence of men and women overlap the most. Our ancestors lived entirely by foraging until 10,000 years ago. If there is any most "natural" form of human society, it is best (although imperfectly—see the box in the chapter "Cultural Change and Adaptation") represented by foragers. Despite the popular stereotype of the club-wielding caveman dragging his mate by the hair, relative gender equality is a much more likely ancestral pattern.

GENDER ISSUES AMONG HORTICULTURALISTS

Gender roles and stratification among cultivators vary widely, depending on specific features of the economy and social structure. Demonstrating this, Martin and Voorhies (1975) studied a sample of 515 horticultural societies, representing all parts of the world. They looked at several variables, including descent and postmarital residence, the percentage of the diet derived from cultivation, and the productivity of men and women.

Women were found to be the main producers in horticultural societies. In 50 percent of those societies, women did most of the cultivating. In 33 percent, contributions to cultivation by men and women were equal. In only 17 percent did men do most of the work. Women tended to do a bit more cultivating in matrilineal compared with patrilineal societies. They dominated horticulture in 64 percent of the matrilineal societies versus 50 percent of the patrilineal ones.

Reduced Gender Stratification— Matrilineal, Uxorilocal Societies

Cross-cultural variation in gender status is related to rules of descent and postmarital residence (Martin and Voorhies 1975; Friedl 1975). Among horticulturalists with matrilineal descent and **uxorilocality** (residence after marriage with the wife's relatives), female status tends to be high. Matriliny and uxorilocality disperse related males, rather than consolidating them. By contrast, patriliny and **virilocality** (residence after marriage with the husband's kin) keep male relatives together.

Women tend to have high status in matrilineal, uxorilocal societies for several reasons. Descent-group membership, succession to political posi-

Women have high status in matrilineal, uxorilocal societies because descent-group membership, succession to political positions, allocation of land, and overall social identity come through female links. Among these Minangkabau of Negeri Sembilan (Malaysia), matriliny gave women sole inheritance of ancestral rice fields and promoted clusters of female kin.

tions, allocation of land, and overall social identity all come through female links. Among the Minangkabau in Malaysia (Peletz 1988), matriliny gave women sole inheritance of ancestral rice fields. Uxorilocality created solidary clusters of female kin. Minangkabau women had considerable influence beyond the household (Swift 1963). In such matrilineal contexts, women are the basis of the entire social structure. Although public authority may be (or may appear to be) assigned to the men, much of the power and decision making may actually belong to the senior women.

Anthropologists have never discovered a **matriarchy,** a society ruled by women. Still, some matrilineal societies, including the **Iroquois** (Brown 1975), a confederation of tribes in aboriginal New York, show that women's political and ritual influence can rival that of the men.

We saw that among foragers gender status was most equal when there was no sharp separation of male and female activities and of public and domestic spheres. However, gender stratification can also be reduced by roles that remove men from the local community. We now refine our generalizations: It is the sharp contrast between male and female roles *within the local community* that promotes gender stratification. Gender stratification may be reduced when women play prominent local roles, while men pursue activities in a wider, regional system. Iroquois women, for example, played a major

subsistence role, while men left home for long periods. As is usual in matrilineal societies, *internal* warfare was uncommon. Iroquois men waged war only on distant groups; this could keep them away for years.

Iroquois men hunted and fished, but women controlled the local economy. Women did some fishing and occasional hunting, but their major productive role was in horticulture. Women owned the land, which they inherited from matrilineal kinswomen. Women controlled the production and distribution of food.

Iroquois women lived with their husbands and children in the family compartments of a communal longhouse. Women born in a longhouse remained there for life. Senior women, or **matrons,** decided which men could join the longhouse as husbands, and they could evict incompatible men. Women therefore controlled alliances between descent groups, an important political job in tribal society.

Iroquois women thus managed production and distribution. Social identity, succession to office and titles, and property all came through the female line, and women were prominent in ritual and politics. Related tribes made up a confederacy, the League of the Iroquois, with chiefs and councils.

A council of male chiefs managed military operations, but chiefly succession was matrilineal. The matrons of each longhouse nominated a man as their representative. If the council rejected their first nominee, the women proposed others until one was accepted. Matrons constantly monitored the chiefs and could impeach them. Women could veto war declarations, withhold provisions for war, and initiate peace efforts. In religion, too, women shared power. Half the tribe's religious practitioners were women, and the matrons helped select the others.

Reduced Gender Stratification— Matrifocal Societies

Nancy Tanner (1974) also found that the combination of male travel and a prominent female economic role reduced gender stratification and promoted high female status. She based this finding on a survey of the **matrifocal** (mother-centered, often

In many parts of Africa, including Yaounde, Cameroon (shown here), women are active in commerce. Polygyny may even help the aspiring woman trader, who can leave her children with cowives while she pursues a business career.

with no resident husband-father) organization of certain societies in Indonesia, West Africa, and the Caribbean. Matrifocal societies are not necessarily matrilineal. A few are even patrilineal.

For example, Tanner (1974) found matrifocality among the Igbo of eastern Nigeria, who are patrilineal, virilocal, and polygynous (men have multiple wives). Each wife had her own house, where she lived with her children. Women planted crops next to their houses and traded surpluses. Women's associations ran the local markets, while men did the long-distance trading.

In a case study of the Igbo, Ifi Amadiume (1987) noted that either sex could fill male gender roles. Before Christian influence, successful Igbo women and men used wealth to take titles and acquire wives. Wives freed husbands (male and female) from domestic work and helped them accumulate wealth. Female husbands were not considered masculine but preserved their femininity. Igbo women asserted themselves in women's groups, including those of lineage daughters, lineage wives, and a community-wide women's council led by titled women. The high status and influence of Igbo women rested on the separation of males from local subsistence and on a marketing system that allowed women to leave home and gain prominence in distribution and—through these accomplishments—in politics.

Increased Gender Stratification— Patrilineal-Virilocal Societies

The Igbo are unusual among patrilineal-virilocal societies, many of which have marked gender stratification. Martin and Voorhies (1975) link the decline of matriliny and the spread of the **patrilineal-virilocal** complex (consisting of patrilineality, virilocality, warfare, and male supremacy) to pressure on resources. Faced with scarce resources, patrilineal-virilocal cultivators such as the Yanomami often wage warfare against other villages. This favors virilocality and patriliny, customs that keep related men together in the same village, where they make strong allies in battle. Such societies tend to have a sharp domestic-public dichotomy, and men tend to dominate the prestige hierarchy. Men may use their public roles in warfare and trade and their greater prestige to symbolize and reinforce the devaluation or oppression of women.

The patrilineal-virilocal complex characterizes many societies in highland Papua–New Guinea. Women work hard growing and processing subsistence crops, raising and tending pigs (the main domesticated animal and a favorite food), and doing domestic cooking, but they are isolated from the public domain, which men control. Men grow and distribute prestige crops, prepare food for feasts, and arrange marriages. The men even get to trade the pigs and control their use in ritual.

In densely populated areas of the Papua–New Guinea highlands, male-female avoidance is associated with strong pressure on resources (Lindenbaum 1972). Men fear all female contacts, including sex. They think that sexual contact with women will weaken them. Indeed, men see everything female as dangerous and polluting. They segregate themselves in men's houses and hide their precious ritual objects from women. They delay marriage, and some never marry.

By contrast, the sparsely populated areas of Papua–New Guinea, such as recently settled areas, lack taboos on male-female contacts. The image of woman as polluter fades, heterosexual intercourse is valued, men and women live together, and reproductive rates are high.

Etoro Homosexuality

One of the most extreme examples of male-female sexual antagonism in Papua–New Guinea comes from the **Etoro** (Kelly 1976), a group of 400 people who subsist by hunting and horticulture in the Trans-Fly region. The Etoro also illustrate the power of culture in molding human sexuality. The following account applies only to Etoro males and their beliefs. Etoro cultural norms prevented the male anthropologist who studied them from gathering comparable information about female attitudes. Etoro opinions about sexuality are linked to their beliefs about the cycle of birth, physical growth, maturity, old age, and death.

The Etoro believe that semen is necessary to give life force to a fetus, which is said to be placed within a woman by an ancestral spirit. Because men are believed to have a limited supply of semen, sexuality saps male vitality. The birth of children, nurtured by semen, symbolizes a necessary (and unpleasant) sacrifice that will lead to the husband's eventual death. Heterosexual intercourse, which is

In some parts of Papua–New Guinea, the patrilineal-virilocal complex has extreme social repercussions. Regarding females as dangerous and polluting, men may segregate themselves in men's houses (such as this one, located near the Sepik River), where they hide their precious ritual objects from women.

needed only for reproduction, is discouraged. Women who want too much sex are viewed as witches, hazardous to their husbands' health. Etoro culture permits heterosexual intercourse only about 100 days a year. The rest of the time it is tabooed. Seasonal birth clustering shows that the taboo is respected.

So objectionable is heterosexuality that it is removed from community life. It can occur neither in sleeping quarters nor in the fields. Coitus can happen only in the woods, where it is risky because poisonous snakes, the Etoro say, are attracted by the sounds and smells of sex.

Although coitus is discouraged, homosexual acts are viewed as essential. Etoro believe that boys cannot produce semen on their own. To grow into men and eventually give life force to their children, boys must acquire semen orally from older men. From the age of ten until adulthood, boys are inseminated by older men. No taboos are attached to this. Homosexual activity can go on in the sleeping area or garden. Every three years a group of boys around the age of twenty are formally initiated into manhood. They go to a secluded mountain lodge, where they are visited and inseminated by several older men.

Etoro homosexuality is governed by a code of propriety. Although homosexual relationships between older and younger males are culturally essential, those between boys of the same age are discouraged. A boy who gets semen from other youths is believed to be sapping their life force and stunting their growth. When a boy develops very rapidly, this suggests that he is ingesting semen from other boys. Like a sex-hungry wife, he is shunned as a witch.

Etoro homosexuality rests not on hormones or genes but on cultural traditions. The Etoro represent one extreme of a male-female avoidance pattern that is widespread in Papua–New Guinea and in patrilineal-virilocal societies.

GENDER ISSUES AMONG AGRICULTURALISTS

As horticulture evolved into agriculture, women lost their role as primary cultivators. Certain agricultural techniques, particularly plowing, were assigned to men because of their greater average size and strength (Martin and Voorhies 1975). Except when irrigation was used, plowing eliminated the need for constant weeding, an activity usually done by women.

Cross-cultural data illustrate these changes in productive roles. Women were the main workers in 50 percent of the horticultural societies surveyed but in only 15 percent of the agricultural groups. Male

subsistence labor dominated 81 percent of the agricultural societies but only 17 percent of the horticultural ones (Martin and Voorhies 1975) (see Table 18.1).

With agriculture, women were cut off from production for the first time in human history. Belief systems started contrasting men's valuable extra-domestic labor with women's domestic role, now viewed as inferior. (**Extradomestic** means outside the home; within or pertaining to the public domain.) Changes in kinship and postmarital residence patterns also hurt women. Descent groups and polygyny declined with agriculture, and the nuclear family became more common. Living with her husband and children, a woman was isolated from her kinswomen and cowives. Female sexuality is carefully supervised in agricultural economies; men have easier access to divorce and extramarital sex, reflecting a "double standard."

Still, female status in agricultural societies is not inevitably bleak. Gender stratification is associated with plow agriculture rather than with intensive cultivation per se. Studies of peasant gender roles and stratification in France and Spain (Harding 1975; Reiter 1975), which have plow agriculture, show that people think of the house as the female sphere and the fields as the male domain. However, such a dichotomy is not inevitable, as my own research among Betsileo agriculturalists in Madagascar shows.

Betsileo women play a prominent role in agriculture, contributing a third of the hours invested in rice production. They have their customary tasks in the division of labor, but their work is more seasonal than men's is.

No one has much to do during the ceremonial season, between mid-June and mid-September. Men work in the rice fields almost daily the rest of the year. Women's cooperative work occurs during

Table 18.1 *Male and female contributions to production in cultivating societies*

	Horticulture (Percentage of 104 Societies)	Agriculture (Percentage of 93 Societies)
Women are primary cultivators	50	15
Men are primary cultivators	17	81
Equal contributions to cultivation	33	3

Source: Martin and Voorhies 1975, p. 283.

transplanting (mid-September through November) and harvesting (mid-March through early May). Along with other members of the household, women do daily weeding in December and January. After the harvest, all family members work together winnowing the rice and transporting it to the granary.

If we consider the strenuous daily task of husking rice by pounding (a part of food preparation rather than production per se), women actually contribute slightly more than 50 percent of the labor devoted to producing and preparing rice before cooking.

Not just women's prominent economic role but traditional social organization enhances female status among the Betsileo. Although postmarital residence is mainly virilocal, descent rules permit married women to keep membership in and a strong allegiance to their own descent groups. Kinship is broadly and bilaterally (on both sides—as in contemporary North America) calculated. The Betsileo exemplify Aihwa Ong's (1989) generalization that bilateral (and matrilineal) kinship systems, combined with subsistence economies in which the sexes have complementary roles in food production and distribution, are characterized by reduced gender stratification. Such societies are common among South Asian peasants (Ong 1989).

The Betsileo woman has obligations to her husband and his kin, but they are also obligated to her and her relatives. Often accompanied by their husbands and children, women pay regular visits to their home villages. The husband and his relatives help the wife's kin in agriculture and attend ceremonials hosted by them. When a woman dies, she is normally buried in her husband's ancestral tomb. However, a delegation from her own village always comes to request that she be buried at home. Women often marry into villages where some of their kinswomen have previously married; thus, even after marriage a woman lives near some of her own relatives.

Betsileo men do not have exclusive control over the means of production. Women can inherit rice fields, but most women, on marrying, relinquish their shares to their brothers. Sometimes a woman and her husband cultivate her field, eventually passing it on to their children.

Traditionally, Betsileo men participate more in politics, but women also hold political office. Women sell their produce and products in markets, invest in cattle, sponsor ceremonials, and are mentioned during offerings to ancestors. Arranging marriages, an important extradomestic activity, is more women's concern than men's. Sometimes Betsileo women seek their own kinswomen as wives for their sons, reinforcing their own prominence in village life and continuing kin-based female solidarity in the village.

The Betsileo illustrate the idea that intensive cultivation does not necessarily entail sharp gender stratification. We can see that gender roles and stratification reflect not just the type of adaptive strategy but also specific environmental variables and cultural attributes. Betsileo women continue to play a significant role in their society's major economic activity, rice production.

Bilateral kinship systems, combined with subsistence economies in which the sexes have complementary roles in food production and distribution, have reduced gender stratification. Such features are common among Asian rice cultivators, such as the Ifugao of the Philippines (shown here).

HIDDEN WOMEN, PUBLIC MEN—PUBLIC WOMEN, HIDDEN MEN

For the past few years, one of Brazil's top sex symbols has been Roberta Close, whom I first saw in a furniture commercial. Roberta, whose looks reminded me of those of the young Natalie Wood, ended her pitch with an admonition to prospective furniture buyers to accept no substitute for the advertised product. "Things," she warned, "are not always what they seem."

Nor was Roberta. This petite and incredibly feminine creature was actually a man. Nevertheless, despite the fact that he—or she (speaking as Brazilians do)—is a man posing as a woman, Roberta has won a secure place in Brazilian mass culture. Her photos decorate magazines. She has been a panelist on a TV variety show and has starred in a stage play in Rio with an actor known for his super-macho image. Roberta even inspired a well-known, apparently heterosexual, pop singer to make a "video" honoring her. In it she pranced around Rio's Ipanema Beach in a bikini, showing off her ample hips and buttocks.

Things aren't always what they seem. Roberta Close, a known transvestite (a transsexual as of 1989) who for years has been one of Brazil's top sex symbols, is genetically male.

The video depicted widespread male appreciation of Roberta's beauty. As confirmation, one heterosexual man told me that he had recently been on the same plane as Roberta and had been struck by her looks. Another man said he wanted to have sex with her. These comments, it seemed to me, illustrated striking cultural contrasts about gender and sexuality. In Brazil, a Latin American country noted for its *machismo*, heterosexual men do not feel that attraction toward a transvestite blemishes their masculine identities.

Roberta Close exists in relation to a gender-identity scale that jumps from extreme femininity to extreme masculinity, with little in between. Masculinity is stereotyped as active and public, femininity as passive and domestic. The male-female contrast in rights and behavior is much stronger in Brazil than it is in North America. Brazilians confront a more rigidly defined masculine role than North Americans do.

The active-passive dichotomy also provides a stereotypical model for male homosexuality: One man is supposed to be the active, masculine (inserting) partner, whereas the other is the passive, effeminate one. The latter man is derided as a *bicha* (intestinal worm), but little stigma at-

---

Plowing has become prominent in Betsileo agriculture only recently, but irrigation makes weeding, in which women participate, a continued necessity. If new tools and techniques eventually reduce women's roles in transplanting, harvesting, and weeding, gender stratification may develop. In the meantime, several features of the economy and social organization continue to shield the Betsileo from the gender hierarchies found in many agricultural and virilocal societies.

We have seen that virilocality is usually associated with gender stratification. However, some cultures with these institutions, including the Betsileo and the matrifocal Igbo of eastern Nigeria, offer contrasts to the generalization. The Igbo and Betsileo are not alone in allowing women a role in trade.

Many patrilineal, polygynous societies in West Africa also allow women to have careers in commerce. Polygyny may even help an aspiring woman trader, who can leave her children with her cowives while she pursues a business career. She repays them with cash and other forms of assistance.

GENDER ISSUES AMONG PASTORALISTS

Because it rarely occurs as a "pure" adaptive strategy, pastoralism has diverse social correlates, including gender roles and stratification. Most pastoralists also cultivate, using either horticultural or agricultural techniques. They are classified as pas-

taches to the inserter. However, for Brazilian men who are unhappy with active masculinity or passive effeminacy there is one other choice— active femininity. For Roberta Close and others like her, the cultural demand of ultramasculinity has yielded to a performance of ultrafemininity. These men-women form a third gender in relation to Brazil's more polarized male-female identity scale.

Transvestites such as Roberta are particularly prominent in Rio's annual Carnival, when an ambience of inversion rules the city. In the culturally accurate words of the American popular novelist Gregory McDonald, who sets one of his books in Brazil at Carnival time:

Everything goes topsy-turvy.... Men become women; women become men; grown-ups become children; rich people pretend they're poor; poor people, rich; sober people become drunkards; thieves become generous. Very topsy-turvy. (McDonald 1984, p. 154)

Most notable in this costumed inversion (DaMatta 1991), men dress as women. Carnival reveals and expresses normally hidden tensions and conflicts as social life is turned upside down. Reality is illuminated through a dramatic presentation of its opposite.

This is the final key to Roberta's cultural meaning. She emerged in a setting in which male-female inversion is part of the year's most popular festival. Transvestites are the pièces de résistance at Rio's Carnival balls, where they dress as scantily as the real women do. They wear postage-stamp bikinis, sometimes with no tops. Photos of real women and transformed ones vie for space in the magazines. It is often impossible to tell the born women from the hidden men. Roberta Close is a permanent incarnation of Carnival—a year-round reminder of the spirit of Carnivals past, present, and yet to come.

Roberta emerges from a Latin culture whose gender roles contrast strongly with those of the United States. From small village to massive city, Brazilian males are public and

Brazilian females are private creatures. Streets, beaches, and bars belong to the men. Although bikinis adorn Rio's beaches on weekends and holidays, there are many more men than women there on weekdays. The men revel in their ostentatiously sexual displays. As they sun themselves and play soccer and volleyball, they regularly stroke their genitals to keep them firm. They are living publicly, assertively, and sexually in a world of men.

Brazilian men must work hard at this public image, constantly acting out their culture's definition of masculine behavior. Public life is a play whose strong roles go to men. Roberta Close, of course, is a public figure. Given that Brazilian culture defines the public world as male, we can perhaps better understand now why the nation's number one sex symbol is a man who excels at performing in public as a woman.

toralists, however, when dairy products and meat provide more than 50 percent of their diet. Among pastoralists who practice intensive agriculture (like the Balkan case discussed below) or who are descended from agricultural parent communities, the gender hierarchy reflects the domestic-public dichotomy characteristic of intensive cultivators. The patrilineal-virilocal complex also characterizes pastoralists. Both of these factors contribute to gender stratification within this strategy of adaptation.

In fact, the transhumant pastoralists of the Balkan peninsula (Greece, the former Yugoslavia, Albania, and Bulgaria) provide an extreme illustration of gender stratification. Balkan men have followed a transhumant pattern between summer and winter pastures, and they practice plow agriculture. Herding and plowing are male activities, although women do some cultivating in addition to domestic work and crafts. Women also carry firewood and water. The domestic-public dichotomy and the patrilineal-virilocal complex are fully expressed in "patricentric" Balkan social organization (Denich 1974). Men control all property. Women inherit neither land nor livestock.

The Balkan pastoralists belong to patrilineal-virilocal tribes and descent groups. Traditionally, the father was the patriarch in a joint household that included his wife, his married sons, their wives and children, and his own unmarried children. Joint households split up after the patriarch's death. The sons become patriarchs in their own right.

Gender stratification involving low female pres-

Among transhumant pastoralists of the Balkan peninsula (Greece, the former Yugoslavia, Albania, and Bulgaria) the domestic-public dichotomy and the patrilineal-virilocal complex are expressed in "patricentric" social organization. Balkan men, like this Albanian shepherd, move their flocks between summer and winter pastures.

tige and subordination was extreme. When identifying their children, men mentioned only sons. Male ancestors, but never female ones, were remembered—for as many as twenty generations. Men arranged all marriages. Brothers' wives had to come from different villages. Therefore, when they married, women had to enter a totally alien social world where they had no relatives.

Men held authority and power. A woman had to defer to her husband and his kinsmen. Women could be beaten and, if adulterous, killed. Female sexual activity was rigidly controlled. Exclusion of women from a major role in production helped maintain patricentric organization in the Balkans.

We have seen that tribal society, under some conditions, discriminates against women. In stratified society, not only does discrimination against women continue but some women join some men in discriminating against other men, women, and children.

In tribal societies, the patrilineal-virilocal complex can promote gender stratification and act to isolate and devalue women. In chiefdoms and states (including industrial nations), new possibilities are opened for some women. With general social stratification, some men, women, and children have privileged access to resources while other strata have more limited opportunities. In such contexts elite women may manipulate wealth and power as effectively as men do. They can become queens, chiefs, headwomen, presidents, and prime ministers. They can direct rituals, convoke, sponsor, and lead events, trade, exchange, arrange marriages, and run businesses.

GENDER ISSUES AND INDUSTRIALISM

The domestic-public dichotomy, which is developed most fully among patrilineal-virilocal food producers and plow agriculturalists, has also affected gender stratification in industrial societies, including the United States and Canada. However, gender roles have been changing rapidly in North America. The "traditional" idea that "a woman's place is in the home" actually emerged in the United States as industrialism spread after 1900. Earlier, pioneer women in the Midwest and West had been recognized as fully productive workers in farming and home industry. Under industrialism attitudes about gendered work came to vary with class and region. In early industrial Europe, men, women, and children had flocked to factories as wage laborers. American slaves of both sexes had done grueling work in cotton fields. With abolition, southern African-American women continued working as field hands and domestics. Poor white women labored in the South's early cotton mills. In the 1890s more than 1 million American women held menial, repetitious, and unskilled factory positions (Margolis 1984; Martin and Voorhies 1975).

After 1900 European immigration produced a

male labor force willing to work for wages lower than those of American-born men. Those immigrant men moved into factory jobs that previously had gone to women. As machine tools and mass production further reduced the need for female labor, the notion that women were biologically unfit for factory work began to gain ground (Martin and Voorhies 1975).

Maxine Margolis (1984) has shown how gendered work, attitudes, and beliefs have varied in response to American economic needs. For example, wartime shortages of men have promoted the idea that work outside the home is women's patriotic duty. During the world wars the notion that women are biologically unfit for hard physical labor faded. Inflation and the culture of consumption have also spurred female employment. When prices and/or demand rise, multiple paychecks help maintain family living standards.

The steady increase in female paid employment since World War II also reflects the baby boom and industrial expansion. American culture has traditionally defined clerical work, teaching, and nursing as female occupations (see Table 18.4). With rapid population growth and business expansion after World War II, the demand for women to fill such jobs grew steadily. Employers also found that they could increase their profits by paying women less wages than they would have to pay returning male veterans.

Margolis (1984) contends that changes in the economy lead to changes in attitudes toward and about women. Woman's role in the home is stressed during periods of high unemployment, although if wages fall or inflation occurs simultaneously, female employment may still be accepted. Between 1970 and 1989 the proportion of women in the American work force increased from 38 to 45 percent, and more than 56 million American women now work at paid jobs (Cowan 1989). Figures on the ever-increasing cash employment of American mothers and wives are given in Table 18.2.

The average American man employed full-time earned $27,430 in 1989, versus $18,778 for the average woman (68 percent of the male rate, up from 62 percent in 1982 and 65 percent in 1987) (Barringer 1989). Table 18.3 details employment in the United States in 1989 by gender and job type. Notice that the income gap between women and men was least marked—but still evident—in professional jobs, where women averaged 71 percent of the male income (up from 68 percent in 1987). The gap was widest in sales, where women averaged barely more than half the male salary.

According to political scientist Andrew Hacker (1984), American women are replacing men in certain occupations for three reasons. First, because of increasing automation, physical strength is less necessary for many jobs. Second, American women tend to be better educated than American men are. Employers prefer to hire more literate people, particularly when—and here is Hacker's third reason—women will accept lower wages.

In particular, many American men between fifty-five and sixty are encouraged to retire earlier, and less-expensive female workers are replacing them. (Later, many of those men will accept lower-paying part-time jobs.) There is also a group of younger

Table 18.2 *Cash employment of American mothers, wives and husbands, 1950–1989**

Year	Percentage of Women with Children Under 18	Percentage of All Married Women[†]	Percentage of All Married Men[‡]
1950	19	N/A	N/A
1960	28	32	89
1970	40	40	86
1975	45	44	83
1980	54	50	81
1985	61	54	79
1989	66	58	78

*Civilian population sixteen years and older.
[†]Husband present.
[‡]Wife present.
Source: Statistical Abstract of the United States, 1991, pp. 390–391.

Table 18.3 *Earnings in the United States (1989) by gender and job type**

	AVERAGE ANNUAL SALARY		Ratio of Earnings, Female/Male
	Men	**Women**	
Median earnings	$27,430	$18,778	68
By job type:			
Managerial/executive/administrative	40,103	24,589	61
Professional	39,449	27,933	71
Sales	29,696	16,057	54
Service	18,903	11,669	62

*Year-round, full-time workers.
Source: Statistical Abstract of the United States, 1991, p. 417.

men, including many ethnic minorities, who are too poorly educated to find work in an economy that increasingly stresses services and information over farm and factory.

Table 18.4, which shows the percentage of female workers in certain occupations in 1950 and 1989, seems to support Hacker's contention that women are replacing men in certain professions, particu-

Table 18.4 *Employment of women in selected occupations, 1950 and 1989*

Occupation	WOMEN AS PERCENT OF ALL WORKERS IN THE OCCUPATION	
	1950	1989
Professional workers	40	50
Engineers	1	8
Lawyers and judges	4	22
Physicians	7	18
Dentists	N/A	9
Registered nurses	98	94
College teachers	23	39
Other teachers	75	73
Managers	14	40
Sales workers	35	49
Clerical workers	62	85
Artisans	3	9
Operatives	34	41
Transport operatives	1	9
Service workers	57	60

N/A: Not available.
Source: Statistical Abstract of the United States, 1991, pp. 395–397; Schaefer 1989, p. 283.

larly in fields that require an advanced education: engineering, medicine, law, and college teaching. Still, certain positions with less prestige and income (e.g., clerical workers) also continue to have a higher proportion of women (Bourque and Warren 1987).

Economist George Gilder (1984) contends that women aren't actually taking jobs away from men. Rather, as the American economy expanded during the 1980s, there were more jobs for both men and women. During the 1980s the number of full-time jobs held by women rose by 28 percent, compared with 12 percent for jobs held by men (*Statistical Abstract,* 1991, p. 393). (The American male population aged twenty and older grew by 15 percent in the same period: *Statistical Abstract,* 1991, p. 13.)

Today's jobs are not especially demanding in terms of physical labor. With machines to do the heavy work, the smaller average body size and lesser average strength of women are no longer impediments to blue-collar employment. The main reason we don't see more modern-day Rosies working alongside male riveters is that the U.S. work force itself is abandoning heavy-goods manufacture. In the 1950s two-thirds of American jobs were blue-collar, compared with 16 percent today. The location of those jobs has shifted within the world capitalist economy. Third World countries with cheaper labor produce steel, automobiles, and other heavy goods less expensively than the United States can, but the United States excels at services. The American mass education system has many inadequacies, but it does train millions of people for service- and information-oriented jobs, from sales clerks to computer operators.

THE SATURDAY EVENING

POST

MAY 29, 1943   10¢

BEGINNING—A NEW
KELLAND SERIAL
Heart on Her Sleeve

EDGAR SNOW
REPORTS ON GERMAN
ATROCITIES

Wartime shortages of men have promoted the idea that extradomestic labor is women's patriotic duty. During the world wars the notion that women were biologically unfit for hard physical labor faded. Shown here is World War II's famous Rosie the Riveter.

The Feminization of Poverty

Alongside the economic gains of many American women, particularly professionals, stands an opposite extreme: the feminization of poverty. This refers to the increasing proportion of America's poor who are women. More than half of U.S. households with sub-poverty-level incomes (3.6 of 6.9 million families) have female heads. The feminization of poverty accounts for almost all the increase (53 percent) in poverty in the United States since 1970 (Barringer 1989).

Feminine poverty has been a trend in the United States since World War II, but it has accelerated recently. In 1959 female-headed households accounted for 26 percent of the American poor. That figure has more than doubled. About half the female

poor are "in transition," facing an economic crisis caused by the departure, disability, or death of a husband. The other half are more permanently dependent on the welfare system or on friends or relatives living nearby (Schaefer and Lamm 1992). The feminization of poverty and its consequences in regard to living standards and health are widespread even among wage earners. Many American women, especially African-American women, work part time for low wages and meager benefits. Fourteen percent of the American population, some 35 million people, had no health insurance in 1991 (Pear 1992).

The fate of America's less fortunate children, whose poverty has increased by 25 percent since 1970, is linked to the feminization of poverty. Almost 40 percent of poor people in the United States are children under age eighteen. More than 20 percent of American children now live with one parent, usually the mother. Among single mothers with children under eighteen, the 1988 poverty rate was 38 percent for whites, 56 percent for African-Americans, and 59 percent for Hispanics (Schaefer and Lamm 1992, p. 252).

WHAT DETERMINES VARIATION IN GENDER ISSUES?

We see that gender roles and stratification have varied widely across cultures and through history. Among the causes of this variation are the needs of particular economies and, more generally, the level of sociopolitical complexity and the degree of participation in the world capitalist economy. Among many foragers and matrilineal cultivators, there is little gender stratification. Competition for resources leads to warfare and the intensification of production. These conditions favor patriliny and virilocality. To the extent that women lose their productive roles in agricultural and pastoral societies, the domestic-public dichotomy is accentuated and gender stratification is sharpened. With industrialism, attitudes about gender vary in the context of female extradomestic employment. Gender is flexible and varies with cultural, social, political, and economic factors. The variability of gender in time and space suggests that it will continue to change. The biology of the sexes is not a narrow enclosure limiting humans but a broad base upon which a variety of structures can be built (Friedl 1975).

SUMMARY

In recent years anthropologists have gathered systematic ethnographic data about gender in many cultural settings. Gender roles and gender stratification vary with environment, economy, adaptive strategy, level of social complexity, and degree of participation in the world capitalist economy. *Gender roles* are the tasks and activities that a culture assigns to each sex. Related to gender roles are *gender stereotypes*—oversimplified but strongly held ideas about the characteristics of males and females. *Gender stratification* describes an unequal distribution of rewards (socially valued resources, power, prestige, and personal freedom) between men and women, reflecting their different positions in a social hierarchy. In stateless societies, gender stratification is often much more obvious in regard to prestige than it is in regard to wealth or power.

Where gathering is prominent, gender status is more symmetrical than is the case when hunting or fishing dominates the foraging economy. Gender status is more equal when the domestic and public spheres are not sharply separated. Foragers lack two public arenas that contribute to higher male status among food producers: warfare and organized interregional trade. Among foragers, hierarchy is least marked, aggression and competition are most discouraged, and the rights, activities, and spheres of influence of men and women overlap the most.

Gender stratification, which tends to increase as cultivation intensifies, is also linked to descent and postmarital residence. Matrilineal-uxorilocal systems occur in societies where population pressure on strategic resources is minimal and warfare is infrequent. Women's status is high in such societies because descent-group membership, political succession, land allocation, and overall social identity come through female links. Although there are no matriarchies, women in many societies wield power and make decisions. If women play a major subsistence role while men leave home for long periods, sexual equality is favored. Gender stratification is marked when male and female spheres are sharply differentiated within the local community.

Scarcity of resources promotes intervillage warfare, patriliny, and virilocality. The localization of related males is adaptive for military solidarity. Men may use their public roles in war and extradomestic distribution to symbolize and reinforce their oppression of women.

Agriculture intensifies production and reliance on crops. With plow agriculture, gender stratification increases as men assume responsibility for subsistence. With the advent of plow agriculture, women were removed from production for the first time in human history. The distinction between women's domestic work and men's extradomestic "productive" labor reinforced the contrast between men as public and valuable and women as domestic and inferior. The Betsileo illustrate, however, that intensive cultivation per se does not entail a low status for women. Pastoralism, since it rarely occurs as a "pure" adaptation, has diverse gender roles, but gender stratification is usually present.

Americans' attitudes toward gender vary with class and region. The attitude that woman's place is in the home emerged with early industrialism. When the need for female labor declines, the idea that women are unfit for many jobs increases. Forces such as war, inflation, falling wages, the baby boom, and employment patterns help account for female cash employment and Americans' attitudes toward it. Alongside the economic gains of many American women, particularly professionals, stands an opposite extreme: the feminization of poverty. The *feminization of poverty*, which refers to the increasing proportion of America's poor who are women, accounts for virtually the entire increase in poverty in the United States since 1970. Sharp differences between the public and private spheres and the gender stratification that such a distinction promotes do not appear to be cultural universals.

GLOSSARY

domestic: Within or pertaining to the home.

domestic-public dichotomy: Contrast between women's role in the home and men's role in public life, with a corresponding social devaluation of women's work and worth.

environmentalists: See *nurturists*.

Etoro: Papua–New Guinea culture in which males are culturally trained to prefer homosexuality.

extradomestic: Outside the home; within or pertaining to the public domain.

gender roles: The tasks and activities that a culture assigns to each sex.

gender stereotypes: Oversimplified but strongly held ideas about the characteristics of males and females.

gender stratification: Unequal distribution of rewards (socially valued resources, power, prestige, and personal freedom) between men and women, reflecting their different positions in a social hierarchy.

Iroquois: Confederation of tribes in aboriginal New York;

matrilineal with communal longhouses and a prominent political, religious, and economic role for women.

matriarchy: A society ruled by women; unknown to ethnography.

matrifocal: Mother-centered; often refers to a household with no resident husband-father.

matrons: Senior women, as among the Iroquois.

naturists: Those who argue that human behavior and social organization are biologically determined.

nurturists: Those who relate behavior and social organization to environmental factors. Nurturists focus on vari-

ation rather than universals and stress learning and the role of culture in human adaptation.

patrilineal-virilocal complex: An interrelated constellation of patrilineality, virilocality, warfare, and male supremacy.

sexual dimorphism: Marked differences in male and female biology besides the contrasts in breasts and genitals.

uxorilocality: Customary residence with the wife's relatives after marriage.

virilocality: Customary residence with the husband's relatives after marriage.

STUDY QUESTIONS

1. What is the dominant position in anthropology regarding the argument that the destinies of men and women are linked with their respective anatomies and genetic makeups?
2. What is the difference between gender roles, gender stereotypes, and gender stratification?
3. How do gender roles in traditional !Kung society compare with those in U.S. or Canadian society?
4. How does gender stratification differ in societies that are matrilineal and uxorilocal compared with those that are patrilineal and virilocal?
5. How are Etoro sexual practices related to patterns of male-female relations in Papua–New Guinea and in patrilineal-virilocal cultures generally?
6. How does gender stratification differ in agricultural versus horticultural societies?
7. How have gender roles in the United States changed in the twentieth century? What has caused these changes?
8. What determines variation in gender roles, and what does this variation suggest for societies of the future?

SUGGESTED ADDITIONAL READING

BOSERUP, E.
1970   *Women's Role in Economic Development.* London: Allen & Unwin. An examination of woman's changing role as cultivation intensifies, including plow agriculture and the domestic-public dichotomy.

BOURQUE, S. C., AND K. B. WARREN
1981   *Women of the Andes: Patriarchy and Social Change in Two Peruvian Villages.* Ann Arbor: University of Michigan Press. Comparison of two communities with respect to traditional and modern gender hierarchies, capitalization, and directions of development.

COLLIER, J. F., AND S. J. YANAGISAKO, EDS.
1987   *Gender and Kinship: Essays toward a Unified Analysis.* Stanford, CA: Stanford University Press. Several essays examine women, men, kinship, and marriage in varied cultural settings.

DAHLBERG, F., ED.
1981   *Women the Gatherer.* New Haven, CT: Yale University Press. Female roles and activities

among prehistoric and contemporary foragers.

DI LEONARDO, M., ED.
1991   *Gender at the Crossroads of Knowledge: Feminist Anthropology in the Postmodern Era.* Berkeley: University of California Press. Up-to-date presentation of issues in feminist anthropology. Twelve essays discuss biological anthropology, primate studies, the global economy, reproductive technologies, race, and gender.

ETIENNE, M., AND E. LEACOCK, EDS.
1980   *Women and Colonization: Anthropological Perspectives.* New York: Praeger and J. F. Bergin. Women and the growth of the world system.

GILMORE, D.
1991   *Manhood in the Making: Cultural Concepts of Masculinity.* New Haven, CT: Yale University Press. Cross-cultural study of manhood as an achieved status.

MARGOLIS, M.
1984   *Mothers and Such: American Views of Women and How They Changed.* Berkeley: University of

California Press. The evolution of the female role, women's work, and attitudes about female nature and activities in the United States since its settlement.

MORGEN, S., ED.

1989   *Gender and Anthropology: Critical Reviews for Research and Teaching.* Washington, DC: American Anthropological Association. Most up-to-date review of scholarship on gender in many areas of the world and in a biosocial perspective.

MUKHOPADHYAY, C., AND P. HIGGINS

1988   Anthropological Studies of Women's Status Revisited: 1977–1987. *Annual Review of Anthropology* 17: 461–495. Extensive review of the cross-cultural literature on the subject.

NASH, J., AND P. FERNANDEZ-KELLY, EDS.

1983   *Women, Men and the International Division of Labor.* Albany: State University of New York Press. Essays on global accumulation; the labor process; production, reproduction, and the household economy; and labor flow and capital expansion, with case studies from electronics and trade.

NASH, J., AND H. SAFA, EDS.

1986   *Women and Change in Latin America.* South Hadley, MA: Bergin and Garvey. Articles by anthropologists on gender, political economy, and social change in Latin America.

REITER, R., ED.

1975   *Toward an Anthropology of Women.* New York:

Monthly Review Press. Classic anthology, with a particular focus on peasant societies.

ROSALDO, M. Z.

1980   *Knowledge and Passion: Notions of Self and Social Life.* Stanford, CA: Stanford University Press. Role of travel, experience, knowledge, and emotion in the gender hierarchy of a stateless society in the Philippines.

ROSALDO, M. Z., AND L. LAMPHERE, EDS.

1974   *Woman, Culture, and Society.* Stanford, CA: Stanford University Press. Another classic anthology, covering many areas of the world.

SILVERBLATT, I.

1988   Women in States. *Annual Review of Anthropology* 17: 427–460. Issues of gender stratification and politics in ancient and modern states.

STRATHERN, M.

1988   *The Gender of the Gift: Problems with Women and Problems with Society in Melanesia.* Berkeley: University of California Press. How Western assumptions have influenced the interpretation of gender relations in Melanesia; considers sexual antagonisms and other issues.

WOLF, M.

1985   *Revolution Postponed: Women in Contemporary China.* Stanford, CA: Stanford University Press. One of the few studies of women based on anthropological field research in China; discusses urban and rural women, marriage, and China's controversial birth control policy.

C H A P T E R 1 9

RELIGION

Anthropologist Anthony F. C. Wallace has defined **religion** as "belief and ritual concerned with supernatural beings, powers, and forces" (1966, p. 5). In studying religion cross-culturally, anthropologists pay attention to religious acts, actions, events, processes, settings, practitioners, specialists, and organizations. We also consider such verbal manifestations of religious beliefs as prayers, chants, invocations, myths, fables, tales, texts, and statements about ethics, standards, and morality.

The supernatural is the extraordinary realm outside (but believed to touch on) the observable world. It is nonempirical, unverifiable, mysterious, and inexplicable in ordinary terms. Supernatural beings—gods and goddesses, ghosts, and souls—are not of the material world. Neither are supernatural forces, some of which are wielded by beings. Other sacred forces are impersonal—they simply exist. In many societies, however, people believe they can benefit from, become imbued with, or manipulate supernatural forces.

Religion, as defined here, exists in all human societies. It is a cultural universal. However, we'll see that it isn't always easy to distinguish the supernatural from the natural and that different cultures conceptualize supernatural entities very differently.

ORIGINS, FUNCTIONS, AND EXPRESSIONS OF RELIGION

When did religion begin? Neandertal burials provide the earliest archeological suggestion of religion. The fact that Neandertals buried their dead and put objects in graves has convinced many anthropologists that they conceived of an afterlife. However, we have no way of knowing the specifics of Neandertal religion or determining whether religion predates them. Any statement about when, where, why, and how religion arose or any description of its original nature is pure speculation. Nevertheless, although such speculations are inconclusive, many of them have revealed important functions and effects of religious behavior. Several theories will be examined now.

Animism

The Englishman Sir Edward Burnett Tylor (1871/1958) was a founder of the anthropology of religion.

Religion was born, Tylor thought, as people tried to comprehend conditions and events they could not explain by reference to daily experience. Tylor believed that our ancestors—and contemporary non-industrial peoples—were particularly intrigued with death, dreaming, and trance. In dreams and trances people experience a form of suspended animation. On waking, they recall images from the dream world.

Tylor concluded that attempts to explain dreams and trances led early humans to believe that two entities inhabit the body, one active during the day and the other—a double or soul—active during sleep and trance states. Although these entities never meet, they are vital to each other. When the double permanently leaves the body, the person dies. Death is departure of the soul. From the Latin for soul, *anima*, Tylor called this belief **animism.**

Tylor thought that religion had evolved through stages, beginning with animism. Polytheism and then monotheism came later. Because religion originated to explain things people didn't understand, Tylor thought it would decline as science offered better explanations. To an extent, he was right. We now have scientific explanations for many things that once were accepted "on faith." Nevertheless, because religion persists, it must do something more than explain the mysterious. It must, and does, have other functions.

Animatism, Mana, and Taboo

There was a competing view to Tylor's theory of animism as the first religion. The alternative was that early humans saw the supernatural as a domain of impersonal power, or force, which people could control under certain conditions. Such a conception of the supernatural, called **animatism,** is particularly prominent in Melanesia, the area of the South Pacific that includes Papua–New Guinea and adjacent islands. Melanesians (like the ancient Hawaiians discussed in the chapter "Marriage") believed in **mana,** a sacred impersonal force existing in the universe. Mana can reside in people, animals, plants, and objects.

Melanesian mana was similar to our notion of luck. Melanesians attributed success to mana, which people could acquire or manipulate in different ways, such as through magic. Objects with mana could change someone's luck. For example, a charm

Beliefs in mana—a supernatural force or power, which people may manipulate for their own ends—are widespread. Mana can reside in people, animals, plants, and objects, such as the skull held here by a member of the head-hunting Iban tribe of Malaysia.

belonging to a successful hunter might transmit the hunter's mana to the next person who held it. A woman might put a rock in her garden, see her yields improve dramatically, and attribute the change to the force contained in the rock.

Beliefs in manalike forces are widespread, although the specifics of the religious doctrines vary. The contrast between mana in Melanesia and Polynesia, for example, reflects the difference between Melanesian tribes and Polynesian chiefdoms and states (such as ancient Hawaii). In Melanesia, one could acquire mana by chance, or by working hard to get it. In Polynesia, however, mana was not potentially available to everyone but was attached to political offices. Rulers and nobles had more mana than ordinary people did.

So charged with mana were the highest chiefs that

contact with them was dangerous to commoners. The mana of chiefs flowed out of their bodies wherever they went. It could infect the ground, making it dangerous for others to walk in the chief's footsteps. It could permeate the containers and utensils chiefs used in eating. Contact between chief and commoners was dangerous because mana could have an effect like an electric shock. Because high chiefs had so much mana, their bodies and possessions were **taboo** (set apart as sacred and off-limits to ordinary people). Contact between a high chief and commoners was forbidden. Because ordinary people couldn't bear as much sacred current as royalty could, when commoners were accidentally exposed, purification rites were necessary.

We see that one function of religion is to explain. The belief in souls explains what happens in sleep, trance, and death. Melanesian mana explains success that people can't understand in ordinary, natural terms. People fail at hunting, warfare, or gardening not because they are lazy, stupid, or inept but because success comes—or doesn't come—from the supernatural world. Animism, animatism, and mana all fit into the definition of religion given at the beginning of this chapter. Most religions include both spirits and impersonal forces. Likewise the supernatural beliefs of contemporary North American people include beings (gods, saints, souls, demons) and forces (charms, talismans, and sacred objects).

Magic and Religion

Magic refers to supernatural techniques intended to accomplish specific aims. These techniques include spells, formulas, and incantations used with deities or with impersonal forces. Magicians use *imitative magic* to produce a desired effect by imitating it. If magicians wish to injure or kill someone, they may imitate that effect on an image of the victim. Sticking pins in "voodoo dolls" is an example. With *contagious magic*, whatever is done to an object is believed to affect a person who once had contact with it. Sometimes practitioners of contagious magic use body products from prospective victims—their nails or hair, for example. The spell performed on the body product is believed to reach the person eventually and work the desired result.

We find magic in cultures with diverse religious beliefs. It can be associated with animism, animatism, polytheism, and even monotheism. Magic is neither simpler nor more primitive than animism or animatism.

Anxiety, Control, Solace

Religion and magic don't just explain things and help people accomplish goals. They also enter the domain of feelings. In other words, they do not have just explanatory (cognitive) functions but have emotional ones as well. For example, supernatural beliefs and practices can help reduce anxiety. Magical techniques can dispel doubts that arise when outcomes are beyond human control. Similarly, religion helps people face death and endure life crises.

Although all societies have techniques to deal with everyday matters, there are certain aspects of people's lives over which they lack control. When people face uncertainty and danger, according to Malinowski, they turn to magic.

> [H]owever much knowledge and science help man in allowing him to obtain what he wants, they are unable completely to control chance, to eliminate accidents, to foresee the unexpected turn of natural events, or to make human handiwork reliable and adequate to all practical requirements. (1931/1978, p. 39)

Malinowski found that the Trobriand Islanders used magic when sailing, a hazardous activity. He proposed that because people can't control matters such as wind, weather, and the fish supply, they turn to magic. People may call on magic when they come to a gap in their knowledge or powers of practical control yet have to continue in a pursuit (Malinowski 1931/1978).

According to Malinowski, magic is used to establish control, but religion "is born out of . . . the real tragedies of human life" (Malinowski 1931/1978, p. 45). Religion offers emotional comfort, particularly when people face a crisis. Malinowski saw tribal religions as concerned mainly with such crises of life as birth, puberty, marriage, and death.

The Social Functions of Ritual Acts

Magic and religion can reduce anxiety and allay fears. Ironically, rituals and beliefs can also *create* anxiety and a sense of insecurity and danger (Radcliffe-Brown 1962/1965). Anxiety may arise *because* a rite exists. Indeed, participation in a rite may build up a common stress whose reduction, through completion of the rite, enhances the solidarity of participants.

Rites of Passage

The traditional vision quests of Native Americans, particularly the Plains Indians, illustrate **rites of passage** (customs associated with the transition from one place or stage of life to another), which are found throughout the world. Among the Plains Indians, to move from boyhood to manhood, a youth temporarily separated from his community. After a period of isolation in the wilderness, often featuring fasting and drug consumption, the young man

Liminal people, like these Mandji girls in Gabon, West Africa, who are temporarily confined to a menstrual hut, exist apart from ordinary distinctions and expectations, living in a time out of time. They are cut off from normal social contacts. A variety of contrasts, such as their body paint, may demarcate liminality from regular social life.

would see a vision, which would become his guardian spirit. He would then return to his community as an adult.

The rites of passage of contemporary cultures include confirmations, baptisms, bar and bat mitzvahs, and fraternity hazing. Passage rites involve changes in social status, such as from boyhood to manhood and from nonmember to sorority sister. More generally, a rite of passage may mark any change in place, condition, social position, or age.

All rites of passage have three phases: separation, margin, and aggregation. In the first phase, people withdraw from the group and begin moving from one place or status to another. In the third phase, they reenter society, having completed the rite. The *margin* phase is the most interesting. It is the period between states, the limbo during which people have left one place or state but haven't yet entered or joined the next. We call this the liminal phase of the passage rite (Turner 1974).

Liminality always has certain characteristics. Liminal people occupy ambiguous social positions. They exist apart from ordinary distinctions and expectations, living in a time out of time. They are cut off from normal social contacts. A variety of contrasts may demarcate liminality from regular social life. For example, among the Ndembu of Zambia, a chief had to undergo a passage rite before taking office. During the liminal period, his past and future positions in society were ignored, even reversed. He was subjected to a variety of insults, orders, and humiliations.

Unlike the vision quest and the Ndembu initiation, which are individual experiences, passage rites are often collective. A group—boys being circumcised, fraternity or sorority initiates, men at military boot camps, football players in summer training camps, women becoming nuns—pass through the rites together. Table 19.1 summarizes the contrasts or oppositions between liminality and normal social life.

Most notable is a social aspect of *collective liminality* called **communitas** (Turner 1978), an intense community spirit, a feeling of great social solidarity, equality, and togetherness. People experiencing liminality together form a community of equals. The social distinctions that have existed before or will exist afterward are temporarily forgotten. Liminal people experience the same treatment and conditions and must act alike. Liminality may be marked

Table 19.1 *Oppositions between liminality and normal social life*

Liminality	Normal Social Structure
transition	state
homogeneity	heterogeneity
communitas	structure
equality	inequality
anonymity	names
absence of property	property
absence of status	status
nakedness or uniform dress	dress distinctions
sexual continence or excess	sexuality
minimization of sex distinctions	maximization of sex distinctions
absence of rank	rank
humility	pride
disregard of personal appearance	care for personal appearance
unselfishness	selfishness
total obedience	obedience only to superior rank
sacredness	secularity
sacred instruction	technical knowledge
silence	speech
simplicity	complexity
acceptance of pain and suffering	avoidance of pain and suffering

Source: Adapted from Victor W. Turner, *The Ritual Process.* Copyright © 1969 by Victor W. Turner. By permission of Aldine de Gruyter, New York.

ritually and symbolically by *reversals* of ordinary behavior. For example, sexual taboos may be intensified or, conversely, sexual excess may be encouraged.

Liminality is part of every passage rite. Furthermore, in certain societies, it can become a permanent feature of particular groups. This happens most notably in state-organized societies. Religious groups often use liminal characteristics to set themselves off from others. Humility, poverty, equality, obedience, sexual abstinence, and silence may be conditions of membership in a sect. Liminal features may also signal the sacredness of persons, settings, and events by setting them off as extraordinary—outside normal social space and regular time.

Totems: Symbols of Society

Thus rituals may serve the social function of creating temporary or permanent solidarity between people—forming a social community. We see this

Passage rites are often collective. A group—such as these initiates in Togo and Marine recruits in South Carolina— pass through the rites together. Such liminal people experience the same treatment and conditions and must act alike. They share communitas, an intense community spirit, a feeling of great social solidarity or togetherness.

also in religious practices known as totemism. Totemism was important in the religions of the Native Australians. *Totems* could be animals, plants, or geographical features. In each tribe, groups of people had particular totems. Members of each totemic group believed themselves to be descendants of their totem. They customarily neither killed nor ate it, but this taboo was lifted once a year, when people assembled for ceremonies dedicated to the totem. These annual rites were believed to be necessary for the totem's survival and reproduction.

Totemism is a religion that uses nature as a model for society. The totems are usually animals and plants, which are part of nature. People relate to nature through their totemic association with natural species. Because each group has a different totem, social differences mirror natural contrasts. Diversity in the natural order becomes a model for separation in the social order. However, although totemic plants and animals occupy different niches in nature, on another level they are united because they all are part of nature. The unity of the human social order is enhanced by symbolic association with and imitation of the natural order (Durkheim 1912/1961; Radcliffe-Brown 1962/1975; Lévi-Strauss 1963).

One role of religious rites and beliefs is to affirm, and thus maintain, the solidarity of a religion's adherents. ("A family that prays together stays together.") Totems are sacred emblems symbolizing common identity. In totemic rites, people gather together to honor their totem. In so doing, they use ritual to maintain the social oneness that the totem symbolizes.

The Nature of Ritual

Several features distinguish **rituals** from other kinds of behavior (Rappaport 1974). Rituals are formal—stylized, repetitive, and stereotyped. People perform them in special (sacred) places and at set times. Rituals include **liturgical orders**—sequences of words and actions invented prior to the current performance of the ritual in which they occur.

These features link rituals to plays, but there are important differences. Plays have audiences rather than participants. Actors merely *portray* something, but ritual performers—who make up congregations—are *in earnest*. Rituals convey information about the participants and their traditions. Repeated year after year, generation after generation, rituals translate enduring messages, values, and sentiments into action.

Rituals are *social* acts. Inevitably, some participants are more committed than others are to the beliefs that lie behind the rites. However, just by taking part in a joint public act, the performers signal that they accept a common social and moral order, one that transcends their status as individuals.

ANALYSIS OF MYTH

Cross-cultural research has documented a rich variety of ideas about the supernatural, including animism, mana, taboo, and totemism. We have seen that participation in a ritual creates solidarity. Regardless of their particular thoughts and varied degrees of commitment, the participants temporarily submerge their individuality in a community. Like descent, marriage, gender, and the other social forces we have examined, religion can be a powerful molder of social solidarity.

Nevertheless, the anthropological study of religion is not limited to religion's social effects or its expression in rites and ceremonies. Anthropology also studies religious and quasi-religious stories about supernatural entities—the myths and tales of long ago or far away that are retold across the generations in every society.

Myths often include people's own account of their creation, of the beginning of their world and the extraordinary events that affected their ancestors. They may also tell of the continuing exploits and activities of deities or spirits either in an alternative world or as they come into occasional contact with mortals. Myths, legends, and folk tales express cultural beliefs and values. They offer hope, excitement, and escape. They also teach lessons that society wants taught.

Structural Analysis

One way of studying myth is structural analysis, or **structuralism,** developed by Claude Lévi-Strauss, a prolific French anthropologist. Lévi-Straussian structuralism (1967) aims not at *explaining* relations, themes, and connections among aspects of culture but at *discovering* them. It differs in its goals and results from the methods of gathering and interpreting data usually used in the sciences. Because structuralism is as close to the humanities as it is to science, structuralist methods have been used in analyzing literature and art as well as in anthropology.

Myths and folk tales are the (oral) literature of nonliterate societies. Lévi-Strauss used structuralism to analyze the cultural creations of such societies, including their myths. Structuralism rests on Lévi-Strauss's belief that human minds have certain characteristics which originate in features of the *Homo sapiens* brain. These common mental structures lead people everywhere to think similarly regardless of their society or cultural background. Among these universal mental characteristics are the need to classify: to impose order on aspects of nature, on people's relation to nature, and on relations between people.

According to Lévi-Strauss, a universal aspect of classification is opposition, or contrast. Although many phenomena are continuous rather than discrete, the mind, because of its need to impose order, treats them as being more different than they are. Things that are quantitatively rather than qualitatively different are made to seem absolutely dissimilar. Scientific classification is the Western academic outgrowth of the universal need to impose order. One of the most common means of classifying is by using **binary opposition.** Good and evil, white and black, old and young, high and low are oppositions that, according to Lévi-Strauss, reflect the human need to convert differences of degree into differences of kind.

Lévi-Strauss has applied his assumptions about classification and binary opposition to myths and folk tales. He has shown that these narratives have simple building blocks—elementary structures or "mythemes." Examining the myths of different cultures, Lévi-Strauss shows that one tale can be converted into another through a series of simple operations, for example, by doing the following:

1. Converting the positive element of a myth into its negative
2. Reversing the order of the elements
3. Replacing a male hero with a female hero
4. Preserving or repeating certain key elements

Through such operations, two apparently dissimilar myths can be shown to be variations on a common structure, that is, to be transformations of each other. One example is Lévi-Strauss's analysis of "Cinderella" (1967), a widespread tale whose elements vary between neighboring cultures. Through reversals, oppositions, and negations, as the tale is told, retold, diffused, and incorporated within the traditions of successive societies, "Cinderella" becomes "Ash Boy," after a series of contrasts related to the change in hero's gender.

Structuralism has been widely applied to the myths of nonindustrial cultures, but we can also use it to analyze narratives in our own society. Interested students may wish to read the Appendix, which includes several examples—including *Star Wars* and *The Wizard of Oz*—drawn from contemporary popular culture.

Fairy Tales

In his book *The Uses of Enchantment: The Meaning and Importance of Fairy Tales* (1975) the psychologist Bruno Bettelheim drew a useful distinction between two kinds of tale: the tragic myth and the hopeful folk tale. Tragic myths include many Biblical accounts (that of Job, for example) and Greco-Roman myths that confront humans with powerful, capricious, and awesome supernatural entities. Such tales, characteristic of state-organized societies, focus on the huge gap between mortals and the supernatural. In contrast, the folk or fairy tales found in many cultures use fantasy to offer hope and to suggest the possibility of growth and self-realization. Bettelheim argues that this message is particularly important for children. The characters in the myths and tales of bands and tribes are not powerful beings but plants, animals, humans, and nature spirits who use intelligence, physical prowess, or cunning to accomplish their ends. State societies retain hopeful tales along with the tragedies.

Bettelheim urges parents to read or tell folk or fairy tales to their children. He chides American parents and librarians for pushing children to read "realistic" and "prosocial" stories, which often are dull, complex, and psychologically empty. Folk or fairy tales, in contrast, allow children to identify with heroes who win out in the end. These stories offer confidence that no matter how bad things seem now, they will improve. They give reassurance that although small and insignificant now, the child will eventually grow up and achieve independence from parents and siblings.

Similar to the way Lévi-Strauss focuses on binary oppositions, Bettelheim analyzes how fairy tales permit children to deal with their ambivalent feelings (love and hate) about their parents and siblings. Fairy tales often split the good and bad aspects of the parent into separate figures of good and evil. Thus, in "Cinderella," the mother is split in two, an evil stepmother and a fairy go(o)dmother. Cinderella's two evil stepsisters disguise hostile and rivalrous feelings toward real siblings. A tale such as "Cinderella" permits the child to deal with hostile feelings toward parents and siblings, since positive feelings are preserved in the idealized good figure.

Bettelheim contends that it doesn't matter much whether the hero is male or female, because children of both sexes can usually find psychological satisfaction of some sort in a fairy tale. However, traditional male heroes usually slay dragons, giants, or monsters (representing the father) and free princesses from captivity, whereas female characters accomplish something, such as spinning straw into gold or capturing a witch's broomstick, and then return home or establish a home of their own.

HALLOWEEN: AN AMERICAN RITUAL OF REBELLION

Brazil is famous for *Carnaval*, a pre-Lenten festival celebrated the four days before Ash Wednesday. Carnival occurs, but has a limited distribution, in the United States. Here we know it as the Mardi Gras for which New Orleans is famous. Mardi Gras (Fat Tuesday) is part of a Latin tradition that New Orleans, because of its French background, shares with Brazil. France and Italy also have carnival. Nowhere, however, do people invest as much in carnival—in money, costumes, time, and labor—as they do in Rio de Janeiro. There, on the Saturday and Sunday before Mardi Gras, a dozen samba schools, each with thousands of members, take to the streets to compete in costumes, rhythmic dancing, chanting, singing, and overall presentation.

The United States lacks any national celebration that is exactly equivalent to carnival, but we do have Halloween, which is similar in some respects. Even if Americans don't dance in the street on Halloween, children do go out ringing bells and demanding "trick or treat." As they do things they don't do on ordinary nights, they also disguise themselves in costumes, as Brazilians do at carnival.

The common thread in the two events is that they are times of culturally permitted *inversion*—carnival much more strongly and obviously than Halloween (see the box in the chapter, "Gender"). In the United States Halloween is the only nationally celebrated occasion that dramatically inverts the normal relationship between children and adults. Halloween is a night of disguises and reversals. Normally, children are at home or in school, taking part in supervised activities. Kids are domesticated and diurnal—active during the day. Halloween permits them to become—once a year—nocturnal invaders of public space. Furthermore, *they can be bad*. Halloween's symbolism is potent. Children love to cloak themselves in evil as they enjoy special privileges of naughtiness. Darth Vader and Freddy Krueger are much more popular Halloween figures than are Luke Skywalker and the Smurfs.

Properly enculturated American kids aren't normally let loose on the streets at night. They aren't usually permitted to ask their neighbors for doles. They don't generally walk around the neighborhood dressed as witches, goblins, or vampires. Traditionally, the expectation that children be good little boys and girls has been overlooked on Halloween. "Trick or treat" recalls the days when children who didn't get treats would pull tricks such as soaping windows, turning over flower boxes, and setting off firecrackers on a grouch's porch.

Halloween is like the "rituals of rebellion" that anthropologists have described in African societies, times when normal power relations are inverted, when the powerless turn on the powerful, expressing resentments they suppress during the rest of the year. Halloween lets kids meddle with the dark side of the force. Children can command adults to do their bidding and punish the adults if they don't. Halloween behavior inverts the scoldings and spankings that adults inflict on kids. For adults, Halloween is a minor occasion, not even a holiday. For children, however, it's a favorite time, a special night. Kids know what rituals of rebellion are all about.

Halloween is therefore a festival that inverts two oppositions important in American life: the adult-child power balance and expectations about good and evil. Halloween's origin can be traced back 2,000 years to Samhain, the Day of the Dead, the most significant holiday in the Celtic religion (Santino 1983). Given its historical development through pagan rites, church suppression, and beliefs about witches and demons, Halloween continues to turn the distinction between good and bad on its head. Innocent children dress as witches and demons and act out their fantasies of rebellion and destruction. Once during the year, real adult witches are interviewed on talk shows, where they have a chance to describe their beliefs as solemnly as orthodox religious figures do. Puritan morality and the need for proper public behavior are important themes in American society. The rules are in abeyance on Halloween, and normal things are inverted. This is why Halloween, like *Carnaval* in Brazil, persists as a ritual of reversal and rebellion, particularly as an escape valve for the frustrations and resentments that build during enculturation.

IN THE NEWS: A JAPANESE RITUAL OF REBELLION

A ritual of rebellion is an institutionalized way for people to express resentments they usually suppress. The Japanese New Year's Eve ritual described here is like Halloween (see the Box in this chapter) and Carnival (see the box in the chapter "Gender"). It is a formal relief-valve that lets people reverse, temporarily, their ordinary "polite" behavior and vent their frustrations.

Ashikaga, Japan, Jan. 1—The life of a typical Japanese—working endless hours, enduring long commutes on packed trains and adhering to rigid rules of behavior—would drive many Americans to the brink of rage. But Japanese seem to bottle up any anger and maintain their world-famous politeness.

Except just before midnight on New Year's Eve in Ashikaga.

In this city about 50 miles north of Tokyo, people take this one occasion to let it all hang out and say what they really think about the year gone by. In one of the strangest festivals in a country full of festivals, they walk up a dark mountain road to a temple screaming curses into the starry night sky that they would never say directly to their fellow man.

"Once a year, we can get rid of our pent-up frustrations," said Ryoken Numajiri, the head priest of the Saishoji Temple. The temple is the headquarters for the Akutare Matsuri, which might best be translated as the "naughty festival" or perhaps the "festival of abusive language."

This year, of course, there was plenty for the roughly 400 participants to be abusive about, what with a national political scandal, the economy in the dumps and the stock market continuing its three-year slide. This city of 170,000 did not escape the pain, with the nearby electronics and automobile factories reducing overtime hours and part-time jobs. . . .

But other marchers complained about daily life, about too much schoolwork, or poor grades on tests. For some it was just an opportunity to escape from normal social strictures. "Women are not allowed to say such words," said Miyoko Kuwako, a housewife. "But it's O.K. tonight."

The festival, which is the only one of its kind in Japan, originated more than 200 years ago as a relief valve for repressed workers, Mr. Numajiri said. At that time, he said, women were brought in from the surrounding countryside to work in factories making material for kimonos. The work was arduous, and the hours were long. But in return for persevering through the year, their boss would take them to the temple once a year so they could let off steam.

Japanese place a high value on patience and perseverance. Even when they do let loose, Japanese curses are mild by American standards, with a more limited se-

---

Secular Rituals

We must recognize certain problems in the cross-cultural study of religion and in the definition of religion given earlier. The first problem: If we define religion with reference to supernatural beings, powers, and forces, how do we classify rituallike behavior that occurs in secular contexts? Some anthropologists believe that there are both sacred and secular rituals. Secular rituals include formal, invariant, stereotyped, earnest, repetitive behavior that takes place in nonreligious settings.

A second problem: If the distinction between the ordinary and the supernatural is not consistently made in certain societies, how can we tell what is religion and what is not? The Betsileo of Madagascar, for example, view witches and dead ancestors as real people who play roles in ordinary life. Nevertheless, their powers are not empirically demonstrable.

A third problem: The kind of behavior considered appropriate for religious occasions varies tremendously from culture to culture. One society may consider drunken frenzy the surest sign of faith, whereas another may inculcate quiet reverence. Who is to say which is "more religious"?

RELIGION AND CULTURE TYPE

Religion is a cultural universal because it has so many causes, effects, and meanings for the people who take part in it. But religions are parts of particular cultures, and cultural differences show up systematically in religious beliefs, practices, and institutions. Religious forms do not vary randomly from society to society. State religions are unlike those of tribes, just as foragers' religions differ from those of food producers. We focus now on the religious

lection of swear words.

The main word shouted by the festival participants was "bakayaro!" which might be literally translated as "you idiot" but sometimes has the connotation of "God damn it." It is the expletive a Japanese driver might yell out the window when another car suddenly cuts in front of his. It might not seem so bad, but it is one of the closest things here to a four-letter word.

New Year's Eve and New Year's Day are traditionally times when millions of Japanese, some clad in traditional kimonos, flock to Buddhist temples or Shinto shrines. But not in the way they do it in Ashikaga.

At 11 P.M., about 200 people began walking up a mountain road to the Saishoji temple led by a man blowing a shell known as a hora-gai, which is supposed to fend off bad tidings. Many were carrying lanterns and wearing cardboard hats bearing the picture of Bisha-monten, one of the seven gods of fortune in Japanese Buddhism and

the god in whose honor Mr. Nu-majiri's temple was built 1,200 years ago. Another 200 people or so followed in buses.

Cries of "bakayaro!" split the night, the extended final "o" sound trailing off into the sky like a coyote's howl. Occasionally there was a more specific complaint like "My teacher is an idiot!" or "Give me a raise!"

After a 40-minute walk, the crowd stormed up the steps to the temple, which is situated atop a 1,000-foot-high hill. The crowd rang the temple bell, clapped their hands and prayed, and bellowed a few more lusty bakayaro's to exorcise the year gone by.

But at the stroke of 12, the insults turned to cries of "congratulations" and "Happy New Year." Many of the worshipers went inside for another ceremony that is unique to this temple, in which people drink sake that is poured onto their foreheads and drips down their faces. The ceremony is supposed to insure that happiness will flow in the year ahead.

Mr. Numajiri, wearing a billowing green robe, called out the name of each worshiper and read aloud his or her wishes for the new year, which the visitors had conveniently circled on multiple-choice lists handed them at the door.

The person whose name was called knelt on the floor and raised a wide red lacquer bowl to his or her lips. As a big taiko drum was pounded, Mr. Numajiri poured the sake onto the person's forehead, and the sake ran down the nose and into the bowl and was consumed.

After venting their anger over the year past and drinking to the year to come, participants said they felt relieved, ready once again to do battle in the factories and offices and crowded trains of modern Japan.

Source: Andrew Pollack, "A Festival That Permits Japanese to Be Impolite," *The New York Times,* January 2, 1993, p. A4.

expressions of different types of society, and we see how such forms of religious expression have causes and effects right here on earth.

State Religions

Many nonindustrial states have had a state religion managed by specialized religious officials. In ancient Mesopotamia, for example, literate priests preserved sacred lore and texts along with utilitarian information about agricultural production, exchanges, and other economic transactions. But while priests manage a state religion, folk beliefs and rites may persist in the countryside. Folk religion often coexists with monotheistic or polytheistic state religions.

State religion has been used to maintain social order and stratification. Misfortune, conquest, and slavery can be borne more easily if the oppressed believe that an afterlife holds better things. Tragic myths portraying awesome deities warn people not to question the authority of the gods or of the rulers and religious leaders who represent them on earth.

Deities

Leslie White (1959) pointed out differences between the religions of foragers and those of food producers. Foragers have *zoomorphic gods*—animals and plants (as in totemism)—or worship natural phenomena such as the sun, moon, and stars. Actually, foragers tend to *identify with* rather than worship spiritual beings. Rituals enact events associated with mythical people and animals, as participants assume their identities.

As people gain more control over the environment through food production, new kinds of gods appear—*anthropomorphic*, or humanlike, ones. Just

IN THE NEWS: *SANTERÍA* AND THE STATE

Religions of indigenous states of Africa, Polynesia, Mexico, Peru, China, India, and the Middle East had powerful deities and priests, with rituals requiring worship and sacrifice. Like Haitian *vodun* ("voodoo") and Brazilian *candomblé*, *santería* is a *syncretic* religion—that is, a cultural blend—of Roman Catholic and West African elements. But *santería*, which is of growing importance in a multiethnic United States, is still viewed as a questionable "alternative" to familiar organized religions, such as Christianity and Judaism. This article examines the complex issue of *santería* animal sacrifice, which has been opposed by state officials and animal rights groups.

Hialeah, Fla., Nov. 2—To Ernesto Pichardo, a Santería priest and devotee of the warrior god of thunder Changó, the occasional sacrifice of a goat or chicken is a religious rite sanctioned by the Constitution and centuries of tradition. But to the city of Hialeah, the practice is a public health hazard that is cruel to animals and violates local zoning laws.

For five years, ever since Mr. Pichardo tried to open the Church of the Lukumí Babalú Ayé Inc. on a used-car lot a few blocks from City Hall, municipal officials and Santería followers have been debating the issue, first in the chambers of the City Council and then in a succession of courtrooms. On Wednesday, the dispute will go before the United States Supreme Court in what legal and religious experts say could clarify the extent to which the state can regulate religion, and on what ground.

The legal experts say the decision may further refine the meaning of a 1990 ruling in which the Court held that the government did not violate the First Amendment right to the free exercise of religion by applying "neutral" laws of general applicability to religious practices.

But Mr. Pichardo and some religious experts take a more sweeping view.

"What needs to be resolved here is the restoration of religious freedom into the Constitution," Mr. Pichardo said during an interview on Friday, shortly before departing for Washington. "This is not a local issue any longer, any more than it is just about Santería or offering animals. It has become about all religions."

In Mr. Pichardo's view, the city of Hialeah, a Miami suburb whose population of 200,000 is 88 percent Hispanic, illegally prevented him from practicing his religion when it passed an ordinance prohibiting animal sacrifice in 1987, after residents and religious leaders complained about his plans to open a church. It is absurd, he said, that hunters are allowed to kill animals for sport while he is barred from engaging in a ritual that is common to many religions around the world, including Judaism and Islam.

"It is very rare that we offer animals," Mr. Pichardo said. "But the problem is that offerings are a vital part of our rites of passage. That's where the theological issue is. If there are no rites, there are no priests. So we have to defend this all the way."

The lawyer who will argue the city's case, which has already been upheld in lower courts, calls that argument nonsense. "The city is not interested in targeting any religion by name," said Richard G. Garrett. "Our position is that animal sacrifice is a legitimate governmental problem, and an ordinance banning it is neutral, because it is aimed at preventing the practice whether engaged in by a religion or for secular purposes."

Santería, which is Spanish for "the worship of saints," blends elements of Roman Catholicism with religious beliefs brought to the Caribbean from West Africa by Yoruba slaves. Each Yoruba "orisha," or deity, for example, is identified with a figure from Christianity. Ritual sacrifices are made to the deities when their help is being sought or any time that a "santero," or priest, is initiated.

Mr. Pichardo estimated there are about 70,000 devotees of Santería in the Miami area, where ritual altars are often seen on lawns, and where several restau-

as food producers manage the reproduction of plants and animals, their deities control such natural phenomena as thunder, lightning, and soil fertility.

State religions have more powerful gods (and officials) than do tribes. Many indigenous states of Africa, Polynesia, Mexico, Peru, China, India, and the Middle East had powerful deities and priests, with rituals requiring worship and sacrifice. In some states, kings were considered divine and rulers assumed priestly duties. A hierarchy of gods might control various aspects of nature. Religious doctrine

rants, taxi services and plant nurseries bear the names of deities like Elegba, a god of the crossroads who is associated with the Christ child, and Yemayá, goddess of the sea. Experts who study the religion put the number of devotees at around a million nationwide, with the largest concentrations in New York, Chicago and other large cities with large Caribbean Hispanic populations. Other cities have laws severely restricting the slaughter of animals, but Hialeah is believed to be the first to pass such a law in response to the appearance of a Santería church.

Many santeros here and elsewhere have hesitated to take Mr. Pichardo's side publicly, saying they fear persecution. But Mr. Pichardo and his congregation have received the support of the Presbyterian Church, the American Jewish Committee, the Catholic League for Religious and Civil Rights and organizations representing Mormons, Seventh-day Adventists and Mennonites.

Those religious groups are among those who see the case not only as a question of rights but as a vehicle that could be used to weaken or overturn a 1990 Supreme Court ruling that the state no longer need prove a "compelling interest" when it limits religious freedom. In that case, Employment Division of Oregon v. Smith, an American Indian was fired from his job for chewing peyote that he said was part of a religious ritual, and he was turned down when he sought unemployment benefits from the state.

The ruling was widely criticized by religious groups, and questions about its scope still linger. However, if the Supreme Court takes the view that the Hialeah ordinance is not a neutral law of general applicability but rather that it is aimed at curbing a specific religious practice, the Justices could strike it down without revisiting the ruling in the Oregon case.

But Mr. Pichardo, a former Roman Catholic altar boy who was born in Cuba in 1954 and came to Miami four years later, said the Supreme Court's willingness to hear his case is a good omen. "They wouldn't have taken this case if they didn't see it as a chance to re-examine the Smith issues," he said. "I think they are really going to try and clean up that decision."

He said he hoped the Court would be persuaded by the legal arguments his lawyers mustered, most notably the contention that his "offerings" were specifically excluded from Florida's animal cruelty statute.

The law states, "To protect freedom of religion, ritual slaughter and the handling or preparation of livestock for ritual slaughter are exempted from the terms of this act."

But city officials and their lawyers say that exception was written for the benefit of rabbis who supervise preparation of foods for observant Jews and they argue that the Santería priests follow different procedures that do not qualify for protection from the ordinance. "It's not like kosher slaughter," Mr. Garrett said of Santería sacrifices. "These animals would experience pain and not die instantly. There is a problem with inhumane treatment."

Hialeah's position has been supported by a number of animal rights groups here and around the nation. They contend that Santería sacrifices are inherently cruel and they complain that parts of animal carcasses are often found in canals or on street corners in South Florida, posing a threat to the public health.

"There is no evidence whatsoever of any threat to safety, health or welfare in any way, shape or form," said Mr. Pichardo's lawyer, Jorge Duarte. Santeros either eat the animals they have slaughtered or dispose of them in accordance with existing laws, he said. In addition, he said, "It is against principles to offer any unhealthy, mistreated or suffering animal to a god."

Mr. Pichardo hoped a favorable decision by the Supreme Court would allow him to proceed with his original plan: to bring out into "the light of day" a religion that has had to operate in secrecy. (In June 1993 the Supreme Court ruled in favor of Mr. Pichardo.)

Source: Larry Rohter, "Court to Weigh Law Forbidding Animal Sacrifice," *The New York Times,* November 3, 1992, p. A3.

and organization have mirrored the political structure of chiefdoms and states.

Throughout history, nation-states have used religion to promote and justify political policy. Religious fervor inspired Christians on crusades against the infidel and led Moslems to undertake *jihads,* holy wars against non-Islamic peoples. Fueling Iran's Islamic revolution was opposition to the "Great Satan," the ayatollahs' term for the United States. Guy Swanson's carefully documented study

The Birth of the Gods (1960), based on cross-cultural research, shows that high gods, believed to be omnipresent (present everywhere), all-knowing, and all-powerful, are present in states, absent in bands and tribes.

Religious Practitioners and Types

In developing a typology of religions of the world, Wallace (1966) defined religion as consisting of all a society's **cult institutions**—rituals and associated beliefs. Considering several cultures, Wallace proposed that there are four types of religion: shamanic, communal, Olympian, and monotheistic (Figure 19.1).

The simplest type is shamanic religion. Unlike priests, **shamans** aren't full-time religious officials but part-time religious figures who mediate between people and supernatural beings and forces. Nevertheless, along with hunter and gatherer, shaman completes the trio of "the world's oldest professions." All cultures have medico-magico-religious specialists. *Shaman* is the general term encompassing curers ("witch doctors"), mediums,

In this historic photo, an Alaskan shaman, wearing a spirit mask and wielding a spirit knife, attempts to cure a man. Shamans often adopt special patterns of dress and behavior. Hunter, gatherer, and shaman are the world's oldest professions. Shamanic religions are typically found among foragers.

Figure 19.1 *Wallace's typology of religions. Associations with sociopolitical types (bands, tribes, chiefdoms, and states) and adaptive strategies (foraging, food production) are only approximate. Communal religions, for example, are found among Australian foragers as well as tribal food producers, where such religions are most typical.*

Type of religion (Wallace)	Religious practitioners; conception of supernatural	Culture type
Monotheistic	priesthood; supreme being	State
Olympian	priesthood; hierarchical pantheon with powerful high gods	
		Chiefdom
Communal	occasional, community-sponsored rituals; several major deities with some control over nature	Food-producing tribe
Shamanic	part-time practitioners	Foraging band

spiritualists, astrologers, palm readers, and other diviners. Wallace found shamanic religions to be most characteristic of foragers, particularly those living in the northern latitudes, such as the Eskimos and the native peoples of Siberia.

Although they are only part-time specialists, shamans often set themselves off symbolically from ordinary people by assuming a different sex or gender role. (In states, priests, nuns, and vestal virgins do something similar by taking vows of celibacy and chastity. The ambiguous sexuality of religious figures continues to fascinate North Americans, as media accounts of televangelists in the late 1980s confirmed.)

Transvestism is one way of being sexually ambiguous. Among the Chukchee of Siberia (Bogoras

1904), where coastal populations fished and interior groups hunted, male shamans copied the dress, speech, hair arrangements, and life styles of women. These shamans took other men as husbands and sex partners and received respect for their supernatural and curative expertise. Female shamans could join a fourth gender, copying men and taking wives.

Among the Crow Indians of the North American Plains, certain ritual duties were reserved for **berdaches,** men who rejected the male role of bison hunter, raider, and warrior and joined a third gender (Lowie 1935). *Berdaches* dressed, spoke, and styled their hair like women and pursued such traditionally female activities as cooking and sewing. The fact that certain key rituals could be done only by *berdaches* indicates their regular and normal place in Crow social life.

Each of Wallace's four types of religion retains the cult institutions of each simpler type while developing distinctive ones of its own. **Communal religions** have, in addition to shamanic cults, cults in which people organize community rituals, such as harvest ceremonies and rites of passage. Although communal religions lack *full-time* religious specialists, they believe in several deities (**polytheism**) who control aspects of nature. Although some foragers, including Australian totemites, have communal religions, these religions are more typical of food producers.

Olympian religions, which appeared with state organization, add full-time religious specialists—professional priesthoods. Like the state itself, the priesthood is hierarchically and bureaucratically organized. The term *Olympian* comes from Mount Olympus, home of the classical Greek gods. Olympian religions are polytheistic. They include powerful anthropomorphic gods with specialized functions, for example, gods of love, war, the sea, and death. Olympian **pantheons** (collections of supernatural beings) were prominent in the religions of many nonindustrial states, including the Aztecs and Incas of the Americas, several African and Asian kingdoms, and classical Greece and Rome.

Wallace's fourth type—**monotheism**—also has priesthoods and notions of divine power, but it views the supernatural differently. In monotheism, all supernatural phenomena are manifestations of, or are under the control of, a single eternal, omniscient, omnipotent, and omnipresent supreme being. Such religions occur in states and empires and survive in modern organized religions. Islam, Judaism, and Christianity are all examples. Table 19.2 compares the numbers of adherents of contemporary religions.

World-Rejecting Religions

A distinctive type of religion (usually monotheistic), the **world-rejecting religion** (Bellah 1978), arose in ancient states along with literacy and a specialized priesthood. For the first time religion rejected the natural world and focused on a different realm of

As part of the Burmese shinbyu *ceremony boys renounce earthly pomp (and their hair) and live a monk's life for up to two months. World-rejecting religions arose in ancient states along with literacy and a specialized priesthood. For the first time religion rejected the natural world; the divine became a domain of exalted morality to which humans could only aspire.*

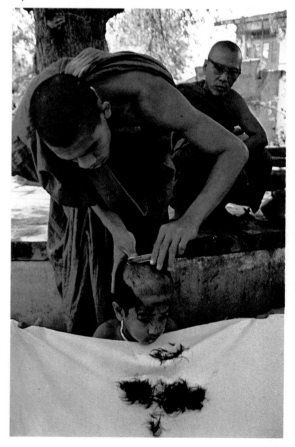

Table 19.2 *Adherents of all religions by seven continental areas*

	Africa	Asia	Europe	Latin America	Northern America	Oceania	U.S.S.R.	World	%	Countries
Christians	293,547,000	236,700,000	410,310,000	410,240,000	234,600,000	21,700,000	104,800,000	1,711,897,000	32.9	251
Roman Catholics	110,264,000	111,028,000	260,450,000	381,800,000	95,200,000	7,660,000	5,300,000	971,702,000	18.7	242
Protestants	77,327,000	73,563,000	73,330,000	15,500,000	94,600,000	7,600,000	9,300,000	351,220,000	6.7	230
Orthodox	26,262,000	3,300,000	35,860,000	1,660,000	5,900,000	540,000	90,100,700	163,622,700	3.1	98
Anglicans	24,108,000	645,000	32,690,000	1,230,000	7,200,000	5,336,000	300	71,209,300	1.4	148
Other Christians	55,586,000	48,164,000	7,980,000	10,050,000	31,700,000	564,000	99,000	154,143,000	3.0	110
Muslims	263,132,000	608,500,000	12,360,000	1,200,000	5,220,000	99,500	34,100,000	924,611,500	17.8	172
Nonreligious	1,700,000	690,000,000	52,158,000	16,000,000	21,700,000	3,100,000	84,855,500	869,513,500	16.7	220
Hindus	1,450,000	685,000,000	594,000	750,000	1,100,000	310,000	1,100	689,205,100	13.2	88
Buddhists	14,000	310,000,000	222,000	495,000	400,000	17,000	290,000	311,438,000	6.0	86
Atheists	250,000	150,000,000	18,460,000	2,900,000	1,200,000	530,000	58,500,000	231,840,000	4.5	130
Chinese folk religionists	10,000	170,000,000	50,000	60,000	101,000	15,000	200	170,236,200	3.3	56
New-Religionists	15,000	125,000,000	35,000	460,000	1,300,000	9,000	500	126,819,500	2.4	25
Tribal religionists	66,240,000	23,500,000	200	950,000	50,000	70,000	0	90,810,200	1.7	98
Sikhs	23,000	17,350,000	217,000	7,000	230,000	8,000	100	17,735,100	0.3	20
Jews	300,000	4,310,000	1,447,000	1,010,000	7,100,000	90,000	3,100,000	17,357,000	0.3	125
Shamanists	900	10,500,000	400	200	500	200	200,000	10,702,200	0.2	10
Confucians	800	5,800,000	1,000	800	18,000	300	500	5,821,400	0.1	3
Baha'is	1,310,000	2,510,000	85,000	750,000	340,000	71,000	6,000	5,072,000	0.1	205
Jains	45,000	3,520,000	10,000	3,000	2,500	1,000	0	3,581,500	0.1	10
Shintoists	300	3,200,000	400	1,000	3,000	500	100	3,205,300	0.1	3
Other religionists	279,000	5,719,000	736,000	4,237,000	405,000	87,500	7,000	11,570,500	0.2	170
Total Population	628,317,000	3,051,609,000	496,686,000	439,064,000	273,770,000	26,109,000	285,861,000	5,201,416,000	100.0	251

Source: Reprinted with permission from the 1990 *Britannica Book of the Year,* copyright © 1990, Encyclopaedia Britannica, Inc., Chicago, Illinois.

reality. The supernatural world was no longer viewed as superior simply because it was more powerful. The divine became a domain of exalted *morality* to which humans could only aspire. Salvation through fusion with the supernatural was the main goal.

In *modern* monotheistic religions, such as Protestantism, the hierarchical structure of previous monotheistic religions has collapsed. Salvation is directly available to individuals, who, regardless of social status, have unmediated access to the supernatural. The role of the priest declines. Protestantism and other forms of Christianity are world-rejecting religions. In contrast to the primitive fusion of nature and religion, they sharply separate the world of here and now from the sacred realm. Notions of the afterlife and of the salvation that it offers dominate their ideologies.

RELIGION, STABILITY, AND CHANGE

Revitalization Movements

Religion helps maintain social order, but it can also be an instrument of change, sometimes even of revolution. As a response to conquest or foreign domination, religious leaders often undertake to alter or revitalize a society. We call such movements *nativistic movements* (Linton 1943) or **revitalization movements** (Wallace 1956).

Christianity originated as a revitalization movement. Jesus was one of several prophets who preached new religious doctrines while the Middle East was under Roman rule. It was a time of social unrest, when a foreign power ruled the land. Jesus inspired a new, enduring, and major religion. His contemporaries were not so successful.

The Handsome Lake religion arose around 1800 among the Iroquois of New York State (Wallace 1970b). Handsome Lake, the founder of this revitalization movement, was a chief of one of the Iroquois tribes. The Iroquois had suffered because of their support of the British against the American colonials. After the colonial victory and a wave of immigration to their homeland, the Iroquois were dispersed on small reservations. Unable to pursue traditional horticulture and hunting in their homeland, the Iroquois became heavy drinkers and quarreled among themselves.

Handsome Lake was an alcoholic who started having visions from heavenly messengers. The spirits warned him that unless the Iroquois changed their ways, they would be destroyed. His visions offered a plan for coping with the new order. Witchcraft, quarreling, and drinking would end. The Iroquois would copy European farming techniques, which, unlike traditional Iroquois horticulture, stressed male rather than female labor. Handsome Lake preached that the Iroquois should also abandon their communal longhouses and matrilineal descent groups for more permanent marriages and individual family households. The teachings of Handsome Lake produced a new church and religion, one that still has members in New York and Ontario. This revitalization movement helped the Iroquois survive in a modified environment. They eventually gained a reputation among their non-Indian neighbors as sober family farmers.

RELIGION AND CULTURAL ECOLOGY

We have considered religious beliefs, practices, institutions, and personnel in different types of society. We have seen, for example, that state religions differ markedly from those of egalitarian societies. We now turn to the cultural ecology of religion. How does behavior motivated by beliefs in supernatural beings, powers, and forces help people survive in their material environments? In this section we will see how beliefs and rituals function as part of a group's cultural adaptation to its environment.

The Adaptive Significance of Sacred Cattle in India

The people of India worship zebu cattle, which are protected by the Hindu doctrine of *ahimsa,* a principle of nonviolence that forbids the killing of animals generally. Western economic development experts occasionally (and erroneously) cite the Hindu cattle taboo to illustrate the idea that religious beliefs can stand in the way of rational economic decisions. Hindus seem to be irrationally ignoring a valuable food (beef) because of their cultural or religious traditions. The economic developers also comment that Indians don't know how to raise proper cattle. They point to the scraggly zebus that wander about town and country. Western tech-

India's zebu cattle are protected by the doctrine of ahimsa, *a principle of nonviolence that forbids the killing of animals generally. This Hindu doctrine puts the full power of organized religion behind the command not to destroy a valuable resource even in times of extreme need.*

niques of animal husbandry grow bigger cattle that produce more beef and milk. Western planners lament that Hindus are set in their ways. Bound by culture and tradition, they refuse to develop rationally.

However, these assumptions are both ethnocentric and wrong. Sacred cattle actually play an important adaptive role in an Indian ecosystem that has evolved over thousands of years (Harris 1974, 1978). Peasants' use of cattle to pull plows and carts is part of the technology of Indian agriculture. Indian peasants have no need for large, hungry cattle of the sort that economic developers, beef marketers, and North American cattle ranchers prefer. Scrawny animals pull plows and carts well enough but don't eat their owners out of house and home. How could peasants with limited land and marginal diets feed supersteers without taking food away from themselves?

Indians use cattle manure to fertilize their fields. Not all the manure is collected, because peasants don't spend much time watching their cattle, which wander and graze at will during certain seasons. In the rainy season, some of the manure that cattle deposit on the hillsides washes down to the fields. In this way, cattle also fertilize the fields indirectly. Furthermore, in a country where fossil fuels are scarce, dry cattle dung, which burns slowly and evenly, is a basic cooking fuel.

Far from being useless, as the development ex-

perts contend, sacred cattle are essential to Indian cultural adaptation. Biologically adapted to poor pasture land and a marginal environment, the scraggly zebu provides fertilizer and fuel, is indispensable in farming, and is affordable for peasants. The Hindu doctrine of *ahimsa* puts the full power of organized religion behind the command not to destroy a valuable resource even in times of extreme need.

The Cultural Ecology of Ceremonial Feasts

In previous chapters we saw that feasts hosted by big men and chiefs bring people together from several places and thus forge regional communities and political alliances. We saw that potlatching on the Pacific Coast of North America evened out variations in local production by distributing resources throughout the region. Potlatching also prevented economic differentiation, because wealth was either destroyed or given away (and thus converted into prestige) rather than being hoarded or reinvested to create additional wealth.

In many tribes, intercommunity feasting is a leveling, redistributive mechanism, helping to even out imbalances in access to strategic resources. Although intercommunity feasting is often done for religious purposes, particularly to fulfill obligations to dead ancestors, this religious behavior has real-world effects that may be more obvious to anthropologists than to natives, as the following two cases illustrate.

The first example comes from my own field work among the Betsileo, who grow rice and use cattle as draft animals. The Betsileo live in dispersed hamlets and villages. Hamlets begin as small settlements with two or three households. Over time many grow into villages. All the settlements have ancestral tombs, which are very important in Betsileo culture. It costs much more to build a tomb than to build a house. It's right to spend more on the tomb, say the Betsileo, because one spends eternity in it. A house is just a temporary home.

Betsileo may be buried in the same tomb as any one of their eight great-grandparents. When a woman has children, she also earns burial rights in her husband's tomb. Most men belong to their father's descent group, live in his village, and will be buried in his tomb. Nevertheless, Betsileo attend ceremonies at all their ancestral tombs, in all of which they have burial rights.

After the annual rice harvest in April and May comes the ceremonial season, when agricultural work is least taxing. Ceremonies honor the ancestors as the Betsileo open the tombs. Sometimes they simply rewrap corpses and bones in new shrouds. Sometimes, in more elaborate ceremonies, they take the bodies and bones outside, dance with them, wrap them in new cloth, and return them to the tomb. Whenever a tomb is built, bodies and bones are moved in from an older family tomb.

During their ceremonies, the Betsileo kill cattle. They offer a small part of the beef to the ancestors; living people eat the rest. After offering meat to the ancestors, people remove it from the altar and eat it as well. The custom of cattle sacrifice arose at a time when there were no markets and the Betsileo lived in small hamlets. At that time, ceremonial distribution was the Betsileo's only source of beef. It was not feasible to kill and eat an entire animal in a small hamlet, because there were too few people to consume it. Nor could the Betsileo buy meat in markets. They got beef by attending ceremonials in villages where they had kinship, descent, and marriage links.

Betsileo also kill cattle for funerals. Again, some beef is dedicated to the ancestors but eaten by the living. People attend the funerals of neighbors, kin, in-laws, and fictive kin. Because funerals occur throughout the year, the Betsileo eat beef and thus

obtain animal protein regularly. However, although people can die at any time, Betsileo deaths cluster in certain seasons—especially November to February, the rainy season. This is a period of food shortages, when much of the rice harvested the previous April has been eaten. Many funerals, occasions on which beef and rice are distributed, occur at precisely the time of year (the preharvest season of food scarcity) when people are hungriest. In Betsileo cultural adaptation, funerals distribute food beyond the local group and to the poorest people, helping them survive the lean season.

Today, settlements are larger and the Betsileo have markets. Ceremonies persist, but there are fewer big feasts than there once were. Naturally, any discussion of the adaptive functions of Betsileo religion raises the question whether the Betsileo started the ceremonies because they recognized their potential adaptive usefulness. The answer is no, but the question is instructive.

The Betsileo maintain these rituals because they honor, commemorate, or appease ancestors, relatives, fictive kin, in-laws, and neighbors. The tomb ceremonies serve many of the social and psychological functions of religion we have discussed. However, although Betsileo receive invitations to several ceremonies each year, they don't attend them all. What determines the individual's decision to attend? If a distant relative or acquaintance dies when people are eating well, they may decide not to go or to send someone junior in their place. However, if an equally distant relative dies during the season of scarcity, many Betsileo, especially poorer people, opt for a day or two of feasting. Some of my Betsileo friends, usually those with small rice fields, became funeral hoppers during the lean season. They used a series of personal connections to attend every available funeral and ceremony. Betsileo ceremonies do not simply maintain social solidarity. They also play a role in cultural adaptation by regulating access to strategic resources, including the nutrients that people need to resist disease and infection and to survive (Kottak 1980).

Ritual Regulation
of Environmental Relations

In a classic study Roy Rappaport (1966, 1984) documented another example of the adaptive functions of ritual, among the Tsembaga Maring of the

Papua–New Guinea highlands. This time it is the ceremonial slaughter of pigs that has adaptive significance. Pig sacrifice functions within two levels of ecosystems. The first is the local ecosystem, consisting of the Tsembaga, their territory, and its plants and animals. The second is a wider, or regional, ecosystem that consists of the Tsembaga and other Maring groups, along with the territory and resources of a wider geographical region.

Until the Australian government brought them under control in 1962, the Maring engaged in intratribal warfare. Local groups such as the Tsembaga fought their neighbors. Usually, the fighting ended in a truce. Occasionally, however, one group prevailed and the other vacated its ancestral territory. When the fighting stopped, the group or groups remaining in ancestral territory carried out a ritual known as planting the rumbim plant. They sacrificed all their adult pigs, feasted, and gave pork to their allies to repay them for their aid. The pig feast also thanked the ancestors for their help in the victory.

But obligations to allies and ancestors didn't end with this sacrifice. As they planted the rumbim, the Tsembaga vowed that they would hold a *kaiko,* a larger pig festival, when the pig herd grew back to its original size. This might take as long as twenty years.

Fighting was taboo as long as the rumbim stayed planted, a custom that limited the frequency of hos-tilities. The taboo brought occasional peace to a society that lacked state organization.

When the big festival did come, the Tsembaga had to kill pigs throughout the entire *kaiko* year, which ended when the rumbim was uprooted. This symbolic gesture announced the full repayment of ancestors and allies. The group was also signaling its readiness to fight again.

Besides the occasional slaughter of the entire herd, the Maring also sacrificed individual pigs when people were ill or injured. Afflicted people and their close kin and neighbors ate this pork. This custom provided pork, which helped the sick person recover, while also providing protein to other members of the local group, whose diets might have been suffering as well. Demands of this sort affected the growth of the pig herd. The herds of healthier populations grew faster.

Maring pigs normally ate substandard yams and sweet potatoes. Pigs roamed the village and its territory during the day and were rounded up at night. As the herd grew, however, Maring women had to start giving the pigs food intended for people. They also had to plant extra gardens. At this point, the Maring, especially Maring women, were working harder, laboring for their surplus pigs.

Besides the additional work, the pig herd created other problems as pigs started invading gardens. Garden owners sometimes shot pigs that uprooted their crops. This usually provoked retaliation by the

Among the Maring of Papua–New Guinea ritual prohibitions regulate relationships in local and regional ecosystems. During the kaiko *festival the rumbim plant is uprooted and dozens of pigs are slaughtered. Here a man holds a pig for another man to kill with a blow to the snout.*

pig owner, who might shoot the garden owner or the garden owner's spouse or pig. Disputes became frequent, and women complained to their husbands that they had more pigs than they could handle. It was time for the *kaiko*.

Women's complaints pushed the men to plan the festival. Throughout the year of the *kaiko*, groups of allies visited. They danced, talked, traded things, and arranged marriages. They stuffed themselves with pork and took leftovers home. When all the adult pigs had been sacrificed, the rumbim was uprooted. The men could again wage war.

After uprooting its rumbim, a group could occupy any territory vacated by its opponents during the last fighting period. Because the enemies had dispersed, joining relatives in other local groups, they had been unable to plant rumbim. It was a rule of Maring culture that if one group could uproot its

rumbim before its opponents could plant theirs, the first group could occupy the second group's territory (Rappaport 1984). The ancestors of the defeated group, like its living members, were believed to have left the territory.

In these ways, the ritual cycle gradually redistributed people over Maring territory. Significantly, the time between warfare's end, rumbim planting, and the *kaiko* was twelve to twenty years. This was exactly the time it normally took gardens, in the cycle of Maring shifting horticulture, to recover their productivity. The twelve- to twenty-year taboo against occupying enemy territory allowed precisely the time needed for the losers' fields to regain their fertility. The timing of the Maring ritual cycle was adapted to the optimal functioning of the productive system.

SUMMARY

Religion, a cultural universal, consists of belief and behavior concerned with supernatural beings, powers, and forces. Cross-cultural studies have revealed many functions of religion. Tylor focused on religion's explanatory role, suggesting that animism—the belief in souls—is religion's most primitive form. He argued that religion evolved from animism through polytheism to monotheism. As science provided better explanations, Tylor thought that religion would eventually disappear. However, a different view of the supernatural also occurs in nonindustrial societies. This is animatism, which sees the supernatural as a domain of raw, impersonal power or force (called *mana* in Polynesia and Melanesia). People can manipulate and control mana under certain conditions.

When ordinary technical and rational means of doing things fail, people may turn to magic, using it when they lack control over outcomes. Religion offers comfort and psychological security at times of crisis. However, rites can also create anxiety. Rituals are formal, invariant, stylized, earnest acts that require people to subordinate their particular beliefs to a social collectivity. Rites of passage have three stages: separation, liminality or margin, and aggregation. Passage rites can mark any change in social status, age, place, or social condition. Collective rites are often cemented by communitas, a feeling of intense solidarity.

The study of religion also leads anthropologists to the cross-cultural analysis of myths and folk tales. These forms of creative expression reveal native theories about the creation of the world and supernatural entities. Myths

express cultural values, offer hope, and teach enculturative lessons. The myths of state-organized societies include cautionary tragedies as well as hopeful tales typical of bands and tribes. Lévi-Strauss, the inventor of the structural analysis of myth, has argued that people universally classify aspects of nature and culture by means of binary opposition. Such opposition makes phenomena that are continuous seem more distinct. Structural analysis aims not to explain but to discover otherwise hidden connections among aspects of culture. This approach links anthropology to the humanities.

Religion varies with culture type. The religions of state-organized societies often have high gods—all-knowing, all-powerful deities—and state religion supports secular authority. Wallace defines four types of religion: shamanic, communal, Olympian, and monotheistic. Each has characteristic ceremonies and practitioners. Shamans are part-time, priests full-time, religious specialists. World-rejecting religions, which appeared more recently, are well represented among the organized religions of contemporary North America. Unlike the religions of bands, tribes, and chiefdoms, they view the supernatural realm as morally superior to the real world.

Religion helps maintain the social and ecological order, but it can also promote change. Revitalization movements incorporate old and new beliefs and have helped people adapt to changing environments.

Besides their psychological and social functions, religious beliefs and practices play a role in the adaptation of human populations to their environments. The Hindu doctrine of *ahimsa,* which prohibits harm to living things, makes cattle sacred and beef a tabooed food. The taboo's force stops peasants from killing their draft cattle even in times of extreme need. This preserves a vital resource for Indian agriculture. Western economic planners should investigate the adaptive significance of a religious prohibition before condemning it as economically irrational.

Intercommunity feasting also falls within a cultural ecological framework. Betsileo tomb ceremonies redistribute food and other scarce resources. The ceremonial slaughter of pigs among the Maring of New Guinea shows that ritual prohibitions help regulate relationships in local and regional ecosystems.

GLOSSARY

ahimsa: Hindu doctrine that prohibits harming life, and thus cattle slaughter.

animatism: Concept of the supernatural as an impersonal power.

animism: Belief in souls or doubles.

berdaches: Among the Crow Indians, members of a third gender, for whom certain ritual duties were reserved.

binary opposition: Pairs of opposites, such as good-evil and old-young, produced by converting differences of degree into qualitative distinctions; important in structuralism.

communal religions: In Wallace's typology, these religions have, in addition to shamanic cults, communal cults in which people organize community rituals such as harvest ceremonies and rites of passage.

communitas: Intense community spirit, a feeling of great social solidarity, equality, and togetherness; characteristic of people experiencing liminality together.

cult institutions: A society's rituals and associated beliefs; basis of Wallace's typology of world religions.

kaiko: Pig festival among the Maring of Papua–New Guinea.

liminality: The critically important marginal or in-between phase of a rite of passage.

liturgical order: A set sequence of words and actions invented prior to the current performance of the ritual in which it occurs.

magic: Use of supernatural techniques to accomplish specific aims.

mana: Sacred impersonal force in Melanesian and Polynesian religions.

monotheism: Worship of an eternal, omniscient, omnipotent, and omnipresent supreme being.

Olympian religions: In Wallace's typology, develop with state organization; have full-time religious specialists—professional priesthoods.

pantheon: A collection of supernatural beings in a particular religion.

polytheism: Belief in several deities who control aspects of nature.

religion: Belief and ritual concerned with supernatural beings, powers, and forces.

revitalization movements: Movements that occur in times of change, in which religious leaders emerge and undertake to alter or revitalize a society.

rites of passage: Culturally defined activities associated with the transition from one place or stage of life to another.

ritual: Behavior that is formal, stylized, repetitive, and stereotyped, performed earnestly as a social act; rituals are held at set times and places and have liturgical orders.

shaman: A part-time religious practitioner who mediates between ordinary people and supernatural beings and forces.

structuralism: Structural analysis; technique developed by Lévi-Strauss not to explain sociocultural similarities and differences but to uncover themes, relations, and other cross-cultural connections.

taboo: Set apart as sacred and off-limits to ordinary people; prohibition backed by supernatural sanctions.

world-rejecting religions: Religions that sharply separate the material world from the sacred; include notions of an afterlife and salvation.

STUDY QUESTIONS

1. How do anthropologists define religion, and what are the problems with this definition?
2. What are the cognitive (explanatory), psychological (emotional), and social functions of religion?
3. What are rituals, and how do they differ from other acts?
4. What is a rite of passage, and what are its phases?
5. Can you give examples of rites of passage from your

own experience or from North American culture in general?

6. What is structural analysis, and how do its aims differ from those of science?

7. Can you suggest an aspect of your culture that might be appropriate for a structural analysis? Sketch such an analysis.

8. How do state religions differ from those of nonstate societies?

9. What are shamans? How are they similar to and different from priests?

10. How do world-rejecting religions differ from those found in bands and tribes?

11. How do revitalization movements function as an instrument of social change?

12. What ethnographic example could illustrate how religious beliefs and practices have material consequences or ecological functions?

SUGGESTED ADDITIONAL READING

BETTELHEIM, B.
1975 *The Uses of Enchantment: The Meaning and Importance of Fairy Tales.* New York: Vintage. Neo-Freudian perspective on fairy tales and myths.

BROWN, K. M.
1991 *Mama Lola: A Vodou Priestess in Brooklyn.* Berkeley: University of California Press. Ethnographic study of a religious community and its leader.

COMBS-SCHILLING, E.
1989 *Sacred Performances: Islam, Sexuality, and Sacrifice.* New York: Columbia University Press. Historical ethnography of the Moroccan state, focusing on its use of Islamic concepts and ideals, placed in the context of Islam as a world religion.

FRIED, M. N., AND M. H. FRIED
1980 *Transitions: Four Rituals in Eight Cultures.* New York: W. W. Norton. Rituals surrounding birth, adolescence, marriage, and death compared cross-culturally.

HARGROVE, E. C.
1986 *Religion and Environmental Crisis.* Athens: University of Georgia Press. Religion and ecological issues.

LESSA, W. A., AND E. Z. VOGT, EDS.
1978 *Reader in Comparative Religion: An Anthropological Approach,* 4th ed. New York: Harper & Row. Excellent collection of major articles on the origins, functions, and expressions of religion in comparative perspective.

MAIR, L.
1969 *Witchcraft.* New York: McGraw-Hill. Analysis of the social contexts and functions of witchcraft and witchcraft accusations; relies heavily on African data.

METCALF, P.
1991 *Celebrations of Death: The Anthropology of Mortuary Ritual, 2nd ed.* New York: Cambridge University Press. Cross-cultural study of rituals surrounding death.

MOORE, S. F., AND B. G. MYERHOFF, EDS.
1978 *Secular Ritual.* Atlantic Highlands, NJ: Humanities Press. Political rallies, carnivals, athletic contests, theater, and national celebrations in several cultures.

MORRIS, B.
1987 *Anthropological Studies of Religion: An Introductory Text.* New York: Cambridge University Press. Up-to-date text on religion cross-culturally.

RAPPAPORT, R. A.
1979 *Ecology, Meaning, and Religion.* Richmond, CA: North Atlantic Books. Various essays on religion in cultural and ecological perspective.

TURNER, V. W.
1974 *The Ritual Process.* Harmondsworth, United Kingdom: Penguin. Liminality among the Ndembu discussed in a comparative perspective.

VECSEY, C., ED.
1990 *Religion in Native North America.* Moscow, Idaho: University of Idaho Press. Essays on Native American religions, including reevaluations of past interpretations.

WALLACE, A. F. C.
1966 *Religion: An Anthropological View.* New York: Random House. Survey of anthropological approaches to religion.

PERSONALITY AND WORLDVIEW

Culture is both public and individual, both in the world and in people's minds. Anthropologists are interested not only in public and collective behavior but also in how *individuals* think, feel, and act. The individual and culture are linked because human social life is a process in which individuals internalize the meanings of *public* (i.e., cultural) messages. Then, alone and in groups, people influence culture by converting their private understandings into public expressions (D'Andrade 1984). We may study this process by focusing on shared, public aspects of culture or by focusing on individuals. Anthropology and psychology intersect in **psychological anthropology,** the ethnographic and cross-cultural study of differences and similarities in human psychology. Focusing on the individual, psychological anthropology exists because a complete account of cultural process requires both perspectives—private and public.

THE INDIVIDUAL AND CULTURE

One area of psychological anthropology is **cognitive anthropology**—the ethnographic and cross-cultural study of cognition—which includes learning, ways of knowing, and the organization of knowledge, perceptions, and meaning. Cognitive anthropology examines private understanding by analyzing aspects of individual behavior, including speech. (This links it to some areas of linguistic anthropology, including the study of meaning, as discussed in the next chapter.)

Drawing on cognitive science, Naomi Quinn and Claudia Strauss (1989/1994) propose an approach that explicitly links the individual and culture. They start with the assumption that every culture is both (1) a network of shared understandings and (2) a changing product involving negotiation by its individual members. Quinn and Strauss draw on **schema theory,** which is prominent in modern cognitive science (Casson 1983). According to this theory, the mind builds schemata (the plural of *schema*) to filter new experience and reconstruct past experience, shaping memories to conform to current expectations. Linked to schema theory is **connectionism**—the idea that things that consistently occur together in an individual's experience become strongly associated in that person's mind. A schema

develops when a set of linked experiences forms a network of strong mental associations.

Schemata produce simplified versions of experience, so that we remember the typical, or modal, event rather than the unusual one. Remembering typical events, we fill in missing information according to expectations created by strong associations. To describe how a child internalizes associations—develops and uses schemata—Quinn and Strauss use the example of a middle-class American girl born just after World War II. During childhood this girl builds up a chain of associations in which mother goes with "food, kitchen, home, indoors, everyday routine. Father goes with basement, garage, office, outdoors, special occasions" (Quinn and Strauss 1989, pp. 6–7). These associations are strengthened because the girl's experience constantly reinforces them. The tendency to remember the typical rather than the unusual can lead individuals to forget or misremember (mistakenly reconstruct in memory) times when the father cooked or the mother worked in the garage.

Diversity among the world's cultures reflects the fact that babies have malleable neural networks, permitting varied learning paths during enculturation. However, as individuals grow, their schemata harden. They make new experiences fit the established pattern more than they change with new experience. One reason why schemata are shared by people in the same culture is the tendency to rely on modal mental images. Although my experience has differed from yours, if we both have experienced the same broad pattern, our schemata retain it. As we enact our shared schemata in our public behavior, the typical pattern is reinforced further in our separate minds.

Cognition and emotions develop together as part of schema formation. Thus if a child learns that mother goes with food, he or she also builds associations of feelings around motherhood and food. Schemata explain not only the shared aspect of culture but also its openness to diverse individual interpretations and the possibility of cultural change. To illustrate this, Quinn and Strauss (1989/1994) add a second middle-class American girl to their example. Both girls may have learned that mother goes with kitchen and father goes with office, but beyond that there may be great differences. One girl may associate her father's arrival home

As members of a culture enact their shared mental schemata in public behavior, the typical pattern is reinforced further in their separate minds. If children learn that extended family goes with Sunday and food, they build associations of feelings around Sundays, kinship, and food. Shown here, a Sunday dinner in Provence, France.

with anticipation; the other, with dread. Individual experiences and feelings give rise to differences in schemata among people who grow up in the same culture.

Society has both unifying and divisive forces. Unique schemata arise from distinct individual experiences, while shared schemata are built up from common experience. In modern nations some schemata are shared by millions because of people's exposure to the mass media. Other schemata are shared by smaller groups—ethnic and regional subcultures, people who accidentally share similar experiences, and experts with the same formal training (such as anthropologists). Schemata are like the *levels of culture* discussed in Chapter 3 in that both are associated with a continuum of shared experience and learning. However, schema theory focuses on the cognitive attributes of the *individuals* who share understandings.

Schema theory leaves room for individual creativity, disagreement, resistance, and change. People aren't doomed to re-create all the patterns they observed in childhood. New social options can provide fresh models for adult behavior. New experiences can create new associations, and associations may be altered by conscious intervention. In such ways behavior (and culture) can change. Our children's schemata and behavior will be both like and unlike our own.

PERSONALITY

Psychological anthropology is sometimes described as the study of "culture and personality." According to one definition, **personality**

> is a more or less enduring organization of forces within the individual associated with a complex of fairly consistent attitudes, values, and modes of perception which account in part for the individual's consistency of behavior. (Barnouw 1985, p. 10)

The consistency of an individual's personality reveals itself in varied settings—work, rest, play, creative activities, and interaction with others. Thus, we can think of personality as an individual's characteristic ways of thinking and acting.

People have different personalities because, except for identical twins, everyone is genetically unique. Furthermore, from conception on, no two people encounter exactly the same environment. The experiences of childhood and later life combine with genetic predispositions to form the psychological attributes of the adult. However, as we saw in the discussion of schema theory, personality attributes can change as adults encounter new problems, situations, and experiences or through conscious intervention.

Psychologists are correct in assuming that despite

cultural diversity, all humans share certain mental traits. These similarities aren't necessarily genetic but may arise from universal or nearly universal experiences—birth itself; stages of physiological development; interaction with parents, siblings, and others; and experiences with light and dark, heat and cold, and wet and dry objects.

Anthropologists only occasionally comment on—usually to question—the existence of psychological universals. Instead, the study of culture and personality pursues anthropology's characteristic interest in diversity by examining psychological data cross-culturally. Psychological anthropologists draw on techniques developed by psychologists to examine personality variation within a society and between societies. Research methods include observing behavior in varied settings, conversing about wide-ranging topics, administering psychological tests, analyzing dreams, and collecting life histories. Because child rearing is crucial in personality formation, anthropologists have investigated this process in many societies. As a result, we can generalize about factors that produce certain personalities.

In modern nations, regional, ethnic, and socioeconomic variation influences child-rearing patterns, individual opportunities, and thus personality formation. In studying relationships between personality and culture, anthropologists must examine (1) personality traits common to all or most members of a society and (2) those associated only with social subdivisions. We also consider personality variation that is *not* typical of either society at large or its subgroups, which we call *deviant* behavior.

EARLY CULTURE AND PERSONALITY RESEARCH

Margaret Mead: Child Training and Gender Roles

Margaret Mead (profiled in Chapter 1) did several studies of culture and personality in the Pacific islands, focusing on childhood and adolescence. Her early book *Coming of Age in Samoa* (1928/1961), based on a nine-month study of Samoan girls, compared Samoan and American adolescence. Mead's hypothesis was that the psychological changes associated with puberty are not biologically based but culturally determined. She described Samoan adolescence as a relatively easy period, lacking the sexual frustrations and stresses characteristic of American adolescence.

Later researchers in other Samoan villages reached different conclusions. A study by Derek Freeman (1983) offers a particularly harsh judgment of Mead's ethnography. Rather than the carefree sexual experimentation Mead described, Freeman found a strict virginity complex. Instead of casual and friendly relations between the sexes, Freeman

Margaret Mead's controversial book Coming of Age in Samoa *(1928/1961), based on a nine-month study, compared Samoan and American adolescence. Samoan personality and culture have changed since Mead did her field work. These young women are celebrating Flag Day in Pago Pago, American Samoa.*

found male-female hostility. His Samoan boys competed in macho contests that involved sneaking up on girls and raping them with their fingers.

How do other anthropologists evaluate Freeman's findings and his criticisms of Mead? We know that in any culture, customs vary from village to village and decade to decade. Mead and Freeman worked at different times (fifteen years apart) and in different villages. Freeman's Samoans may well have differed from the people Mead observed in 1930. Furthermore, different anthropologists have particular interests, skills, and biases, which affect their interpretations.

Besides their own biases, ethnographers should be aware of variation within any culture they are studying. They must avoid the tendency to imply that a particular village is homogeneous or that it represents the entire culture. Freeman's attack on Mead is merely the most publicized in a series of disagreements between anthropologists who offer contrasting interpretations of a given culture (see also Solway and Lee 1990; Wilmsen 1989). Ethnographers need to be more sensitive to variation within a culture as well as to ways in which their particular interests may influence their field work.

Culture and personality research has been criticized more than most other aspects of ethnography. Long before Freeman's attack, anthropologists (e.g., Harris 1968) had faulted Mead's work for being too impressionistic. Mead relied heavily on her own impressions about the emotions of Samoan girls. Although she did report deviant cases, Mead claimed to focus on the *typical* adolescent experience. However, because she presented little statistical data, the ratio of normal to deviant could not be established. In defending her research, Mead stated that "the student of the more intangible and psychological aspects of human behavior is forced to illuminate rather than demonstrate a thesis" (1928/1961, p. 260). More recent approaches to culture and personality research that are less impressionistic than Mead's are discussed below.

Ruth Benedict: Cultures as Individuals

Like Mead's work, Ruth Benedict's widely read book *Patterns of Culture* (1934/1959) influenced research on culture and personality. Using published sources rather than personal field experiences, Benedict contrasted the cultural orientations of the

Kwakiutl of the Northwest Coast of North America and the Zuni of the American Southwest. The Kwakiutl, whose potlatch system was described in the chapter "Economic Systems," are unusual foragers. They inhabit a rich environment and have tribal or chiefdom rather than band organization. The Zuni, tribal agriculturalists, are one of the Pueblo peoples of American Southwest.

Benedict proposed that particular cultures are integrated by one or two dominant psychological themes and that entire cultures—here the Zuni and the Kwakiutl—can be labeled by means of their psychological attributes. Thus, she called the Kwakiutl *Dionysian* and the Zuni *Apollonian*, from the Greek gods of wine and light, respectively. Benedict portrayed the Dionysian Kwakiutl as striving to escape limitations, achieve excess, and break into another order of experience. Given these goals, they valued drugs and alcohol, fasting, self-torture, and frenzy. In contrast, Benedict's Apollonian Zuni were noncompetitive, gentle, and peace-loving. She found no Dionysian traits (strife, factionalism, painful ceremonies, disruptive psychological states) among the Zuni. They valued a middle-of-the-road existence and distrusted excess.

Benedict's approach was **configurationalism.** In this view, cultures are integrated wholes, each uniquely different from all others. She thought that cross-cultural comparison of particular features is less feasible than demonstrating each culture's distinctive patterning. However, later scholars have faulted Benedict for stereotyping cultures—by ignoring cooperative features of Kwakiutl life and strife, suicide, and alcoholism among the Zuni. Unfortunately, Benedict's risky use of individual psychological labels to characterize whole cultures influenced later descriptions of national character.

National Character

Studies of **national character** were popular in the United States from World War II until the early 1950s. These studies were flawed because they used a few informants to generalize about the psychological features of entire nations. Several anthropologists tried to help the American war effort by describing Japanese culture and personality structure (Benedict 1946; Gorer 1943). Because the war precluded field work in Japan, American anthropologists had to do "studies of culture at a distance."

VARIETIES OF HUMAN SEXUALITY

Margaret Mead called attention to the fact that sexual behavior varies from culture to culture. A later, more systematic cross-cultural study (Ford and Beach 1951) found wide variation in attitudes about masturbation, bestiality (sex with animals), and homosexuality. Even in a single culture, such as the United States, attitudes about sex differ with socioeconomic status, region, and rural versus urban residence. However, even in the 1950s, before the "age of sexual permissiveness" (the late 1960s and 1970s) began, research showed that almost all American men (92 percent) and more than half of American women (54 percent) admitted to masturbation. Between 40 and 50 percent of American farm boys had sex with animals. In the famous Kinsey report (Kinsey, Pomeroy, and Martin 1948), 37 percent of the men surveyed admitted having had at least one homosexual experience leading to orgasm. In a later study of 1,200 unmarried women, 26 percent reported homosexual activities.

Attitudes toward homosexuality, masturbation, and bestiality in other cultures differ strikingly, as I find when I contrast the cultures I know best—the United States, urban and rural Brazil, and Madagascar. During my first stay in Arembepe, Brazil, when I was nineteen years old and unmarried, young men told me details of their experiences with prostitutes in the city. In Arembepe, a rural community, sex with animals was common. Targets of the male sex drive included cattle, horses, sheep, goats, and turkeys. Arembepe's women were also more open about their sex lives than their North American counterparts were.

Arembepeiros talked about sex so willingly that I wasn't prepared for the silence and avoidance of sexual subjects that I encountered in Madagascar. My wife's and my discreet attempts to get the Betsileo to tell us at least the basics of their culture's sexual practices led nowhere. I did discover from city folk that, as in many non-Western cultures, traditional ceremonies were times of ritual license, when normal taboos lapsed and Betsileo men and women engaged in what Christian missionaries described as "wanton" sexuality. Only during my last week in Madagascar did a young man in the village of Ivato, where I had spent a year, take me aside and offer to write down the words for genitals and sexual intercourse. He could not say these tabooed words, but he wanted me to know them so that my knowledge of Betsileo culture would be as complete as possible.

I have never worked in a culture with institutionalized homosexuality of the sort that exists among several tribes in Papua–New Guinea, such as the Kaluli (Schieffelin 1976) or Sambia (Herdt 1981, 1987). The

They interviewed Japanese people in the United States, watched Japanese films, and read books, magazines, and histories. Because their aim was to describe *common* behavior patterns and personality traits, these anthropologists often ignored variation. They assumed that each individual represented groupwide patterns, at least partially. However, these national character researchers never used samples that properly encapsulated the range of variation in a complex nation.

Sigmund Freud's psychoanalytic influence was apparent in national character studies. The most famous example was the purported relationship between Japanese toilet training, said to be severe and early, and a "compulsive" Japanese personality preoccupied with ritual, order, and cleanliness (Benedict 1946; Gorer 1943; LaBarre 1945). Some anthropologists even argued that the compulsion engendered by strict toilet training made the Japanese particularly aggressive in warfare. However, later research showed that modal Japanese were actually *less* preoccupied with toilet training than Americans were.

Many early descriptions of personality and national character contained ethnocentric and personal impressions. Without careful field work, objectivity and cultural relativism faded. (From the perspective of cultural relativism, the values and moral standards of one culture shouldn't be used to evaluate another.) It's difficult to believe that anthropologist Ralph Linton, a contributor to culture and personality research, wrote in a professional report about tribes of Madagascar that

the Betsimisaraka are stupid and lazy, and insolent unless kept in check. . . . The Tsimahety are moderately

Kaluli believe that semen has a magical quality that promotes knowledge and growth. Before traveling into alien territory, boys must eat a mixture of ginger, salt, and semen to enhance their ability to learn a foreign language. At age eleven or twelve, a Kaluli boy forms a homosexual relationship with an older man chosen by his father. (This man cannot be a relative, because that would violate their incest taboo.) The older man has anal intercourse with the boy. The Kaluli cite the boy's peach-fuzz beard, which appears thereafter, as evidence that semen promotes growth. Young Kaluli men also have homosexual intercourse at hunting lodges, where they spend an extended period learning the lore of the forest and the hunt from older bachelors.

Homosexual activities were absent, rare, or secret in only 37 percent of seventy-six societies for which data were available (Ford and Beach 1951). In the others, various forms of homosexuality were considered normal and acceptable. Sometimes sexual relations between people of the same sex involved transvestism on the part of one of the partners. However, this was not true of homosexuality among the Sudanese Azande, who valued the warrior role (Evans-Pritchard 1970). Prospective warriors—boys aged twelve to twenty—left their families and shared quarters with adult fighting men, who paid bridewealth for, and had sex with, them. During this apprenticeship, the boys performed the domestic duties of women. Upon reaching warrior status, young men took their own boy brides. Later, retiring from the warrior role, Azande men married women. Flexible in their sexual expression, Azande men had no difficulty shifting to heterosexual coitus.

There appears to be greater cross-cultural acceptance of homosexuality than of bestiality or masturbation. Most societies in the Ford and Beach (1951) study discouraged masturbation, and only five allowed human-animal sex. However, these figures measure only the social approval of sexual practices, not their actual frequency. As in our own society, socially disapproved sex acts are more widespread than people admit.

We see nevertheless that flexibility in human sexual expression is an aspect of our primate heritage. Both masturbation and homosexual behavior exist among chimpanzees and other primates (White 1989). Primate sexual potential is molded both by the environment and by reproductive necessity. Heterosexuality is practiced in all human societies—which, after all, must reproduce themselves—but alternatives are also widespread (Davis and Whitten 1987). The sexual component of personality—just how humans express their "natural" sexual urges—is a matter that culture and environment determine and limit.

straightforward and courageous, and are courteous to whites, but indifferent. . . . The Sakalava are by far the bravest of the . . . tribes, and are also fairly intelligent. (1927, pp. 296–297)

If some anthropologists find it difficult to maintain scholarly objectivity during an ethnographic survey, it is much more difficult to provide a balanced description of an enemy nation. This reveals major flaws—impressionism and ethnocentrism—in national character studies, which are rarely done today.

CROSS-CULTURAL STUDIES

In the late 1930s, in a series of seminars at Columbia University, the psychoanalyst Abram Kardiner (1939) developed the idea of **basic personality structure** (fundamental shared personality traits acquired by adapting to a culture). Several anthropologists gave accounts of societies they had studied, which Kardiner interpreted psychoanalytically. Kardiner's theoretical framework is more useful than those of other early culture and personality researchers. He believed that a basic personality structure typifies people in any society. Basic personality exists in the context of cultural institutions—patterned ways of doing things in that society.

Cultural institutions fall into two categories: primary and secondary. *Primary institutions* include kinship, child care, sexuality, and subsistence. In adapting to primary institutions, the individual develops his or her personality. Because the primary patterns are similar throughout the society, many personality traits are shared. These shared traits make up the society's basic personality structure.

Primary institutions, such as kinship, child care, and subsistence, are often combined, as in this scene in rural Eritrea. Because primary patterns are similar throughout the society, many personality traits are also shared. According to Kardiner, these shared traits make up that society's basic personality structure.

Secondary institutions arise as individuals deal with the primary ones. Images of the gods, for example, may be modeled on a primary institution—children's relationship to their parents. Secondary institutions encompass religion, rituals, and folk tales.

Kardiner's framework also linked personality changes to changes in basic institutions. In this view, an alteration in a primary institution, such as subsistence, changes basic personality structure and secondary institutions. Kardiner compared the Tanala and Betsileo of Madagascar—closely related cultures that differed in types of economy. The Tanala were horticulturalists; the Betsileo, intensive cultivators of irrigated rice. Kardiner argued that certain

Betsileo secondary institutions, such as an emphasis on magic and spirit possession, came from anxieties that the demands of irrigated agriculture produced in their basic personality structure. Kardiner also recognized that the diversity of personality types in a culture increases with that culture's social and political complexity. He identified some of the anxieties associated with social stratification, private property, warfare, and state organization.

Since the 1950s, culture and personality studies have tended to follow a comparative strategy like Kardiner's, using data from several societies rather than one or two. There have been noteworthy attempts to improve data quality, to permit accurate cross-cultural generalization about personality formation. For example, one project (Whiting, ed. 1963) dispatched six teams for a coordinated investigation of child rearing in northern India, Mexico, Okinawa, the Philippines, New England, and East Africa. The teams used a common field guide and research techniques. Focusing on 50 to 100 families in each culture, the teams studied interactions between mothers and young children. They interviewed and observed behavior, paying attention to nurturing, self-reliance, responsibility, achievement orientation, dominance, obedience, aggression, and sociability. The teams rated the societies on the basis of psychological tones of child rearing. For example, mothers in some societies were rated more affectionate than were those in others. Child-rearing patterns were then linked to certain culture traits, such as the presence or absence of warfare.

Also in the 1960s, Walter Goldschmidt (1965) organized a project to investigate cultural, psychological, and ecological variation among four groups in East Africa: the Hehe, Kamba, Pokot, and Sebei. All four had mixed economies. In each group, some communities cultivated, others herded, and some did both. Project researcher Robert Edgerton (1965) gathered psychological information in eight communities, one pastoral and one agricultural for each group. He drew a sample of at least thirty adults of each gender for each community and interviewed a total of 505 people.

To assess personality differences between the groups, Edgerton (1965) analyzed responses to questions, inkblot plates, and color slides. What kinds of conclusions did he reach? He found the Kamba to have male dominance, fear of poverty, and restrained emotions. The Hehe were aggressive, formal, mistrusting, and secretive. Different personality traits marked the Pokot and the Sebei.

Some similarities correlated with language. The Pokot and Sebei spoke languages of the Kalenjin group, and the Hehe and Kamba spoke Bantu languages. The Kalenjin speakers valued both sons and daughters; the Bantu speakers, just sons. The Bantus worried about sorcery and witchcraft and valued land over cattle. The Bantu groups respected wealthy people; the Kalenjins, prophets.

Economic contrasts also were found to influence personality. The cultivators consulted sorcerers and made group decisions, whereas the pastoralists were more individualistic. The farmers valued hard work; the herders didn't. The cultivators were more hostile and suspicious, indirect, abstract, and anxious and less able to control their emotions and impulses. The herders, by contrast, were more direct, open, and realistic.

Unlike earlier, more impressionistic culture and personality studies, this one used statistical data, collected in accordance with objective standards. This made it possible to evaluate the respective contributions of culture, language, history, and economy to personality formation. If personality traits correlate with economic systems in East Africa, do similar associations exist on a worldwide scale? Several anthropologists have answered yes.

WORLDVIEW

Peasants and Limited Good

George Foster (1965), for example, found that a distinctive cognitive orientation, ideology, or **worldview** characterizes "classic" peasant economies—nonindustrial farming communities within nation-states. (A *worldview* is a culture's characteristic way of perceiving, interpreting, and explaining the world.) Foster cited several ethnographic cases to illustrate this peasant worldview, which he called the **image of limited good.** In this ideology everything is perceived as finite: land, wealth, health, love, friendship, honor, respect, status, power, influence, safety, and security. Viewing everything as scarce, peasants believe that individuals can excel only by taking more than their fair share from a common pool, therefore depriving others.

If someone does manage to increase his or her wealth, there are several possible responses. Peasants accept differential wealth that comes from outside the village and clearly hasn't required dipping into the finite local pool. Thus peasants may prosper from wage work outside or favors from external patrons. Profit also may come from sheer luck (winning a lottery, finding a treasure). In all these cases the community supply of good remains intact.

When the image of limited good operates, peasants try to hide differences in wealth. Their dress, homes, and diet remain ordinary. George Foster found the image of limited good to be most obvious among Latin American and European peasants, such as the couple shown here near Avila, Spain.

If, however, wealth comes from local activity, forces of public opinion act as leveling mechanisms. Prosperous people may be forced to sponsor ceremonies, which reduce differential wealth, leaving only prestige, which isn't dangerous. Prosperous peasants may also become targets of gossip, envy, ostracism, and physical violence. Given such community responses, peasants try to hide good fortune. Their dress, homes, and diet remain ordinary. Furthermore, people who have had bad luck and sink below the community norm are also distrusted, for they are thought to be envious of everyone else.

Foster found the image of limited good to be most obvious among Latin American and European peasants. African peasants were less individualistic; their competition and rivalry occurred between descent groups rather than between individuals or families. The image of limited good develops when peasant societies emphasize nuclear family organization but not when corporate descent groups are important. Foster also pointed out that the image of limited good is a response to the subordinate position of peasants within a larger society. Often, good really is limited by land-ownership patterns, poor health care, and inadequate government services. Foster suggested—and there is considerable evidence to support him—that when access to wealth, power, and influence is more open, the image of limited good declines.

The (Sub)Culture of Poverty

Anthropologist Oscar Lewis (1959) described another constellation of values, the "subculture of poverty," which he often shortened to "culture of poverty." Economically, the **culture of poverty** is marked by low incomes, unemployment, unskilled occupations, little saving, and frequent pawning. Its social attributes include crowded living quarters, lack of privacy, alcoholism, violence, early sex, informal and unstable marriages, and mother-centered households. Psychologically, Lewis argued, the culture of poverty has a distinctive set of values and feelings. These include marginality, insecurity, fatalism, desperation, aggression, gregariousness, sensuality, adventurousness, spontaneity, impulsiveness, absence of planning, and distrust of government.

Lewis argued that these values and customs marginalize people, limiting their chances for success and social mobility. He was explicit about the conditions that give rise to the culture of poverty: a cash economy, unemployment, low wages, and a certain set of values in the dominant class—stressing wealth and property accumulation and regarding poverty as resulting from personal inferiority. According to Lewis, poverty doesn't always produce the culture of poverty. For example, when poor people become class-conscious or active in labor unions,

Oscar Lewis argued that the culture of poverty developed when the poor lacked a sense of social solidarity. Its values, he contended, limited their chances for success and social mobility. Among the conditions leading to the culture of poverty were a cash economy, unemployment, and low wages. Shown here, impoverished Filipinos forage in a garbage dump in Manila.

they may escape the culture of poverty—although they may still be poor.

Before he began to study the culture of poverty in Mexico City and San Juan, Puerto Rico, Lewis had done field work in India, where he found poverty but no subculture of poverty. Although Hindu villages were poorer than the slums of Mexico City and San Juan, the caste system gave people a sense of social identity and solidarity that was missing in Latin America. Lewis argued that the culture of poverty developed in the absence of such a feeling of belonging and in the context of bilateral kinship systems. In areas with corporate descent groups, such as India and Africa, the subculture would not develop, even though poverty might be great. Lewis saw something positive in descent-group organization—the feeling that a corporate body continues to exist while individuals come and go. This feeling offers a sense of past and future even to the desperately poor.

Although the culture of poverty first emerged in Europe, with capitalism, industrialization, and urban migration, Lewis found the best contemporary examples in Latin America. It was less marked in the United States, where the welfare system had eliminated many of its causes. Critics have suggested that the poor really don't have a separate subculture (Valentine 1968; Stack 1975); they are merely unable to live up to dominant norms because of their economic disadvantages. Others have suggested that the poor hold two sets of values simultaneously, one shared with the larger society and the other a response to poverty (Parker and Kleiner 1970). The second value set helps the poor adjust psychologically and thus preserves their mental health. Lewis and his critics agreed that if poverty were totally eradicated, the culture of poverty, with its values and feelings of marginality, would disappear as well.

The Protestant Ethic and Capitalism

Consider now the emergence of a worldview and personality structure—the **Protestant ethic**—valuing hard work, thrift, wealth, and capital accumulation. In *The Protestant Ethic and the Spirit of Capitalism* (1920/1958), sociologist Max Weber argued that capitalism demanded an entrepreneurial personality type, which he linked to the values preached by early Protestant leaders. Weber observed that European Protestants tended to be more successful financially than Catholics were, and he attributed this contrast to values stressed by their religion. Weber characterized Catholics as more concerned with immediate happiness and security, Protestants as more ascetic and future-oriented.

Capitalism required that the attitudes of Catholic peasants be replaced by values more compatible with an industrial economy fueled by capital accumulation. Protestantism offered a worldview that valued profit seeking and work. Early Protestants believed that success on earth is a sign of divine favor. According to some Protestant credos, individuals can gain favor through good works. Other sects stressed predestination, the doctrine that only a few mortals are selected for eternal life and that people cannot change their fates. However, material success, achieved through work, can signal that an individual is one of the elect. Here, hard work was valued because success helped convince individuals of their salvation.

The English Puritan variety of Protestantism stressed physical and mental labor; it discouraged leisure and the enjoyment of life. Waste of time was the deadliest sin because work was a duty demanded by God. The Puritans valued the simplicity of the middle-class home and condemned ostentation as worldly enjoyment. Profits, the fruits of successful labor, could be given to the church or reinvested. However, they could not be hoarded, because excess wealth might lead to temptation. People could increase their profit-making activity as long as they kept in mind the common good and didn't engage in harmful, illegal, greedy, or dishonest activity.

According to Weber, the change in worldview promoted by the Protestant Reformation fueled the growth of modern industrial capitalism. However, residues of the traditional Catholic peasant mentality slowed the pace of change. Early Protestants who produced more than they needed for subsistence—who tried to make a profit—stirred up the mistrust, hatred, and moral indignation of others. Successful innovators were people of strong character who could persevere despite resistance and command the confidence of customers and workers.

Weber also argued that rational business organization entailed removing production from the household, its setting in peasant societies. Protestant doctrines made such a split possible by emphasizing individualism: individuals rather than families would be saved or not. The family was a secondary matter for Weber's Protestants.

Controversy surrounds Weber's ideas, mainly because he paid insufficient attention to economic forces, historical events, and political structures—all of which are known causes of capitalism's emergence and spread (see the chapter "The World System, Industrialism, and Stratification"). Today, people of many religions and worldviews are successful capitalists. Furthermore, the old Protestant emphasis on honesty and hard work often has little relationship to modern economic maneuvers. Still, there is no denying that the individualistic focus of Protestantism was compatible with the severance of ties to land and extended family that the Industrial Revolution demanded. Might a similar worldview exist in nonindustrial areas, specifically among foragers, as an example of convergent evolution? In the case that follows, I argue that it does.

Personality and Cognition among Fishermen

One cross-cultural study (Barry, Bacon, and Child 1959) found that foragers, like Weber's Protestant capitalists, tended to emphasize achievement, competition, self-reliance, and independence. Arembepe, a fishing community in Brazil (Kottak 1992), illustrates this orientation toward achievement among foragers. (Remember that foraging encompasses fishing as well as hunting and gathering.)

When I began to study Arembepe in the mid-1960s, the basis of the village economy was Atlantic Ocean fishing. However, Arembepe was not an isolated foraging community; it was tied to the Brazilian nation economically, politically, and socially. Arembepeiros sold their fish to marketers from outside, often to the detriment of their own subsistence needs.

Although Arembepeiros lacked a peasantlike, land-based economy, their behavior and ideology and their economic and political ties to the nation-state were similar to those of peasants. Since Arembepeiros were like peasants in some important ways, one might expect them to have some of the features of the image of limited good, and they did. However, since most men fished—a form of foraging—they might also be expected to be independent and achievement-oriented.

Arembepe's main social unit was the household, generally inhabited by a nuclear family. Local social organization was individualistic and atomistic, though not to the extent that Foster (1965) leads us to expect in a peasant community. Arembepe was a fairly homogeneous community socially and economically. Everyone belonged to the national lower class, with only minor differences in wealth and status. Ambitious young men had a relatively equal chance to climb the local ladder of achievement.

Success came through fishing. Sailboats fished with crews of four or five men, one of whom was the captain, who usually was also the owner of the boat. Arembepe's fishermen formed four groups: (1) successful young captains, (2) older captains, who had once belonged to the first group, (3) the least successful captains, who fished irregularly, primarily because of alcoholism, and (4) ordinary fishermen.

These groups had different opinions about what determines success in fishing. Ordinary fishermen said that captains needed good *eyesight* to see distant landmarks that marked profitable fishing spots. They mentioned their own poor eyesight as a reason why they weren't captains. They also said that *luck* helped some people catch more fish than others did. Older, formerly successful captains blamed their declining catches on their failing eyesight, which prevented them from fishing as effectively as in the past. The third group of captains attributed differential success only to luck, refusing to admit that some captains were better than others.

The most successful captains (the first group) explained success differently, linking it to personality traits recalling Weber's Protestant ethic. They cited their hard and constant work and sobriety, rarely mentioning luck or eyesight. My analysis of success in fishing supports this explanation. The traits and behavior of successful captains differed from those of less successful fishermen. Because they were in their twenties and thirties, they had good health, which permitted them to fish regularly. They attracted hard-working crew members because they were dependable and could remain at sea longer. Like Weber's Protestant entrepreneurs, successful captains took calculated risks. They sometimes traveled to farther fishing zones during the season of storms and rough seas. They experimented more, seeking out new fishing areas. Often their risks paid off in the form of larger catches.

Although they weren't teetotalers, they drank

only on festive occasions, and they preferred beer to the rum that ordinary fishermen and less successful captains drank. Young captains missed no fishing because of drunkenness. They commanded better crew allegiance and attracted more energetic crew members. They were respected within the community and became officers of the fishermen's society. Other villagers were aware of their success and eager to join their crews. Like Protestant entrepreneurs, successful captains reinvested their profits to produce additional wealth. They bought livestock, planted coconut trees, and invested in new technology to increase fishing productivity.

Unlike peasants, Arembepeiros did not depend on the land, an easily limitable resource. Their subsistence came from the sea, a more open frontier where it's harder to assign and maintain property rights. Hard work at sea does pay off. Furthermore, the high rate of inflation that plagued Brazil also promoted reinvestment. With continual devaluation, hoarding would have been disastrous.

Arembepeiros didn't restrict their kin ties as severely as Weber's Protestant capitalists did. Because fishing required hard work and vigor, even the most successful fishermen knew that their productivity would eventually decline. They planned for their declining years by building up sources of income on the land. However, because there was no social security system, successful people knew they might eventually depend on their kin for help. Anticipating this, good fishermen shared some of their wealth with relatives.

Arembepeiros didn't think of good as limited. No doubt this reflected the combination of an open local economy and ties to the external world. However, social mechanisms similar to those Foster (1965) described for peasant societies did operate to ensure that individuals acted appropriately. Consider the case of Laurentino, Arembepe-born son of an immigrant. Like his father, Laurentino never fished but ran a store. His store prospered, he bought four boats, and he inherited his father's store. Arembepeiros attributed Laurentino's business success to a pact they believed he had made with the devil.

Between 1962 and 1965 I observed the social gap between Laurentino and other Arembepeiros widen steadily. Villagers warned me about devil worship in his house and about a demon he had caged in his store. They distrusted Laurentino because unlike other local storekeepers, he refused to give credit.

Successful sea fishing requires hard work, discipline, vigor, and risk-taking—traits also associated with Max Weber's "Protestant ethic." Shown here is a lobster fisherman from New Brunswick, Canada.

Laurentino cultivated social distance, perhaps in an effort to free himself from the community obligations that all other Arembepeiros had to face. He found it amusing that other villagers thought of him as a witch or devil worshiper. Flouting Catholic doctrine and local practice, he bought birth control pills for his wife and demanded that she take them. When she did get pregnant, he let it be known that his child wouldn't be baptized.

Laurentino eventually suffered because of his unconventional behavior. Villagers started avoiding his stores. More important, he could no longer find men to serve as captains of his boats. Eventually, all four boats rotted and he chopped them up for firewood. Not only did he become the most isolated man in Arembepe, his efforts to increase his wealth were blocked by public opinion. The lesson is that one can prosper in Arembepe only within limits set by community opinion.

Arembepe illustrates that many different cognitive orientations and ideological themes can coexist in a fairly homogeneous community. The explanations for success that people offer, like other aspects of their worldview, reflect their reference groups.

Yet certain ideologies, for example, that of sharing with less fortunate villagers, can override differences in outlook among subgroups. This analysis of one village suggests that despite the value of cross-cultural studies of relationships between personality and culture, we also need to study particular cases intensively in order to understand the subtle influences of culture on cognition and personality. Internal variation within a community or society may turn out to be as interesting as variation between cultures.

SUMMARY

Anthropologists are interested in public and collective behavior and in how individuals, think, feel, and act. The individual and culture are linked in a process by which individuals internalize, express, and influence the meanings of public messages. Anthropology and psychology intersect in psychological anthropology. With its focus on the individual, psychological anthropology exists because a complete account of cultural processes requires both perspectives—private and public.

One area of psychological anthropology is cognitive anthropology—the ethnographic and cross-cultural study of cognition (the organization of knowledge, perceptions, and meaning). A culture is both a network of shared understandings and a changing product involving negotiation by its individual members.

According to schema theory, the mind builds schemata to filter new experience and reconstruct past experience. Schemata construct simplified versions of experience; we remember the typical (modal) rather than the unusual. Cognition and emotions develop together as part of people's schemata. As individuals grow, their schemata harden. In a given culture, if people experience the same typical pattern, their schemata retain it. However, individual feelings and experiences give rise to differences in schemata among people who grow up in the same culture. Like the idea of levels of culture, schema theory recognizes a continuum of shared experience and learning.

Culture and personality studies examine the personality types that characterize different cultures. Early students of culture and personality, such as Margaret Mead, were criticized for relying too heavily on personal impressions in gathering field data. Assuming that individuals in a culture would share personality traits, certain anthropologists tried to define basic personality structures and national character. National character studies, which were popular during World War II, were criticized on several grounds, including their impressionistic basis and overemphasis on childhood determinism.

Kardiner proposed that a culture's basic personality structure results from individual adaptation to primary institutions, including family organization and type of economy. The basic personality structure then influences secondary institutions, including religion and ideology. More recent, less impressionistic culture and personality generalizations have emerged from problem-oriented field work that uses more objective techniques to get data on personality formation.

Several studies have suggested or documented correlations between economic systems and personality type or worldview. Foster found an "image of limited good" to be part of the cognitive orientation of "classic" peasant societies. Lewis identified a gregarious, spontaneous, fatalistic, marginalizing subculture of poverty associated with real poverty, capitalism, and bilateral kinship. Weber attributed the emergence of industrial capitalism to asceticism, emphasis on hard and constant work, and profit seeking, all of which he associated with Protestantism.

The case of Arembepe, a Brazilian fishing community, shows that cognition varies with a person's reference group even in a fairly homogeneous village. Nevertheless, all Arembepeiros have a general ideology of sharing. Both ethnographic and comparative studies promise to increase our understanding of psychological and cognitive variation between cultures and social groups.

GLOSSARY

basic personality structure: According to Abram Kardiner, personality traits shared by members of a society; acquired in adapting to a culture's primary institutions.

cognitive anthropology: Area of psychological anthropology; the ethnographic and cross-cultural study of cognition, including learning, ways of knowing, and the organization of knowledge, perceptions, and meaning.

configurationalism: View associated with Ruth Benedict. Cultures are integrated wholes, each uniquely different from all others.

connectionism: Linked to schema theory; the idea that things that consistently occur together in an individual's experience become strongly associated in that person's mind.

culture of poverty: Coined by Oscar Lewis; has economic, social, and psychological characteristics—gregariousness, spontaneity, fatalism, marginality; associated with real poverty, capitalism, and bilateral kinship.

image of limited good: Peasant worldview in which all desired things are considered finite; belief that when one person takes too much, everyone else is deprived.

national character: Personality traits shared by the inhabitants of a nation.

personality: An individual's characteristic ways of think-ing and acting and the underlying structure that produces this consistency.

Protestant ethic: Worldview associated with early ascetic Protestantism; values hard and constant work as a sign of salvation; concept developed by Max Weber.

psychological anthropology: Ethnographic and cross-cultural study of differences and similarities in human psychology.

schema theory: Theory that the mind builds schemata (the plural of schema) to filter new experience and recon-struct past experience, shaping memories to conform to current expectations.

worldview: A culture's characteristic way of perceiving, interpreting, and explaining the world.

STUDY QUESTIONS

1. What is psychological anthropology, and why is it necessary?
2. What is cognitive anthropology, and what is its value?
3. What is schema theory, and how does it deal with similarities and differences within cultures?
4. How does schema theory deal with cultural change?
5. What does Derek Freeman's criticism of Margaret Mead teach us about ethnography and psychological anthropology?
6. What were the contributions and shortcomings of the studies of culture and personality by Mead, Benedict, and Kardiner?
7. What were the aims and limitations of national char-acter studies?
8. What kinds of correlations between ecology-economy and personality have been discovered?
9. What is Foster's concept of the image of limited good, and how does it help us understand peasant behavior?
10. What is the culture of poverty, and under what conditions does it emerge and persist?
11. How did Weber relate the Protestant ethic to the development of capitalism?
12. Why and how is the case analysis of Arembepe fish-ermen relevant to the discussion (in the section on Mead and Freeman) of the need to pay attention to variation in a culture?

SUGGESTED ADDITIONAL READING

BARNOUW, V.
  1985 *Culture and Personality*, 4th ed. Homewood, IL: Dorsey Press. One of the most readable and complete introductions to the field.
BOCK, P. K.
  1980 *Continuities in Psychological Anthropology*. San Francisco: W. H. Freeman. Overview of psy-chological anthropology.
BOURGUIGNON, E.
  1979 *Psychological Anthropology: An Introduction to Human Nature and Cultural Differences*. New York: Holt, Rinehart & Winston. Textbook with a focus on child development and social-ization.

BRADY, I., ED.
  1983 Special Section: Speaking in the Name of the Real: Freeman and Mead on Samoa. *American Anthropologist* 85: 908–947. Several anthropol-ogists evaluate Freeman's charges, Mead's work, and the implications of the controversy for psychological anthropology and ethnog-raphy.
DAVIS, D. L., AND R. G. WHITTEN
  1987 The Cross-Cultural Study of Human Sexual-ity. *Annual Review of Anthropology* 16: 69–98. Review of recent research.

FREEMAN, D.

1983 *Margaret Mead and Samoa: The Making and Un-making of an Anthropological Myth.* Cambridge, MA: Harvard University Press. Controversial work criticizing the renowned anthropologist.

FREILICH, M., D. RAYBECK, AND J. SAVISHINSKY

1991 *Deviance: Anthropological Perspectives.* Westport, CT: Bergin and Garvey. Cross-cultural case studies shed light on the cultural construction of what is "normal" and what isn't.

HOLLAND, D., AND N. QUINN, EDS.

1987 *Cultural Models in Language and Thought.* Cambridge: Cambridge University Press. Cognition through linguistic examples.

JODELET, D.

1991 *Madness and Social Representations: Living with the Mad in One French Community.* Translated from the French by Gerard Duveen. Berkeley: University of California Press. Ethnographic study of a French community where the mentally ill have played a prominent role for seventy years; a reconsideration of madness in society.

LEVINE, R. A.

1982 *Culture, Behavior, and Personality: An Introduction to the Comparative Study of Psychosocial Adaptation,* 2nd ed. Chicago: Aldine. Original, sophisticated text of psychological anthropology by an anthropologist-psychoanalyst.

MEAD, M.

1961 (orig. 1928). *Coming of Age in Samoa.* New York: New American Library. Popular report of Mead's first field work, a study of female adolescents in a Polynesian society.

SCHWEDER, R. A., AND R. A. LEVINE, EDS.

1984 *Culture Theory: Essays on Mind, Self, and Emotion.* Cambridge: Cambridge University Press. Papers on social and emotional development during childhood.

SPINDLER, G. D., ED.

1978 *The Making of Psychological Anthropology.* Berkeley: University of California Press. Various anthropologists describe their personal experiences in contributing to culture and personality research.

LANGUAGE

Anthropologists study language in its social and cultural context, and in linguistic anthropology, we again encounter anthropology's characteristic interest in comparison, variation, and change. Some linguistic anthropologists reconstruct ancient languages by comparing their contemporary descendants and in so doing make discoveries about history. Others make inferences about universal features of language, linking them to uniformities in the human brain. Still others study linguistic differences to discover varied worldviews and patterns of thought in a multitude of cultures. Sociolinguists examine dialects and styles in a single language to show how speech reflects social differences (Fasold 1990; Labov 1972a, b). Linguistic anthropologists also explore the role of language in colonization, capitalist expansion, state formation, class relations, and political and economic dependence (Geis 1987).

THE STRUCTURE OF LANGUAGE

Until the late 1950s linguists thought that the study of a language should proceed through a sequence of stages of analysis. The first stage was **phonology,** the study of sounds used in speech. Phonological analysis would determine which speech sounds (**phones**) were present and significant in that language. Speech sounds can be recorded using the International Phonetic Alphabet, a series of symbols devised to describe dozens of sounds that occur in different languages. The next stage was **morphology,** the study of the forms in which sounds combine to form **morphemes**—words and their meaningful constituents. Thus, the word *cats* would be analyzed as containing two morphemes—*cat,* the name for a kind of animal, and *-s,* a morpheme indicating plurality. The language's **lexicon** was a dictionary containing all its morphemes and their meanings. The next step was to study **syntax,** the arrangement and order of words in phrases and sentences. This stage-by-stage analysis sometimes created the erroneous impression that phonology, morphology, lexicon, and syntax were unconnected. All this was revolutionized by an approach known as *transformational-generative grammar,* to which we shall return after a brief consideration of phonology.

Phonemes and Phones

No language includes all the sounds designated by the symbols in the International Phonetic Alphabet. Nor is the number of **phonemes**—significant sound contrasts in a given language—infinite. Phonemes lack meaning in themselves, but they are the smallest sound *contrasts* that distinguish meaning. We discover them by comparing **minimal pairs,** words that resemble each other in all but one sound. An example is the minimal pair *pit/bit*. These two words are distinguished by a single sound contrast between /p/ and /b/ (we enclose phonemes in slashes). Thus /p/ and /b/ are phonemes in English. Another example is the different vowel sound of *bit* and *beat* (Figure 21.1). This contrast serves to distinguish these two words and the two phonemes /I/ and /i/ in English.

Standard (American) English (SE), the "region-free" dialect of TV network newscasters, has about

Figure 21.1 *Vowel phonemes in Standard American English shown according to height of tongue and tongue position at front, center, or back of mouth. Phonetic symbols are identified by English words that include them; note that most are minimal pairs. (Adaptation of excerpt and Figure 2-1 from* Aspects of Language, *Third Edition, by Dwight Bolinger and Donald Sears, copyright © 1981 by Harcourt Brace Jovanovich, Inc., reprinted by permission of the publisher.)*

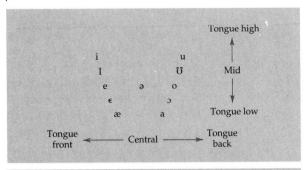

high front (spread)	[i]	as in *beat*
lower high front (spread)	[I]	as in *bit*
mid front (spread)	[e]	as in *bait*
lower mid front (spread)	[ɛ]	as in *bet*
low front	[æ]	as in *bat*
central	[ə]	as in *butt*
low back	[a]	as in *pot*
lower mid back (rounded)	[ɔ]	as in *bought*
mid back (rounded)	[o]	as in *boat*
lower high back (rounded)	[ʊ]	as in *put*
high back (rounded)	[u]	as in *boot*

thirty-five phonemes—at least eleven vowels and twenty-four consonants. The number of phonemes varies from language to language—from fifteen to sixty, averaging between thirty and forty. The number of phonemes also varies between dialects of a given language. In American English, for example, vowel phonemes vary noticeably from dialect to dialect. Readers should pronounce the words in Figure 21.1, paying attention to (or asking someone else) whether they distinguish each of the vowel sounds. Most Americans don't pronounce them all.

Phonetics is the study of speech sounds in general, what people actually say in various languages. **Phonemics** studies the significant sound contrasts (phonemes) of a *particular* language. In English, /b/ and /v/ are phonemes, occurring in minimal pairs such as *bat* and *vat*. In Spanish, however, the contrast between [b] and [v] doesn't distinguish meaning, and they are therefore not phonemes (we enclose phones that are not phonemic in brackets). Spanish speakers normally use the [b] sound to pronounce words spelled with either *b* or *v*.

In any language a given phoneme extends over a phonetic range. In English the phoneme /p/ ignores the phonetic contrast between the [pʰ] in *pin* and the [p] in *spin*. Most English speakers don't even notice that there is a phonetic difference. [pʰ] is aspirated, so that a puff of air follows the [p]. The [p] in *spin* is not. (To see the difference, light a match and watch the flame as you pronounce the two words.) However, the contrast between [pʰ] and [p] is phonemic in some languages. That is, there are words whose meaning is distinguished only by the contrast between an aspirated and an unaspirated [p].

Native speakers vary in their pronunciation of certain phonemes. This variation is important in the evolution of language. With no shifts in pronunciation, there can be no linguistic change. The section on sociolinguistics below considers phonetic variation and its relationship to social divisions and the evolution of language.

TRANSFORMATIONAL-GENERATIVE GRAMMAR

Noam Chomsky's influential book *Syntactic Structures* (1957) advocated a new method of linguistic analysis—**transformational-generative grammar.**

In Chomsky's view, a language is more than the surface phenomena just discussed (sounds, words, and word order). Beneath the surface features discovered through stage-by-stage analysis of particular languages, all languages share a limited set of organizing principles.

Chomsky views language as a uniquely human possession, qualitatively different from the communication systems of other animals, including those of nonhuman primates. Every normal child who grows up in a society develops language easily and automatically. Chomsky thinks that this occurs because the human brain contains a genetically transmitted blueprint, or basic linguistic plan, for building language. He calls this plan a **universal grammar.** When children learn a language, they don't start from scratch, because they already have the outline. As they learn their native language, children experiment with different parts of the blueprint. In so doing, they discover that their language uses some sections but not others. They gradually reject principles used in other languages and accept only the ones in their own.

The fact that children everywhere begin to speak at about the same age buttresses Chomsky's theory. Furthermore, people master features of language at similar rates. There are universals in language acquisition, such as improper generalizations (*foot, foots; hit, hitted*), which are eventually corrected. Children experiment with linguistic rules, accepting and refining some while rejecting others.

As we learn to speak, we master a specific **grammar,** a *particular* set of rules—the ones our language has taken from the universal set. These rules let us convert what we want to say into what we do say. People who hear us and speak our language understand our meaning. Our knowledge of the rules enables us to use language creatively, to *generate* an infinite number of sentences according to a finite number of rules. We can produce sentences that no one has ever uttered before, and we can understand other people's original statements.

Chomsky distinguishes between a native speaker's linguistic **competence** (what the speaker must—and does—know about his or her language in order to speak and understand) and **performance** (what the person actually says in social situations). Competence develops during childhood and becomes an unconscious structure. The linguist's job is to discover this structure by looking at deep struc-

According to Noam Chomsky the human brain contains a genetically transmitted blueprint, or basic linguistic plan, for building language. As they learn their native language, children experiment with different parts of that blueprint. They gradually reject principles used in other languages and accept only the ones in their own—Japanese in this case.

tures, surface structures, and the transformational rules that link them.

When a speaker wishes to express a thought, a sentence is formed at what Chomsky calls the level of **deep structure** (the mental level) in the speaker's mind. That sentence rises to **surface structure** (actual speech)—expressed in sound—and passes from speaker to hearer. When a *sentence* (roughly defined as a complete thought) is spoken, the hearer figures out its meaning by translating it back into his or her own deep structure (Figure 21.2).

On the surface—the object of traditional linguistics—languages seem more different than they really are. Similarities are more evident at the level of deep structure. Chomsky proposed that by studying the deep structures of many languages, linguists might eventually discover the grammatical building blocks on which all languages are based.

LANGUAGE, THOUGHT, AND CULTURE

According to Chomsky, the human brain contains a limited set of rules for organizing language. The fact that people can learn foreign languages and that words and ideas can be translated from one language into another tends to support Chomsky's position that all humans have similar linguistic abilities and thought processes.

The Sapir-Whorf Hypothesis

Other linguists and anthropologists take a different approach to the relationship between language and thought. Rather than seeking universal linguistic structures as clues to universal mental processes, they believe that different languages produce different ways of thinking. This position is sometimes

Figure 21.2 *How a message passes from speaker to hearer according to Chomsky's model. The speaker translates meaning (the semantic component) into sound (the phonological component) through grammar (deep structure, a transformation rule, and a surface-structure sentence). The hearer decodes in reverse order to find meaning.*

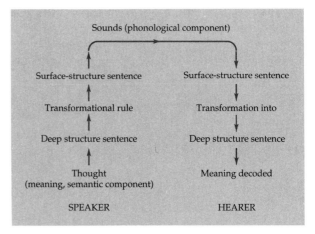

known as the **Sapir-Whorf hypothesis** after Edward Sapir (1931) and Benjamin Lee Whorf (1956), its prominent early advocates. They argued that languages lead their speakers to think about things in particular ways. For example, the third-person singular pronouns of English (*he, she; him, her; his, hers*) distinguish gender, whereas those of the Palaung, a small tribe in Burma, do not (Burling 1970). Gender exists in English, although a fully developed noun-gender and adjective-agreement system, as in French and other Romance languages (*la belle fille, le beau fils*), does not. The Sapir-Whorf hypothesis therefore might suggest that English speakers can't help paying more attention to differences between males and females than do the Palaung and less than do French or Spanish speakers.

English divides time into past, present, and future. Hopi, a language of the Pueblo region of the Native American Southwest, does not. However, Hopi distinguishes between events that exist or have existed (what we use past and present to discuss) and those which don't or don't yet (our future events, along with imaginary and hypothetical events). Whorf argued that this difference gives English and Hopi speakers different perceptions of time and reality. Language thus causes differences in thought.

Focal Vocabulary

A lexicon (or vocabulary) is a language's dictionary, its set of names for things, events, and ideas. Lexicon influences perception. Thus, Eskimos have several distinct words for different types of snow that in English are all called *snow*. Most English speakers never notice the differences between these types of snow and might have trouble seeing them even if someone pointed them out. Eskimos recognize and think about differences in snow that English speakers don't see because our language provides us with just one word.

Similarly, the Nuer of the Sudan have an elaborate vocabulary to describe cattle. Eskimos have several words for snow and Nuer have dozens for cattle because of their particular histories, economies, and environments (Eastman 1975; Brown 1958). When the need arises, English speakers can also elaborate their snow and cattle vocabularies. For example, skiers name varieties of snow with words that are missing from the lexicons of Florida retirees. Simi-

A lexicon, or vocabulary, is a language's dictionary, its set of names for things, events, and ideas. Eskimos have several distinct words for different types of snow that in English are all called "snow." Eskimos recognize and think about differences in snow that English speakers don't see because our language provides us with just one word.

larly, the cattle vocabulary of Texas ranchers is much more extensive than that of a salesperson in a New York City department store. Such specialized sets of terms and distinctions that are particularly important to certain groups (those with particular *foci* of experience or activity) are known as **focal vocabulary.**

Vocabulary and lexical distinctions belong to the area of language that changes most readily. New words and distinctions, when needed, appear and spread. For example, who would have "faxed" anything a decade ago? Often-used words tend to be or become simple (*monolexemes*) rather than compound expressions (*rain* versus *tropical storm*) (Brown 1958).

Names for items get simpler as they become common and important. A television has become a *TV*, an automobile a *car*, and a videocassette recorder a *VCR*.

Language, culture, and thought are interrelated. However, it would be more accurate to say that changes in culture produce changes in language and thought than the reverse. Consider differences between female and male Americans in regard to the color terms they use (Lakoff 1975). Distinctions implied by such terms as *salmon, rust, peach, beige, teal, mauve, cranberry,* and *dusky orange* aren't in the vocabularies of most American men. However, many of them weren't even in American women's lexicons fifty years ago. These changes reflect changes in American economy, society, and culture. Color terms and distinctions have increased with the growth of the fashion and cosmetic industries. A similar contrast in Americans' lexicons shows up in football, basketball, and hockey vocabularies. Sports fans, more often males than females, use more terms in reference to and make more elaborate distinctions between the games they watch. Thus cultural contrasts and changes affect lexical distinctions (for instance, *peach* versus *salmon*) within semantic domains (for instance, color terminology). **Semantics** refers to a language's meaning system.

Meaning

Speakers of particular languages use sets of terms to organize, or categorize, their experiences and perceptions. Linguistic terms and contrasts encode (embody) differences in meaning that people perceive. **Ethnoscience,** or **ethnosemantics,** studies such classification systems in various languages. Well-studied ethnosemantic *domains* (sets of related things, perceptions, or concepts named in a language) include kinship terminology and color terminology. When we study such domains, we are examining how those people perceive and distinguish between kin relationships or colors. Other ethnosemantic domains include ethnomedicine—the terminology for causes, symptoms, and cures of disease (Frake 1961); ethnobotany—native classification of plant life (Conklin 1954; Berlin, Breedlove, and Raven 1974); and ethnoastronomy (Goodenough 1953).

The ways in which people divide up the world—the contrasts they perceive as meaningful or signifi-cant—reflect their experiences. Anthropologists have discovered that certain lexical domains and vocabulary items evolve in a determined order. For example, after studying color terminology in more than 100 languages, Berlin and Kay (1969/1992) discovered ten basic color terms: *white, black, red, yellow, blue, green, brown, pink, orange,* and *purple* (they evolved in more or less that order). The number of terms varied with cultural complexity. Representing one extreme were Papua–New Guinea cultivators and Australian hunters and gatherers, who used only two basic terms, which translate as *black* and *white* or *dark* or *light*. At the other end of the continuum were European and Asian languages with all the color terms. Color terminology was most developed in areas with a history of using dyes and artificial coloring.

SOCIOLINGUISTICS

No language is a homogeneous system in which everyone speaks just like everyone else. Linguistic *performance* (what people actually say) is the concern of sociolinguists. The field of **sociolinguistics** investigates relationships between social and linguistic variation, or language in its social context. How do different speakers use a given language? How do linguistic features correlate with social stratification, including class, ethnic, and gender differences (Tannen 1986, 1990)? How is language used to express, reinforce, or resist power (Geis 1987)?

Sociolinguists don't deny that people who speak the same language share deep structures and rules which permit mutually intelligible communication. However, sociolinguists focus on features that vary systematically with social position and situation. To study variation, sociolinguists must do field work in order to define, observe, and measure variable aspects of language. Different aspects of variable speech must be quantified. To show that linguistic features correlate with social, economic, and political differences, the social attributes of speakers must also be measured and related to speech (Fasold 1990; Labov 1972*a*).

Variation within a language at a given time is historical change in progress. According to the principle of **linguistic uniformitarianism,** the same forces that have produced large-scale linguistic changes over the centuries, working gradually, are still at

Ethnic and linguistic diversity characterizes many nations, especially in big cities, as is illustrated by this multilingual advertising on New York's Lower East Side.

In stratified societies, people constantly shift linguistic styles. Linguistic performance varies in formal and informal contexts. The Portuguese woman on the left uses an animated, informal style with her neighbor in Lisbon's Alfama.

work and can be observed in linguistic events taking place today (Labov 1972b). Linguistic change doesn't occur in a vacuum but in society. Only when new ways of speaking are associated with social factors can they be imitated, spread, and play a role in linguistic change.

Linguistic Diversity in Nation-States

As an illustration of the linguistic variation encountered in all nation-states, consider the contemporary United States. Ethnic diversity is revealed by the fact that millions of Americans learn first languages other than English. Spanish is the most common. Most of these people eventually become bilinguals, adding English as a second language. In many multilingual (including colonized) nations, people use two languages on different occasions—one in the home, for example, and the other on the job or in public.

Whether bilingual or not, we all vary our speech in different contexts; we engage in **style shifts.** In certain parts of Europe, people regularly switch dialects. This phenomenon, known as **diglossia,** applies to "high" and "low" variants of the same language, for example, in German and Flemish (spoken in Belgium). People employ the "high" variant at universities and in writing, professions, and the mass media. They use the "low" variant for ordinary conversation with family members and friends.

Just as social situations influence our speech, so do geographical, cultural, and socioeconomic differences. Many dialects coexist in the United States with Standard (American) English (SE). SE itself is a dialect that differs, say, from "BBC English," which is the preferred dialect in Great Britain. According to the principle of **linguistic relativity,** all dialects are equally effective as systems of commu-

JOCKS, BURNOUTS, AND RUNTS

Depending on where we live, Americans have certain stereotypes about how people in other regions talk. Some stereotypes, spread by the mass media, are more generalized than others. Most Americans think they can imitate a "southern accent." We also have nationwide stereotypes about speech in New York City (the pronunciation of *coffee*, for example) and Boston ("I pahked the kah in Hahvahd Yahd").

Many Americans also believe that midwesterners don't have accents. This belief stems from the fact that midwestern dialects don't have many stigmatized linguistic variants—speech patterns that people in other regions recognize and look down on, such as *r*lessness and *dem*, *dese*, and *dere* (instead of *them*, *these*, and *there*).

Actually, regional patterns influence the way all Americans speak. Midwesterners do have detectable accents. College students from out of state easily recognize that their instate classmates speak differently. In-state students, however, have difficulty hearing their own speech peculiarities, because they are accustomed to them and view them as normal.

In Detroit-area high schools, sociolinguist Penelope Eckert, as described in her book *Jocks and Burnouts* (1990), studied variation in speech correlated with high school social categories. Eckert's study has revealed links between speech and social status—the high school manifestation of a larger and underlying American social class system. Social variation showed up most clearly in the division of the high school population into two main categories—"jocks" and "burnouts."

Along with teachers, administrators, and parents (particularly "jock parents"), jocks helped maintain the school's formal and traditional social structure. They participated more in athletics, student government, and organized school-based activities. In contrast, burnouts (a social label derived from their tendency to smoke cigarettes) had their main social networks in their neighborhoods. They took school social structure less seriously.

A comparable split exists in many public high schools, although the specific names of the two categories vary from place to place. Jocks have also been called "preppies" or "tweeds," and burnouts have been called "freaks," "greasers," "hoods," and "rednecks." This social division correlates with linguistic differences. Many adult speech habits are set when people are teens, as adolescents copy the speech of people they like and admire. Because jocks and burnouts move in different social systems, they come to talk differently. Eckert is still analyzing the specific differences.

The first step in a sociolinguistic study is to find out which speech forms vary. In New York City, the pronunciation of *r* varies systematically with social class and thus can be used in studies of sociolinguistic variation. However, this feature doesn't vary much among midwesterners, most of whom are adamant *r* pronouncers. However, vowel pronunciation does vary considerably among midwesterners and can be used in a sociolinguistic study.

Far from having no accents, midwesterners, even in the same high school, exhibit sociolinguistic variation. Furthermore, dialect differences in Michigan are immediately obvious to people, like myself, who come from other parts of the country. One of the best examples of variable vowel pronunciation is the /e/ phoneme, which occurs in words like *ten*, *rent*, *French*, *section*, *lecture*, *effect*, *best*, and *test*. In southeastern Michigan there are four different ways of pronouncing this phoneme. Speakers of Black English and immigrants from Appalachia often pronounce *ten* as *tin*, just as southerners habitually do. Some Michigans say *ten*, the correct pronunciation in Standard English. However, two other pronunciations are more common. Instead of *ten*, many Michiganians say *tan*, or *tun* (as though they were using the word *ton*, a unit of weight).

My students often astound me with their pronunciation. One day I met one of my Michigan-raised teaching assistants in the hall. She was deliriously happy. When I asked why, she replied, "I've just had the best suction."

"What?" I said.

"I've just had a wonderful suction," she repeated.

"What?" I still wasn't understanding.

She finally spoke more precisely. "I've just had the best saction." She considered this a clearer pronunciation of the word *section*.

Another TA complimented me, "You luctured to great effuct today." After an exam a student lamented that she hadn't been able to do her "bust on the tust." Once I lectured about uniformity in fast-food restaurant chains. One of my students had just vacationed in Hawaii, where, she told me, hamburger prices were higher than they were on the mainland. It was, she said, because of the runt. Who, I wondered, was this runt? The very puny owner of Honolulu's McDonald's franchise? Perhaps he advertised on television "Come have a hamburger with the runt." Eventually I figured out that she was talking about the high cost of *rent* on those densely packed islands.

nication, which is language's main job. Our tendency to think of particular dialects as better or worse than others is a social rather than a linguistic judgment. We rank certain speech patterns because we recognize that they are used by groups that we also rank. People who say *dese*, *dem*, and *dere* instead of *these*, *them*, and *there* communicate perfectly well with anyone who recognizes that the *d* sound systematically replaces the *th* sound in their speech. However, this form of speech has become an indicator of low social rank. We call it, like the use of *ain't*, "uneducated speech." The use of *dem*, *dese*, and *dere* is one of many phonological differences that Americans recognize and look down on.

Gender Speech Contrasts

Women's speech tends to be more similar to the standard dialect than men's is. Consider the data in Table 21.1, gathered in Detroit. In all social classes, but particularly in the working class, men were more apt to use double negatives (e.g., "I don't want none"). Women are more careful about "uneducated speech." This trend shows up in both the United States and England. Men may adopt working-class speech because they associate it with masculinity. Perhaps women pay more attention to the media, where standard dialects are employed. Also, women may compensate for the socioeconomic barriers they have faced by copying the linguistic norms of upper-status groups.

According to Robin Lakoff (1975), the use of certain types of words and expressions has reflected women's lesser power in American society (see also Coates 1986; Tannen 1990). For example, *Oh dear*, *Oh fudge*, and *Goodness!* are less forceful than *Hell* and *Damn*. Men's customary use of "forceful" words re-

Table 21.1 *Multiple negation ("I don't want none") according to gender and class (in percentages)*

	Upper Middle Class	Lower Middle Class	Upper Working Class	Lower Working Class
Male	6.3	32.4	40.0	90.1
Female	0.0	1.4	35.6	58.9

Source: From *Sociolinguistics: An Introduction to Language and Society* by Peter Trudgill (London: Pelican Books, 1974, revised edition 1983), p. 85, copyright © Peter Trudgill, 1974, 1983. Reproduced by permission of Penguin Books Ltd.

flects their traditional public power and presence. Furthermore, men can't normally use certain "women's words" (*adorable, charming, sweet, cute, lovely, divine*) without raising doubts about their masculinity.

Stratification and Symbolic Domination

We use and evaluate speech—and language changes—in the context of *extralinguistic* forces—social, political, and economic. Mainstream Americans evaluate the speech of low-status groups negatively, calling it "uneducated." This is not because these ways of speaking are bad in themselves but because they have come to symbolize low status. Consider variation in the pronunciation of *r*. In some parts of the United States *r* is regularly pronounced, and in other (*r*less) areas it is not. Originally, American *r*less speech was modeled on the fashionable speech of England. Because of its prestige, *r*lessness was adopted in many areas and continues as the norm around Boston and in the South.

New Yorkers sought prestige by dropping their *r*'s in the nineteenth century, after having pronounced them in the eighteenth. However, contemporary New Yorkers are going back to the eighteenth-century pattern of pronouncing *r*'s. What matters, and what governs linguistic change, is not the reverberation of a strong midwestern *r* but *social evaluation*, whether *r*'s happen to be "in" or "out."

Studies of *r* pronunciation in New York City have clarified the mechanisms of phonological change. William Labov (1972b) focused on whether *r* was pronounced after vowels in such words as *car, floor, card*, and *fourth*. To get data on how this linguistic variation correlated with social class, he used a series of rapid encounters with employees in three New York City department stores, each of whose prices and locations attracted a different socioeconomic group. Saks Fifth Avenue (68 encounters) catered to the upper middle class, Macy's (125) attracted middle-class shoppers, and S. Klein's (71) had predominantly lower-middle-class and working-class customers. The class origins of store personnel tended to reflect those of their clients.

Having already determined that a certain department was on the fourth floor, Labov approached ground-floor salespeople and asked where that department was. After the salesperson had answered, "Fourth floor," Labov repeated his "Where?" in order to get a second response. The second reply was more formal and emphatic, the salesperson presumably thinking that Labov hadn't heard or understood the first answer. For each salesperson, therefore, Labov had two samples of /r/ pronunciation in two words.

Labov calculated the percentages of workers who pronounced /r/ at least once during the interview. These were 62 percent at Saks, 51 percent at Macy's, but only 20 percent at S. Klein's. He also found that personnel on upper floors, where he asked "What floor is this?" (and where more expensive items were sold), pronounced *r* more often than ground-floor salespeople did.

In Labov's study, *r* pronunciation was clearly associated with prestige. Certainly the job interviewers who had hired the salespeople never counted *r*'s before offering employment. However, they did use speech evaluations to make judgments about how effective certain people would be in selling particular kinds of merchandise. In other words, they practiced sociolinguistic discrimination, using linguistic features in deciding who got certain jobs.

In stratified societies, our speech habits help determine our access to employment and other material resources. Because of this, "proper language" itself becomes a strategic resource—and a path to wealth, prestige, and power (Gal 1989). Illustrating this, many ethnographers have described the importance of verbal skill and oratory in politics (Beeman 1986; Bloch, ed. 1975; Brenneis 1988; Geis 1987). Remember, too, that a "great communicator," Ronald Reagan, dominated American society in the 1980s as a two-term President.

The French anthropologist Pierre Bourdieu views linguistic practices as *symbolic capital* which properly trained people may convert into economic and social capital. The value of a dialect—its standing in a "linguistic market"—depends on the extent to which it provides access to desired positions in the labor market. In turn, this reflects its legitimation by formal institutions—the educational establishment, state, church, and prestige media. In stratified societies, even people who don't use the prestige dialect accept its authority and correctness, its "symbolic domination" (Bourdieu 1982, 1984). Thus, linguistic forms, which lack power in themselves, take on the power of the groups and relationships they symbolize. The education system, however (defending its own worth), denies this, misrepresenting prestige speech as being inherently better. The linguistic insecurity of lower-class and minority speakers is a result of this symbolic domination.

Black English Vernacular (BEV)

Many linguists have analyzed variation based on ethnic background. In particular, Labov and several associates, both white and black, have conducted detailed studies of what they call **Black English Vernacular (BEV). (Vernacular** means ordinary, casual speech.) BEV is the

> relatively uniform dialect spoken by the majority of black youth in most parts of the United States today, especially in the inner city areas of New York, Boston, Detroit, Philadelphia, Washington, Cleveland, . . . and other urban centers. It is also spoken in . . . rural areas and used in the casual, intimate speech of many adults. (Labov 1972a, p. xiii)

Researchers have collected data from adolescent and adult BEV speakers in New York and other cities.

Contrary to popular belief, BEV, which is usually called simply Black English, is not an ungrammatical hodge-podge but a complex linguistic system with its own rules. It developed as a variant of southern speech, with a phonology and a syntax similar to those of southern dialects. Nearly every feature distinguishing BEV from SE (Standard English) also characterizes the speech of some southern whites, although less often than is the case among speakers of BEV.

Among the phonological differences between BEV and SE, BEV speakers are less likely to pronounce *r*. Although many SE speakers fail to pronounce *r* before other consonants (ca*r*d) or at the end of words (ca*r*), most do pronounce *r* before a vowel, either at the end of a word (fou*r* o'clock) or within a word (Ca*r*ol). BEV speakers are more likely to omit the *r* before a vowel or between vowels. The result is that speakers of the two dialects have different **homonyms** (words that sound the same but have different meanings). If they don't pronounce *r* between vowels, BEV speakers have the following homonyms: *Carol/Cal; Paris/pass.*

Because of phonological contrasts between BEV and SE, BEV speakers pronounce certain words differently than SE speakers do. This has relevance for teaching in multiethnic classrooms. The homonyms of BEV-speaking students differ from those of SE-speaking teachers and students. To evaluate reading accuracy, teachers must take care to determine whether students are recognizing the different meanings of such BEV homonyms as *Paris, passed, past,* and *pass.* Teachers need to make sure that students grasp what they are reading, which is more important than whether they are pronouncing words "correctly" according to the SE norm.

Phonological contrasts between BEV and SE speakers often have grammatical consequences. One of these is **copula deletion,** the absence of SE forms of the verb *to be.* For example, any of the following may contrast BEV and SE:

BEV	SE
you tired	you are tired
he tired	he is tired
we tired	we are tired
they tired	they are tired

In its deletion of the present tense of *to be,* BEV is similar to many languages, including Russian, Hungarian, and Hebrew, but it contrasts with SE. BEV copula deletion is a grammatical result of BEV's phonological rules. Notice that BEV omits the copula only where SE has contractions. SE contracts "you are tired" to "you're tired." Through contraction, SE produces "he's," "we're," and "they're." The phonological rules of BEV dictate that r's and word-final s's be dropped. However, BEV speakers do pronounce *m.* The BEV first-person singular is "I'm tired," just as in SE. When BEV omits the copula, it is merely carrying contraction one step further. This is a result of BEV's phonological rules.

Also, phonological rules may lead BEV speakers to omit *-ed* as a past-tense marker and *-s* as a marker of plurality. These, however, are differences in surface structure rather than deep structure. BEV speakers *do* understand the difference between past and present verbs and singular and plural nouns. Confirming this are irregular verbs (for instance, *tell, told*) and irregular plurals (for instance, *child, children*), in which BEV works the same as SE.

BEV, like SE, is a complex, rule-governed dialect. SE is not superior to BEV as a linguistic system, but it does happen to be the dialect used in the mass media, in writing, and in most public and professional contexts. In areas of Germany where there is diglossia, speakers of Plattdeusch (Low German) learn the High German dialect to communicate ap-

propriately in the national context. Similarly, upwardly mobile BEV-speaking students learn SE.

Language is not learned from remote experience (such as the mass media) but from an individual's personal social network, particularly from peers. Speech responds to primary influences, people who make a difference in your life, such as supervisors, coworkers, and classmates. Urban ghetto existence tends to isolate blacks from whites. Many black children have never talked to white children before entering school. Despite the use of SE on radio and television, American dialect variance is actually growing, not just between blacks and whites but also between whites in different cities. Dialect divergence has the effect of "locking" blacks out of "important networks that lead to jobs, housing, and basic rights and privileges" (Williams 1985, p. 10).

Although BEV is diverging from SE, the dialects are still close. This means that teachers of multiethnic classrooms need to know something about the phonology and grammar of both dialects if they are to teach successfully. Schoolteachers should be able to show BEV-speaking students exactly how SE differs in phonology and syntax.

Many Americans who spoke other regional and ethnic dialects as children have eventually learned to shift their linguistic styles outside the home. Since BEV is a bit more different from SE than other American English dialects are, mastery of the prestige dialect requires more effort. If learning and teaching SE are to be goals of blacks and whites within our educational system, school personnel need linguistic knowledge and sensitivity.

HISTORICAL LINGUISTICS

Sociolinguists study contemporary variation in speech—language change in progress. **Historical linguistics** deals with longer-term change. Historical linguists can reconstruct many features of past languages by studying contemporary **daughter languages.** These are languages that descend from the same parent language and that have been changing separately for hundreds or even thousands of years. We call the original language from which they diverge the **protolanguage** (Figure 21.3). French and Spanish, for example, are daughter languages of Latin, their common protolanguage. Historical linguists also classify languages according to their degree of relationship.

Language changes over time. It evolves—varies, spreads, divides into **subgroups** (languages within a taxonomy of related languages that are most closely related). Dialects of a single parent language become distinct daughter languages, especially if they are isolated from one another. Some of them split, and new "granddaughter" languages develop. If people remain in the ancestral homeland, their speech patterns also change. The evolving speech in the ancestral homeland should be considered a daughter language like the others. Language may also unify people when groups that once spoke different languages occupy a new homeland, develop a national identity, or come under a common system of political domination (Bourdieu 1982; Gal 1989; Weber 1976).

A close relationship between languages doesn't necessarily mean that their speakers are closely related biologically or culturally, because people can adopt new languages. In the equatorial forests of Africa, "pygmy" hunters have discarded their ancestral languages and now speak those of the cultivators who have migrated to the area. Immigrants to the United States spoke many different languages on arrival, but their descendants now speak fluent English. People with very different customs may speak a single language, and people who are culturally similar over a large area, such as Central Af-

rican hunters and gatherers, may speak different languages.

How does linguistic evolution differ from biological evolution? Biological species originate in reproductive isolation, and gene sharing or borrowing is not possible after speciation. In language and in culture, however, complete isolation never occurs. Diffusion, borrowing, conquest, and consolidation go on all the time. In the world system, linguistic and cultural items keep passing from group to group. Linguistic change is influenced by contact between languages and cultures.

Historical Linguistics and Other Anthropological Concerns

Knowledge of linguistic relationships is often valuable to anthropologists interested in history, particularly events during the past 5,000 years. Cultural features may (or may not) correlate with the distribution of language families. Groups that speak related languages may (or may not) be more culturally similar to each other than they are to groups whose speech derives from different linguistic ancestors. Of course, cultural similarities aren't limited to speakers of related languages. Even groups whose members speak unrelated languages have contact through trade, intermarriage, and warfare. Ideas and inventions diffuse widely among human groups. Many items of vocabulary in contemporary

Breughel's Tower of Babel. The Bible traces the origin of different languages to God's punishment of humans who dared approach heaven by building the tower of Babel: all at once, the tower builders started speaking mutually incomprehensible languages. The actual explanation is linguistic uniformitarianism, which states that new languages evolve out of old ones as minor linguistic variations, of the sort observable in any language today, gradually accumulate. This gradual process is illustrated by differences and similarities between Middle and modern English.

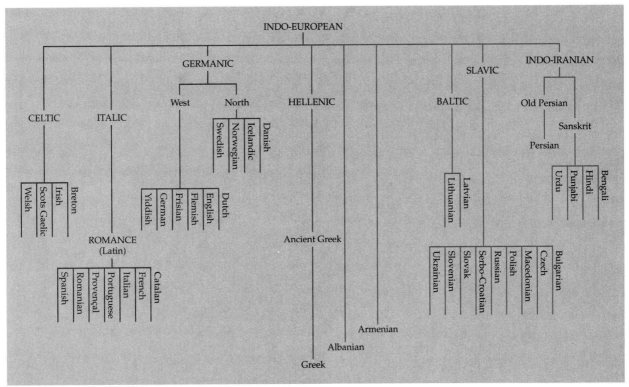

Figure 21.3 *Main languages and subgroups of the Indo-European language stock. All these daughter languages have developed out of the protolanguage (Proto-Indo-European) spoken in northern Europe about 5,000 years ago. Note subgrouping: English, a member of the Germanic branch, is more closely related to German and Dutch than it is to Italic (or Romance) languages such as French and Spanish. However, English shares many linguistic features with French through borrowing and diffusion. (Figure 8.6 from* An Introduction to Language, *Fourth Edition, by Victoria Fromkin and Robert Rodman, copyright © 1988 by Holt, Rinehart & Winston, Inc., reprinted by permission of the publisher.)*

English come from French. Even without written documentation of France's influence after the Norman Conquest of England in 1066, linguistic evidence in contemporary English would reveal a long period of important firsthand contact with France. Similarly, linguistic evidence may confirm cultural contact and borrowing when written history is lacking. By considering which words have been borrowed, we can also make inferences about the nature of the contact.

Language and Adaptation

Language is a major adaptive advantage that differentiates *Homo sapiens* from other species and has been partially responsible for the evolutionary success of humans. Just as there are no documented

differences in brain complexity or intelligence between contemporary human populations, no one has ever shown the superiority of any language or dialect to any other. The doctrine of linguistic relativity states that all known languages and dialects are effective means of communication. This contradicts popular stereotypes. Many French people believe that theirs is the only appropriate language for civilized conversation. Many British and Americans assert the superiority of their language for commercial negotiations.

These claims, however, reflect cultural rather than linguistic facts. They originate in world politics and economy rather than in inherent linguistic properties. In creating a nation-state, and thereafter a world empire, the French spread their culture through their language. They asserted to the prov-

IN THE NEWS: USING MODERN TECHNOLOGY TO PRESERVE LINGUISTIC DIVERSITY

Linguistic diversity is reduced when people abandon their ancestral tongue for a dominant or national language. The anthropologist H. Russell Bernard has been a pioneer in teaching speakers of endangered languages how to write their language using a computer. Bernard's work permits the preservation of languages and cultural memories. Native peoples from Mexico to Cameroon are using their mother tongue to express themselves as individuals and to provide insiders' accounts of different cultures.

Jesús Salinas Pedraza, a rural schoolteacher in the Mexican state of Hidalgo, sat down to a word processor a few years back and produced a monumental book, a 250,000-word description of his own Indian culture written in the Nähñu language. Nothing seems to be left out: folktales and traditional religious beliefs, the practical uses of plants and minerals and the daily flow of life in field and village.

But it is more than the content that makes the book a remarkable publishing event, for Mr. Salinas is neither a professional anthropologist nor a literary stylist. He is, though, the first person to write a book in Nähñu (NYAW-hnyu), the native tongue of several hundred thousand Indians but a previously unwritten language.

Such a use of microcomputers and desktop publishing for languages with no literary tradition is now being encouraged by anthropologists for recording ethnographies from an insider's perspective. They see this as a means of preserving cultural diversity and a wealth of human knowledge. With even greater urgency, linguists are promoting the techniques as a way of saving some of the world's languages from imminent extinction.

Half of the world's 6,000 languages are considered by linguists to be endangered. These are the languages spoken by small societies that are dwindling with the encroachment of larger, more dynamic cultures. Young people feel economic pressure to learn only the language of the dominant culture, and as the older people die, the non-written language vanishes, unlike languages with a history of writing, like Latin.

Dr. H. Russell Bernard, the anthropologist at the University of Florida at Gainesville who taught Mr. Salinas to read and write his native language, said: "Languages have always come and gone. Neither the language of Jesus nor that of Caesar are spoken today. But languages seem to be disappearing faster than ever before."

In 30 years of field studies, Dr. Kenneth Hale, a linguist at the Massachusetts Institute of Technology and a leader in efforts to preserve endangered languages, said he had worked with at least eight that have become extinct and many others that are "seriously imperiled."

Dr. Michael E. Krauss, the director of the Alaska Native Language Center at the University of Alaska in Fairbanks, estimates that 300 of the 900 indigenous languages in the Americas are moribund. That is, they are no longer being spoken by children, and so could disappear in a generation or two. Only two of the 20 native languages in Alaska are still being learned by children.

"Languages no longer being learned as mother-tongue by children are beyond endangerment," Dr. Krauss said. Unless the current course is somehow reversed, he added, these languages "are already doomed to extinction, like species lacking reproductive capacity."

Dr. Krauss asks: "Should we mourn the loss of Eyak or Ubykh any less than the loss of the panda or California condor?"

At a symposium a few years ago in Mexico on "The Politics of Linguistic Revitalization," representatives of Latin American Indians passed a resolution saying, "The loss of a language in the world means the disappearance of the cultural heritage transmitted by it, and the truncation of an alternate route of cultural development for humankind."

In an effort to preserve language diversity in Mexico, Dr. Bernard and Mr. Salinas decided in 1987 on a plan to teach the Indian people to read and write their own language using microcomputers. They established a native literacy center in Oaxaca, Mexico, where others could follow in the footsteps of Mr. Salinas and write books in other Indian languages.

The Oaxaca center goes beyond most bilingual education programs, which concentrate on teaching people to speak and read their native languages. Instead, it operates on the premise that, as Dr. Bernard decided, what most native languages lack is native authors who write books in their own languages.

"Without popular literacy, all but a few endangered languages will soon disappear," Dr. Bernard said. "And when non-written languages disappear, they disappear forever."

Mr. Salinas set the example. He had grown up speaking both Spanish and Nähñu, one of the more widely spoken of the 56 Indian languages in Mexico. The Nähñu Indians are also known as the Otomí, a name they now reject because of its pejorative connotations in Mexican Spanish.

While conducting research in Mexico in the 1970's, Dr. Bernard taught Mr. Salinas to read and write the Nähñu language, using a modified version of an alphabet that had been developed by mis-

Anthroplogists have taught speakers of diverse languages to write their language using a computer, permitting the preservation of linguistic and cultural diversity. Native peoples from Mexico to Bali, Indonesia—shown here—are writing their mother tongue to express themselves as individuals and provide insiders' accounts of their culture.

sionaries. The Summer Institute of Linguistics, a world-wide evangelical Protestant organization based in Dallas, has for decades developed the alphabets for hundreds of Indian languages.

Virtually all indigenous languages now have rudimentary writing systems, including alphabets, a dictionary and some grammar. In Nähñu and many other languages, however, the only book is a Bible translation.

Next Dr. Bernard adapted computer software for writing Nähñu on a word processor and for printing manuscripts and books, which would not have been affordable through traditional publishing. In this way, Mr. Salinas first produced a book of Nähñu folktales and, two years ago, his magnum opus on Nähñu culture. A translation in English, by Dr. Bernard, is entitled, "Native Ethnography: A Mexican Indian Describes His Culture."

There is a long tradition of training people of a remote culture to be what anthropologists call informants. These people would describe the legends and customs and sometimes dictate their autobiographies. But these were usually taped interviews with an anthropologist and not the direct work of an indigenous person.

The Oaxaca project's influence is spreading. Impressed by the work of Mr. Salinas and others, Dr. Norman Whitten, an anthropologist at the University of Illinois, arranged for schoolteachers from Ecuador to visit Oaxaca and learn the techniques.

Now Ecuadorian Indians have begun writing about their cultures in the Quechua and Shwara languages. Others from Bolivia and Peru are learning to use the computers to write their languages, including Quecha, the tongue of the ancient Incas, still spoken by about 12 million Andean Indians.

Anthropologists in Cameroon have introduced the technology in that African country of more than 200 tribal languages. At the end of a two-week training course, Dr. Bernard said, each of the five speakers of the Kom language would turn on the computer in the morning and start typing Kom without hesitation. Anything they could say, they could write.

Dr. Bernard emphasized that these native literacy programs are not intended to discourage people from learning the dominant language of their country as well. "I see nothing useful or charming about remaining monolingual in any Indian language if that results in being shut out of the national economy," he said.

Anthropologists acknowledge that bilingualism can be a sensitive political issue. In places struggling to create a workable nation, the preservation of separate languages can be seen as potentially divisive, setting one group against another.

But anthropologists and leaders of native cultures generally favor bilingualism because it preserves a distinctive culture, which often gives the people more power than if they were completely assimilated. A distinctive language can be a strong force in establishing cultural uniqueness, or ethnicity, which in turn can reinforce a group's claim to a share of power.

Such efforts may be too late for hundreds of languages and dwindling cultures, anthropologists and linguists say, but in time to help preserve some of the cultural heterogeneity of the planet.

Source: John Noble Wilford, "In a Publishing Coup, Books in 'Unwritten' Languages," *The New York Times*, December 31, 1991, pp. B5, 6.

The geographic distribution of a language has nothing to do with intrinsic features of that language. Thus French is spoken by millions of people because of French colonization, conquest, and colonialism—not because of special qualities of the French language per se. In creating a nation-state, then a colonial empire, the French spread their culture through their language—to places like Haiti, where a creole language based on French is the native language.

inces they attached and the people they conquered that they were engaged in a civilizing mission. They came to equate the French language with civilization itself.

The contemporary use and distribution of a language reflect factors other than features of the language itself. One language spoken in China has more native speakers than English does not because it is a better language but because the population that speaks it has multiplied as a result of nonlinguistic factors. English is the native language of British people, North Americans, Australians, New Zealanders, and many South Africans because of English colonization and conquest. The success of this colonization and conquest had nothing to do with language. Weapons, ships, commerce, and sociopolitical organization played decisive roles.

Between 2,000 and 3,000 years ago a West African (proto-Bantu) population lived in a small area of what is now Nigeria and Cameroon. Today the linguistic descendants of the proto-Bantu cover most of Central Africa and southern Africa. Speakers of **Bantu** did not expand because their languages were superior means of communication. Rather, they

grew, prospered, and spread because they developed a highly competitive cultural adaptation based on iron tools and weapons and productive food crops.

We have seen that no language or dialect can confer, because of its purely linguistic qualities, a differential advantage on its speakers. Only the social evaluation of its speakers and, by extension, of the language itself can do this. Languages are flexible and—at least at the surface level—constantly changing systems. They easily admit and adopt new items and new terms. Speakers modify old forms, borrow foreign words, and create entirely new expressions.

Through surface changes, languages adjust to rapid cultural changes. However, the core of a language—its deep structure—may remain virtually intact while its speakers' lives are revolutionized. In many respects the daily lives of rural Europeans before the Industrial Revolution were more similar to those of precolonial West Africans than to those of their contemporary European descendants. Yet linguistic change in English or in French has proceeded very slowly compared with the rate of economic, political, and social change.

SUMMARY

Linguistic anthropologists share anthropology's general interest in uniformity and diversity in time and space. Linguistic anthropology examines meaning systems, relationships between language and culture, linguistic universals, sociolinguistics, and linguistic change.

No language includes all the sounds (phones) that the human vocal apparatus can make. Phonology—the study of speech sounds—focuses on sound contrasts (phonemes) that distinguish meaning in a given language. In sociolinguistics, variation among speakers of the same language correlates with social contrasts and exemplifies linguistic change in progress.

In his transformational-generative approach, Chomsky argues for an innate blueprint for building language in the human brain. All people share this genetically determined capacity for language, though not for any particular language. Each language's grammar is a particular set of rules taken from the universal set. Once we master our language's rules, we can generate an infinite number of statements. Surface structures, the object of traditional linguistic study, make languages seem more different than they are. The similarities lie deeper, at the level of deep structure.

There are culturally distinctive as well as universal relationships between language and mental processes. The lexicons and grammars of particular languages can lead speakers to perceive and think in particular ways. Studies of domains such as kinship, color terminologies, and pronouns show that speakers of different languages categorize their experiences differently. However, language does not tightly restrict thought, because cultural changes can produce changes in thought and in language, particularly in surface structure.

Sociolinguistics investigates relationships between social and linguistic variation. It focuses on performance (the actual use of language) rather than competence (rules shared by all speakers of a given language). Sociolinguists do field work with several informants and quantify their observations. Only when features of speech acquire social meaning are they imitated. If they are valued, they spread.

People vary their speech on different occasions, shifting styles, dialects, and languages, particularly in the modern world system. As linguistic systems, all languages and dialects are equally complex, rule-governed, and effective for communication. However, speech is used, is evaluated, and changes in the context of political, economic, and social forces. The linguistic traits of a low-status group are negatively evaluated (often even by members of that group) not because of their *linguistic* features but because they are associated with and symbolize low *social* status. One dialect, supported by the dominant institutions of the state, exercises symbolic domination over the others.

Black English Vernacular, a dialect of contemporary English, shares, despite certain surface differences, most of its deep structural rules with Standard English and other American English dialects. Both SE and BEV are complex, rule-governed systems. Neither dialect communicates more effectively than the other.

Historical linguistics is useful for anthropologists interested in historical relationships between populations. Cultural similarities and differences often correlate with linguistic ones. Linguistic clues can suggest past contacts between cultures. Related languages—members of the same language family—descend from an original protolanguage. Relationships between languages don't necessarily mean that there are biological ties between their speakers, because people can learn new languages.

Linguistic relativity views each language as a communication system that is as adequate as any other for the exchange of information.

GLOSSARY

Bantu: Group of related languages spoken over a large area of Central Africa and eastern and southern Africa.

Black English Vernacular (BEV): Like Standard English, a rule-governed dialect of contemporary English; spoken by many inner-city African-Americans.

competence: What native speakers must (and do) know about their language in order to speak and understand it.

copula deletion: Absence of the verb *to be*.

daughter languages: Languages developing out of the same parent language; for example, French and Spanish are daughter languages of Latin.

deep structure: In transformational grammar, the mental level; a sentence is formed in the speaker's mind and then interpreted by the hearer.

diglossia: The existence of "high" (formal) and "low" (informal, familial) dialects of a single language, such as German.

ethnoscience: See *ethnosemantics*.

ethnosemantics: The study of lexical (vocabulary) contrasts and classifications in various languages.

focal vocabulary: A set of words and distinctions that are particularly important to certain groups (those with particular foci of experience or activity), such as types of snow to Eskimos or skiers.

grammar: The formal organizing principles that link sound and meaning in a language; the set of abstract rules that makes up a language.

historical linguistics: Subdivision of linguistics that studies languages over time.

homonyms: Words that sound the same but have different meanings, such as *bear* and *bare.*

lexicon: Vocabulary; a dictionary containing all the morphemes in a language and their meanings.

linguistic relativity: Notion that all languages and dialects are equally effective as systems of communication.

linguistic uniformitarianism: Belief that explanations for long-term change in language should be sought in ordinary forces that continue to work today; thus, the forces that have produced linguistic changes over the centuries are observable in linguistic events (variation) taking place today.

minimal pairs: Words that resemble each other in all but one sound; used to discover phonemes.

morpheme: Minimal linguistic form (usually a word) with meaning.

morphology: The study of form; used in linguistics (the study of morphemes and word construction) and for form in general—for example, biomorphology relates to physical form.

performance: What people actually say; the use of speech in social situations.

phone: Any speech sound.

phoneme: Significant sound contrast in a language that serves to distinguish meaning, as in minimal pairs.

phonemics: The study of the sound contrasts (phonemes) of a particular language.

phonetics: The study of speech sounds in general; what people actually say in various languages.

phonology: The study of sounds used in speech.

protolanguage: Language ancestral to several daughter languages.

Sapir-Whorf hypothesis: Theory that different languages produce different ways of thinking.

semantics: A language's meaning system.

sociolinguistics: Study of relationships between social and linguistic variation; study of language (performance) in its social context.

style shifts: Variations in speech in different contexts.

subgroups: Languages within a taxonomy of related languages that are most closely related.

surface structure: In transformational grammar, the message that passes from speaker to hearer; an actual speech event.

syntax: The arrangement and order of words in phrases and sentences.

transformational-generative grammar: Approach associated with Noam Chomsky; views language as set of abstract rules with deep and surface structures.

universal grammar: According to Chomsky, a genetically transmitted blueprint for language, that is, a basic linguistic plan in the human brain.

vernacular: Ordinary, casual speech.

STUDY QUESTIONS

1. Why is linguistic anthropology a subdiscipline of anthropology? What does it share with the other subdisciplines? How does it link up with cultural anthropology?
2. What is Chomsky's transformational-generative grammar, and how does it relate to the issue of "human nature"?
3. What is the Sapir-Whorf hypothesis, and how does it relate to cultural diversity?
4. What is sociolinguistics, and how does it relate to the distinction between competence and performance?
5. Several examples of interrelationships between social and linguistic variation have been given. Can you cite comparable sociolinguistic examples from your own experience?
6. How do men and women differ in their use of language?
7. What is historical linguistics, and what are the issues it studies?
8. What is linguistic relativity, and how does it relate to symbolic domination by prestige dialects?

SUGGESTED ADDITIONAL READING

APPEL, R., AND P. MUYSKEN
1987   *Language Contact and Bilingualism.* London: Edward Arnold. Issues of linguistic contact.

BARON, D.
1986   *Grammar and Gender.* New Haven: Yale University Press. Differences in grammatical patterns and strategies of men and women.

BEEMAN, W.
1986   *Language, Status, and Power in Iran.* Bloomington, IN: Indiana University Press. Informative case study using sociolinguistic analysis to examine issues of speech, performance, and power.

BURKE, P., AND R. PORTER
1987   *The Social History of Language.* Cambridge: Cambridge University Press. Language in society through history.

BURLING, R.
1970   *Man's Many Voices: Language in Its Cultural Context.* New York: Holt, Rinehart & Winston. Readable introduction to sociolinguistics and language and culture.

COATES, J.
1986   *Women, Men, and Language.* London: Longman. Gender differences in language.

COOK-GUMPERZ, J.
1986   *The Social Construction of Literacy.* Cambridge: Cambridge University Press. Literacy in its social and cultural context.

FASOLD, R. W.
1990   *The Sociolinguistics of Language.* Oxford: Basil Blackwell. Recent text with up-to-date examples.

FERGUSON, C. A., AND S. B. HEATH, EDS.
1981   *Language in the U.S.A.* New York: Cambridge University Press. Bilingualism, professional jargon, languages of Native Americans, Spanish, and varieties of American English.

GEIS, M. L.
1987   *The Language of Politics.* New York: Springer-Verlag. Thorough examination of political uses of speech and oratory and the manipulation of language in power relations.

GUMPERZ, J. J.
1982   *Language and Social Identity.* Cambridge: Cambridge University Press. Well-known sociolinguist discusses language and social identification.

HELLER, M.
1988   *Codeswitching: Anthropological and Sociolinguistic Perspectives.* Berlin: Mouton de Gruyter. Style shifting and diglossia.

HEWITT, R.
1986   *White Talk, Black Talk.* Cambridge: Cambridge University Press. Black English Vernacular and its relationship to Standard English and white dialects.

KRAMARAE, R., M. SHULZ, AND M. O'BARR, EDS.
1984   *Language and Power.* Beverly Hills, CA: Sage. Issues of language, politics, and symbolic domination.

LAKOFF, R.
1975   *Language and Woman's Place.* New York: Harper & Row. Influential nontechnical discussion of how women use and are treated in Standard American English.

MUHLHAUSLER, P.
1986   *Pidgin and Creole Linguistics.* London: Basil Blackwell. New languages of travel, trade, and colonialism.

STEEDMAN, C., C. URWIN, AND V. WALKERDINE, EDS.
1985   *Language, Gender, and Childhood.* London: Routledge and Kegan Paul. The learning of gender differentiation through language.

TANNEN, D.
1986   *That's Not What I Meant! How Conversational Style Makes or Breaks Your Relations with Others.* New York: William Morrow. How sociolinguistic variation based on region, class, and gender affects interpersonal relations.
1990   *You Just Don't Understand: Women and Men in Conversation.* New York: Ballantine. Popular book on gender differences in speech and conversational styles.

THOMASON, S. G., AND T. KAUFMAN
1988   *Language Contact, Creolization, and Genetic Linguistics.* Berkeley: University of California Press. Language in the world system.

TRUDGILL, P.
1983   *Sociolinguistics: An Introduction to Language and Society, rev. ed.* Harmondsworth, United Kingdom: Penguin. Readable short introduction to the role and use of language in society.

WOOLARD, K. A.
1989   *Double Talk: Bilingualism and the Politics of Ethnicity in Catalonia.* Stanford, CA: Stanford University Press. Field study of diglossia.

CHAPTER 22

APPLIED ANTHROPOLOGY

Anthropology reduces ethnocentrism by instilling an appreciation of cultural diversity. This broadening, educational role affects the knowledge, values, and attitudes of people exposed to anthropology. Now we focus on the question: What contributions can anthropology make in identifying and solving problems stirred up by contemporary currents of economic, social, and cultural change?

Applied anthropology refers to the application of anthropological data, perspectives, theory, and methods to identify, assess, and solve social problems. There are two important professional groups of applied anthropologists (also called *practicing anthropologists*). The older is the independent Society for Applied Anthropology, founded in 1941. The second, the National Association for the Practice of Anthropology, was established as a unit of the American Anthropological Association in 1983. (Many people belong to both groups.) Practicing anthropologists work, regularly or occasionally, for nonacademic clients: governments, **nongovernmental organizations (NGOs),** tribal and ethnic associations, interest groups, businesses, and social-service and educational agencies. Practicing anthropologists make it their business to apply their specialized knowledge and skills to problem solving.

There was a time—the 1940s—when most anthropologists focused on practical problems. Many anthropologists worked for governments during World War II. American anthropologists studied Japanese and German culture "at a distance" and aided the war effort. Applied anthropology did not disappear during the 1950s and 1960s, but academic anthropology did most of the growing after World War II.

ACADEMIC AND APPLIED ANTHROPOLOGY

The baby boom, which began in 1945 and peaked in 1957, fueled expansion of the American educational system and thus of academic jobs. New junior, community, and four-year colleges opened. Anthropology became a standard part of the college curriculum. During the 1950s and 1960s most American anthropologists were professors, although some still worked in agencies and museums.

This era of academic anthropology continued through the early 1970s. Especially during the Vietnam War, undergraduates flocked to anthropology classes to learn about the cultures of the Third World. Students were especially interested in the peoples and cultures of Southeast Asia, whose traditional lives were threatened by war. Many anthropologists protested the superpowers' blatant disregard for the values, customs, social systems, and lives of Third World peoples.

During the Vietnam War, many anthropologists protested the superpowers' blatant disregard for the values, customs, social systems, and lives of Third World peoples. Several anthropologists, including the author (nearer of two men with glasses and chin-in-hand, on lower level), attended this all-night Columbia University "teach-in" against the war in 1965.

A shift in the interests of college students and in the jobs available to anthropologists occurred during the 1970s with the end of the Vietnam War and the baby boom. Students started turning away from a broad liberal education and toward a curriculum that seemed more practical. Computer science, engineering, business, accounting, economics, and even psychology seemed more likely to lead to a job than did anthropology, philosophy, history, or literature.

Anthropology itself followed this shift toward the practical. Anthropologists sought jobs in international organizations, government, business, hospitals, and schools. The shift toward application, though only partial, benefitted the profession. It forced anthropologists to consider the wider social values and implications of their research.

Massive changes in human life are going on today, and many anthropologists feel obliged not simply to study but also to try to solve contemporary problems. Applied anthropologists work in diverse settings. Some hold academic positions but also consult for firms and organizations. Some do independent research on the social context and effects of planned and unplanned changes. Still others work full-time as nonacademic anthropologists. Recognizing their increasing importance, the American Anthropological Association (AAA) now publishes a directory of applied anthropologists that parallels the long-published AAA guide [to departments of anthropology]. This is called the *NAPA Directory of Practicing Anthropologists* (1991).

Theory and Practice

One of the applied anthropologist's most valuable research tools is the ethnographic method. Ethnographers study societies firsthand, living with and learning from ordinary people. Ethnographers are participant-observers, taking part in the events they study in order to understand native thought and behavior. Ethnographic techniques guide applied anthropologists in both foreign and domestic settings.

Other "expert" participants in social-change programs may be content to converse with officials, read reports, and copy statistics. However, the applied anthropologist's likely early request is some variant of "take me to your villagers." We know that local people must play an active role in the changes that affect them and that "the people" have information that "the experts" lack.

Anthropological theory—the body of findings and generalizations of the subdisciplines—also guides applied anthropology. Anthropology's holistic perspective—its interest in biology, society, culture, and language—permits the evaluation of many issues that affect people. Anthropology's **systemic perspective** recognizes that changes don't occur in a vacuum. A project or program always has multiple effects, some unforeseen. For example, dozens of economic development projects intended to increase productivity through irrigation have worsened public health by creating waterways where diseases thrive. In an American example of unintended consequences, a program aimed at enhancing teachers' appreciation of cultural differences led to ethnic stereotyping (Kleinfeld 1975). Specifically, Native American students did not welcome teachers' frequent comments about their Indian heritage. The students felt set apart from their classmates and saw this attention to their ethnicity as patronizing and demeaning.

Theory aids practice, and application fuels theory. As we compare social-change policy and projects, our understanding of cause and effect increases. We add new generalizations about culture change to those discovered in traditional and ancient cultures.

Applied Anthropology and the Subdisciplines

Applied anthropologists come from all four subdisciplines. Biological anthropologists work in public health, nutrition, genetic counseling, substance abuse, epidemiology, aging, and mental illness. They apply their knowledge of human anatomy and physiology to the improvement of automobile safety standards and to the design of airplanes and spacecraft. In forensic work, biological anthropologists help police identify skeletal remains. Similarly, forensic archeologists reconstruct crimes by analyzing physical evidence.

An important role for applied archeologists has been created by legislation requiring surveys of prehistoric and historic sites threatened by dams, highways, and other projects supported by federal funds. To save as much as possible of the past when actual sites cannot be preserved is the work of **salvage archeology.** Applied cultural anthropologists

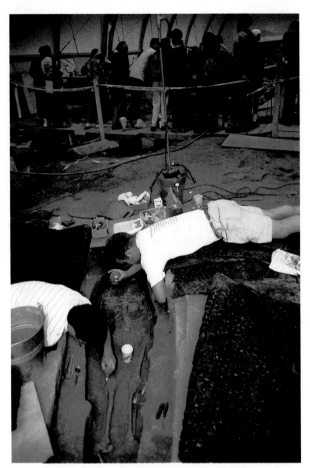

An important role for applied archeologists has been created by legislation requiring surveys of historic sites. To save as much as possible of the past when actual sites cannot be preserved is the work of salvage archeology. New York City has yielded one of the largest African-American archeological sites in the United States.

sometimes work with the applied archeologists, assessing the human problems generated by the change and determining how they can be reduced.

Cultural anthropologists work with social workers, business people, media researchers, advertising professionals, factory workers, gerontologists, nurses, physicians, mental-health professionals, school personnel, and economic development experts. Linguistic anthropology, particularly sociolinguistics, aids education. Knowledge of linguistic differences is important in an increasingly multicultural society whose populace grows up speaking many languages and dialects. Because linguistic differences may affect children's schoolwork and

teachers' evaluations, many schools of education now require courses in sociolinguistics.

ANTHROPOLOGY AND EDUCATION

Ethnography brings a novel perspective to education, with practical applications (Eddy 1978). **Anthropology and education** refers to anthropological research in classrooms, homes, and neighborhoods. Some of the most interesting research has been done in classrooms, where anthropologists observe interactions between teachers, students, parents, and visitors. Jules Henry's classic account of the American elementary school classroom (1955) shows how students learn to conform to and compete with their peers. Anthropologists also follow students from classrooms into their homes and neighborhoods, viewing children as total cultural creatures whose enculturation and attitudes toward education belong to a context that includes family and peers.

Sociolinguists and cultural anthropologists work side by side in education research, for example, in a study of Puerto Rican seventh-graders in the urban Midwest (Hill-Burnett 1978). In classrooms, neighborhoods, and homes, anthropologists uncovered some misconceptions by teachers. For example, the teachers had mistakenly assumed that Puerto Rican parents valued education less than did non-Hispanics. However, in-depth interviews revealed that the Puerto Rican parents valued it more.

Researchers also found that certain practices were preventing Hispanics from being adequately educated. For example, the teachers' union and the board of education had agreed to teach "English as a foreign language." However, they had not provided bilingual teachers to work with Spanish-speaking students. The school started assigning all students (including non-Hispanics) with low reading scores and behavior problems to the English-as-a-foreign-language classroom.

This educational disaster brought together a teacher who spoke no Spanish, children who barely spoke English, and a group of English-speaking students with reading and behavior problems. The Spanish speakers were falling behind not just in reading but in all subjects. They could at least have kept up in the other subjects if a Spanish speaker had been teaching them science, social studies, and math until they were ready for English-language instruction in those areas.

Sociolinguists and ethnographers have worked side by side in education research, for example, in bilingual and multiethnic settings. Here Canadian students learn bilingually (in French and English) on an outing to the Cap Tourmente National Wildlife Reserve on the Saint Lawrence River in Quebec.

The researchers also found that Anglo-Americans and Hispanics reacted differently to humor and teasing. Many Hispanic youths believed that teachers' kidding comments went too far. They heard the remarks as insults and slurs rather than jokes. The Hispanics who adapted best were those who had learned the general American norm about kidding, so that teachers' attempts at humor didn't damage their self-esteem.

A dramatic illustration of the relevance of sociolinguistics to education comes from Ann Arbor, Michigan. In 1979 the parents of several black students at the predominantly white Dr. Martin Luther King, Jr., Elementary School sued the board of education. They claimed that their children faced linguistic discrimination in the classroom.

The children, who lived in a neighborhood housing project, spoke Black English Vernacular (BEV, see the preceding chapter) at home. At school, most had encountered problems with their classwork. Some had been labeled "learning impaired" and placed in remedial reading courses. (Consider the embarrassment that children suffer and the effect on self-image of such labeling.)

The African-American parents and their attorney contended that the children had no intrinsic learning disabilities but simply did not understand everything their teachers said. Nor did their teachers always understand them. The lawyer argued that because BEV and Standard English (SE) are so similar, teachers often misinterpreted a child's correct pronunciation (in BEV) of an SE word as a reading error.

The children's attorney recruited several sociolinguists to testify on their behalf. The school board, by contrast, could not find a single qualified linguist to support its argument that there was no linguistic discrimination.

The judge ruled in favor of the children and ordered the following solution: Teachers at the King School had to attend a full-year course designed to improve their knowledge of nonstandard dialects, particularly BEV. The judge did not advocate that the teachers learn to speak BEV or that the children do their assignments in BEV. The school's goal remained to teach the children to use SE, the standard dialect, correctly. Before this could be accomplished, however, teachers and students alike had to learn how to recognize the differences between these similar dialects. At the end of the year most of the teachers interviewed in the local newspaper said the course had helped them.

In a diverse, multicultural populace, teachers should be sensitive to and knowledgeable about linguistic and cultural differences. Children need to be protected so that their ethnic or linguistic background is not used against them. That happens when a social variation is regarded as a learning disability.

URBAN ANTHROPOLOGY

By the twenty-first century, most people will be descendants of the non-Western groups that anthropologists have traditionally studied. By 2025 the developing countries will account for 85 percent of the

Most African cities have ethnic associations that link rural and urban social systems. In Kampala, Uganda, shown here, urban members of the Luo tribe are organized by traditional clan ties and rural areas of origin. Luo associations provide economic and moral support, including transportation of destitute people back to the country.

world's population, compared with 77 percent in 1992 (Stevens 1992). Solutions to future problems will depend increasingly on understanding non-Western cultural backgrounds. The Southern Hemisphere is steadily increasing its share of world population, and the fastest population growth rates are in Third World cities. The world had only 16 cities with more than a million people in 1900, but there were 276 such cities in 1990. By 2025, 60 percent of the global population will be urban, compared with 37 percent in 1990 (Stevens 1992). Rural migrants usually move to slums, where they live in hovels, without utilities and public sanitation facilities.

If current trends continue, urban population in-

crease and the concentration of people in slums will be accompanied by rising rates of crime and water, air, and noise pollution. These problems will be most severe in the less-developed countries. Almost all (97 percent) of the projected world population increase will occur in developing countries, 34 percent in Africa alone (Lewis 1992). Still, global population growth will also affect the Northern Hemisphere, through international migration.

As social complexity, industrialization, and urbanization spread globally, anthropologists increasingly study these processes and the social problems they create. Urban anthropology, which has theoretical (basic research) and applied dimensions, is the cross-cultural and ethnographic study of global urbanization and life in cities. The United States and Canada have also become popular arenas for urban anthropological research on topics such as ethnicity, poverty, class, and subcultural variations (Mullings, ed. 1987).

Urban versus Rural

Recognizing that a city (even a preindustrial one) is a social context that is very different from a tribal or peasant village, an early student of Third World urbanization, the anthropologist Robert Redfield, focused on contrasts between rural and urban life. He contrasted rural communities, whose social relations are on a face-to-face basis, with cities, where impersonality characterizes many aspects of life. Redfield (1941) proposed that urbanization be studied along a rural-urban continuum. He described differences in values and social relations in four sites that spanned such a continuum. In Mexico's Yucatán peninsula, Redfield compared an isolated Maya-speaking Indian community, a rural peasant village, a small provincial city, and a large capital. Several studies in Africa (Little 1971) and Asia were influenced by Redfield's view that cities are centers through which cultural innovations spread to rural and tribal areas.

In any nation, urban and rural represent different social systems. However, cultural diffusion occurs as people, products, and messages move from one to the other. Migrants bring rural practices and beliefs to town and take urban patterns back home. The experiences and social forms of the rural area affect adaptation to city life. For example, principles of tribal organization, including descent, provide migrants to African cities with coping mechanisms that Latin American peasants lack. City folk also develop new institutions to meet specific urban needs (Mitchell 1966).

African urban groups include ethnic associations, occupational groups, social clubs, religious groups, and burial societies. Through membership in these groups, urban Africans have networks of personal support. Ethnic or "tribal" associations, which build a bridge between one social system and another (rural and urban), are common both in West and East Africa (Little 1965; Banton 1957).

City dwellers from the Luo tribe in Kampala, Uganda (Parkin 1969), for example, are organized by migrants' clan ties and rural areas of origin. Luo associations provide economic and moral support, including transportation of destitute people back to the country. Nigerian associations also use a tribal-descent model to organize city dwellers, with extended families and lineages grouped into clans. The urban clans belong to district groups, which combine to make up the entire urban ethnic association. Although most members of such Nigerian urban associations are laborers, some are doctors, lawyers, and other professionals.

The ideology of such associations is that of a gigantic kin group. Members call one another "brother" and "sister." As in an extended family, rich members help their poor relatives. When members fight among themselves, the group acts as judge. A member's improper behavior can lead to expulsion—an unhappy fate for a migrant in an ethnically heterogeneous city.

Modern North American cities also have kin-based ethnic associations. One example comes from Los Angeles, which has the largest Samoan immigrant community (12,000 people) in the United States. Samoans in Los Angeles draw on their traditional system of *matai* (respect for elders) to deal with modern urban problems. For example, in 1992, a white policeman shot and killed two unarmed Samoan brothers. When a judge dismissed charges against the officer, local leaders used the *matai* system to calm angry youths (who have formed gangs, like other ethnic groups in the Los Angeles area). Clan leaders and elders organized a well-attended community meeting, in which they urged young members to be patient. Los Angeles Samoans aren't just traditionalists; they also use the American judicial system. They brought a civil case against the officer in question and pressed the U.S. Justice Department to initiate a civil-rights case in the matter (Mydans 1992b).

Urban Ethnic Groups, Poverty, and Crime

Kin-modeled, ethnic, and voluntary associations help reduce the stress of urban life on migrants. In North American cities such groups even play a role in organizing crime. Francis Ianni (1977) has studied

Kin-modeled, ethnic, and voluntary associations help reduce the stress of urban life on migrants. In the Los Angeles area, youths of many national backgrounds, like these Cambodians, have formed gangs.

criminal organizations among African-Americans and Hispanics. He views organized crime as a long-established feature of American economic life—a response to poverty and differential power. Ianni sees criminal organizations as representing one end of an economic continuum, with legitimate businesses at the other end.

Most African-Americans and Hispanics, even those who face severe poverty, don't become criminals. Historically, however, some poor ethnics have used crime as a route to financial and psychological security. Crime appears when legitimate economic opportunities are limited by unemployment, which is caused by state organization and industrialization. In nonstate societies people derive their subsistence from land, livestock, and natural resources. Everyone who wants to work can do so. Only states have joblessness.

Crime is also a creation of state organization. By definition, a crime is an illegal act, and only states have legal codes. According to Ianni, poverty and powerlessness rather than ethnic background cause crime. After all, in American history successive ethnic groups with very different cultural backgrounds (but facing similar conditions of poverty) have used crime to better themselves economically.

Ianni found that several types of personal relationships introduce African-American and Hispanic criminals to each other and to crime. Links between adult criminals often grow out of childhood friendships or membership in a gang. Commonly, however, boys begin their careers in crime as apprentices to older men. Established criminals, who become role models, recruit boys for criminal ventures. Links established in prison also lead to later criminal association. Women occasionally join criminal groups through male friends or husbands.

Once people are committed to crime, their common activity holds the networks together. Networks link partners, employers and employees, and buyers and sellers of goods and services. Social solidarity—an *esprit de corps*—cements criminal networks. The stronger this spirit is, the more successful the ventures in crime tend to be.

One kind of criminal association is the entrepreneurial organization, which Ianni compares to a legitimate business. Consisting of a head and the head's agents in illegality, it has a code of rules designed to protect itself and its activities. The rules stress secrecy (don't tell the police or nonmembers), honesty (don't cheat on members), and competence.

Ianni discusses the ethnic succession of crime in American cities. Segments of Italian, Cuban, Puerto Rican, African-American, and other ethnic groups have all used crime to escape poverty and powerlessness. However, the networks of each group have differed. Kinship is one of the most obvious differences. Kinship has played a stronger role in organizing Italian-American and Cuban-American criminals than it has in organizing African-American and Puerto Rican criminals.

Homelessness

In 1989 almost 13 percent of the American population (31.5 million people) lived below the official poverty level (*Statistical Abstract* 1991, p. 462). The poverty rate grew from 11.4 percent in 1978 to 12.8 percent in 1989. In that period the number of poor people—whom we meet every day on the streets of American cities—rose from 24.5 million to 31.5 million.

Middle-class and poorer American earners—rural and urban—lost ground in the 1980s. Seventy percent of the rise in family income between 1977 and 1989 went to the top 1 percent of the population (Nasar 1992). The top 5 percent got 24 percent of total national income in 1989, up from 18 percent in 1977. The share of national income received by the bottom 60 percent declined from 34 to 29 percent in the same period (Nasar 1992).

Much of the poverty in industrial nations is caused by unemployment. The ongoing North American economic shift from manufacturing to services and information processing demands a better-educated and more skillful work force. Poorly educated people find it harder to make a living. In the United States and throughout the world, members of the **underclass** (the abjectly poor) lack jobs, adequate food, medical care, even shelter.

Poverty and homelessness are obvious on the streets of big cities. For example, millions of rural Brazilians have migrated to burgeoning urban shanty towns (*favelas*). Abandoned children camp in the streets, bathe in fountains, beg, rob, and scavenge like their homeless counterparts in North America.

Homelessness in North America is an extreme form of downward mobility, which may follow job loss, layoffs, or situations in which women and children flee from domestic abuse. The causes of homelessness are varied—psychological, economic, and

Poverty is particularly obvious in big cities throughout the world. Millions of rural Brazilians have settled in burgeoning urban shanty towns (favelas), *such as this one in Rio de Janeiro.*

social. They include inability to pay rent, eviction, sale of urban real estate to developers, and mental illness. In New York City many of the urban poor sleep in cardboard cartons and at train stations, on sidewalks and near warm-air gratings. They feed themselves by begging, scavenging, and raiding garbage (particularly that of restaurants) for food. The homeless are the foragers of modern society. They are poorly clad urban nomads, shaggy men and bag ladies who carry their meager possessions with them as they move.

Today's most extreme socioeconomic contrasts within the world capitalist economy are between the richest people in core nations and the poorest people on the periphery. However, as the gap between rich and poor has widened in North America, the social distance between the underclasses of core and periphery has shrunk. The road to Bangladesh passes through Times Square.

MEDICAL ANTHROPOLOGY

Both biological and cultural, both academic and applied, anthropologists work in **medical anthropology**. This growing field considers the sociocultural context and implications of disease and illness. **Disease** refers to an etic or scientifically identified health threat caused by a bacterium, virus, fungus, parasite, or other pathogen. **Illness** is an emic condition of poor health felt by an individual (Inhorn

and Brown 1990). Cross-cultural research shows that perceptions of good and bad health, along with health threats and problems, are culturally constructed. Different ethnic groups and cultures recognize different illnesses, symptoms, and causes and have developed different health-care systems and treatment strategies.

Disease also varies among cultures and with culture type. Traditional and ancient foragers, because of their small numbers, mobility, and relative isolation from other groups, lacked most of the epidemic infectious disease that affect agrarian and urban societies (Inhorn and Brown 1990; Cohen and Armelagos, eds. 1984). Epidemic diseases like cholera, typhoid, and bubonic plague thrive in dense populations, and thus among farmers and city dwellers. The spread of malaria has been linked to population growth and deforestation associated with food production.

Certain diseases have spread with economic development. **Schistosomiasis** (liver flukes) is probably the fastest-spreading and most dangerous parasitic infection now known (Heyneman 1984). It is propagated by snails that live in ponds, lakes, and waterways, usually ones created by irrigation projects. A study done in a Nile Delta village in Egypt (Farooq 1966) illustrated the role of culture (religion) in the spread of schistosomiasis. The disease was more common among Muslims than among Christians because of an Islamic practice called *wudu*, ritual ablution (bathing) before prayer.

IN THE NEWS: AIDS AND GENDER IN AFRICA

In Africa AIDS and other sexually transmitted diseases are spreading along highways and rivers, mainly via encounters between male travelers and female prostitutes. AIDS is also spread as men move from rural areas to cities, where they engage in wage work—and casual sex. Later the men infect their wives. Focusing on the increasing threat to women, this article reports on the heterosexual transmission of AIDS in the Third World.

Amsterdam, July 20—Women throughout the world are becoming infected with the virus that causes AIDS about as often as men, and by the year 2000 most new infections will be in women, the World Health Organization's leading official on the disease told an international meeting here today.

Worldwide since Jan. 1, "close to half of the one million newly infected adults have been women," said Dr. Michael H. Merson, who heads W.H.O.'s global program on AIDS. He added that "women's rising infection rates have been accompanied by a corresponding rise in the number of children born to them infected with H.I.V.," the virus that causes AIDS.

Also, millions of infants may escape infection but are destined to become AIDS orphans when their mothers die.

In the first few years after the discovery of AIDS in 1981, gay men in urban areas accounted for about two-thirds of all AIDS cases in adults in the United States, Europe and parts of Latin America. But more recently, that proportion has fallen due to an increasing trend for heterosexual women to become infected through sexual intercourse with infected men.

"The disease is now everywhere, and we want to get home the point that the AIDS epidemic is becoming heterosexual everywhere," Dr. Merson said in an interview.

The growing number of H.I.V.-infected women reflects the surge in the epidemic in third world countries. W.H.O. estimates that from 10 million to 12 million adults and 1 million children have been infected. The overwhelming majority are in Africa and Asia. By the year 2000, W.H.O. estimates, up to 40 million people will be infected. But the Global AIDS Policy Coalition, based at Harvard University, has said the number could reach 110 million.

"The virus is following roads and navigable rivers deeper and deeper into the countryside," Dr. Merson said. "Tomorrow we can expect little difference between urban and rural areas."

To combat AIDS, health workers must find out what has worked in some areas and apply it on a wider basis, Dr. Merson said, echoing remarks made a month ago by Dr. Jonathan Mann, the director of the International AIDS Center at Harvard.

Dr. Merson and others said that women had to be empowered to have more control over their health. Women at the meeting have urged quick licensing of female condoms and greater research efforts to develop germicides that kill H.I.V. and other microbes that are spread by sex while still allowing the option of pregnancy.

The meeting participants, who number more than 11,000, were told of a recent study of women attending a clinic in Rwanda in Africa where one-fourth of those with only one lifetime sex partner had been infected with H.I.V., pre-

---

In eastern Africa AIDS and other sexually transmitted diseases (STDs) have spread along highways, via encounters between male truckers and female prostitutes. STDs are also spread through prostitution as young men from rural areas seek wage work in cities, labor camps, and mines. When the men return to their natal villages, they infect their wives (Larson 1989; Miller and Rockwell, eds. 1988). Cities have also been prime sites of STD transmission in Europe, Asia, and North and South America.

We see that the incidence of particular diseases varies between societies, and cultures interpret and treat illness differently. Standards for sick and healthy bodies are cultural constructions that vary in time and space (Martin 1992). Still, all societies have what George Foster and Barbara Anderson (1978) call "disease-theory systems" to identify, classify, and explain illness. According to Foster and Anderson (1978), there are three basic theories about the causes of illness: personalistic, naturalistic, and emotionalistic. **Personalistic disease theories** blame illness on agents (often malicious), such as sorcerers, witches, ghosts, or ancestral spirits. **Naturalistic disease theories** explain illness in impersonal terms. One example is Western medicine or **biomedicine,** which links illness to scientifically demonstrated agents, which bear no personal malice toward their victims. Thus Western medicine attributes illness to

sumably by their steady partner.

Dr. Mann, who is chairman of the international AIDS meeting here, said in an interview that the AIDS epidemic had shown that "male-dominated societies are a threat to public health" because women have less power to protect themselves from disease.

Even though the infection rate for women is increasing, surprising new evidence from studies reported today shows that women do not die of AIDS faster than men, as had been thought, and that there are no gender differences in the occurrence of H.I.V.-related illnesses. The findings came from teams in Atlanta, Chicago, New York City and the National Institutes of Health, a Federal agency in Bethesda, Md., and run counter to studies reported several years ago.

W.H.O. has urged the wider distribution of condoms as well as campaigns to motivate behavioral change as two chief ways to combat the spread of H.I.V. infections.

Population Services International, a nonprofit organization in Washington, said it had been successful in increasing the use of condoms in Zaire in Africa, one of the countries hit hardest by AIDS, through a Madison Avenue tech-nique called social marketing. Condoms are distributed through pharmacies, grocery stores, bars, restaurants, movie theaters and clinics.

Last August, 3.6 million condoms were sold through that group's program, compared with 300,000 condoms for the entire year of 1988. Richard A. Frank, president of Population Services International, said such condom use had averted an estimated 7,200 cases of H.I.V. infection.

The program has been expanded to include 10 other African countries, and an additional program is targeted at prostitutes in Bombay, India.

Mr. Frank cited United States Census Bureau figures estimating that a 20 percent increase in condom use in the cities of developing countries could reduce the level of H.I.V. infection in those areas in the year 2015 by approximately one-half.

Anke A. Ehrhardt of the New York State Psychiatric Institute and Columbia University criticized the meager data about sexual behavior and changes in such behavior in the United States. She said, "Efforts to assess sexual behavior, design prevention programs, and to rigorously assess their effectiveness have been hampered by a battle between social scientists and representatives of religious and moralizing groups."

She told the participants that prevention messages to women and men needed to be gender-specific. "To make condom use the norm, we must particularly target heterosexual men," she said. "At the same time, women need to be given messages and tools that they can truly control." She said condom use was not a method that women could control.

Dr. Stephen Mills of the San Francisco Department of Health reported findings from a study showing "compelling evidence that Magic Johnson's H.I.V. diagnosis had the profound behavioral effect of motivating men and women to get tested for H.I.V." The effect was most profound among women, Dr. Mills said. He suggested that the influence of publicity about celebrities was underutilized in preventing AIDS.

Source: Lawrence K. Altman, "Women Worldwide Nearing Higher Rate for AIDS Than Men," *The New York Times,* July 21, 1992, pp. C1, C3.

---

organisms (e.g., bacteria, viruses, fungi, or parasites) or toxic materials. Other naturalistic ethnomedical systems blame poor health on unbalanced body fluids. Many Latin cultures classify food, drink, and environmental conditions as "hot" or "cold." People believe their health suffers when they eat or drink hot or cold substances together or under inappropriate conditions. One shouldn't drink something cold after a hot bath or eat a pineapple (a "cold" fruit) when one is menstruating (a "hot" condition).

Emotionalistic disease theories assume that emotional experiences cause illness. For example, Latin Americans may develop *susto,* an illness caused by anxiety or fright (Bolton 1981; Finkler et al. 1984). Its symptoms (lethargy, vagueness, distraction) are similar to those of "soul loss," a diagnosis of similar symptoms made by people in Madagascar. Modern psychoanalysis also focuses on the role of the emotions in physical and psychological well-being.

All societies have **health-care systems**—beliefs, customs, specialists, and techniques aimed at ensuing health and preventing, diagnosing, and curing illness. A society's illness-causation theory is important for treatment. When illness has a personalistic cause, shamans and other magicoreligious specialists may be good curers. They draw on varied techniques (occult and practical), which comprise their special expertise. A shaman may cure soul loss by enticing the spirit back into the body. Shamans may ease difficult childbirths by asking spirits to travel up the vagina and guide the baby out (Lévi-Strauss 1967). A shaman may cure a cough by counteracting a curse or removing a substance introduced by a sorcerer.

All cultures have health-care specialists. If there is a "world's oldest profession" besides hunter and gatherer, it is **curer,** or shaman. The curer's role has some universal features (Foster and Anderson 1978). Thus curers emerge through a culturally defined process of selection (parental prodding, inheritance, visions, dream instructions) and training (apprentice shamanship, medical school). Eventually, the curer is certified by older practitioners and acquires a professional image. Patients believe in the skills of the curer, whom they consult and compensate.

Non-Western systems (traditional medicine) offer some lessons for Western medicine. For example, traditional practitioners may have more success treating certain mental conditions than psychiatrists or psychotherapists do. Non-Western systems may explain mental illness by causes that are easier to identify and combat. Thus it may be simpler to rid a body of a spirit possessor than to undo all the damage that a Freudian might attribute to an Oed-

ipus complex. Curing may be an intense community ritual in which the shaman heals by temporarily taking on and then rejecting the patient's illness (Lévi-Strauss 1967). In modern mental institutions, by contrast, no prior social ties link patients to each other or to doctors and nurses. Mental illness is viewed as the patient's individual burden. The context of treatment is often one of isolation and alienation—separation of the afflicted person from society—rather than participation by a group in a common ritual.

We should not lose sight, ethnocentrically, of the difference between **scientific medicine** and Western medicine per se (Lieban 1977). Despite advances in pathology, microbiology, biochemistry, surgery, diagnostic technology, and applications, many Western medical procedures have little justification in logic or fact. Overprescription of tranquilizers and drugs, unnecessary surgery, and the impersonality and inequality of the physician-patient relationship are questionable features of Western medical systems.

Still, biomedicine surpasses tribal treatment in many ways. Although medicines like quinine, coca, opium, ephedrine, and rauwolfia were discovered in nonindustrial societies, traditional medicines aren't as effective against bacteria as antibiotics are. Preventive health care has improved during the twentieth century. Today's surgical procedures are

Western medicine and scientific medicine are not the same thing. Many Western medical procedures have no clear justification, but scientific medicine surpasses tribal health-care systems in several ways. Clinics such as this one bring antibiotics, minor surgery, and preventive medicine to the Masai of Kenya.

safer and more effective than those of traditional societies.

But industrialization has spawned its own health problems. Modern stressors include noise, air and water pollution, poor nutrition, dangerous machinery, impersonal work, isolation, poverty, homelessness, and substance abuse. Health problems in industrial nations are due as much to economic, social, political, and cultural factors as to pathogens. In modern North America, for example, poverty contributes to many illnesses, including arthritis, heart conditions, back problems, and hearing and vision impairment. Poverty is even a factor in the differential spread of infectious diseases.

Medical anthropology, which is based on biological, sociocultural, and cross-cultural research, has theoretical and applied dimensions. Anthropologists have served as cultural interpreters in public health programs, which must pay attention to native theories about the nature, causes, and treatment of illness. Successful health interventions are not forced on communities; they must fit into local cultures and be accepted by local people. When Western medicine is introduced, people usually retain many of their old methods while also accepting new ones (see Green 1987). Native curers may go on treating certain conditions (like *susto* or spirit possession), whereas M.D.s may deal with others. If both modern and traditional specialists are consulted and the patient is cured, the native curer may get more credit than the physician.

A more personal treatment of illness that emulates the non-Western curer-patient-community relationship could help Western systems. Western medicine tends to draw a rigid line between biological and psychological causation. Non-Western theories usually lack this sharp distinction, recognizing that poor health has intertwined physical, emotional, and social causes. The mind-body opposition is part of Western folk taxonomy, not of science.

Non-Western practitioners typically treat symptoms, instead of seeking causes, and their aim—and often their result—is an immediate cure. Traditional curers often succeed with health problems that biomedicine classifies as "psychosomatic" (not a disease, therefore not an illness) and dismisses as not requiring treatment—despite the feelings of the ill patient. Non-Western systems tell us that patients can be treated effectively as whole beings, using any combination of methods that prove beneficial.

SOCIAL WORK, BUSINESS, AND MEDIA ANTHROPOLOGY

A program of study linking anthropology and social work began at the University of Michigan in Ann Arbor in 1981. After obtaining master's degrees in both fields, students use anthropological techniques in their doctoral research. One recent example involves the design and evaluation of a culturally appropriate alcoholism treatment strategy for a Native American community. The main difference between this kind of research and traditional doctoral research in anthropology is that anthropology–social work dissertations use research to guide social policy.

Carol Taylor (1978) discusses the value of an "anthropologist-in-residence" in a complex organization such as a hospital. A free-ranging ethnographer can be a perceptive oddball when information and decisions usually move through a rigid hierarchy. If allowed to converse freely with all levels of personnel, from orderly to chief surgeon, the anthropologist may acquire a unique perspective on organizational conditions and problems.

For many years anthropologists have used ethnography to study businesses (Arensberg 1978), working directly with workers, managers, planners, and executives (Serrie, ed. 1986). For example, ethnographic research in an auto factory views workers, managers, and executives as different social categories participating in a common social system. Each group has characteristic attitudes, values, and behavior patterns. These are transmitted through **microenculturation**, the process by which people learn particular roles in a limited social system. The free-ranging nature of ethnography takes the anthropologist from worker to executive. Each of these people is both an individual with a personal viewpoint and a cultural creature whose perspective is, to some extent, shared with other members of a group. Applied anthropologists have acted as "cultural brokers," translating managers' goals or workers' concerns to the other group.

Not just ethnography but the cross-cultural perspective is of interest to business, especially when other nations have higher productivity than we do (Ferraro 1990). The reasons for differential productivity are cultural, social, and economic. To find them, anthropologists must focus on key features in the organization of production. For example, Japanese auto workers earn less but have more secure jobs than do their American counterparts. The salary differential between worker and executive is greater in the United States. There is less of an economic basis for an adversary relationship between workers and management in Japan.

Furthermore, Japanese businesses use varied techniques to increase productivity (McGraw, ed. 1986). Profit sharing enhances company loyalty. More subtle social and symbolic techniques also strengthen the social fiber. Solidarity enhancers vary from culture to culture but may include common meals, agreeable working conditions, distinctive costumes or work uniforms, and joint participation in special company events and "rituals."

Because cultural anthropologists have always studied values, attitudes, and opinions, anthropology links up with media research and advertising (Eiselein and Topper 1976; Kottak 1990). The media play a powerful integrative role in contemporary culture (see the chapter "Cultural Exchange and Survival" and the Appendix). The popularity, themes, and content of television, films, and literature reflect underlying culture. It is obvious to many anthropologists that advertising uses techniques borrowed from religion to sell products (Arens and Montague 1981; Kottak, ed. 1982). Similarly, contemporary religion—particularly televangelism—uses techniques borrowed from advertising to propagate religion. The media both reflect and influence the beliefs, attitudes, opinions, and behavior of the natives at whom they are aimed.

CAREERS IN ANTHROPOLOGY

Many students find anthropology interesting and consider majoring in it. However, their parents or friends may discourage them by asking, "What kind of job are you going to get with an anthropology major?" The purpose of this section is to answer that question. You may want to show it to your parents and other skeptics if you decide to take additional anthropology courses or to major in the field.

The first step in answering "What do you do with an anthropology major?" is to consider the more general question "What do you do with any college major?" The answer is "Not much, without a good bit of effort, thought, and planning." A survey of graduates of the literary college of the University of Michigan showed that few had jobs that were clearly linked to their majors. Medicine, law, and many other professions require advanced degrees. Although many colleges offer bachelor's degrees in engineering, business, accounting, and social work, master's degrees are often needed to get the best jobs in those fields.

A broad college education, and even a major in anthropology, can be an excellent basis for success

Solidarity-enhancers used by businesses include common meals, distinctive costumes or work uniforms, and joint participation in special company events and "rituals." In Japan, this sake distillery uses calisthenics to promote physical fitness and social solidarity among its employees.

in many fields. A recent survey of women executives showed that most had not majored in business but in the social sciences or humanities. Only after graduating did they study business, obtaining a master's degree in business administration. These executives felt that the breadth of their college educations had contributed to their business careers. Anthropology majors go on to medical, law, and business schools and find success in many professions that often have little explicit connection to anthropology.

Anthropology's breadth provides knowledge and an outlook on the world that are useful in many kinds of work. For example, an anthropology major combined with a master's degree in business is excellent preparation for work in international business and economic development. However, job seekers must convince employers that they have a special and valuable "skillset."

Breadth is anthropology's hallmark. Anthropologists study people biologically, culturally, socially, and linguistically, in time and space, in developed and underdeveloped nations, in simple and complex settings. Most colleges have anthropology courses that compare cultures and others that focus on particular world areas, such as Latin America, Asia, and Native North America. The knowledge of foreign areas acquired in such courses can be useful in many jobs. Anthropology's comparative outlook, its longstanding Third World focus, and its appreciation of diverse life styles combine to provide an excellent foundation for overseas employment.

Even for work in North America, the focus on culture is valuable. Every day we hear about cultural differences, about social problems whose solutions require a multicultural viewpoint—an ability to recognize and reconcile ethnic differences. Government, schools, and private firms constantly deal with people from different social classes, ethnic groups, and tribal backgrounds. Physicians, attorneys, social workers, police officers, judges, teachers, and students can all do a better job if they understand social differences in a part of the world that is one of the most ethnically diverse in history.

The cross-cultural perspective is one reason why many North American businesses have become interested in anthropology. Business practices in other cultures can suggest techniques that improve efficiency here. A trend in many business schools is to recognize that organizations include **microcul-**tures—several restricted social circles and traditions of particular social groups within a complex organization. (In a plant these might involve assembly-line workers, union representatives, professionals, middle managers, engineers, and top management.) Microcultures have different viewpoints, goals, and perceptions. Along with organizational psychologists, anthropologists have worked to increase communication between levels and microcultures. Often there is a need to reduce social distinctions and enhance company loyalty in order to increase worker productivity and profits. An ethnographic focus on behavior in the daily social setting can help locate problems that plague American businesses, which tend to be overly hierarchical.

Attention to the social dimension of business can only gain importance. More and more executives recognize that proper human relations are as important as economic forecasts are in maximizing productivity. Applied anthropologists design plans for deploying employees better and increasing job satisfaction. This is part of "the new humanism," which is of growing importance as a management strategy. A noted proponent of this approach, James O'Toole, a management professor in southern California and editor of *New Management* magazine, has a Ph.D. in anthropology from Oxford.

Anthropologists also work to help natives threatened by external systems. As highways and power-supply systems cross tribal boundaries, the "modern" world comes into conflict with historic land claims and traditions. An anthropological study is often considered necessary before permission is granted to extend a public system across native lands.

Because dams, reservoirs, and other works may threaten archeological sites, fields such as salvage archeology and cultural resource management have developed. Government agencies, engineering firms, and construction companies now have jobs for people with an anthropological background because of legislation to protect historic and prehistoric sites.

Knowledge about the traditions and beliefs of subgroups within a nation is important in planning and carrying out programs that affect those subgroups. Attention to social background and cultural categories helps ensure the welfare of affected ethnic groups, communities, and neighborhoods. Experience in planned social changes—whether

CULTURE AND INTERNATIONAL MARKETING

Innovation succeeds best when it is culturally appropriate. This axiom of applied anthropology could guide the international spread of businesses, such as fast food. Each time McDonald's or Burger King expands to a new nation, it must devise a culturally appropriate strategy for fitting into the new setting.

McDonald's has been successful internationally, with a quarter of its sales outside the United States. One area where McDonald's is expanding successfully is Brazil, where 30 to 40 million middle-class people, most living in densely packed cities, provide a concentrated market for a fast-food chain. Still, it took McDonald's some time to find the right marketing strategy for Brazil.

In 1980 I visited Brazil after a seven-year absence. One manifestation of Brazil's growing participation in the world economy was the appearance of two McDonald's restaurants in Rio de Janeiro. There wasn't much difference between Brazilian and American McDonald's. The restaurants looked alike. The menu was more or less the same, as was the taste of the quarter-pounders. I picked up an artifact, a white paper bag with yellow lettering, exactly like the take-out bags then used in American McDonald's. An advertising device, it carried several messages about how Brazilians could bring McDonald's into their lives. However, it seemed to me that McDonald's Brazilian ad campaign was missing some important points about how fast food should be marketed in a culture that values large, leisurely lunches.

The bag proclaimed, "You're going to enjoy the [McDonald's] difference," and listed several "favorite places where you can enjoy McDonald's products." This list confirmed that the marketing people were trying to adapt to Brazilian middle-class culture, but they were making some mistakes. "When you go out in the car with the kids" transferred the uniquely developed North American cultural combination of highways, affordable cars, and suburban living to the very different context of urban Brazil. A similar suggestion was "traveling to the country place." Even Brazilians who own country places can't find McDonald's, still confined to the cities, on the road. The ad creator had apparently never attempted to drive up to a fast-food restaurant in a neighborhood with no parking spaces.

Several other suggestions pointed customers toward the beach, where *cariocas* (Rio natives) do spend much of their leisure time. One could eat McDonald's products "after a dip in the ocean," "at a picnic at the beach," or "watching the surfers." These suggestions ignored the Brazilian custom of consuming cold things, such as beer, soft drinks, ice cream,

---

community organization in North America or economic development overseas—shows that a proper social study should be done before a project begins. When local people want the change and it fits their life style and traditions, it will be more successful, beneficial, and cost-effective. There will be not only a more humane but a more economical solution to a real social problem.

Some agencies working overseas place a special value on anthropological training. Others seek employees with certain skills without caring much about specific academic backgrounds. Among the government agencies that hire anthropologists are **USAID** (the United States Agency for International Development) and **USDA** (the United States Department of Agriculture). These organizations hire anthropologists both full-time and as short-term consultants.

Several consulting firms with "social experts" are located near Washington, D.C. Although these firms have regular staffs, they also use outside experts for particular projects. For instance, I was once offered a part-time consultancy requiring fluency in French and Portuguese and research experience among rice cultivators and fishermen. My work among fishermen in Brazil and rice farmers in Madagascar made me one of a limited number of people qualified to do the social planning for a group of development projects in two African nations. The **World Bank** (the International Bank for Reconstruction and Development, or **IBRD**), along with USAID, USDA, and other such organizations, often hires anthropologists for this type of work abroad.

Private voluntary organizations working overseas offer other opportunities. These **PVOs** (a kind of NGO) include Care, Save the Children, Catholic

and ham and cheese sandwiches, at the beach. Brazilians don't consider a hot, greasy hamburger proper beach food. They view the sea as "cold" and hamburgers as "hot"; they avoid "hot" foods at the beach.

Also culturally dubious was the suggestion to eat McDonald's hamburgers "lunching at the office." Brazilians prefer their main meal at midday, often eating at a leisurely pace with business associates. Many firms serve ample lunches to their employees. Other workers take advantage of a two-hour lunch break to go home to eat with the spouse and children. Nor did it make sense to suggest that children should eat hamburgers for lunch, since most kids attend school for half-day sessions and have lunch at home. Two other suggestions— "waiting for the bus" and "in the beauty parlor"—did describe common aspects of daily life in a Brazilian city. However, these settings have not proved especially inviting to hamburgers or fish filets.

The homes of Brazilians who can afford McDonald's products have cooks and maids to do many of the things that fast-food restaurants do in the United States. The suggestion that McDonald's products be eaten "while watching your favorite television program" is culturally appropriate, because Brazilians watch TV a lot. However, Brazil's consuming classes can ask the cook to make a snack when hunger strikes. Indeed, much televiewing occurs during the light dinner served when the husband gets home from the office.

Most appropriate to the Brazilian life style was the suggestion to enjoy McDonald's "on the cook's day off." Throughout Brazil, Sunday is that day. The Sunday pattern for middle-class families is a trip to the beach, liters of beer, a full midday meal around 3 P.M., and a light evening snack. McDonald's has found its niche in the Sunday evening meal, when families flock to the fast-food restaurant, and it is to this market

that its advertising is now appropriately geared.

McDonald's is expanding rapidly in Brazilian cities, and in Brazil as in North America, teenage appetites are fueling the fast-food explosion. As McDonald's outlets appeared in urban neighborhoods, Brazilian teenagers used them for after-school snacks, while families had evening meals there. As an anthropologist could have predicted, the fast-food industry has not revolutionized Brazilian food and meal customs. Rather, McDonald's is succeeding because it has adapted to preexisting Brazilian cultural patterns.

The main contrast with North America is that the Brazilian evening meal is lighter. McDonald's now caters to the evening meal rather than to lunch. Once McDonald's realized that more money could be made by fitting in with, rather than trying to Americanize, Brazilian meal habits, it started aiming its advertising at that goal.

Relief Services, Foster Parents Plan International, and Oxfam (a hunger-relief organization operating out of Boston and Oxford). Some of these groups employ anthropologists full-time. Anthropologists, including anthropology majors seeking overseas employment, should consult the book *Who Owns Whom in North America* (1984), which lists organizations with international divisions.

Anthropologists apply their expertise in diverse areas. They negotiate business deals, suggest organizational changes, and testify as expert witnesses. Anthropologists have also worked for pharmaceutical firms interested in potential conflicts between traditional and Western medicine and in culturally appropriate marketing of their products in new settings. Other anthropologists are working to help native peoples get a share of the profits when their traditional remedies, including medicinal plants, are marketed by drug companies.

People with anthropology backgrounds are doing well in many fields. Furthermore, even if the job has little or nothing to do with anthropology in a formal or obvious sense, anthropology is always useful when we work with fellow human beings. For most of us, this means every day of our lives.

SUMMARY

Applied anthropology is the application of anthropological data, perspectives, theory, and methods to identify, assess, and solve contemporary social problems. Applied (or practicing) anthropologists work for governments, nongovernmental organizations, tribal, ethnic, and interest groups, businesses, social services, and educational agencies. In the 1940s most anthropologists focused on practical problems, but academic anthropology grew substantially in the 1950s and 1960s, as the baby boom fueled educational expansion. Applied anthropology started growing again in the 1970s, after the end of the Vietnam War.

Applied anthropology draws its practitioners from biological, archeological, linguistic, and cultural anthropology. Ethnography has become one of applied anthropology's most valuable research tools, along with the comparative, cross-cultural perspective. Holism allows applied anthropologists to perceive the biological, social, cultural, and linguistic dimensions of policy issues. A systemic perspective helps anthropologists recognize that all changes have multiple consequences, some unintended.

Applied anthropology has many domains. Anthropology and education researchers work in classrooms, homes, neighborhoods, and other settings relevant to education. Some of their research leads to policy recommendations. Courses in cultural anthropology and sociolinguistics are making teachers more aware of how linguistic and ethnic differences should be handled in the classroom.

As complex societies expand, anthropologists increasingly study such societies and the issues involved in their expansion. Urban anthropology includes the study of life in cities and the process of urbanization that affects people throughout the world. The United States has become a popular arena for urban anthropological research on topics such as ethnicity, poverty, class, and subcultural variation.

Rural social relations are personal and face to face, but impersonality characterizes many aspects of life in cities. Although urban and rural are different social systems, there is cultural diffusion from one to the other. Rural and tribal social forms affect adjustment to the city. For example, principles of tribal organization, including descent, provide migrants to African cities with adaptive mechanisms. Urban associations have also been important in organizing crime among segments of certain ethnic groups in the United States. Crime has been linked to poverty and powerlessness rather than to the subcultural norms of ethnic groups.

Medical anthropology unites biological and cultural, theoretical and applied, anthropologists in the cross-cultural study of health problems and conditions, disease, illness, disease theories, and health-care systems. Characteristic diseases reflect diet, population density, economy, and social complexity. The three main native theories of illness are personalistic, naturalistic, and emotionalistic. *Personalistic causes* refer to such agents as witches and sorcerers. In this context, shamans can be effective curers. Western medicine, or biomedicine, is not the same as scientific medicine. The latter has made many advances, particularly in bacterial diseases and surgery. However, a non-Western treatment of psychosomatic illness is often more effective, because it occurs in a personal, community-support context with no rigid distinction drawn between mind and body.

Ethnography has also proved useful in studying businesses, factories, and hospitals. Free-ranging anthropologists translate messages and viewpoints between microcultures and hierarchical levels in complex organizations. Research on work organization in other countries can enlighten North American businesses. Anthropologists also study the mass media, showing their reflection of cultural themes and their role in enculturating and in promoting social change.

A broad college education, including anthropology and foreign-area courses, offers excellent preparation for many fields. Anthropology's comparative outlook, long-standing Third World focus, and cultural relativism provide an excellent basis for overseas employment. Among the agencies that hire anthropologists are USAID, USDA, independent consulting firms, the World Bank, and such private voluntary organizations as Care, Save the Children, Catholic Relief Services, Foster Parents Plan International, and Oxfam.

Even for work in North America, a focus on culture is valuable. Anthropological training is useful in dealing with issues that reflect cultural contrasts and problems whose solutions require an ability to recognize and reconcile social or ethnic differences. The cross-cultural perspective and the focus on daily social life of anthropologists help locate problems that plague American businesses, which tend to be too hierarchical. Anthropologists have worked for and with natives threatened by external systems. Anthropology majors attend medical, law, and business schools and succeed in many fields, some of which have little explicit connection with anthropology.

Experience with social-change programs, whether community organization in North America or economic development abroad, offers a common lesson. If local people want the change and if the change fits their life style and traditions, the change will be more successful, beneficial, and cost-effective.

GLOSSARY

anthropology and education: Anthropological research in classrooms, homes, and neighborhoods, viewing students as total cultural creatures whose enculturation and attitudes toward education belong to a larger context that includes family, peers, and society.

applied anthropology: The application of anthropological data, perspectives, theory, and methods to identify, assess, and solve contemporary social problems.

biomedicine: Western medicine, which attributes illness to scientifically demonstrated agents—biological organisms (e.g., bacteria, viruses, fungi, or parasites) or toxic materials.

curer: Specialized role acquired through a culturally appropriate process of selection, training, certification, and acquisition of a professional image; the curer is consulted by patients, who believe in his or her special powers, and receives some form of special consideration; a cultural universal.

disease: An etic or scientifically identified health threat caused by a bacterium, virus, fungus, parasite, or other pathogen.

emotionalistic disease theories: Theories that assume that illness is caused by intense emotional experiences.

health-care systems: Beliefs, customs, and specialists concerned with ensuring health and preventing and curing illness; a cultural universal.

IBRD: See *World Bank.*

illness: An emic condition of poor health felt by an individual.

medical anthropology: Unites biological and cultural anthropologists in the study of disease, health problems, health-care systems, and theories about illness in different cultures and ethnic groups.

microculture: Restricted traditions of particular social groups within a complex organization. See *microenculturation.*

microenculturation: The process by which people learn particular roles in a limited social system; creates microcultures.

naturalistic disease theories: Includes scientific medicine; theories that explain illness in impersonal systemic terms.

nongovernmental organizations (NGOs): Subsumes PVOs.

personalistic disease theories: Theories that attribute illness to sorcerers, witches, ghosts, or ancestral spirits.

private voluntary organizations (PVOs): Nongovernmental organizations such as Care, Save the Children, Catholic Relief Services, Foster Parents Plan International, and Oxfam.

salvage archeology: Branch of applied archeology aimed at preserving sites threatened by dams, highways, and other projects.

schistosomiasis: Disease caused by liver flukes transmitted by snails inhabiting ponds, lakes, and waterways, often created by irrigation projects.

scientific medicine: As distinguished from Western medicine, a health-care system based on scientific knowledge and procedures, encompassing such fields as pathology, microbiology, biochemistry, surgery, diagnostic technology, and applications.

systemic perspective: View that changes have multiple consequences, some unforeseen.

underclass: The abjectly poor.

USAID: The United States Agency for International Development.

USDA: The United States Department of Agriculture.

World Bank: Also called the *International Bank for Reconstruction and Development (IBRD);* a major international lending organization that funds development projects.

STUDY QUESTIONS

1. What is applied anthropology? Is is the same as practicing anthropology?
2. What are the main professional groups of applied anthropologists?
3. How did the baby boom affect academic and applied anthropology?
4. What is the ethnographic method? What is its relevance for modern society, contemporary problems, and applied anthropology?
5. Why have many anthropologists turned from academic to applied work?
6. What is educational anthropology, and what are its applications?
7. What is urban anthropology, and what are its applications?
8. What causes crime? Why is crime a creation of the state?

9. What is medical anthropology, and what are its applications?
10. How can anthropology be relevant to business?
11. How can anthropology be relevant to the study of the media?
12. What is the relevance of anthropological training to employment opportunities abroad?
13. How has federal legislation concerning historic and prehistoric sites affected anthropologists?
14. What governmental, international, and private organizations concern themselves with socioeconomic change abroad?

SUGGESTED ADDITIONAL READING

DOUGLAS, M., AND A. WILDAVSKY
1982   *Risk and Culture: An Essay on the Selection of Technological and Environmental Dangers.* Berkeley: University of California Press. Controversial analysis and comparison of ideologies concerning environmental threats and risk perception in tribal and industrial societies.

EDDY, E. M., AND W. L. PARTRIDGE, EDS.
1978   *Applied Anthropology in America.* New York: Columbia University Press. Historical review of applications of anthropological knowledge in the United States.

FERRARO, GARY
1990   *The Cultural Dimension of International Business.* Englewood Cliffs, NJ: Prentice-Hall. Culture matters; Ferraro applies this to international business and intercultural communication.

FOSTER, G. M., AND B. G. ANDERSON
1978   *Medical Anthropology.* New York: Wiley. Thorough introduction to this field.

HUMAN ORGANIZATION
The quarterly journal of the Society for Applied Anthropology. An excellent source for articles on applied anthropology and development.

JANES, C. R., R. STALL, AND S. M. GIFFORD, EDS.
1986   *Anthropology and Epidemiology: Interdisciplinary Approaches to the Study of Health and Disease.* Dordrecht: D. Reidel. Eleven articles explore historical and theoretical perspectives, infectious diseases (e.g., AIDS), noninfectious diseases (e.g., hypertension), and psychosocial conditions (e.g., colonial stress, alcohol use).

JOHNSON, T. J., AND C. F. SARGENT, EDS.
1990   *Medical Anthropology: A Handbook of Theory and Method.* New York: Greenwood. Nineteen articles cover theoretical perspectives, medical systems, health issues, methods in medical anthropology, and issues of policy and advocacy.

McGRAW, T. K., ED.
1986   *America versus Japan.* Boston: Harvard Business School Press. A collection of articles dealing with Japanese and American business interactions.

MILLER, N., AND R. C. ROCKWELL, EDS.
1988   *AIDS in Africa: The Social and Policy Impact.* Lewiston: Edwin Mellen. Articles describe AIDS in Africa in terms of its history, ecological implications, management, policy, political, social and educational issues, and study resources available for the central and eastern African AIDS epidemic.

MOFFATT, M.
1989   *Coming of Age in New Jersey: College and American Culture.* New Brunswick, NJ: Rutgers University Press. Participant observation on a contemporary college campus.

MULLINGS, L., ED.
1987   *Cities of the United States: Studies in Urban Anthropology.* New York: Columbia University Press. Includes several case studies and argues for more applied and advocacy research in American cities.

MURPHY, R.
1990   *The Body Silent.* New York: W. W. Norton. An anthropologist's personal journey into the world of people with disabilities.

SERRIE, H., ED.
1986   *Anthropology and International Business.* Studies in Third World Societies, No. 28. Williamsburg, VA: Department of Anthropology, College of William and Mary. Introduction to business anthropology—national and international.

SPINDLER, G., ED.
1982   *Doing the Ethnography of Schooling: Educational Anthropology in Action.* New York: Holt, Rinehart & Winston. Efforts by anthropologists to throw light on the sources of inequality and other problems found in schools.

VAN WILLINGEN, J.

1993   *Applied Anthropology: An Introduction.* Revised edition. South Hadley, MA: Bergin and Garvey. Excellent review of the growth of applied anthropology and its links to general anthropology.

1987   *Becoming a Practicing Anthropologist: A Guide to Careers and Training Programs in Applied Anthropology.* NAPA Bulletin 3. Washington, DC: American Anthropological Association/National Association for the Practice of Anthropology. Useful brief guide for students contemplating a career in applied anthropology.

WEAVER, T., GEN. ED.

1973   *To See Ourselves: Anthropology and Modern Social Issues.* Glenview, IL: Scott, Foresman. Classic anthology of articles on the social responsibility of the anthropologist, anthropology and the Third World, race and racism, poverty and culture, education, violence, environment, intervention, and anthropology in the contemporary United States.

WULFF, R. M., AND S. J. FISKE, EDS.

1987   *Anthropological Praxis: Translating Knowledge into Action.* Boulder, CO: Westview Press. Cases illustrating the use of anthropology in solving human problems in various areas.

CHAPTER 23

COLONIALISM AND DEVELOPMENT

Anthropologists have held three different positions about applying anthropology and using it to identify and solve social problems. People who hold the **ivory tower view** contend that anthropologists should concentrate on research, publication, and teaching and not make policy recommendations. Those who favor the **schizoid view** think that anthropologists should help carry out, but not make or criticize, policy (Piddington 1970). In this view, personal "value judgments" should be kept separate from scientific investigation. The third view is **advocacy**. Its proponents assert that precisely because anthropologists are experts on human problems and social change and because they study, understand, and respect cultural values, they should make policy affecting people. In this view, proper roles for applied anthropologists include (1) identifying needs for change that local people perceive, (2) working with those people to design socially appropriate intervention strategies, and (3) protecting local people from harmful development schemes.

I join many other anthropologists in favoring advocacy. I share the belief that no one is better qualified to propose and evaluate guidelines for society than are those who study anthropology. To be effective advocates, anthropologists must present their views clearly, thoughtfully, and forcefully to policy makers and the public (Gough 1968/1973). Many anthropologists do serve as social commentators, problem solvers, and policy makers, advisers, and evaluators. We express our policy views in books and journals, through participation in social and political movements, and through professional associations, such as the Society for Applied Anthropology and the National Association of Practicing Anthropologists. NAPA, part of the AAA, is designed to help applied anthropologists refine their skills and market their services. NAPA fosters information sharing among practitioners, publishes materials useful to them, helps train them, and works to support their interests in and outside of academic settings.

An increasing number of anthropologists work for groups that promote, manage, and assess programs aimed at influencing social conditions. The scope of applied anthropology includes change and development abroad and social problems and policies in North America. Modern applied anthropology (Kimball 1978) differs from an earlier version that mainly served the goals of colonial regimes. Before turning to the new, we should consider some dangers of the old.

ANTHROPOLOGY AND COLONIALISM

Colonialism refers to the political, social, economic, and cultural domination of a territory and its people by a foreign power for an extended time (W. Bell, 1981). The British and French colonial empires are the most familiar examples. The British Empire ruled parts of North America, Africa, and Asia (e.g., India). France's colonial regime included parts of North Africa (e.g., Algeria and Tunisia), Africa (e.g., Senegal, Madagascar), and the Pacific.

In the context of the British empire, Bronislaw Malinowski (1929a) proposed that "practical anthropology" (his term for colonial applied anthropology) should focus on the westernization of African societies. The diffusion of European culture into tribal societies was of special interest to Malinowski. He argued that anthropologists could avoid politics by concentrating on facts and processes. However, he was actually expressing his own political views, because he questioned neither the legitimacy of colonialism nor the anthropologist's role in making it work. He saw nothing wrong with aiding colonial regimes by studying land tenure and land use to decide how much land natives should keep and how much Europeans should get. Malinowski's views exemplify a historical association between anthropology, particularly in Europe, and colonialism (Maquet 1964).

DEVELOPMENT

During the Industrial Revolution, a strong current of thought viewed industrialization as a beneficial process of organic development and progress. Many economists still assume that industrialization increases production and income. They seek to create in Third World ("developing") countries a process like the one that first occurred spontaneously in eighteenth-century Great Britain.

Development plans usually are guided by some kind of **intervention philosophy**, an ideological justification for outsiders to guide native peoples in specific directions. Bodley (1988) argues that the basic belief behind interventions—whether by colonialists, missionaries, governments, or development planners—has been the same for more than 100 years. This belief is that industrialization, modernization, westernization, and individualism are desirable evolutionary advances and that development schemes that promote them will bring long-term benefits to natives. In a more extreme form, intervention philosophy may pit the assumed wisdom of enlightened colonial or other First World planners against the conservatism, ignorance, or "obsolescence" of "inferior" natives.

Anthropologists dispute such views. We know that for thousands of years bands and tribes have done "a reasonable job of taking care of themselves" (Bodley 1988, p. 93). Indeed, because of their low energy needs, they have managed their resources better than we manage our own. Many problems that people face today are due to their position within nation-states and their increasing dependence on the world cash economy.

Sometimes when natives are reluctant to change, it isn't because they have unduly conservative attitudes but because powerful interest groups oppose reform. Many Third World governments are reluctant to tamper with existing socioeconomic conditions in their countries (Manners 1956/1973). The attempt to bring the "green revolution" to Java that is analyzed below illustrates this situation. Resistance by elites to land reform is a reality throughout the Third World. Millions of people in colonies and underdeveloped nations have learned from bitter experience that if they increase their incomes, their taxes and rents also rise.

Conflicts between governments (colonial or postcolonial) and natives often arise when outside interests exploit resources on tribal lands. Driven by deficits and debts, governments seek to wrest as much wealth as possible from the territory they administer. This goal helps explain the worldwide intrusion on indigenous peoples and their local ecosystems by highway construction, mining, hydroelectric projects, ranching, lumbering, agribusiness, and planned colonization (Bodley 1988).

Studying people at the local level, ethnographers have a unique view of the impact of national and international planning on intended "beneficiaries." Local-level research often reveals inadequacies in the measures that economists use to assess development and a nation's economic health. For example, per capita income and gross national product don't measure the distribution of wealth. Because the first is an average and the second is a total, they may rise as the rich get richer and the poor get poorer.

Today, many government agencies, international groups, and private foundations encourage attention to local-level social factors and the cultural dimension of development. Anthropological expertise is important because social problems can doom projects to failure. A study of fifty development projects (Lance and McKenna 1975) judged only twenty-one to be successes. Social and cultural incompatibilities had doomed most of the failed projects.

For example, a 1981 anthropological study of a multimillion-dollar development project in Madagascar uncovered several reasons for its failure. The project had been planned and funded by the World Bank in the late 1960s. The planners (no anthropologists among them) anticipated none of the problems that emerged. The project was aimed at draining and irrigating a large plain to increase rice production. Its goal was to raise production through machinery and double cropping—growing two crops annually on the same plot. However, the planners disregarded several things, including the unavailability of spare parts and fuel for the machines. The designers also ignored the fact, well known to anthropologists, that cross-culturally, intensive cultivation is associated with dense populations. If there are no machines to do the work, there have to be people around to do it. However, population densities in the project area (15 per square kilometer) were much too low to support intensive cultivation without modern machinery.

Planners should have known that labor and machinery for the project were unavailable. Furthermore, many local people were understandably hostile toward the project because it gave their ancestral land away to outsiders. (Unfortunately, this is a common occurrence in development projects.) Many land-grant recipients were members of regional and national elites who used their influence to get fields that were intended for poor farmers. The project also suffered from technical problems. The foreign firm hired to dig the irrigation canals dug them lower than the land they had to irrigate, and so the water couldn't flow up into the fields.

An anthropological study of an irrigated rice project in Madagascar found several reasons for its failure. The designers ignored the fact that intensive cultivation is associated with dense populations. If there are no machines to do the work, there have to be people around to do it— like these Betsileo women who are transplanting rice in the traditional manner.

Hundreds of millions of dollars of development funds could have produced greater human benefits if anthropologists had helped plan, supervise, and evaluate the projects. Planners who are familiar with the language and customs of a country can make better forecasts about project success than can those who are not. Accordingly, anthropologists increasingly work in organizations that promote, manage, and assess programs that influence human life in the United States and abroad.

However, ethical dilemmas often confront applied anthropologists (Escobar 1991). Our respect for cultural diversity is often offended because efforts to extend industry and technology may entail profound cultural changes. Foreign aid doesn't usually go where need and suffering are greatest. It is spent on political, economic, and strategic priorities as national leaders and powerful interest groups perceive them. Planners' interests don't always coincide with the best interests of the local people. Although the aim of most development projects is to enhance the quality of life, living standards often decline in the target area (Bodley 1988).

The Brazilian Sisal Scheme

A well-studied case in which development harmed the intended beneficiaries occurred in an arid area of Brazil's northeastern interior called the *sertão*. Here development increased dependence on the world economy, ruined the local subsistence economy, and worsened local health and income distribution. Until the 1950s the *sertão*'s economy was based on corn, beans, manioc, and other subsistence crops. The *sertão* was also a grazing region for cattle, sheep, and goats. Most years peasants subsisted on their crops. However, about once every decade a major drought drastically reduced yields and forced people to migrate to the coast to seek jobs. To develop the northeast and dampen the effects of drought, the Brazilian government began encouraging peasants to plant **sisal**, a fibrous plant used to make rope, as a cash crop.

To ready sisal for export, preparation in the field was necessary. Throughout the *sertão* there arose local centers with decorticating machines, devices that strip water and residue from sisal leaf, leaving only the fiber. These machines were expensive. Small-scale farmers couldn't afford them and had to use machines owned by the elite.

Small teams of workers were in charge of decorticating. Two jobs were especially hard, both done by adult men. One was that of disfiberer, the person who fed the sisal leaf into the machine. This was a demanding and dangerous job. The machine exerted a strong pull, making it possible for the disfiberers to get their fingers caught in the press. The other job was that of residue man, who shoveled away the residue that fell under the machine and brought new leaves to the disfiberer.

Anthropologist Daniel Gross (1971*a*) studied the effects of sisal on the people of the *sertão*. Most sisal growers were people who had converted most of their land to the cash crop, completely abandoning subsistence cultivation. Because sisal takes four years to mature, peasants had to seek wage work, often as members of a decorticating team, until they could harvest their crop. When they did harvest, they often found that the price of sisal on the world market was less than it had been when they planted the crop. Moreover, once sisal was planted, its strong root system made it almost impossible for the peasants to return to other crops. The land and people of the *sertão* became hooked on sisal.

A nutritionist, Barbara Underwood, collaborated with Gross in studying the new economy's effects on nutrition. For people to subsist, they must consume sufficient calories to replace those they expend in daily activity. Gross calculated the energy expended in two of the jobs on the decorticating team: disfiberer and residue man. The former expended an average of 4,400 calories per day; the latter, 3,600 calories.

Gross then examined the diets of the households headed by each man. The disfiberer earned the equivalent of $3.65 per week, whereas the residue man made less—about $3.25. The disfiberer's household included just himself and his wife. The residue man had a pregnant wife and four children, aged three, five, six, and eight. By spending most of his income on food, the disfiberer was getting at least 7,100 calories a day for himself and his wife. This was ample to supply his daily needs of 4,400 calories. It also left his wife a comfortable 2,700 calories.

However, the residue man's household was less fortunate. With more than 95 percent of his tiny income going for food, he could provide himself, his wife, and his four children with only 9,400 calories per day. Of this, he consumed 3,600 calories—enough to go on working. His wife ate 2,200 calories. His children, however, suffered nutritionally. Table 23.1 compares the minimum daily requirements for his children with their actual intake.

Long-term malnutrition has results that are reflected in body weight. Table 23.1 shows that the weights of the residue man's malnourished children compared poorly with the standard weights for their ages. The longer malnutrition continues, the greater is the gap between children with poor diets and those with normal diets. The residue man's oldest children had been malnourished longest. They compared least favorably with the standard body weight.

The children of sisal workers were being malnourished to enable their fathers to go on working for wages that were too low to feed them. However, the children of business people and owners of decorticating machines were doing better; malnutrition was much less severe among them. Finally, the

In Petrolina, Bahia, Brazil, workers tie up bundles of decorticated sisal fiber. Since most sisal is grown for export, variation in its price on the world market has brought a boom and a bust to the Brazilian sertão.

Table 23.1 *Malnutrition among the children of a Brazilian sisal residue man*

Age of Child	CALORIES		Percentage of Standard Body Weight
	Minimum Daily Requirement	Actual Daily Allotment	
8 (M)	2,100	1,100	62
6 (F)	1,700	900	70
5 (M)	1,700	900	85
3 (M)	1,300	700	90

Source: Gross and Underwood 1971, p. 733.

nutrition of sisal workers was also worse than that of traditional cultivators in the *sertão*. People who had reached adulthood before sisal cultivation began had more normal weights than did those who grew up after the shift.

This study is important for understanding problems that beset many people today. A shift from a subsistence economy to a cash economy led neither to a better diet nor to more leisure time for most people. The rich merely got richer and the poor got poorer. Badly planned and socially insensitive economic development projects often have such unforeseen consequences.

The Greening of Java

Like Gross in Brazil, anthropologist Richard Franke (1977) conducted an independent study of discrepancies between goals and results in a scheme to promote social and economic change in Java, Indonesia. Experts and planners of the 1960s and 1970s assumed that as small-scale farmers got modern technology and more productive crop varieties, their lives would improve. The media publicized new, high-yielding varieties of wheat, maize, and rice. These new crops, along with chemical fertilizers, pesticides, and new cultivation techniques, were hailed as the basis of a **green revolution**. This "revolution" was expected to increase the world's food supply and thus improve the diets and living conditions of victims of poverty, particularly in land-scarce, overcrowded regions.

The green revolution was an economic success. It did increase the global food supply. New strains of wheat and rice doubled or tripled farm supplies in many Third World countries (except for Sub-Saharan Africa). Thanks to the green revolution, world food prices declined by more than 20 percent during the 1980s (Stevens 1992). But its social effects were not what its advocates had intended, as we learn from Javanese experience.

Governments throughout southern Asia, including Indonesia, have encouraged cultivation of new rice varieties and use of chemical fertilizers and pesticides. Shown here are experimental seedlings at Java's Rice Research Center.

Java received a genetic cross between rice strains from Taiwan and Indonesia—a high-yielding "miracle" rice known as IR-8. This hybrid could raise the productivity of a given plot by at least half. Governments throughout southern Asia, including Indonesia, encouraged the cultivation of IR-8, along with the use of chemical fertilizers and pesticides.

The Indonesian island of Java, one of the most densely populated places in the world (over 700 people per square kilometer), was a prime target for the green revolution. Java's total crop was insufficient to supply its people with minimal daily requirements of calories (2,150) and protein (55 grams). In 1960 Javanese agriculture supplied 1,950 calories and 38 grams of protein per capita. By 1967 these already inadequate figures had fallen to 1,750 calories and 33 grams. Could miracle rice, by increasing crop yields 50 percent, reverse the trend?

Java shares with many other underdeveloped nations a history of socioeconomic stratification and colonialism. Indigenous contrasts in wealth and power were intensified by Dutch colonialism. Although Indonesia gained political independence from the Netherlands in 1949, internal stratification continued. Today, contrasts between the wealthy (government employees, business people, large landowners) and the poor (small-scale peasants) exist even in small farming communities. Stratification led to problems during Java's green revolution.

In 1963 the University of Indonesia's College of Agriculture launched a program in which students went to live in villages. They worked with peasants in the fields and shared their knowledge of new agricultural techniques while learning from the peasants. The program was a success. Yields in the affected villages increased by half. The program, directed by the Department of Agriculture, was expanded in 1964; nine universities and 400 students joined. These intervention programs succeeded where others had failed because the outside agents recognized that economic development rests not only on technological change but on political change as well. Students could observe firsthand how interest groups resisted attempts by peasants to improve their lot. Once, when local officials stole fertilizer destined for peasant fields, students got it back by threatening in a letter to turn evidence of the crime over to higher-level officials.

The combination of new work patterns and political action was achieving promising results when, in 1965–1966, there was an insurrection against the government. In the eventual military takeover, Indonesia's President Sukarno was ousted and replaced by President Suharto. Efforts to increase agricultural production resumed soon after Suharto took control. However, the new government assigned the task to multinational corporations based in Japan, West Germany, and Switzerland rather than to students and peasants. These industrial firms were to supply miracle rice and other high-yielding seeds, fertilizers, and pesticides. Peasants adopting the whole green revolution kit were eligible for loans that would allow them to buy food and other essentials in the lean period just before harvesting.

Java's green revolution soon encountered problems. One pesticide, which had never been tested in Java, killed the fish in the irrigation canals and thus destroyed an important protein resource. One development agency turned out to be a fraud, set up to benefit the military and government officials.

Java's green revolution also encountered problems at the village level because of entrenched interests. Traditionally, peasants had fed their families by taking temporary jobs, or borrowing, from wealthier villagers before the harvest. However, having accepted loans, the peasants were obliged to work for wages lower than those paid on the open market. Low-interest loans would have made peasants less dependent on wealthy villagers, thus depriving local patrons of cheap labor.

Local officials were put in charge of spreading information about how the program worked. Instead they limited peasant participation by withholding information. Wealthy villagers also discouraged peasant participation more subtly: They raised doubts about the effectiveness of the new techniques and about the wisdom of taking government loans when familiar patrons were nearby. Faced with the thought that starvation might follow if innovation failed, peasants were reluctant to take risks—an understandable reaction.

Production increased, but wealthy villagers rather than small-scale farmers reaped the benefits of the green revolution. Just 20 percent of one village's 151 households participated in the program. However, because they were the wealthiest households, headed by people who owned the most land,

40 percent of the land was being cultivated by means of the new system. Some large-scale land-owners used their green revolution profits at the peasants' expense. They bought up peasants' small plots and purchased labor-saving machinery, including rice-milling machines and tractors. As a result, the poorest peasants lost both their means of subsistence—land—and local work opportunities. Their only recourse was to move to cities, where a growing pool of unskilled laborers depressed already low wages.

In a complementary view of the green revolution's social effects, Ann Stoler (1977) focused on gender and stratification. She took issue with Esther Boserup's (1970) contention that colonialism and development inevitably hurt Third World women more than men by favoring commercial agriculture and excluding women from it. Stoler found that the green revolution had permitted some women to gain power over other women and men. Javanese women were not a homogeneous group but varied by class. Stoler found that whether the green revolution helped or harmed Javanese women depended on their position in the class structure. The status of landholding women rose as they gained control over more land and the labor of more poor women. The new economy offered wealthier women higher profits, which they used in trading. However, poor women suffered along with poor men as traditional economic opportunities declined. Nevertheless, the poor women fared better than did the poor men, who had no access at all to off-farm work.

Like Gross's analysis of the Brazilian sisal scheme, these studies of the local effects of the green revolution reveal results different from those foreseen by policy makers, planners, and the media. Again we see the unintended and undesirable effects of development programs that ignore traditional social, political, and economic divisions. New technology, no matter how promising, does not inevitably help the intended beneficiaries. It may very well hurt them if vested interests interfere. The Javanese student-peasant projects of the 1960s worked because peasants need not just technology but also political clout. Two ambitious development programs in Brazil and Java, although designed to alleviate poverty, actually increased it. Peasants stopped relying on their own subsistence production and started depending on a more volatile pursuit—cash sale of labor. Agricultural production became profit-oriented, machine-based, and chemical-dependent. Local autonomy diminished as linkages with the world system increased. Production rose, as the rich got richer and poverty increased.

Equity

A common goal, in theory at least, of development policy is to promote equity. **Increased equity** means reduced poverty and a more even distribution of wealth. However, a conflict between production goals and equity goals arises in many stratified nations. In such countries, if projects are to increase equity, they must have the support of reform-minded governments. Peasants oppose projects that interfere too much with their basic economic activities. Similarly, wealthy and powerful people resist projects that threaten their vested interests, and their resistance is usually more difficult to combat.

Some types of projects, particularly irrigation schemes, are more likely than others to widen wealth disparities, that is, to have a negative equity impact. An initial uneven distribution of resources (particularly land) often becomes the basis for greater skewing after the project. The social impact of new technology tends to be more severe, contributing negatively to quality of life and to equity, when inputs are channeled to or through the rich, as in Java's green revolution.

Many fisheries projects have also had negative equity results. In Bahia, Brazil (Kottak 1992), sailboat owners (but not nonowners) got loans to buy motors for their boats. To repay the loans, the owners increased the percentage of the catch they took from the men who fished in their boats. Over the years, they used the rising profits to buy larger and more expensive boats. The result was stratification—the creation of a group of wealthy people within a formerly egalitarian community. These events hampered individual initiative and interfered with further development of the fishing industry. With new boats so expensive, ambitious young men who once would have sought careers in fishing no longer had any way to obtain their own boats. To avoid such results, credit-granting agencies must seek out enterprising young fishers rather than giving loans only to owners and established business people.

The Third World Talks Back

In the postcolonial world, anthropologists from industrial core nations have paid attention to criticisms leveled against them by Third World colleagues. For example, the late Mexican anthropologist Guillermo Batalla (1966) decried certain "conservative and essentially ethnocentric assumptions" of applied anthropology in Latin America. He criticized the heavy psychological emphasis of many studies. These studies, he argued, focused too much on attitudes and beliefs about health and nutrition rather than on the material causes of poor health and malnutrition. Another problem he mentioned was the misuse of cultural relativism by certain anthropologists. Batalla faulted those researchers for refusing to interfere in existing social situations because they considered it inappropriate to judge and to promote change.

Batalla also criticized the multiple causation theory, which assumes that any social event has countless small and diverse causes. Such a theory does not perceive major social and economic inequities as targets for attack. Batalla also faulted anthropologists who see communities as isolated units, because local-level changes are always accepted or opposed in a larger context. He argued that applied anthropologists should pay more attention to regional, national, and international contexts. Finally, Batalla criticized anthropologists for thinking that diffusion, usually of technical skills and equipment from the First World, is the most significant process involved in change.

Batalla didn't argue that all applied anthropology suffers from these faults. However, his points are generally valid, and many Third World social scientists agree with him. Those scholars have also criticized American anthropology for the links that have existed between some anthropologists and government agencies that don't promote the best interests of the people.

The Code of Ethics

Largely in response to critics like Batalla, in 1971 the AAA adopted a code of ethics entitled "AAA: Principles of Professional Responsibility." Its preamble suggests that anthropologists should avoid research that can damage either the people studied or the scholarly community. The code covers six areas of professional responsibility.

1. Responsibility to Those Studied. Anthropologists' main responsibility is to the people they study. Anthropologists should do all they can to protect their informants' welfare and to respect their dignity and privacy. If interests conflict, these people come first. Their rights and interests must be protected. Specifically, anthropologists should let informants know the aims and anticipated consequences of their research. They should ensure that informants preserve their anonymity in data collection. Informants should not be exploited for personal gain. Anthropologists must anticipate and take steps to avoid damaging effects of the publication of their result. Reflecting the AAA's disapproval of secret research, reports should be available to the public.

2. Responsibility to the Public. As scholars who devote their lives to understanding human diversity, anthropologists should speak out about what they know and believe because of their professional expertise. They should contribute to an adequate definition of social reality, upon which public opinion and policy can be based. Anthropologists should also be aware of the limitations of their expertise.

3. Responsibility to the Discipline. Anthropologists are responsible for the reputations of their discipline and their colleagues. They should maintain their integrity in the field so that their behavior will not jeopardize future research by others.

4. Responsibility to Students. Professors should be fair, candid, and committed to the welfare and academic progress of their students. They should make students aware of ethical problems in research.

5. Responsibility to Sponsors. Anthropologists should be honest about their qualifications, capabilities, and aims. They should not accept employment that violates professional ethics. They should retain the right to make their own decisions on ethical issues during research.

6. Responsibility to One's Own and to Host Governments. Anthropologists should demand assurance that agreements with governments don't require them to compromise professional responsibilities and ethics in order to pursue their research.

This statement of principles of professional responsibility was designed to offer guidelines. However, the code also provides for censure of unprofessional conduct. When the actions of one anthropologist jeopardize others or appear unethical, colleagues may examine those actions and take measures that lie within the mandate of the AAA. A committee on ethics is now a permanent part of the AAA.

STRATEGIES FOR INNOVATION

In a comparative study of sixty-eight development projects from all over the world, I found the **culturally compatible economic development projects** to be twice as successful financially as the incompatible ones (Kottak 1990, 1991). This finding shows that using anthropological expertise in planning, to ensure cultural compatibility, is cost-effective. To maximize social and economic benefits, projects must (1) be culturally compatible, (2) respond to locally perceived needs, (3) involve people in planning and carrying out the changes that affect them, (4) harness traditional organizations, and (5) be flexible. Applied anthropologists should not just implement (carry out) development policies; they are as qualified as economists are to make policy.

Anthropological input is valuable during all the stages of a development project: identification, appraisal, design, implementation, and evaluation. Together these stages make up the **project cycle.**

During identification, needs for potential projects in particular places are assessed. At appraisal, background studies are done to decide project feasibility. If the project seems viable and funding is approved, design begins. Carrying out the project is known as *implementation*. After this comes *evaluation*, the last stage. Later, some projects get an *ex post facto* evaluation, to assess their ongoing success.

Too many true local needs cry out for a solution to waste money by funding projects that are inappropriate in area A but needed in area B or unnecessary anywhere. Social expertise can sort out the A's and B's and fit the projects accordingly. Projects that put people first by responding to the needs for change they perceive must be identified. After that, social expertise is needed to ensure efficient and socially compatible ways of carrying out the projects.

Overinnovation

In my comparative study, the compatible and successful projects avoided the fallacy of **overinnovation** (too much change). Instead, they (intuitively) applied Romer's rule, which was used in the chapter "The World System, Industrialism, and Stratification," to explain why the Industrial Revolution took place in England. Recall that Romer (1960) developed his rule to explain the evolution of land-dwelling vertebrates from fish. The ancestors of land animals lived in pools of water that dried up seasonally. Fins evolved into legs to enable those animals to get back to water when particular pools

To maximize social and economic benefits, development projects should: (1) be culturally compatible, (2) respond to locally perceived needs for change, (3) harness traditional organizations, and (4) have a proper (and flexible) social design for carrying out the project. This Zambian farm club, which draws on traditional social organization, plants cabbages.

dried up. Thus an innovation (legs) that later proved essential to land life originated to maintain life in the water.

Romer's lesson is that an innovation that evolves to *maintain* a system can play a major role in *changing* that system. Evolution occurs in increments. Systems take a series of small steps to maintain themselves, and they gradually change. Romer's rule can be applied to economic development, which, after all, is a process of (planned) socioeconomic evolution. To apply Romer's rule to development is not to argue against change. The emergence of legs, which prompted Romer's rule, was a very important change. It offered the vertebrates many paths of diversification and development.

Applying Romer's rule to development, we would expect people to resist projects that require major changes in their daily lives, especially ones that interefere with subsistence pursuits. People usually want to change just enough to keep what they have. Motives for modifying behavior come from the traditional culture and the small concerns of ordinary life. Peasants' values are not such abstract ones as "learning a better way," "progressing," "increasing technical know-how," "improving efficiency," or "adopting modern techniques." (Those phrases exemplify intervention philosophy.) Instead, their objectives are down-to-earth and specific ones. People want to improve yields in a rice field, amass resources for a ceremony, get a child through school, or pay taxes. The goals and values of subsistence producers differ from those of people who produce for cash, just as they differ from the intervention philosophy of development planners. Different value systems must be considered during planning.

Note that development guided by Romer's rule can even be compatible with social "revolutions" that reallocate land in highly stratified nations. If land reform permits peasants to go on farming their fields and get more of the product, it can be very successful.

Failed projects usually work in opposition to Romer's rule. For example, one South Asian project promoted the cultivation of onions and peppers, expecting this practice to fit into a preexisting labor-intensive system of rice-growing. Cultivation of these cash crops wasn't traditional in the area. It conflicted with existing crop priorities and other interests of farmers. The labor peaks for pepper and onion production coincided with those for rice, to which farmers gave priority.

Throughout the world, project problems have arisen from inadequate attention to, and consequent lack of fit with, local culture. Another naive and incompatible project was an overinnovative scheme in Ethiopia. Its major fallacy was to try to convert nomadic herders into sedentary cultivators. It ignored traditional land rights. Outsiders—commercial farmers—were to get much of the herders' territory. The pastoralists were expected to settle down and start farming. This project neglected social and

Applying Romer's rule to development, people usually want to change just enough to keep what they have. Motives for modifying behavior come from the traditional culture and the small concerns of ordinary life. For example, understanding that deforestation causes local shortages of firewood and water can lead people to reforest. These people in Rwanda tend tree seedlings, which they will plant as part of a reforestation project.

IN THE NEWS: A CASE OF SUCCESSFUL AND CULTURALLY APPROPRIATE DEVELOPMENT

To maximize social and economic benefits, development should be culturally compatible, respond to locally perceived needs, involve people in planning and carrying out the changes that affect them, harness traditional organizations, and be flexible. The Santa Ana Indians of New Mexico have chosen a path of economic change that satisfies all these conditions. Their organic farming system also minimizes environmental destruction. The people of Santa Ana have adopted a multi-pronged development strategy, stressing improvements in their traditional agriculture, without seeking to hide from larger systems and the world cash economy.

Bernalillo, N.M., Nov. 18—The fields north of Albuquerque farmed by the Santa Ana Indians have turned brown, and 19 remaining acres of blue corn are being harvested. But already the tribe has reaped a profit from its agricultural operations.

The corn will be ground in a new grain mill financed with help from a British concern that is turning Santa Ana's organically grown corn into a sophisticated line of cosmetics for international marketing. The tribe recently received a $20,000 prize for enterprise from the Ford Foundation, one of 25 winners picked from 1,600 competitors. Along with the prize came national recognition and a raft of requests for advice.

That a small tribe of 110 households with 629 people has revitalized itself without selling land or depending on income from casino gambling has made the Santa Ana one of the uncommon success stories among the country's 300 tribes.

Yet the tribal leaders tend to regard their financial accomplishments as a secondary achievement. "The driving force behind everything we do is to insure the tribe has all it needs in the future to survive as a tribe," said Roy Montoya, the tribal administrator. Six years ago he gave up a job as a

computer analyst and took a sizable pay cut to manage the tribe's once rich but neglected farmlands along the Rio Grande.

Most of the acreage had been allowed to go fallow, partly because income from farming was shrinking, credit was drying up and workers were finding jobs away from the reservation. By the early 1980's, the decline threatened to undercut the ancestral culture and religion practiced for centuries, a culture in which the cultivation of blue corn and its use in ceremonies is a major element. As a tribal rite, corn powder is rubbed on the newborn.

To rekindle interest in farming and to maintain the Santa Ana as a viable community, the Tribal Council adopted a plan in the mid-1980's to preserve land east of the river for traditional agriculture while developing property on the western bank for commercial and recreational use. (A separate but wholly owned tribal concern has attracted outside investors and built a golf course

---

cultural issues. It helped wealthy outsiders instead of the natives. The planners naively expected free-ranging herders to give up a generations-old way of life to work three times harder growing rice and picking cotton.

Sometimes development agencies ignore good initial advice and go on with overinnovative projects anyway. In one African cattle project, the planners ignored the appraisal team's advice not to establish ranches in the project area because they would conflict with land-use patterns. The designers ignored the most basic (and easily available) census data and maps for the project area. When the project began, a few thousand local people, whose existence the planners had failed to notice, tore down fences, burned pasture, and rustled cattle. Lo-

cal people continued guerrilla actions against the ranches being built on their ancestral lands. These problems diminished when foreign managers were replaced with nationals, who used traditional pacts (blood brotherhood) between villages to end the rustling.

Underdifferentiation

The fallacy of **underdifferentiation** is the tendency to view "the less-developed countries" as more alike than they are. Development agencies have often ignored cultural diversity (e.g., between Brazil and Burundi) and adopted a uniform approach to deal with very different sets of people. Neglecting cultural diversity, many projects also have tried to

and restaurant and has plans for a hotel.)

The agricultural program was developed in three parts: a 100-acre farm was created with Government financial help; a mill was established so the tribe could earn higher profits for grinding and roasting corn, including corn from other tribes, or pueblos, and a native plant nursery was set up to cultivate trees and bushes for sale to golf courses and homebuilders.

All crops are organically grown, and other sound environmental practices are observed, like rotation of crops. Keeping the land under cultivation and controlling its seven miles of irrigation ditches protect the tribe's legal claims to water rights, Mr. Montoya said.

The pueblo's households buy most of the vegetables, although some are sold to outsiders.

The turning point in the tribe's revitalization came two years ago, when its organically grown crops attracted the attention of Anita Roddick, founder of the Body Shop, a chain of 830 stores in 40 countries that markets cosmetic products made of natural ingredi-

ents. Mrs. Roddick said her aim is to promote trade with people in third-world countries in the hope of "building human values into the products we sell."

Looking for a link with an American group, she flew to Albuquerque to meet Mr. Montoya and Gerald Kinsman, the pueblo's agricultural coordinator. She returned home with a rucksack of blue corn and directed her research chemists to come up with a product line.

Because the pueblo had only a primitive mill, the Body Shop gave it a $2,000 advance on an order for six tons of cornmeal so it could buy a more advanced mill. The new mill has raised grinding capacity to 300 pounds an hour from 60 pounds.

"They were very up front with us," Mr. Montoya said. "They really worried about not taking advantage of this little Indian tribe."

Agricultural progress did not come easily. Besides overcoming initial doubts of the tribal elders, Mr. Montoya, aided by Mr. Kinsman, had to deal with rapacious

grasshoppers, asparagus that required too much labor and unexpected weather swings that flooded the alfalfa one season.

"That we could get 100 acres under farming, have no debts and own $80,000 in equipment in six years is unheard of," said Mr. Kinsman, one of several non-Indian members of the administrative team.

Agriculture will always remain the tribe's major aim, Mr. Montoya said, but he does not disdain pursuing other ventures, even a casino, if they are combined with other recreational activities like golf.

"After all," he said, "what is more of a gamble than farming?"

Source: Kathleen Teltsch, "A Tiny Tribe Preserves Itself by Returning to Farming Tradition," *The New York Times*, November 22, 1992, p. A14.

impose incompatible property notions and social units. Most often, the faulty social design assumes either (1) individualistic productive units that are privately owned by an individual or couple and worked by a nuclear family or (2) cooperatives that are at least partially based on models from the former Eastern bloc and Socialist countries.

Often development aims at generating *individual* cash wealth through exports. This goal contrasts with the tendency of bands and tribes to share resources and depend on local ecosystems and renewable resources (Bodley 1988). Development planners commonly emphasize benefits that will accrue to individuals; more concern with the effects on communities is needed (Bodley 1988).

One example of faulty Euro-American models

(the individual and the nuclear family) was a West African project designed for an area where the extended family was the basic social unit. The project succeeded despite its faulty social design because the participants used their traditional extended family networks to attract additional settlers. Eventually, twice as many people as planned benefitted as extended family members flocked to the project area. This case shows that local people are not helpless victims of the world system. Settlers modified the project design that had been imposed on them by using the principles of their traditional society.

The second dubious foreign social model that is common in development strategy is the cooperative. In my comparative study of development projects, new cooperatives fared badly. Coopera-

Project problems often arise from inadequate attention to, and consequent lack of fit with, local culture. In Ethiopia, overinnovative planners wanted to convert nomadic herders into sedentary farmers. The planners naively expected free-ranging herders to give up a generations-old way of life to work three times harder plowing, growing rice, and picking cotton.

tives succeeded only when they harnessed preexisting local-level communal institutions. This is a corollary of a more general rule: Participants' groups are most effective when they are based on traditional social organization or on a socioeconomic similarity among members.

Neither foreign social model—the nuclear family farm or the cooperative—has an unblemished record in development. An alternative is needed: greater use of Third World social models for Third World development. These are traditional social units, such as the clans, lineages, and other extended kinship groups of Africa, Oceania, and many other nations, with their communally held estates and resources. The most humane and productive strategy for change is to base the social design for innovation on traditional social forms in each target area.

Third World Models and Culturally Appropriate Development

Many governments lack a genuine commitment to improving the lives of their citizens. Interference by major powers has also kept governments from enacting needed reforms. In many highly stratified societies, particularly in Latin America, the class structure is very rigid. Movement of individuals into the middle class is difficult. It is equally hard to raise the living standards of the lower class as a whole. These nations have a long history of control of government by powerful interest groups that tend to oppose reform.

In some nations, however, the government acts more as an agent of the people. Madagascar provides an example. As in many areas of Africa, precolonial states had developed in Madagascar before its conquest by the French in 1895. The people of Madagascar, the Malagasy, had been organized into descent groups before the origin of the state. Imerina, the major precolonial state of Madagascar, wove descent groups into its structure, making members of important groups advisers to the king and thus giving them authority in government. Imerina made provisions for the people it ruled. It collected taxes and organized labor for public works projects. In return, it redistributed resources to peasants in need. It also granted them some protection against war and slave raids and allowed them to cultivate their rice fields in peace. The government maintained the water works for rice cultivation. It opened to ambitious peasant boys the chance of becoming, through hard work and study, state bureaucrats.

Throughout the history of Imerina—and continuing in modern Madagascar—there have been strong relationships between the individual, the descent group, and the state. Local Malagasy communities, where residence is based on descent, are more cohesive and homogeneous than are communities in Java or Brazil. Madagascar gained political inde-

Third World models for Third World development include traditional cultural and social units, such as the extended kinship groups of Africa and Oceania. The social design for innovation should be based on existing groups and institutions in each target area. A traditional system of planning and management by Buddhist temples has been harnessed for culturally appropriate agricultural development in Bali, Indonesia.

pendence from France in 1960. Although it was still economically dependent on France when I first did research there in 1966–1967, the new government was committed to a form of socialist development. Its economic development schemes were increasing the ability of the Malagasy to feed themselves. Government policy emphasized increased production of rice, a subsistence crop, rather than cash crops. Furthermore, local communities, with their traditional cooperative patterns and solidarity based on kinship and descent, were treated as partners in, not obstacles to, the development process.

In a sense, the corporate descent group is pre-adapted to equitable national development. In Madagascar, members of local descent groups have customarily pooled their resources to educate their ambitious members. Once educated, these men and women gain economically secure positions in the nation. They then share the advantages of their new positions with their kin. For example, they give room and board to rural cousins attending school and help them find jobs.

Malagasy administrations appear generally to have shared a commitment to democratic economic development. Perhaps this is because government officials are of the peasantry or have strong personal ties to it. By contrast, in Latin American countries, the elites and the lower class have different origins and no strong connections through kinship, descent, or marriage.

Furthermore, societies with descent-group organization contradict an assumption that many social scientists and economists seem to make. It is not inevitable that as nations become more tied to the world capitalist economy, native forms of social organization will break down into nuclear family organization, impersonality, and alienation. Descent groups, with their traditional communalism and corporate solidarity, have important roles to play in economic development.

The use of descent groups in Malagasy rice production exemplifies culturally appropriate innovation. So does an East African cattle project judged to be one of the most successful livestock projects in Africa (Kottak 1990, 1991). It introduced cattle herding to a region recently freed of tsetse fly infestation. (These flies transmit African sleeping sickness to people and animals.) The project made good use of local and regional conditions. Some examples:

1. Cattle grazing was a culturally appropriate activity in the region. Previously, people in the project area had not herded only because of tsetse flies. With this barrier removed, people simply extended their practice to fill a new niche.
2. Livestock came from a neighboring country; the cattle were adapted to the regional ecology.
3. Project aims fit the traditional land tenure system. Fences and small farms were customary

and compatible with the project's private property and grazing goals.

4. The project used a mixture of productive units: government ranches, a cooperative ranch, and private ranches.

5. The population was dense enough for effective supervision, animal health care, marketing, and delivery.

Consider a final case of culturally appropriate innovation. Here, in a successful Papua–New Guinea resettlement project, participants used their profits just as—in Romer's study—the ancestors of land vertebrates had used their finlike legs. They changed (began producing palm oil for sale) not to forge a brand-new life style but to keep their ties with home. The settlers constantly revisited their homelands and invested in its social life and ceremonies. This cash crop project fit Oceanian values and customs involving competition for wealth and capital, such as big-man systems. The settlers came from different tribes, but intertribal mingling was already part of local experience. Marriage between people who speak different dialects and languages is common in Papua–New Guinea, as is participation in common religious movements.

Realistic development promotes change but not overinnovation. Many changes are possible if the aim is to preserve local systems while making them work better. Successful projects respect, or at least don't attack, local cultural patterns. Effective development draws on indigenous cultural practices and social structures.

SUMMARY

Anthropologists have different opinions about the relationship between research and its application. In the ivory tower view, anthropologists should teach, do independent research, and publish but avoid applications and political issues. In the schizoid view, anthropologists may work for agencies; however, their role is not to set but to carry out policies or to investigate reasons for the acceptance or rejection of changes. Advocates believe that anthropologists, as experts on social life and cultural diversity, should seek to influence policy and should participate only in projects they approve.

In the applied anthropology of earlier periods, anthropologists supported colonialism by working on projects aimed at economic and cultural change. Colonial anthropologists faced, and modern applied anthropologists may still face, problems posed by their inability to set or influence policy and the difficulty of criticizing programs in which they have participated. Anthropology's professional organizations have addressed these problems with codes of ethics and ethics committees.

Modern applied anthropologists keep ethical guidelines in mind as they try to help people facing economic and social changes. The American Anthropological Association (AAA) has issued a statement of professional conduct that lays out the responsibilities of anthropologists to informants, universities, colleagues, students, sponsors, and governments. The AAA has also committed itself to taking action against breaches of professional ethics.

Development plans are usually guided by some kind of intervention philosophy, an ideological justification for outsiders to direct native peoples toward particular goals. Development is usually justified by the belief that industrialization, modernization, westernization, and individualism are desirable and beneficial evolutionary advances. However, bands and tribes, with their low-energy adaptations, usually manage resources better than industrial states do. Many problems that Third World people face today are due to their position within nation-states and their increasing dependence on the world cash economy.

Conflicts between governments and natives may arise when outsiders claim resources on tribal lands. There has been worldwide intrusion on indigenous peoples and their local ecosystems by roads, mining, hydroelectric projects, ranching, lumbering, agribusiness, and planned colonization.

Increasingly, government agencies, international groups, and private foundations are encouraging attention to local-level social factors and the cultural dimension of social change and economic development. Anthropologists work in organizations that promote, manage, and assess programs that affect human life in the United States and abroad.

Development projects that replace subsistence pursuits with economies dependent on the unpredictable alternations of the world capitalist economy can be especially damaging. Following a shift from subsistence to cash cropping in northeastern Brazil, local material conditions worsened. Research on the socioeconomic effects of sisal cultivation reveals some unforeseen consequences (e.g., negative equity) that many accompany development. Similarly, research in Java found that the green revolution was failing because it stressed new technology rather than a combination of technology and peasant political organization. Java's green revolution was increasing poverty rather than ending it, although women were not as hard hit by the new economy as men were. Because so many projects have failed for social and political reasons, development organizations are increasingly using anthropologists in planning, supervision, and evaluation.

Governments are not equally committed to eradicating poverty and increasing equity. Local interest groups often oppose reform, and resistance by elites is especially hard to combat. Culturally compatible projects tend to be more financially successful than incompatible ones are. This means that the use of anthropological expertise in development not only promotes more humane changes but is also cost-effective. An anthropological perspective is valuable throughout the project cycle: identification, appraisal, design, implementation, and evaluation.

Compatible and successful projects avoid the fallacy of overinnovation and apply Romer's rule: An innovation that evolves to maintain a system can play a major role in changing that system. Natives are unlikely to cooperate with projects that require major changes in their daily lives, especially ones that interfere too much with customary subsistence pursuits. People usually want to change just enough to keep what they have. Peasants' motives to change come from their traditional culture and the small concerns of everyday existence. Peasant values are not abstract and long-term and thus differ from those of development planners.

The fallacy of underdifferentiation refers to the tendency to see less-developed countries as an undifferentiated group. Neglecting cultural diversity and the local context, many projects impose culturally biased and incompatible property notions and social units on the intended beneficiaries. The most common flawed social models are the nuclear family farm and the cooperative, neither of which has an unblemished record in development. A more promising alternative is to harness Third World social units for purposes of development. These traditional social forms include the clans, lineages, and other extended kinship groups of Africa and Oceania, with their communally held resources. The most productive strategy for change is to base the social design for innovation on traditional social forms in each target area.

GLOSSARY

advocacy: View that because anthropologists are experts on human problems and social change, they should make and influence policies affecting people.

colonialism: Political, social, economic, and cultural domination of a territory and its people by a foreign power for an extended time.

culturally compatible economic development projects: Projects that harness traditional organizations and locally perceived needs for change and that have a culturally appropriate design and implementation strategy.

equity, increased: A reduction in absolute poverty and a fairer (more even) distribution of wealth.

green revolution: Agricultural development based on chemical fertilizers, pesticides, twentieth-century cultivation techniques, and new crop varieties such as IR-8 ("miracle rice").

intervention philosophy: Guiding principle of colonialism, conquest, missionization, or development; an ideological justification for outsiders to guide native peoples in specific directions.

ivory tower view: View that anthropologists should avoid practical matters and concentrate on research, publication, and teaching.

overinnovation: Characteristic of projects that require major changes in natives' daily lives, especially ones that interfere with customary subsistence pursuits.

project cycle: A development project through all its stages; identification, appraisal, design, implementation, and evaluation.

sertão: Arid interior of northeastern Brazil; backlands.

schizoid view: View that anthropologists can collect facts for development agencies but should neither make nor criticize policy because personal value judgments should be kept strictly separate from scientific investigation.

sisal: Plant adapted to arid areas; its fiber is used to make rope.

underdifferentiation: Planning fallacy of viewing less-developed countries as an undifferentiated group; ignoring cultural diversity and adopting a uniform approach (often ethnocentric) for very different types of project beneficiaries.

STUDY QUESTIONS

1. What are the three viewpoints on anthropology's role in practical affairs?
2. Which of these viewpoints do you prefer, and why?
3. What was the relationship between the old applied anthropology and colonialism? What's different about modern applied anthropology?
4. What were Batalla's criticisms of applied anthropology?
5. How do anthropologists deal with the matter of professional ethics?
6. What are some common reasons for the failure of economic development programs?
7. What are equity goals, and what were the equity results of the Brazilian sisal scheme and Java's green revolution?
8. How did the equity results of Java's green revolution differ for men and for women?
9. What does it mean to say that an economic development project is "culturally compatible"? What are the advantages of ensuring that projects are culturally compatible?
10. What is Romer's rule, and how does it apply to development strategy?
11. What are some examples of the fallacy of overinnovation?
12. What is the fallacy of underdifferentiation? What are some possible alternatives to it?
13. How might descent-group organization contribute to economic development?
14. In your opinion, what criteria should be used to evaluate the success of an economic development program?

SUGGESTED ADDITIONAL READING

BARLETT, P. F., ED.
1980 *Agricultural Decision Making: Anthropological Contribution to Rural Development.* New York: Academic Press. How farmers choose what to plant and decide how to plant it in various cultures.

BENNETT, J. W., AND J. R. BOWEN, EDS.
1988 *Production and Autonomy: Anthropological Studies and Critiques of Development.* Monographs in Economic Anthropology, No. 5, Society for Economic Anthropology. New York: University Press of America. Twenty-three recent articles on many social aspects of economic development.

BODLEY, J. H.
1985 *Anthropology and Contemporary Human Problems,* 2nd ed. Mountain View, CA: Mayfield. Overview of major problems of today's industrial world: overconsumption, the environment, resource depletion, hunger, overpopulation, violence, and war.
1988 *Tribal Peoples and Development Issues: A Global Overview.* Mountain View, CA: Mayfield. Overview of case studies, policies, assessments, and recommendations concerning tribal peoples and development.

CERNEA, M., ED.
1990 *Putting People First: Sociological Variables in Rural Development,* 2nd ed. New York: Oxford University Press (published for the World Bank). First collection of articles by social scientists based on World Bank files and project experiences. Examines development successes and failures and the social and cultural reasons for them.

HART, K.
1982 *The Political Economy of West African Agriculture.* Cambridge: Cambridge University Press. Examines the origins of West African underdevelopment.

HUMAN ORGANIZATION
The quarterly journal of the Society for Applied Anthropology. An excellent source for articles on applied anthropology and development.

KORTEN, D. C.
1980 Community Organization and Rural Development: A Learning Process Approach. *Public Administration Review,* September–October, pp. 480–512. People-oriented development strategies as opposed to the "blueprint" approach used by most development agencies.

SELIGSON, M. A.
1984 *The Gap between Rich and Poor: Contending Perspectives on the Political Economy of Development.* Boulder, CO: Westview Press. Equity issues in development.

WORSLEY, P.
1984 *The Three Worlds: Culture and World Development.* Chicago: University of Chicago Press. Examines the nature of development processes and critiques existing theories.

CULTURAL EXCHANGE AND SURVIVAL

In a global culture that heralds diversity, the linkages in the modern world system have both enlarged and erased old boundaries and distinctions. Arjun Appadurai (1990, p. 1) characterizes today's world as a "translocal" "interactive system" that is "strikingly new." Whether as refugees, migrants, tourists, pilgrims, proselytizers, laborers, business people, development workers, employees of nongovernmental organizations (NGOs), politicians, soldiers, sports figures, or media-borne images, people travel more than ever.

So important is transnational migration that many Mexican villagers find "their most important kin and friends are as likely to be living hundreds or thousands of miles away as immediately around them" (Rouse 1991). Most migrants maintain their ties with their native land (phoning, visiting, sending money, watching "ethnic TV"), so that, in a sense, they live multilocally—in different places at once. Dominicans in New York City, for example, have been characterized as living "between two islands"—Manhattan and the Dominican Republic (Grasmuck and Pessar 1991). Many Dominicans—like migrants from other countries—migrate to the United States temporarily, seeking cash to transform their life styles when they return to the Caribbean.

PEOPLE IN MOTION

With so many people "in motion," the unit of anthropological study expands from the local community to the **diaspora**—the offspring of an area who have spread to many lands. Anthropologists increasingly follow descendants of the villages we have studied as they move from rural to urban areas and across national boundaries. For the 1991 annual meeting of the American Anthropological Association in Chicago, the anthropologist Robert Van Kemper organized a session of presentations about long-term ethnographic field work. Kemper's own long-time research focus has been the Mexican village of Tzintzuntzan, which, with his mentor George Foster, Kemper has studied for decades. However, their database now includes not just Tzintzuntzan, but its descendants all over the world (one of whom reached Alaska in 1990). Given the Tzintzuntzan diaspora, Kemper was even able to use some of his time in Chicago to visit people from

Tzintzuntzan who had established a colony there. In today's world, as people move, they take their traditions and their anthropologists along with them.

Postmodernity describes our time and situation—today's world in flux, these people on the move who have learned to manage multiple identities depending on place and context. In its most general sense, **postmodern** refers to the blurring and breakdown of established canons (rules or standards), categories, distinctions, and boundaries. The word is taken from **postmodernism**—a style and movement in architecture that succeeded modernism, beginning in the 1970s. Postmodern architecture rejected the rules, geometric order, and austerity of modernism. Modernist buildings were expected to have a clear and functional design. Postmodern design is "messier" and more playful. It draws on a diversity of styles from different times and places—including popular, ethnic, and nonwestern cultures. Postmodernism extends "value" well beyond classic, elite, and Western cultural forms. *Postmodern* is now used to describe comparable developments in music, literature, and visual art. From this origin, *postmodernity* describes a world in which traditional standards, contrasts, groups, boundaries, and identities are opening up, reaching out, and breaking down.

Globalization describes the accelerating links between nations and people in a world system connected economically, politically, and by modern media and transportation. Globalization promotes intercultural communication, including travel and migration, which bring people from different cultures into direct contact. The world is more integrated than ever. Yet *dis*integration also surrounds us. Nations dissolve (Yugoslavia, Czechoslovakia, the Soviet Union), as do political blocs (the Warsaw Pact nations), and ideologies ("Communism"). The notion of a "Free World" collapses because it existed mainly in opposition to a group of "Captive Nations"—a label that has lost much of its meaning.

Simultaneously new kinds of political and ethnic units are emerging. Ethnicity, "once a genie contained in the bottle of some sort of locality . . . has now become a global force, forever slipping in and through the cracks between states and borders" (Appadurai 1990, p. 15). For example, not only do Native American cultures survive, there is a growing Panindian identity, and an international Pantribal movement as well. Thus in June 1992 the

World Conference of Indigenous Peoples met in Rio de Janeiro concurrently with UNCED (the United Nations Conference on the Environment and Development). Along with diplomats, journalists, and environmentalists came 300 representatives of the tribal diversity that survives in the modern world— from Lapland to Mali (Brooke 1992*a* and *b*).

Postmodern Moments in the World System

Increasingly anthropologists experience what I call "postmodern moments in the world system." Some of my most vivid ones can be traced back to Ambalavao, Madagascar. In 1966–67 my wife and I rented a house in that town in southern Betsileo country. We spent weekends there when we came in from the rural villages where our field work was based.

By 1966 Madagascar was independent from France, but its towns still had foreigners to remind them of colonialism. Besides us, Ambalavao had at least a dozen world system agents, including an Indian cloth merchant, Chinese grocers, and a few French people. A French consultant was there to help develop the tobacco industry, and two young men in the French equivalent of the Peace Corps were teaching school.

One of them, Noel, served as principal of the junior high school. He lived across the street from a prominent local family (who served as our sponsors in a rural village, their ancestral community, we were studying). Since Noel often spoke disparagingly of the Malagasy, I was surprised to see him courting a young woman from this family. She was Lenore, the sister of Leon, a schoolteacher who became one of my best friends. My wife and I left Ambalavao in December 1967. Noel and the other world system agents stayed on.

Each of my revisits to Madagascar has brought postmodern moments—encounters with people and products on the move, in multilocal and unexpected contexts. After 1967, my next trip to Madagascar came in February 1981. I was doing applied anthropology as a consultant for the World Bank. This work took me to a new area, the Lake Alaotra region, where I was to evaluate the social and cultural reasons for the failure of an expensive irrigation project. Near Alaotra (Madagascar's largest lake), I had no choice but to stay at the Water Lily Hotel. I shared the hotel with a dozen prostitutes, my Malagasy collaborator (a professor of geography), an American World Bank officer, and a Russian technician assigned to this desolate region (instead of Siberia, we joked), perhaps for life. For breakfast I drank Orange Crush (the only bottled drink available) and watched a rat run through the dining room.

During my 1981 stay in Antananarivo, the capital, I was confined each evening to the newly built Hilton hotel by a curfew imposed after a civil insurrection. I shared the hotel with a group of Russian MIG pilots (and their wives), there to teach the Malagasy to defend their island, strategically placed in the Indian Ocean, against imagined enemies. Later, I went down to Betsileo country to visit Leon, my schoolteacher friend from Ambalavao, who had become a prominent politician. Unfortunately for me, he was in Moscow, participating in a three-month Soviet exchange program.

My next visit to Madagascar was in summer 1990. Again I was doing applied anthropology, this time for the United States Agency for International Development (USAID). My job was to help design a socially sound conservation project, aimed at preserving Madagascar's rich biodiversity. This time a postmodern moment occurred when I met Emily, the twenty-two-year-old daughter of Noel and Lenore, whose courtship I had witnessed in 1967. One of her aunts brought Emily to meet me at my hotel in Antananarivo, where Emily was participating in a program organized by USAID.

Emily was about to visit several cities in the United States, where she planned to study marketing. I met her again just a few months later in Gainesville, Florida, where she was taking a course at Santa Fe Community College. As we lunched in a Mexican restaurant, Emily sold me some woodwork she had brought from Madagascar. She asked my wife and me to help her market other Malagasy crafts. Finally she asked us about her father, whom she had never met. She told us she had sent several letters to France, but Noel had never responded.

Descendants of Ambalavao (and thus of rural Betsileo villages) now live all over the world. Emily, a child of colonialism, has two aunts in France (married to French men) and another in Germany (working as a diplomat). Members of her family, which is not especially wealthy, although regionally prominent, have traveled to Russia, Canada, the United States, France, Germany and West Africa.

Cultural Contact in Larger Systems

This book has examined many aspects of increasing participation by local cultures in wider systems—regional, national, and global. The main forces influencing cultural interaction for the past 500 years have been commercial expansion and industrialization. These globalizing forces have also contributed to the destruction of indigenous economies, ecologies, and populations. Two centuries ago, 50 million people lived in bands, tribes, and chiefdoms—accounting for half the world's inhabited area and 20 percent of its population. Industrialization tipped the balance in favor of nation-states, in which all surviving bands and tribes now live. Alterations in the wider environments of human groups—that is, in their relations with other groups—are changes to which people continue to adapt, at an accelerating rate.

Since the 1920s anthropologists have been investigating the changes that arise from contact between industrial and nonindustrial societies. Studies of "social change" and "acculturation" are abundant. British and American ethnographers, respectively, have used these terms to describe the same process. Acculturation was defined in the chapter "Ethnicity and Ethnic Relations." It refers to changes that result when groups come into continuous firsthand contact—changes in the cultural patterns of either or both groups (Redfield, Linton, and Herskovits 1936, p. 149).

Acculturation differs from diffusion, or cultural borrowing, which can occur without firsthand contact. For example, most North Americans who eat hot dogs ("frankfurters") have never been to Frankfurt, nor have most North American Sony owners or sushi eaters ever visited Japan. Although *acculturation* can be applied to any case of cultural contact and change, the term has most often described **westernization**—the influence of Western expansion on native cultures. Thus natives who wear store-bought clothes, learn Indo-European languages, and otherwise adopt Western customs are called acculturated.

DOMINATION

Different degrees of destruction, domination, resistance, survival, adaptation, and modification of native cultures may follow interethnic contact. In the most destructive encounters native and subordinate cultures face obliteration. Yet in many modern arenas the contact leads to cultural exchange. Today many non-Western cultures are making important contributions to an emerging world culture.

In cases where contact between indigenous cultures and more powerful outsiders leads to destruction—a situation most characteristic of colonialist and expansionist eras—a "shock phase" often follows the initial encounter (Bodley, ed. 1988). Traders and settlers may exploit the native people. Such exploitation may increase mortality, disrupt subsistence, fragment kin groups, damage social support systems, and inspire new religious movements (Bodley, ed. 1988). There may be civil repression backed by military force. Such factors may lead to the tribe's cultural collapse (*ethnocide*) or its physical extinction (*genocide*).

More recently, in the development/modernization era, native landscapes and their traditional management systems have been attacked and often destroyed. Outsiders often attempt to remake native landscapes and cultures in their own image. A name for this process—"terraforming"—can be borrowed from science fiction. Anticipating space exploration and planetary colonization, science fiction writers have imagined a policy of **terraforming.** This refers to the use of technology to make other worlds as much like earth (*terra*) as possible—so that earth colonists can feel at home.

By analogy, we can say that dominant nations and cultures have "terraformed" right here on earth. Political and economic colonialists have tried to redesign conquered and dependent lands, peoples, and cultures, imposing their cultural standards on others. The aim of many agricultural development projects, for example, seems to have been to make the world as much like Iowa as possible, complete with mechanized farming and nuclear family ownership—despite the fact that these models may be inappropriate for settings outside the North American heartland.

Development and Environmentalism

Today it is often multinational corporations, usually based in core nations, rather than the governments of those nations, who are changing the nature of Third World economies. However, nations do tend to support the predatory enterprises that seek cheap labor and raw materials in countries outside the core, such as Brazil, where economic development has contributed to ecological devastation.

Simultaneously, environmentalists from core nations increasingly preach ecological morality to the rest of the world. This doesn't play very well in Brazil, whose Amazon is a focus of environmentalist attention. Brazilians complain that northerners talk about global needs and saving the Amazon after having destroyed their own forests for First World economic growth. Akbar Ahmed (1992) finds the non-Western world to be cynical about western ecological morality, seeing it as yet another imperialist message. "The Chinese have cause to snigger at the Western suggestion that they forgo the convenience of the fridge to save the ozone layer" (Ahmed 1992, p. 120).

In the last chapter we saw that development projects usually fail if they try to replace native forms with culturally alien property concepts and productive units. A strategy that incorporates the native forms is more effective than the fallacies of overinnovation and underdifferention. To those fallacies in promoting cultural diffusion, we may add "the fallacy of the noble global." This refers to a modern intervention philosophy that seeks to impose global ecological morality without due attention to cultural variation and autonomy. Countries and cultures may resist interventionist philosophies aimed at either development or globally oriented environmentalism.

A clash of cultures related to environmental change may occur when *development threatens indigenous peoples and their environments.* Native groups like the Kayapó Indians of Brazil and the Kaluli of Papua–New Guinea (see box) may be threatened by regional, national, and international development plans (such as a dam or commercially driven deforestation) that would *destroy* their homelands.

A second clash of cultures related to environmental change occurs when *external regulation threatens indigenous peoples.* Thus native groups, like the Tanosy of southeastern Madagascar, may be harmed by regional, national, and international environmental plans that seek to *save* their homelands. Sometimes outsiders expect local people to give up many of their customary economic and cultural activities without clear substitutes, alternatives, or incentives. The traditional approach to conservation has been to restrict access to protected areas, hire park guards, and punish violators.

Native peoples, such as these Tanala ("Forest people") of eastern Madagascar, may be threatened by development plans that would destroy their homelands. Ironically, native groups may also be harmed by environmental plans that seek to save their homelands. Because environmental preservation depends on local cooperation, conservation schemes must be culturally appropriate.

Problems often arise when external regulation replaces the native system. Like development projects, conservation schemes may ask people to change the way they have been doing things for generations to satisfy planners' goals rather than local goals. In locales as different as Madagascar, Brazil, and the Pacific Northwest of North America people are being asked, told, or forced to change or abandon basic economic activities because to do so is good for "nature" or "the globe." Ironically, well-meaning conservation efforts can be as insensitive as development schemes that promote radical changes without involving local people in planning and carrying out the policies that affect them. When people are asked to give up the basis of their livelihood, they usually resist.

VOICES OF THE RAINFOREST

The government of Papua–New Guinea has approved oil exploration by American, British, Australian, and Japanese companies in the rainforest habitat of the Kaluli and other indigenous peoples. The forest degradation that usually accompanies logging, ranching, road building, and drilling endangers plants, animals, peoples, and cultures. Lost along with trees are songs, myths, words, ideas, artifacts, and techniques—the cultural knowledge and practices of rainforest people like the Kaluli, whom the anthropologist and ethnomusicologist Steven Feld has been studying for fifteen years.

Recently Feld teamed up with Mickey Hart of the Grateful Dead in a project designed to promote the cultural survival of the Kaluli through their music. For years Hart has worked to preserve musical diversity through educational funding, concert promotion, and recording, including a successful series called "The World" on the Rykodisc label. *Voices of the Rainforest*, released in

that series in April 1991, is the first CD completely devoted to indigenous music from Papua–New Guinea. In one hour it encapsulates twenty-four hours of a day in Kaluli life in Bosavi village. The recording permits a form of cultural survival and diffusion in a high-quality commercial product. Bosavi is presented as a "soundscape" of blended music and natural environmental sounds. Kaluli weave the natural sounds of birds, frogs, rivers and streams into their texts, melodies, and rhythms. They sing and whistle with birds and waterfalls. They compose instrumental duets with birds and cicadas.

The rock star Sting, known for his support of the Amazon rainforest and the Kayapó Indians, isn't the only media figure working to save endangered habitats, peoples, and cultures. The Kaluli project was launched on Earth Day 1991 at *Star Wars* creator George Lucas's Skywalker Ranch. There Randy Hayes, the Executive Director of the Rainforest Action Network, and musician

Mickey Hart spoke about the linked issues of rainforest destruction and musical survival. Next came a San Francisco benefit dinner for the Bosavi People's Fund. This is the trust established to receive royalties from the Kaluli recording—a financial prong in Steven Feld's strategy to foster Kaluli cultural survival.

Voices of the Rainforest is being marketed as "world music." This term is intended to point up musical diversity, the fact that musics originate from all world regions and cultures. Our postmodern world recognizes more than one canon (standard for excellence). (As used here, *postmodern* refers to the blurring and breakdown of established canons, categories, distinctions, and boundaries. Postmodernism reaches out to include less formal, precise, and restricted standards—extending "value" well beyond Western and elite culture.) In the postmodern view, "tribal" music joins Western "classical" music as a form of artistic expression worth performing, hear-

Consider the case of a Tanosy man who lives on the edge of the Andohahela Reserve of southeastern Madagascar. For years he has relied on rice fields and grazing land inside a reserve. Now external agencies are trying to get him to abandon this land for the sake of conservation. This man is a wealthy *ombiasa* (traditional sorcerer-healer). With four wives, a dozen children, and twenty head of cattle, he is an ambitious, hard-working and productive peasant. With money, social support, and supernatural authority, he is mounting effective resistance against the park ranger who has been trying to get him to abandon his fields. The *ombiasa* claims he has already left some of his land, but he is waiting for compensatory land. His most effective resistance has been supernatural. The death in July 1990 of the ranger's son was attributed to the *ombi-*

asa's magical power. Since then the ranger has been less vigilant in his enforcement efforts.

Like development plans, the most effective conservation strategies pay attention to the needs and wishes of the people living in the affected area. Conservation depends on local cooperation. In the Tanosy case, the guardians of the reserve must do more to satisfy the *ombiasa* and other affected people, through boundary adjustments, negotiation, and compensation. For effective conservation (as for development) the task is to devise culturally appropriate strategies. Neither development agencies nor NGOs (nongovernmental organizations) will succeed if they try to impose their goals without considering the practices, customs, rules, laws, beliefs, and values, of the people to be affected.

ing, and preserving. Hart's series offers musics of non-Western origin as well as those of ethnically dominated groups of the Western world. Like Paul Simon's recordings *Graceland* and *Rhythm of the Saints*, which draw on African and Brazilian music, a "world music" record series helps blur the boundaries between the exotic and the familiar. The local and the global unite in a transnational popular culture.

Hart's record series aims at preserving "endangered music" against the artistic loss suffered by indigenous peoples. Its intent is to give a "world voice" to people who are being silenced by the dominant world system. In 1993, Hart launched a new series, *The Library of Congress Endangered Music Project*, which will include digitally remastered field recordings collected by the American Folklife Center. The first of this series, "The Spirit Cries," concentrates on music from a broad range of cultures in South and Central America and the Caribbean. Proceeds from this project will be used

to support the performers and their cultural traditions.

In "Voices of the Rainforest," Feld and Hart excised all "modern" and "dominant" sounds from their recording. Gone are the world system sounds that Kaluli villagers now hear every day. The recording temporarily silences "machine voices": the tractor that cuts the grass on the local airstrip, the gas generator, the sawmill, the helicopters and light planes buzzing to and from the oil-drilling areas. Gone, too, are the village church bells, Bible readings, evangelical prayers and hymns, and the voices of teachers and students at an English-only school.

Initially, Feld anticipated criticism for attempting to create an idealized Kaluli "soundscape" insulated from invasive forces and sounds. Among the Kaluli he expected varied opinions about the value of his project:

It is a soundscape world that some Kaluli care little about, a world that other Kaluli momentarily choose to forget, a world that some

Kaluli are increasingly nostalgic and uneasy about, a world that other Kaluli are still living and creating and listening to. It is a sound world that increasingly fewer Kaluli will actively know about and value, but one that increasingly more Kaluli will only hear on cassette and sentimentally wonder about. (Feld 1991, p. 137)

Despite these concerns, Feld was met with an overwhelmingly positive response when he returned to Papua New Guinea in 1992 armed with a boombox and the recording. The Education Department has put copies of the recording into every high school library. The people of Bosavi also reacted very favorably. Not only did they appreciate the recording, they have also been able to build a much-needed community school with the "Voices of the Rainforest" royalties that have been donated to the Bosavi Peoples Fund.

Source: Based on Steven Feld, "Voices of the Rainforest," *Public Culture* 4(1): 131–140 (1991).

Religious Domination

In the movie *Raiders of the Lost Ark* Indiana Jones, anthropologist extraordinaire, faces an assassin armed with a scimitar. The Middle-Easterner displays an elaborate series of moves showing his skills in traditional weaponry. Impressed by the demonstration, as the audience appreciates the threat, Jones takes out a pistol and shoots the man dead. This sequence makes a point about dominance and cultural diversity, interethnic encounters, the world system, resistance, and survival. The scimitar-wielding Mid-Easterner can be seen as symbolizing traditional culture against the world system. We should not forget that anthropologists, too, are agents of the world system. A century ago the anthropologist tended to arrive after the traders (the

economic proselytizers), but around the same time, and often competing with, the missionaries (the religious proselytizers). The Christians came to "save souls." The anthropologists were there to salvage cultures. But all were Western presences among the natives.

Religious proselytizing can promote ethnocide, as native beliefs and practices are replaced by Western ones. Sometimes a religion and associated customs are completely replaced by ideology and behavior more compatible with Western culture. One example is the Handsome Lake religion (as described in the chapter on religion), which led the Iroquois Indians to copy European farming techniques, stressing male rather than female labor. The Iroquois also gave up their communal longhouses and matrilineal descent groups for nuclear family households. The

Like development projects, conservation schemes may ask people to change their traditional economy to satisfy planners' goals rather than local goals. People who fear the loss of their livelihood, like these California loggers, are likely to resist.

teachings of Handsome Lake led to a new church and religion. This revitalization movement helped the Iroquois survive in a drastically modified environment, but much ethnocide was involved.

Handsome Lake was a native who created a new religion, drawing on Western models. More commonly, missionaries and proselytizers representing the major world religions, especially Christianity and Islam, are the proponents of religious change. Protestant and Catholic missionization continues even in remote corners of the world. Evangelical Protestantism, for example, is advancing in Peru, Brazil, and other parts of Latin America. It challenges a jaded Catholicism that has too few priests and that is sometimes seen mainly as women's religion.

Sometimes the political ideology of a nation-state (for example, "godless communism") is pitted against traditional religion. Officials of the former Soviet empire discouraged both Catholicism and Islam. In Central Asia, Soviet dominators destroyed Muslim mosques and discouraged religious practice.

On the other hand, governments often use their power to advance a religion, such as Islam in Iran or Sudan. A military government seized power in Sudan in 1989. It immediately launched a campaign to change that country of 25 million people, where one-third are not Muslims, into an Islamic nation. Sudan adopted a policy of religious, linguistic, and cultural imperialism. The government sought to extend Islam and the Arabic language to the non-Muslim south. This was an area of Christianity and tribal religions that had resisted the central government for a decade. The new government declared a *jihad* (holy war) against non-Muslims. It persecuted Catholic leaders and purged the military, the civil service, the judiciary, and the educational system of non-Muslims. Students in the south were forced to take their exams in Arabic, for them a foreign language (Hedges 1992*a*).

During a long civil war, which began in 1983, many villagers had fled the south and moved north, to slums outside Khartoum, Sudan's capital. In 1992 the Islamic government began a forced relocation program to rid Khartoum of 1 million squatters. Half a million were moved at gunpoint from the slums to relocation camps. Those who resisted were beaten or shot. The camps had no jobs, clinics, or schools, and international NGOs were banned from working there. The government promoted conversion to Islam by allowing only Islamic charities to operate in the camps. Loudspeakers invited camp dwellers to turn to Islam in return for food, money, and a place to live (Hedges 1992*b*).

RESISTANCE AND SURVIVAL

Systems of domination—political, cultural, or religious—always have their more muted aspects along with their public dimensions. In studying apparent cultural domination, or actual political domination, we must pay careful attention to what lies beneath the surface of evident, public, behavior. In public the oppressed may seem to accept their own domination, but they always question it offstage. James Scott (1990) uses "**public transcript**" to describe the open, public interactions between dominators and oppressed—the outer shell of power relations. He uses "**hidden transcript**" to describe the critique of power that goes on offstage, where the power holders can't see it.

In public the oppressed and the elites observe the etiquette of power relations. The dominants act like haughty masters while their subordinates show humility and defer. Antonio Gramsci (1971) developed the concept of **hegemony** for a stratified social order in which subordinates comply with domination by internalizing its values and accepting its "naturalness" (this is the way things were meant to be). According to Pierre Bourdieu (1977, p. 164) every social order tries to make its own arbitrariness (including its oppression) seem natural. All hegemonic ideologies offer explanations about why the existing order is in everyone's interest. Often promises are made (things will get better if you're patient). Gramsci and others use the idea of hegemony to explain why people conform even without coercion, why they knuckle under when they don't really have to.

Hegemony, the internalization of a dominant ideology, is one way to curb resistance. Another way is to let subordinates know they will eventually gain power—as young people usually forsee when they let their elders dominate them. Another way of curbing resistance is to separate or isolate subordinates and supervise them closely. According to Michel Foucault (1979), describing control over prisoners, solitude (as in solitary confinement) is an effective way to induce submission. Subordinates may conclude that the severity of punishment makes open resistance too risky.

Weapons of the Weak

Often, situations that seem to be hegemonic do have active resistance, but it is individual and disguised rather than collective and defiant. Scott (1985) uses Malay peasants, among whom he did field work, to illustrate small-scale acts of resistance—which he calls "weapons of the weak." The Malay peasants used an indirect strategy to resist a corrupt Islamic tithe (religious tax). The goods (usually rice) that peasants had to give went to the provincial capital. In theory, the tithe would come back as charity, but it never did. Peasants didn't resist the tithe by rioting, demonstrating, or protesting. Instead they used a "nibbling" strategy, based on small acts of resistance. For example, they failed to declare their land or lied about the amount they farmed. They underpaid or delivered rice paddy contaminated with water, rocks, or mud, to add weight. Because of this resistance, only 15 percent of what was due was actually paid (Scott 1990, p. 89).

Subordinates also use various strategies to resist

Illustrating a policy of religious, linguistic, and cultural imperialism, the Sudanese government has sought to extend Islam and the Arabic language to the non-Muslim south. This area of Christianity and tribal religions has resisted the central government for a decade. Shown here are members of the resistance, the Sudan People's Liberation Army.

publicly, but again, usually in disguised form. Discontent may be expressed in public rituals and language, including metaphors, euphemisms, and folk tales. For example, trickster tales (like the Brer Rabbit stories told by slaves in the southern United States) celebrate the wiles of the weak as they triumph over the strong.

Resistance is most likely to be expressed openly when the oppressed are allowed to assemble. The hidden transcript may be publicly revealed on such occasions. People see their dreams and anger shared by others with whom they haven't been in direct contact. The oppressed may draw courage from the crowd, from its visual and emotional impact and its anonymity. Sensing danger, the elites discourage such public gatherings. They try to limit and control holidays, funerals, dances, festivals, and other occasions that might unite the oppressed. Thus in the southern United States gatherings of five or more slaves were forbidden unless a white person was present.

Factors that interfere with community formation—such as geographic, linguistic, and ethnic separation—also work to curb resistance. Consequently, southern U.S. plantation owners sought slaves with diverse cultural and linguistic backgrounds. But such divisive factors can be overcome. Despite the measures used to divide them, the slaves resisted, developing their own popular culture, linguistic codes, and religious vision. The masters taught portions of the Bible that stressed compliance, but the slaves seized on the story of Moses, the promised land, and deliverance. As in Melanesian cargo cults (see below), the cornerstone of slave religion became the idea of a reversal in the conditions of whites and blacks. According to Scott (1990, pp. 80–81) it is easy to visualize a reversal of the existing distribution of status and rewards. People can always imagine an end to oppressive conditions. Slaves also resisted directly, through sabotage and flight. In many New World areas slaves managed to establish free communities in the hills and other isolated areas (Price, ed. 1973).

Hidden transcripts tend to be publicly expressed at certain times (festivals and Carnivals) and in certain places (for example, markets). Because of its costumed anonymity and its ritual structure (reversal), Carnival is an excellent arena for expressing normally suppressed speech and aggression—antihegemonic discourse. (**Discourse** includes talk, speeches, gestures, and actions.) Carnivals, public rituals of reversal, celebrate freedom through immodesty, dancing, gluttony, and sexuality (DaMatta 1991). Carnival may begin as a playful outlet for frustrations built up during the year. Over time it may evolve into a powerful annual critique of domination and a threat to the established order (Gilmore 1987). (Recognizing that ceremonial license could turn into political defiance, the Spanish dictator Francisco Franco outlawed Carnival.)

Because of its costumed anonymity and its ritual structure (reversal), Carnival is an excellent arena for expressing normally suppressed speech. This is vividly symbolized by these Carnival headdresses in Trinidad.

In medieval Europe, according to Mikhail Bakhtin (1984), the market was the main place where the dominant ideology was questioned. The anonymity of the crowd and of commerce put people on an equal footing. The rituals and deference used with lords and clergy didn't apply to the marketplace. Later in Europe the hidden transcript also went public in pubs, taverns, inns, cabarets, beer cellars, and gin mills. These places fostered a popular culture—in games, songs, gambling, blasphemy, and disorder—which was at odds with the official culture. People met in an atmosphere of freedom encouraged by alcohol. Church and state alike condemned these activities as subversive.

Resistance through Nongovernmental Organizations

Domination continues in today's world, and the dominated continue to find new forms of resistance. For example, thousands of nongovernmental organizations (NGOs) have formed worldwide. NGOs, representing an increasingly significant form of political organization, have emerged to foster various objectives. Often, as in the Mexican case discussed below, NGOs organize resistance to forms of domination and exploitation.

NGOs can be local, regional, national, or international in their goals and membership. One prominent international NGO is *Cultural Survival* (see below) whose goal is to foster the survival of native peoples. Other international NGOs include Care, Save the Children, Catholic Relief Services, Foster Parents Plan International, and Oxfam (a hunger relief organization). WWF (the World Wildlife Fund) and IUCN (the International Union for the Conservation of Nature) are international NGOs that promote the conservation of animals, plants, and ecosystems. Large modern nations have hundreds or thousands of NGOs. In Brazil, for example, more than 400 such groups have formed around various national, regional, and local ecological issues.

NGOs formed at the local level are also known as "grassroots" organizations. In Mexico such groups play an increasing role in resisting government policies that have forced people off their ancestral lands. These policies pose a particular threat to indigenous peoples who rely on communally held lands known as *ejidos*.

In Chiapas, a state in southern Mexico, there has been a recent change—toward greater inequality and domination—in traditional peasant communities. Formerly, communal lands and a strong feeling of local solidarity and cooperation provided a common social identity for indigenous peasants. Recently, however, wealth contrasts have widened into class divisions in many communities (Nash and Sullivan, 1992). Community leaders (*caciques*) now draw substantial profits by selling alcohol, beer, soft drinks, and candles, and from money lending and fines. Increasingly the Indian leaders have used an ideology of community solidarity to advance their own interests at the expense of less powerful community residents. Claiming that tradition is on their side, *caciques* expel dissidents from communal lands and seize their assets.

The leaders justify their actions by claiming that those who are expelled are people who refuse to follow custom. Converts from the traditional Catholicism to Protestantism are their main targets, but *caciques* also expel Catholics who challenge them. The expelled people have denounced the elites, but the government has done little to stop these land grabs. In fact, regional and national leaders usually back the *caciques*, because they work to ensure electoral victories for the dominant political party. State and federal agents ignore the expulsions since the *caciques* deliver the vote.

Mexico's population continues to grow as its available farmland shrinks. One way the government has responded to peasant demands for more land is by encouraging multiethnic colonization in the jungle homeland of the Lacandon Maya. These government land grants have threatened Maya autonomy and promoted interethnic conflict in this area. But recently, multiethnic coalitions have emerged to resist dominance and the division of the oppressed. New peasant organizations are bridging the contrasts in language and customs.

Despite government policies that promote ethnic divisions, ethnic groups have joined in NGOs. One of their aims is to resist the *caciques*. Organized resistance to land grabs by the *caciques* began in 1982 when Protestants formed the Committee for the Defense of the Threatened, Persecuted, and Expelled of Chamula. This was followed by the interdenominational Organization of the Indians of the Chiapas Highlands (ORIACH). These groups work to defend Indians against the state, large landowners, and other Indians (Nash and Sullivan 1992).

IN THE NEWS: "THINGS HAVE HAPPENED TO ME AS IN A MOVIE"

In 1992 Rigoberta Menchú, a 33-year-old Quiché Indian, received the Nobel Peace Prize for her fight on behalf of Indians and human rights in Guatemala. Ms. Menchú has continued her father's leadership role in a grassroots organization, the Committee of Peasant Unity. Her work has also been assisted by a Mexican NGO—a liberal Catholic group called "the Guatemalan Church in Exile." Ms. Menchú's father and brother were tortured (as is described in this autobiographical selection) during the ongoing Guatemalan civil war. Most of the 100,000 people believed to have been killed in that war, which has lasted three decades, have been unarmed Indian peasants. Ms. Menchú's father, mother, and brother were eventually killed in separate incidents. Rigoberta Menchú planned to use her $1.2 million prize to campaign for peace in Guatemala and the rights of Indians throughout the hemisphere.

I am a native of the Quiché people of Guatemala. My life has been a long one. Things have happened to me as in a movie. My parents were killed in the repression. I have hardly any relatives living. It has been the lot of many, many Guatemalans.

We were a very poor family. My parents worked cutting cotton, cutting coffee. Two of my brothers died on the plantation. One of them got sick and died. The other died when the landowner ordered cotton sprayed while we were in the field. My brother was poisoned, and we buried him on the plantation.

My father was a catechist, and in Guatemala a catechist is a leader of the community, preaching the Gospel. We began to evolve in the Catholic religion and became catechists.

We grew up—and really you can't say we started fighting only a short time ago, because it has been 22 years since my father fought over the land. The landowners wanted to take away our little bit of land, and so my father fought for it. So he went to speak with the mayors and judges in various parts of Guatemala. For many years, he was tricked because he did not speak Spanish. None of us spoke Spanish. So they made my father travel all over to sign papers, letters, telegrams, which meant that not only he, but the whole community, had to sacrifice to pay the expenses.

My father was imprisoned many times. First, he was accused of causing unrest among the population. When he was in jail, the army kicked us out of our houses. They burned our clay pots. It was really hard for us to understand this situation. Then my father was sentenced to 18 years in prison, but we were able to work with lawyers to get him released. After a year and two months, he returned home with more courage to go on fighting and angrier because of what had happened.

A short time later, he was tortured by the landowners' bodyguards. Some armed men took him away. We found him lying in the road, about two kilometers from home, barely alive. The priests had come out to take him to the hospital. He had been in the hospital for six months when he heard he was going to be taken out and killed. The landowners had been discussing it loudly. We had to find a private clinic so he would heal.

In 1977, my father was in jail again. The military told us it didn't want us to see him, because he had committed many crimes. From lawyers we learned he was going to be executed. Many union workers, students, peasants and some priests demonstrated. My father was freed, but he was told he was going to be killed anyway for being a Communist.

In 1979, five armed men, their faces covered, kidnapped one of my little brothers. He was 16. Since my father couldn't go out, we went with my mother and members of the community to make a complaint to the army, but they said they didn't know anything. We went to City Hall, to all the jails in Guatemala. My mother was very upset. It had taken a lot for

Armed Resistance

Besides NGOs, other forms of mobilization have emerged to express resentment against domination and exploitation. There has been collective action aimed at preserving or regaining tribal or ethnic autonomy in Africa, the Philippines, India, North America, Central America, Indonesia, and Australia.

Collective armed resistance can be an effective response to state intervention in tribal life. For example, tribes in the Philippines and in Sudan have used armed resistance to stop development projects that would have destroyed cultures, economies, and ecosystems. In the Philippines a hydroelectric project promoted by the Ferdinand Marcos government would have devastated the terraced irrigation-

Rigoberta Menchú, the winner of the 1992 Nobel Peace Prize, is shown here in Mexico City with her friend Rosalina Tuyuc.

my brother to survive, and so it was very hard to accept his disappearance.

At that time the army published a bulletin saying that they had some guerrillas in their custody and that they were going to punish them in public. My mother said: "I hope to God my son is there. I want to know what has happened to him." We walked for one day and almost the whole night to get to the town. Hundreds of soldiers had gathered the people to witness what they were going to do. After a while a truck arrived with 20 people who had been tortured in different ways.

Among them we recognized my brother. We had to calm my mother down, telling her that if she gave herself away she was going to die right there for being family of a guerrilla. We were crying, but almost all the rest of the people were crying also at the sight of the tortured people. The army had pulled my little brother's fingernails out, cut off parts of his ears and other parts of his body, his lips, and he was covered with scars and swollen all over. Among the prisoners was a woman and parts of her breasts and other parts of her body were cut off.

An army captain gave a very long speech, saying that if we got involved with Communism the same things would happen to us. Then he explained the various types of torture they had applied to the prisoners. After three hours, the officer ordered the troops to strip the prisoners and said, "Part of the punishment is still to come." He ordered them tied to some posts. The people didn't know what to do, and my mother was overcome with despair. And none of us knew how we could bear the situation. The officer ordered the prisoners covered with gasoline and they set fire to them, one by one.

Source: Rigoberta Menchú, "Things Have Happened to Me as in a Movie," *The New York Times,* October 17, 1992, A25. Adapted from an autobiographical chapter in *You Can't Drown the Fire: Latin American Women Writing in Exile,* Cleis Press, 1989.

based native economy of the Igorots, who are mountain people (Drucker 1988). Igorot political action and armed resistance halted the project. Otherwise, the dams would have ruined a highly productive, generations-old engineering system of water and soil management that supported 90,000 people.

Armed resistance in Sudan has been less effective, as of this writing. In 1974 the government started digging the Jonglei canal in southern Sudan, across the homelands of Nilotic peoples, including the Nuer and the Dinka. Building stopped in 1984 after armed attacks on construction camps. Calling themselves the Sudan People's Liberation Army, many resisters were Nilotes who considered the canal an invasion from the Muslim north. With a planned length of 360 kilometers (225 miles), the Jonglei

In 1974 the national government started digging the Jonglei canal in southern Sudan, across the homelands of Nilotic peoples, including the Nuer and the Dinka. The Jonglei Dam would have helped northern farmers and hurt southern herders. Building was halted in 1984 after armed attacks on construction camps by the Sudan People's Liberation Army.

canal was an ambitious engineering project. Its purpose was to bypass the great bend in the Nile to reduce "water loss" and to channel water northward for export crops such as cotton.

The Jonglei Dam would have helped northern farmers and hurt southern herders. Behind this scheme was an old evolutionary assumption—that agriculture is a higher (more advanced) stage than pastoralism. The expectation was that herders should and would want to "progress" by becoming sedentary farmers. But the people of southern Sudan resisted the project because it would have destroyed pasture, which depends on seasonal flooding. The government tried to justify the project by claiming that half the annual flood was lost to evaporation anyway. But the government ignored the fact that the Nuer, the Dinka, and their herds depended on that water and the pasture and plants it nourished.

An explicit government goal in building the canal was to increase the herders' involvement with the national economy. Sudan's government cared little about the Nuer and Dinka cattle because they were "merely" the basis of a subsistence economy. Unlike the cash crops the canal would have irrigated, those cattle did not enter the marketplace (Lako 1988).

Tribal and Human Rights

National and international NGOs have emerged to support native populations threatened by development programs. One of the most prominent NGOs is **Cultural Survival,** founded in 1972 by David and Pia Maybury-Lewis. Its goal is to help native peoples—such as the Yanomami, who have been threatened by development in Brazil—to survive as successful ethnic minorities within nation-states.

When I first wrote this section, I had just learned of a decree signed by a former Brazilian President, José Sarney, limiting Yanomami use of their ancestral lands. The decree gave Brazilian miners and ranchers the right to exploit much of Yanomami territory. Responding to international criticism (including a well-publicized report commissioned by the American Anthropological Association), Sarney's successor, Fernando Collor, rescinded his predecessor's decision. In March 1992, Collor signed a decree recognizing Yanomami rights to a huge area and restricting outsiders' access to it. The Yanomami had won an immediate victory, but it remains unclear whether it will be a permanent one since Collor is no longer president. Even if he were, many Brazilian laws and decrees go unenforced, and federal laws often face opposition at the state level.

Facing the world system, people may resist, fight, and sometimes win. Some native peoples manage to survive and flourish. The Kayapó Indians of Brazil have become their own advocates, ethnographers, and historians. Kayapó use camcorders to record their fights against outside encroachment. They take the machines with them wherever they go, to record what they see and bring the images back so that others may participate in their experi-

The Kayapó Indians of Brazil have become their own advocates, ethnographers, and historians. Also to ensure their cultural survival, they have enlisted Brazilian and foreign anthropologists, and the world media. The rock star Sting, shown here with Chief Raoni, was part of the Kayapós' successful campaign to stop the construction of a dam that would have flooded their homeland.

ences. The Kayapó also creatively enlisted Brazilian and foreign anthropologists, and the world media. The rock star Sting was part of their successful campaign to stop the construction of a dam that would have flooded their homeland.

Indigenous peoples, such as the Kayapó and the Inuit of Canada, go on fighting to preserve their cultural diversity. The Inuit have recently won a major victory. Following up an agreement signed in December 1991, Canada is setting the boundaries for a self-governing Inuit homeland. On May 5, 1992, voters in Canada's "Northwest Territories" authorized its split into two separate territories. Extending almost to Greenland, the eastern territory covers an area a third larger than Alaska. It is inhabited by 17,500 "Eskimos," who call themselves Inuit. The Inuit will administer this area, which they call Nunavut, "Our Land." They will receive title to about 20 percent of the land in Nunavut. As an economic jump-start for their new homeland, they will also get at least $1.4 billion over fourteen years (Farnsworth 1992).

SYNCRETISMS, BLENDS, AND ACCOMMODATION

Many new forms of popular expression have emerged from the interplay of local, regional, national, and international cultural forces. **Syncretisms,** for example, are cultural *blends* that emerge

Following up an agreement signed in December 1991, Canada is setting the boundaries for a self-governing Inuit homeland. The Inuit will administer this area, which they call Nunavut, "Our Land."

from acculturation. One example is the mixture of African, Native American, and Roman Catholic saints and deities in Caribbean vodun, or "voodoo," cults. This blend is also present in **candomblé,** an "Afro-Brazilian" cult. Another syncretism is the blend of Melanesian and Christian beliefs in cargo cults.

Cargo Cults

Many religious movements (like the Handsome Lake religion discussed earlier) have arisen in response to the spread of colonialism, European domination, and the world capitalist economy. Revitalization movements may emerge when natives have regular contact with industrial societies but are denied their wealth, technology, and living standards. Some such movements attempt to *explain* European domination and wealth and to achieve similar success magically by mimicking European behavior and manipulating symbols of the desired life style. Some of the best-known examples are the syncretic **cargo cults** of Melanesia and Papua–New Guinea, which weave Christian doctrine with aboriginal beliefs. They take their name from their focus on cargo–European goods of the sort natives have seen unloaded from the cargo holds of ships and airplanes.

In one early cult, members believed that the spirits of the dead would arrive in a ship. These ghosts would bring manufactured goods for the natives and would kill all the whites. More recent cults replaced ships with airplanes (Worsley 1959/1985). Many cults have used elements of European culture as sacred objects. The rationale is that Europeans use these objects, have wealth, and therefore must know the "secret of cargo." By mimicking how Europeans use or treat objects, natives hope also to come upon the secret knowledge needed to gain cargo.

For example, having seen Europeans' reverent treatment of flags and flagpoles, the members of one cult began to worship flagpoles. They believed the flagpoles were sacred towers that could transmit messages between the living and the dead. Other natives built airstrips to entice planes bearing canned goods, portable radios, clothing, wristwatches, and motorcycles. Near the airstrips they made effigies of towers, airplanes, and radios. They talked into the cans in a magical attempt to establish radio contact with the gods.

Some cargo cult prophets proclaimed that success would come through a reversal of European domination and native subjugation. The day was near, they preached, when natives, aided by God, Jesus, or native ancestors, would turn the tables. Native skins would turn white, and those of Europeans would turn brown; Europeans would die or be killed.

As syncretisms, cargo cults blend aboriginal and Christian beliefs. Melanesian myths told of ancestors shedding their skins and changing into powerful beings and of dead people returning to life. Christian missionaries, who had been in Melanesia since the late nineteenth century, also spoke of resurrection. The cults' preoccupation with cargo is related to traditional Melanesian big-man systems. Previously we saw (in the chapter "Bands and Tribes") that a Melanesian big man had to be generous. People worked for the big man, helping him amass wealth, but eventually he had to give a feast and give away all that wealth. Because of their experience with big-man systems, Melanesians believed that all wealthy people eventually had to give their wealth away. For decades they had attended Christian missions and worked on plantations. All the while they expected Europeans to return the fruits of their labor as their own big men did. When the Europeans refused to distribute the wealth or even to let natives know the secret of its production and distribution, cargo cults developed.

Like arrogant big men, Europeans would be leveled, by death if necessary. However, natives lacked the physical means of doing what their traditions said they should do. Thwarted by well-armed colonial forces, natives resorted to magical leveling. They called on supernatural beings to intercede, to kill or otherwise deflate the European big men and redistribute their wealth.

Cargo cults are religious responses to the expansion of the world capitalist economy. However, this religious mobilization had political and economic results. Cult participation gave Melanesians a basis for common interests and activities and thus helped pave the way for political parties and economic interest organizations. Previously separated by geography, language, and customs, Melanesians started forming larger groups as members of the same cults and followers of the same prophets. Cargo cults paved the way for political action through which indigenous peoples eventually regained their autonomy.

Cultural Imperialism, Stimulus Diffusion, and Creative Opposition

Cultural imperialism refers to the rapid spread or advance of one culture at the expense of others, or its imposition on other cultures, which it modifies, replaces, or destroys—usually because of differential economic or political influence. Thus children in the French colonial empire learned French history, language, and culture from standard textbooks also used in France. Tahitians, Malagasy, Vietnamese, and Senegalese learned the French language by reciting from books about "our ancestors the Gauls." Ironically, modern French intellectuals, seemingly forgetting France's colonialist past, are quick to complain about American cultural imperialism. Thus in 1992 French intellectuals protested the opening of Euro Disney as a threat to French (and European) culture. The French minister of culture Jack Lang has lamented the extent to which American films and TV programs (purportedly) dominate popular culture in many countries. Lang has decried an "intellectual imperialism" that "grabs consciousness, ways of thinking, ways of living" (Gutis 1987).

The matter isn't as simple as the French intellectuals imagine. People aren't passive victims of cultural imperialism. Contemporary people—often with considerable creativity—constantly revise, rework, resist, and reject the messages they get from external systems.

Some critics worry that modern technology, including the mass media, is killing off traditional cultures by homogenizing products to reach more people. But others see an important role for modern technology in allowing social groups (local cultures) to express themselves and thus in disseminating particular subcultures (Marcus and Fisher 1986, p. 122). Modern radio and TV, for example, constantly bring local happenings (for example, a "chicken festival" in Iowa) to the attention of a larger public. The North American media play a role in stimulating local activities of many sorts. Similarly in Brazil, local practices, celebrations, and performances are changing in the context of outside forces, including the mass media and tourism.

In the town of Arembepe TV coverage has stimulated participation in a traditional annual performance, the *Chegança*. This is a fishermen's dance-play that reenacts the Portuguese discovery of Brazil. Arembepeiros have traveled to the state capital to perform the *Chegança* before television cam-

eras, for a TV program featuring traditional performances from many rural communities. Here one sees television's role in allowing social groups to express themselves and in disseminating local cultures.

One national Brazilian Sunday-night variety program (*Fantástico*) is especially popular in rural areas because it shows such local events. In several towns along the Amazon River, annual folk ceremonies are now staged more lavishly for TV cameras. In the Amazon town of Parantíns, for example, boatloads of tourists arriving any time of year are shown a videotape of the town's annual Bumba Meu Boi festival. This is a costumed performance mimicking bull-fighting, parts of which have been shown on *Fantástico*. This pattern, in which communities preserve, revive, and intensify the scale of traditional ceremonies to perform for TV and tourists, is expanding.

However, Brazilian television has also played a "top-down" role, by spreading the popularity of national (and international) holidays, like Carnival and Christmas (Kottak 1990). TV has aided the national spread of Carnival beyond its traditional urban centers, especially Rio de Janeiro. Still, local reactions to the nation-wide broadcasting of Carnival and its trappings (elaborate parades, costumes, and frenzied dancing) are not simple or uniform responses to external stimuli. Like syncretisms, these new forms of popular expression are cultural creations that develop from the interplay of local, regional, national, and international forces.

Rather than direct adoption of Carnival, or rote imitation of it, local Brazilians respond in various ways. These reactions include "stimulus diffusion" and "creative opposition." **Stimulus diffusion** describes the process by which a group modifies a custom by adopting images and behavior associated with an external practice, without borrowing the practice itself. We see stimulus diffusion when Brazilians don't take up Carnival itself but modify their local festivities to fit Carnival images. **Creative opposition** occurs when people change their behavior as they consciously and actively avoid or spurn an external image or practice. We see creative opposition when local Brazilians deliberately reject Carnival, sometimes by celebrating traditional local festivals on a previously unimagined scale, sometimes by rejecting certain local practices perceived as similar to the disdained external practice.

In Brazilian towns national Carnival coverage

seems more often to inspire stimulus diffusion than direct borrowing through simple imitation. Local groups work hard not on Carnival per se but on incorporating its elements and themes in their own ceremonies. Some of these have grown in scale, in imitation of Carnival celebrations shown on national TV. But local reactions can also be negative, even hostile. One example is Arembepe, where Carnival has never been important, probably because of its calendrical closeness to the main local festival, which is held in February to honor Saint Francis of Assisi. In the past, villagers couldn't afford to celebrate both occasions. Now, not only do the people of Arembepe reject Carnival, they are also increasingly hostile to their own main festival. Arembepeiros resent the fact that Saint Francis has become "an outsiders' event," because it draws thousands of tourists to Arembepe each February. The villagers think that commercial interests and outsiders have appropriated Saint Francis.

In creative opposition, many Arembepeiros now say they like and participate more in the traditional June festivals honoring Saint John, Saint Peter, and Saint Anthony. In the past these were observed on a much smaller scale than was Saint Francis. Arembepeiros celebrate them now with a new vigor and enthusiasm, as they react to outsiders and their celebrations, real and televised.

MAKING AND REMAKING CULTURE

Any media-borne image, such as Carnival, can be considered a **text**—something that is creatively "read," interpreted, and assigned meaning by each person who receives it. Carnival images in Brazil illustrate some ways in which "readers" produce their own meanings from a text. Such meanings may be very different from what the creators of the text imagined. (The reading or meaning that the creators intended—or the one that the elites consider to be the intended or correct meaning—can be called the **hegemonic reading**.)

"Readers" of media messages constantly produce their own meanings. They may resist or creatively oppose the hegemonic meaning of a text, or they may seize on the antihegemonic aspects of a text. We saw this process when American slaves preferred the Biblical story of Moses and deliverance to

the hegemonic lessons of obedience that their masters taught.

Popular Culture

In his book *Understanding Popular Culture* (1989), John Fiske views each individual's use of popular culture as a creative act (an original "reading" of a text). (For example, Madonna, the Grateful Dead, or *Star Wars* mean something different to each of their fans.) As Fiske puts it, ". . . the meanings I make from a text are pleasurable when I feel that they are *my* meanings and that they relate to *my* everyday life in a practical, direct way" (1989, p. 57). All of us can creatively "read" magazines, books, music, television, films, celebrities, and other popular culture products.

Individuals also draw on popular culture to express resistance. Through their use of popular culture, people can symbolically resist the unequal power relations they face each day—in the family, at work, and in the classroom. Forms and readings of popular culture (from rap music to sitcoms) can express discontent and resistance by groups that are or feel oppressed.

Indigenizing Popular Culture

To understand culture change, it is important to recognize that meaning is not inherent or imposed but locally manufactured. People assign their own meanings and value to the texts, messages, and products they receive. Those meanings reflect their cultural backgrounds and experiences. When forces from world centers enter new societies, they are **indigenized**—modified to fit the local culture. This is true of cultural forces as different as fast food, music, housing styles, science, terrorism, celebrations, and political ideas and institutions (Appadurai 1990).

The notion of cultural imperialism is flawed because it views people as victims rather than as creative agents in their own transformation. For example, Michaels (1986) found *Rambo* to be a popular movie among aborigines in the deserts of central Australia, who had manufactured their own meanings from the film. Their "reading" was very different from the one imagined by the movie's creators, and by most Americans. The Native Australians saw Rambo as a representative of the Third World

The notion of cultural imperialism is flawed because it views people as victims rather than as creative agents in their own transformation. Native Australians saw Rambo *as a representative of the Third World battling the white officer class. This "reading" of* Rambo *expressed their hostility toward white paternalism and existing race relations. Shown here, a* Rambo *poster in Jakarta, Indonesia.*

battling the white officer class. This reading expressed their negative feelings about white paternalism and existing race relations. The Native Australians also created tribal ties and kin links between Rambo and the prisoners he was rescuing. All this made sense, based on their experience. Native Australians are disproportionately represented in Australian jails, and their most likely liberator would be someone with a personal link to them. These readings of *Rambo* were relevant meanings produced *from* the text, not *by* it (Fiske 1989).

Something comparable has happened in the Philippines, where a long history of American missionization and political intervention has helped create a nation of "make-believe Americans" (Appadurai 1990, p. 5). Most specifically, Filipinos use American songs, especially from the 1950s and 1960s, as an important part of their popular culture (Iyer 1988). In fact, Filipino renditions of those songs are more widespread there and more faithful to the originals than are the same songs in the United States today. "An entire nation seems to have learned to mimic Kenny Rogers and the Lennon sisters" (Appadurai 1990, p. 5). But Appadurai thinks it would be improper to call this process "Americanization" because there is not now, nor has there ever been, anything quite like it in the United States. The Filipinos have not recreated American culture as it was a generation ago, when the music and lyrics of those songs were intertwined with other American cultural themes. The rest of Filipino culture is dramat-

ically out of sync with the world that first produced those songs. American music has found a new—not a borrowed—meaning and context within Filipino popular culture.

A World System of Images

Also, in Appadurai's view (1990, p. 4) the United States has lost its role as principal "puppeteer of a world system of images" (a media-saturated world in which the imagination plays a growing role in social life). All cultures express imagination—in dreams, songs, fantasies, myths, and stories. Today, however, more people in many more places imagine "a wider set of 'possible' lives than they ever did before. One important source of this change is the mass media, which present a rich, ever-changing store of possible lives . . ." (Appadurai 1991, p. 197). The United States remains a media center, but one among many. It has been joined by Canada, Japan, Western Europe, Brazil, Mexico, Nigeria, Egypt, India, and Hong Kong.

Film industries in Hong Kong and Hollywood have worked together to spread images of masculinity and violence across nations. Old martial arts traditions have been reformulated to meet the fantasies of contemporary male youth, especially in Asia. This, in turn, has fueled violence in national and international politics, through a worldwide arms trade (Appadurai 1990).

As print has done for centuries (Anderson 1990),

the electronic mass media can also spread, and even create, national and ethnic identities. Like print, television and radio can diffuse the cultures of different countries within their own boundaries, thus enhancing national cultural identity. For example, millions of Brazilians who were formerly cut off (by geographic isolation or illiteracy) from urban and national events and information now join in a national communication system, thanks to the national TV network called *Globo*. Through television modern Brazilians have a sense of regular participation in national events (Kottak 1990).

Cross-cultural studies of television contradict a belief Americans ethnocentrically hold about televiewing in other countries. This misconception is that American programs inevitably triumph over local products. This doesn't happen when there is appealing local competition. In Brazil, for example, the most popular network (TV Globo) relies heavily on native productions. American imports like *Dallas* and *Dynasty* have drawn small audiences. TV Globo's most popular programs are *telenovelas*, locally made serials that are similar to American soap operas. Globo plays each night to the world's largest and most devoted audience (60 to 80 million viewers throughout the nation). The programs that attract this horde are made by Brazilians, for Brazilians. Thus it is not North American culture but a new pan-Brazilian national culture, which Brazilian TV is propagating. Brazilian productions also compete internationally. They are exported to over 100 countries, spanning Latin America, Europe, Asia, and Africa.

We may generalize that American programming that is culturally alien won't do very well anywhere, when a quality local choice is available. Confirmation comes from many countries. National productions are highly popular in Japan, Mexico, India, Egypt, and Nigeria. In a survey during the mid-1980s, 75 percent of Nigerian viewers preferred local productions. Only 10 percent favored imports, and the remaining 15 percent liked the two options equally. Local productions are successful in Nigeria because "they are filled with everyday moments that audiences can identify with. These shows are locally produced by Nigerians" (Gray 1986). Thirty million people watched one of the most popular series, *The Village Headmaster*, each week. That program brought rural values to the screens of urbanites who had lost touch with their rural roots (Gray 1986).

The electronic mass media also play a key role in preserving ethnic and national identities among people who lead transnational lives. As groups move, they stay linked to each other and to their homeland through the media. Diasporas have enlarged the markets for media and travel services targeted at specific ethnic, national, or religious audiences. In 1992, for a fee, a PBS station in Fairfax, Virginia, offered more than thirty hours a week to immigrant groups in the D.C. area, to make programs in their own languages. *Somali Television*, for instance, is a half-hour program with about 5,000 Somali viewers, who can see their flag and hear their language on TV each week. Starting the program is a reading from the Koran, with clips of mosques from around the world (thus contributing, too, to a transnational Islamic identity). Formerly, an entertainment segment featured folk dances and Somali music. As Somalia's civil war dragged on, the entertainment segment was replaced in 1992 by images of bony children and parched countryside. *Somali Television* also features obituaries, rallies, and a segment called "Somalia Today," which has interviews with diplomats, immigration lawyers, and travel agents discussing air fares. Guests represent various tribes and subclans. *Somali Television* became a vital link between emigrant Somalis and their homeland. This was particularly true before images of Somalia became widespread on network news in late 1992 and early 1993 (*The New York Times*, December 18, 1992).

A Transnational Culture of Consumption

Another key transnational force is finance. Money makers look beyond national boundaries for places to invest. As Appadurai (1991, p. 194) puts it, "money, commodities, and persons unendingly chase each other around the world." Many Latin American communities have lost their autonomy because their residents now depend on cash derived from international labor migration. The United States also relies more on foreign cash. Long dominated by domestic capital, the economy of the United States is increasingly influenced by foreign investment, especially from Britain, Canada, Germany, the Netherlands, and Japan (Rouse 1991). The American economy has also increased its dependence on foreign labor—through both the immigration of laborers and the export of jobs.

Transnational finance and labor modify the economic control and the ethnic mix of local life. For example, by the mid-1980s, 75 percent of the buildings in downtown Los Angeles were owned at least in part by foreign capital. Up to 90 percent of multistory construction was being financed from abroad. Forty percent of the Angeleno metropolitan population consisted of ethnic minorities, mainly from Latin America and Asia. This figure is estimated to grow to 60 percent by 2010 (Rouse 1991).

Contemporary global culture is driven by flows of people, technology, finance, information, and ideology (Appadurai 1990). Business, technology, and the media have increased the craving for commodities and images throughout the world. This has forced nation-states, including "Iron Curtains," to open to a global culture of consumption. Almost everyone today participates in this culture. Few people have never seen a T-shirt advertising a Western product. Michael Jackson's *Beat It* blasts through the streets of Rio de Janeiro, while taxi drivers from Toronto to Madagascar play Brazilian *lambada* tapes. Peasants and tribal people participate in the modern world system not only because they (willingly or unwillingly) work for cash but also because their products and images are appropriated by world capitalism. They are commercialized by others (like the San in the movie *The Gods Must Be Crazy*). And, seizing their own destinies, often helped by outsiders, indigenous peoples also market their own images and products through outlets like the Body Shop and Cultural Survival. David Maybury-Lewis's ten-program 1992 TV series *Millennium (Tribal Wisdom and the Modern World)* was designed to remedy misconceptions about tribal people, to help ensure their autonomy and survival.

Some social commentators see contemporary flows of people, technology, finance, information, and ideology as a cultural imperialist steamroller. This view ignores the selective, synthesizing activity of human beings as they deal with external forces, images, and messages. Anthropological studies show that domination is usually met by resistance and that cultural diffusion is a creative process.

THE CONTINUANCE OF DIVERSITY

Anthropology has a crucial role to play in promoting a more humanistic vision of social change, one that respects the value of cultural diversity. The existence of anthropology is itself a tribute to the continuing need to understand social and cultural differences. Anthropology teaches us that the adaptive responses of humans can be more flexible than can those of other species because our main adaptive means are sociocultural. However, the cultural forms, institutions, values, and customs of the past always influence subsequent adaptation, producing continued diversity and giving a certain uniqueness to the actions and reactions of different groups.

Let us hope that vigorous cultural differences will

Business, technology, and the media have increased the worldwide craving for commodities and images. Various forms of domination have collapsed in a media-saturated world. Here Soviet Muslims watch Mikhail Gorbachev, who, through the media, became more popular in North America than in his own Soviet Union, before its breakdown.

continue to prevent what some social scientists see as a bland convergence in the future, so that free and open investigation of human diversity can continue. With our knowledge and our awareness of our professional responsibilities, let us work to keep anthropology, the study of humankind, the most humanistic of all the disciplines.

SUMMARY

The linkages in the modern world system have both enlarged and erased old boundaries and distinctions. People travel more than ever, but migrants maintain their ties with home, so that they live multilocally. With so many people "in motion," the unit of anthropological study expands from the local community to the diaspora. *Post-modernity* describes this world in flux, these people on the move who have learned to manage multiple social identities depending on place and context. *Globalization* describes the accelerating links between nations and people in a world system connected economically, politically, and by modern media and transportation. New kinds of political and ethnic units are emerging as others break down or disappear.

The main forces influencing cultural interaction for the past 500 years have been commercial expansion and industrialization. These globalizing forces have also contributed to the destruction of indigenous economies, ecologies, and populations. *Acculturation* refers to changes that result when groups come into continuous firsthand contact—changes in the cultural patterns of either or both groups. Acculturation differs from *diffusion*, or cultural borrowing, which can occur without firsthand contact.

Different degrees of destruction, domination, resistance, survival, adaptation, and modification of native cultures may follow interethnic contact. This may lead to the tribe's cultural collapse (*ethnocide*) or its physical extinction (*genocide*). The native landscape and its traditional management system may be attacked. Outsiders often attempt to remake native landscapes and cultures in their own image, a process called *terraforming*.

Multinational business corporations are a major force in the modern world system. Core nations continue to send predatory enterprises to noncore nations, where multinationals have fueled economic development and ecological devastation. Countries and cultures may resist interventionist philosophies aimed at either development or globally oriented environmentalism. The non-Western world tends to be cynical about Western ecological morality, seeing it as yet another imperialist message.

A clash of cultures related to environmental change may occur when development threatens indigenous peoples and their environments. Another clash may occur when external regulation threatens indigenous peoples. Native groups may be harmed by regional, national, and international environmental plans that seek to *save* their homelands. Like development projects, conservation schemes may ask people to change the way they have been doing things for generations to satisfy planners' goals rather than local goals. When people are asked to give up the basis of their livelihood, they usually resist. Like development plans, the most effective conservation strategies pay attention to the needs and wishes of the people living in the affected area.

Religious proselytizing can promote ethnocide, as native beliefs and practices are replaced by Western ones. Sometimes the political ideology of a nation-state is pitted against traditional religion. Governments often use their power to advance a religion, such as Islam in Iran or Sudan.

Systems of domination have their muted aspects along with their public dimensions. "Public transcript" describes the open, public interactions between dominators and oppressed. "Hidden transcript" describes the critique of power that goes on offstage, where the power holders can't see it. *Hegemony* describes a stratified social order in which subordinates comply with domination by internalizing its values and accepting its "naturalness."

Often, situations that appear hegemonic have active resistance, but it is individual and disguised rather than collective and defiant. Subordinates also use various strategies to resist publicly, but again, usually in disguised form. Discontent may be expressed in public rituals and language. Resistance is most likely to be expressed openly when the oppressed are allowed to assemble. Sensing danger, the elites discourage such public gatherings. Factors that interfere with community formation—such as geographic, linguistic, and ethnic separation—work to curb resistance. But such divisive factors can be overcome. Hidden transcripts tend to be publicly expressed at certain times (festivals and Carnivals) and in certain places (markets).

Multiethnic NGOs have emerged in Mexico to resist land grabs and oppressive government policies. Other forms of mobilization, including armed resistance, express resentment against domination and exploitation. Facing the world system, people resist, fight, and sometimes win. There has been collective action aimed at preserving or regaining tribal or ethnic autonomy in Africa, the Philippines, India, North America, Central America, Indonesia, and Australia. National and international NGOs such as Cultural Survival have emerged to support native populations threatened by development programs.

Many forms of popular expression have emerged from

the interplay of local, regional, national, and international cultural forces. *Syncretisms* are cultural blends that emerge from acculturation. *Cargo cults* developed in an acculturative context produced by expansion of the world capitalist economy and colonialism. These cults blend native expectations about tribal big men with magical explanations for the wealth of foreign overlords. Cargo cults have forged people into larger communities that have gained political and economic influence.

Cultural imperialism refers to the rapid spread or advance of one culture at the expense of others, or its imposition on other cultures, which it modifies, replaces, or destroys—usually because of differential economic or political influence. But people aren't passive victims of cultural imperialism. Contemporary people—often with considerable creativity—constantly revise, rework, resist, and reject the messages they get from external systems.

Some critics worry that modern technology, including the mass media, is killing off traditional cultures by homogenizing products to reach more people. But others see an important role for modern technology in allowing local cultures to express themselves. *Stimulus diffusion* describes the process by which a group modifies a custom by adopting images and behavior associated with an external practice, without borrowing the practice itself. *Creative opposition* occurs when people change their behavior as they consciously and actively avoid or spurn an external image or practice.

Any media-borne image can be considered a *text*—something that is creatively "read," interpreted, and assigned meaning by each person who receives it. People may resist or creatively oppose the hegemonic meaning of a text, or they may seize on the antihegemonic aspects of a text. Forms and readings of popular culture can express discontent and resistance by groups that are or feel oppressed. Meaning is not inherent or imposed but locally manufactured. When forces from world centers enter new societies, they are *indigenized*—modified to fit the local culture.

All cultures express imagination, but today, through the mass media, people imagine a wider set of possible lives than they ever did before. The electronic mass media can spread, even create, national and ethnic identities. Like print, television and radio can diffuse the cultures of different countries within their own boundaries, thus enhancing national cultural identity. The electronic mass media also play a key role in preserving ethnic and national identities among people who lead transnational lives.

Contemporary global culture is driven by flows of people, technology, finance, information, and ideology. Transnational finance and labor modify the economic control and the ethnic mix of local life. Business, technology, and the media have increased the craving for commodities and images throughout the world, creating a global culture of consumption. Anthropological studies show that domination is usually met by resistance and that cultural diffusion is a creative process.

GLOSSARY

candomblé: A syncretic "Afro-Brazilian" cult.

cargo cults: Postcolonial, acculturative religious movements, common in Melanesia, that attempt to explain European domination and wealth and to achieve similar success magically by mimicking European behavior.

creative opposition: Process in which people change their behavior as they consciously and actively avoid or spurn an external image or practice.

cultural imperialism: The rapid spread or advance of one culture at the expense of others, or its imposition on other cultures, which it modifies, replaces, or destroys—usually because of differential economic or political influence.

Cultural Survival: NGO founded in 1972 by David and Pia Maybury-Lewis, with the goal of helping native peoples to survive as successful ethnic minorities within nation-states.

diaspora: The offspring of an area who have spread to many lands.

discourse: Talk, speeches, gestures, and actions.

hegemonic reading (of a "text"): The reading or meaning that the creators intended, or the one the elites consider to be the intended or correct meaning.

hegemony: As used by Antonio Gramsci, a stratified social order in which subordinates comply with domination by internalizing its values and accepting its "naturalness."

hidden transcript: As used by James Scott, the critique of power by the oppressed that goes on offstage—in private—where the power holders can't see it.

indigenized: Modified to fit the local culture.

postmodern: In its most general sense, describes the blurring and breakdown of established canons (rules, standards), categories, distinctions, and boundaries.

postmodernism: A style and movement in architecture that succeeded modernism. Compared with modernism, postmodernism is less geometric, less functional, less austere, more playful, and more willing to include elements from diverse times and cultures; *postmodern* now describes comparable developments in music, literature, and visual art.

postmodernity: Condition of a world in flux, with people on the move, in which established groups, boundaries, identities, contrasts, and standards are reaching out and breaking down.

public transcript: As used by James Scott, the open, public interactions between dominators and oppressed—the outer shell of power relations.

stimulus diffusion: The process by which a group modifies a custom by adopting images and behavior associated with an external practice, without borrowing the practice itself.

syncretisms: Cultural blends, or mixtures, that emerge from acculturation, particularly under colonialism, such as African, Native American, and Roman Catholic saints and deities in Caribbean vodun, or "voodoo," cults.

terraforming: From science fiction, the use of technology to make other worlds as much like earth (*terra*) as possible; applied by analogy to results of political and economic domination on earth.

text: Something that is creatively "read," interpreted, and assigned meaning by each person who receives it; includes any media-borne image, such as Carnival.

westernization: The acculturative influence of Western expansion on native cultures.

STUDY QUESTIONS

1. What does it mean to say that linkages in today's world system have both enlarged and erased old boundaries and distinctions?
2. What does it mean to say that people live multilocally?
3. What is the difference between postmodernity and postmodernism? How has postmodernity affected the units of anthropological study?
4. What are the main forces influencing interaction between cultures?
5. What is the difference between acculturation and diffusion?
6. What is terraforming, and how does it relate to political and economic domination?
7. What are some of the similarities between development and environmentalism as interventionist philosophies?
8. How may external regulation harm indigenous peoples, and what is the best strategy for effective environmentalism?
9. What are some ways in which religious proselytizing has led to forms of ethnocide?
10. What is meant by the hidden and public transcripts in situations of domination?
11. What strategies do the oppressed use to resist publicly, and at what times and places is this usually done?
12. What are some of the roles that NGOs (local, national, and international) play in resistance?
13. What are some examples of effective resistance, including armed resistance?
14. What are some examples of syncretisms?
15. How are cargo cults related both to traditional social structure and to the expansion of the world capitalist economy?
16. What are some of the arguments for and against the interpretation of the mass media as forms of cultural imperialism?
17. What are examples of stimulus diffusion and creative opposition?
18. What is a "text," and how does its reading relate to the role of the individual in popular culture?
19. What are some examples of the indigenization of popular culture?
20. What does it mean to say that there is a new world system of images?
21. What contributions do the media make to national and ethnic identity?
22. What are examples of contemporary global flows of people, technology, finance, information, and ideology?

SUGGESTED ADDITIONAL READING

AHMED, A. S.
1992 *Postmodernism and Islam: Predicament and Promise.* New York: Routledge. Clear presentation of postmodernism, in relation to the media and to images of Islam.

BODLEY, J. H.
1985 *Anthropology and Contemporary Human Problems,* 2nd ed. Mountain View, CA: Mayfield. Overview of major problems of today's industrial world: overconsumption, the environ-

ment, resource depletion, hunger, overpopulation, violence, and war.

1988 *Tribal Peoples and Development Issues: A Global Overview*. Mountain View, CA: Mayfield. Overview of case studies, policies, assessments, and recommendations concerning tribal peoples and development.

CULTURAL SURVIVAL

1992 *At the Threshold*. Cambridge, MA: Cultural Survival. Originally published as the spring 1992 issue of *Cultural Survival Quarterly*. Manual for the promotion of the rights of indigenous peoples. Highlights activist successes, gives instructions for affecting policy, working in schools and communities, directly helping native societies, and using the media as a human-rights ally.

DAMATTA, R.

1991 *Carnivals, Rogues, and Heroes: An Interpretation of the Brazilian Dilemma*. Translated from the Portuguese by John Drury. Notre Dame, IN: University of Notre Dame Press. Classic study of Brazilian Carnival in relation to Brazilian national culture.

FELD, S.

1990 "Sound and Sentiment: Birds, Weeping, Poet-ics, and Song in Kaluli Expression," 2d Ed. Philadelphia: University of Pennsylvania Press. Ethnographic study of sound as a cultural system among the Kaluli people of Papua New Guinea.

FISKE, J.

1989 *Understanding Popular Culture*. Boston: Unwin Hyman. The role of the individual in using popular culture, constructing meaning, and resisting everyday power relations.

IYER, P.

1988 *Video Night in Kathmandu*. New York: Knopf. The transformation of global popular culture in local contexts.

PUBLIC CULTURE

Journal published by the University of Chicago. Articles deal with the anthropology of the modern and postmodern world system.

SCOTT, JAMES C.

1990 *Domination and the Arts of Resistance*. New Haven, CT: Yale University Press. A study of institutionalized forms of domination, such as colonialism, slavery, serfdom, racism, caste, concentration camps, prisons, and old-age homes—and the forms of resistance that oppose them.

AMERICAN POPULAR CULTURE

Although culture is shared, all cultures have divisive as well as unifying forces. Tribes are divided by residence in different villages and membership in different descent groups. Nations, though united by government, are divided by class, region, ethnicity, religion, and political party. Unifying forces in tribal cultures include marriage, trade, and segmentary lineage structure. In any society, of course, a common cultural tradition also provides a basis for uniformity.

Whatever unity contemporary American culture has doesn't rest on a particularly strong central government. Nor is our national unity based on segmentary lineage structure or marital exchange networks. In fact, many of the commonalities of experience, belief, behavior, and activity that enable us to speak of "contemporary American culture" are relatively new. Like the globalizing forces discussed in the chapter "Cultural Exchange and Survival," they are founded on and perpetuated by twentieth-century developments, particularly in business, transportation, and the mass media.

ANTHROPOLOGISTS AND AMERICAN CULTURE

When anthropologists study urban ethnic groups or relationships between class and household organization, they focus on variation, a very important topic. When we look at the creative use that each individual makes of popular culture, as we did in the chapter "Cultural Exchange and Survival," we are also considering variation. However, anthropology traditionally has been concerned as much with uniformity as with variation. "National character" studies of the 1940s and 1950s foreshadowed anthropology's interest in unifying themes in modern nations. Unfortunately, those studies, of such countries as Japan and Russia, focused too much on the psychological characteristics of individuals.

Contemporary anthropologists interested in national culture realize that culture is an attribute of groups. Despite increasing ethnic diversity in the United States, we can still talk about an "American national culture." Through common experiences in their enculturation, especially through the media, most Americans do come to share certain knowledge, beliefs, values, and ways of thinking and acting (as was discussed in the chapter "Culture"). The shared aspects of national culture override differences between individuals, genders, regions, or ethnic groups.

The chapter "Cultural Exchange and Survival" examined the creative use that individuals and cultures make of introduced cultural forces, including media images. That chapter discussed how, through different "readings" of the same media "text," individuals and cultures constantly make and remake popular culture. Here we take a different approach, focusing on some of the "texts" that have diffused most successfully in a given national culture. Such "texts" spread because they are culturally appropriate and—for various cultural reasons—able to carry some sort of meaning to millions of Americans. Previous chapters have focused on variation and diversity, but this Appendix stresses unifying factors—common experiences, actions, and beliefs in American culture.

Anthropologists *should* study American society and culture. Anthropology, after all, deals with universals, generalities, and uniqueness. A national culture is a particular cultural variant, as interesting as any other. Although survey research is traditionally used to study modern nations, techniques developed to interpret and analyze smaller-scale societies, where sociocultural uniformity is more marked, can also contribute to an understanding of American life.

Native anthropologists are those who study their own cultures—for example, American anthropologists working in the United States, Canadian anthropologists working in Canada, or Nigerians working in Nigeria. Anthropological training and field work abroad provide an anthropologist with a certain degree of detachment and objectivity that most natives lack. However, life experience as a native gives an advantage to anthropologists who wish to study their own cultures. Nevertheless, more than when working abroad, the native anthropologist is both participant and observer, often emotionally and intellectually involved in the events and beliefs being studied. Native anthropologists must be particularly careful to resist their own emic biases (their prejudices as natives). They must strive to be as objective in describing their own cultures as they are in analyzing others.

Natives often see and explain their behavior very differently than anthropologists do. For example, most Americans have probably never considered the possibility that apparently secular, commercial, and recreational institutions such as sports, movies, Walt Disney enterprises, and fast-food restaurants have things in common with religious beliefs, symbols, and behavior. However, these similarities can be demonstrated anthropologically. Anthropology helps us understand ourselves. By studying other cultures, we learn both to appreciate and to question aspects of our own. Furthermore, the same techniques that anthropologists use in describing and analyzing other cultures can be applied to American culture.

American readers may not find the analyses that

follow convincing. In part this is because you are natives, who know much more about your own culture than you do about any other. Also, as we saw in the chapter "Cultural Exchange and Survival," people in a culture may "read" that culture differently. Furthermore, American culture assigns a high value to differences in individual opinion—and to the belief that one opinion is as good as another. Here I am trying to extract *culture* (widely shared aspects of behavior) from diverse *individual* opinions, actions, and experiences.

The following analyses depart from areas that can be easily quantified, such as demography or economics. We are entering a more impressionistic domain, where cultural analysis sometimes seems more like philosophy or humanities than like science. You will be right in questioning some of the conclusions that follow. Some are surely debatable; some may be wrong. However, if they illustrate how anthropology can be used to shed light on aspects of your own life and experience and to revise and broaden your understanding of your own culture, they will have served a worthwhile function.

A reminder (from the chapter "Culture") about culture, ethnocentrism, and native anthropologists is needed here. For anthropologists, *culture* means much more than refinement, cultivation, education, and appreciation of "classics" and "fine arts"—its popular usage. Curiously, however, when some anthropologists confront their own culture, they forget this. They carry an image of themselves as adventurous and broad-minded specialists in the unusual, the ethnic, and the exotic. Like other academics and intellectuals, they may regard American "pop" culture as trivial and unworthy of serious study. In doing so, they demonstrate ethnocentrism and reveal a bias that comes with being members of an academic-intellectual subculture.

In examining American culture, native anthropologists must be careful to overcome the bias associated with the academic subculture. Although some academics discourage their children from watching television, the fact that TVs outnumber toilets in American households is a significant cultural fact that anthropologists can't afford to ignore. My own research on Michigan college students may be generalizable to other young Americans. They visit McDonald's more often than they visit houses of worship. I found that almost all had seen a Walt Disney movie and had attended rock concerts or football games. If these observations are true of young Americans generally, as I suspect they are, such shared experiences are major features of American enculturation patterns. Certainly any extraterrestrial anthropologist doing field work in the United States would stress them. Within the United States the mass media and the culture of consumption have created major themes in contemporary national culture. These themes merit anthropological study.

From the popular domains of sports, TV, movies, theme parks, and fast food, I have chosen certain very popular "texts." I could have used other texts (for example, blue jeans, baseball, or pizza) to make the same points—that there are powerful shared aspects of contemporary American national culture and that anthropological techniques can be used to interpret them.

FOOTBALL

Football, we say, is only a game, yet it has become a popular spectator sport. On fall Saturdays millions of people travel to and from college football games. Smaller congregations meet in high school stadiums. Millions of Americans watch televised football. Indeed, more than half the adult population of the United States watches the Super Bowl. Because football is of general interest to Americans, it is a unifying cultural institution that merits anthropological attention. Our most popular sports manage to attract people of diverse ethnic backgrounds, regions, religions, political parties, jobs, social statuses, wealth levels, and genders.

The popularity of football, particularly professional football, depends directly on the mass media, especially television. Is football, with its territorial incursion, hard hitting, and violence—occasionally resulting in injury—popular because Americans are violent people? Are football spectators vicariously realizing their own hostile, violent, and aggressive tendencies? Anthropologist W. Arens (1981) discounts this interpretation. He points out that football is a peculiarly American pastime. Although a similar game is played in Canada, it is less popular there. Baseball has become a popular sport in the Caribbean, parts of Latin America, and Japan. Basketball and volleyball are also spreading. However, throughout most of the world, soccer is the most popular sport. Arens argues that if football were a particularly effective channel for expressing aggression, it would have spread (like soccer and baseball)

to many other countries, where people have as many aggressive tendencies and hostile feelings as Americans do. Furthermore, he suggests that if a sport's popularity rested simply on a bloodthirsty temperament, boxing, a far bloodier sport, would be America's national pastime. Arens concludes that the explanation for the sport's popularity lies elsewhere, and I agree.

He contends that football is popular because it symbolizes certain key features of American life. In particular, it is characterized by teamwork based on elaborate specialization and division of labor, which are pervasive features of modern life. Susan Montague and Robert Morais (1981) take the analysis a step further. They argue that Americans appreciate football because it presents a miniaturized and simplified version of modern organizations. People have trouble understanding organizational bureaucracies, whether in business, universities, or government. Football, the anthropologists argue, helps us understand how decisions are made and rewards are allocated in organizations.

Montague and Morais link football's values, particularly teamwork, to those associated with business. Like corporate workers, ideal players are diligent and dedicated to the team. Within corporations, however, decision making is complicated, and workers aren't always rewarded for their dedication and good job performance. Decisions are simpler and rewards are more consistent in football, these anthropologists contend, and this helps explain its popularity. Even if we can't figure out how Citibank and IBM run, any fan can become an expert on football's rules, teams, scores, statistics, and patterns of play. Even more important, football suggests that the values stressed by business really do pay off. Teams whose members work hardest, show the most spirit, and best develop and coordinate their talents can be expected to win more often than other teams do.

STAR TREK AS A SUMMATION OF DOMINANT CULTURAL THEMES*

Star Trek, a familiar, powerful, and enduring force in American popular culture, can be used to illustrate the idea that popular media content often is

*This section is adapted from *Prime-Time Society: An Anthropological Analysis of Television and Culture* by Conrad Phillip Kottak. © 1990 by Wadsworth, Inc. Used by permission of the publisher.

derived from prominent values expressed in many other domains of culture. Americans first encountered the Starship *Enterprise* on NBC in 1966. *Star Trek* was shown in prime time for just three seasons. However, the series not only survives but thrives today in reruns, books, cassettes, and theatrical films. Revived as a regular weekly series with an entirely new cast in 1987, *Star Trek: The Next Generation* became the third most popular syndicated program in the United States (after *Wheel of Fortune* and *Jeopardy*).

What does the enduring mass appeal of *Star Trek* tell us about American culture? I believe the answer to be this: *Star Trek* is a transformation of a fundamental American origin myth. The same myth shows up in the image and celebration of Thanksgiving, a distinctively American holiday. Thanksgiving sets the myth in the past, and *Star Trek* sets it in the future.

When they encounter the word *myth*, most Americans probably think of stories about Greek, Roman, or Norse gods and heroes. However, all societies have myths. Their central characters need not be unreal, superhuman, or physically immortal. Such tales may be rooted in actual historical events.

> The popular notion that a "myth" is . . . "untrue"—indeed that its untruth is its defining characteristic—is not only naive but shows misunderstanding of its very nature. Its "scientific truth" or otherwise is irrelevant. A myth is a statement about society and man's place in it and the surrounding universe. (Middleton, ed. 1967, p. x)

Myths are hallowed stories that express fundamental cultural values. They are widely and recurrently told among, and have special meaning to, people who grow up in a particular culture. Myths may be set in the past, present, or future or in "fantasyland." Whether set in "real time" or fictional time, myths are always at least partly fictionalized.

The myths of contemporary America are drawn from a variety of sources, including such popular-culture fantasies as *Star Wars*, *The Wizard of Oz* (see below), and *Star Trek*. Our myths also include real people, particularly national ancestors, whose lives have been reinterpreted and endowed with special meaning over the generations. The media, schools, churches, communities, and parents teach the national origin myths to American children. The story of Thanksgiving, for example, continues to be important. It recounts the origin of a national holiday

celebrated by Protestants, Catholics, and Jews. All those denominations share a belief in the Old Testament God, and they find it appropriate to thank God for their blessings.

Again and again Americans have heard idealized retellings of that epochal early harvest. We have learned how Indians taught the Pilgrims to farm in the New World. Grateful Pilgrims then invited the Indians to share their first Thanksgiving. Native American and European labor, techniques, and customs thus blended in that initial biethnic celebration. Annually reenacting the origin myth, American public schools commemorate "the first Thanksgiving" as children dress up as Pilgrims, Indians, and pumpkins.

More rapidly and pervasively as the mass media grow, each generation of Americans writes its own revisionist history. Our culture constantly reinterprets the origin, nature, and meaning of national holidays. The collective consciousness of contemporary Americans includes TV-saturated memories of "the first Thanksgiving" and "the first Christmas." Our mass culture has instilled widely shared images of a *Peanuts*-peopled Pilgrim-and-Indian "love-in."

We also conjure up a fictionalized Nativity with Mary, Joseph, Jesus, manger animals, shepherds, three oriental kings, a little drummer boy, and, in some versions, Rudolph the Red-Nosed Reindeer. Note that the interpretation of the Nativity that American culture perpetuates is yet another variation on the same dominant myth. We remember the Nativity as a Thanksgiving involving interethnic contacts (e.g., the three kings) and gift giving. It is set in Bethlehem rather than Massachusetts.

We impose our present on the past as we reinterpret quasi-historic and actual events. For the future we do it in our science-fiction and fantasy creations. *Star Trek* places in the future what the Thanksgiving story locates in the past—*the myth of the assimilationist, incorporating, melting-pot society.* The myth says that America is distinctive not just because it is assimilationist but because it is *founded* on unity in diversity. (Our *origin* is unity in diversity. After all, we call ourselves "the United States.") Thanksgiving and *Star Trek* illustrate the credo that unity through diversity is essential for survival (whether of a harsh winter or of the perils of outer space). Americans survive by sharing the fruits of specialization.

Star Trek proclaims that the sacred principles that

validate American society, because they lie at its foundation, will endure across the generations and even the centuries. The Starship *Enterprise* crew is a melting pot. Captain James Tiberius Kirk is symbolic of real history. His clearest historical prototype is Captain James Cook, whose ship, the *Endeavor,* also sought out new life and civilizations. Kirk's infrequently mentioned middle name, from the Roman general and eventual emperor, links the captain to the earth's imperial history. Kirk is also symbolic of the original Anglo-American. He runs the *Enterprise* (America is founded on free enterprise), just as laws, values, and institutions derived from England continue to run the United States.

McCoy's Irish (or at least Gaelic) name represents the next wave, the established immigrant. Sulu is the successfully assimilated Asian-American. The African-American female character Uhura, "whose name means freedom," indicates that blacks will become full partners with all other Americans. However, Uhura was the only major female character in the original crew. This reflects the fact that female extradomestic employment was less characteristic of American society in 1966 than it is now.

One of *Star Trek's* constant messages is that strangers, even enemies, can become friends. Less obviously, this message is about cultural imperialism, the assumed irresistibility of American culture and institutions. Soviet nationals (Chekhov) could be seduced and captured by an expansive American culture. Spock, although from Vulcan, is half human, with human qualities. We learn, therefore, that our assimilationist values will eventually not just rule the earth but extend to other planets as well. By "the next generation," Klingons, even more alien than Vulcans, and personified by Bridge Officer Worf, have joined the melting pot.

Even God is harnessed to serve American culture, in the person of Scotty. His role is that of the ancient Greek *deus ex machina.* He is a stage controller who "beams" people up and down, back and forth, from earth to the heavens. Scotty, who keeps society going, is also a servant-employee who does his engineering for management—illustrating loyalty and technical skill.

The Next Generation contains many analogues of the original characters. Several "partial people" are single-character personifications of particular human qualities represented in more complex form by the original *Star Trek* crew members. Kirk, Spock, and McCoy have all been split into multiple char-

acters. Captain Jean-Luc Picard has the intellectual and managerial attributes of James T. Kirk. With his English accent and French name, Picard, like Kirk, draws his legitimacy from symbolic association with historic Western European empires. First Officer Riker replaces Kirk as a romantic man of action.

Spock, an alien (strange ears) who represents science, reason, and intellect, has been split in two. One half is Worf, a Klingon bridge officer whose cranial protuberances are analogous to Spock's ears. The other is Data, an android whose brain contains the sum of human wisdom. Two female characters, an empath and the ship's doctor, have replaced Dr. McCoy as the repository of healing, emotion, and feeling.

Mirroring contemporary American culture, *The Next Generation* features prominent black, female, and physically handicapped characters. An African-American actor plays the Klingon Mr. Worf. Another, LeVar Burton, appears as Geordi La Forge. Although blind, Geordi manages, through a vision-enhancing visor, to see things that other people cannot. His mechanical vision expresses the characteristic American faith in technology. So does the android, Data.

During its first year, *The Next Generation* had three prominent female characters. One was the ship's doctor, a working professional with a teenage son. Another was an empath, the ultimate "helping professional." The third was the ship's security officer.

America is more specialized, differentiated, and professional than it was in the sixties. The greater role specificity and diversity of *Next Generation* characters reflect this. Nevertheless, both series convey the central *Star Trek* message, one that dominates the culture that created them: Americans are diverse. Individual qualities, talents, and specialties divide us. However, we make our livings and survive as members of cohesive, efficient groups. We explore and advance as members of a crew, a team, an enterprise, or, most generally, a society. Our nation is founded on and endures through assimilation—effective subordination of individual differences within a smoothly functioning multiethnic team. The team is American culture. It worked in the past. It works today. It will go on working across the generations. Orderly and progressive democracy based on mutual respect is best. Inevitably, American culture will triumph over all others—by convincing and assimilating rather than conquering them. Unity in diversity guarantees human survival, and for this we should be thankful.

FANTASY FILMS AS MYTH

Techniques that anthropologists use to analyze myths can be extended to two fantasy films that most students have seen. *The Wizard of Oz* has been telecast annually for decades. *Star Wars* is one of the most popular films of all time. Both are familiar and significant cultural products with obvious mythic qualities. The contributions of French structuralist anthropologist Claude Lévi-Strauss and neo-Freudian psychoanalyst Bruno Bettelheim (as discussed in the religion chapter) permit the following analysis of visual fairy tales that contemporary Americans know well. I will show that *Star Wars* is a systematic

structural transformation of *The Wizard of Oz*. I cannot say how many of the resemblances were conscious and how many merely express a collective unconscious that *Star Wars* writer and director George Lucas shares with other Americans through common enculturation.

The Wizard of Oz and *Star Wars* both begin in arid country, the first in Kansas and the second on the desert planet Tatooine (Table A.1). *Star Wars* changes *The Wizard*'s female hero into a boy, Luke Skywalker. Fairy tale heroes usually have short, common first names and second names that describe their origin or activity. Thus Luke, who travels aboard spaceships, is a Skywalker, while Dorothy Gale is swept off to Oz by a cyclone (a gale of wind). Dorothy leaves home with her dog, Toto, who is pursued by and has managed to escape from a woman who in Oz becomes the Wicked Witch

Table A.1 Star Wars *as a structural transformation of* The Wizard of Oz

Star Wars	*The Wizard of Oz*
Male hero (Luke Skywalker)	Female hero (Dorothy Gale)
Arid Tatooine	Arid Kansas
Luke follows R2D2: R2D2 flees Vader	Dorothy follows Toto: Toto flees witch
Luke lives with uncle and aunt: Primary relationship with uncle (same sex as hero) Strained, distant relationship with uncle	Dorothy lives with uncle and aunt: Primary relationship with aunt (same sex as hero) Warm, close relationship with aunt
Tripartite division of same-sex parent: 2 parts good, 1 part bad father Good father dead at beginning Good father dead (?) at end Bad father survives	Tripartite division of same-sex parent: 2 parts bad, 1 part good mother Bad mother dead at beginning Bad mother dead at end Good mother survives
Relationship with parent of opposite sex (Princess Leia Organa): Princess is unwilling captive Needle Princess is freed	Relationship with parent of opposite sex (Wizard of Oz): Wizard makes impossible demands Broomstick Wizard turns out to be sham
Trio of companions: Han Solo, C3PO, Chewbacca	Trio of companions: Scarecrow, Tin Woodman, Cowardly Lion
Minor characters: Jawas Sand People Stormtroopers	Minor characters: Munchkins Apple Trees Flying Monkeys
Settings: Death Star Verdant Tikal (rebel base)	Settings: Witch's castle Emerald City
Conclusion: Luke uses magic to accomplish goal (destroy Death Star)	Conclusion: Dorothy uses magic to accomplish goal (return to Kansas)

of the West. Luke follows his "Two-Two" (R2D2), who is fleeing Darth Vader, the witch's structural equivalent.

Dorothy and Luke both live with an uncle and an aunt. However, because of the gender change of the hero, the primary relationship is reversed and inverted. Thus Dorothy's relationship with her aunt is primary, warm, and loving, whereas Luke's relationship with his uncle, though primary, is strained and distant. Aunt and uncle are in the tales for the same reason. They represent home (the nuclear family of orientation), which children (according to American culture norms) must eventually leave to make it on their own. As Bettelheim (1975) points out, fairy tales often disguise parents as uncle and aunt, and this establishes social distance. The child can deal with the hero's separation (in *The Wizard of Oz*) or the aunt's and uncle's death (in *Star Wars*) more easily than with the death of or separation from real parents. Furthermore, this permits the child's strong feelings toward his or her real parents to be represented in different, more central characters, such as the Wicked Witch of the West and Darth Vader.

Both films focus on the child's relationship with the parent of the same sex, dividing that parent into three parts. In *The Wizard*, the mother is split into two parts bad and one part good. They are the Wicked Witch of the East, dead at the beginning of the movie; the Wicked Witch of the West, dead at the end; and Glinda, the good mother, who survives. The first *Star Wars* film reversed the proportion of good and bad, giving Luke a good father (his own), the Jedi knight who is proclaimed dead at the film's beginning. There is another good father, Ben Kenobi, who is ambiguously dead when the movie ends. Third is a father figure of total evil, Darth Vader. As the good-mother third survives *The Wizard of Oz*, the bad-father third lives on after *Star Wars*, to strike back in the sequel.

The child's relationship with the parent of the opposite sex is also represented in the two films. Dorothy's father figure is the Wizard of Oz, an initially terrifying figure who later is proved to be a fake. Bettelheim notes that the typical fairy tale father is disguised as a monster or giant or else (when preserved as a human) is weak, distant, or ineffective. Children wonder why Cinderella's father lets her be treated badly by her stepmother and stepsisters, why the father of Hansel and Gretel does not throw

out his new wife instead of his children, and why Snow White's father doesn't tell the queen she's narcissistic. Dorothy counts on the wizard to save her but finds that he makes seemingly impossible demands and in the end is just an ordinary man. She succeeds on her own, no longer relying on a father who offers no more than she herself possesses.

In *Star Wars* (although not in the later films in the trilogy), Luke's mother figure is Princess Leia Organa. Bettelheim notes that boys commonly fantasize their mothers to be unwilling captives of their fathers, and fairy tales often disguise mothers as princesses whose freedom the boy-hero must obtain. In graphic Freudian imagery, Darth Vader threatens Princess Leia with a needle the size of the witch's broomstick. By the end of the film, Luke has freed Leia and defeated Vader.

There are other striking parallels in the structure of the two films. Fairy tale heroes are often accompanied on their adventures by secondary characters who personify the virtues needed in a successful quest. Dorothy takes along wisdom (the Scarecrow), love (the Tin Woodman), and courage (the Lion). *Star Wars* includes a structurally equivalent trio—Han Solo, C3PO, and Chewbacca—but their association with particular qualities is not as precise. The minor characters are also structurally parallel: Munchkins and Jawas, Apple Trees and Sand People, Flying Monkeys and Stormtroopers. And compare settings—the witch's castle and the Death Star, the Emerald City and the rebel base. The endings are also parallel. Luke accomplishes his objective on his own, using the Force (Oceanian mana, magical power). Dorothy's aim is to return to Kansas. She does that by tapping her shoes together and drawing on the Force in her ruby slippers.

All successful cultural products blend old and new, drawing on familiar themes. They rearrange them in novel ways and thus win a lasting place in the imaginations of the culture that creates or accepts them. *Star Wars* successfully used old cultural themes in novel ways, and it drew on *the* American fairy tale, one that had been available in book form since the turn of the century.

DISNEY MYTH AND RITUAL

Just as anthropological techniques developed to analyze myths also fit fantasy films, anthropology can show how an ostensibly secular activity, a visit to Walt Disney World, takes on some of the attributes of a religious pilgrimage. The North American Disney "shrines"—Disneyland in California and Walt Disney World in Florida—owe their success not just to the amusement they offer but to years of preprogramming that have influenced Americans for over half a century. Disney's creations—films, television programs, a cable channel, cartoons, comics, toys, and amusement parks—have been important forces in American enculturation. I will examine the Disney mythology and then look at what happens during a visit to Walt Disney World. We shall see that certain observations about religion also apply to this quasi-religious dimension of contemporary American culture.

Walt Disney, who died in 1966, was a highly successful businessman whose commercial empire was built on movies, television programs, and amusement parks. Disney products have cultural as well as commercial significance. Specifically, exposure to Disney creations (just as to *Star Wars* and *The Wizard of Oz*) has been part of Americans' common enculturation, particularly since 1937, when *Snow White and the Seven Dwarfs,* Disney's first full-length cartoon, was released. Disney products, transmitted through the mass media, provide a set of quasi-mythological symbols. Diffused worldwide, they have affected enculturation in many nations. Particularly important are the images of childhood fantasy, the cartoon characters—unusual humans and humanlike animals—that continue to be part of the mythology of American childhood.

Disney mythology shows similarities with myths of other cultures and can be analyzed in the same terms. In myths, binary oppositions (polar contrasts) are often resolved by mediating figures, entities that somehow link opposites. Consider the binary opposition between nature and culture, which is a concern of people everywhere. We know scientifically that many differences between humans and other animals are differences of degree rather than kind. However, religions and myths, for thousands of years and throughout the world, have been concerned with demonstrating just the opposite—that people stand apart from nature, that humans are unique. The opposition between people and nature has been symbolized by major attributes of culture, such as speech ("In the beginning was the word"), technology (Prometheus stole fire from the

gods), thought (the soul), and knowledge (the Fall of Adam and Eve). Human knowledge of good and evil is opposed to animal innocence.

Myths often use mediating figures to resolve oppositions. Animals, for example, are given human abilities, thus bridging the opposition between culture and nature. In Genesis, a humanlike animal (a bipedal, talking, lying snake) brings culture and nature closer together. In the beginning, Adam and Eve are innocent parts of nature, yet they are unique because of their creation in God's image. The snake encourages Original Sin, which keeps humans unique, but in a far less exalted way. The punishment for eating forbidden fruit is a destiny of physical labor, a struggle with nature. That humans are a part of nature while also being different from other animals is explained by the serpent-mediator's role in the Fall. The fall of humanity is paralleled in the fall of the serpent—from culture-bearing creature to belly-crawling animal.

According to Lévi-Strauss (1967), myths often resolve an apparent contradiction. Mediating figures and events may resolve such oppositions as culture versus nature by showing that just as mythical animals can have human abilities and thus be cultural, people, while different from nature, are also part of nature. People are like animals in many ways, dependent on natural resources and participants in natural systems.

Disney creations address the culture-nature opposition. Disney conferred human attributes on his animated (from *anima,* Latin for "soul") characters. These qualities include talking, laughing, tricking, bumbling, lying, singing, making friends, and participating in family life. In most of his movies, the animals—and witches, dwarfs, fairies, mermaids, and other not-quite-human characters—deny the opposition of culture and nature by having more human qualities than the stereotypically perfect heroes and heroines do.

In *Cinderella,* for example, the nature-culture opposition is inverted (turned over, reversed). Mice—natural (undomesticated) animals that are ordinarily considered pests—are endowed with speech and other cultural attributes and become Cinderella's loyal friends. The cat, ordinarily a part of culture (domesticated), becomes a dark creature of evil who almost blocks Cinderella's transformation from domestic servant into princess. The reversal of the normal opposition—that is, cat-culture-good versus mouse-nature-bad—shows how Disney characterization overcomes the opposition between culture and nature. Similarly, just as natural animals in Disney films are depicted as cultural creatures, people are often represented as being closer to nature than they normally are. In several Disney films human actors are used to portray close relationships between children and undomesticated animals such as raccoons, foxes, bears, and wolves. Disney's choice of Kipling's *The Jungle Book* as the subject matter for a cartoon feature also illustrates this second means of dealing with the nature-culture opposition.

A Pilgrimage to Walt Disney World

With Disney as creator and myth maker for so many Americans, his shrines could hardly fail. In many cultures, religion focuses on sacred sites. Infertile women in Madagascar seek fecundity by spilling the blood of a rooster in front of phallic stones. Australian totems are associated with holy sites where, in mythology, totemic beings first emerged from the ground. Sacred groves provide symbolic unity for dispersed clans among the Jie of Uganda (Gulliver 1965/1974). A visit to Mecca (*haj*) is an obligation of Islam. Pilgrims seek miraculous cures at shrines such as Lourdes and Fátima, which are associated with Roman Catholicism. In the arid *sertão* of northeastern Brazil, thousands of pilgrims journey each August 6 to fulfill their vows to a wooden statue in a cave—Bom Jesus da Lapa. Similarly, but virtually every day of the year, thousands of American families travel long distances and invest significant amounts of money to experience Disneyland and Walt Disney World.

A conversation with anthropologist Alexander Moore, then of the University of Florida, first prompted me to think of Walt Disney World as analogous to religious pilgrimage centers. The behavior of the millions of Americans who visit it is comparable to that of religious pilgrims. Moore pointed out that like other shrines, Walt Disney World has an inner, sacred center and an outer, more secular domain. At Walt Disney World, appropriately enough, the inner, sacred area is known as "the Magic Kingdom."

Motels, restaurants, and campgrounds dot the approach to Disney World, becoming increasingly concentrated near the park. You enter Walt Disney World on "World Drive." You can choose between the Magic Kingdom or turnoffs to Epcot Center and the MGM Theme Park. The following analysis applies only to the Magic Kingdom. A sign on World Drive instructs you to turn to a specified radio station. A recording played continuously throughout the day gives information about where and how to park and how to proceed on the journey to the Magic Kingdom. It also promotes new Magic Kingdom activities and special attractions, such as "America on Parade" and "Senior American Days."

Travelers enter the mammoth parking lot by driving through a structure like a turnpike toll booth. As they pay the parking fee, they receive a brochure describing attractions both inside and outside the central area. (Campgrounds, lakes, islands, and an "international shopping village" are in the park's outlying areas.) Sections of the parking lot have totemlike designations—Minnie, Goofy, Pluto, and Chip 'n' Dale—each with several numbered rows. Uniformed attendants direct motorists to parking places. They make sure that cars park within the marked spaces and that every space is filled in order. As visitors emerge from their cars, they are directed to open-air trainlike buses called trams. Lest they forget where their cars are parked, they are told as they board the tram to "remember" Minnie, Pluto, or whichever mythological figure has become the temporary guardian of their vehicle. Many travelers spend the first minute of the tram ride reciting "Minnie 30, Minnie 30," memorizing the automobile's row number. Leaving the tram, visitors hurry to booths where they purchase entrance to the Magic Kingdom and its attractions ("adventures"). They then pass through turnstiles behind the ticket sales booths and prepare to be transported, by "express" monorail or ferryboat, to the Magic Kingdom itself.

Because the approach to the central area occurs in gradual stages, the division of Walt Disney World into outer, secular space and inner, sacred space is not clear-cut. Moving concentrically inward, the zones become gradually rather than abruptly more sacred. Even after one passes the parking lot and turnstiles, a zone that is still secular, with hotels, beaches, and boating areas, comes before the Magic Kingdom. This is the obviously more ordinary part of Walt Disney World, where visitors can check into hotels and eat in restaurants that recall similar places throughout the United States. The "Polynesian" architecture and decor of one of the hotel complexes aren't unusual for Sun Belt condominium communities. Nor do the white beaches, paddle boats, and water sports visible in this peripheral area suggest anything other than a typical vacationland. Although visitors have the option of taking a "local" monorail to one of the hotels, most pilgrims board the express monorail directly to the Magic Kingdom. The alternative to this futuristic mode of transportation is a more sedate ferryboat.

On the express monorail, which bridges the opposition between the secular areas and the Magic Kingdom, similarities between Disney pilgrims and participants in rites of passage are especially obvious. (Rites of passage may be transitions in space, age, or social status.) Disney pilgrims who ride the express monorail exhibit, as one might expect in a transition from secular to sacred space (a magic kingdom), many of the attributes associated with liminal states, as discussed in the chapter "Religion." Like liminal periods in other passage rites, aboard the monorail all prohibitions that apply everywhere else in Disney World are intensified. In the secular areas and in the Magic Kingdom itself people may smoke and eat, and in the secular areas they can consume alcohol and go shoeless, but all these things are taboo on the monorail. Like ritual passengers, monorail riders temporarily relinquish control over their destinies. Herded like cattle into the monorail, passengers move out of ordinary space and into a time out of time in which social distinctions disappear and everyone is reduced to a common level. As the monorail departs, a disembodied voice prepares the pilgrims for what is to come, enculturating them in the lore and standards of Walt Disney World.

Symbols of rebirth at the end of liminality are typical of liminal periods. Rebirth symbolism is an aspect of the monorail ride. As the monorail speeds through the Contemporary Resort Hotel, travelers facing forward observe and pass through an enormous tiled mural that covers an entire wall. Just before the monorail reaches the hotel, but much more clearly after it emerges, travelers see Walt Disney World's primary symbol—Cinderella's castle. The sudden emergence from the mural into full view of the Magic Kingdom is a simulation of rebirth.

Within the Magic Kingdom

Once the monorail pulls into the Magic Kingdom station, the transition is complete. Passengers are on their own. Attendants, so prominent at the other end of the line, are conspicuously absent. Walking down a ramp, travelers pass through another turnstile; a transit building where lockers, phones, rest rooms, strollers, and wheelchairs are available; and a circular open area. Soon they are in the Magic Kingdom, walking down "Main Street, U.S.A."

The Magic Kingdom itself invites comparison with shrines and rites. Pilgrims agree implicitly to constitute a temporary community, to spend a few hours or days observing the same rules, sharing experiences, and behaving alike. They share a common social status as pilgrims, waiting for hours in line and partaking in the same "adventures." Several anthropologists have argued that the major social function of rituals is to reaffirm, and thus to maintain, solidarity among members of a congregation. Victor Turner (1974) suggested that certain rituals among the Ndembu of Zambia serve a mnemonic function (they make people remember). Women's belief that they can be made ill by the spirits of their deceased matrilineal kinswomen leads them to take part in rites that remind them of their ancestors.

Similar observations can be made about Walt Disney World. Frontierland, Liberty Square, Main Street, U.S.A., Tomorrowland, Fantasyland, and Mickey's Birthdayland—the major sections of the Magic Kingdom—make us remember departed presidents (our national ancestors) and American history. They also juxtapose and link together the past, present, and future; childhood and adulthood; the real and the unreal. Many of the adventures, or rides, particularly the roller coasters, can be compared to anxiety-producing rites. Anxiety is dispelled when the pilgrims realize that they have survived simulated speeds of 90 miles an hour.

Detaching oneself from American culture, one might ask how a visitor from Madagascar would view Disney World adventures, particularly those based on fantasy. In Madagascar, as in many nonindustrial societies, witches are actual people—part of reality rather than fantasy. Peasants in Brazil and elsewhere believe in witches, werewolves, and nefarious creatures of the night. A villager from Madagascar would find it hard to understand why Americans voluntarily take rides designed to produce uncertainty and fright.

Yet the structure and attractions of the Magic Kingdom also relate to higher levels of sanctity. They represent, recall, and reaffirm not only Walt

Disney's creative acts but the values of American society at large. In Liberty Square's Hall of Presidents, pilgrims silently and reverently view moving, talking lifelike dummies. Like Tanzanian rites, the Magic Kingdom makes us remember not just presidents and history but characters in children's literature such as Tom Sawyer. And, of course, we meet the cartoon characters who, in the person of costumed humans, walk around the Magic Kingdom, posing for photographs with children.

The juxtaposition of past, present, future, and fantasy symbolizes eternity. It argues that our nation, our people, our technological expertise, our beliefs, myths, and values will endure. Dress codes for employees reaffirm the stereotype of the clean-cut American. Disney propaganda uses Walt Disney World itself to illustrate what American creativity joined with technical know-how can accomplish. Students in American history are told how our ancestors carved a new land out of wilderness. Similarly, Walt Disney is presented as a mythic figure, creator of cosmos out of chaos—a structured world from the undeveloped chaos of Florida's central interior.

A few other links between Walt Disney World and religious and quasi-religious symbols and shrines should be examined. Disney World's most potent symbol is Cinderella's castle, complete with a moat where pilgrims throw coins and make wishes. On my first visit I was surprised to discover that the castle has a largely symbolic function as a trademark or logo for Walt Disney World. The castle has little utilitarian value. A few shops on the ground floor were open to the public, but the rest of the building was off limits. In interpreting Cinderella's castle, I recalled a lecture given in 1976 by British anthropologist Sir Edmund Leach. In describing the ritual surrounding his dubbing as a knight, Leach noted that Queen Elizabeth stood in front of the British throne and did not, in accordance with our stereotype of monarchs, sit on it. Leach surmised that the primary value of the throne is to represent, to make concrete, something enduring but abstract—the British sovereign's right to rule. Similarly, the most important thing about Cinderella's castle is its symbolism. It offers concrete testimony to the eternal aspects of Disney creations.

A Pilgrimage to a "Religious" Shrine

A comparison of Walt Disney World to a shrine in Brazil reveals further similarities between Disney World and "religious" pilgrimage sites. As described by Daniel Gross (1971b), the Brazilian shrine Bom Jesus da Lapa is also located in the interior of a state. It receives an annual influx of more than 20,000 pilgrims, mostly on August 6. The patron saint, Bom ("Good") Jesus, is a wooden statue atop an altar in a cave. Like Cinderella's castle, a well-known landmark—a gray limestone outcrop pitted with caves—identifies Bom Jesus to pilgrims.

Most pilgrims go to Bom Jesus to fulfill vows, usually vows concerned with health. They promise to make the pilgrimage if a prayer is answered. Bom Jesus may be asked to help cure a specific malady, guarantee a safe journey, or help lovers stop quarreling. To fulfill their vows, pilgrims make offerings at the altar. If the prayer concerned a successful marriage, a photograph of the happy couple may be offered. People who have prayed for a broken leg to heal may leave an X-ray or cast at the altar.

The reasons why people make pilgrimages vary from shrine to shrine. Brazilians go to Bom Jesus to fulfill vows. Miraculous cures are sought and reported at Lourdes in France. Visitors to Disney World have various motives for the trip. "Pleasing the children" is a frequent reason. Also, parents offer a trip to Disney World as a reward for children's good behavior and achievements or perhaps as an incentive to help them recover from an illness.

Most Americans probably visit Walt Disney World for amusement, recreation, and vacation. In this sense, they differ from pilgrims to religious shrines. Americans don't appear to believe that a Disney visit has curative properties, although they may feel that vacations promote health. Nonetheless, television news programs occasionally run stories about communities pooling their resources to send terminally ill children to Disneyland. Thus, even though a visit to a Disney park is not regarded as curative, it is an appropriate last wish.

Furthermore, even when people undertake "religious" pilgrimages, their motives may not be exclusively or even primarily "religious" as the Bom Jesus da Lapa pilgrimage illustrates. Because there are so many pilgrims, most have no chance to worship the wooden statue. Chapel attendants rapidly herd them past the altar, just as Disney visitors are corralled into tram and monorail. Many Bom Jesus pilgrims must make way for others before they have a chance to kneel.

Bom Jesus da Lapa and Disney World also have similar commercial and recreational aspects. A variety of souvenirs, not limited to church-related icons, are sold to Bom Jesus pilgrims, just as in Disney World. In fact, the Bom Jesus pilgrim spends little time in religious contemplation. Several kinds of entertainment come to Bom Jesus along with the pilgrims, including traveling circuses, trained boa constrictors, vaudeville acts, gambling devices, and singing troubadours. During the height of the pilgrimage, Bom Jesus also has more than a dozen brothels. Most Americans would probably find Walt Disney World purer than Bom Jesus da Lapa. Similar nonreligious activities and a similar representation of other-than-religious motives characterize popular shrines and pilgrims elsewhere.

RECOGNIZING RELIGION

Some anthropologists think that rituals are distinguished from other behavior by special emotions, nonutilitarian intentions, and supernatural entities. However, other anthropologists define ritual more broadly. Writing about football, Arens (1981) pointed out that behavior can simultaneously have sacred and secular aspects. On one level, football is "simply a sport"; on another, it is a public ritual. Similarly, Walt Disney World, an amusement park, is on one level a mundane, secular place, but on another it assumes some of the attributes of a sacred place.

In the context of comparative religion, this isn't surprising. The French sociologist/anthropologist Émile Durkheim (1912/1961) pointed out long ago that almost everything from the sublime to the ridiculous has in some societies been treated as sacred. The distinction between sacred and profane doesn't depend on the intrinsic qualities of the sacred symbol. In Australian totemism, for example, sacred beings include such humble creatures as ducks, frogs, rabbits, and grubs, whose inherent qualities could hardly have given rise to the religious sentiment they inspire. If frogs and grubs can be elevated to a sacred level, why not Disney creations?

Many Americans believe that recreation and religion are separate domains. From my field work in Brazil and Madagascar and my reading about other societies, I believe that this separation is both ethnocentric and false. Madagascar's tomb-centered ceremonies are times when the living and the dead are joyously reunited, when people get drunk, gorge themselves, and enjoy sexual license. Perhaps the gray, sober, ascetic, and moralistic aspects of many religious events in the United States, in taking the "fun" out of religion, force us to find our religion in fun. Many Americans seek in such apparently secular contexts as amusement parks, rock concerts, and sports what other people find in religious rites, beliefs, and ceremonies.

Standing back from the native explanations provided by my culture, I perceive Walt Disney not merely as a commercial figure and view his amusement parks not simply as recreational domains. There is a deeper level of attachment between Americans and Disney creations. The implication is not that this constitutes a religion, although there are parallels with passage rites and religious pilgrimages. There is no doubt, however, that Disney, his parks, and his creations do constitute powerful enculturative forces in the contemporary United States.

RITUALS AT McDONALD'S

Each day, on the average, a new McDonald's restaurant opens somewhere in the world. The number of McDonald's outlets today surpasses the total number of fast-food restaurants in the United States in 1945. McDonald's has grown from a single hamburger stand in San Bernardino, California, into today's international web of thousands of outlets. Have factors less obvious to American natives than relatively low cost, fast service, and taste contributed to McDonald's success? Could it be that natives—in consuming the products and propaganda of McDonald's—are not just eating but experiencing something comparable in certain respects to participation in religious rituals? To answer this question we must briefly review the nature of ritual.

Rituals, we know, are formal—stylized, repetitive, and stereotyped. They are performed in special places at set times. Rituals include liturgical orders—set sequences of words and actions laid down by someone other than the current performers. Rituals also convey information about participants and their cultural traditions. Performed year after year, generation after generation, rituals translate messages, values, and sentiments into action. Rituals are social acts. Inevitably, some participants are more strongly committed than others are to the beliefs on which the rituals are founded. However, just by taking part in a joint public act, people signal that they accept an order that transcends their status as mere individuals.

For several years, like many other Americans, I have occasionally eaten at McDonald's. Eventually I began to notice certain ritual-like aspects of Americans' behavior at these fast-food restaurants. Tell your fellow Americans that going to McDonald's is similar in some ways to going to church and their bias as natives will reveal itself in laughter, denial, or questions about your sanity. Just as football is a game, *Star Wars* a movie, and Walt Disney World an amusement park, McDonald's, for natives, is just a place to eat. However, an analysis of what natives do at McDonald's will reveal a very high degree of formal, uniform behavior by staff members and customers alike. It is particularly interesting that this invariance in word and deed has developed without any theological doctrine. McDonald's ritual aspect is founded on twentieth-century technology, particularly automobiles, television, work away from home, and the short lunch break. It is striking nevertheless that one commercial organization should be so much more successful than other businesses, the schools, the military, and even many religions in producing behavioral invariance. Factors other than low cost, fast service, and the taste of the food—all of which are approximated by other chains—have contributed to our acceptance of McDonald's and adherence to its rules.

Remarkably, when Americans travel abroad, even in countries noted for good food, many visit the local McDonald's outlet. The same factors that lead us to frequent McDonald's at home are responsible. Because Americans are thoroughly familiar with how to eat and more or less what they will pay at McDonald's, in its outlets overseas they have a home away from home. In Paris, whose people aren't known for making tourists, particularly Americans, feel at home, McDonald's offers sanctuary. It is, after all, an American institution, where natives, programmed by years of prior experience, can feel completely at home. Americans, if they wish, can temporarily reverse roles with their hosts. If American tourists can't be expected to act like the French, neither can the French be expected to act in a culturally appropriate manner at McDonald's.

This devotion to McDonald's rests in part on uni-

formities associated with its outlets, at least in the United States: food, setting, architecture, ambience, acts, and utterances. The McDonald's symbol, the golden arches, is an almost universal landmark, as familiar to Americans as Mickey Mouse, Mr. Rogers, and the flag. The McDonald's nearest my university is a brick structure whose stained-glass windows have golden arches as their central theme. Sunlight floods in through a skylight that is like the clerestory of a church.

Americans enter a McDonald's restaurant for an ordinary, secular act—eating. However, the surroundings tell us that we are somehow apart from the variability of the world outside. We know what we are going to see, what we are going to say, and what will be said to us. We know what we will eat, how it will taste, and how much it will cost. Behind the counter, agents wear similar attire. Permissible utterances by customer and worker are written above the counter. Throughout the United States, with only minor variation, the menu is in the same place, contains the same items, and has the same prices. The food, again with only minor regional variation, is prepared according to plan and varies little in taste. Obviously, customers are limited in what they can choose. Less obviously, they are limited in what they can say. Each item has its appropriate designation: "large fry," "quarter pounder with cheese." The novice who innocently asks, "What kind of hamburgers do you have?" or "What's a Big Mac?" is out of place.

Other ritual phrases are uttered by the person behind the counter. After the customer has completed his order, if no potatoes are requested, the agent ritually asks, "Any fries?" Once food is presented and picked up, the agent conventionally says, "Have a nice day." Nonverbal behavior is also programmed. As customers request food, agents look back to see if the desired sandwich item is available. If not, they tell you, "That'll be a few minutes," and prepare your drink. After this a proper agent will take the order of the next customer in line. McDonald's lore and customs are even taught at a "seminary" called Hamburger University in Illinois. Managers who attend the program pass on what they learn to the people who work in their restaurants.

It isn't simply the formality and regularity of behavior at McDonald's but its total ambience that invites comparison with sacred places. Like the

Disney organization, McDonald's image makers stress clean living and draw on an order of values—"traditional American values"—that transcends McDonald's itself. Agents submit to dress codes. Kitchens, grills, and counters sparkle. Understandably, as the world's number-one fast-food chain, McDonald's has also evoked hostility. In 1975 the Ann Arbor campus McDonald's was the scene of a ritual rebellion—desecration by the Radical Vegetarian League, which held a "puke-in." Standing on the second-story balcony just below the clerestory, a dozen vegetarians gorged themselves on mustard and water and vomited down on the customer waiting area. McDonald's, defiled, lost many customers that day.

The formality and invariance of behavior in a demarcated setting suggest analogies between McDonald's and rituals. Furthermore, as in a ritual, participation in McDonald's occurs at specified times. In American culture our daily food consumption is supposed to occur as three meals: breakfast, lunch, and dinner. Americans who have traveled abroad are aware that cultures differ in which meal they emphasize. In many countries, the midday meal is primary. Americans are away from home at lunchtime because of their jobs and usually take less than an hour for lunch. They view dinner as the main meal. Lunch is a lighter meal symbolized by the sandwich. McDonald's provides relatively hot and fresh sandwiches and a variety of subsidiary fare that many American palates can tolerate.

The ritual of eating at McDonald's is confined to ordinary, everyday life. Eating at McDonald's and religious feasts are in complementary distribution in American life. That is, when one occurs, the other doesn't. Most Americans would consider it inappropriate to eat at a fast-food restaurant on Christmas, Thanksgiving, Easter, or Passover. Our culture regards these as family days, occasions when relatives and close friends get together. However, although Americans neglect McDonald's on holidays, television reminds us that McDonald's still endures, that it will welcome us back once our holiday is over. The television presence of McDonald's is particularly obvious on such occasions—whether through a float in the Macy's Thanksgiving Day parade or through sponsorship of special programs, particularly "family entertainment."

Although Burger King, Wendy's, and Arby's compete with McDonald's for the fast-food business, none rivals McDonald's success. The explanation may lie in the particularly skillful ways in which McDonald's advertising plays up the features just discussed. Its commercials are varied to appeal to different audiences. On Saturday morning television, with its steady stream of cartoons, McDonald's is a ubiquitous sponsor. The commercials for children's shows usually differ from the ones adults see in the evening and on sports programs. Children are reminded of McDonald's through fantasy characters, headed by clown Ronald McDonald. Children can meet "McDonaldland" characters again at outlets. Their pictures appear on cookie boxes and plastic cups. Children also have a chance to meet Ronald McDonald as actors scatter visits throughout the country. One can even rent a Ronald for a birthday party.

Adult advertising has different but equally effective themes. Breakfast at McDonald's has been promoted by a fresh-faced, sincere, happy, clean-cut young woman. Healthy, clean-living Americans gambol on ski slopes or in mountain pastures. The single theme, however, that for years has run through the commercials is personalism. McDonald's, the commercials drone on, is something other than a fast-food restaurant. It's a warm, friendly place where you are graciously welcomed and feel at home, where your children won't get into trouble. McDonald's commercials tell you that you aren't simply an anonymous face in an amorphous crowd. You find respite from a hectic and impersonal society, the break you deserve. Your individuality and dignity are respected at McDonald's.

McDonald's advertising tries to deemphasize the fact that the chain is a commercial organization. One jingle proclaimed "You, you're the one; we're fixin' breakfast for ya"—not "We're making millions off ya." Commercials make McDonald's seem like a charitable organization by stressing its program of community good works. "Family" television entertainment such as the film *The Sound of Music* is "brought to you by McDonald's." McDonald's commercials regularly tell us that it supports and works to maintain the values of American family life.

As with the Disney organization, the argument here is not that McDonald's has become a religion. Rather, I am suggesting that specific ways in which Americans participate in McDonald's bear analogies to religious systems involving myth, symbol, and ritual. Just as in rituals, participation in Mc-

Donald's requires temporary subordination of individual differences in a social and cultural collectivity. In a land of ethnic, social, economic, and religious diversity, we demonstrate that we share something with millions of other Americans. Furthermore, as in rituals, participation in McDonald's is linked to a cultural system that transcends the chain itself. By eating there, we say something about ourselves as Americans, about our acceptance of certain collective values and ways of living. By returning to McDonald's, we affirm that certain values and life styles, developed through the collective experience of Americans before us, will continue.

ANTHROPOLOGY AND AMERICAN "POP" CULTURE

In the chapter "Religion" we saw that ritual pig slaughter in New Guinea and taboos on beef eating in India have material causes and effects. Correspondingly, we see here that consumption of the propaganda and products of commercial organizations can entail ritual behavior and mythological and symbolic components that go unrecognized by native participants. Just as rituals can have material consequences, businesses can share features with rituals and myths.

This Appendix has stressed not variation but experiences and enculturative forces that are common to most Americans, particularly the young. I have emphasized several points. Techniques developed for studying other cultures can be used in interpreting our own. Studying their own cultures, native anthropologists can contribute by coupling professional detachment and objectivity with personal experience and understanding.

Anthropology's structural and symbolic analyses share as much with the humanities as with science. These approaches seek primarily to discover, interpret, and illuminate otherwise hidden dimensions of phenomena rather than to explain them. Structural and symbolic analyses are therefore difficult to confirm or disprove. They can be evaluated emically: Do natives accept them or prefer them to other interpretations? Do they enable natives to make more sense of familiar phenomena? They can also be evaluated etically: Do they fit within a comparative framework provided by data and analyses

from other societies? In previous chapters we have discussed correlations between, say, population density and political organization. Such relationships, which can be evaluated statistically, can be confirmed by researchers who independently examine the same data. However, structural and symbolic hypotheses, although relying more on impressions, can be revealing as well. They may enlighten us about otherwise unsuspected coherence and contradictions in cultural forms.

The examples considered in this Appendix are shared cultural forms that have appeared and spread rapidly during the twentieth century because of major changes in the material conditions of American life—particularly work organization, communication, and transportation. Most contemporary Americans deem at least one automobile a necessity. Televisions outnumber toilets in American households. Through the mass media, institutions such as sports, movies, TV shows, amusement parks, and fast-food restaurants have become powerful elements of American national culture. They provide a framework of common expectations, experiences, and behavior overriding differences in region, class, formal religious affiliation, political sentiments, gender, ethnic group, and place of residence. Although some of us may not like these changes, it's difficult to deny their significance.

The rise of these institutions is linked not just to the mass media but also to decreasing participation in traditional religion and the weakening of ties based on kinship, marriage, and community within industrial society. Neither a single church, a strong central government, nor segmentary lineage organization unites most Americans. Unification through the mass media and consumption opens a new chapter in the exploration of cultural diversity.

These dimensions of contemporary culture are dismissed as passing, trivial, or "pop" by some. However, because millions of people share them, they deserve and are receiving scholarly attention. Such studies help fulfill the promise that by studying anthropology, we can learn more about ourselves. Americans can view themselves not just as members of a varied and complex nation but also as a population united by distinctive shared symbols, customs, and experiences. American culture takes its place within the realm of cultural diversity. That, after all, is the subject matter of anthropology.

BIBLIOGRAPHY

ADAMS, R. M.
1981   *Heartland of Cities.* Chicago: Aldine.

AGAR, M. H.
1980   *The Professional Stranger: An Informal Introduction to Ethnography.* New York: Academic Press.

AHMED, A. S.
1992   *Postmodernism and Islam: Predicament and Promise.* New York: Routledge.

AKAZAWA, T.
1980   *The Japanese Paleolithic: A Techno-Typological Study.* Tokyo: Rippo Shobo.

AKAZAWA, T., AND C. M. AIKENS, EDS.
1986   *Prehistoric Hunter-Gatherers in Japan: New Research Methods.* Tokyo: University of Tokyo Press.

ALBERT, B.
1989   Yanomami 'Violence': Inclusive Fitness or Ethnographer's Representation? *Current Anthropology* 30: 637–640.

AMADIUME, I.
1987   *Male Daughters, Female Husbands.* Atlantic Highlands, NJ: Zed.

AMERICAN ANTHROPOLOGICAL ASSOCIATION
AAA Guide: A Guide to Departments, a Directory of Members. (Formerly *Guide to Departments of Anthropology.*) Published annually by the American Anthropological Association, Washington, DC.
Anthropology Newsletter. Published 9 times annually by the American Anthropological Association, Washington, DC.

ANDERSON, B.
1991   *Imagined Communities: Reflections on the Origin and Spread of Nationalism,* rev. ed. London: Verso.

ANN ARBOR NEWS
1985   Testimony of Linda Tarr-Whelan of the National Education Association to the House Committee on Science, Research and Technology; quoted in Karen Grassmuck, Local Educators Join Push for "A Computer in Every Classroom." February 10, p. A11.
1985   Poverty Affecting More Children, Government Study Finds. May 23, p. C5.
1985   More Young Adults Are Postponing Marriage, Living with Their Parents (from UPI), November 10, p. C2.
1989   Census Shows Big Change in Families. September 5, p. C2.
1989   College Costs for Year 2000: Save Up Now. September 5, p. D2.
1989   Population Control Key to World Hunger, Economist Says. September 10, p. C1.

ANN ARBOR OBSERVER
1985   Surveys of Black Americans: Most Feel Oppressed. May, pp. 42–43.

AOKI, MICHIKO Y., AND M. B. DARDESS, EDS.
1981   *As the Japanese See It: Past and Present.* Honolulu: University Press of Hawaii.

APPADURAI, A.
1990   Disjuncture and Difference in the Global Cultural Economy. *Public Culture* 2(2): 1–24.

1991   Global Ethnoscapes: Notes and Queries for a Transnational Anthropology. In *Recapturing Anthropology: Working in the Present*, ed. R. G. Fox, pp. 191–210. Santa Fe: School of American Research Advanced Seminar Series.

APPEL, R., AND MUYSKEN, P.
1987   *Language Contact and Bilingualism*. London: Edward Arnold.

APPELL, G. N.
1978   *Ethical Dilemmas in Anthropological Inquiry: A Case Book*. Waltham, MA: Crossroads Press.

APPIAH, K. A.
1990   Racisms. In *Anatomy of Racism*, ed. David Theo Goldberg, pp. 3–17. Minneapolis: University of Minnesota Press.

ARDREY, R.
1961   *African Genesis*. New York: Atheneum.
1966   *The Territorial Imperative*. New York: Atheneum.

ARENS, W.
1981   Professional Football: An American Symbol and Ritual. In *The American Dimension: Cultural Myths and Social Realities*, 2nd ed., eds. W. Arens and S. B. Montague, pp. 1–10. Sherman Oaks, CA: Alfred.

ARENS, W., AND S. P. MONTAGUE
1981   *The American Dimension: Cultural Myths and Social Realities*, 2nd ed. Sherman Oaks, CA: Alfred.

ARENSBERG, C.
1978   Theoretical Contributions of Industrial and Development Studies. In *Applied Anthropology in America*, eds. E. M. Eddy and W. L. Partridge, pp. 49–78. New York: Columbia University Press.

BAILEY, R. C.
1990   *The Behavioral Ecology of Efe Pygmy Men in the Ituri Forest, Zaire*. Ann Arbor, MI: Anthropological Papers, Museum of Anthropology, University of Michigan, no. 86.

BAILEY, R. C., G. HEAD, M. JENIKE, B. OWEN, R. RECHTMAN, AND E. ZECHENTER
1989   Hunting and Gathering in Tropical Rain Forests: Is It Possible? *American Anthropologist* 91:59–82.

BAKER, P. T.
1978   *The Biology of High Altitude Peoples*. New York: Cambridge University Press.

BAKER, P. T., AND J. S. WEINER, EDS.
1966   *The Biology of Human Adaptability*. Oxford: Oxford University Press.

BAKHTIN, M.
1984   *Rabelais and His World*, trans. Helen Iswolksy. Bloomington: Indiana University Press.

BANTON, M.
1957   *West African City. A Study in Tribal Life in Freetown*. London: Oxford University Press.

BARASH, D. P.
1977   *Sociobiology and Behavior*. Amsterdam: Elsevier.

BARLETT, P. F., ED.
1980   *Agricultural Decision Making: Anthropological Contributions to Rural Development*. New York: Academic Press.

BARNABY, F., ED.
1984   *Future War: Armed Conflict in the Next Decade*. London: M. Joseph.

BARNARD, A.
1979   Kalahari Settlement Patterns. In *Social and Ecological Systems*, eds. P. Burnham and R. Ellen. New York: Academic Press.

BARNES, J. A.
1954   Class and Committees in a Norwegian Island Parish. *Human Relations* 7: 39–58.

BARNOUW, V.
1985   *Culture and Personality*, 4th ed. Belmont, CA: Wadsworth.

BARON, D.
1986   *Grammar and Gender*. New Haven: Yale University Press.

BARRINGER, F.
1989   32 Million Lived in Poverty in '88, a Figure Unchanged. *The New York Times*, October 19, p. 18.
1992   New Census Data Show More Children Living in Poverty. *The New York Times*, May 29, pp. A1, A12, A13.

BARRY, H., M. K. BACON, AND I. L. CHILD
1959   Relation of Child Training to Subsistence Economy. *American Anthropologist* 61: 51–63.

BARTH, F.
1968   (Orig. 1958). Ecologic Relations of Ethnic Groups in Swat, North Pakistan. In *Man in Adaptation: The Cultural Present*, ed. Yehudi Cohen, pp. 324–331. Chicago: Aldine.
1969   *Ethnic Groups and Boundaries: The Social Organization of Cultural Difference*. London: Allyn and Unwin.

BAR-YOSEF, O.
1987   Pleistocene Connections between Africa and Southwest Asia: An Archaeological Perspective. *African Archaeological Review* 5: 29–38.

BATALLA, G. B.
1966   Conservative Thought in Applied Anthropology: A Critique. *Human Organization* 25: 89–92.

BATESON, M.
1984   *With a Daughter's Eye: A Memoir of Margaret*

Mead and Gregory Bateson. New York: William Morrow.

BEEMAN, W.
1986   *Language, Status, and Power in Iran.* Bloomington: Indiana University Press.

BELL, WENDELL
1981   Neocolonialism. In *Encyclopedia of Sociology,* p. 193. Guilford, CT.: DPG Publishing.

BELLAH, R. N.
1978   Religious Evolution. In *Reader in Comparative Religion: An Anthropological Approach,* 4th ed., eds. W. A. Lessa and E. Z. Vogt, pp. 36–50. New York: Harper & Row.

BELSHAW, C. S.
1978   The Significance of Modern Cults in Melanesian Development. In *Reader in Comparative Religion: An Anthropological Approach,* 4th ed., eds. W. A. Lessa and E. Z. Vogt, pp. 523–527. New York: Harper & Row.

BENEDICT, BURTON
1970   Pluralism and Stratification. In *Essays in Comparative Social Stratification,* eds. L. Plotnicov and A. Tuden, pp. 29–41. Pittsburgh: University of Pittsburgh Press.

BENEDICT, R.
1946   *The Chrysanthemum and the Sword.* Boston: Houghton Mifflin.
1959   (Orig. 1934). *Patterns of Culture.* New York: New American Library.

BENNETT, J. W.
1969   *Northern Plainsmen: Adaptive Strategy and Agrarian Life.* Chicago: Aldine.

BENNETT, J. W., AND BOWEN, J. R., EDS.
1988   *Production and Autonomy: Anthropological Studies and Critiques of Development.* Monographs in Economic Anthropology, no. 5, Society for Economic Anthropology. New York: University Press of America.

BERLIN, B. D., E. BREEDLOVE, AND P. H. RAVEN
1974   *Principles of Tzeltal Plant Classification: An Introduction to the Botanical Ethnography of a Mayan-Speaking People of Highland Chiapas.* New York: Academic Press.

BERLIN, B., AND P. KAY
1992   *Basic Color Terms: Their Universality and Evolution,* 2nd ed. Berkeley: University of California Press.

BERNARD, H. R.
1988   *Research Methods in Cultural Anthropology.* Newbury Park, CA: Sage.

BERNARD, H. R., AND W. E. SIBLEY
1975   *Anthropology and Jobs: A Guide for Undergraduates.* A Special Publication of the American Anthropological Association. Washington, DC: American Anthropological Association.

BERNOR, R. L.
1983   Geochronology and Zoogeographic Relationships of Miocene Hominoidea. In *New Interpretations of Ape and Human Ancestry,* eds. R. L. Ciochon and R. S. Corruccini, pp. 21–64. New York: Plenum.

BERREMAN, G. D.
1962   Pahari Polyandry: A Comparison. *American Anthropologist* 64: 60–75.
1973   (Orig. 1969). Academic Colonialism: Not So Innocent Abroad. In *To See Ourselves: Anthropology and Modern Social Issues,* gen. ed. T. Weaver, pp. 152–156. Glenview, IL: Scott, Foresman.
1975   Himalayan Polyandry and the Domestic Cycle. *American Ethnologist* 2: 127–138.

BETTELHEIM, B.
1975   *The Uses of Enchantment: The Meaning and Importance of Fairy Tales.* New York: Vintage.

BINFORD, L. R.
1968   Post-Pleistocene Adaptations. In *New Perspectives in Archeology,* eds. S. R. Binford and L. R. Binford, pp. 313–341. Chicago: Aldine.
1981   *Bones. Ancient Men and Modern Myths.* New York: Academic Press.

BINFORD, L. R., AND S. R. BINFORD
1979   Stone Tools and Human Behavior. In *Human Ancestors, Readings from* Scientific American, eds. G. L. Isaac and R. E. F. Leakey, pp. 92–101. San Francisco: W. H. Freeman.

BIRD-DAVID, N.
1992   Beyond "The Original Affluent Society": A Culturalist Reformulation. *Current Anthropology* 33(1): 25–47.

BIRDSELL, J. B.
1981   *Human Evolution: An Introduction to the New Physical Anthropology,* 3rd ed. Boston: Houghton Mifflin.

BLANTON, R. E., S. A. KOWALEWSKI, G. FEINMAN, AND J. APPEL
1981   *Ancient Mesoamerica.* New York: Cambridge University Press.

BLOCH, M.
1971   *Placing the Dead: Tombs, Ancestral Villages, and Kinship in Madagascar.* New York: Seminar Press.

BLOCH, M., ED.
1975   *Political Language and Oratory in Traditional Societies.* London: Academic Press.

BLUM, H. F.
1961   Does the Melanin Pigment of Human Skin

Have Adaptive Value? *Quarterly Review of Biology* 36: 50–63.

BOAS, F.
1966   (Orig. 1940). *Race, Language, and Culture*. New York: Free Press.

BOCK, P. K.
1980   *Continuities in Psychological Anthropology*. San Francisco: W. H. Freeman.

BODLEY, J. H.
1985   *Anthropology and Contemporary Human Problems*, 2nd ed. Palo Alto, CA: Mayfield.

BODLEY, J. H., ED.
1988   *Tribal Peoples and Development Issues: A Global Overview*. Palo Alto, CA: Mayfield.

BODMER, W. F., AND L. L. CAVALLI-SFORZA
1976   *Genetics, Evolution, and Man*. San Francisco: W. H. Freeman.

BOGORAS, W.
1904   The Chukchee. In *The Jesup North Pacific Expedition*, ed. F. Boas. New York: Memoir of the American Museum of Natural History.

BOGUCKI, P. I.
1988   *Forest Farmers and Stockherders: Early Agriculture and Its Consequences in Northcentral Europe*. New York: Cambridge University Press.

BOHANNAN, P.
1955   Some Principles of Exchange and Investment among the Tiv. *American Anthropologist* 57: 60–70.
1963   *Social Anthropology*. New York: Holt, Rinehart & Winston.

BOHANNAN, P., AND J. MIDDLETON, EDS.
1968   *Marriage, Family, and Residence*. Garden City, NY: Natural History Press.

BOLTON, R.
1981   Susto, Hostility, and Hypoglycemia. *Ethnology* 20(4): 227–258.

BOSERUP, E.
1965   *The Conditions of Agricultural Growth*. Chicago: Aldine.
1970   *Women's Role in Economic Development*. London: Allen and Unwin.

BOTT, E.
1957   *Family and Social Network*. London: Tavistock.

BOURDIEU, P.
1977   *Outline of a Theory of Practice*, trans. Richard Nice. Cambridge: Cambridge University Press.
1982   *Ce Que Parler Veut Dire*. Paris: Fayard.
1984   *Distinction: A Social Critique of the Judgment of Taste*, trans. Richard Nice. Cambridge: Harvard University Press.

BOURGUIGNON, E.
1979   *Psychological Anthropology: An Introduction to Human Nature and Cultural Differences*. New York: Holt, Rinehart & Winston.

BOURQUE, S. C., AND KAY B. WARREN
1981   *Women of the Andes: Patriarchy and Social Change in Two Peruvian Villages*. Ann Arbor: University of Michigan Press.
1987   Technology, Gender and Development. *Daedalus* 116(4): 173–197.

BOUVIER, L. F., AND C. B. DAVIS
1980   The Future Racial Composition of the United States. Washington, DC: Demographic Information Services Center of the Population Reference Bureau.

BOWER, J., AND D. LUBELL, EDS.
1988   *Prehistoric Cultures and Environments in the Late Quaternay of Africa*. Cambridge Monographs in African Archaeology, 26. Oxford, England: B.A.R.

BOYD, R., AND P. J. RICHERSON
1985   *Culture and the Evolutionary Process*. Chicago: University of Chicago Press.

BRACE, C. L.
1964   A Nonracial Approach towards the Understanding of Human Diversity. In *The Concept of Race*, ed. A. Montagu, pp. 103–152. New York: Free Press.
1973   Sexual Dimorphism in Human Evolution. In *Man in Evolutionary Perspective*, ed. C. L. Brace and J. Metress, pp. 238–254. New York: Wiley.
1991   *The Stages of Human Evolution*, 4th ed. Englewood Cliffs, NJ: Prentice-Hall.

BRACE, C. L., AND F. B. LIVINGSTONE
1971   On Creeping Jensenism. In *Race and Intelligence*, eds. C. L. Brace, G. R. Gamble, and J. T. Bond, pp. 64–75. Anthropological Studies, no. 8. Washington, DC: American Anthropological Association.

BRADLEY, C., C. MOORE, M. BURTON, AND D. WHITE
1990   A Cross-Cultural Historical Analysis of Subsistence Change. *American Anthropologist* 92(2): 447–457.

BRADY, I., ED.
1983   Special Section: Speaking in the Name of the Real: Freeman and Mead on Samoa. *American Anthropologist* 85: 908–947.

BRAIDWOOD, R. J.
1975   *Prehistoric Men*, 8th ed. Glenview, IL: Scott, Foresman.

BRAUDEL, FERNAND
1973   *Capitalism and Material Life, 1400–1800*, trans. M. Kochan. London: Weidenfeld and Nicolson.
1977   *Afterthoughts on Material Civilization and Capi-*

talism. Baltimore: Johns Hopkins University Press.

1981   *Civilization and Capitalism, 15th-18th Century Volume I: The Structure of Everyday Life: The Limits*, trans. S. Reynolds. New York: Harper & Row.

1982   *Civilization and Capitalism, 15th–18th Century Volume II: The Wheels of Commerce*. New York: Harper & Row.

1984   *Civilization and Capitalism 15th–18th Century, Volume III: The Perspective of the World*. New York: Harper & Row.

BRENNEIS, D.

1988   Language and Disputing. *Annual Review of Anthropology* 17: 221–237.

BRIM, J. A., AND D. H. SPAIN

1974   *Research Design in Anthropology*. New York: Holt, Rinehart & Winston.

BRONFENBRENNER, U.

1975   Nature with Nurture: A Reinterpretation of the Evidence. In *Race and IQ*, ed. A. Montagu, pp. 114–144. New York: Oxford University Press.

BROOKE, J.

1992   Rio's New Day in Sun Leaves Laplander Limp. *The New York Times*, June 1, p. A7.

BROWN, J. K.

1975   Iroquois Women: An Ethnohistoric Note. In *Toward an Anthropology of Women*, ed. R. Reiter, pp. 235–251. New York: Monthly Review Press.

BROWN, K. M.

1991   *Mama Lola: A Vodou Priestess in Brooklyn*. Berkeley: University of California Press.

BROWN, R. W.

1958   *Words and Things*. Glencoe, IL: Free Press.

BRYANT, BUNYAN, AND PAUL MOHAI

1991   Race, Class, and Environmental Quality in the Detroit Area. In *Environmental Racism: Issues and Dilemmas*, eds. Bunyan Bryant and Paul Mohai. Ann Arbor: The University of Michigan Office of Minority Affairs.

BUCHLER, I. R., AND H. A. SELBY

1968   *Kinship and Social Organization: An Introduction to Theory and Method*. New York: Macmillan.

BUNZEL, R.

1952   *Chichicastenango: A Guatemalan Village*. New York: J. J. Augustin.

BURKE, P., AND R. PORTER

1987   *The Social History of Language*. Cambridge: Cambridge University Press.

BURLING, R.

1970   *Man's Many Voices: Language in Its Cultural Context*. New York: Holt, Rinehart & Winston.

BURNS, J. F.

1992a   Bosnian Strife Cuts Old Bridges of Trust. *The New York Times*, May 22, pp. A1, A6.

1992b   Winds of Yugoslavia's War Threaten to Engulf Ethnic Enclave in Serbia. *The New York Times*, May 26, p. A5.

1992c   Replay of the 40's in Hills of Bosnia. *The New York Times*, May 31, p. 11.

1992d   In Sarajevo, Anger and Grief amid Ruins. *The New York Times*, June 1, p. A1, A6.

1992e   Serbian Recruits Fight for the Road to Sarajevo. *The New York Times*, June 3, p. A4.

1992f   A Serb, Fighting Serbs, Defends Sarajevo. *The New York Times*, July 12, Section 4, p. E-3.

CAMPBELL, B. G.

1985   *Human Evolution: An Introduction to Man's Adaptations*, 3rd ed. New York: Aldine.

1988   *Humankind Emerging*, 5th ed. Glenview, IL: Scott, Foresman.

CANN, R. L., M. STONEKING, AND A. C. WILSON

1987   Mitochondrial DNA and Human Evolution. *Nature* 325: 31–36.

CARNEIRO, R. L.

1956   Slash-and-Burn Agriculture: A Closer Look at Its Implications for Settlement Patterns. In *Men and Cultures, Selected Papers of the Fifth International Congress of Anthropological and Ethnological Sciences*, ed. A. F. C. Wallace, pp. 229–234. Philadelphia: University of Pennsylvania Press.

1968   (Orig. 1961). Slash-and-Burn Cultivation among the Kuikuru and Its Implications for Cultural Development in the Amazon Basin. In *Man in Adaptation: The Cultural Present*, ed. Y. A. Cohen, pp. 131–145. Chicago: Aldine.

1970   A Theory of the Origin of the State. *Science* 69: 733–738.

1990   Chiefdom-Level Warfare as Exemplified in Figi and the Cauca Valley. In *The Anthropology of War*, ed. J. Haas, pp. 190–211. Cambridge: Cambridge University Press.

CARTER, J.

1988   Freed from Keepers and Cages, Chimps Come of Age on Baboon Island. *Smithsonian* June, pp. 36–48.

CASSON, R.

1983   Schemata in Cognitive Anthropology. *Annual Review of Anthropology* 12: 429–462.

CERNEA, M., ED.

1990   *Putting People First: Sociological Variables in Rural Development*, 2nd ed. New York: Oxford University Press (published for The World Bank).

CHAGNON, N.
1974 *Studying the Yanomamo.* New York: Holt, Rinehart & Winston.
1988 Life Histories, Blood Revenge and Warfare in a Tribal Population. *Science* 239: 985–991.
1992 *Yanomamo: The Fierce People,* 4th ed. New York: Holt, Rinehart & Winston.

CHAGNON, N. A., AND W. IRONS, EDS.
1979 *Evolutionary Biology and Human Social Behavior: An Anthropological Perspective.* North Scituate, MA: Duxbury.

CHAMPION, T., AND C. GAMBLE, EDS.
1984 *Prehistoric Europe.* New York: Academic Press.

CHANG, K. C.
1977 *The Archaeology of Ancient China.* New Haven: Yale University Press.

CHILDE, V. G.
1951 *Man Makes Himself.* New York: New American Library.

CHOMSKY, N.
1957 *Syntactic Structures.* The Hague: Mouton.

CIOCHON, R. L.
1983 Hominoid Cladistics and The Ancestry of Modern Apes and Humans. In *New Interpretations of Ape and Human Ancestry.* eds. R. L. Ciochon and R. S. Corruccini, pp. 783–843. New York: Plenum.

CIOCHON, R. L., AND R. S. CORRUCCINI, EDS.
1983 *New Interpretations of Ape and Human Ancestry.* New York: Plenum.

CLAMMER, J., ED.
1976 *The New Economic Anthropology.* New York: St. Martin's Press.

CLARK, J. D., AND S. A. BRANDT
1984 *From Hunter to Farmers: The Causes and Consequences of Food Production in Africa.* Berkeley: University of California Press.

CLIFFORD, J.
1982 *Person and Myth: Maurice Leenhardt in the Melanesian World.* Berkeley: University of California Press.
1988 *The Predicament of Culture: Twentieth-Century Ethnography, Literature and Art.* Cambridge: Harvard University Press.

CLIFTON, J. A.
1970 *Applied Anthropology: Readings in the Uses of the Science of Man.* Boston: Houghton Mifflin.

COATES, J.
1986 *Women, Men, and Language.* London: Longman.

COE, M. D.
1962 *Mexico.* New York: Praeger.

COE, M. D., AND K. FLANNERY
1964 Microenvironments and Mesoamerican Prehistory. *Science* 143: 650–654.

COHEN, M. N.
1979 *The Food Crisis in Prehistory: Overpopulation and the Origins of Agriculture.* New Haven: Yale University Press.

COHEN, M. N., AND G. J. ARMELAGOS, EDS.
1984 *Paleopathology at the Origins of Agriculture.* New York: Academic Press.

COHEN, R.
1967 *The Kanuri of Bornu.* New York: Holt, Rinehart & Winston.

COHEN, R., AND E. R. SERVICE, EDS.
1978 *Origins of the State: The Anthropology of Political Evolution.* Philadelphia: Institute for the Study of Human Issues.

COHEN, Y.
1974 *Man in Adaptation: The Cultural Present,* 2nd ed. Chicago: Aldine.
1974 Culture as Adaptation. In *Man in Adaptation: The Cultural Present,* 2nd ed., ed. Y. A. Cohen, pp. 45–68. Chicago: Aldine.

COLE, S.
1975 *Leakey's Luck: The Life of Louis Bazett Leakey, 1903–1972.* New York: Harcourt Brace Jovanovich.

COLLIER, J. F., ED.
1988 *Marriage and Inequality in Classless Societies.* Stanford: Stanford University Press.

COLLIER, J. F., AND S. J. YANAGISAKO, EDS.
1987 *Gender and Kinship: Essays Toward a Unified Analysis.* Stanford: Stanford University Press.

COLLINS, T. W.
1989 Rural Economic Development in Two Tennessee Counties: A Racial Dimension. Paper presented at the annual meetings of the American Anthropological Association, Washington, D.C.

COLSON, E.
1971 *The Social Consequences of Resettlement: The Impact of the Kariba Resettlement on the Gwembe Tonga.* Manchester: Manchester University Press.

COLSON, E., AND T. SCUDDER
1975 New Economic Relationships Between the Gwembe Valley and the Line of Rail. In *Town and Country in Central and Eastern Africa,* ed. David Parkin, pp. 190–210. London: Oxford University Press.
1988 *For Prayer and Profit: The Ritual, Economic, and Social Importance of Beer in Gwembe District, Zambia, 1950–1982.* Stanford, CA: Stanford University Press.

COMAROFF, J.
1982 Dialectical Systems, History and Anthropology: Units of Study and Questions of Theory.

The Journal of Southern African Studies 8: 143–172.

COMAROFF, J., ED.

1980 *The Meaning of Marriage Payments.* New York: Academic Press.

COMBS-SCHILLING, E.

1989 *Sacred Performances: Islam, Sexuality, and Sacrifice.* New York: Columbia University Press.

COMTE, A.

1880 *A General View of Positivism.* London: Trbuer.

CONKLIN, H. C.

1954 *The Relation of Hanuno Culture to the Plant World.* Unpublished Ph.D. dissertation, Yale University.

CONNAH, G.

1987 *African Civilizations.* New York: Cambridge University Press.

CONNOR, W.

1972 Nation-building or Nation destroying. *World Politics* 24(3).

COOK-GUMPERZ, J.

1986 *The Social Construction of Literacy.* Cambridge: Cambridge University Press.

COOPER, F., AND A. L. STOLER

1989 Introduction, Tensions of Empire: Colonial Control and Visions of Rule. *American Ethnologist* 16: 609–621.

COWAN, A. L.

1989 Poll Finds Women's Gains Have Taken Personal Toll, *The New York Times*, August 21, 1989, pp. 1, 8.

COX, V.

1976 Jane Goodall: Learning from the Chimpanzee. *Human Behavior*, March, pp. 25–30.

CRANE, L. B., E. YEAGER, AND R. L. WHITMAN

1981 *An Introduction to Linguistics.* Boston: Little, Brown.

CRICK, F. H. C.

1968 (Orig. 1962). The Genetic Code. In *The Molecular Basis of Life: An Introduction to Molecular Biology, Readings from* Scientific American, pp. 198–205. San Francisco: W. H. Freeman.

CROSBY, A. W., JR.

1972 *The Columbian Exchange: Biological and Cultural Consequences of 1492.* Westport, CT: Greenwood Press.

1986 *Ecological Imperialism: The Biological Expansion of Europe 900–1900.* Cambridge: Cambridge University Press.

CULTURAL SURVIVAL

1992 *At the Threshold.* Cambridge, MA: Cultural Survival. Originally published as the Spring 1992 issue of *Cultural Survival Quarterly.*

CULTURAL SURVIVAL QUARTERLY

Quarterly journal. Cambridge, MA: Cultural Survival, Inc.

DAHLBERG, F., ED.

1981 *Woman the Gatherer.* New Haven: Yale University Press.

DALTON, G., ED.

1967 *Tribal and Peasant Economies.* Garden City, NY: The Natural History Press.

1968 *Primitive, Archaic and Modern Economies: Essays of Karl Polanyi.* Garden City, NY: Anchor Books.

DaMATTA, R.

1981 *Carnavais, Malandros, e Heróis.* Rio de Janeiro: Zahar.

1991 *Carnivals, Rogues, and Heroes: An Interpretation of the Brazilian Dilemma*, trans. from the Portuguese by John Drury. Notre Dame, IN: University of Notre Dame Press.

D'ANDRADE, R.

1984 Cultural Meaning Systems. In *Culture Theory: Essays on Mind, Self, and Emotion*, eds. R. A. Shweder and R. A. Levine, pp. 88–119. Cambridge, England: Cambridge University Press.

DARWIN, C.

1958 (Orig. 1859). *The Origin of Species.* New York: Dutton.

DARWIN, E.

1796 (Orig. 1794). *Zoonomia, Or the Laws of Organic Life*, 2nd ed. London: J. Johnson.

DAVIS, D. L., AND R. G. WHITTEN

1987 The Cross-Cultural Study of Human Sexuality. *Annual Review of Anthropology* 16: 69–98.

DAVIS, S. E.

1989 Twilight Zone of the Tech World. *Washington Post*, August 22, pp. 8–9.

DEGLER, C.

1970 *Neither Black nor White: Slavery and Race Relations in Brazil and the United States.* New York: Macmillan.

DELSON, ERIC, ED.

1985 *Ancestors: The Hard Evidence.* New York: Alan R. Liss.

DeLUMLEY, H.

1976 (Orig. 1969). A Paleolithic Camp at Nice. In *Avenues to Antiquity, Readings from* Scientific American, ed. B. M. Fagan, pp. 36–44. San Francisco: W. H. Freeman.

DENICH, B. S.

1974 Sex and Power in the Balkans. In *Woman, Culture, and Society*, eds. M. Z. Rosaldo and L. Lamphere, pp. 243–262. Stanford, CA: Stanford University Press.

DENTAN, R. K.
1968 *The Semai: A Nonviolent People of Malaya.* New York: Harcourt Brace.
1979 *The Semai: A Nonviolent People of Malaya.* Fieldwork edition. New York: Harcourt Brace.

DESPRES, L., ED.
1975 *Ethnicity and Resource Competition.* The Hague: Mouton.

DE VOS, G. A., AND H. WAGATSUMA
1966 *Japan's Invisible Race: Caste in Culture and Personality.* Berkeley: University of California Press.

DE VOS, G. A., W. O. WETHERALL, AND K. STEARMAN
1983 *Japan's Minorities: Burakumin, Koreans, Ainu and Okinawans.* Report no. 3. London: Minority Rights Group.

DIAMOND, J.
1989 Blood, Genes, and Malaria. *Natural History,* February, pp. 8–18.
1990 A Pox upon Our Genes. *Natural History,* February, pp. 26–30.

DI LEONARDO, M., ED.
1990 *Toward a New Anthropology of Gender.* Berkeley: University of California Press.

DIVALE, W. T., AND M. HARRIS
1976 Population, Warfare, and the Male Supremacist Complex. *American Anthropologist* 78: 521–538.

DOBZHANSKY, T., F. J. AYALA, G. L. STEBBINS, AND J. W. VALENTINE
1977 *Evolution.* San Francisco: W. H. Freeman.

DOUGLAS, M., AND A. WILDAVSKY
1982 *Risk and Culture: An Essay on the Selection of Technological and Environmental Dangers.* Berkeley: University of California Press.

DRAPER, P.
1975 !Kung Women: Contrasts in Sexual Egalitarianism in Foraging and Sedentary Contexts. In *Toward an Anthropology of Women,* ed. R. Reiter, pp. 77–109. New York: Monthly Review Press.

DRENNAN, R. D., AND C. A. URIBE, EDS.
1987 *Chiefdoms in the Americas.* Landon, MD: University Press of America.

DRUCKER, C.
1988 (Orig. 1985). Dam the Chico: Hydropower, Development and Tribal Resistance. In *Tribal Peoples and Development Issues: A Global Overview,* ed. J. H. Bodley, pp. 151–165. Palo Alto, CA: Mayfield.

DURKHEIM, E.
1951 (Orig. 1897). *Suicide: A Study in Sociology.* Glencoe, IL: Free Press.
1961 (Orig. 1912). *The Elementary Forms of the Religious Life.* New York: Collier Books.

DWYER, K.
1982 *Moroccan Dialogues: Anthropology in Question.* Baltimore: Johns Hopkins University Press.

EAGLETON, T.
1983 *Literary Theory: An Introduction.* Minneapolis: University of Minnesota Press.

EARLE, T.
1987 Chiefdoms in Archaeological and Ethnohistorical Perspective. *Annual Review of Anthropology* 16: 279–308.

EASTMAN, C. M.
1975 *Aspects of Language and Culture.* San Francisco: Chandler and Sharp.

ECKERT, P.
1989 *Jocks and Burnouts: Social Categories and Identity in the High School.* New York: Teachers College Press, Columbia University.

EDDY, E. M., AND W. L. PARTRIDGE, EDS.
1978 *Applied Anthropology in America.* New York: Columbia University Press.

EDGERTON, R.
1965 "Cultural" versus "Ecological" Factors in the Expression of Values, Attitudes and Personality Characteristics. *American Anthropologist* 67: 442–447.

EDWARDS, J.
1985 *Language, Society and Identity.* London: Basil Blackwell. Self and speech in society.

EISELEIN, E. B., AND M. TOPPER
1976 Media Anthropology: A Symposium. *Human Organization* 35: 111–192.

EISELEY, L.
1961 *Darwin's Century.* Garden City, NY: Doubleday, Anchor Books.

ELDREDGE, N.
1985 *Time Frames: The Rethinking of Darwinian Evolution and the Theory of Punctuated Equilibria.* New York: Simon & Schuster.

ERLANGER, S.
1992 An Islamic Awakening in Central Asian Lands. *The New York Times,* June 9, pp. A1, A7.

ERRINGTON, F., AND D. GEWERTZ
1987 *Cultural Alternatives and a Feminist Anthropology: An Analysis of Culturally Constructed Gender Interests in Papua New Guinea.* New York: Cambridge University Press.

ESCOBAR, A.
1991 Anthropology and the Development Encounter: The Making and Marketing of Development Anthropology. *American Ethnologist* 18: 658–682.

ETIENNE, M., AND E. LEACOCK, EDS.
1980 *Women and Colonization: Anthropological Perspectives.* New York: Praeger and J. F. Bergin.

EVANS-PRITCHARD, E. E.
1940   *The Nuer: A Description of the Modes of Livelihood and Political Institutions of a Nilotic People.* Oxford: Clarendon Press.
1970   Sexual Inversion among the Azande. *American Anthropologist* 72: 1428–1433.

FAGAN, B. M.
1987   *The Great Journey: The Peopling of Ancient America.* London: Thames and Hudson.
1988   *Archeology: A Brief Introduction*, 2nd ed. Glenview, IL: Scott, Foresman.
1989   *People of the Earth: An Introduction to World Prehistory*, 6th ed. Glenview, IL: Scott, Foresman.

FARNSWORTH, C. H.
1992   Canada to Divide Its Northern Land. *The New York Times*, May 6, p. A7.

FAROOQ, M.
1966   Importance of Determining Transmission Sites in Planning Bilharziasis Control: Field Observations from the Egypt-49 Project Area. *American Journal of Epidemiology* 83: 603–612.

FASOLD, R. W.
1990   *The Sociolinguistics of Language.* Oxford: Basil Blackwell.

FEDIGAN, L.
1982   *Primate Paradigms: Sex Roles and Social Bonds.* Montreal: Eden Press.

FELD, S.
1991   Voices of the Rainforest. *Public Culture* 4(1): 131–140.

FENLASON, L.
1990   Wolpoff Questions 'Eve's' Origin Date, Says It Ignores Contradictory Fossil Data. *The University Record* (University of Michigan, Ann Arbor) 45(21): 12.

FERGUSON, C. A., AND S. B. HEATH, EDS.
1981   *Language in the U.S.A.* New York: Cambridge University, Press.

FERGUSON, R. B.
1989*a*   Game Wars?: Ecology and Conflict in Amazonia. *Journal of Anthropological Research* 45(2): 179–207.
1989*b*   Ecological Consequences of Amazonian Warfare. *Ethnology* 28(3): 249–264.
1989*c*   Do Yanomamo Killers Have More Kids? *American Ethnologist* 16: 564–565.

FERRARO, G. P.
1990   *The Cultural Dimension of International Business.* Englewood Cliffs, NJ: Prentice-Hall.

FINKLER, K.
1985   *Spiritualist Healers in Mexico: Successes and Failures of Alternative Therapeutics.* South Hadley, MA: Bergin and Garvey.

FISHER, A.
1988   The More Things Change. *MOSAIC* 19(1): 22–33.
1988   On the Emergence of Humanness. *MOSAIC* 19(1): 34–45.

FISKE, J.
1989   *Understanding Popular Culture.* Boston: Unwin Hyman.

FLANNERY, K. V.
1969   Origins and Ecological Effects of Early Domestication in Iran and the Near East. In *The Domestication and Exploitation of Plants and Animals*, eds. P. J. Ucko and G. W. Dimbleby, pp. 73–100. Chicago: Aldine.
1972   The Cultural Evolution of Civilizations. *Annual Review of Ecology and Systematics* 3: 399–426.
1973   The Origins of Agriculture. *Annual Review of Anthropology* 2: 271–310.

FLANNERY, K. V., ED.
1986   *Guila Naquitz: Archaic Foraging and Early Agriculture in Oaxaca, Mexico.* Orlando: Academic Press.

FLANNERY, K. V., J. MARCUS, AND R. G. REYNOLDS
1989   *The Flocks of the Wamani: A Study of Llama Herders on the Punas of Ayacucho, Peru.* San Diego: Academic Press.

FORD, C. S., AND F. A. BEACH
1951   *Patterns of Sexual Behavior.* New York: Harper Torchbooks.

FOSSEY, D.
1981   The Imperiled Mountain Gorilla. *National Geographic*, 159: 501–523.
1983   *Gorillas in the Mist.* Boston: Houghton Mifflin.

FOSTER, G. M.
1965   Peasant Society and the Image of Limited Good. *American Anthropologist* 67: 293–315.

FOSTER, G. M., AND B. G. ANDERSON
1978   *Medical Anthropology.* New York: McGraw-Hill.

FOUCAULT, M.
1979   *Discipline and Punish: The Birth of the Prison*, trans. Alan Sheridan. New York: Vintage Books.

FOUTS, R. S., D. H. FOUTS, AND T. E. VAN CANTFORT
1989   The Infant Loulis Learns Signs from Cross-Fostered Chimpanzees. In *Teaching Sign Language to Chimpanzees*, eds. R. A. Gardner, B. T. Gardner and T. E. Van Cantfort, pp. 280–292. Albany, NY: State University of New York Press.

FOX, J. W.
1987   *Maya Postclassic State Formation.* Cambridge: Cambridge University Press.

1989   On the Rise and Fall of Tuláns and Maya Segmentary States. *American Anthropologist* 91: 656–681.

FOX, R.
1985   *Kinship and Marriage.* New York: Viking Penguin.

FOX, R. G., ED.
1990   *Nationalist Ideologies and the Production of National Cultures.* American Ethnological Society Monograph Series, no. 2. Washington, DC: American Anthropological Association.

FRAKE, C. O.
1961   The Diagnosis of Disease among the Subanun of Mindanao. *American Anthropologist* 63: 113–132.

FRANKE, R.
1977   Miracle Seeds and Shattered Dreams in Java. In *Readings in Anthropology*, pp. 197–201. Guilford, CT: Dushkin.

FRASER, D.
1980   Industrial Revolution. *Academic American Encyclopedia*, pp. 158–160. Princeton, NJ: Arête.

FREEMAN, D.
1983   *Margaret Mead and Samoa: The Making and Unmaking of an Anthropological Myth.* Cambridge, MA: Harvard University Press.

FREILICH, M., D. RAYBECK, AND J. SAVISHINSKY
1991   *Deviance: Anthropological Perspectives.* Westport, CT: Bergin and Garvey.

FRENCH, H. W.
1992   Unending Exodus from the Caribbean, with the U.S. a Constant Magnet. *The New York Times*, May 6, pp. A1, A8.

FREUD, S.
1950   (Orig. 1918). *Totem and Taboo*, trans. J. Strachey. New York: W. W. Norton.

FRICKE, T.
1986   *Himalayan Households: Tamang Demography and Domestic Processes.* Ames: Iowa State University Press.

FRIED, M. H.
1960   On the Evolution of Social Stratification and the State. In *Culture in History*, ed. S. Diamond, pp. 713–731. New York: Columbia University Press.
1967   *The Evolution of Political Society: An Essay in Political Anthropology.* New York: McGraw-Hill.

FRIED, M. N., AND M. H. FRIED
1980   *Transitions: Four Rituals in Eight Cultures.* New York: W. W. Norton.

FRIEDL, E.
1975   *Women and Men: An Anthropologist's View.* New York: Holt, Rinehart & Winston.

FRIEDMAN, J., AND M. J. ROWLANDS, EDS.
1978   *The Evolution of Social Systems.* Pittsburgh: University of Pittsburgh Press.

FRISANCHO, A. R.
1975   Functional Adaptation to High Altitude Hypoxia. *Science* 187: 313–319.

FURNIVALL, J. S.
1944   *Netherlands India: A Study of Plural Economy.* New York: Macmillan.

FUTUYMA, D. J.
1983   *Science on Trial.* New York: Pantheon.

GAL, S.
1989   Language and Political Economy. *Annual Review of Anthropology* 18: 345–367.

GAMST, F. C., AND E. NORBECK, EDS.
1976   *Ideas of Culture: Sources and Uses.* New York: Holt, Rinehart & Winston.

GARDNER, R. A., B. T. GARDNER, AND T. E. VAN CANTFORT, EDS.
1989   *Teaching Sign Language to Chimpanzees.* Albany, NY: State University of New York Press.

GARGAN, E. A.
1992   A Single-Minded Man Battles to Free Slaves. *The New York Times*, June 4, p. A7.

GEERTZ, C.
1973   *The Interpretation of Cultures.* New York: Basic Books.
1980   Blurred Genres: The Refiguration of Social Thought. *American Scholar* 29(2): 165–179.
1983   *Local Knowledge.* New York: Basic Books.

GEIS, M. L.
1987   *The Language of Politics.* New York: Springer-Verlag.

GELLNER, ERNEST
1983   *Nations and Nationalism.* Ithaca, NY: Cornell University Press.

GELMAN, D.
1985   Who's Taking Care of Our Parents? *Newsweek*, May 6, pp. 60–64, 68.

GIBBS, N.
1989   How America Has Run Out of Time, *Time*, April 24, pp. 59–67.

GIDDENS, A.
1973   *The Class Structure of the Advanced Societies.* New York: Cambridge University Press.

GILDER, G.
1984   *The Spirit of Enterprise.* New York: Simon and Schuster.

GILMORE, D.
1987   *Aggression and Community: Paradoxes of Andalusian Culture.* New Haven: Yale University Press.
1990   *Manhood in the Making: Cultural Concepts of*

Masculinity. New Haven: Yale University Press.

GISH, D. T.

1982 It Is Either "In the Beginning, God"—or ". . . Hydrogen," *Christianity Today*, October 8, 1982, p. 29.

GLICK-SCHILLER, N., AND G. FOURON

1990 "Everywhere We Go, We Are in Danger": Ti Manno and the Emergence of Haitian Transnational Identity. *American Ethnologist* 17(2): 329–347.

GOLDBERG, D. T., ED.

1990 *Anatomy of Racism*. Minneapolis: University of Minnesota Press.

GOLDSCHMIDT, W.

1965 Theory and Strategy in the Study of Cultural Adaptability. *American Anthropologist* 67: 402–407.

GOLDSCHMIDT, W., ED.

1979 *The Uses of Anthropology*. Washington, DC: American Anthropological Association.

GOLEMAN, D.

1989 New Measure Finds Growing Hardship for Youth. *The New York Times*, October 19, p. 26.

GOODALL, J.

1968a A Preliminary Report on Expressive Movements and Communication in Gombe Stream Chimpanzees. In *Primates: Studies in Adaptation and Variability*, ed. P. C. Jay, pp. 313–374. New York: Holt, Rinehart & Winston.

1968b The Behavior of Free Living Chimpanzees in the Gombe Stream Reserve. *Animal Behavior Monographs* 1: 161–311.

1971 *In the Shadow of Man*. Boston: Houghton Mifflin.

1986 *The Chimpanzees of Gombe: Patterns of Behavior*. Cambridge, MA: Belknap Press of Harvard University Press.

1988 *In the Shadow of Man*, rev. ed. Boston: Houghton Mifflin.

GOODENOUGH, W. H.

1953 *Native Astronomy in the Central Carolines*. Philadelphia: University of Pennsylvania Press.

GOODMAN, M., M. L. BABA, AND L. L. DARGA

1983 The Bearings of Molecular Data on the Cladograms and Times of Divergence of Hominoid Lineages. In *New Interpretations of Ape and Human Ancestry*, eds. R. L. Ciochon and R. S. Corruccini, pp. 67–87. New York: Plenum.

GOODY, J.

1977 *Production and Reproduction: A Comparative Study of the Domestic Domain*. New York: Cambridge University Press.

GOODY, J., AND S. T. TAMBIAH

1973 *Bridewealth and Dowry*. Cambridge: Cambridge University Press.

GORER, G.

1943 Themes in Japanese Culture. *Transactions of the New York Academy of Sciences* (Series II) 5: 106–124.

GORMAN, C. F.

1969 Hoabinhian: A Pebble-Tool Complex with Early Plant Associations in Southeast Asia. *Science* 163: 671–673.

GOUGH, K.

1973 (Orig. 1968). World Revolution and the Science of Man. In *To See Ourselves: Anthropology and Modern Social Issues*, gen. ed. T. Weaver, pp. 156–165. Glenview, IL: Scott, Foresman.

GOWLETT, J. M.

1984 *Ascent to Civilization: The Archaeology of Early Man*. New York: McGraw-Hill.

GRABURN, N., ED.

1971 *Readings in Kinship and Social Structure*. New York: Harper & Row.

GRAMSCI, A.

1971 *Selections from the Prison Notebooks*. Eds. and trans. Quenten Hoare and Geoffrey Nowell Smith. London: Wishart.

GRASMUCK, S., AND P. PESSAR

1991 *Between Two Islands: Dominican International Migration*. Berkeley: University of California Press.

GRAY, J.

1986 With a Few Exceptions, Television in Africa Fails to Educate and Enlighten. *Ann Arbor News*, December 8.

GRAY, J. P.

1985 *Primate Sociobiology*. New Haven, CT: HRAF Press.

GREEN, E. C.

1992 (Orig. 1987). The Integration of Modern and Traditional Health Sectors in Swaziland. In *Applying Anthropology*, eds. A. Podolefsky and P. J. Brown, pp. 246–251. Mountain View, CA: Mayfield.

GROSS, D.

1971a The Great Sisal Scheme. *Natural History*, March, pp. 49–55.

1971b Ritual and Conformity: A Religious Pilgrimage to Northeastern Brazil. *Ethnology* 10: 129–148.

GROSS, D., AND B. UNDERWOOD

1971 Technological Change and Caloric Costs: Sisal Agriculture in Northeastern Brazil. *American Anthropologist* 73: 725–740.

GULLIVER, P. H.

1955 *The Family Herds: A Study of Two Pastoral Peoples in East Africa, the Jie and Turkana*. New York: Humanities Press.

1974 (Orig. 1965). The Jie of Uganda. In *Man in Adaptation: The Cultural Present*, 2nd ed., ed. Y. A. Cohen, pp. 323–345.

GUMPERZ, J. J.

1982 *Language and Social Identity*. Cambridge: Cambridge University Press.

GUTIS, P. S.

1987 American TV Isn't Traveling So Well. *The New York Times*.

HACKER, A.

1983 *U/S: A Statistical Portrait of the American People*. New York: Viking Press.

HALL, E. T.

1966 *The Hidden Dimension*. Garden City, NY: Doubleday.

HAMBURG, D. A., AND E. R. McCOWN, EDS.

1979 *The Great Apes*. Menlo Park, CA: Benjamin Cummings.

HARCOURT, A. H.

1979 Social Relationships between Adult Male and Female Mountain Gorillas in the Wild. *Animal Behavior* 27: 325–342.

HARCOURT, A. H., D. FOSSEY, AND J. SABATER-PI

1981 Demography of Gorilla gorilla. *Journal of Zoology* 195: 215–233.

HARDING, S.

1975 Women and Words in a Spanish Village. In *Toward an Anthropology of Women*, ed. R. Reiter, pp. 283–308. New York: Monthly Review Press.

HARGROVE, E. C.

1986 *Religion and Environmental Crisis*. Athens, GA: University of Georgia Press.

HARLAN, J. R., AND D. ZOHARY

1966 Distribution of Wild Wheats and Barley. *Science* 153: 1074–1080.

HARNER, M.

1977 The Ecological Basis for Aztec Sacrifice. *American Ethnologist* 4: 117–135.

HARRIS, M.

1964 *Patterns of Race in the Americas*. New York: Walker.

1968 *The Rise of Anthropological Theory*. New York: Crowell.

1970 Referential Ambiguity in the Calculus of Brazilian Racial Identity. *Southwestern Journal of Anthropology* 26(1): 1–14.

1974 *Cows, Pigs, Wars, and Witches: The Riddles of Culture*. New York: Random House.

1978 *Cannibals and Kings*. New York: Vintage.

1979 *Cultural Materialism: The Struggle for a Science of Culture*. New York: Random House.

1987 *Why Nothing Works: The Anthropology of Daily Life*. New York: Simon and Schuster.

1989 *Our Kind: Who We Are, Where We Came from, Where We Are Going*. New York: Harper & Row.

HARRIS, M., AND C. P. KOTTAK

1963 The Structural Significance of Brazilian Racial Categories. *Sociologia* 25: 203–209.

HARRIS, N. M., AND HILLMAN, G.

1989 *Foraging and Farming: The Evolution of Plant Exploitation*. London: Unwin Hyman.

HARRISON, G. G., W. L. RATHJE, AND W. W. HUGHES

1992 Food Waste Behavior in an Urban Population. In *Applying Anthropology: An Introductory Reader*, eds. A. Podolefsky and P. J. Brown, pp. 99–104. Mountain View, CA: Mayfield.

HART, C. W. M., AND A. R. PILLING

1960 *The Tiwi of North Australia*. New York: Holt, Rinehart & Winston.

HART, K.

1982 *The Political Economy of West African Agriculture*. Cambridge: Cambridge University Press.

HARTL, D.

1983 *Human Genetics*. New York: Harper & Row.

HAUSFATER, G., AND S. HRDY, EDS.

1984 *Infanticide: Comparative and Evolutionary Perspectives*. Hawthorne, NY: Aldine.

HAWKES, K., J. O'CONNELL, AND K. HILL

1982 Why Hunters Gather: Optimal Foraging and the Aché of Eastern Paraguay. *American Ethnologist* 9: 379–398.

HAYDEN, B.

1981 Subsistence and Ecological Adaptations of Modern Hunter/Gatherers. In *Omnivorous Primates: Gathering and Hunting in Human Evolution*, eds. R. S. Harding and G. Teleki, pp. 344–421. New York: Columbia University Press.

HEADLAND, T. N., AND L. A. REID

1989 Hunter-gatherers and Their Neighbors from Prehistory to the Present. *Current Anthropology* 30: 43–66.

HEDGES, C.

1992a Sudan Presses Its Campaign to Impose Islamic Law on Non-Muslims. *The New York Times*, June 1, p. A7.

1992b Sudan Gives Its Refugees a Desert to Contemplate. *The New York Times*, June 3, p. A4.

HEIDER, K.

1988 The Rashomon Effect: When Ethnographers Disagree. *American Anthropologist* 90: 73–81.

HELLER, M.
1988 *Codeswitching: Anthropological and Sociolinguistic Perspectives*. Berlin: Mouton deGruyter.

HENDRY, J.
1981 *Marriage in Changing Japan*. London: Croom Helm Ltd.

HENRY, D. O.
1989 *From Foraging to Agriculture: The Levant at the End of the Ice Age*. Philadelphia: University of Pennsylvania Press.

HENRY, J.
1955 Docility, or Giving Teacher What She Wants. *Journal of Social Issues* 2: 33–41.

HERDT, G.
1981 *Guardians of the Flutes*. New York: McGraw-Hill.
1987 *Sambia: Ritual and Gender in New Guinea*. New York: Harcourt Brace.

HERRNSTEIN, R. J.
1971 I.Q. *The Atlantic* 228(3): 43–64.

HEWITT, R.
1986 *White Talk, Black Talk*. Cambridge: Cambridge University Press.

HEYERDAHL, T.
1971 *The Ra Expeditions*, trans. P. Crampton. Garden City, NY: Doubleday.

HEYNEMAN, D.
1984 Development and Disease: A Dual Dilemma. *Journal of Parasitology* 70: 3–17.

HILL, C. E., ED.
1986 *Current Health Policy Issues and Alternatives: An Applied Social Science Perspective*. Southern Anthropological Society Proceedings. Athens: University of Georgia Press.

HILL, J. H.
1978 Apes and Language. *Annual Review of Anthropology* 7: 89–112.

HILL, K., H. KAPLAN, K. HAWKES, AND A. HURTADO
1987 Foraging Decisions among Aché Hunter-gatherers: New Data and Implications for Optimal Foraging Models. *Ethology and Sociobiology* 8: 1–36.

HILL-BURNETT, J.
1978 Developing Anthropological Knowledge through Application. In *Applied Anthropology in America*, eds. E. M. Eddy and W. L. Partridge, pp. 112–128. New York: Columbia University Press.

HINDE, R.A.
1974 *Biological Bases of Human Social Behavior*. New York: McGraw-Hill.
1983 *Primate Social Relationships: An Integrated Approach*. Sunderland: Sinaeur Associates.

HOBHOUSE, L. T.
1915 *Morals in Evolution*, rev. ed. New York: Holt.

HOBSBAWM, E. J.
1990 *Nations and Nationalism since 1780: Programme, Myth, Reality*. New York: Cambridge University Press.

HOEBEL, E. A.
1954 *The Law of Primitive Man*. Cambridge, MA: Harvard University Press.
1968 (Orig. 1954). The Eskimo: Rudimentary Law in a Primitive Anarchy. In *Studies in Social and Cultural Anthropology*, ed. J. Middleton, pp. 93–127. New York: Crowell.

HOLE, F., K. V. FLANNERY, AND J. A. NEELY
1969 *The Prehistory and Human Ecology of the Deh Luran Plain*. Memoir no. 1. Ann Arbor, MI: University of Michigan Museum of Anthropology.

HOLLAND, D., AND N. QUINN, EDS.
1987 *Cultural Models in Language and Thought*. Cambridge: Cambridge University Press.

HOLLOWAY, R. L.
1975 (Orig. 1974). The Casts of Fossil Hominid Brains. In *Biological Anthropology, Readings from Scientific American*, ed. S. H. Katz, pp. 69–78. San Francisco: W. H. Freeman.

HOLMES, L. D.
1987 *Quest for the Real Samoa: The Mead/Freeman Controversy and Beyond*. South Hadley, MA: Bergin and Garvey.

HOPKINS, T., AND I. WALLERSTEIN
1982 Patterns of Development of the Modern World System. In *World Systems Analysis: Theory and Methodology*, by T. Hopkins, I. Wallerstein, R. Bach, C. Chase-Dunn, and R. Mukherjee, pp. 121–141. Beverly Hills, CA: Sage.

HOWELL, F. C.
1967 *Early Man*, rev. ed. New York: Time-Life Books.

HOWELLS, W. W.
1976 Explaining Modern Man: Evolutionists versus Migrationists. *Journal of Human Evolution* 5: 477–496.

HRDY, S. B.
1981 *The Woman That Never Evolved*. Cambridge, MA: Harvard University Press.

HUGHES, J. D.
1983 *American Indian Ecology*. El Paso: Texas Western Press.

HUMAN ORGANIZATION
Quarterly journal. Oklahoma City: Society for Applied Anthropology.

HYMES, D., ED.
1964 *Language in Culture and Society: A Reader in Lin-*

guistics and Anthropology. New York: Harper & Row.

IANNI, F.
1977   New Mafia: Black, Hispanic and Italian Styles. In *Readings in Anthropology*, pp. 66–78. Guilford, CT.: Dushkin.

INHORN, M. C., AND P. J. BROWN
1990   The Anthropology of Infectious Disease. *Annual Review of Anthropology* 19: 89–117.

IRVING, W. N.
1985   Context and Chronology of Early Man in the Americas. *Annual Review of Anthropology* 14: 529–555.

ISAAC, G. L.
1972   Early Phases of Human Behavior: Models in Lower Paleolithic Archaeology. In *Models in Archaeology*, ed. D. L. Clarke, pp. 167–199. London: Methuen.
1978   Food Sharing and Human Evolution: Archaeological Evidence from the Plio-Pleistocene of East Africa. *Journal of Anthropological Research* 34: 311–325.

IYER, P.
1988   *Video Night in Kathmandu*. New York: Knopf.

JAMESON, F.
1984   Postmodernism, or the Cultural Logic of Late Capitalism. *New Left Review* 146: 53–93.
1988   *The Ideologies of Theory: Essays 1971–1986*. Minneapolis: University of Minnesota Press.

JANES, C. R., R. STALL, AND S. M. GIFFORD, EDS.
1986   *Anthropology and Epidemiology: Interdisciplinary Approaches to the Study of Health and Disease*. Dordrecht: D. Reidel.

JANSON, C. H.
1986   Capuchin Counterpoint: Divergent Mating and Feeding Habits Distinguish Two Closely Related Monkey Species of the Peruvian Forest, *Natural History* 95: 44–52.

JENSEN, A.
1969   How Much Can We Boost I.Q. and Scholastic Achievement? *Harvard Educational Review* 29: 1–123.

JODELET, D.
1991   *Madness and Social Representations: Living with the Mad in One French Community*. Trans. from the French by Gerard Duveen. Berkeley: University of California Press.

JOHANSON, D. C., AND M. EDEY
1981   *Lucy: The Origins of Humankind*. New York: Simon & Schuster.

JOHANSON, D. C., AND T. D. WHITE
1979   A Systematic Assessment of Early African Hominids. *Science* 203: 321–330.

JOHNSON, A. W.
1978   *Quantification in Cultural Anthropology: An Introduction to Research Design*. Stanford, CA: Stanford University Press.

JOHNSON, A. W., AND T. EARLE
1987   *The Evolution of Human Societies: From Foraging Group to Agrarian State*. Stanford, CA: Stanford University Press.

JOHNSON, J.
1989   Childhood Is Not Safe for Most Children, Congress Is Warned. *The New York Times*, October 2, pp. 1, 10.

JOHNSON, T. J., AND C. F. SARGENT, EDS.
1990   *Medical Anthropology: A Handbook of Theory and Method*. New York: Greenwood.

JOLLY, A.
1985   *The Evolution of Primate Behavior*, 2d ed. New York: Macmillan.

JOLLY, C. J.
1970   The Seed-Eaters: A New Model of Hominid Differentiation Based on a Baboon Analogy. *Man* 5: 1–26.

JOLLY, C. J., AND F. PLOG.
1986   *Physical Anthropology and Archeology*, 3rd ed. New York: McGraw-Hill.

JOLLY, C. J., AND R. WHITE
1994   *Physical Anthropology and Archeology*, 5th ed. New York: McGraw-Hill.

JONES, G., AND R. KRAUTZ
1981   *The Transition to Statehood in the New World*. Cambridge: Cambridge University Press.

KAGAN, J.
1975   The Magical Aura of I.Q. In *Race and IQ*, ed. A. Montagu, pp. 55–58. New York: Oxford University Press.

KAHN, J.
1981   Explaining Ethnicity: A Review Article. *Critique of Anthropology* 4(16): 340–356.

KAN, S.
1986   The 19th-Century Tlingit Potlatch: A New Perspective. *American Ethnologist* 13: 191–212.
1989   *Symbolic Immortality: The Tlingit Potlatch of the Nineteenth Century*. Washington: Smithsonian Institution Press.

KANO, T.
1992   *The Last Ape: Pygmy Chimpanzee Behavior and Ecology*. Trans. E. O. Vineburg. Stanford, CA: Stanford University Press.

KARDINER, A., ED.
1939   *The Individual and His Society*. New York: Columbia University Press.

KELLY, R. C.
1976   Witchcraft and Sexual Relations: An Exploration in the Social and Semantic Implications of

the Structure of Belief. In *Man and Woman in the New Guinea Highlands*, eds. P. Brown and G. Buchbinder, pp. 36–53. Special Publication, no. 8. Washington, DC: American Anthropological Association.

KENT, S.
1992 The Current Forager Controversy: Real Versus Ideal Views of Hunter-gatherers. *Man* 27: 45–70.

KENT, S., AND H. VIERICH
1989 The Myth of Ecological Determinism: Anticipated Mobility and Site Organization of Space. In *Farmers as Hunters: The Implications of Sedentism*, ed. S. Kent, pp. 96–130. New York: Cambridge University Press.

KIMBALL, S. T.
1978 Anthropology as a Policy Science. In *Applied Anthropology in America*, eds. E. M. Eddy and W. L. Partridge, pp. 277–291. New York: Columbia University Press.

KINSEY, A. C., W. B. POMEROY, AND C. E. MARTIN
1948 *Sexual Behavior in the Human Male*. Philadelphia: W. B. Saunders.

KIRSCH, P. V.
1984 *The Evolution of the Polynesian Chiefdoms*. Cambridge: Cambridge University Press.

KLEINFELD, J.
1975 Positive Stereotyping: The Cultural Relativist in the Classroom. *Human Organization* 34: 269–274.

KLINEBERG, O.
1951 Race and Psychology. In *The Race Question in Modern Science*. Paris: UNESCO.

KLUGE, A. G.
1983 Cladistics and the Classification of the Great Apes. In *New Interpretations of Ape and Human Ancestry*, eds. R. L. Ciochon and R. S. Corruccini, pp. 151–177. New York: Plenum.

KORTEN, D. C.
1980 Community Organization and Rural Development: A Learning Process Approach. *Public Administration Review*, September–October, pp. 480–512.

KOTTAK, C. P.
1971 Social Groups and Kinship Calculation among the Southern Betsileo. *American Anthropologist* 73: 178–193.
1972 Ecological Variables in the Origin and Evolution of African States: The Buganda Example. *Comparative Studies in Society and History* 14: 351–380.
1980 *The Past in the Present: History, Ecology, and Social Organization in Highland Madagascar*. Ann Arbor: University of Michigan Press.

1985 When People Don't Come First: Some Sociological Lessons from Completed Projects. In *Putting People First: Sociological Variables in Rural Development*, ed. Michael Cernea, pp. 325–356. New York: Oxford University Press.
1990 *Prime-Time Society: An Anthropological Analysis of Television and Culture*. Belmont, CA: Wadsworth.
1992 *Assault on Paradise: Social Change in a Brazilian Village*, 2nd ed. New York: McGraw-Hill.

KOTTAK, C. P., ED.
1982 *Researching American Culture: A Guide for Student Anthropologists*. Ann Arbor: University of Michigan Press.

KRAMARAE, R., M. SHULZ, AND M. O'BARR, EDS.
1984 *Language and Power*. Beverly Hills, CA: Sage.

KRETCHMER, N.
1975 (Orig. 1972). Lactose and Lactase. In *Biological Anthropology, Readings from* Scientific American, ed S. H. Katz, pp. 310–318. San Francisco: W. H. Freeman.

KROEBER, A. L., AND C. KLUCKHOLN
1963 *Culture: A Critical Review of Concepts and Definitions*. New York: Vintage.

LABARRE, W.
1945 Some Observations of Character Structure in the Orient: The Japanese. *Psychiatry* 8: 326–342.

LAFONTAINE, J. S., ED.
1978 *Sex and Age as Principles of Social Differentiation*. New York: Academic Press.

LABOV, W.
1972a *Language in the Inner City: Studies in the Black English Vernacular*. Philadelphia: University of Pennsylvania Press.
1972b *Sociolinguistic Patterns*. Philadelphia: University of Pennsylvania Press.

LAGUERRE, M.
1984 *American Odyssey: Haitians in New York*. Ithaca, NY: Cornell University Press.

LAKO, G. T.
1988 (Orig. 1985). The Impact of the Jonglei Scheme on the Economy of the Dinka. In *Tribal Peoples and Development Issues: A Global Overview*, ed. J. H. Bodley, pp. 135–150. Palo Alto, CA: Mayfield.

LAKOFF, R.
1975 *Language and Woman's Place*. New York: Harper & Row.

LAMBERG-KARLOVSKY, C. C., ED.
1989 *Archeological Thought in America*. New York: Cambridge University Press.

LANCE, L. M., AND E. E. MCKENNA
1975 Analysis of Cases Pertaining to the Impact

of Western Technology on the Non-Western World. *Human Organization* 34: 87–94.

LARSEN, C. S., AND R. W. MATTER
1985 *Human Origins: The Fossil Record.* Prospect Heights IL: Waveland.

LARSON, A.
1989 Social Context of Human Immunodeficiency Virus Transmission in Africa: Historical and Cultural Bases of East and Central African Sexual Relations. *Review of Infectious Diseases* 11: 716–731.

LAWRENCE, P.
1964 *Road Belong Cargo.* Manchester: Manchester University Press.

LAYTON, R., R. FOLEY, AND E. WILLIAMS
1991 The Transition between Hunting and Gathering and the Specialized Husbandry of Resources: A Socioecological Approach. *Current Anthropology* 32: 255–274.

LEACH, E. R.
1955 Polyandry, Inheritance and the Definition of Marriage. *Man* 55: 182–186.
1961 *Rethinking Anthropology.* London: Athlone Press.
1985 *Social Anthropology.* New York: Oxford University Press.

LEAKEY, R. E. F., AND A. WALKER
1985 New Higher Primates from the Early Miocene of Buluk, Kenya. *Nature* 318: 173–175.

LEAKEY, R. E. F., LEAKEY, M. G., AND A. C. WALKER
1988 Morphology of *Afropithecus turkanensis* from Kenya. *American Journal of Physical Anthropology* 76: 289–307.

LeCLAIR, E. E., AND H. K. SCHNEIDER, EDS.
1968 (Orig. 1961). *Economic Anthropology: Readings in Theory and Analysis.* New York: Holt, Rinehart & Winston.

LEE, R. B.
1974 (Orig. 1968). What Hunters Do for a Living, or, How to Make Out on Scarce Resources. In *Man in Adaptation: The Cultural Present*, 2nd ed., ed. Y. A. Cohen, pp. 87–100. Chicago: Aldine.
1979 *The !Kung San: Men, Women, and Work in a Foraging Society.* New York: Cambridge University Press.
1984 *The Dobe !Kung.* New York: Harcourt Brace.

LEE, R. B., AND I. DeVORE, EDS.
1977 *Kalahari Hunter-Gatherers: Studies of the !Kung San and Their Neighbors.* Cambridge, MA: Harvard University Press.

LENSKI, G.
1966 *Power and Privilege: A Theory of Social Stratification.* New York: McGraw-Hill.

LESSA, W. A., AND E. Z. VOGT, ED.
1978 *Reader in Comparative Religion: An Anthropological Approach*, 4th ed. New York: Harper & Row.

LEVINE, N.
1988 *The Dynamics of Polyandry: Kinship, Domesticity, and Population in the Tibetan Border.* Chicago: University of Chicago Press.

LEVINE, R. A.
1982 *Culture, Behavior, and Personality: An Introduction to the Comparative Study of Psychosocial Adaptation*, 2nd ed. Chicago: Aldine.

LEVINE, R. A., ED.
1974 *Culture and Personality: Contemporary Readings.* Chicago: Aldine.

LEWIS, H. S.
1989 *After the Eagles Landed: The Yemenites of Israel.* Boulder, CO: Westview.

LEWIS, O.
1959 *Five Families.* New York: Basic Books.

LEWIS, P.
1992 U.N. Sees a Crisis in Overpopulation. *The New York Times*, April 30, p. A6.

LÉVI-STRAUSS, C.
1963 *Totemism*, trans. R. Needham. Boston: Beacon Press.
1967 *Structural Anthropology.* New York: Doubleday.
1969 (Orig. 1949). *The Elementary Structures of Kinship.* Boston: Beacon Press.

LIEBAN, R. W.
1977 The Field of Medical Anthropology. In *Culture, Disease, and Healing: Studies in Medical Anthropology*, ed. D. Landy, pp. 13–31. New York: Macmillan.

LIGHT, D., S. KELLER, AND C. CALHOUN
1994 *Sociology*, 6th ed. New York: McGraw-Hill.

LIJPHART, A.
1977 *Democracy in Plural Societies.* New Haven, CT: Yale University Press.

LINDENBAUM, S.
1972 Sorcerers, Ghosts, and Polluting Women: An Analysis of Religious Belief and Population Control. *Ethnology* 11: 241–253.

LINTON, R.
1927 Report on Work of Field Museum Expedition in Madagascar. *American Anthropologist* 29: 292–307.
1936 *The Study of Man: An Introduction.* New York: D. Appleton-Century.
1943 Nativistic Movements. *American Anthropologist* 45: 230–240.

LITTLE, K.
1965 *West African Urbanization: A Study of Voluntary*

Associations in Social Change. Cambridge: Cambridge University Press.

1971   Some Aspects of African Urbanization South of the Sahara. Reading, MA: Addison-Wesley, McCaleb Modules in Anthropology.

LIVINGSTONE, F. B.

1958   Anthropological Implications of Sickle Cell Gene Distribution in West Africa. *American Anthropologist* 60: 533–562.

1969   Gene Frequency Clines of the &β Hemoglobin Locus in Various Human Populations and Their Similarities by Models Involving Differential Selection. *Human Biology* 41: 223–36.

LIZOT, J.

1985   *Tales of the Yanomami: Daily Life in the Venezuelan Forest.* New York: Cambridge University Press.

LOOMIS, W. F.

1967   Skin-pigmented Regulation of Vitamin-D Biosynthesis in Man. *Science* 157: 501–506.

LOWIE, R. H.

1935   *The Crow Indians.* New York: Farrar and Rinehart.

1961   (Orig. 1920). *Primitive Society.* New York: Harper & Brothers.

LYELL, C.

1969   (Orig. 1830–33). *Principles of Geology.* New York: Johnson reprint.

MacDOUGLAS, A. K.

1984   Yawning Chasms Between Classes Widen in the Third World. *Ann Arbor News,* November 4, p. B14.

MacKINNON, J.

1974   *In Search of the Red Ape.* New York: Ballantine.

MAIR, L.

1969   *Witchcraft.* New York: McGraw-Hill.

MALINOWSKI, B.

1927   *Sex and Repression in Savage Society.* London and New York: International Library of Psychology, Philosophy and Scientific Method.

1929a   Practical Anthropology. *Africa* 2: 23–38.

1929b   *The Sexual Life of Savages in North-Western Melanesia.* New York: Harcourt, Brace, and World.

1948   *Magic, Science and Religion, and Other Essays.* Boston: Beacon Press.

1961   (Orig. 1922). *Argonauts of the Western Pacific.* New York: Dutton.

1978   (Orig. 1931). The Role of Magic and Religion. In *Reader in Comparative Religion: An Anthropological Approach,* 4th ed., eds. W. A. Lessa and E. Z. Vogt, pp. 37–46. New York: Harper & Row.

MANN, A.

1975   *Paleodemographic Aspects of the South African Australopithecines.* Philadelphia: University of Pennsylvania Publications in Anthropology, No. 1.

MANNERS, R.

1973   (Orig. 1956). Functionalism, Realpolitik and Anthropology in Underdeveloped Areas. America Indigena 16. In *To See Ourselves: Anthropology and Modern Social Issues,* gen. ed. T. Weaver, pp. 113–126. Glenview, IL: Scott, Foresman.

MAQUET, J.

1964   Objectivity in Anthropology. *Current Anthropology* 5: 47–55 (also in Clifton, ed. 1970).

MARCUS, G. E., AND D. CUSHMAN

1982   Ethnographies as Texts. *Annual Review of Anthropology* 11:25–69.

MARCUS, G. E., AND M. M. J. FISCHER

1986   *Anthropology as Cultural Critique: An Experimental Moment in the Human Sciences.* Chicago: University of Chicago Press.

MARGOLIS, M.

1984   *Mothers and Such: American Views of Women and How They Changed.* Berkeley: University of California Press.

MARSHACK, A.

1972   *Roots of Civilization.* New York: McGraw-Hill.

MARTIN, E.

1987   *The Woman in the Body: A Cultural Analysis of Reproduction.* Boston: Beacon Press.

MARTIN, K., AND B. VOORHIES

1975   *Female of the Species.* New York: Columbia University Press.

MARX, K., AND F. ENGELS

1976   (Orig. 1948). *Communist Manifesto.* New York: Pantheon.

MAUSS, M.

1954   *The Gift: Forms and Functions of Exchange in Archaic Societies.* New York: Free Press.

MAYESKE, G. W.

1971   *On the Explanation of Racial-Ethnic Group Differences in Achievement Test Scores.* Washington, DC: U.S. Government Printing Office, Office of Education.

MAYR, E.

1970   *Animal Species and Evolution.* Cambridge: Harvard University Press.

McDONALD, G.

1984   *Carioca Fletch.* New York: Warner Books.

McGRAW, T. K., ED.

1986   *America versus Japan.* Boston: Harvard Business School Press.

McGREW, W. C.

1979   Evolutionary Implications of Sex Differences in Chimpanzee Predation and Tool Use. In *The*

Great Apes, eds. D. A. Hamburg and E. R. McCown, pp. 441–463. Menlo Park, CA: Benjamin Cummings.

McKUSICK, V.
1966   *Mendelian Inheritance in Man.* Baltimore: Johns Hopkins University Press.
1990   *Mendelian Inheritance in Man: Catalogs of Autosomal Dominant, Autosomal Recessive, and X-Linked Phenotypes*, 9th ed. Baltimore: Johns Hopkins University Press.

MEAD, M.
1930   *Growing Up in New Guinea.* New York: Blue Ribbon.
1950   (Orig. 1935). *Sex and Temperament in Three Primitive Societies.* New York: New American Library.
1961   (Orig. 1928). *Coming of Age in Samoa.* New York: Morrow Quill.
1972   *Blackberry Winter; My Earlier Years.* New York: Simon and Schuster.

MEADOW, R., ED.
1991   *Harappa Excavations 1986–1990: A Multidisciplinary Approach to Third Millennium Urbanism.* Monographs in World Archeology, no. 3. Madison, WI: Prehistory Press.

MERCER, J. R.
1971   Pluralistic Diagnosis in the Evaluation of Black and Chicano Children: A Procedure for Taking Sociocultural Variables into Account as Clinical Assessment. Paper presented at the meetings of the American Psychological Association, Washington, DC.

METCALF, P.
1991   *Celebrations of Death: The Anthropology of Mortuary Ritual*, 2nd ed. New York: Cambridge University Press.

MICHAELS, E.
1986   Aboriginal Content. Paper presented at the meeting of the Australian Screen Studies Association. Sydney, December.

MIDDLETON, J.
1967   Introduction. In John Middleton, ed. *Myth and Cosmos: Readings in Mythology and Symbolism*, pp. ix–xi. Garden City, NY: The Natural History Press.

MIDDLETON, J., ED.
1967   *Gods and Rituals.* Garden City, NY: The Natural History Press.

MILES, H. L.
1983   Apes and Language: The Search for Communicative Competence. In *Language in Primates*, eds. J. de Luce and H. T. Wilder, pp. 43–62. New York: Springer Verlag.

MILLER, N., AND R. C. ROCKWELL, EDS.
1988   *AIDS in Africa: The Social and Policy Impact.* Lewiston: Edwin Mellen.

MINTZ, S.
1985   *Sweetness and Power: The Place of Sugar in Modern History.* New York: Viking Penguin.

MITCHELL, J. C.
1966   Theoretical Orientations in African Urban Studies. In *The Social Anthropology of Complex Societies*, ed. M. Banton, pp. 37–68. London: Tavistock.

MITTERMEIER, R. A., AND M. J. POLTKIN, EDS.
1982   *Primates and the Tropical Forest.* Washington, DC: World Wildlife Fund.

MOERMAN, MICHAEL
1965   Ethnic Identification in a Complex Civilization: Who Are the Lue? *American Anthropologist* 67(5 Part I): 1215–1230.

MOFFATT, M.
1989   *Coming of Age in New Jersey: College and American Culture.* New Brunswick, NJ: Rutgers University Press.

MONTAGU, A.
1975   *The Nature of Human Aggression.* New York: Oxford University Press.

MONTAGU, A., ED.
1975   *Race and IQ.* New York: Oxford University Press.

MONTAGUE, S., AND R. MORAIS
1981   Football Games and Rock Concerts: The Ritual Enactment. In *The American Dimension: Cultural Myths and Social Realities*, 2nd ed., eds. W. Arens and S. B. Montague, pp. 33–52. Sherman Oaks, CA: Alfred.

MOORE, A. D.
1985   The Development of Neolithic Societies in the Near East. *Advances in World Archaeology.* 4: 1–69.

MOORE, S. F.
1986   *Social Facts and Fabrications.* Cambridge MA: Cambridge University Press.

MOORE, S. F., AND B. G. MYERHOFF, EDS.
1978   *Secular Ritual.* Atlantic Highlands, NJ: Humanities Press.

MORAN, E.
1979   *Human Adaptability: An Introduction to Ecological Anthropology.* North Scituate, MA: Duxbury.

MORGAN, L. H.
1963   (Orig. 1877). *Ancient Society.* Cleveland: World Publishing.

MORGEN, S., ED.
1989   *Gender and Anthropology: Critical Reviews for*

Research and Teaching. Washington, DC: American Anthropological Association.

MORRIS, B.

1987 *Anthropological Studies of Religion: An Introductory Text.* New York: Cambridge University Press.

MORRIS, C. R.

1989 The Coming Global Boom. *Atlantic Monthly,* October, pp. 51–64.

MOWAT, F.

1987 *Woman in the Mists: The Story of Dian Fossey and the Mountain Gorillas of Africa.* New York: Warner Books.

MUHLHAUSLER, P.

1986 *Pidgin and Creole Linguistics.* London: Basil Blackwell.

MUKHOPADHYAY, C., AND P. HIGGINS

1988 Anthropological Studies of Women's Status Revisited: 1977–1987. *Annual Review of Anthropology* 17: 461–495.

MULLINGS, L., ED.

1987 *Cities of the United States: Studies in Urban Anthropology.* New York: Columbia University Press.

MURDOCK, G. P.

1934 *Our Primitive Contemporaries.* New York: Macmillan.

1949 *Social Structure.* New York: Macmillan.

1957 World Ethnographic Sample. *American Anthropologist* 59: 664–687.

MURPHY, E. M.

1984 *Food and Population: A Global Concern.* Washington, DC: U.S. Government Printing Office, Office of Education.

MURPHY, R. F.

1990 *The Body Silent.* New York: W. W. Norton.

MURPHY, R. F., AND L. KASDAN

1959 The Structure of Parallel Cousin Marriage. *American Anthropologist* 61: 17–29.

MYDANS, S.

1992a Criticism Grows over Aliens Seized during Riots. *The New York Times,* May 29, pp. A8.

1992b Judge Dismisses Case in Shooting by Officer. *The New York Times,* June 4, p. A8.

NAISBITT, J., AND P. ABURDENE

1990 *Megatrends 2000: Ten New Directions for the 1990's.* New York: William Morrow.

NASAR, S.

1992a Federal Report Gives New Data on Gains by Richest in 80's; Concentration of Assets; Top 1% Had Greater Net Worth than Bottom 90% of U.S. Households by 1989. *The New York Times,* April 21, p. A1.

1992b However You Slice the Data, the Richest Did Get Richer. *The New York Times,* May 11, p. C1.

NASH, D.

1988 *A Little Anthropology.* Englewood Cliffs, NJ: Prentice-Hall.

NASH, J.

1981 Ethnographic Aspects of the World Capitalist System. *Annual Review of Anthropology* 10: 393–423.

NASH, J., AND P. FERNANDEZ-KELLY, EDS.

1983 *Women, Men and the International Division of Labor.* Albany: State University of New York Press.

NASH, J., AND H. SAFA, EDS.

1986 *Women and Change in Latin America.* South Hadley, MA: Bergin and Garvey.

NASH, J., AND K. SULLIVAN

1992 Return to Porfirismo. *Cultural Survival Quarterly* 16(2): 13–16.

NATIONAL ASSOCIATION FOR THE PRACTICE OF ANTHROPOLOGY

1991 *NAPA Directory of Practicing Anthropologists.* Washington: American Anthropological Association.

NELSON, H., AND R. JURMAIN

1991 *Introduction to Physical Anthropology,* 5th ed. St. Paul, MN: West.

NETTING, R. M. C., R. R. WILK, AND E. J. ARNOULD, EDS.

1984 *Households: Comparative and Historical Studies of the Domestic Group.* Berkeley, CA: University of California Press.

NEWMAN, K.

1983 *Law and Economic Organization: A Comparative Study of Pre-Industrial Societies.* New York: Cambridge University Press.

1988 *Falling from Grace: The Experience of Downward Mobility in the American Middle Class.* New York: The Free Press.

NEWMAN, M.

1992 Riots Bring Attention to Growing Hispanic Presence in South-Central Area. *The New York Times,* May 11, p. A10.

NEW YORK TIMES

1989 Black and White Death Rates Continue to Differ, Study Says. September 27, p. 11.

1990 Tropical Diseases on March, Hitting 1 in 10. March 28, p. A3.

1992 Married with Children: The Waning Icon. August 23, section 4, p. E2.

1992 Alexandria Journal: TV Program for Somalis Is a Rare Unifying Force. December 18, p. A14.

NIELSSON, G. P.
1985 States and Nation-Groups: A Global Taxonomy. In *New Nationalisms of the Developed World*, eds. E. A. Tiryakian and R. Rogowski, pp. 27–56. Boston: Allen and Unwin.

NIETSCHMANN, B.
1987 The Third World War. *Cultural Survival Quarterly* 11(3): 1–16.

OAKLEY, K. P.
1976 *Man the Tool-Maker*, 6th ed. Chicago: University of Chicago Press.

ONG, A.
1987 *Spirits of Resistance and Capitalist Discipline: Factory Women in Malaysia*. Albany: State University of New York Press.
1989 Center, Periphery, and Hierarchy: Gender in Southeast Asia. In *Gender and Anthropology: Critical Reviews for Research and Teaching*, ed. S. Morgen, pp. 294–312. Washington: American Anthropological Association.

OTTERBEIN, K. F.
1968 (Orig. 1963). Marquesan Polyandry. In *Marriage, Family and Residence*, eds. P. Bohannan and J. Middleton, pp. 287–296. Garden City, NY: Natural History Press.

PARKER, S., AND R. KLEINER
1970 The Culture of Poverty: An Adjustive Dimension. *American Anthropologist* 72: 516–527.

PARKIN, D.
1969 *Neighbours and Nationals in an African City Ward*. London: Routledge and Kegan Paul.

PARSONS, J. R.
1974 The Development of a Prehistoric Complex Society: A Regional Perspective from the Valley of Mexico. *Journal of Field Archaeology* 1: 81–108.
1976 The Role of Chinampa Agriculture in the Food Supply of Aztec Tenochtitlan. In *Cultural Change and Continuity: Essays in Honor of James Bennett Griffin*, ed. C. E. Cleland, pp. 233–262. New York: Academic Press.

PATTERSON, F.
1978 Conversations with a Gorilla. *National Geographic*, October, pp. 438–465.

PAUL, R.
1989 Psychoanalytic Anthropology. *Annual Review of Anthropology* 18: 177–202.

PEAR, R.
1992 Ranks of U.S. Poor Reach 35.7 Million, the Most since '64. *The New York Times*, September 3, pp. A1, A12.

PEEBLES, S.
1985 Preschool: A Headstart toward Academic Success? *Ann Arbor News*, May 5, p. A4.

PELETZ, M.
1988 *A Share of the Harvest: Kinship, Property, and Social History among the Malays of Rembau*. Berkeley: University of California Press.

PELTO, P.
1973 *The Snowmobile Revolution: Technology and Social Change in the Arctic*. Menlo Park, CA: Cummings.

PELTO, P. J., AND G. H. PELTO
1978 *Anthropological Research: The Structure of Inquiry*. 2nd ed. New York: Cambridge University Press.

PFEIFFER, J.
1977 *The Emergence of Society*. New York: McGraw-Hill.
1985 *The Emergence of Humankind*. 4th ed. New York: Harper & Row.

PIDDINGTON, R.
1970 Action Anthropology. In *Applied Anthropology: Readings in the Uses of the Science of Man*, ed., James Clifton, pp. 127–143. Boston: Houghton Mifflin.

PIDDOCKE, S.
1969 The Potlatch System of the Southern Kwakiutl: A New Perspective. In *Environment and Cultural Behavior*, ed. A. P. Vayda, pp. 130–156. Garden City, NY: Natural History Press.

PLATTNER, S., ED.
1989 *Economic Anthropology*. Stanford, CA: Stanford University Press.

PODOLEFSKY, A., AND P. J. BROWN, EDS.
1992 *Applying Anthropology: An Introductory Reader*, 2nd ed. Mountain View, CA: Mayfield.

POLANYI, K.
1968 *Primitive, Archaic and Modern Economies: Essays of Karl Polanyi*, ed. G. Dalton. Garden City, NY: Anchor Books.

POPULATION TODAY
1984 Now it Costs $98,000 to Raise a Child, September, p. 3.

POSPISIL, L.
1963 *The Kapauku Papuans of West New Guinea*. New York: Holt, Rinehart & Winston.

POTASH, B., ED.
1986 *Widows in African Societies: Choices and Constraints*. Stanford, CA: Stanford University Press.

PRICE, R., ED.
1973 *Maroon Societies*. New York: Anchor Press/Doubleday.

QUINN, N., AND C. STRAUSS
1989 A Cognitive Cultural Anthropology. Paper presented at the Invited Session "Assessing Developments in Anthropology," American

Anthropological Association 88th Annual Meeting, November 15–19, Washington, DC.

1994   A Cognitive Cultural Anthropology. In *Assessing Cultural Anthropology*, ed. Robert Borofsky. New York: McGraw-Hill.

RADCLIFFE-BROWN, A. R.

1950   Introduction to *African Systems of Kinship and Marriage*, eds. A. R. Radcliffe-Brown and D. Forde, pp. 1–85. London: Oxford University Press.

1965   (Orig. 1962). *Structure and Function in Primitive Society*. New York: Free Press.

RAK, Y.

1986   The Neandertal: A New Look at an Old Face. *Journal of Human Evolution*, 15(3): 151–164.

RAMOS, A.

1987   Reflecting on the Yanomami: Ethnographic Images and the Pursuit of the Exotic. *Cultural Anthropology* 2: 284–304.

RAPPAPORT, R. A.

1974   Obvious Aspects of Ritual. *Cambridge Anthropology* 2: 2–60.

1979   *Ecology, Meaning, and Religion*. Richmond, CA: North Atlantic Books.

1984   *Pigs for the Ancestors: Ritual in the Ecology of a New Guinea People*, 2nd ed. New Haven: Yale University Press.

READ-MARTIN, C. E., AND READ, D. W.

1975   Australopithecine Scavenging and Human Evolution: An Approach from Faunal Analysis. *Current Anthropology* 16: 359–368.

REDFIELD, R.

1941   *The Folk Culture of Yucatan*. Chicago: University of Chicago Press.

REDFIELD, R., R. LINTON, AND M. HERSKOVITS

1936   Memorandum on the Study of Acculturation. *American Anthropologist* 38: 149–152.

REITER, R.

1975   Men and Women in the South of France: Public and Private Domains. In *Toward an Anthropology of Women*, ed. R. Reiter, pp. 252–282. New York: Monthly Review Press.

REYNOLDS, V.

1971   *The Apes*. New York: Harper Colophon.

RICHARDS, P.

1973   The Tropical Rain Forest. *Scientific American* 229(6): 58–67.

RICOEUR, P.

1971   The Model of the Text: Meaningful Action Considered as a Text. *Social Research* 38: 529–562.

ROBERTS, D. F.

1953   Body Weight, Race and Climate. *American Journal of Physical Anthropology* 11: 533–558.

ROBERTS, S.

1979   *Order and Dispute: An Introduction to Legal Anthropology*. New York: Penguin Books.

ROBERTSON, J.

1992   Koreans in Japan. Paper presented at the University of Michigan Department of Anthropology, Martin Luther King Jr. Day Panel, January 1992. Ann Arbor: University of Michigan Department of Anthropology (unpublished).

RODSETH, L., R. W. WRANGHAM, A. M. HARRIGAN, AND B. SMUTS

1991   The Human Community as a Primate Society. *Current Anthropology* 32: 221–254.

ROMER, A. S.

1960   *Man and the Vertebrates*, 3rd ed., vol. 1. Harmondsworth, England: Penguin, 1960.

ROSALDO, M. Z.

1980a *Knowledge and Passion: Notions of Self and Social Life*. Stanford, CA: Stanford University Press.

1980b The Use and Abuse of Anthropology: Reflections on Feminism and Cross-Cultural Understanding. *Signs* 5(3): 389–417.

ROSALDO, M. Z., AND L. LAMPHERE

1974   Introduction to *Woman, Culture, and Society*, eds. M. Z. Rosaldo and L. Lamphere, pp. 1–16. Stanford, CA: Stanford University Press.

ROSEBERRY, W.

1988   Political Economy. *Annual Review of Anthropology* 17: 161–185.

ROUSE, R.

1991   Mexican Migration and the Social Space of Postmodernism. *Diaspora* 1(1): 8–23.

ROYAL ANTHROPOLOGICAL INSTITUTE

1951   *Notes and Queries on Anthropology*, 6th ed. London: Routledge and Kegan Paul.

RYAN, S.

1990   *Ethnic Conflict and International Relations*. Brookfield, MA: Dartmouth.

SADE, D.

1972   A Longitudinal Study of Social Behavior of Rhesus Monkeys. In *The Functional and Evolutionary Biology of Primates*, ed. R. Tuttle. Chicago: University of Chicago Press.

SAGGS, H.

1989   *Civilization before Greece and Rome*. New Haven: Yale University Press.

SAHLINS, M. D.

1961   The Segmentary Lineage: An Organization of Predatory Expansion. *American Anthropologist* 63: 322–345.

1968   *Tribesmen*. Englewood Cliffs, NJ: Prentice-Hall.

1972   *Stone Age Economics*. Chicago: Aldine.

1978 Culture for Protein and Profit, *New York Review of Books*, November 23, pp. 45–53.

1988 (Orig. 1968). Notes on the Original Affluent Society. In *Tribal Peoples and Development Issues: A Global Overview*, ed. J. H. Bodley, pp. 15–21. Palo Alto, CA: Mayfield.

SAHLINS, M. D., AND E. R. SERVICE
1960 *Evolution and Culture*. Ann Arbor: University of Michigan Press.

SALZMAN, P. C.
1974 Political Organization among Nomadic Peoples. In *Man in Adaptation: The Cultural Present*, 2nd ed., ed. Y. A. Cohen, pp. 267–284. Chicago: Aldine.

SANDAY, P. R.
1974 Female Status in the Public Domain. In *Woman, Culture, and Society*, eds. M. Z. Rosaldo and L. Lamphere, pp. 189–206. Stanford, CA: Stanford University Press.

SANDERS W. T., AND B. J. PRICE
1968 *Mesoamerica: The Evolution of a Civilization.* New York: Random House.

SANDERS, W. T., J. R. PARSONS, AND R. S. SANTLEY
1979 *The Basin of Mexico: Ecological Processes in the Evolution of a Civilization.* New York: Academic Press, 1979.

SANKOFF, G.
1980 *The Social Life of Language.* Philadelphia: University of Pennsylvania Press.

SANTINO, J.
1983 Night of the Wandering Souls. *Natural History*, 92(10): 42.

SAPIR, E.
1931 Conceptual Categories in Primitive Languages. *Science* 74: 578–584.

SCHAEFER, R.
1989 *Sociology*, 3rd ed. New York: McGraw-Hill.

SCHAEFER, R., AND R. P. LAMM
1992 *Sociology*, 4th ed. New York: McGraw-Hill.

SCHALLER, G.
1963 *The Mountain Gorilla: Ecology and Behavior.* Chicago: University of Chicago Press.

SCHMEMANN, S.
1992 Ethnic Battles Flaring in Former Soviet Fringe. *The New York Times*, May 24, p. 7.

SCHEPER-HUGHES, N.
1987 Culture, Scarcity, and Maternal Thinking: Mother Love and Child Death in Northeast Brazil. In *Child Survival*, ed. N. Scheper-Hughes, pp. 187–208. Boston: D. Reidel.

1992 *Death Without Weeping: The Violence of Everyday Life in Brazil.* Berkeley: University of California Press.

SCHIEFFELIN, E.
1976 *The Sorrow of the Lonely and the Burning of the Dancers.* New York: St. Martin's Press.

SCHNEIDER, J.
1977 Was There a Pre-capitalist World System? *Peasant Societies* 6: 20–28.

SCOTT, J. C.
1985 *Weapons of the Weak.* New Haven, CT: Yale University Press.

1990 *Domination and the Arts of Resistance.* New Haven, CT: Yale University Press.

SCUDDER, T.
1982 The Impact of Big Dam-building on the Zambezi River Basin. In *The Careless Technology: Ecology and International Development*, eds. M. T. Farvar and J. P. Milton, pp. 206–235. New York: Natural History Press.

SCUDDER, T., AND E. COLSON
1980 *Secondary Education and the Formation of an Elite: The Impact of Education on Gwembe District, Zambia.* London: Academic Press.

SCUDDER, T., AND J. HABARAD
1991 Local Responses to Involuntary Relocation and Development in the Zambian Portion of the Middle Zambezi Valley. In *Migrants in Agricultural Development*. ed. J. A. Mollett, pp. 178–205. New York: New York University Press.

SEBEOK, T. A., AND J. UMIKER-SEBEOK, EDS.
1980 *Speaking of Apes: A Critical Anthropology of Two-Way Communication with Man.* New York: Plenum.

SELIGSON, M. A.
1984 *The Gap between Rich and Poor: Contending Perspectives on the Political Economy of Development.* Boulder: Westview.

SERRIE, H., ED.
1986 *Anthropology and International Business.* Studies in Third World Societies, no. 28. Williamsburg, VA: Department of Anthropology, College of William and Mary.

SERVICE, E. R.
1962 *Primitive Social Organization: An Evolutionary Perspective.* New York: Random House.

1966 *The Hunters.* Englewood Cliffs, NJ: Prentice-Hall.

1971 *Primitive Social Organization: An Evolutionary Perspective*, 2nd ed. New York: Random House.

1975 *Origins of the State and Civilization: The Process of Cultural Evolution.* New York: W. W. Norton.

SEYFARTH, R. M., D. L. CHENEY, AND P. MARLER
1980　Monkey Responses to Three Different Alarm Calls. *Science* 210: 801–803.

SHABECOFF, P.
1989a　Ivory Imports Banned to Aid Elephant, *The New York Times*, June 7, p. 15.
1989b　New Lobby Is Helping Wildlife of Africa, *The New York Times*, June 9, p. 14.

SHANNON, T. R.
1989　*An Introduction to the World System Perspective.* Boulder: Westview.

SHOSTAK, M.
1981　*Nisa: The Life and Words of a !Kung Woman.* Cambridge, MA: Harvard University Press.

SHREEVE, J.
1992　The Dating Game: How Old Is the Human Race? *Discover* 13(9): 76–83.

SHWEDER, R., AND H. LEVINE, EDS.
1984　*Culture Theory: Essays on Mind, Self, and Emotion.* Cambridge: Cambridge University Press.

SIBLEY, C. G., AND AHLQUIST, J. E.
1984　The Phylogeny of the Hominoid Primates, as Indicated by DNA-DNA Hybridization. *Journal of Molecular Evolution* 20: 2–15.

SILBERBAUER, G.
1981　*Hunter and Habitat in the Central Kalahari Desert.* New York: Cambridge University Press.

SILVERBLATT, I.
1988　Women in States. *Annual Review of Anthropology* 17: 427–460.

SIPES, R. G.
1973　War, Sports, and Aggression: An Empirical Test of Two Rival Theories. *American Anthropologist* 75: 64–86.

SKODAK, M., AND H. M. SKEELS
1949　A Final Follow-up Study of One Hundred Adopted Children. *Journal of Genetic Psychology* 75: 85–125.

SLADE, M.
1984　Displaying Affection in Public. *The New York Times*, December 17, p. B14.

SMALL, M., ED.
1984　*Female Primates: Studies by Women Primatologists.* New York: Alan R. Liss.

SMITH, B.
1982　Upper Pleistocene Hominid Evolution in South-Central Europe. *Current Anthropology* 23: 667–703.
1984　Fossil Hominids from the Upper Pleistocene of Central Europe and the Origin of Modern Europeans. In *The Origins of Modern Humans*, eds. F. H. Smith and F. Spencer, pp. 187–209. New York: Alan R. Liss.

SMITH, C. A.
1990　The Militarization of Civil Society in Guatemala: Economic Reorganization as a Continuation of War. *Latin American Perspectives* 17: 8–41.

SMITH, M. G.
1965　*The Plural Society in the British West Indies.* Berkeley: University of California Press.

SMUTS, B. B.
1985　*Sex and Friendship in Baboons.* New York: Aldine.

SOLHEIM, W. G., II.
1976　(Orig. 1972). An Earlier Agricultural Revolution. In *Avenues to Antiquity, Readings from Scientific American*, ed. B. M. Fagan, pp. 160–168. San Francisco: W. H. Freeman.

SOLWAY, J., AND R. LEE
1990　Foragers, Genuine and Spurious: Situating the Kalahari San in History (with CA treatment). *Current Anthropology* 31(2): 109–146.

SONNEVILLE-BORDES, D. DE
1963　Upper Paleolithic Cultures in Western Europe. *Science* 142: 347–355.

SPINDLER, G. D., ED.
1978　*The Making of Psychological Anthropology.* Berkeley: University of California Press.
1982　*Doing the Ethnography of Schooling: Educational Anthropology in Action.* New York: Holt, Rinehart & Winston.

SPRADLEY, J. P.
1979　*The Ethnographic Interview.* New York: Holt, Rinehart & Winston.

STACEY, J.
1990　*Brave New Families: Stories of Domestic Upheaval in Late Twentieth Century America.* New York: Basic Books.

STACK, C. B.
1975　*All Our Kin: Strategies for Survival in a Black Community.* New York: Harper Torchbooks.

STATISTICAL ABSTRACT OF THE UNITED STATES
1991　111th ed. Washington, DC: U.S. Bureau of the Census, U.S. Government Printing Office.

STAUB, S.
1989　*Yemenis in New York City: The Folklore of Ethnicity.* Philadelphia: The Balch Institute Press.

STEEDMAN, C., URWIN, C., AND V. WALKERDINE, EDS.
1985　*Language, Gender and Childhood.* London: Routledge and Kegan Paul.

STEEGMAN, A. T., JR.
1975　Human Adaptation to Cold. In *Physiological Anthropology*, ed. A. Damon, pp. 130–166. New York: Oxford University Press.

STEPONAITIS, V.
1986   Prehistoric Archaeology in the Southeastern United States. *Annual Review of Anthropology* 15:363–404.

STEVENS, W. K.
1992   Humanity Confronts Its Handiwork: An Altered Planet. *The New York Times*, May 5, pp. B5–B7.

STEVENSON, R. F.
1968   *Population and Political Systems in Tropical Africa.* New York: Columbia University Press.

STEWARD, J. H.
1949   Cultural Causality and Law: A Trial Formulation of the Development of Early Civilizations. *American Anthropologist* 51: 1–27.
1955   *Theory of Culture Change.* Urbana: University of Illinois Press.

STOCKING, G. W., ED.
1986   *Malinowski, Rivers, Benedict and Others: Essays on Culture and Personality.* Madison, WI: University of Wisconsin Press.

STOLER, A. L.
1977   Class Structure and Female Autonomy in Rural Java. *Signs* 3: 74–89.

STRATHERN, M.
1988   *The Gender of the Gift: Problems with Women and Problems with Society in Melanesia.* Berkeley: University of California Press.

SUDETIC, C.
1992   Serbian Gunners Pound Sarajevo. *The New York Times*, May 30, pp. A1, A3.

SUSMAN, R. L.
1987   Pygmy Chimpanzees and Common Chimpanzees: Models for the Behavioral Ecology of the Earliest Hominids. In *The Evolution of Human Behavior: Primate Models.* ed. W. G. Kinzey, pp. 72–86. Albany: State University of New York Press.

SWANSON, G. E.
1960   *The Birth of the Gods: The Origin of Primitive Beliefs.* Ann Arbor: University of Michigan Press.

SWIFT, M.
1963   Men and Women in Malay Society. In *Women in the New Asia*, ed. B. Ward, pp. 268–286. Paris: UNESCO.

SZALAY, F. S., AND E. DELSON
1980   *Evolutionary History of the Primates.* New York: Academic Press.

TAGUE, R. G., AND C. O. LOVEJOY
1986   The Obstetric Pelvis of A. L. 288-1 (Lucy). *Journal of Human Evolution* 15: 237–255.

TAINTER, J.
1987   *The Collapse of Complex Societies.* New York: Cambridge University Press.

TANAKA, J.
1980   *The San Hunter-Gatherers of the Kalahari.* Tokyo: University of Tokyo Press.

TANNEN, D.
1986   *That's Not What I Meant! How Conversational Style Makes or Breaks Your Relations with Others.* New York: William Morrow.
1990   *You Just Don't Understand: Women and Men in Conversation.* New York: Ballantine.

TANNER, N.
1974   Matrifocality in Indonesia and Africa and among Black Americans. In *Women, Culture, and Society*, eds. M. Z. Rosaldo and L. Lamphere, pp. 129–156. Stanford, CA: Stanford University Press.

TAYLOR, C.
1978   Anthropologist-in-Residence. In *Applied Anthropology in America*, eds. E. M. Eddy and W. L. Partridge, pp. 229–244. New York: Columbia University Press.

TELEKI, G.
1973   *The Predatory Behavior of Wild Chimpanzees.* Lewisburg, PA: Bucknell University Press.

TERRACE, H. S.
1979   *Nim.* New York: Knopf.

THOMASON, S. G., AND KAUFMAN, T.
1988   *Language Contact, Creolization and Genetic Linguistics.* Berkeley: University of California Press.

THOMSON, A., AND L. H. D. BUXTON
1923   Man's Nasal Index in Relation to Certain Climatic Conditions. *Journal of the Royal Anthropological Institute* 53: 92–112.

THOMPSON, W.
1983   Introduction: World System with and without the Hyphen. In *Contending Approaches to World System Analysis*, ed. W. Thompson, pp. 7–26. Beverly Hills, CA: Sage.

TONER, R.
1992   Los Angeles Riots Are a Warning, Americans Fear. *The New York Times*, May 11, pp. A1, A11.

TRUDGILL, P.
1983   *Sociolinguistics: An Introduction to Language and Society*, rev. ed. Baltimore: Penguin.

TURNBULL, C.
1965   *Wayward Servants: The Two Worlds of the African Pygmies.* Garden City, NY: Natural History Press.

TURNER, V. W.
1974   *The Ritual Process.* Harmondsworth, England: Penguin.

TYLOR, E. B.
1889   On a Method of Investigating the Development of Institutions: Applied to Laws of Mar-

riage and Descent. *Journal of the Royal Anthropological Institute* 18: 245–269.

1958 (Orig. 1871). *Primitive Culture*. New York: Harper Torchbooks.

UCKO, P. J., AND G. W. DIMBLEBY, EDS.

1969 *The Domestication and Exploitation of Plants and Animals*. Chicago: Aldine.

UCKO, P., AND A. ROSENFELD

1967 *Paleolithic Cave Art*. London: Weidenfeld and Nicolson.

UNITED STATES BUREAU OF THE CENSUS

1991 *Statistical Abstract of the United States*, 111th ed. Washington, DC: U.S. Government Printing Office.

VALENTINE, C.

1968 *Culture and Poverty*. Chicago: University of Chicago Press.

VALLADAS, H., J. L. REYSS, J. L. JORON, G. VALLADAS, O. BAR-JOSEPH, AND B. VANDERMEERSCH

1988 Thermoluminescence Dating of Mousterian "Proto-Cro-Magnon" Remains from Israel and the Origin of Modern Man. *Nature* 331: 614–616.

VAN BAAL, J.

1966 *Dema, Description and Analysis of Marindanim Culture (South New Guinea)*. The Hague: M. Nijhoff.

VAN CANTFORT, T. E., AND J. B. RIMPAU

1982 Sign Language Studies with Children and Chimpanzees. *Sign Language Studies* 34: 15–72.

VAN DANIKEN, E.

1971 *Chariots of the Gods*. New York: Bantam.

VAN SCHAIK, C. P., AND G. A. R. A. M. VAN HOOFF

1983 On the Ultimate Causes of Primate Social Systems. *Behaviour* 85: 91–117.

VAN WILLINGEN, J.

1986 *Applied Anthropology: An Introduction*. South Hadley, MA: Bergin and Garvey.

1987 *Becoming a Practicing Anthropologist: A Guide to Careers and Training Programs in Applied Anthropology*. NAPA Bulletin 3. Washington, DC: American Anthropological Association/ National Association for the Practice of Anthropology.

VAYDA, A. P.

1968 (Orig. 1961). Economic Systems in Ecological Perspective: The Case of the Northwest Coast. In *Readings in Anthropology*, 2nd ed., vol. 2, ed. M. H. Fried, pp. 172–178. New York: Crowell.

VECSEY, C., ED.

1990 *Religion in Native North America*. Moscow: Idaho: University of Idaho Press.

VIOLA, H. J., AND C. MARGOLIS

1991 *Seeds of Change: Five Hundred Years since*

Columbus, a Quincentennial Commemoration. Washington, DC: Smithsonian Institution Press.

WAGLEY, C. W.

1968 (Orig. 1959). The Concept of Social Race in the Americas. In *The Latin American Tradition*, ed. C. Wagley, pp. 155–174. New York: Columbia University Press.

1968 *The Latin American Tradition*. New York: Columbia University Press.

1977 *Welcome of Tears: The Tapirapé Indians of Central Brazil*. New York: Oxford University Press.

WAGNER, R.

1981 *The Invention of Culture*, rev. ed. Chicago: University of Chicago Press.

WALLACE, A. F. C.

1956 Revitalization Movements. *American Anthropologist* 58: 264–281.

1966 *Religion: An Anthropological View*. New York: Random House.

1970a *Culture and Personality*, 2nd ed. New York: Random House.

1970b *The Death and Rebirth of the Seneca*. New York: Knopf.

WALLERSTEIN, I.

1974 *The Modern World-System: Capitalist Agriculture and the Origins of the European World-Economy in the Sixteenth Century*. New York: Academic Press.

1980 *The Modern World System II: Mercantilism and the Consolidation of the European World-Economy, 1600–1750*. New York: Academic Press.

1982 The Rise and Future Demise of the World Capitalist System: Concepts for Comparative Analysis. In *Introduction to the Sociology of "Developing Societies,"* eds. H. Alavi and T. Shanin, pp. 29–53. New York: Monthly Review Press.

WALLMAN, S., ED.

1977 *Perceptions of Development*. New York: Cambridge University Press.

WASHBURN, S. L., AND R. MOORE

1980 *Ape into Human: A Study of Human Evolution*, 2nd ed. Boston: Little, Brown.

WATSON, J. D.

1970 *Molecular Biology of the Gene*. New York: Benjamin.

WATSON, P.

1972 Can Racial Discrimination Affect IQ? In *Race and Intelligence: The Fallacies Behind the Race-IQ Controversy*, eds. K. Richardson and D. Spears, pp. 56–67. Baltimore: Penguin.

WATSON, P. J., S. A. LeBLANC, AND C. L. REDMAN

1984 *Archeological Explanation: The Scientific Method*

in Archeology. New York: Columbia University Press.

WATSON, R. S., AND P. B. EBREY

1991   *Marriage and Inequality in Chinese Society.* Berkeley: University of California Press.

WAX, M. L., AND J. CASSELL, EDS.

1979   *Federal Regulations: Ethical Issues and Social Research.* Boulder: Westview.

WEAVER, T., GEN. ED.

1973   *To See Ourselves: Anthropology and Modern Social Issues.* Glenview, IL: Scott, Foresman.

WEBER, M.

1947   *The Theory of Social and Economic Organization.* London: Hodge.

1958   (Orig. 1904). *The Protestant Ethic and the Spirit of Capitalism.* New York: Scribner's.

1968   (Orig. 1922). *Economy and Society.* Trans. E. Fischoff et al. New York: Bedminster Press.

WEBER, W.

1976   *Peasants into Frenchman.* Stanford: Stanford University Press.

WEINER, J. S.

1954   Nose Shape and Climate. *American Journal of Physical Anthropology* 12: 1–4.

1992   *Human Biology and Behavior: An Anthropological Perspective,* 6th ed. Glenview, IL: Scott, Foresman.

WEISS, M. L., AND A. E. MANN

1989   *Human Biology and Behavior: An Anthropological Perspective,* 5th ed. Glenview, IL: Scott, Foresman.

1992   *Human Biology and Behavior: An Anthropological Perspective,* 6th ed. Glenview, IL: Scott, Foresman.

WENKE, R.

1990   *Patterns in Prehistory,* 3rd ed. New York: Oxford University Press.

WESTERMARCK, E.

1894   *The History of Human Marriage.* London: Macmillan.

WHITE, L. A.

1959   *The Evolution of Culture: The Development of Civilization to the Fall of Rome.* New York: McGraw-Hill.

WHITING, B. E., ED.

1963   *Six Cultures: Studies of Child Rearing.* New York: Wiley.

WHO OWNS WHOM

Annual directories of parent, associate, and subsidiary companies, by region. London: O. W. Roskill.

WHO OWNS WHOM IN NORTH AMERICA

1984   16th ed. Philadelphia: International Publications Service.

WHORF, B. L.

1956   A Linguistic Consideration of Thinking in Primitive Communities. In *Language, Thought, and Reality: Selected Writings of Benjamin Lee Whorf,* ed. J. B. Carroll, pp. 65–86. Cambridge, MA: MIT Press.

WILLIAMS, B.

1989   A Class Act: Anthropology and the Race to Nation across Ethnic Terrain. *Annual Review of Anthropology* 18: 401–444.

WILLIAMS, J.

1985   What They Say, Home? English Dialects Are Adding to Racial Misunderstandings. *The Washington Post National Weekly Edition,* May 6, p. 10.

WILMSEN, E.

1989   *Land Filled with Flies: A Political Economy of the Kalahari.* Chicago: University of Chicago Press.

WINSLOW, J. H., AND A. MEYER

1983   The Perpetrator at Piltdown. *Science 83,* September, pp. 33–43.

WITTFOGEL, K. A.

1957   *Oriental Despotism: A Comparative Study of Total Power.* New Haven, CT: Yale University Press.

WOLCOTT, H. F.

1977   *Teachers versus Technocrats: An Educational Innovation in Anthropological Perspective.* Eugene: Center for Educational Policy and Management, University of Oregon.

WOLF, E. R.

1955   Types of Latin American Peasantry. *American Anthropologist* 57: 452–471.

1966   *Peasants.* Englewood Cliffs, NJ: Prentice-Hall.

1982   *Europe and the People without History.* Berkeley: University of California Press.

WOLF, M.

1985   *Revolution Postponed: Women in Contemporary China.* Stanford, CA: Stanford University Press.

WOLPOFF, M. H.

1980a   *Paleoanthropology.* New York: McGraw-Hill.

1980b   Cranial Remains of Middle Pleistocene Hominids. *Journal of Human Evolution* 9: 339–358.

1988   Divergence between Early Hominid Lineages: The Roles of Competition and Culture. In *Evolutionary History of the "Robust" Australopithecines,* ed. F. E. Grine, pp. 485–497. New York: Aldine de Gruyter.

1989   Multiregional Evolution: The Fossil Alternative to Eden. In *The Human Revolution: Behavioral and Biological Perspectives on the Origins of Modern Humans,* eds. R. P. Mellars and C. Stringer, pp. 62–108. Princeton, NJ: Princeton University Press.

WOOLARD, K. A.
  1989   *Double Talk: Bilingualism and the Politics of Ethnicity in Catalonia.* Stanford, CA: Stanford University Press.

WORLD ALMANAC & BOOK OF FACTS
  1985   New York: Newspaper Enterprise Association.
  1992   New York: Pharos Books.

WORSLEY, P.
  1970   *The Trumpet Shall Sound: A Study of Cargo Cults in Melanesia.* New York: Schocken.
  1984   *The Three Worlds: Culture and World Development.* Chicago: University of Chicago Press.
  1985   (orig. 1959). Cargo Cults. In *Readings in Anthropology 85/86.* Guilford, CN: Dushkin.

WRANGHAM, R.
  1980   An Ecological Model of Female-Bonded Primate Groups. *Behavior* 75: 262–300.
  1987   The Significance of African Apes for Reconstructing Human Social Evolution. In *The Evolution of Human Behavior: Primate Models.* ed. W. G. Kinzey, pp. 51–71. Albany: State University of New York Press.

WRIGHT, H. T., AND G. A. JOHNSON
  1975   Population, Exchange, and Early State Formation in Southwestern Iran. *American Anthropologist* 77: 267–289.

WULFF, R. M., AND S. J. FISKE, EDS.
  1987   *Anthropological Praxis: Translating Knowledge into Action.* Boulder, CO: Westview Press.

YETMAN, N.
  1991   *Majority and Minority: The Dynamics of Race and Ethnicity in American Life,* 5th ed. Boston: Allyn and Bacon.

ZEUNER, F. E.
  1963   *A History of Domesticated Animals.* London: Hutchinson.

ACKNOWLEDGMENTS

PHOTO CREDITS

Chapter 1
1 Tadao Kimura/The Image Bank
5 Jerald T. Milanich
6 Top, Mark Edwards/Still Pictures; bottom, Robert Phillips/The Image Bank
8 Lowell Georgia/Photo Researchers
10 Ian Berry/Magnum
11 Irven De Vore/Anthro-Photo File
12 Lisa Gezon
15 UPI/Bettmann Newsphotos
17 Malcolm S. Kirk/Peter Arnold

Chapter 2
21 David Gillison/Peter Arnold
24 Yoram Kahana/Peter Arnold
25 Top left, Thomas L. Kelley, from "Millennium: Tribal Wisdom and the Modern World" (c) Biniman Productions Limited; top right, H. Uible/Photo Researchers
26 American Folklife Center/Library of Congress
30 Michal Heron/Woodfin Camp & Associates
32 P.F. Bentley/Time Magazine, Time Warner
33 Arlene Burns/Peter Arnold

Chapter 3
37 Juergen Schmitt/The Image Bank
38 Top, Tom McHugh/Photo Researchers; bottom, Marc & Evelyne Bernheim/Woodfin Camp & Associates

39 Fran Allan/The Picture Cube
41 Left, Howard Dratch/The Image Works; right, Jeff Rotman/Peter Arnold
43 Top, H. Armstrong Roberts; bottom, Ralf-Finn Hestoft/SABA

Chapter 4
51 Giboux/Gamma Liaison
53 Abbas/Magnum
55 Abbas/Magnum
57 Stephanie Maze/Woodfin Camp & Associates
58 Zachmann/Magnum
60 Tibor Bognar/The Stock Market
67 Jon Jones/Sygma
68 Alexandra Avakian/Woodfin Camp & Associates

Chapter 5
75 Sebastião Barbosa/The Image Bank
76 Gerd Ludwig/Woodfin Camp & Associates
78 Donna Binder/Impact Visuals
79 P.J. Griffiths/Magnum
83 Terry Madison/The Image Bank
84 Claude Coivault, from "Millennium: Tribal Wisdom and the Modern World" (c) Biniman Productions Limited.
87 Jan Spieczny/Peter Arnold
87 Jocelyn Boutin/The Picture Cube
88 David Madison/Duomo
89 Bruce Byers/FPG International

Chapter 6
95 Peter Menzel
97 Noah's Ark by Edward Hicks, 1846, 26 ½″ × 30 ½″,

Oil on canvas, Philadelphia Museum of Art, Bequest of Lisa Norris Elkins
101 Alexander Tsiaras/Science Source/Photo Researchers
104 Merrim/Monkmeyer Press
105 Michael Abbey/Photo Researchers
111 Philippe Plailly/Science Photo Library/Photo Researchers
113 Top left, Robert Caputo/Stock, Boston; right, Clyde H. Smith/Peter Arnold

Chapter 7
119 John Cancalogi/Peter Arnold
120 Left, David Agee/Anthro-Photo File; right, UPI/Bettmann Newsphotos
123 Evelyn Gallardo/Peter Arnold
127 Ralph Morse/Life Magazine, Time Warner
129 Peter Veit/DRK Photo
133 Peter Davey/Bruce Coleman
134 Roger S. Fouts
135 Cartoon by Sidney Harris
136 Robert Caputo/Photo Researchers
139 Gregory G. Dimijian, M.D./Photo Researchers

Chapter 8
145 Africapix/Peter Arnold
147 Kunto Owaki/The Stock Market
153 Morton Beebe/The Image Bank
154 Bill Stover/New York Times Pictures
157 John Reader/Science Photo Library/Photo Researchers
160 John Reader/Science Photo Library/Photo Researchers
163 Des Bartlett/Photo Researchers
165 Top left, Alan Walker, Johns Hopkins University/(c) National Museums of Kenya, Kalakol Account; bottom right, Gary Larson, Universal Press Syndicate
168 John Shea/Anthro-Photo File

Chapter 9
173 Sylvian Julienne/Woodfin Camp & Associates
177 Drawing by Handelsman; © 1990, *The New Yorker* Magazine, Inc.
178 Neg. no 315446. Courtesy of the American Museum of Natural History. Photo by Charles H. Coles
182 Musee de L'Homme, Paris
189 Left, David R. Austen/Stock, Boston; right, Gordon Cahan/Photo Researchers
190 Gamma Liaison

Chapter 10
197 Harvey Lloyd/The Stock Market
201 Hinterleitner/Gamma Liaison

204 J. Scherschel/Photo Researchers
206 Mike Yamashita/Woodfin Camp & Associates
207 Earth Scenes
210 Martha Cooper/Peter Arnold
217 Jacques Jangoux/Peter Arnold

Chapter 11
221 Thomas L. Kelly from "Millenium: Tribal Wisdom and the Modern World" (c) Biniman Productions Limited
222 Steele-Perkins/Magnum
224 Irven DeVore/Anthro-Photo File
228 Steve McCurry/Magnum
231 Victor Englebert
232 Charles Gupton/The Stock Market
233 Victor Englebert
234 Martha Cooper/Peter Arnold
237 Kazuyoshi Nomachi/Photo Researchers

Chapter 12
241 George Holton/Photo Researchers
244 The Bettmann Archive
248 George Holton/Photo Researchers
251 Burt Glinn/Magnum
254 Dr. J.F.E. Bloss/Anthro-Photo File
255 Roland & Sabrina/Woodfin Camp & Associates
256 Historical Pictures Service/Stock Montage
257 Douglas Kirkland/The Image Bank
258 Mike Schneps/The Image Bank

Chapter 13
263 Lisl Dennis/The Image Bank
264 Louis H. Jawitz/The Image Bank
265 Diane Lowe/Stock, Boston
266 Photo by R.H. Beck. Courtesy Department Library Services, American Museum of Natural History
269 Left, T. Graham/Sygma; right, R. Bossu/Sygma
271 Alon Reininger/Contact Press Images
277 Robert Frerck/The Stock Market
278 Sean Sprague/Impact Visuals

Chapter 14
285 Chuck O'Rear/Westlight
286 Paul Van Riel/Black Star
292 Carl Frank/Photo Researchers
294 Culver Pictures
298 Top, Dilip Mehta/Woodfin Camp & Associates; bottom, Picture Collection, New York Public Library
299 Keith Dannemiller/SABA
302 Nick Nichols/Magnum

Chapter 15
307 Victor Englebert
310 Top, Victor Englebert; bottom, Bill Gillette/Stock, Boston

312 Michael Salas/The Image Bank
313 Left, John Eastcott/Yva Momatiuk/The Image Works; right, Richard Kalvar/Magnum
315 John Eastcott/Yva Momatiuk/Woodfin Camp & Associates
319 Mathew McVay/New York Times Pictures
320 Courtesy of the American Museum of Natural History

Chapter 16
325 Joel Gordon
328 FJ Dean/The Image Works
330 Grant Faint/The Image Bank
331 Eastcott/Momatiuk/Woodfin Camp & Associates
332 Terry E. Eiler/Stock Boston
335 Left, The Memory Shop; right, Richard Cartwright/CBS
336 Claudia Parks/The Stock Market

Chapter 17
345 Frank Fournier/Contact Press Images
347 C.S. Perkins/Magnum
349 Courtesy Dr. Victor A. McKusick, The Johns Hopkins Hospital
350 Lila Abu-Lughod/Anthro-Photo File
354 Mike Yamashita/Woodfin Camp & Associates
356 Top, Cary Wolinsky/Stock, Boston; bottom, Gerard Rancinan/Sygma
360 Emil Muench/Photo Researchers
361 Thomas L. Kelly

Chapter 18
365 Steve McCurry/Magnum
367 Carleton Ray/Photo Researchers
368 Jeff Isaac Greenberg/Photo Researchers
371 Michael Peletz, Hamilton, N.Y.
372 S. Salgado/Magnum
373 George Holton/Photo Researchers
375 Martha Cooper/Peter Arnold
376 AMIGA TV TUDO Magazine, Rio de Janeiero, Brazil, 1/26/90
378 Nicholas Jallot/Cosmos 1990/Woodfin Camp & Associates
381 © 1943 The Curtis Publishing Company

Chapter 19
385 Abbas/Magnum
387 David Alan Harvey/Woodfin Camp & Associates
388 Bruno Barbey/Magnum
390 Top left, Thierry Secretan Cosmos/Woodfin Camp & Associates; bottom right, Michael Minardi/Peter Arnold

398 Courtesy of The American Museum of Natural History
399 Bruno Barbey/Magnum
402 Michele Burgess/The Stock Market
404 Philip Jones Griffiths/Magnum

Chapter 20
408 Thomas L. Kelly, from "Millennium: Tribal Wisdom and the Modern World" (c) Biniman Productions Limited
411 Richard Lucas/The Image Works
412 John Lewis Stage/The Image Bank
416 Dan Connell/Impact Visuals
417 Joseph Nettis/Photo Researchers
418 Misha Erwitt/Magnum
421 Richard & Mary Magruder/The Image Bank

Chapter 21
425 Robbi Newman/The Image Bank
428 Bruno Barbey/Magnum
429 David Hiser/The Image Bank
431 Bottom left, Burt Glinn/Magnum; bottom right, Spencer Grant/The Picture Cube
436 Bruegel, Pieter (the Elder) The Tower of Babel, Oil on oakwood (1563), Kunsthistorisches Museum, Gemaeldegalerie, Vienna, Austria/Art Resource
439 Dr. Stephen Lansing
440 Owen Franken/Stock Boston

Chapter 22
445 Steele Perkins/Magnum
446 Charles Harbutt/Actuality
448 John Giordano/SABA
449 Robert Fried/Stock, Boston
450 Robert Caputo/Stock, Boston
451 Alon Reininger/Woodfin Camp & Associates
453 Peter Frey/The Image Bank
456 Yoram Kahana/Peter Arnold
458 Alon Reininger/Contact Press Images

Chapter 23
467 Peter Frey/The Image Bank
470 Alexander Low/Woodfin Camp & Associates
471 United Nations
472 Andrea Brizzi/The Stock Market
476 Marc & Evelyne Bernheim/Woodfin Camp & Associates
477 Sean Sprague/Impact Visuals
480 John Moss/Photo Researchers
481 Dr. Steven Lansing/Abbas/Magnum

Chapter 24

485 Ricardo Funari/Impact Visuals
489 M. Gunther/Bios/Peter Arnold
492 Michael Schumann/SABA
493 Peterson/Gamma Liaison
494 Rob Crandall/Stock, Boston

497 Gary Payne/Gamma Liaison
498 Klaus D. Francke/Peter Arnold
499 Top, G. Dambier/Sygma; bottom, Eugene Fisher/Gamma Liaison
503 Michael Nichols/Magnum
505 Abbas/Magnum

ILLUSTRATION AND TEXT CREDITS

4–5: Excerpt from *Assault on Paradise: Social Change in a Brazilian Village* by Conrad Kottak. Copyright (c) 1992. Reprinted by permission of McGraw Hill, Inc.

31: Table 2.1 From "Portrait of the Electorate," *The New York Times*, November 5, 1992. Copyright (c) 1992 by The New York Times Company. Reprinted by permission.

59: Figure 4.1 From *The Future Racial Composition of the U.S.*, by L. F. Bouvier and C. B. Davis, Population Reference Bureau, 1982.

65: In the News From Veronica Byrd, "Easing the Cultural Tension at the Neighborhood Store," *The New York Times*, October 25, 1992. Copyright (c) 1992 by The New York Times Company. Reprinted by permission.

77: Table 5.1 From Felicity Barringer, "New Census Data Show More Children Living in Poverty," *The New York Times*, May 29, 1992. Copyright (c) 1992 by The New York Times Company. Reprinted by permission.

86: Figure 5.1 From *Evolution and Human Origins* by B. J. Williams. Copyright (c) 1979 by B. J. Williams. Reprinted by permission of HarperCollins Publishers.

108: Figure 6.6 From *Human Evolution: An Introduction to the New Physical Anthropology* by Joseph B. Birdsell. Copyright (c) 1975, 1981 by HarperCollins, Publishers, Inc. Reprinted by permission of HarperCollins Publishers.

110: From Daniel Q. Haney, "Bad News Borne," as it appeared in *Ann Arbor News*, November 12, 1992. Reprinted by permission of Associated Press.

122: Table 7.2 From D. L. Cheney, R. M. Seyfarth, B. B. Smuts, and R. W. Wrangham, "The Study of Primate Societies," in *Primate Societies* edited by B. B. Smuts, D. L. Cheney, R. M. Seyfarth, R. W. Wrangham, and T. T. Struhsaker. Copyright (c) 1987. Reprinted by permission of The University of Chicago Press.

135: Cartoon (c) 1993 by Sidney Harris.

154–155: In the News From John Noble Wilford, "Jawbone Offers Clue in Search for 'Missing Link,' " *The New York Times*, March 17, 1992. Copyright (c) 1992 by The New York Times Company. Reprinted by permission.

190–191: In the News From Marlise Simons, "Stone Age Art Shows Penguins at Mediterranean," *The New York Times*, October 20, 1992. Copyright (c) 1992 by The New York Times Company. Reprinted by permission.

200–201: In the News From Boyce Rensberger, "A Man Who Lived 5,300 Years Ago," *The Washington Post*, November 26, 1992. (c) 1992, *The Washington Post*. Reprinted with permission.

208: In the News From John Noble Wilford, "Clues to Food Crops Are Found in Africa," *The New York Times*, October 27, 1992. Copyright (c) 1992 by The New York Times Company. Reprinted by permission.

217: Figure 10.7 From *Physical Anthropology and Archeology*, 4th Edition, by C. Jolly and F. Plog. Copyright (c) 1986. Reprinted by permission of McGraw-Hill Inc.

230: Table 11.1 From R. Layton, R. Foley, and E. Williams, "The Transition between Hunting and Gathering and the Specialized Husbandry of Resources: A Socioecological Approach," *Current Anthropology*, Vol. 32, No. 3, June 1991. Copyright (c) 1991. Reprinted by permission of The University of Chicago Press.

236: In the News From Jane Perlez, "Dinkaland, Where Cattle Are Treated Like Equals," *The New York Times*, January 18, 1991. Copyright (c) 1991 by The New York Times Company. Reprinted by permission.

253: Figure 12.4 Reprinted by permission from E. E. Evans-Pritchard, *The Nuer: A Description of the Modes of Livelihood and Political Institutions of a Nilotic People* (Oxford: Clarendon Press, 1940).

289: Figure 14.1 Reprinted from *An Introduction to the World-System Perspective* by Thomas Richard Shannon, 1989, by permission of Westview Press, Boulder, Colorado.

301: Table 14.2 From *Anthropology and Contemporary Human Problems* by John H. Bodley, 1985. Reprinted by permission of Mayfield Publishing.

318–319: In the News From Timothy Egan, "Indians and Salmon: Making Nature Whole," *The New York Times*, November 26, 1992. Copyright (c) 1992 by The New York Times Company. Reprinted by permission.

333: Figure 16.3 From "Family Arrangements," *The New*

York Times, August 23, 1992. Copyright (c) 1992 by The New York Times Company. Reprinted by permission.

334: Table 16.2 From *The World Almanac & Book of Facts*, 1992 edition, copyright Pharos Books 1991, New York, New York 10166.

354–355: In the News From Daniel Goleman, "Anthropology Goes Looking for Love in All the Old Places," *The New York Times*, November 24, 1992. Copyright (c) 1992 by The New York Times Company. Reprinted by permission.

369: In the News From Jane Perlez, "Woman's Work Is Never Done (Not by Masai Men)," *The New York Times*, December 1, 1991. Copyright (c) 1991 by The New York Times Company. Reprinted by permission.

374: Table 18.1 From *Female of the Species* by K. Martin and B. Voorhies, 1975, (c) Columbia University Press, New York. Reprinted by permission of the publisher.

380: Table 18.4 From *Sociology*, Third Edition, by R. Schaefer. Copyright (c) 1989. Reprinted by permission of McGraw-Hill, Inc.

389: Table 19.1 Adapted from *The Ritual Process* by V. W. Turner, Aldine de Gruyter, 1969. Reprinted by permission of the Estate of Victor W. Turner.

394–395: In the News From Andrew J. Pollack, "A Festival That Permits Japanese to be Impolite," *The New York Times*, January 2, 1993. Copyright (c) 1993 by The New York Times Company. Reprinted by permission.

396–397: In the News From Larry Rohter, "Court to Weigh Law Forbidding Animal Sacrifice," *The New York Times*, November 3, 1992. Copyright (c) 1993 by The New York Times Company. Reprinted by permission.

400: Table 19.2 Reprinted with permission from the 1990 *Britannica Book of the Year*, copyright 1990, Encyclopaedia Britannica, Inc., Chicago, Illinois.

433: Table 21.1 "Multiple Negation Table" from *Sociolinguistics: An Introduction to Language and Society* by Peter Trudgill (Penguin Books 1974, Revised edition 1983) copyright (c) Peter Trudgill, 1974, 1983.

437: Figure 21.3 From *An Introduction to Language*, Fourth Edition by Victoria A. Fromkin and Robert Rodman, copyright (c) 1988 by Holt, Rinehart and Winston, Inc., reprinted by permission of the publisher.

438–439: In the News From John Noble Wilford, "In a Publishing Coup, Books in 'Unwritten' Languages," *The New York Times*, December 31, 1991. Copyright (c) 1991 by The New York Times Company. Reprinted by permission.

454–455: In the News From Lawrence K. Altman, "Women Worldwide Nearing Higher Rate for AIDS Than Men," *The New York Times*, July 21, 1992. Copyright (c) 1992 by The New York Times Company. Reprinted by permission.

472: Table 23.1 From D. Gross and B. Underwood, "Technological Change and Calorie Costs: Sisal Agriculture in Northeastern Brazil." Reproduced by permission of the American Anthropological Association from *American Anthropologist* 73:3, June 1971. Not for further reproduction.

478–479: In the News From Kathleen Teltsch, "Tiny Tribe Preserves Itself by Returning to Farming Tradition," *The New York Times*, November 22, 1992. Copyright (c) 1992 by The New York Times Company. Reprinted by permission.

496–497: In the News From Rigoberta Menchu, "Things Have Happened to Me as If in a Movie," in *You Can't Drown the Fire: Latin American Women Writing in Exile*, Cleis Press, 1989.

INDEX

Cultivation of plants (*see* Food
    production; Plant cultivation)
Cultural adaptation, 3
Cultural anthropology, 4–5, 7–8
    sociology and, 12, 14–15
Cultural colonialism, 69–70
Cultural continuity, as explanation for
    incest taboo, 349–350
Cultural diversity:
    continuance of, 505–506
    development and, 478–479
Cultural ecology, 9
Cultural evolution, 224–225
    archeological inference of, 9
Cultural exchange, 485–507
    continuance of diversity and, 505–506
    domination and, 488–492
    making and remaking culture and,
        502–505
    migration and, 486–488
    syncretisms, blends, and
        accommodation and, 499–502
    (*See also* Survival)
Cultural imperialism, 501
    flaws in assumptions about, 502–503
Cultural institutions, 415–416
Cultural learning, 39–41
Cultural materialism, 273
Cultural relativism, 45–46
Cultural Survival, 495, 498, 505
Cultural transmission of communication
    systems, 134
Culturally compatible economic
    development projects, 476
Culture:
    adaptive and maladaptive, 44
    all-encompassing nature of, 39
    creative use of, 44
    definition of, 2
    evolution of, 224–225
    ideal, 44
    individual and, 410–411
    international, 45
    international marketing and, 460–461
    language and, 428–430
    national, 44–45
    patterns of, 43–44
    personality and, 16–17
    popular, 502–503
    of poverty, 418–419
    real, 44
    symbolic nature of, 41–42
    (*See also* Acculturation; Enculturation;
        Subcultures)
Curer, 456
Customs, manifest and latent functions of,
    351–352

Dallas (television program), 503–504
Dances with Wolves (film), 256, 319
Dar (chimpanzee), 133
Dart, Raymond, 159
Darwin, Charles, 6, 166
Dating methods, 146–151
Daughter languages, 435
Davis, Susan, 355

Deep structure, 428
Deforestation, endangered primates and,
    131
Deities, 395–398
Demonstrated descent, 245
Dentition (*see* Teeth)
Dependent variables, 30
Descent:
    genealogical method and, 25
    (*See also* Kinship)
Descent groups, 245–246
    flexibility in organization of, 338
    local, 246
    matrilineal, 245, 246, 330
    nuclear families compared with,
        327–329
    patrilineal, 245, 246, 348, 372–373
    segmentary lineage organization and,
        252–255
    status in, 251
    unilineal, 245, 337
    (*See also* Clans; Lineages)
Descriptive linguistics, 10
Development, 468–476
    culturally appropriate, 478, 480–482
    culturally compatible projects for, 476
    environmentalism and, 488–490
    equity and, 474
Developmental type, 225
Dialects, 431–433
    (*See also* Black English Vernacular)
Dialogic ethnographies, 29
Diary, ethnography and, 22–23
Diasporas, 486, 503–504
Dickens, Charles, 293
Diet:
    fertility and, 249
    of primates, 136
Differential access, 267
Diffusion, 45
Digit (gorilla), 131
Diglossia, 431
Dinka culture (Sudan), 236–237, 497–498
Dinkins, David, 62
Directional selection, 103–104
Discourse, 494
Discrimination, 62–63
    attitudinal, 63
    in Brazil, 81
    cultural construction of race and, 77
    de facto, 62
    de jure, 62–63
    ethnic conflict and, 66–70
    institutional, 63
    in Japan, 78–81
    (*See also* Stratification)
Disease:
    blood type and, 112
    definition of, 453
    food production and, 216
    (*See also* Medical anthropology)
Disease-theory systems, 454–455
Disney, Walt, 518
Disneyland, 60, 518
Displacement, linguistic, 135
Dispute resolution, segmentary descent
    and, 254

Division of labor, gender-based, 229–230,
    249, 309–310, 368
    among foraging populations, 139
    among primates, 137
Divorce rate, in United States, 332–333
DNA (deoxyribonucleic acid),
    mitochondrial, 184, 185
Domestic-public dichotomy, 368
Domestic sphere, 367
Domestic system, 288
Domestication of animals (*see* Animal
    domestication; Food production)
Dominance hierarchies:
    among chimpanzees, 132
    among monkeys, 127
Domination, religious, 491–492
Dowry, 353
Draper, Patricia, 370
Dry farming, 198
Dryopith(s), 151
Dryopithecine pattern, 151
Dubois, Eugene, 178
Durkheim, Émile, 22, 522
Dynasty (television program), 503–504

Early village farming community, 213
Eckert, Penelope, 432
Ecocide, 301
Ecological diversity, origins of state and,
    274
Ecology, 9
    of food production, 202
Economic development, disease and,
    453–454
Economic specialization, 279
Economic status, stratification and, 267
Economic systems, 307–322
    ancient, 8
    in chiefdoms, 264–266
    distribution and exchange and,
        314–316
    economizing and maximization and,
        308–309
    money and spheres of exchange and,
        317
    in periphery nations, 288
    potlatching and, 317, 320–321
    production and, 309–310, 312–314
    world, 299
    (*See also* Capitalism)
Economic typology, 243
Economics, 308
    anthropology and, 7, 15–16
    comparative, 16
    of nuclear family, 330
    personality and, 417
Economizing, 15, 308–309
    alternative ends and, 308–309
Economy:
    attitudes toward women and, 379
    broad-spectrum revolution and, 188
    cargo cults and, 500
    definition of, 308
    glacial retreat and, 187–188
    Mayan, 273
    Mesopotamian, 206

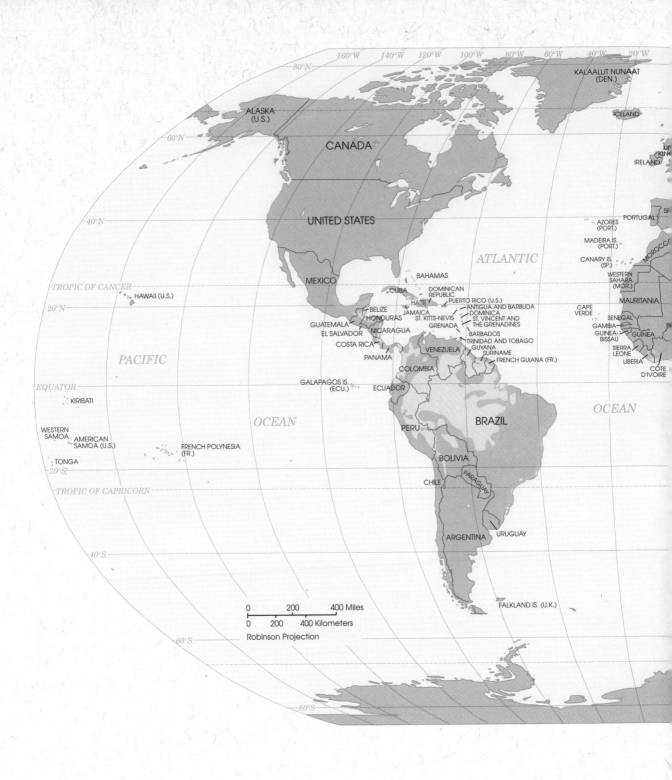

80°N

160°W   140°W   120°W   100°W   80°W   60°W   40°W   20°W

KALAALLIT NUNAAT
(DEN.)

ALASKA
(U.S.)

ICELAND

60°N

CANADA

UN
KIN
IRELAND

40°N

UNITED STATES

ATLANTIC

AZORES
(PORT.)

PORTUGAL

SF

MADEIRA IS.
(PORT.)

CANARY IS.
(SP.)

MOROCC

MEXICO

BAHAMAS

WESTERN
SAHARA
(MOR.)

TROPIC OF CANCER

HAWAII (U.S.)

CUBA

DOMINICAN
REPUBLIC

PUERTO RICO (U.S.)

MAURITANIA

20°N

BELIZE
HONDURAS

HAITI
JAMAICA
ST. KITTS-NEVIS

ANTIGUA AND BARBUDA
DOMINICA
ST. VINCENT AND
THE GRENADINES

CAPE
VERDE

SENEGAL

GUATEMALA
EL SALVADOR
NICARAGUA

GRENADA

GAMBIA
GUINEA-
BISSAU

GUINEA

BI

COSTA RICA

BARBADOS
TRINIDAD AND TOBAGO
GUYANA
SURINAME

SIERRA
LEONE

PANAMA

VENEZUELA

FRENCH GUIANA (FR.)

LIBERIA

CÔTE
D'IVOIRE

PACIFIC

COLOMBIA

GALAPAGOS IS.
(ECU.)

ECUADOR

OCEAN

EQUATOR

KIRIBATI

PERU

BRAZIL

WESTERN
SAMOA

AMERICAN
SAMOA (U.S.)

FRENCH POLYNESIA
(FR.)

BOLIVIA

TONGA

PARAGUAY

20°S

CHILE

TROPIC OF CAPRICORN

ARGENTINA

URUGUAY

40°S

FALKLAND IS. (U.K.)

0   200   400 Miles

0   200   400 Kilometers

60°S

Robinson Projection

80°S